THE HISTORY OF SHELBURNE FARMS

A Changing Landscape, An Evolving Vision

THE HISTORY OF SHELBURNE FARMS

A Changing Landscape, An Evolving Vision

Erica Huyler Donnis

Erica Donnis

THE VERMONT HISTORICAL SOCIETY
Barre, Vermont

SHELBURNE FARMS
Shelburne, Vermont

Copyright 2010 by Shelburne Farms.

All rights reserved. No part of this book may be reproduced in any form or by any electronic or mechanical means including information storage and retrieval systems without permission in writing from Shelburne Farms, except by a reviewer who may quote brief passages in a review. Inquiries should be addressed to: Shelburne Farms, 1611 Harbor Road, Shelburne, VT 05482.

Frontispiece: View of the north turret of the Farm Barn, with the Green Mountains in the background, by Marshall C. Webb, c. 2002. Shelburne Farms Collections.

Book design by Ann Aspell.

The paper used in this book is certified by the Forest Stewardship Council™, a non-governmental, non-profit organization that promotes the responsible management of the world's forests.

Printed in the United States of America by Queen City Printers Inc., certified by the Forest Stewardship Council.

12 11 10   1 2 3

Library of Congress Cataloging-in-Publication Data

Donnis, Erica Huyler.
The history of Shelburne Farms : a changing landscape, an evolving vision / by Erica Huyler Donnis.
     p. cm.
ISBN 978-0-934720-55-7 (pb : alk. paper) -- ISBN 978-0-934720-56-4 (hc : alk. paper)
1. Shelburne Farms (Shelburne, Vt.)--History. 2. Webb family. I. Title.
F59.S49D66 2010
974.3'17--dc22
                    2009001933

First Printing, May 2010
ISBN: 978-0-934720-55-7 (pb), 978-0-934720-56-4 (hc)

CONTENTS

Foreword — *vii*
Preface — *xv*
Author's Acknowledgments — *xvii*
With Thanks — *xix*
Genealogy — *xx*

1. BEGINNINGS — 1
2. SEWARD AND LILA WEBB — 17
3. DESIGNING A COUNTRY ESTATE — 31
4. SHELBURNE HOUSE — 43
5. FARM AND FOREST — 55
6. THE ESTATE — 79
7. INFRASTRUCTURE — 95
8. EMPLOYEES — 105
9. TRIALS — 117
10. TRANSITIONS — 133
11. INCORPORATION — 157
12. THE NEXT GENERATION — 179
13. THE POSTWAR YEARS — 205
14. TURNING POINTS — 221
15. A FARM AND EDUCATION CENTER — 255

Afterword — *275*
Final Acknowledgment — *277*
Maps
    Shelburne Farms, 1886–1942 and 2009 — *278–79*
    Breeding Barn and Farm Barn — *280–81*
    Shelburne House, the Coach Barn, and Surroundings — *282*
Notes — *283*
Bibliography — *327*
Index — *337*

FOREWORD

Shelburne Farms, located beside Lake Champlain in Shelburne, Vermont, is one of America's great pastoral landscapes. Spectacularly sited on a hilly promontory overlooking a vast swath of the lake, the Green Mountains, and the Adirondacks, the visual panorama of the Farms evokes a dream of environmental wholeness that began centuries ago and still resonates in the human heart.

The Farms was founded in 1886, as the private estate of the Webb/Vanderbilt family. It was also designed to be a grand and expansive model farm. Today, more than a century later, much of the original estate is open to the public, and the ideal of environmental wholeness is being pursued through educational programs promoting environmental sustainability on those same lands. Shelburne Farms has been transformed into a public entity, yet an echo of the original vision remains in today's mission.

The Farms' story, as told in this book by historian Erica Donnis, constitutes a quiet drama that shows how a particular place—in this case, a very beautiful place on the shores of Lake Champlain—can inform, shape, and nurture a dream, and how both the place and the dream change and mature through the years.

Entering this 1,400-acre park-like farm today, one leaves behind the traffic and bustle of suburban South Burlington, less than a mile away, and enters a quieter world of broad meadows, gently rounded hills, and winding gravel lanes. At the first bend in the entry road, off to the left, there's a huge four-story, Norman-style barn, stone-walled, shingled and turreted. It looks vaguely medieval, like something out of a fairy tale. The road winds on through a copse of trees, passes a more conventional dairy barn, and emerges onto another broad field with an enormous view of Lake Champlain and the distant Adirondacks.

A handsome brick mansion with multiple chimneys and spacious porches sits atop a rise overlooking the lakeside panorama, and a Romanesque brick coach barn sits just down the way. Unpaved lanes and trails lead off to other meadows, other forested hills, and further vistas.

It all seems slightly dreamlike, something translated from an earlier time. And that is not an entirely inaccurate first impression. For when Shelburne Farms was created as a private country retreat, it was envisioned as a model farm—a dream you could say, of agricultural wholeness.

High ideals and a grand vision were part of the founding of Shelburne Farms in 1886. And now, 130 years later, idealism and vision are still an important part of what makes Shelburne Farms the magical place it is.

Something about this carefully designed landscape draws viewers in and speaks to them on a deeper level than everyday reality. That same something also calls to us from other places in Vermont's traditional farmed landscape. It is a major reason for Vermont's appeal. People exclaim about the beauty of this small state's classic open fields, dotted with barns and farmhouses, backed by mountains. Both in rural Vermont and at Shelburne Farms, they feel something that is attractive and deeply satisfying. The basis of that something is the pastoral myth.

As any reader of classical literature knows, myths embody profound truths about human nature and life. They touch us in a different way than ordinary reality. The pastoral myth—the idea that working the land is a noble and restorative occupation—emerged on the hillsides of rural Greece centuries ago and only grew stronger as cities developed and urban life became more complicated. It represents our eternal yearning for a simpler, more meaningful life, a golden age.

The myth's abiding flaw is that it ignores the grittier realities of farming: the unending toil, the smells of sweat and manure, the thousand-and-one mishaps that make farming tedious and difficult. And yet the myth endures, because we need it to endure. It lives on in the farmed meadows and hillsides of Vermont, even as those farms struggle to survive economically and the nearby urban sprawl of Chittenden County becomes as complex and unpleasant as urban sprawl anywhere.

Undeveloped land around Burlington is now worth more money as real estate than as productive farmland. As a result, open fields and working farms are at a premium in Chittenden County and housing developments seem to crop up daily throughout the region. Examples of suburban sprawl begin on the outskirts of Burlington and spread in all directions along every major highway.

The broad, green meadows of Shelburne Farms offer a respite from the mind-numbing commercial development creeping outward from Vermont's largest city. Those fields and meadows are a gentle reminder of the restorative power of open land. Small wonder that the place attracts a constant stream of visitors—walkers, young families out to visit farm animals, and others. By keeping a significant piece of Chittenden County's working landscape open and productive, Shelburne Farms provides green space, and a striking example of pastoral Vermont, for the city dwellers who live nearby.

It is more than slightly ironic that the original estate that swallowed up 32 small farms around Shelburne Point in the late 1800s has become the means of that same land's agricultural preservation. But ironies abound in the story of Shelburne Farms, as Erica Donnis shows us in the pages that follow.

Briefly, the historical trajectory of Shelburne Farms begins with Seward and Lila (Vanderbilt) Webb, who founded the estate in 1886. They inherited a huge fortune, and with money, ambition, and a bit of hubris, they aimed to have their property showcase the most modern, scientific farming methods of the day. Seward's special love was English Hackney horses and he specifically designed the southern part of the estate as a large—very large—breeding and training complex, involving hundreds of horses.

Yet their vision was much broader than simply running a very grand horse farm. They took on a great range of agricultural endeavors, from a state-of-the-art dairy operation to huge flocks of poultry, hundreds of sheep, pigs, and an enormous greenhouse complex producing both vegetables and flowers year-round. The Farms even hatched and fledged hundreds of wild pheasants for the Webbs' guests to hunt.

The estate that supported this large, multi-faceted operation was monumental in both size and complexity. At its largest extent, it encompassed nearly 4,000 acres and occupied most of Shelburne Point, a substantial promontory that juts northward into Lake Champlain. The Webbs engaged a well-known architect, Robert H. Robertson, to design farm buildings and a mansion to fit the scale of the huge landscape they envisioned. And then they hired the most famous American landscape architect of the day, Frederick Law Olmsted, to make it all beautiful.

They were interested in the emerging science of forestry, and began establishing substantial plantations of trees. Between 1887 and 1900, as many as 155,000 trees were planted each year on the Shelburne Farms property by a staff of up to 400 men. Like the other activities Seward and Lila Webb undertook, their forestry was not minor in scale.

A huge Farm Barn (the turreted "fairy tale" barn) was built as the focus of all those activities. Four stories high and more than 400 feet long, it was equipped with gas lighting, a tower with a chiming clock, steam-driven hayforks, and an elevator. Its haylofts and granaries could hold 1,500 tons of crops. Its only rival in size on the estate was the Breeding Barn a half-mile to the south, which was the center of a complex of buildings devoted to Seward Webb's extensive horse raising and breeding operation. When it was completed in 1891, the Breeding Barn was said to enclose the "largest unsupported interior space in the United States."

Despite their interest in scientific forestry and agriculture and innovative technology, there is no direct evidence that the Webbs were influenced by the turn-of-the-century conservation movement that was just then emerging. Instead, it seems likely that in devoting their huge new estate to improving farming and forestry, they were, in fact, following the widespread sense of duty that many wealthy people of the day felt to contribute to the advance of American society. They were part of an informal movement that aimed to make American agriculture great—or at least, better than it had been. The presence of the landscape architect Olmsted in their planning suggests that connection, since he was an important transitional figure during the Gilded Age: He shuttled back and forth between the great estates, promoting (especially) improved scientific forestry, designing landscapes that would be both beautiful and ecologically sound, and espousing the ideals of land conservation.

Gradually, as the Progressive Era dawned and government took on more responsibility for improving farming and forestry, the role that the large estates had played just a few years earlier was forgotten, and the estates themselves began to be seen as white elephants.

∼

EVEN THE GREATEST VISION can topple from its own weight. Vast as it was, Shelburne Farms was never profitable. In fairness, it was not intended to operate purely as a business enterprise. The Webbs' original intention was to farm scientifically, to test and experiment with the best agricultural practices of the day, and to pass the resulting improvements on to farmers in Vermont and elsewhere. Making a profit on their operations was probably never possible, given the lavishness of their original vision.

Shelburne Farms' enormous size and overpowering complexity—along with the Webbs' growing financial difficulties, Seward Webb's declining health, new patterns of taxation, and social changes brought by the 20th century—led to the Farms' eventual decline.

By the early 1900s, the estate began to strain the Webb family's finances. Its farm operations did not generate any significant profit, and the investment and upkeep required to keep the farms going was very large—more, in fact, than even their substantial fortunes could support.

Over the next half-century or so, three generations of Webbs tried to make Shelburne Farms economically viable. Their hope was that it could become financially self-supporting, or at least not demand so much of their family money to keep it intact and operating. Some farm enterprises, notably dairying and beef production, turned a profit, but never enough to pay the ever-growing cost of owning and maintaining the sprawling estate and its buildings.

The capable farm management of third-generation owner, Derick V. Webb, was a turning point. His determination to make the farm operations profitable was, in fact, a milestone in the Farms' history, an important turn away from the idea that the Farms was primarily a luxurious, fabulously expensive family retreat. He wanted to run the place as a farm and enjoyed the hard work that farming always entails.

And he made some decisions that seemed to underline his rejection of the estate concept—such as locating the new dairy barn smack in the middle of what had been the family's private golf course! Derick Webb came as close as any member of the family had to turning Shelburne Farms into an actual operating farm, and his children grew up appreciating both the difficulties and benefits of a farm life.

Nevertheless, by the 1960s, the estate's great buildings had fallen into disrepair, and the overwhelming expenses of the operation continued to grow. It began to seem inevitable that the estate, which began with such a grand vision, would have to be subdivided and sold off.

But then something almost unbelievable happened. A new generation of Webbs had a different idea.

~

THE YOUNGEST WEBBS did not possess the immense wealth that Seward and Lila Webb had commanded. But they did have resources, chief among them the great estate itself and their strong commitment to it. They had grown up there—the first generation to live year-round on their family's pastoral estate—and they loved the place. Moreover, they were endowed with the idealism of youth, and coming of age at the dawn of the environmental movement of the 1960s and 1970s, were convinced that if they could keep Shelburne Farms intact, they could find a way to use the beautiful property to address the Earth's growing environmental problems. In the process, they hoped that they could make the Farms economically viable.

The environmental devastation wrought by an increasingly commercial society, warnings from scientists and naturalists, and the advocacy of environmental and conservation groups had raised the consciousness of the American public to the value of a whole, natural environment. At the same time, Vermont was attracting young idealists who wanted to live more simply, in closer contact with the land. Many of these urban refugees tried farming, and some actually stayed with it.

The younger generation of Webbs was inspired by both the new environmentalism and the back-to-the land movement. They discussed these ideas extensively, and eventually decided that they should use Shelburne Farms as a place to educate people about the intimate connection between people and the natural world.

"We were doing the planet in, and felt a place like this should be used for some higher purpose," Alec Webb said later. "We were coming out of a concern for the environment. It was more that than trying to preserve the family heritage."

They began small: a one-month educational summer camp in the early 1970s with about 15 youngsters sleeping in tents on one of the Farms' forested hillsides. They tended a garden and staffed a produce booth at the Burlington Farmers' Market on weekends. It grew from there.

Although the Webbs' vision faced large fiscal challenges throughout the 1970s and 1980s, their energy, resourcefulness, and a strong determination to keep the Farms together—plus hard work, generous supporters, and a few lucky breaks—ultimately proved to be enough.

Derick Webb's decision to bequeath his interests in the Farms to the nonprofit corporation his children established helped enormously. And fortuitously, two new Shelburne Farms enterprises became profitable and began to return income to the Farms as a whole. Those were the prize-winning cheddar cheeses produced from the herd of Brown Swiss dairy cows, and the restored and refurbished Shelburne House (the mansion on a hill), which became a high-end country inn. Both enterprises won honors and made money for the Farms.

∼

Today, the Farms' educational mission drives activities there. Shelburne Farms is devoted to promoting the idea—and the practice—of environmental sustainability.

Sustainability is the belief that humans can live and thrive within the earth's ecological limits. Farming, for example, can yield crops and, at the same time, maintain the fertility of the soil. People can live, work, and recreate in energy-efficient communities that conserve open land and are more reliant on renewable resources. Humankind can live carefully while sustaining nature's integrity. Sustainability is a practical environmentalism, akin to pastoralism, that includes human life as part of the equation. It's a new-fangled word for an old-fashioned Vermont value.

How does that play out in actual practice at Shelburne Farms?

On one recent summer morning, the Farms' broad fields were drenched in sunlight, and puffy, fair-weather clouds marched in ranks across the shimmering blue reaches of Lake Champlain. Barn swallows swooped and dove over the red brick walls of Shelburne House and the stately Coach Barn, while a host of gulls patrolled the broad waters beyond.

On the lawn and along the curving gravel roadways of the Farms, small groups of people—schoolteachers, as it turned out—were talking quietly, drawing maps. It was part of an exercise they had been assigned by Matt Dubel and Jen Cirillo, leaders of Shelburne Farms' Education for Sustainability Institute. Mapping, it was explained to them, is a way of expressing both the natural and the man-made features of any landscape. "It allows us to find a deep way into a particular place," Cirillo said. The connection between human activity and the natural world is important at Shelburne Farms because that is where stewardship, or exploitation, happens.

At Shelburne Farms, natural systems and human agricultural systems exist side-by-side. "Human needs are being met," Dubel said, "while the integrity of the ecosystems here are being maintained."

Twenty teachers came to the two-day workshop from all over the United States: Colorado, Hawaii, California, Massachusetts, Rhode Island, as well as Vermont. They were there to learn the practical skills they would need to teach sustainability and a conservation ethic to their students at home.

Young students from Vermont already participate in a wide variety of workshops and classes at Shelburne Farms. But the Education for Sustainability Institute enables Shelburne Farms' staff to share these practices of sustainability much more broadly, across the country and around the world.

"There's a certain number of students we can serve directly at the farms," Dubel said. "We're also trying to use what's done here as an inspiration and model for what these teachers can do back in their own home places."

Shelburne Farms is obviously valuable, not only as a teaching facility, but also as a unique place. Since it has been a working landscape for hundreds of years (and an inhabited landscape by Native Americans for thousands of years before that), it demonstrates implicitly that human life and natural communities cannot be separated.

The fact that it is strikingly beautiful doesn't hurt; in fact that helps make the point. Not only does the Farms' pastoral landscape attract people to come and learn, it also demonstrates the effects of stewardship and conservation: A sustainable landscape is a beautiful landscape. Thus the property is both a tool for teaching sustainability and a working example of that ethic and its benefits.

Less obvious than the beauty of the place, yet just as real and equally important, are the subtler signs of its current mission. At the Farms' sizable organic vegetable gardens in the fall, one is likely to see chickens picking over the cover crops of clover and winter rye. The extra vegetable matter in their diet makes the chickens happier and healthier—and they lay more nutritious eggs! Their manure helps fertilize the garden and is used in the farms' substantial composting operation. Pigs are allowed to root and feed in a fenced area of the forest and, incidentally, they fertilize the forest. Market Gardener Josh Carter says that he regards his primary responsibility as building healthy soil, and that the vegetables he grows are simply a by-product of that process.

Likewise, the grass and hay produced from the carefully tended fields sustains the Farms' Brown Swiss dairy herd. Rotational grazing and natural fertilizing methods, without the use of herbicides and pesticides, exemplify the holistic approach to agriculture. The award-winning cheese made from the fresh, untreated milk of those cows is rbST/rbGH free, a natural product.

The preservation and reuse of the Farms' magnificent set of historic buildings helps preserve the unique history of the land, and also provides space for a variety of small enterprises that are linked to the ideal of sustainability. In the lower reaches of the historic Farm Barn, for instance, the O Bread Bakery bakes its natural and organic breads—and makes the Shelburne Farms' administrative staff upstairs hungry whenever they turn out a fresh and fragrant batch of cinnamon-raisin bread. In the same building, Beeken Parsons furniture makers hand craft wooden furniture—some of the pieces made from wood harvested from the Farms' managed forests. Those forests are also the source each spring of maple sap that is boiled into Vermont maple syrup. This syrup winds up on the tables of The Inn at Shelburne Farms.

In the summer, day campers at the Farms learn the dynamics of organic market gardening—and ride their bikes from place to place along the Farms' gravel roads to help cut down on motor traffic. Guests at the inn and customers at the Welcome Center get a subtle education in the principles of sustainability along with their purchases of the award-winning Shelburne Farms cheddar cheese. Like the teachers trained in the annual Education for Sustainability Institute, when they return home many of those visitors and inn guests will become quiet ambassadors for sustainable farming and simpler, more ecological ways of living.

Thus the beauty of the land on Shelburne Point is being put to use in a practical way that promotes a concept vital to the future of our earth. Thanks to a carefully nurtured vision and strong determination, Shelburne Farms is, in its own way, making a difference in Vermont, and the world. In all this there is a clear echo of the purpose for which the Farms was founded more than a century ago.

To suggest that a piece of land, even a very lovely piece, has a "destiny" is a Romantic notion, and probably a foolish one. But to suggest, conversely, that humankind decides and controls the ultimate fate of any piece of land is to fall prey to a disastrous kind of arrogance.

It is only where we relinquish our false sense of mastery, listen carefully to the land, and work cooperatively with it that its destiny can truly be expressed. We are not separate from the natural world, far less superior to it. We are part of it. That sense of cooperation between humankind and the land is at the heart of the pastoral vision, a vision that has been vital in shaping the destiny of Shelburne Farms.

At the Farms today, we have a clear example of what listening carefully to a piece of land can mean—and accomplish. Here, a vision that shaped the land was itself, ultimately shaped by the land. A private estate that overwhelmed even a vast private fortune has, through an act of creative relinquishment, become a public resource. The Farms' rolling hills and open fields have a clear mission now—one that the world desperately needs.

— *Tom Slayton*
February 2010

PREFACE

It has been said that the special collections of today are the rare books of tomorrow. However, it is unlikely that Edward F. Gebhardt—Shelburne Farms' longtime farm manager and valued employee—ever imagined that the detailed business correspondence and estate records he and his staff created during his forty years of employment would have survived another fifty or more years in the attic and north tower of the Farm Barn to become a vital collection in the Shelburne Farms Archives.

During the 1970s, it was equally unlikely that the fourth-generation Webb family members, their friends, and associates ever contemplated the long-term historical significance of the records they created in the process of forming Shelburne Farms Resources, Inc. They were young and heady with optimism for the future of their fledgling nonprofit, whose complex mission was rooted in environmental education and back-to-the land initiatives.

One of the five articles of association written in 1972 for Shelburne Farms Resources, Inc., read, "To enable maximum realization of the potential of Shelburne Farms' function as an educational resource." Realizing and enabling this potential required utilizing historic resources in the promotion and growth of educational and environmental outreach programs. For example, in 1974 Shelburne House opened for the first time in its history as a place to host public workshops, conferences, and performances. Just five years later, in 1979, Shelburne Farms Resources promoted the first regular public tours of the property. To further the organization's rapidly growing programs and early institutional growth, subsequent historic building and landscape restoration projects were undertaken.

In the early 1980s, as Shelburne Farms launched capital campaigns, cheese-making endeavors, and a host of expanded educational programs, there was a growing awareness of the potential and value of the marvelous yet abandoned records chronicling the long-ago life and stories of Shelburne Farms. Bolstered by support from its trustees and staff, as well as the State Archives of Vermont, in 1988 Shelburne Farms submitted a grant proposal to the NHPRC (National Historical Publications and Records Commission). The project envisioned would "carry out a formal program for the Shelburne Farms archives" that involved preserving, arranging, and describing the large collection of archival gems.

Thanks to the generosity of granting agencies as well as a group of private funders, a climate-controlled Archive officially opened in the basement of the Inn on June 10, 1992. Its purpose was to house a large and important cache of family papers, which included personal journals and photograph albums as well as property records, ledgers, correspondence, photographs, log books, business catalogs, architectural plans, maps, and scrapbooks relevant to the founding of the Shelburne Farms estate.

By creating a repository for such a collection, Shelburne Farms did not simply preserve physical records. It fostered—and continues to foster—the gathering of the stories of Shelburne Farms through recorded oral histories, the donation of manuscripts and objects, and further scholarly research into the collections.

Today, the Shelburne Farms Archives and collections are an invaluable resource to staff and volunteers as well as to students, collectors, researchers, professionals in the field, and the general public. Many are inspired by the completeness of this remarkable collection, and certainly without its completeness, a comprehensive book such as this could not have been written.

Thanks to the commitment of Shelburne Farms and the generosity of donors, the archival collections provide continuity and exactness for preserving and sharing the rich history of a Gilded Age country estate and the evolving story of Shelburne Farms as a nonprofit venture. We must realize that if these stories are not preserved and shared, it will be as if this important place in Vermont never existed at all.

— *Julie Eldridge Edwards*
CURATOR OF COLLECTIONS
FEBRUARY 2010

AUTHOR'S ACKNOWLEDGMENTS

THIS BOOK WAS MADE POSSIBLE by the invaluable assistance and support of many individuals. A debt of gratitude is due to the members of the Webb family who shared memories and photographs and reviewed portions of the manuscript, among them Laura Brown, Megan Camp, Deenie and Steve Galipeau, Kitty Webb Harris, Mary Kelly, Marilyn Neagley, Lisa and John Roberts, Elizabeth Smith, Alec Webb, Marshall Webb, Quentyn Webb, Richard Webb, and Samuel B. Webb Jr. Of these family members, a special debt is owed to Alec Webb, Marshall Webb, and Megan Camp, who shared the vision for the project, spent many hours answering questions and reviewing drafts, and patiently waited more than nine years for the book's successful completion.

Many other members of the Shelburne Farms community, including current and former employees, volunteers, and residents, played an invaluable role. Of special note are David Barash, Rick Bessette, Jane Boisvert, Julie Bressor, Holly Brough, Harriet Elstner, Gerald Francis, Rosalyn Graham, Eileen Growald, Marcia Hawkins, Audrey Lewis, Donald Maynard, Shirley Murray, Rita Myers, Tom Nold, Barbara Steen Paulman, Gordon Paterson, Keenis Patterson, Catherine Quinn, Meredith Scott, Hilary Sunderland, and Lola Van Wagenen. More than anyone else, Julie Eldridge Edwards provided vital assistance to the project.

Numerous other individuals offered assistance, shared advice, reviewed drafts, and facilitated access to materials in their collections, including Bill Alexander and Stephanie Gardener at Biltmore Estate; Martha Briggs at the Newberry Library; Phillip Buffinton; Sylvia Bugbee, Chris Burns, Prudence Doherty, and Connell Gallagher in the Special Collections Department of the University of Vermont's Bailey/Howe Library; Paul Carnahan at the Vermont Historical Society; T. Michele Clark and Michael Daws at the Frederic Law Olmsted National Historic Site; Polly Darnell and Rick Peters at Shelburne Museum; Jane Dorney; Bill Fullerton; Jeff Groff, Maggie Lidz, Helena Richardson, and Neville Thompson at Winterthur Museum; Colleen Haag, Pat Morrow, and Lisa Mann at the Shelburne Town Clerk's Office; Marissa Hendricks at the Rare Books and Manuscript Library of the University of Pennsylvania; Mark Huyler at the University of Massachusetts Amherst; Charles Lacy; Doris Maeck; Marjorie McNinch at Hagley Museum and Library; Jonathan Schoenfeld; Tom Slayton; Sloane Stephens; Richard Tracy; and Mary

Twitchell. Editor Alan Berolzheimer, at the Vermont Historical Society, and copyeditor Judith Bellamy provided excellent guidance. Designer Ann Aspell created a beautiful look for the book, and Carrie Mardorf at Heritage Landscapes expertly prepared its maps.

This book could not have been accomplished without the valuable work of the following historians, whose scholarship paved the way: Julie Bressor, Margaret Campbell, Julie Eldridge Edwards, Alan Emmet, Robbe Foreman, Gerald Francis, Susan Hayward, Gail Henderson King, William Lipke, Patricia O'Donnell, Catherine Quinn, and John Stimson.

On a personal level, I thank my husband, Donald, and son, Jack, for putting up with the many late nights and weekends I spent on this project. And finally, I dedicate this book to the late J. Richard Huyler, who would have been proud.

— *Erica Huyler Donnis*
February 2010

Note on editorial method

In order to preserve the color and tone of the original sources, spelling and grammatical errors in quotations were left intact, except when extreme confusion might result.

WITH THANKS

Shelburne Farms profoundly thanks the benefactors who made this book possible:

For sponsorship of the Shelburne Farms Archives and the publication of this book:
Kitty Webb Harris and the Kate Jennings Charitable Trust

For the initial challenge grant to launch this special project:
Members of the Nash family and The Nash Foundation

For the matching funds to meet The Nash Foundation challenge:
Holly Anne Barany, and Michael, Peter, and Sean Darling, in memory of Holly Webb Froud
Charles Reynolds
Anonymous

We stand on the shoulders of those who came before us and are forever grateful for the continuing care, generosity, expertise, and inspiration of everyone making the vision of Shelburne Farms possible today.

∼

BOARD OF DIRECTORS, FEBRUARY 2010

Julia Alvarez	Will Jackson	Gail Neale
Bob Baird	Nan Jenks-Jay	Lisa Steele
Fred Bay	Steve Johnson	Charlotte Stetson
Birgit Deeds	David Marvin	Lola Van Wagenen
Mary Jane Gentry	Andrew Meyer	Hub Vogelmann
David Hollenbeck	Casey Murrow	Alec Webb

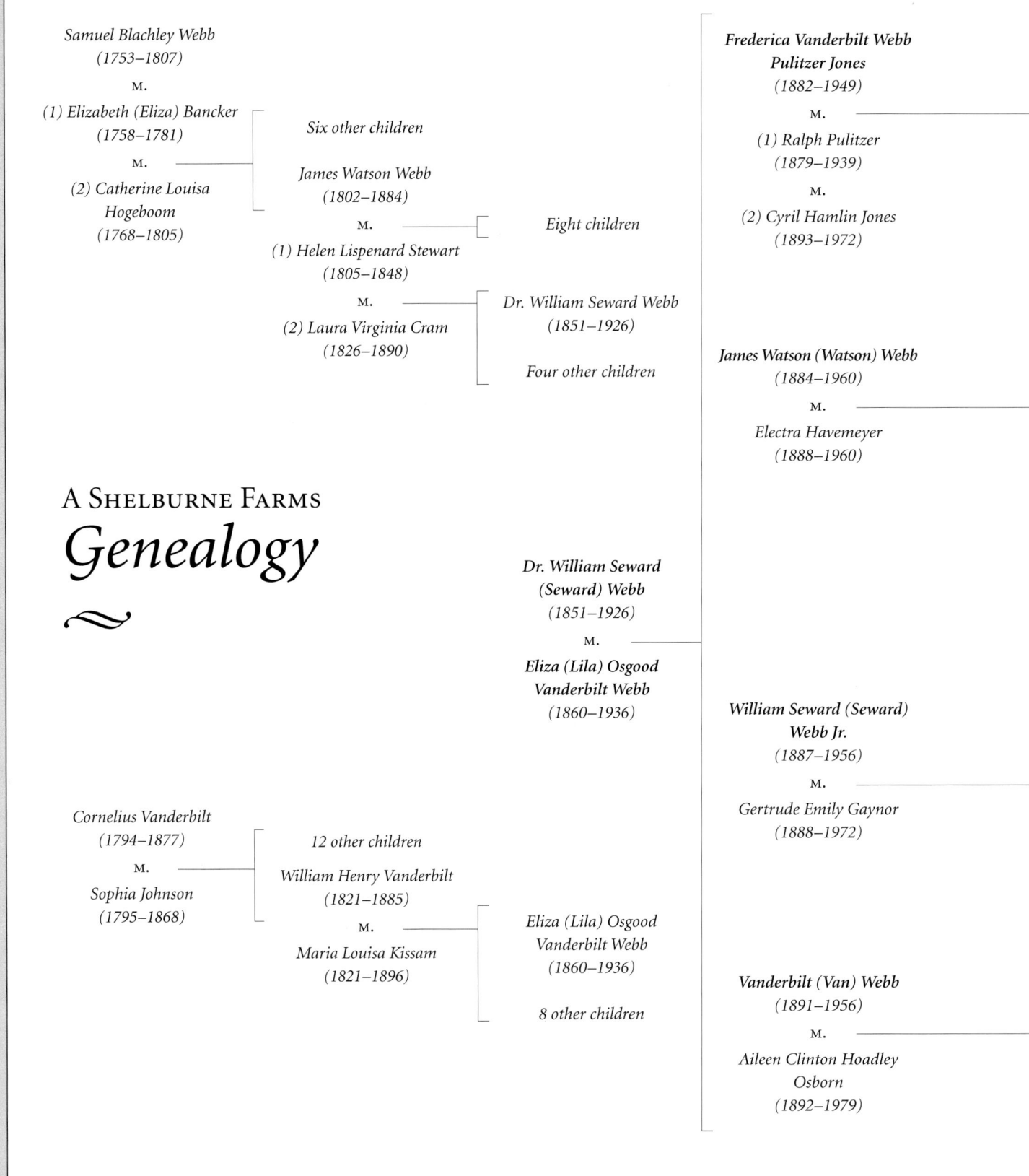

A Shelburne Farms
Genealogy

Ralph Pulitzer Jr. (1906–1965)
Seward Webb Pulitzer (1911–1972) —————— *Sally, Seward, Mary Jane*

Electra Webb Bostwick (1910–1982)
                m.   *Electra, Lillian, Dundeen, Elliot*
Dunbar Wright Bostwick (1908–2006)

Samuel Blachley Webb Sr. (1912–1988)
                m.   *Holly Webb Darling Froud (1936–2001)*
(1) Elizabeth Fiske Johnson (1914–1990)   *Samuel Blachley Webb Jr. (b. 1939)*
                m.
(2) Martha Young (1910–1989)

Lila Vanderbilt Webb Wilmerding (1913–1961)
                m.   *John, Lila, James Watson*
John Currie Wilmerding (1911–1965)

James Watson (Watson) Webb Jr. (1916–2000)

Harry Havemeyer Webb (1922–1975)
                m.   *Kate (Kitty) Brewster Webb Harris (b. 1948)*
Kate DeForest Jennings (1927–2002)   *Laura Havemeyer Webb Brown (b. 1950)*
                                                      Dundeen (Deenie) Cromwell Webb Galipeau (b. 1952)

William Seward Webb III (1912–1984) —— *Susan, William Seward IV*
Frederica Webb Gamble (b. 1913) —— *David, Frederica*
Jacob Louis Webb (1919–1999)
Gertrude (Punchie) Webb Meades (1925–2009) —— *Michael, Jamie*
William Gaynor Webb (1930–2003) —— *Eliza, Electra, Angela*

Frederick (Derick) Vanderbilt Webb (1913–1984)   *Derick (Quentyn) Osborn Webb (b. 1946)*
                m.   *Marshall Canfield Webb (b. 1948)*
(1) Elizabeth Canfield (b. 1924)   *Mary Webb Phillips Kelly (b. 1950)*
                m.   *Alexander (Alec) Stewart Webb (b. 1952)*
(2) Helen (Rusty) Allen (b. 1926)   *Elizabeth (Lisa) Webb Roberts (b. 1955)*
                                                      Robert Maynard Webb (b. 1958)
William Osborn Webb (1914–2002) —— *Killian, Garrett*
Barbara Webb Rockwell Henry (1916–1991) —— *Gael, Martha, Seth, Lynn*
Alexander Stewart Webb (1918–1918)
Richard Humphrey Webb (b. 1921) —— *Richard (Tom), Paul, Bradford, Van, Faith, Bayard*

THE HISTORY OF SHELBURNE FARMS

Chapter 1

BEGINNINGS

Shelburne Farms lies on the edge of Lake Champlain, in the heart of northwestern Vermont's Champlain Valley. The lake laps at the estate's western border, a series of rocky lakeshore cliffs from which the Farm's rolling hills and woodlands stretch inland for approximately one and a half miles. In the distance to the west rise the Adirondack peaks of New York State; to the east, the foothills of Vermont's Green Mountains.

The land that now comprises Shelburne Farms has witnessed tremendous change over the centuries. It was submerged under glaciers and lake water during prehistoric times, heavily forested and used as a hunting ground by Native Americans, cleared for use as farmland by European settlers, and finally consolidated into a single, large agricultural estate. The Shelburne Farms property itself has existed in its present form for only 120 years.

At the heart of Shelburne Farms is the land itself. Breathtakingly scenic and lush, it remains a place of reverence for many. In the nineteenth century, the Morehouse family farmed a parcel of land in the center of the future estate. Jean (Jennie) Morehouse Edwards (1850–1943) recalled a peaceful childhood spent there in the years before the start of the Civil War. Her memories as a young girl of fetching the cows for milking with her brother Clarke on a spring evening are steeped in an appreciation for the land:

We first passed by the apple orchard, filled with blossoms in May, and looked forward to the time when the pipin tree in the nearest corner would be loaded with fruit. We then let down the bars and went down the long lane. Near the foot of it was a basswood tree and…Clarke would jump over the fence and get a branch off it, take his jack knife out of his pocket, and soon we would have two nice basswood whistles, and on we would go blowing our whistles. Then there were more bars to let

Aerial view of Shelburne Farms, by Marshall C. Webb, c. 1998. Shelburne Farms Collections.

down and we were in fine shade all the rest of the way as we passed some beautiful woods…Soon we came to a place where wild flowers grew, and we were over the fence in a hurry. Early in May we found quantities of hepatica, and later there were anemone, violets, bellwort, adder's-tongue, blood-root, trillium, lady's slippers, Solomon's seal, maidenhair and other beautiful ferns. Hastily we gathered our hands full, not forgetting that we had come after the cows. We let down the last bars, climbed a fence and began calling in a loud voice, "Co Boss, Co Boss." The cows away down by the lake in a cedar swamp, where they had gone to keep cool, heard our voices, and soon the leader started and all the rest followed. We kept on calling for the fun of it, and soon Spot and Blackie and Betsy and Peggy and all the rest came trudging up the long lane, as they knew it was milking time.[1]

In April of 1922, some sixty years after Jennie and Clarke Morehouse walked through their family's pastures and woods, estate founder Lila Webb (1860–

1936) climbed to the highest point on the property to admire the panoramic view it afforded. She described her experiences in a letter to her husband, Seward, later that day:

Dearest Seward,
Such a heavenly day, & I walked up to Lone Tree Hill this afternoon, & spent over an hour there, thinking of that day so many many years ago when you & I went up there & decided we would buy this property. My, but it was beautiful this afternoon. I wish you could have seen it, with the snow on Mansfield, & yet the sun so warm & bright, & no wind, so that it was comfortable for over an hour...I wish you could have been here! There is no place in the world to me quite like Shelburne, and there never will be.[2]

PREHISTORY[3]

The qualities of the Shelburne Farms landscape that have attracted many of its residents and admirers—its scenic beauty, rich agricultural soils, and proximity to Lake Champlain—were created by the accidents of geologic change. The Adirondack and Green Mountain ranges, which began their development about 1.3 billion years ago, shelter the land and the freshwater lake in the Champlain Valley, creating some of the best growing conditions in the state of Vermont. As Christopher Klyza and Stephen Trombulak have noted, "The climate of the Champlain Valley is the mildest anywhere in the state. The Adirondack Mountains to the west block much of the snow that would otherwise move into the region during the winter, and [Lake Champlain] itself moderates the temperatures throughout most of the year."[4] The region has one of the longest growing seasons in the state, an average of 150 days.

The Champlain Valley is blessed with rich, fertile soil, created as the landscape evolved. The precursor to Lake Champlain, which developed about 15,000 to 12,500 years ago as the climate warmed and the last glacier melted, filled the valley and lapped at the lower elevations of the Adirondack and Green Mountains. Through its waters filtered eroding mountain sediments, which settled over glacial rock litter on the submerged valley floor. Once exposed as the lake receded to its present size, the earth on the valley floor proved to be exceptionally fertile ground for native plant growth and crop cultivation.

The first human inhabitants of the Champlain Valley probably arrived about 12,000 to 10,000 years ago. Over succeeding generations, they adapted their diet and lifestyle to the species that thrived as the region's landscape progressed from glacier, to tundra, to woodlands. They gradually began to rely on woodland plants and animals, which included "bear, deer, seals, small mammals, turkey and other birds...berries, nuts, roots, seeds, and other edible plants."[5] As the seasons changed, the native peoples capitalized on the availability of their food sources by moving to and from a series of camps located near sources of fresh water.

About 4,000 years ago, Native Americans residing in the broader New England area began to cultivate plants in addition to hunting, fishing, and gathering. This change in focus resulted in the development of larger settled villages around which crops were cultivated. Yet many historians believe that agriculture remained only a supplement to hunting, fishing, and gathering activities in northern Vermont, including the Champlain Valley. The landscape in the Champlain Valley region, and Shelburne Farms in particular, probably remained heavily forested until the arrival of European settlers in the mid- to late eighteenth century.

Archaeological evidence indicates that the Shelburne Farms area was used by Native Americans for seasonal hunting, fishing, and gathering. At least forty-nine archaeological sites are known to exist in the town of Shelburne. Sites within the historic boundaries of Shelburne Farms include ones located on Shelburne Point to the north; the shores of McCabes Brook and the LaPlatte River to the east; the wetlands near Saxton's Point to the west; and an area in the center of the estate, near a small stream leading to the LaPlatte River. (See maps on pages 278–82.) Although further study is required, one archaeologist has speculated that projectile points and other artifacts found at the latter site could indicate either "a very large settlement—one of the largest recorded anywhere in Vermont from this time period—or the site of recurring occupations over an extended period of time."[6]

The descendants of the area's first inhabitants, known today as the Western Abenaki, consider the Champlain Valley fundamental to their sense of being. As historian Jan Albers has commented, "The best evidence that the Champlain Basin is the ancestral home of the Abenaki is that all their most vital myths are centered on its shores."[7] Rock Dunder, a small island in Lake Champlain not

far from Shelburne Farms' northern border, is a sacred point central to the Abenaki creation myth:

> *The creator of Burlington Bay and the surrounding area, Odzihozo (He Who Shapes Himself), molded himself from the dust of the cosmos. As his hands and arms pushed the earth, the Green Mountains and Adirondacks emerged. When he rose to walk around the land, the impression left by his body formed the lake itself, with one leg on either side of the Champlain Islands. Ultimately, he decided to rest from his labors, and settled down to enjoy this beautiful spot for all eternity.*[8]

EUROPEAN ARRIVAL

Historians estimate that approximately 4,000 Abenaki resided in the Champlain Valley when Samuel de Champlain explored the region, later named in his honor, for France in the summer of 1609. However, Champlain did not record any encounters with the Abenaki during the several weeks that he spent in the area. Recent clashes with the Iroquois and Mohawk may have caused them to retreat inland toward the Green Mountains into safer territory. Any Abenaki who were living in the valley during the first decades of the seventeenth century were probably greatly affected by an epidemic of smallpox introduced by European settlers in 1633, which eventually killed an estimated ninety percent of the area's native population.[9]

By the 1630s, Lake Champlain had become an efficient means of transportation for fur traders foraying into the region from French territories to the north and British territories to the south. It had also become a major staging ground for hostilities between the European powers and their Native American allies. Lake Champlain and its shores were frequent battlegrounds in the series of conflicts commonly known as the French and Indian Wars. The Abenaki aligned themselves with the French, a choice that resulted in their retreat to far northern Vermont and the Canadian territories after the British were victorious in 1763. Probably very few native peoples were left in the Champlain Valley by the late eighteenth century.[10]

The end of the conflicts in 1763 opened much of the Champlain Valley to European settlement. In fact, the town of Shelburne, a total of 14,272 acres, was chartered by England's King George III that same year. The charter's terms for land ownership promoted residential settlement, the practice of agriculture, and the harvesting of trees, setting the stage for the land use pattern that continues to this day.[11]

Shelburne's town charter was sponsored by New Hampshire's Royal Governor, Benning Wentworth, as part of his efforts to claim the territory now within Vermont state borders for his colony. Wentworth's activities were in direct opposition to the claims of the neighboring colony of New York. Shel-

Left: Rock Dunder in Lake Champlain, date unknown. Vermont Historical Society.

burne, in fact, was named in honor of the Earl of Shelburne, a chief supporter of Wentworth's claims in British Parliament. The validity of Shelburne's charter was not fully resolved until several years after the end of the Revolutionary War, when an agreement was reached to compensate New York for annexed lands as part of the admission of the state of Vermont into the United States in 1791.[12]

The Onion River Land Company, a speculative venture established by brothers Ethan and Ira Allen and their family, played an important role in developing a substantial portion of Shelburne, as well as numerous other towns in northwestern Vermont. At its height, the Onion River Land Company owned approximately 65,000 acres bordering the Winooski (Onion) River and the shores of Lake Champlain. The Allens promoted the resale of their holdings to settlers in New York and southern New England. A surveyor by trade, Ira Allen (1751–1816) bought up most of the original Shelburne land deeds shortly after the town's establishment. In 1775, he surveyed the town and divided it into plots, which he soon began selling off to new settlers. Allen remained a major landowner in town until the close of the eighteenth century.[13]

Early Settlement

The earliest evidence of European settlement in Shelburne dates to the late 1760s. By the start of the Revolutionary War in 1776, approximately ten families had settled in Shelburne, most likely establishing subsistence-level farms on which they would support themselves, their families, and their livestock. At least two early settlers also harvested oak from their properties for the Canadian lumber market. However, residents all but abandoned Shelburne and the surrounding area when the Revolutionary War began and the Lake Champlain corridor became an active battleground again. One wartime account notes that Shelburne contained "naught but desolation, no living person there."[14]

The end of the war in 1783 brought a return of habitation and redoubled settlement activities to the region at large, including Shelburne. Many former residents returned to their property, and new settlers arrived in large numbers. By the time of the first federal census of 1790, Shelburne's population consisted of 387 people.[15]

The land that became Shelburne Farms was settled by a number of families who arrived in Shelburne in the 1780s and 1790s, among them the Comstocks, Morehouses, Nashes, Saxtons, Smiths, and Tracys. Many of them had ties to Ira Allen, and many arrived in Shelburne after periods of time spent in other pioneer towns. Norwich, Connecticut, native Daniel Comstock (1742–1816), who brought a family of nine children to Shelburne, owned 314 acres by 1798. In the 1840s, Comstock's son Levi (b. circa 1793) built a two-story brick home south of Lone Tree Hill.[16]

Hezekiah Tracy (1746–1827) arrived in town in the 1780s after a brief period in Pawlet, Vermont, and a stint as a private in the Vermont militia during the Revolutionary War, where he served under Ira Allen. He and his wife, Eunice (1750–1808), had thirteen children. Hezekiah's son Ezekiel (1790–1873) farmed about 100 acres on the southwestern side of Shelburne Point, a spit of land jutting north into Lake Champlain.[17]

Another early settler was Quaker blacksmith William Smith, who arrived in Shelburne in about 1783 with his wife, Elizabeth, and their four sons and two daughters. The Smiths resided on a teardrop-shaped peninsula of land that extended west into Lake Champlain and was linked with the mainland by a narrow, marshy isthmus. The area where they lived was commonly known as "Quaker Smith's Point" or "Quaker Smith Point" by the late 1790s. The land may have been so named as a way of distinguishing the Smiths who lived there from other Smith families in town, who practiced other religions.[18]

After serving as a colonel in the Berkshire (Massachusetts) Company during the Revolution-

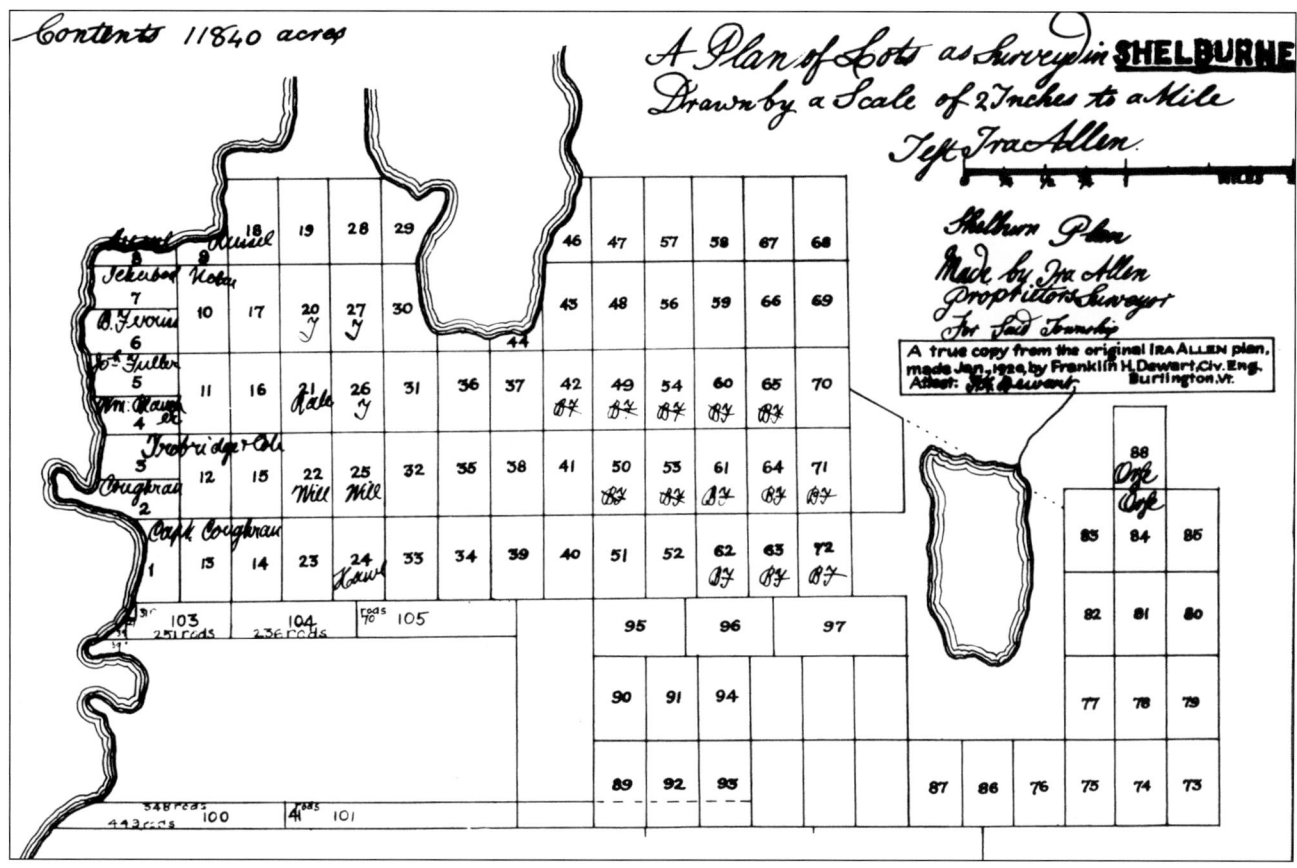

Plan of Lots as Surveyed in Shelburne, a copy of Ira Allen's 1775 plan by Franklin Dewart, 1920. Shelburne Town Clerk's Office.

ary War, Frederick Saxton (1748–96) became a prominent landowner in the city of Burlington, about ten miles north of Shelburne. However, by 1790, he owed both Ira Allen and Allen's brother Levi considerable sums of money. Saxton's 1791 exchange of all his land in Burlington for 375 acres belonging to Ira Allen in Shelburne may have served as a debt settlement.[19]

Saxton's new residence was located north of the Comstock family's land, at the base of a high, rocky outcropping jutting out into Lake Champlain, which became known as Saxton's Point. By the mid-nineteenth century, the Saxton family farm consisted of a complex of buildings, including a two-story Greek Revival style house and a group of barns and outbuildings.[20]

Sturgis Morehouse (1754–1813) arrived in Shelburne in 1783 from the Stamford, Connecticut, area with his wife and six children. He bought acreage in the eastern part of town from several property owners, including Ira Allen. In the 1830s and early 1840s, Sturgis's grandson Franklin Hawley Morehouse (1804–62) purchased farmland within the future Shelburne Farms boundaries. He settled with his family on a parcel south of Lone Tree Hill.[21]

A native of Sheffield, Massachusetts, Asahel Nash (1758–1822) arrived around 1786 after stints in northeastern Pennsylvania, western Massachusetts, and Essex, Vermont. He and his wife, Betsy (1766–21), settled along the lake-

The Saxton family house, while serving as the Webb family coachman's house, c. 1892. Shelburne Farms Collections.

shore just north of the Saxton farm in an area that came to be known as Orchard Point. One of their twelve children, Asahel Jr. (1794–1878), purchased the family's 120-acre homestead farm from them in 1822, just before Asahel Sr. died. Asahel Jr.'s brothers Truman (1789–1860) and John (1796–1889) settled close by.[22]

By the beginning of the nineteenth century, the land that would become Shelburne Farms had been settled by more than seven families that had emigrated from other sections of Vermont and New England. The new settlers' adjoining farms, with their developing fields, woodlots, houses, and barns, would influence the character of the property into the twentieth century.

Farming the Land

By 1800, the town of Shelburne supported two important industries: a sawmill founded by Ira Allen, located in the middle of town on the LaPlatte River at Shelburne Falls; and the Shelburne Shipyard near the tip of Shelburne Point, which would become "the dominant shipyard for building and maintaining steamboats on Lake Champlain" by the 1820s.[23] However, the development of Shelburne at large mirrored that of the state of Vermont: most residents had established farms to support themselves and their families.[24]

Like the Abenaki, the European settlers tended to situate their residences near sources of fresh water, whether it was Lake Champlain itself, the LaPlatte River, or a brook or stream providing a steady, year-round supply. However, while the Abenaki had left the land primarily forested for use as a hunting ground, the European settlers cleared the majority of the property for agricultural pasturage and cropland. Early Vermont historian Abby Hemenway notes that soon after the settlement boom of the late eighteenth century, "The forests began to disappear; cultivated fields were to be seen in almost every part of the township; highways were laid out and opened; bridges erected across the streams;…rail and log fences [replaced] the brush fence which inclosed the clearings originally."[25]

By the mid-nineteenth century, the land that would become Shelburne Farms consisted predominantly of open fields, with only isolated stands of trees left to serve as woodlots for fuel and building materials. The changes to the Shelburne Farms landscape were not an anomaly in the region. "Agriculture was the predominant cause of the dramatic changes to the Vermont landscape that occurred from 1760 to 1870…[A]s of 1861, 4.5 million acres of Vermont—roughly three quarters of the state—were classified farmland, and 3 million of these acres were improved."[26]

An important use for the lumber produced by clearing land was the construction of houses and barns. Hemenway notes that most of Shelburne's early European settlers built log houses. The construction of the first two frame houses in 1784 and 1789, likely made possible by Ira Allen's new sawmill, was momentous enough to be carefully recorded for posterity. However, several decades probably elapsed before frame houses became standard. Connecticut missionary Nathan Perkins, who passed through Shelburne in 1789, found the living conditions in the area to be rather poor: "Set out…to Shelburn through ye wilderness on ye Lake Champlain…mud up to my horse's belly… I got lost…found a little log cabin hut & put up there…no supper—my horse no feed—Slept on a Chaff-bed without covering—a man, wife & 3 children all in ye same nasty stinking room."[27]

Nathan Perkins's memoir notwithstanding, few specifics are known about the lives and livelihoods of settlers on Shelburne Farms land during the late eighteenth and early to mid-nineteenth centuries.

However, some idea may be gleaned from what occurred in Vermont and the Champlain Valley at large. One group of historians has noted that

Vermont farms were, by modern standards, small yet remarkably diverse. While farm properties averaged one hundred acres or more during this era, farm families rarely cultivated more than twenty acres. In part, that reflected the prevailing tendency to rotate lands, allowing fallow land time to regenerate vital nutrients before reusing it. On the cleared acreage itself, farmers labored to produce wheat, rye, and barley for the family's consumption, along with an array of vegetables including peas, turnips, and pumpkins. They raised corn and hay primarily for the livestock, which usually included cattle, pigs, sheep, and horses. Hemp and flax were planted to provide the raw materials for the family's clothing. Orchards were also common, with apple cider deemed more healthy than water.[28]

Champlain Valley farmers of the late eighteenth and early nineteenth centuries managed diverse, primarily self-sufficient operations. They probably raised enough produce and livestock to cover their own food needs, with a small amount of surplus to sell for profit and/or pay their taxes. While many sold or traded that surplus locally, at least some found outside markets in Canada, the Hudson River Valley area of New York State, and even southern New England. Of all long-distance markets, Canada was perhaps the most important to area farmers at this time, as Lake Champlain provided an inexpensive method of transporting their products northward. Indeed, citizens of Shelburne were among those who protested against President Thomas Jefferson's embargo against trade with Canada, which became law in 1808. Some Champlain Valley farmers defied the embargo and secretly shipped goods across the border.

The loss of the Canadian market after 1808 was offset in a few years by the opportunities provided by the outbreak of the War of 1812. Approximately 2,000 soldiers from the 11th United States Infantry were stationed nearby in the city of Burlington, and an additional number of sailors from the fledgling United States Navy established winter quarters in Shelburne Bay and Vergennes, sixteen miles to the south. Although the proximity of American troops and their British counterparts, who were massed along the Canadian border, brought the threat of war home to local residents, it also significantly increased demand for foodstuffs. Champlain Valley farmers found a ready market for their meats and grains, and some area farmers even surreptitiously sold items at huge profit to the British army.[29]

In the 1820s, two external forces provided new prospects to farmers in the region at large. The 1823 completion of the Champlain Canal, which connected Lake Champlain with the Hudson River and the eastern end of the Erie Canal, drastically reduced shipping costs to New York City and upstate New York. Vermont farmers were now able to sell their goods to a much wider market at more competitive prices. As a result, many moved toward commercial agriculture, specializing in one or two main products that would appeal to the demands of their new markets. These included "beef,…grain, live cattle and horses, maple sugar, pork, potash, dairy products, timber products, and wool."[30]

The introduction of tariffs on imported wool in 1824, and their subsequent strengthening during the late 1820s and early 1830s, made American wool much more competitively priced and sheep farming much more profitable. The Merino sheep boom, which reached its zenith during the late 1830s and early 1840s, affected agriculture across Vermont. By 1840, the Champlain Valley was a center of wool production in the state. Sheep farming required an especially large amount of pasturage to be profitable, encouraging the consolidation of farms into the hands of fewer individuals and the clearing of even more land.

Many Shelburne residents had invested heavily in sheep by 1840. In that year, agricultural census records indicate that the town produced 36,677 pounds of wool from 17,636 sheep. Other important cash crops included oats and potatoes. Shelburne farmers also raised cattle, swine, and poultry, as well as the field crops needed to sustain these livestock.[31]

Over the ensuing decades, Shelburne farmers responded to regional and national changes in agricultural markets, adjusting their cash crops accordingly. The wool market declined during the 1840s and 1850s as a result of tariff reductions and increased competition from farmers in the western United States. The advent of railroads, which arrived in Vermont in the late 1840s and 1850s, made the long-distance transportation of perishable dairy products such as butter, cheese, and fluid milk more feasible. While some Shelburne farmers continued to raise fairly large sheep flocks into the 1870s, during the mid- to late nineteenth century, many dramatically increased their dairy herds and focused instead on selling butter and milk.

Farmers in the Shelburne Farms area were luckier than many in Vermont: they cultivated some of the most fertile soil in the region. Many of those farming the more mountainous regions of the state had depleted the productivity of their acreage by the mid- to late nineteenth century. One to three generations of clearing trees from the hilly land and intensive use of the land for pasture and crops resulted in soil erosion and exhaustion. On the contrary, the rich soils of the Champlain Valley continued to produce, and Champlain Valley farmers retained a level of prosperity not often experienced in hill towns.

A Snapshot of the Area in the Mid-Nineteenth Century

By 1850, most residents on the land that would become Shelburne Farms managed farms of about 100 to 250 acres in size. Many focused upon one

Selected Shelburne Farm Data from the 1880 Federal Agricultural Census

Farmer	Acreage	Primary Livestock	Primary Agricultural Produce	Estimated Value of Farm, including land, buildings, implements, and livestock
Mary Holabird	125	6 dairy cattle 70 sheep	400 pounds of butter 300 bushels of apples	$7,650
Edgar Nash	140	8 dairy cattle 50 sheep	1,800 pounds of butter 75 pounds of wool 600 bushels of apples	$12,700
Edward S. Saxton	165	9 dairy cattle	2,000 pounds of fluid milk 240 pounds of butter 1,200 bushels of apples	$7,400
Guy Tracy	460	32 dairy cattle 20 chickens	3,500 pounds of butter 600 dozen eggs 200 bushels of apples	$17,000

to three primary income-producing agricultural products such as butter, cheese, eggs, or apples. They supported their dairy herds by growing field crops such as Indian corn, and they sustained their families by raising additional livestock, such as pigs, and crops, including oats, barley, wheat, rye, potatoes, and garden vegetables. Many owned their own woodlots, from which they heated their homes and built fences, houses, and barns. Most possessed several horses to till their land and pull their vehicles.[32]

At seventy acres, Franklin Morehouse's farm was one of the smallest in the area that became Shelburne Farms. In 1850, the forty-six-year-old farmer's primary sources of income were wool, produced by a flock of sixty sheep, and butter, produced by his four dairy cows. He also possessed a few additional cattle and pigs, and a team of horses to work his fields of wheat, rye, Indian corn, oats, and potatoes. An orchard provided him with a crop of apples. He sold at least some of his agricultural products locally, including beef to a neighbor, grains to the local gristmill, and apples to a Burlington retailer. During the winter months, he supplemented his farm income by working as a carpenter at the Shelburne Shipyard. Between the two occupations, he supported himself, his second wife, Maria, and seven children ranging in age from seventeen to infancy. Among these children was his daughter Jennie, who would later recall fetching her family's cows home for milking.[33]

Daguerreotype portrait of Franklin H. Morehouse, c. 1855. Vermont Historical Society.

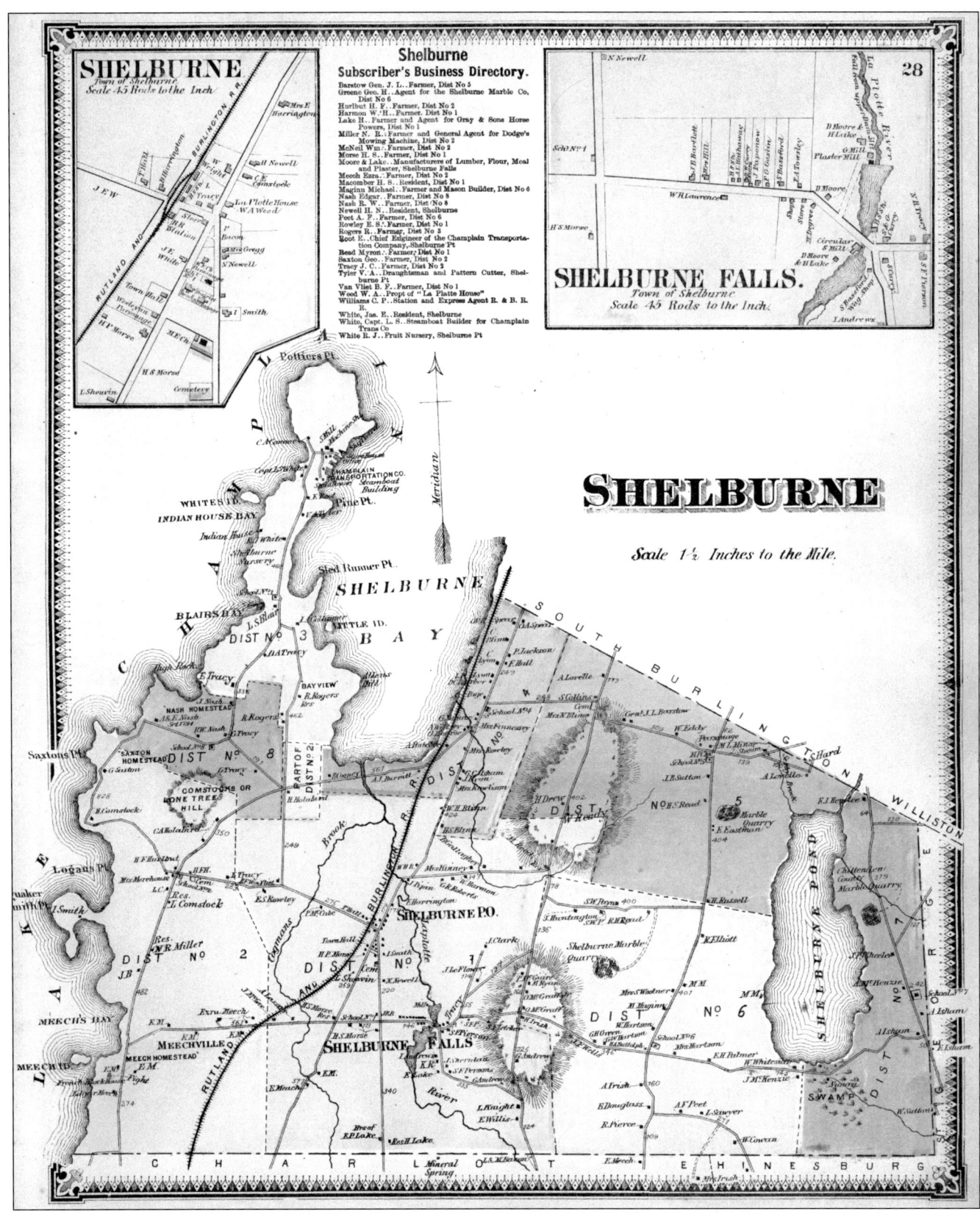

By 1880, Hezekiah Tracy's seventy-year-old grandson, Guy Tracy (1810–?), owned a large and prosperous farm to the northeast of Lone Tree Hill, in the center of what would become Shelburne Farms. His primary source of income was the sale of butter. In 1879, his dairy produced some 3,500 pounds of butter, a substantial amount when compared to the average butter production in the state, which amounted to 711 pounds a decade later. Tracy supplemented his income with a poultry flock and a large orchard. He also owned several teams of horses and oxen to work the land. A widower, Tracy and his two daughters, Caroline and Jennie, managed the farm with the assistance of hired laborers.[34]

Also in 1880, Mary Holabird (1829–?), the fifty-one-year-old widow of Cassius Holabird, ran her family's farm on the northern and eastern flanks of Lone Tree Hill along with her daughters, Harriet (Hattie) and Mary, and the two farm workers she employed. The Holabirds lived in a one-and-a-half-story clapboard farmhouse on the property. Like Guy Tracy, Mrs. Holabird's primary cash crop was butter. She also received some income from her apple orchard and flock of sheep.[35]

On the other side of Lone Tree Hill, Frederick Saxton's thirty-eight-year-old great-grandson, Edward Stevenson Saxton (1842–1920), farmed land on and around Saxton's Point with the assistance of his wife, Sarah, Sarah's sister, and a hired man. The Saxton farm produced fluid milk, butter, and apples.

Edgar Nash (1831–1913) inherited the 140-acre Nash family homestead, located just north of the Saxton farm, when his father, Asahel Nash Jr., died in 1878. Two years later, the sixty-seven-year old Edgar lived in the family's brick farmhouse with his unmarried sixty-six-year-old sister, Louisa (1832–?), and their young servant, Margaret White. A large barn with a cupola stood facing the house. The Nashes' largest sources of income were butter, wool, apples, and cordwood. They also raised a few pigs and chickens and planted barley, Indian corn, oats, wheat, and Irish potatoes.[36]

Area residents formed a tightly knit, interdependent community. Saxtons and Comstocks married Holabirds, Holabirds married Morehouses, Comstocks married Tracys. Neighbors hired each other's daughters to do housework, attended sewing circles together, and served as witnesses for each other's land purchases, executors of each other's wills, and trustees for each other's minor children. Residents buried their dead in a cemetery located south of Lone Tree Hill, established by the 1790s, and attended the Methodist, Congregational, and Episcopal churches located in the center of town. They socialized at gatherings of the local Sons of Temperance society. Generally well-educated themselves, they sent their children to one of three small schoolhouses situated within walking distance of their homes and funded additional secondary schooling for them on occasion.[37]

Franklin Morehouse maintained a close relationship with many of his neighbors—close enough to borrow their farm equipment, arrange to pasture some of his livestock in their fields, and send for a neighbor's wife to nurse his

Left: Map of Shelburne, Vermont, in Frederick Beers, *Atlas of Chittenden County, Vermont* (New York, 1869). Special Collections Library, University of Vermont.

From left to right: William McNeil, Jennie Morehouse, and Lucia (Comstock) McNeil (in carriage), c. 1870. Morehouse Family Papers, Vermont Historical Society.

own ailing spouse. During the winter months, he worked side by side with his neighbors to shovel snow from the public roads they all shared and took turns with them to split and cart wood for the local schoolhouse. In 1861, Morehouse and his wife, Maria, attended a local "Oister and Turkey Dinner" during the holiday season. He later recalled, "we Met there Levi Comstock and all his Family, Mr. Isaac Smith George Saxton Hezekiah Comstock and their Wifes, we had a good social time."[38]

Prosperity and Challenges

While tight-knit, this small community, like others across the state of Vermont, was affected by regional and national events as the nineteenth century progressed. "As Vermont farmers became part of increasingly integrated markets, the less control over their own destinies they had."[39] As area farmers modified their agricultural production to supply external markets, they became more closely tied to the national economy, for better and for worse. The sheep boom of the 1830s and 1840s was a huge opportunity for those who possessed the large amount of pasturage that the animals required or the capital to purchase more land, but it also resulted in pressure on smallholders to sell out. The subsequent collapse of wool prices in the 1840s and 1850s forced farmers who had specialized in sheep farming to seek alternative sources of income. The spreading network of canals and railroads initially opened markets but eventually increased competition from farmers in the western United States. By the 1870s and 1880s, Vermonters were in the midst of a statewide agricultural depression that had its roots in the mid-century decline in the wool market, the flood of agricultural goods entering urban centers from the west, and deflated wheat markets. One historian has noted that "between 1870 and 1890 farm valuations in Vermont receded from [$]135 to 100 million."[40]

The natural progression of generations also took its toll. An average life expectancy of forty to forty-five years during most of the nineteenth century, combined with the untimely deaths of some settlers and their children, sometimes left families without the labor needed to continue to farm their land. When family patriarchs and matriarchs died, their landholdings were often subdivided, leaving smaller portions for each passing generation or opportunities for only one or two family members to stay and farm the land.

As Vermont became more settled, young residents began to leave to explore new opportunities in the West and burgeoning cities throughout the country. The state's population growth had leveled off by 1850, and "in 1860, of those born in Vermont still living in the United States, 42 percent lived outside the state (the largest percentage of any state)."[41]

Of the four sons who settled on Quaker Smith Point with their parents, William and Elizabeth Smith, in the 1780s, one died within ten years of their arrival, and two others emigrated to New York State in the 1790s. Ultimately, only one descendant, grandson Isaac Smith (1792–1870), would remain on the property to manage the farm. After his death, his aging widow, Lucinda (1817–95), leased the farm to a tenant family and then sold it to Seward and Lila Webb in 1886.[42]

Asahel Sr. and Betsy Nash had twelve children. One died in infancy, five emigrated westward, and three settled in other Vermont towns, leaving three remaining in Shelburne. By 1886, Nash descendants who owned land in the Shelburne Farms area consisted of Asahel and Betsy's ninety-year-old son, John, a recent widower; John's son Elbert (1831–1909) and his wife, Jane (1836–1924), ages fifty-five and forty-nine; and Elbert and Jane's unmarried cousins, Louisa, age fifty-four, and Edgar, age fifty-five, who lived in the Nash family homestead on Orchard Point. Louisa and Edgar sold their property to Seward and Lila Webb within days of each other in 1886. At the same time, John, Elbert, and Jane sold two adjoining parcels totaling 135 acres. John sold an additional thirteen acres in 1887, and Elbert and Jane sold their larger, 133-acre home farm near the LaPlatte River in 1889.[43]

Although the Tracy family maintained a strong presence in the Shelburne area throughout the nineteenth century and into the twentieth, a number of founder Hezekiah Tracy's grandchildren and great-grandchildren left to seek their fortunes elsewhere. When grandson Dere Azro Tracy (?–1873) died only a few months after his father, Ezekiel, he left the family's homestead property to his wife, Julia, and their four adult children. However, by the time the estate was settled, the children had all moved to upstate New York, Oregon, and California, and Mrs. Tracy had remarried. The property was sold to Seward and Lila Webb in 1887.[44]

Mary Holabird and her husband, Cassius, lost their only son in 1858 at the age of ten. When Cassius himself died twenty years later, Mary and her daughters, Hattie and Mary, relied upon hired help to run their farm. In the 1880s, the young Mary Holabird married one of the family's farmhands and moved with him to Iowa, and her mother and sister bought her share of the property. The elder Mary and her remaining daughter would sell their property to the Webbs in 1888.[45]

The outbreak of the Civil War in 1861 was an additional blow to many families in the area and across the state of Vermont. "Vermont sent roughly one ninth of its population to fight in the Civil War (34,328 soldiers), causing a labor shortage at home. More than half of these soldiers did not return: over five thousand of them were killed, and many others settled elsewhere after the war."[46] Among the Shelburne men who fought in the war were two members of the Holabird family (Oliver and William), a Tracy (William), a Nash (Edgar), and three sons of Franklin Morehouse (Edward, Roderick, and George).[47]

The Morehouse family was particularly affected. Franklin Morehouse's three eldest sons all fought for the Union and then settled elsewhere. Their absence left the brunt of the farm work to their aging father and younger half-brother, Hawley (1847–65). Another half-brother, Clarke (1855–1935), was too young to share much of the heavy labor. When Franklin died in the midst of the war in 1862, the bulk of his farmland passed to his three absent sons. His second wife, Maria, and her four young children received the small plot of land on which the family's home was situated.[48]

Without enough property or assistance to manage a profitable farm, Hawley was forced to seek outside employment at the age of fifteen to support his mother and siblings. He died in 1865 during a dysentery outbreak in Burlington, and his sister Jennie later wrote that overwork caused by the heavy responsibility of caring for his family had made him susceptible to falling ill. Another sister, Lucia (1845–1931), recalled, "As the eldest at home during those sad days, the iron of the war entered deep into my soul."[49]

The older Morehouse sons sold their portion of the family farm in 1867, and it passed through two other owners before it was purchased by Seward Webb in 1886. The family's homestead descended to Clarke Morehouse after the death of his mother in 1877. He would also sell his parcel to Seward and Lila Webb in 1886.[50]

The tightly knit local community of farmers had already begun to unravel by the time the Webbs started purchasing their property in 1886. However, the sale of the land and the subsequent establishment of Shelburne Farms accelerated the community's deterioration.

According to Tracy family descendants, this disintegration of the community prompted Lee Tracy (1817–97), one of Hezekiah Tracy's grandsons, to sell his property in the area to the Webbs in 1888 and 1889. Lee and his younger sons, Charles (1865–1933) and Henry (1848–1925), had moved by 1882 to a new brick home in the center of Shelburne, from which Lee operated a wool-buying business. After they left the family's 125-acre farm south of Lone Tree Hill, Lee's oldest son, Julius (1846–1916), his wife, Hannah, and their thirteen children continued to occupy the homestead. However, as their close neighbors sold their farms to the Webbs one by one in 1886, 1887, and 1888, Julius and Hannah Tracy felt increasingly isolated. They agreed to allow Lee to sell the family property and then moved to another farm in Shelburne, closer to the village, in 1889.[51]

Thus, by the end of the 1880s, a confluence of factors—personal, regional, and national—eventually resulted in the sale of the land that the Morehouses, Comstocks, Nashes, Saxtons, Tracys, and others had farmed for several generations to Seward and Lila Webb. The Webbs' newly established estate of Shelburne Farms united more than thirty individual farms, replacing one community with a different one. The Webbs came from quite a different background and brought a new perspective and way of life to the area. However, they ultimately shared a common goal with the families from whom they purchased their property: to farm the land.

Chapter 2
SEWARD AND LILA WEBB

The sail from Burlington here was lovely 2 hours and I wanted my Lila so to see it all & the scenery was beautiful. You know it is one of the loveliest lakes in the East. The bold sharp Adirondacks in the West which are grand and the Green mountains in the East. The Lake is full of islands on any one of which I would like to spend a month with my wife, where we could be all alone, far away from all trouble, no one to disturb us, oh how happy we would be.

— W. Seward Webb, July 18, 1879[1]

In 1879, Seward Webb traveled to Burlington, Vermont, on his way to a hunting expedition in the Adirondack Mountains. While crossing Lake Champlain aboard the steamer *Vermont II*, he captured his impressions of the scenery in a journal intended for his future wife, Lila Vanderbilt. Seward was obviously taken with the area during this brief encounter, his earliest recorded visit to the region where he and Lila would soon establish Shelburne Farms, and his statement sheds light on why the Webbs chose the location for their country estate. Not only was the area strikingly beautiful, but it was also situated quite a distance away from New York City, "far away from all trouble," where they could be "all alone." In Vermont, they were free to pursue their own interests as they pleased.[2]

Born on January 31, 1851, William Seward Webb entered a family that had long been nationally prominent in political affairs. His grandfather, Brig. Gen. Samuel Blachley Webb (1753–1807), was an aide to Gen. George Washington during the American Revolution and fought in the Battle of Bunker Hill. Seward's father, Gen. James Watson Webb (1802–84), served in the army as a young man, wrote fiery editorials for the Whig party as the owner and editor of a leading New York newspaper, the *Morning Courier and New-York Enquirer*, and was the American ambassador to Brazil from 1861 to 1869. Gen. Alexander Stewart Webb (1835–1911), Seward's older half-brother, was a West Point graduate and Civil War hero who earned a medal of honor for his performance as a Union leader at the Battle of Gettysburg. He later served as president of the College of the City of New York. Seward himself was named in honor of family friend and future secretary of state William Henry Seward, who negotiated the purchase of the Alaska Territories in 1867 for President Andrew Johnson.[3]

Seward was the ninth of Gen. James Watson Webb's thirteen children and

Gen. James Watson Webb, his second wife, Laura Virginia Cram, and their five children, c. 1866. W. Seward Webb stands behind his father. Shelburne Farms Collections.

the oldest child of his father's union with his second wife, Laura Virginia Cram (1826–90), daughter of a wealthy brewer. His early childhood was spent at the Webb family home on the Hudson River near Tarrytown, New York. He and his siblings grew up in a close-knit, affectionate, and devoutly Episcopalian household. His parents sought to give him and his siblings an excellent education and held high expectations that he would honor the family name by entering military service.[4]

As a young adolescent, Seward accompanied his parents to Rio de Janeiro for the first three years of his father's ambassadorial term. In 1863, in the midst of the American Civil War, he returned to the United States to attend Churchill's Military Academy, a preparatory school in Sing Sing, New York. His studies were focused with an appointment to West Point in mind, possibly with the idea of eventually joining the military if the war continued. However, he performed poorly, apparently more interested in social activities and mischief. Throughout his school years, he received stern admonishments from his disappointed parents, such as this 1868 upbraiding from his father: "You Seward, should and would have done better, if you had not been so fond of society and so neglectful of your studies."[5]

Seward's poor marks thwarted his father's dreams of sending his son to West Point. Despite several attempts, Gen. Webb was unable to obtain an appointment for him. Instead, with the Civil War over, Seward entered Columbia College (now University) in 1869 to study medicine. During the next seven years, he studied at Columbia's College of Physicians and Surgeons and in hospitals in Paris and Vienna, attending classes in anatomy, physiology, pathology, chemistry, obstetrics and gynecology, and surgery. Seward reported to a friend in 1871 while studying in Vienna, "Medicine is getting on finely. I am working very hard at present and will have to during this year. I go to the Hospital here once a day and hear lectures in the wards on the different patients, every thing is in German, but I know enough to understand the sum & substance of the lectures."[6] He received a Doctor of Medicine degree from Columbia in 1875.[7]

Seward selected a career in a field that he enjoyed and at which he excelled. In 1870, the president of Columbia College wrote a letter of recommendation stating that Seward's "scholarship has been eminently creditable and his deportment in all respects exemplary."[8] His skills evidently encompassed treating animals as well as people; in 1876 the periodical *Forest and Stream* published a detailed letter from him describing his success at treating several dogs afflicted with distemper.[9]

After completing his course of study, Seward interned at St. Luke's Hospital in New York City for two years. He was just establishing an independent medical practice in the city when he met Lila Vanderbilt in 1877.[10]

Lila was born Eliza Osgood Vanderbilt on September 20, 1860, the eighth child and youngest daughter of William Henry Vanderbilt (1821–85) and his wife, Maria Louisa Kissam (1821–96). Named after her father's sister, Eliza Osgood, her early attempts to pronounce her first name resulted in the nickname "Lila," which remained for life. Lila was the granddaughter of family patriarch "Commodore" Cornelius Vanderbilt (1794–1877), who had established the family transportation business and fortune.[11]

In less than one hundred years, the Vanderbilts had experienced the ultimate fulfillment of the American dream, a meteoric rise in fortune from their origins as Staten Island farmers to prominence as one of the wealthiest, most famous, and most influential industrialist families in the country. Around 1810, Cornelius Vanderbilt started a ferry business traveling around New York Bay with a small sailboat purchased with funds loaned by his mother. A skilled businessman with a relentless focus on profits and a ruthless disregard for his competitors, he quickly expanded to schooners and steamboats operating up and down the Hudson River, the New England coast, and, by the

"Commodore" Cornelius Vanderbilt, by William Rae Howell, New York, c. 1870–77. Shelburne Farms Collections.

The William H. Vanderbilt Family, by Seymour Guy, 1873. Lila Vanderbilt is seated in the center of the painting. Used with permission from The Biltmore Company, Asheville, North Carolina.

1850s, around Central and South America to California. Vanderbilt began to invest in railroad transportation in the mid-1850s, when the industry was in its infancy. He acquired the New York and Harlem, the New York and Hudson, and the New York Central Railroads, and built the first Grand Central Terminal in New York City. At the time of his death in 1877, he left an estate of some $100 million.[12]

Lila's father, William Henry Vanderbilt, Cornelius's eldest son, inherited the bulk of Cornelius's fortune and assumed the helm of the family businesses. In 1881, William Henry employed some 15,000 men and owned 600 locomotives, 800 passenger cars, and 23,000 freight cars. The family fortune had more than doubled to some $200 million at the time of his death four years later. By the first decade of the twentieth century, the Vanderbilts controlled almost 20,000 miles of railroad track.[13]

Lila spent the first four years of her life on her father's 350-acre farm in Staten Island, New York. She moved with her family to New York City in 1864, when

William Henry Vanderbilt became vice president of his father's Harlem and Hudson Railroad. For most of her childhood, Lila lived in a brownstone townhouse at 459 Fifth Avenue, on the southeast corner of 40th Street.[14]

From 1875 to 1878, Lila attended Miss Porter's School, a young women's boarding school in Farmington, Connecticut. She studied American and European history, literature, German, Greek, French, music, singing, psychology, economics, and bookkeeping. Lila possessed a close circle of friends at Miss Porter's with whom she formed the "Monogram Literary Club," which met weekly to read and discuss members' works. Under the pen names "Vio Vintin" and "Queenie," Lila wrote a series of girlish and romantic novels, poems, and plays.[15]

Good-humored, pious, and kind, Lila was the darling of the Vanderbilt family. Her older sister Emily Vanderbilt Sloane considered Lila to be "one of the brightest, happiest girls she had ever known" and named one of her daughters after her.[16] Lila was devoted to her large family, especially Emily, her brother Frederick, and her parents. As she wrote in 1877, "God has given me such a lovely Mother. I ought to try to be more Christian-like, & to resemble her. Everyone loves her who meets her." She described her father thus: "He is so kind & good to me, dear Papa, and I love him very dearly."[17] Miss Porter's School did not offer a degree-granting program, and although she loved her friends and studies, Lila decided to leave in 1878 in part because of her affection for her mother. She wrote, "Mother is alone, with the exception of Fred and George, my brothers, and I feel after three years of boarding school life, as if I should like to be with her again."[18]

As a young woman, Lila enjoyed attending social gatherings such as dances, concerts, and sledding parties. Vivacious and witty, with brown eyes and hair, she soon attracted the attentions of several suitors. In June 1875, at the young age of fifteen, she described her impressions of a party she

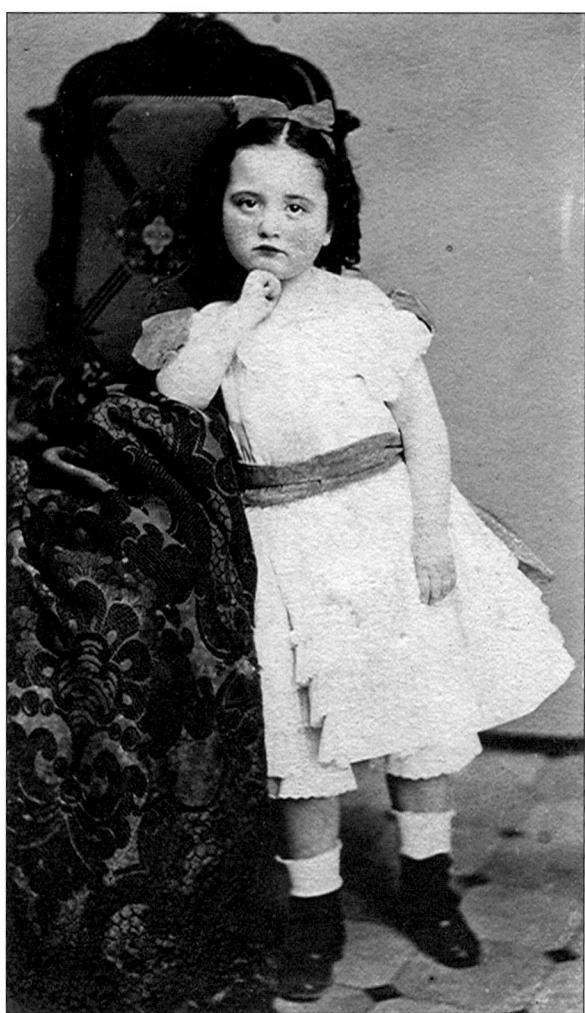

The young Lila Vanderbilt, Studio of George G. Rockwood, New York, c. 1865.

attended: "Had a perfectly gorgeous time. Danced the german with W.B. but had sixteen elegant dances with chow-chow. F.B. danced with Fannie Babcock, and J.H. with Minnie Babcock. F.D. was there, and I had two walks on the piazza with him. Danced until one minute of 12."[19]

Lila Vanderbilt and Seward Webb met in April 1877, while Lila was home in New York on a vacation from Miss Porter's School. In mourning for her grandfather Cornelius Vanderbilt, she could not participate in the usual round of society events. Instead, she and her brother Frederick attended "a little dancing class" together one afternoon, where she later wrote of meeting "Seward Webb (Dr.) there…He was very pleasant."[20]

By the spring of 1878, Seward was visiting Lila at Miss Porter's School regularly. In August of that year, he was one of two mystery guests and potential beaux invited by Lila's brother-in-law Elliott Shepard to a weekend gathering assembled in her honor. Apparently Lila preferred Seward to the other surprise guest, a Mr. Taylor: "Dr. Webb is shorter than Mr. Taylor, and most people think him much handsomer. He is very manly looking and has a good figure. His eyes are blue, too small, his nose very good. One can tell but little about the lower portion of his face, as it is entirely covered with a very handsome full English beard, brown to match his hair."[21] By the end of the weekend, Lila and Seward had exchanged mementos: her scarf pin for a gold pipe that he inscribed "*toujours fideli.*"[22]

Throughout 1878, the romance grew more serious. In November, Seward professed his love for Lila, writing her, as she stated, "*the* loveliest letter I have ever read."[23] However, her father was less than pleased. By June 1879, he had forbidden Lila to see or correspond with Seward, or even to speak his name. In the hopes of pacifying her father, Lila entreated Seward, "1. not to write 2. not to send flowers 3. not to send any thing 4. not to speak to me in the street or join me 5. Not to look up to my windows when passing 6. Not to make any sign 7. to look happy & contented when you pass."[24]

In William Henry Vanderbilt's opinion, Seward was not a suitable match. Lila, his youngest daughter, was just eighteen, and Seward was nine and a half years older. In addition, Seward's profession was unlikely to provide him with an income that would meet Vanderbilt standards. Vanderbilt worried that Seward wanted to marry his daughter for her inheritance.[25]

Despite Vanderbilt's hopes that his daughter's feelings for Seward would wane if she did not see him, the enforced separation only served to strengthen their relationship. Seward and Lila

Lila Osgood Vanderbilt on her wedding day, by Mora Studio, New York, 1881. Shelburne Farms Collections.

resorted to keeping journals and writing lengthy letters that were secretly exchanged with the assistance of her older siblings Emily and Frederick. The forbidden correspondence continued for eighteen months in 1879 and 1880, and by the end of that time, they were deeply in love with each other.[26]

Seward and Lila recorded in detail the trials of their separation in their correspondence. Passionate and sentimental in the Victorian terms of the era, they poured their hearts out to each other. Seward wrote of breaking down in tears at the office and pacing up and down the street in front of Lila's bedroom window in the hopes of catching a glimpse of her. Caught between her loyalty and respect for her parents' wishes and her love for Seward, Lila wrote of being compelled to carry on her social life as if Seward did not exist. They took solace in their journals and letters. As Lila wrote to Seward in her 1879 journal, "I think what a great

great comfort [my journal] will be next winter, for I am sure yours will be to me, and so I will write down all I can tell you is the same dear old sweet story over again. 'I love you, I love you, I love you,' which I shall never be tired of hearing from you, again and again & again."[27]

In the hopes of impressing William Henry Vanderbilt, Seward abandoned his medical practice in 1879 in favor of a more lucrative business career. His actions likely represented a significant sacrifice. A year earlier, he had received glowing recommendations from his supervisors, colleagues, and former teachers for a possible medical position in the military. Upon hearing that Seward would be giving up his practice, one of his former professors at Columbia College stated that he "was very bright and smart and...had [he] remained in the medical profession [he] would have been a great success."[28] Instead, Seward worked briefly for the North West Telegraph Company and then became a partner in the Worden & Company brokerage house on Wall Street in January 1880. Lila's sympathetic brother Frederick gave Seward all of his stock business, and Seward proved successful at his new venture by the spring of 1880.[29]

That same spring, Lila's father relented and reluctantly agreed to a wedding the following year. Their marriage, on December 20, 1881, in St. Bartholemew's Church, was one of the highlights of the New York social season. Among the honored guests were former President Ulysses S. Grant, two former governors of the state of New York, two leading United States senators, several railroad executives, and many members of New York high society.[30]

After a wedding tour through Canada via a private railway car, Seward and Lila took up residence in New York City. They lived first with Lila's parents at their Fifth Avenue townhouse from about 1881 to 1885, and then in a new townhouse William Henry Vanderbilt built for them. One of a series of residences that Vanderbilt commissioned for himself and his daughters in the early to mid-1880s, the

Dr. W. Seward Webb, attributed to Mora Studio, New York, c. 1880. Shelburne Farms Collections.

Gothic-style dwelling was designed by architects John B. Snook and Charles B. Atwood. It stood at 680 Fifth Avenue, in the center of the block between West 53rd and 54th Streets, and it was attached to Lila's sister Florence Twombly's neighboring residence to the north. The fashionable St. Thomas Church occupied the plot directly to the south. Townhouses belonging to Lila's father and other siblings Emily Sloane, Margaret Shepard, Cornelius Vanderbilt II, and William K. Vanderbilt were all located nearby along the section of Fifth Avenue dubbed "Vanderbilt Row."[31]

The Vanderbilt townhouses were at the forefront of the migration of New York's social elite from lower Manhattan to what is now the midtown section of Fifth Avenue. The neighborhoods surrounding lower Fifth Avenue that had served as the center of New York society for much of the nineteenth century were gradually changing as New York's burgeoning commercial centers and the growing crowds of immigrants began to move northward. The city's elite increasingly sought enclaves farther to the north, where they could purchase substantial pieces of land to build large townhouses in the newest fashion and be assured of some isolation from dense commercial development. Fifth Avenue between 50th and 60th Streets, part of an underdeveloped hinterland as late as the 1850s, became "New York's most sumptuous residential district" in the 1880s and 1890s.[32] Residing at 680 Fifth Avenue placed Seward and Lila in the geographical center of the New York social world.[33]

Prominent members of New York society, Seward and Lila were part of the exclusive set known as the "Four Hundred."[34] During the city's annual

Left: The Webbs' Manhattan townhouse at 680 Fifth Avenue (center), c. 1900. Also depicted are St. Thomas Church (left), and the house of Lila Webb's sister Florence Twombly (right). Shelburne Farms Collections.

social season from November to April, the Webbs attended the Charity, Assembly, and Patriarch's Balls and the Madison Square Garden Horse Show and viewed performances from their box at the Metropolitan Opera House. They participated in the now famous 1883 costume ball given by Lila's brother and sister-in-law, William K. and Alva Vanderbilt, which marked the Vanderbilt family's full entrée into conservative "Old New York" society. The Webbs gave fashionable dinner parties and balls at 680 Fifth Avenue, such as an 1888 event for 175 guests catered by the society restaurant Delmonico's, in which the evening's music was provided by an orchestra and a Hungarian band. Lila hosted a series of "literary dinners," including one for which she gave an opening address on the subject of "Which left the greatest impression on the history of the world, the Renaissance or the Reformation?"[35] Seward served as a vestryman at St. Bartholemew's Church and held memberships in numerous gentleman's clubs and special interest societies, including the New York Yacht Club, New York Coaching Club, New York Farmers' Club, Turf and Field Club, and Hackney Horse Association. He also underwrote a $300 prize given to a landscape painter at the annual exhibition of the Society of American Artists.[36]

Soon after they married in 1881, the Webbs established a pattern of spending the winter and spring of each year in New York and the summer and autumn in Vermont. Their schedule ensured that Seward could spend the majority of the year close to his business office and associates, and the couple could participate in the social events of the New York season. However, they could also escape to Vermont and exchange the formality of New York society for an active outdoor lifestyle during the temperate months. As Seward stated in 1895, in Vermont "one can lead an ideal summer existence, far from the heat and noise of the city, yet near enough to be in daily touch with all that transpires."[37]

In 1885, after working in the stock market for five years, Seward was appointed president of the Wagner Palace Car Company, a recent acquisition of Lila's father. Founded in 1866 as the Wagner Sleeping Car Company, the firm built and operated railway cars, competing with the Pullman Company, among others. Seward would soon earn acclaim for improving Wagner's public image by refurbishing the cars it provided to railroad lines across the country.[38]

During the first two summers after their marriage, Seward and Lila rented a relatively small, Georgian-style house in the city of Burlington. In the autumn of 1883, they acquired 245 acres of farmland and shipyard property on the shores of Lake Champlain in the southern part of Burlington, where they created Oakledge Farm.[39]

The Webbs' first country estate, Oakledge reflected their interests in informal country living, agriculture, and horses. Known in the press as a "fine country seat" and "one of the handsomest places in Burlington," the estate consisted of a large Queen Anne–style residence and a large farm.[40] Completed by May 1884, the house was sited on a hill overlooking a broad sweeping lawn, Lake

The Webbs' house at Oakledge Farm, by C. P. Hibbard, Burlington, Vermont, c. 1885. Shelburne Farms Collections.

Below: The barns at Oakledge Farm, by Brown's, Burlington, Vermont, c. 1885. Shelburne Farms Collections.

Champlain, and the Adirondacks. The rambling residence featured a shingled exterior; a roofline punctuated by turrets, gables, and chimneys; and a deep wrap-around veranda; a complex of one- and two-story barns housed horses, Jersey dairy cattle, and sheep. A small, late-eighteenth-century farmhouse, predating the establishment of the estate, was used as a gatehouse.[41]

Seward focused upon developing a horse stud farm at Oakledge that by 1887 included over thirty brood mares and two stallions. In April of that year, the *New York Times* reported: "Dr. Seward Webb, of this city, is establishing a stock farm at 'Oak Ledge,' his Vermont country seat, and last week shipped there a carload of finely bred brood mares and colts, which will be added to the list of well bred ones already quartered there."[42]

Oakledge proved to be an excellent place to raise an active, growing family. By 1884, Seward and Lila had two young children: Frederica Vanderbilt Webb (1882–1949), named after Lila's brother Frederick, and James Watson Webb (1884–1960), named in honor of Seward's father, who had died one month before his birth. Watson, as he was known throughout his life, was born at Oakledge shortly after the Webbs settled into their new home. At their country estate, the Webbs took their children on carriage drives and placed them on horseback at early ages.[43]

Oakledge was ideally suited for swimming, lawn tennis, sailing on the Webbs' newly acquired wooden steam yacht, *Sappho*, and ice sailing and tobogganing in the winter. The Webbs built a large toboggan slide on the lawn near their house and invited many family members up for the winter carnival season in Burlington. Seward offered a personal apology to the city mayor after being caught coasting down a city street, a popular but illegal activity of the time. His misconduct notwithstanding, Seward became the president of the Burlington Coasting Club, a local organization founded in 1885 to promote "outdoor winter sports, such as Coasting, Toboggan Sliding, Snow-Shoeing, Ice Skating, and Curling." He was praised by the local press as "the gentleman who is responsible for the remarkable success of Burlington's winter carnival."[44]

In developing Oakledge Farm, Seward and Lila were strongly influenced by both national trends and family traditions. During the late nineteenth and early twentieth centuries, numerous middle- and upper-class Americans spent winters at their city townhouses and then relocated to the country for all or part of the spring, summer, and autumn months.

Wealthy urban Americans had fled to rural areas to escape disease epidemics for generations. However, the practice of living in the country for part of the year became routine during the latter half of the nineteenth century. As the nation became more and more industrialized, economic

Lila Webb with her two older children, Frederica (right) and J. Watson (left), by W. Kurtz, New York, c. 1885. Shelburne Farms Collections.

prosperity concentrated in metropolitan areas. Residents of rural areas and immigrants flocked to major cities such as New York, Boston, and Chicago seeking opportunity. As one historian has noted, "from 1860 to 1910, America's urban population increased sevenfold."[45] Marked overcrowding and poverty followed, and those affluent enough to avoid it left for the country.

New York society members generally preferred areas within easy traveling distance of the city, including Newport, Rhode Island; Bar Harbor, Maine; Lenox, Massachusetts; the Hudson River Valley; the New Jersey and Long Island coasts; and the Adirondacks. While some favored houses on small lots in resort areas, others built estates on extensive acreage. In 1904, Barr Feree, the author of *American Estates and Gardens,* defined the American country house as "a new type of dwelling, a sumptuous house, built at large expense, often palatial in its dimensions, furnished in the richest manner and placed on an estate, perhaps large enough to admit of independent farming operations, and in most cases with a garden which is an integral part of the architectural scheme."[46]

American country residences and estates of the Gilded Age borrowed many features from their European counterparts. Their architecture, interiors, and landscapes were often influenced by the great houses of the European landed gentry, especially those of the British. They were often sited on expansive properties with farms that yielded produce for the owners' tables. They served as retreats for relaxation and renewal as well as exclusive formal entertaining. They housed collections of fine art, antiques, books, and bibelots. And they

Frederica and J. Watson Webb in a pony cart at Oakledge, with a groom holding the reins, c. 1885. Shelburne Farms Collections.

A tobogganing party at Oakledge Farm, 1885. W. Seward Webb sits at the front of the sleigh; his wife, Lila, and daughter, Frederica, directly behind him; and his son, Watson, in the baby carriage beside him. Shelburne Farms Collections.

supported their owners' particular interests and activities, such as horses, agriculture, hunting, gardening, yachting, tennis, and golf.[47]

However, American country residences and estates possessed a singular difference from their European predecessors: rather than serving as the source of their owners' income, they were created as a symbol of their owners' wealth. The rapid industrialization of the United States in the second half of the nineteenth century produced both a large number of Americans wealthy enough to afford country homes, and also a nostalgic longing for the rapidly disappearing country life. As one historian has noted, "the freedom to cultivate a garden or steward a farm was now a luxury made possible by urban, industrial wealth."[48]

While following many of the standard precepts for an American country estate, Oakledge Farm also reflected the Webbs' own personal experiences and interests. Lila had spent a portion of her childhood on her father's farm on Staten Island, and she grew up surrounded by horse enthusiasts. As a young girl and adolescent, she spent a great deal of time in Saratoga Springs, New York, where her grandfather loved to race trotters. Her father was one of the

29

founding members of the New York Coaching Club. In 1875, Lila had accompanied her family to Louisville, Kentucky, where they witnessed horse races and visited fine stables.[49]

At the turn of the twentieth century, Lila's siblings were in the midst of acquiring and building a series of no fewer than thirteen country residences for themselves in the eastern United States. Several of her siblings possessed more than one country residence, and many were situated near each other in Newport, Bar Harbor, and along the Hudson River, among other sites.[50]

Seward had spent much of his childhood on his father's estate in the Hudson Valley, and he showed an early interest in country properties and pursuits. Among the bad habits for which he was reprimanded by his father was his affection for horses. As the elder Webb wrote in the 1860s,

My dear, dear Seward…In looking at your hours of study and recreation I find 2½ hours on horseback, 2 hours driving! In all 4½ hours with the horse daily! Now to that I object in the most emphatic manner. You are not destined for a groom, coachman, or horse jocky; and the bare idea that a young man studying for college should devote four hours and a half daily to the horse is too absurd for comment.[51]

True to form, Seward focused upon the stables when he visited a Hudson Valley estate in 1879: "I went down to the Rives place and saw Mr. & Mrs. Rives & their fine stable & horses…They have a beautiful stable, the carriage house is 50 x 50 feet & last fall they waxed the floor and had a large ball there."[52]

Seward's idea of indulging his wife was to give her horses and carriages. In an 1880 journal entry addressed to Lila, he vowed, "Oh darling mine you shall have a lovely turn out as soon as we are married."[53]

Oakledge Farm fulfilled Seward's 1879 dream for his and Lila's married life. It accommodated their interests in agriculture, horses, and relaxed country living. In addition, it was located amidst beautiful scenery in northern Vermont, a distance from New York City and the recognized resort areas where many New Yorkers built their country houses and estates. None of the Webbs' family members owned estates in the area, and only two other prominent members of New York society lived nearby. At Oakledge, the Webbs escaped from the familial disapproval that had dogged them for their long courtship and were, at last, "all alone, far away from all trouble, no one to disturb [them]."[54]

CHAPTER 3

DESIGNING A COUNTRY ESTATE

Dr. Webb has purchased 1700 acres on the lakeshore and if justice is done to the situation and conditions it will without doubt be one of the most important and beautiful country places in America.

— ROBERT ROBERTSON TO FREDERICK LAW OLMSTED, JUNE 17, 1886[1]

AT THE CLOSE OF 1885, SEWARD AND LILA WEBB had been married for four years. Their life together centered upon their two small children, Seward's demanding position as the leader of a railroad company, and an active social life involving a large circle of family, friends, and society members. In December of that year, Lila's father, William Henry Vanderbilt, died. His death would have a significant and immediate impact upon the couple, as well as on each of Lila's seven surviving brothers and sisters. Already quite well off, Seward and Lila were suddenly fabulously wealthy. Lila and her three sisters each inherited $10 million; Lila received $5 million in cash and $5 million held in trust during her lifetime, as well as the title to the house on Fifth Avenue. The sum that the four Vanderbilt daughters received was rather small compared to the approximately $50 million inherited by their brothers Cornelius II and William K. Vanderbilt. But it was still an astronomical fortune, worth approximately $237 million in the year 2008.[2]

While Oakledge Farm may have seemed suitable before their windfall, Seward and Lila were now in a position to realize their grandest ambitions for a country estate. They envisioned a property that would include a commodious residence, facilities for their favorite outdoor sporting activities, and a multifaceted model farm incorporating the latest scientific techniques for producing crops and breeding and managing livestock. Shelburne Farms, as their new estate was called, would prove to be just such a place.

LAND ACQUISITION

In January 1886, a little more than a month after the death of William Henry Vanderbilt, the couple began to purchase farmland along Lake Champlain in Shelburne, six miles south of Oakledge. By the end of the year, they had

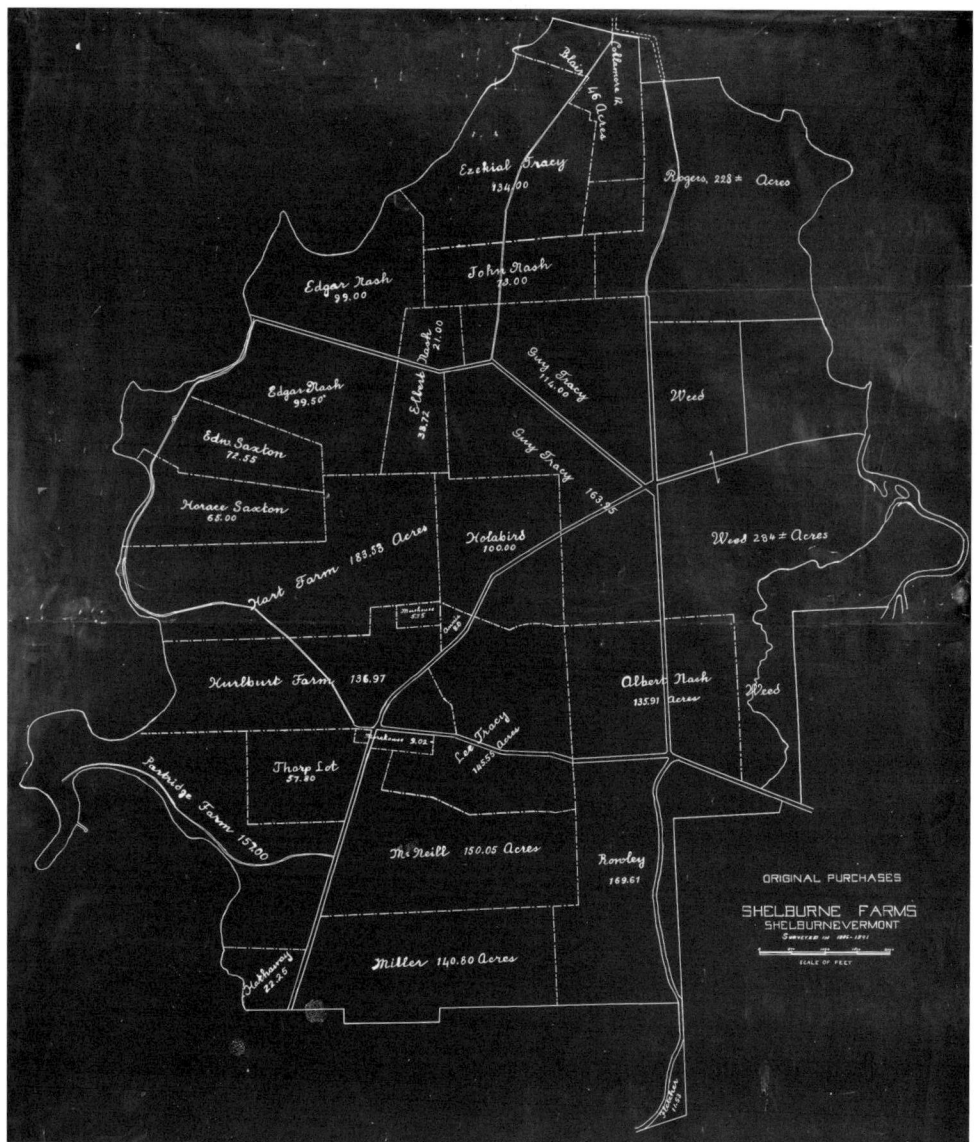

Original Purchases, Shelburne Farms, Shelburne, Vermont, Surveyed 1886–1891, artist unknown. Shelburne Farms Collections.

purchased eleven lakeshore farms containing about 1,000 acres in the Quaker Smith Point and Saxton's Point areas. In 1887, they added 500 acres to the north in the Orchard Point area. By 1891, their holdings consisted of almost 3,000 acres along Lake Champlain and inland to Shelburne Bay and the LaPlatte River. Ten years later, Shelburne Farms had grown to its largest size of approximately 3,800 acres, encompassing some thirty former farmsteads.[3]

The Webbs probably decided upon Shelburne as the site for their extensive country estate for several important reasons. It was ideally sited, with magnificent views of Lake Champlain, the Adirondack Mountains, and the Green Mountains. Lila wrote that the Lone Tree Hill area, in the center of their property, "seems to me like heaven."[4] In addition, the property had proven its worth as productive farmland for several generations. Finally, their close friend Col. LeGrand B. Cannon raised horses and cattle nearby at his Vermont Stock Farm, which was located within the town boundaries.[5]

Four individuals assisted the couple in their land purchases. John J. Flynn, a local real estate agent, "acted as a broker in the sale…of a considerable portion of the estate."[6] George W. Wales, a Burlington attorney, performed the title research, negotiated with at least some of the landowners, and completed the initial purchase agreements. New York City resident William J. Van Arsdale signed many of the deeds for properties purchased in 1886 and then transferred them to the Webbs within a few months. Similarly, Hamilton McK. Twombly, Lila's brother-in-law, held several of the 1887 deeds for a brief period before transferring them to the Webbs.[7]

Van Arsdale may have been involved with the 1886 purchases in order to keep the Webbs' identity under wraps while negotiations were underway. Although extremely wealthy, Seward and Lila likely did not want to pay more than market value for the parcels. According to a story related by generations of family and local community members, the Webbs enlisted a "stranger in a buckboard" to make the rounds of the desired farms and secretly buy out each landowner without the others' knowledge.[8] After the sales were final, the farmers discovered, much to their surprise and dismay, that they had all sold out to the same affluent New York couple. In fact, after word of the Webbs' initial purchases was made public, area real estate prices rose. In August 1886, the *New York Tribune* noted, "Dr. Webb is still buying property around Shelburne's Point to add to his magnificent 1,500-acre tract on Lake Champlain. The price of farm land in that vicinity has gone up since the disclosure of his numerous purchases to make this tract."[9]

Although rumors that Twombly intended to build his own country residence neighboring the Webbs' abounded in the press, he was probably acting on behalf of his sister and brother-in-law. In 1887, Twombly acquired a chunk of land located north of the Webbs' 1886 acquisitions, including a small remaining portion of John Nash's farm and the Ezekiel Tracy property. He then signed them over to Seward and Lila.[10]

In addition, the Webbs' attorney, George Wales, also noted that Twombly was involved "in order to simplify the order of the Selectmen in setting over the discontinued road to the adjoining proprietors."[11] Wales may have thought that the town's governing body, the selectboard, would be more willing to close the road to the public if the land it crossed was owned by one individual.

Although the Webbs' initial method of purchasing land may have been perceived as underhanded by some, most of the sellers received excellent prices for their land. In fact, several may have been able to negotiate sale prices up to $200 per acre. The *New York Tribune* reported the story of one such individual in 1886: "There is one farm of 300 acres that he [Seward Webb] is extremely desirous to acquire, as it makes a corner in his tract. Although he has bought his land at an average of about $60 to $80 an acre, the owner of this property has set a value of $300 an acre as the lowest price for which he will sell. I am told that Dr. Webb has offered him $200 an acre."[12]

However, in many cases, the sales did not occur without a great deal of regret at the loss of family homesteads, neighborly connections, and a way of life, and some resentment at the immediate source of such upheaval: wealthy outsiders Seward and Lila Webb. Within a short period of time, it became clear to community members that the Webbs possessed ambitious plans for their developing country estate, plans that would completely and permanently alter the appearance and use of the land they had owned, as well as the composition of their town. The Webbs would bring with them many new people in the form of visiting friends and family, as well as short- and long-term employees. It was the beginning of a very different era for the town of Shelburne.

Robert Robertson, Architect

Soon after making their initial land purchases in 1886, the Webbs commissioned New York City architect Robert Henderson Robertson (1849–1919) to design the structures they envisioned for their new estate. A native of Philadelphia, Robertson received his architectural training at Rutgers College and apprenticed with Philadelphia architect Henry Sims and New York architects Edward T. Potter and George Post. After several years in private practice in the early 1870s, Robertson worked in partnership with William Appleton Potter, who served as supervising architect of the United States Treasury from 1875 to 1880. From 1880 to 1902, while Robertson was designing most of the estate structures for Shelburne Farms, he owned an independent practice in New York. He took William Potter's nephew, Robert Burnside Potter, as a junior partner in 1902, and the young man assisted with the last of Robertson's design work at Shelburne Farms.[13]

Throughout his career, Robertson utilized the design vocabularies of several late-nineteenth-century architectural movements, including the Victorian Gothic, Richardsonian Romanesque, shingle, Queen Anne, and neoclassical styles. His architectural commissions included ecclesiastical buildings, railroad stations, townhouses, and at least seven public and commercial buildings in New York City. He is perhaps best known today for his New York skyscrapers; his Park Row buildings were the tallest in the city when constructed between 1896 and 1899. In addition to his work at Shelburne Farms, Robertson designed several other country residences and estates in the popular summer resort areas near New York, some in partnership with William Potter.[14]

Seward and Lila were probably familiar with many of Robertson's structures in the New York area. They also moved in some of the same social circles. Seward was a member of the city's Knickerbocker Club, whose headquarters Robertson had

Robert Henderson Robertson, engraving by Finlay & Conn, date unknown. Shelburne Farms Collections.

designed in 1882. Just before receiving the commission for Shelburne Farms in 1886, Robertson had begun work designing two buildings with Vanderbilt family connections: a structure for the Young Women's Christian Association (YWCA), financed by Margaret Shepard, Lila's older sister; and the Mott Haven railroad station for the New York Central and Hudson River Railroad. Several years later, he built the YWCA's Margaret Louisa Home, also funded by Shepard.[15]

Shelburne Farms, however, represented the most extensive architectural commission of Robertson's career. Between 1886 and 1905, he designed approximately thirty-six buildings and structures for Shelburne Farms in a combination of the shingle and Queen Anne styles popular at the time. At least thirty of Robertson's designs were constructed.[16]

On board by June 1886, Robertson immediately set to work. His first order of business was to design two major estate structures: a grand country residence and a barn intended to be the centerpiece of the Webbs' new model farm. Over the next year, Robertson also worked on plans for a temporary house for the family to live in until their permanent dwelling was constructed.[17]

Frederick Law Olmsted, Landscape Architect

Shortly after he was hired, Robertson invited landscape architect Frederick Law Olmsted Sr. to oversee the design of the estate landscape:

> *I am requested by my client Dr. W. Seward Webb for whom I am designing a most important country house, stock Barns, Stables &c to be built upon his property at Burlington to write you asking you…to confer in regard to the Landscape dept Which it gives me much pleasure to believe he will place in your charge if you will undertake it…Dr. Webb has purchased 1700 acres on the lakeshore and if justice is done to the situation and conditions it will without doubt be one of the most important and beautiful country places in America.*[18]

Frederick Law Olmsted (1822–1903) was the preeminent American landscape architect of the late nineteenth century. Born in Hartford, Connecticut,

Frederick Law Olmsted, c. 1890. Courtesy of the National Park Service, Frederick Law Olmsted National Historic Site.

Olmsted had spent his young life drifting from one occupation to another, serving as a clerk, sailor, journalist, editor, and general secretary of the United States Sanitary Commission, the precursor to the American Red Cross. He managed two successive farms as a gentleman farmer from 1847 to 1855. In 1858, Olmsted and architect Calvert Vaux won the commission to design New York City's Central Park. It was Olmsted's first major landscape project and remains his best known.[19]

Over the thirty-year landscape career that ensued, Olmsted planned numerous other public parks and educational campuses, and more than two thousand private property commissions, including many rural private residences and estates. His country estate projects included the 275-acre Moraine Farm in Beverly, Massachusetts, designed for John C. Phillips in 1880, which can be seen as a prototype for Shelburne Farms. At Moraine Farm, Olmsted "proposed to blend scientific farming and experimental forestry with a country retreat." The property featured areas of forest plantations, open pastureland, lawns connected by winding drives, and a country house overlooking a lake.[20]

Olmsted's connection to the Vanderbilt family began in the 1850s. While he was a gentleman farmer on Staten Island, he offered landscaping advice to his neighbors William Henry and Maria Louisa Vanderbilt, Lila's parents. During the last two decades of the nineteenth century, he worked on several Vanderbilt commissions in addition to Shelburne Farms: the family mausoleum on Staten Island (1886–92); Elm Court, the Lenox country house of William and Emily Vanderbilt Sloane (1887–1900); Rough Point, Frederick and Louise Vanderbilt's Newport home (1887–1924); Point D'Acadie, George Vanderbilt's Bar Harbor residence (1890–91); and Biltmore, George Vanderbilt's extensive estate in Asheville, North Carolina (1888–95).[21]

Olmsted and Vaux defined their profession as "landscape architecture," the art of designing a landscape by blending and connecting individual elements to make a unified whole. Olmsted saw landscape as a powerful method of social improvement that could provide refreshment and solace to Americans who were increasingly detached from nature as the nation became more and more urbanized. He sought to work in harmony with and heighten the natural appearance of a landscape. Influenced by informal English landscapes, Olmsted often worked in the pastoral and picturesque styles, creating soothing landscapes with broad pastures, calm bodies of water, and stands of trees. As Olmsted wrote, "the pastoral consists of combinations of trees, standing singly and in groups, and casting their shadows over broad stretches of turf, or repeating their beauty by reflection upon the calm surface of pools, and the predominant associations are in the highest degree tranquilizing and grateful, as expressed by the Hebrew poet: 'He maketh me to lie down in green pastures; he leadeth me beside the still waters.'"[22]

At Shelburne Farms, Olmsted set about implementing his landscape theories. By September 1886, he had visited the area, consulted with Seward, and received civil engineer Joseph P. Cotton's initial topographical map of the Webbs' newly purchased farmland. Divided into the individual farmsteads formerly owned by the Comstocks, Nashes, Saxtons, Tracys, and others, the majority of the Webbs' new land was cleared, fenced, and sprinkled with clusters of farm buildings. Public roads connecting the parcels ran across the topography, and small woodlots and orchard plots stood at the edges of the fields.[23]

Olmsted was excited by the landscape possibilities at Shelburne Farms. As he wrote to a colleague in July 1886, "We have an interesting private work in a great stock farm for Dr. Webb near Burlington, Vermont with a magnificent view over Champlain to the Adirondacks."[24] Olmsted had in fact visited the Shelburne area as a young man in 1845, where he had remarked upon the striking view of the Adirondacks in a letter to his father: "I never saw mountains rise more beautifully one above

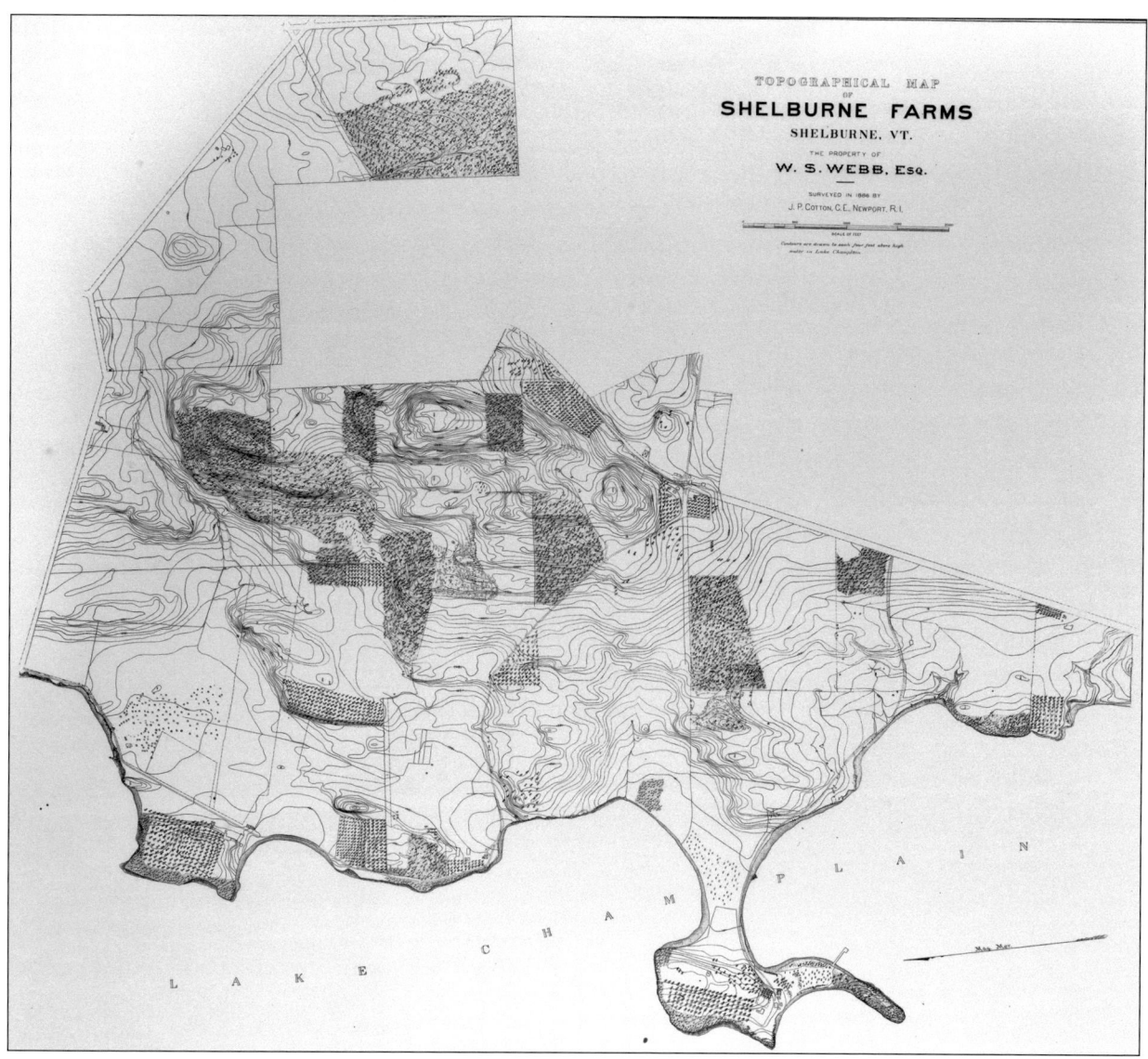

Topographical Map of Shelburne Farms, Shelburne, VT. The Property of W.S. Webb, Esq., by Joseph P. Cotton, 1886. Shelburne Farms Collections.

another the larger ones seeming to cluster round and protect the smaller, nor did the summer veil of haze ever sit on them more sweetly."[25]

By March 1887, Olmsted had developed a plan to replant one portion of the Shelburne Farms landscape as an "arboretum Vermontii" featuring native species of trees and shrubs. His plans followed methodology then being formulated by Charles Sprague Sargent for what would become the Arnold Arboretum in Boston, Massachusetts. As Olmsted wrote, the Shelburne Farms forest would be "a beautiful, interesting and instructive and publicly important arboretum…the present natural woods forming an appropriate and harmonious background for it and adding directly to its scientific value."[26] Olmsted submitted the idea to Seward and Lila with an extensive planting list. Proposed tree species included white, yellow, and paper birch; hemlock;

hickory; American chestnut; American beech; red oak; white and red pine; white, blue, and Oriental spruce; ash; scarlet, sugar, and striped bark maple; and Lombardy poplar. Proposed shrubs included forsythia, arbor vitae, spirea, and viburnum.[27]

The Webbs initially approved of the arboretum plan. Seward wrote Olmsted that he was "very much pleased with your general plan, for the planting of the Vermont Arboritum, and I beg to say I would be very much pleased to have you give Pringle & Horsford an order for the above plants and stock at the price you suggest."[28] By June 1887, a total of $2,882 in plantings had been purchased for the arboretum from the neighboring Pringle & Horsford nursery in Charlotte, Vermont, and other nurseries across the United States. The following year, the *New York Tribune* reported on the progress of the arboretum project:

The year 1888 witnessed the transformation of a score of fine farms located on the shore of Lake Champlain, in Shelburn, into a mammoth park embracing over 2,000 acres, forming one of the most extensive and attractive estates in New England…What was before beautiful by nature has been made more attractive and delightful by changes effected in the park under the supervision of Mr. Frederick Law Olmsted…In different portions of the park there will be collections of trees and shrubs indigenous to the soil. During the past year over 40,000 plants were set out, which are to be transplanted another season in groups and belts on the estate.[29]

Young stock in the estate tree nursery, by Thomas E. Marr, c. 1900. Shelburne Farms Collections.

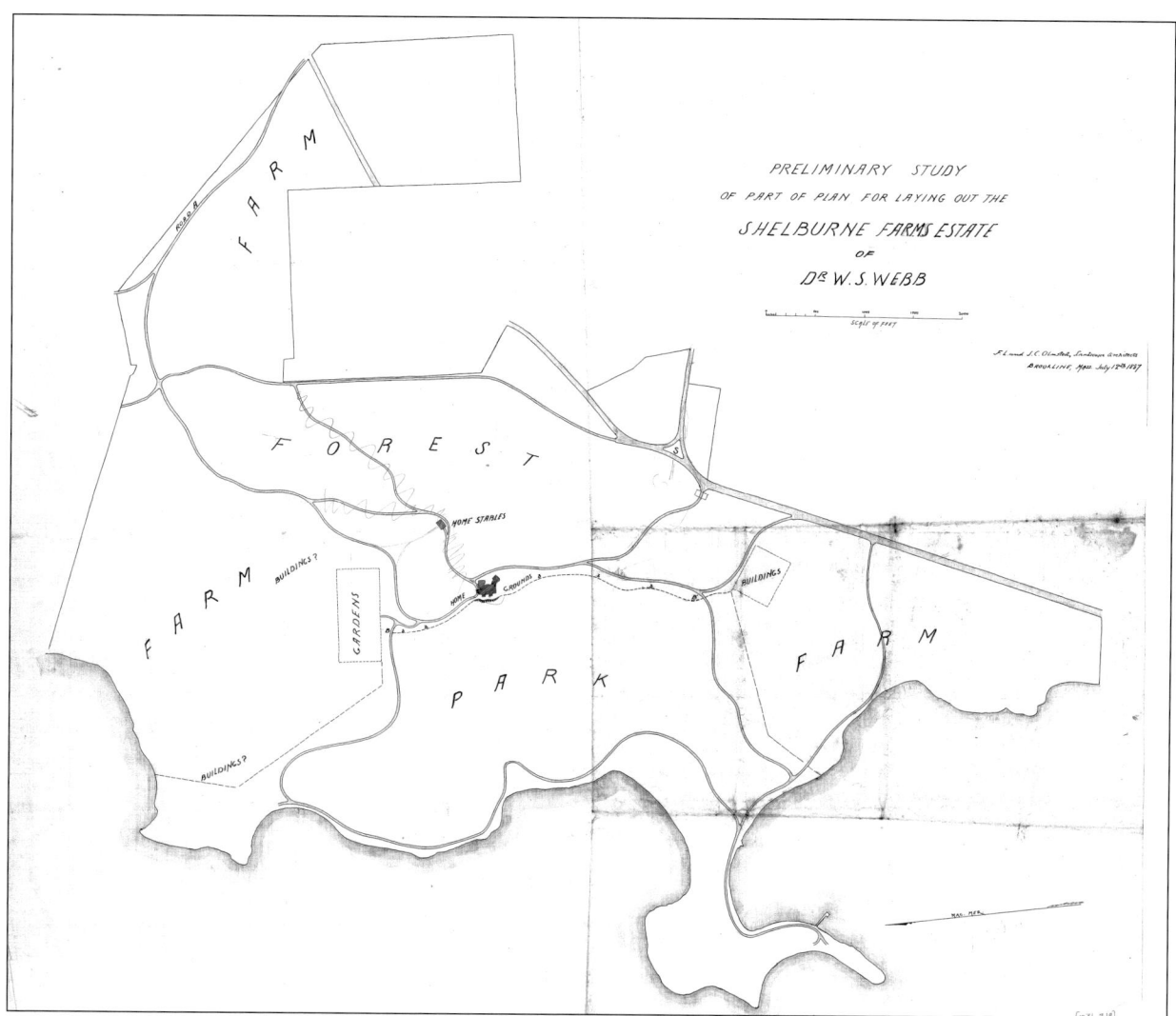

Preliminary Study of Part of Plan for Laying Out the Shelburne Farms Estate of Dr. W. S. Webb, by Frederick Law Olmsted, 1887. Courtesy of the National Park Service, Frederick Law Olmsted National Historic Site.

In July 1887, Olmsted submitted a preliminary plan for the entire Shelburne Farms landscape that divided the estate into "farm, forest, and parklands" sections: "1st Tillage and pasturelands in rotation; 2nd Park or permanent pasturelands; 3rd Forests arboretum Vermontii."[30] According to Olmsted's plan, the existing individual farm parcels were to be replaced by broad divisions in the land based upon function. Two sections of farmland, each containing rotating cropland and pastureland, would flank the Vermont arboretum to the east and a large park to the west bordering Lake Champlain. Olmsted sited the estate's future agricultural buildings inside the southern area of farmland. He placed the planned country house on the flanks of Lone Tree Hill facing west over the parkland: "I propose a perfectly simple park, or pasture field, a mile long on the lake, half a mile deep, the house looking down upon and over it."[31]

However, during the next several years, the Webbs continued to acquire additional parcels, leaving the plans unsettled. Design work was often delayed as they negotiated the purchase of more farms, failed to relay vital information about their newest purchases, and changed their minds about the landscape plans as additional properties were added. They pressed Olmsted to reevaluate and modify his designs to incorporate the new parcels. As Olmsted wrote Seward in January 1887, "I heard that you had a scheme for a large addition to your Shelburne property and would not want us to proceed with plans until you had reached a conclusion, as your proposed new purchases...would involve a general review of previous instructions...Having no instructions from you we have done nothing."[32]

Robert Robertson, deep into designing the estate architecture and close to starting construction on the couple's temporary country house, faced similar problems in getting them to commit to a set plan. As he confided to Olmsted in March 1887, "I find it exceedingly difficult to obtain from the Doctor a final decision upon many of the points in question, and in consequence the whole scheme seems to be held in abeyance."[33]

As it turned out, the Webbs were not willing to implement Olmsted's full vision for Shelburne Farms. First, they wavered about the site for their permanent country residence. Olmsted favored a site known as Windmill Hill, on land formerly belonging to the Comstocks and Morehouses, along the southwestern flank of Lone Tree Hill overlooking Lake Champlain. But Seward and Lila hesitated to commit to that location and eventually focused upon the Saxton's Point promontory bordering Lake Champlain, already the future site of their temporary country house. As one historian has speculated, the Webbs may have chosen Saxton's Point because they did not feel the need for the statement a house would make if more prominently positioned on Windmill Hill.[34]

Olmsted's first indication of Seward and Lila's changing minds came in a letter from the topographer Cotton in September 1886: "I saw Mr. Taylor [the estate's farm manager] and he told me that they [the Webbs] were negotiating for the purchase of more land which if consummated might change the location of the house."[35] Over the next two years, Olmsted unsuccessfully pushed the couple to reconsider their decision to abandon the Windmill Hill site. His farm–forest–parkland sketch of July 1887 placed the house in that location. In the spring of 1888, he visited the property again to consider other options but remained fixed on Windmill Hill. He wrote to Seward again, "I greatly hope that you will come back to the old position for the mansion...I am sure that there is no other site that offers nearly equal advantages. I had thought of three others as promising well but when I came to try to fit a house and grounds to them none proved satisfactory."[36]

The Webbs also retreated from fully implementing Olmsted's Vermont arboretum. Seward was wedded to the idea of planting at least a few nonnative, ornamental species that were often featured on other contemporary American estates, including rhododendrons, tea roses, and gardenias. Olmsted tried to discourage these ideas, replying to one request, "We would advise caution in planting the weeping willow. Hardly any tree is more incongruous with the landscape character of your shore or more difficult to reconcile with it."[37]

Olmsted was quite likely discouraged and frustrated by Seward and Lila's disregard for his advice, especially when it came to the Vermont arboretum. He began to disengage himself from the Shelburne Farms project, first by turning it over to other members of his firm and then ceasing to work on it altogether around 1889. It is unclear exactly when Olmsted stopped consulting for the Webbs, and which party officially severed the ties.[38]

Whatever the case, in the end, Olmsted was probably dissatisfied with his aborted project at Shelburne Farms. As one historian has written, Olmsted "sought to learn his clients' wishes and needs, but his plans often involved considerations of sanitation, psychology, and aesthetics that went beyond their experience and understanding. Once a client accepted a design, Olmsted expected to be

Shelburne Farms employees, c. 1893. In the front row are clerk and future farm manager Edward F. Gebhardt (left), farm manager Archibald Taylor (center), and head farmer W. H. Clarke (right). Shelburne Farms Collections.

free to carry it out in all particulars."[39] The landscape architect was to more fully implement some of the ideas he had proposed for Shelburne Farms, including an arboretum of native species, at another Vanderbilt property, George Vanderbilt's Biltmore, where he and his firm worked from 1888 to 1903.[40]

Seward and Lila, however, were appreciative of Olmsted as a landscape architect and of his overall plans for Shelburne Farms in particular. In 1887, Seward recommended Olmsted to his brother-in-law Frederick Vanderbilt for landscape work at Vanderbilt's home, Rough Point, in Newport, Rhode Island.[41]

The Webbs turned to Archibald Taylor (1826–1908) to continue developing the estate using the majority of Olmsted's design ideas. Born in Scotland, Taylor had assisted his father, the chief forester of a large Scottish nobleman's estate, before immigrating to the United States and settling in Vermont in 1857. Before being hired by the Webbs to manage Oakledge Farm, Taylor first ran a nursery and then laid out the grounds and managed the Burlington estate of Seward and Lila's friend Col. Cannon. Taylor would spend the last twenty-three years of his career as farm manager at Shelburne Farms, the first person to hold that position. As his obituary later noted, "In laying out the grounds and beautifying the landscape, Mr. Taylor did a work which brought him the highest endorsement."[42]

While some details of Olmsted's plan were altered to accommodate new land acquisitions and revised building sites, the landscape architect's farm–

Looking west toward Quaker Smith Point, by Thomas E. Marr, c. 1900. Shelburne Farms Collections.

forest–parkland plan proved to be the guiding template. Under Archibald Taylor's direction, over the next twenty years, the property was divided into agricultural areas containing the estate's model farm buildings, pastures, and cropland; forested areas; and parkland areas for the Webb family's country residence and surrounding lawns, carriage barns, golf course, docks, and boathouse. Many of the public roads were closed and planted over, replaced by a series of winding primary and secondary drives based upon Olmsted's sketches. And most of the preexisting farm buildings were dismantled to make way for architect Robert Robertson's new estate structures.[43]

Chapter 4
SHELBURNE HOUSE

Place looking fine & house in beautiful order, and all so glad to have us home again, as are we to be here!
— Lila Webb, September 6, 1903

Seward & I leave tonight for Shelburne!!! ...We are both glad to get 'home.'
— Lila Webb, May 22 and 23, 1925[1]

For thirty-eight years, Seward and Lila Webb spent most of the spring, summer, and autumn months at Shelburne Farms, often returning for the Thanksgiving and Christmas holidays as well. There, they entertained friends and family members and pursued the same kind of athletic, outdoor-oriented lifestyle they had maintained at Oakledge. While the couple enjoyed their winters in New York, and later in Florida, they always spoke of Shelburne Farms as their "home," the place to which they returned year after year for emotional fulfillment.

A Country Residence

Design work on the Webbs' private residence began soon after architect Robert Robertson had been engaged by the couple. By March 1887, just before Frederick Law Olmsted completed his farm–forest–parkland landscape plan, Robertson had submitted a preliminary design for the family's permanent country house. A rendering of the building was published in the March 19 issue of *American Architect and Building News*, and it appeared in the *New York Daily Graphic* soon thereafter. The latter described it favorably as "a magnificent new country home...The effect of the house is a union of the imposing and superb with the home-like as delightful as it is rare."[2]

Robertson's design consisted of a commanding three-story stone residence with numerous dormers, chimneys, porches, turrets, and multipaned windows. On the interior, formal public spaces included a main hall with a staircase leading to a gallery above, a two-story dining room with a built-in organ, a library, and a formal drawing room. A wing containing a billiard room and a morning room was connected to the massive main block with a curved arcade

passageway. A month after the design was published, Olmsted incorporated its footprint into his landscape plan.³

While Olmsted debated with Seward and Lila on the final location for their permanent residence, Robertson set to work designing the couple's temporary home, Shelburne House. The site selected was Edward Saxton's former apple orchard on Saxton's Point, a high promontory overlooking Lake Champlain and surrounded by water on three sides. Built between the summer of 1887 and May 1888, the rambling, low-slung Shelburne House lay across the top of the point. Robertson designed the three-story structure in the shingle style, one of the most popular architectural styles for dwellings of middle- and upper-class Americans during the 1870s and 1880s. The shingle style represented a distillation and reinterpretation of features drawn from seventeenth-century English Queen Anne and American Colonial architecture. Shelburne House's exterior

Top: A design by Robert Robertson for the Webbs' permanent residence at Shelburne Farms, published in the *New York Daily Graphic*, June 1887. Shelburne Farms Collections. Above: Construction workers in front of the incomplete Shelburne House, attributed to Dr. W. Seward Webb, c. 1887–88. Shelburne Farms Collections.

Shelburne House, c. 1890. Shelburne Farms Collections.

featured clapboards on its first story and shingles above, half-timbered gables, windows with decorative pane patterns, and a broad, unifying shingled roof.[4]

On the interior, Shelburne House was relatively informal and intimate. Numerous windows and exterior doors provided an easy transition between outdoors and indoors. Instead of formal drawing room and reception spaces, Shelburne House contained two first-floor porches, a main hall, a library, a dining room, and a breakfast room as its primary living spaces. In addition to dressing rooms and bedrooms for the master and mistress of the house, the second floor included nurseries for the Webb children and four guest bedrooms. The kitchen and other service spaces were grouped to the north beyond the first-floor public living areas, and open dormitory-style bedrooms on the third floor were set aside for household employees.[5]

Shelburne House was relatively small and casual compared to the size and scale of the permanent residence that Robertson was designing for the family. The *Telegram* of Troy, New York, reported that the building's interiors were "comfortable and luxuriously rustic."[6] They were filled with the elements of a late Victorian aesthetic: oriental rugs, heavy portières (curtains hung across door frames), patterned wallpapers, potted palms, and a mixture of Louis XV–style and wicker furniture piled high with plump pillows. Lila may have served as the primary interior decorator for the house, which the *Boston Home Journal* reported contained "stairways and walls finished in oak, and other apartments in different styles—empire, pink, blue, etc."[7]

However, even as a temporary dwelling, Shelburne House probably began to feel inadequate for the family's requirements soon after its construction. According to the lifestyle to which Seward and Lila were accustomed, four major living spaces and four guest bedrooms were simply not enough to comfortably house their steady stream of guests and friends, and their growing family, which had increased to four children with the birth of their younger sons, William Seward Jr. (1887–1956) and Vanderbilt (1891–1956). The family's requirements and constant entertaining also probably placed a strain on the residence's service areas, which needed to accommodate not only the Webbs' own cooks, housemaids, butlers, footmen, nursemaids, and other household servants, but also the personal servants who accompanied the family's guests. In 1891, a two-story wing was added to Shelburne House for use until the permanent country house was erected. The "annex," as it was called, added several service areas, guest and staff bedrooms, and a smoking room on the northwest end of the building.[8]

While Shelburne House was being enlarged, Robertson prepared several additional palatial designs for the Webbs' permanent country residence. The designs followed a new trend in formal American domestic architecture toward the Beaux-Arts model, which emphasized the

Lila and Vanderbilt Webb on the south porch at Shelburne House, c. 1892. Shelburne Farms Collections.

resplendence of European palaces and country seats rather than the intimacy and informality of shingle style houses. The Beaux-Arts architectural model encompassed a variety of grand styles, such as French Renaissance, Georgian, and Tudor, and featured specialized spaces for family members, guests, and servants.[9]

American residences built and furnished in the Beaux-Arts manner were frequently showy, sacrificing intimacy for a palatial physical and decorative scale. The often-cited paradigm is Marble House, the Newport residence of Lila's brother and sister-in-law William and Alva Vanderbilt, which contained an ornate "gold room" with carved and gilded walls, a ten-ton copy of a screen from Versailles with the couple's monogram in place of that of Louis XIV, and solid bronze dining chairs. While the plans prepared for the Webbs appear to be for a house somewhat less conspicuous than Marble House, or several other Beaux-Arts houses built for

Lila's siblings, they were of the same scale. Seward and Lila's home would have fit well in Newport had they built any of Robertson's Beaux-Arts plans.[10]

Yet they eventually rejected not only their architect's specific Beaux-Arts plans, but also the very idea of a full-fledged palatial residence—just as they had resisted Frederick Law Olmsted's pressure to place their permanent house on Windmill Hill. Instead, by 1893, the Webbs had decided to modify and enlarge Shelburne House on Saxton's Point and turn it into a permanent home. Lila noted in her diary rather matter-of-factly in June 1893, that "this afternoon we cut down a number of trees in the woods near the [Shelburne] house, as we have decided to alter this house, and give up building the other one." Significantly, it was the *barns* at Shelburne Farms that would end up looking like castles, not the country house.[11]

Noteworthy in the decision not to build a formal Beaux-Arts house was the state of the couple's finances. Robertson's Windmill Hill plans indicate that the permanent residence would have been quite expensive, and its costs were estimated by the press to be between $1.5 and $3 million. Seward and Lila could probably have afforded such a house, but only by significantly draining their fortune. A Beaux-Arts residence could have consumed an entire year's income or more, leaving little or nothing for other expenses or projects—of which the Webbs had many.[12]

Thus, Shelburne House was enlarged and transformed in a series of construction projects lasting from 1895 to 1900. A large wing added to the northern end of the building more than doubled the service sections of the house and freed many of the support areas in both the dwelling and its annex for other purposes. The annex was physically detached from the side of the original house, moved approximately 200 feet to the northwest, and placed on a new foundation as a stand-alone structure in order to accommodate additional staff housing and sporting rooms. Then, a brick addition was erected in place of the annex. The new addition contained more formal entertaining

View of a plan for a country house at Shelburne Farms influenced by Warwick Castle, designed by Robert H. Robertson and rendered by J. King James, 1891. Shelburne Farms Collections.

Shelburne House and its formal gardens, by J. Watson Webb Jr., July 1934. Shelburne Farms Collections.

rooms, a porch, a series of guest bedrooms, and a children's playroom. Finally, the original portion of the building was substantially renovated in order to harmonize its appearance and function with the new addition: it was bricked over and reroofed in slate, its chimneys rebuilt, and its top floor enlarged and partitioned into more guest bedrooms.[13]

In its final form, Shelburne House contained vestiges of both the original, temporary structure and the planned Windmill Hill residence, providing it with a dual sense of shingle style comfort and Beaux-Arts stateliness. The renovated and expanded Shelburne House was ideally suited to the kind of luxurious yet comfortable country life that Seward and Lila loved.

Several elements contributed to a new sense of Beaux-Arts formality. Shelburne House now contained more than 40,000 square feet, 22 family and guest bedrooms, 23 fireplaces, 23 bathrooms, and 29 bedrooms for household employees and servants accompanying guests. In addition, the renovation projects added a half-story to the main portion of the house, giving it three full floors, which, combined with the dwelling's expanded footprint, created a much more imposing appearance from the exterior.[14]

Shelburne House's new exterior finishes also provided a heightened sense of formality. In place of the original and more informal cladding and roofing, the house now featured a more imposing Queen Anne–style façade with brick sheathing, decorative half-timbering on the second and third stories, and a slate roof punctuated by numerous turrets, gables, and chimneys with ornamental brick patterns.[15]

On the other hand, several elements of the final Shelburne House maintained ties to the more informal shingle style of the original dwelling. Instead of a formal floor plan featuring one or more straight axes along which the rooms were arranged, the building possessed a rambling, Y-shaped floor plan, which spread the rooms out along long, angled hallways. Second, with its multiple large windows and exterior doors, the entire dwelling remained oriented to the outdoors, allowing the inhabitants to easily extend their living spaces beyond the walls into their surroundings. Third, the interior featured the same warm Victorian aesthetic as the original Shelburne House: the rooms were packed with furniture and potted palms, the walls covered with framed pictures, and the tabletops filled with vases of cut flowers, family photographs, and personal mementos. Layers of curtains, carpets, upholstery fabrics, pillows, and furs covered every available surface with a profusion of patterns, textures, and colors.[16]

The new Shelburne House's dual shingle style and Beaux-Arts allegiances were also manifested in the types and functions of the rooms that the building now contained. On the southern end of the first floor, a group of informal living areas, including a piazza, a library, a main hall, and a "morning/smoking room," provided spaces for the family to carry out everyday activities and informal entertaining. The piazza, which became known as the "south porch," was an especially favored space. The Webbs and their guests spent hours there, conversing, watching nearby lawn games, waiting for arriving friends and family members, and simply enjoying the tremendous 180-degree views of Lake Champlain and the Adirondacks to the south and west. The south porch was available for year-round enjoyment: in the cooler months, it was enclosed by windows and doors and heated, while in the warmer months, the windows and doors were removed and replaced with awnings. Lila, a voracious reader who read as many as three books a day, spent afternoons, or even days at a time, on the south porch reading, writing letters, and relaxing. Seward and Lila's young son Vanderbilt pitched his play tent on the lawn just beyond the porch. His brother Seward Jr. later wrote, "We live there in the summer."[17]

Seward Sr. worked from five o'clock to nine o'clock each morning in his first-floor office, which was located near the family living areas on the east side of Shelburne House to capitalize on the morning sun. Here he met and communicated with business associates, his personal secretary, other Wagner Palace Car Company employees, his farm manager, and estate department leaders such as the stud groom, who was in charge of the horse breeding operation. In 1899, the *Burlington Free Press* reported,

> *Dr. Webb has in his private office, or workroom, telegraph and telephone wires, enabling him to keep in touch with his business affairs in New York. A special railroad service brings him three mail bags every night, made up at his New York offices. This enables him to spend the greater part of his time at his Shelburne home and still attend to the details of his vast business interests in the metropolis.*[18]

The office contained a large desk, several comfortable upholstered chairs, and bookshelves for his personal library. An exterior door leading to the circular drive in front of Shelburne House allowed Seward to step outside and greet business associates. The presence of the exterior door also meant that those arriving to meet with him could come and go without disturbing the social activities occurring in other sections of the residence.[19]

The Webb family's second-floor bedrooms and dressing rooms were located directly above the living and office areas on the southern end of the house. Seward and Lila occupied a suite of rooms, which after about 1905 consisted of adjoining bedrooms, dressing/sitting rooms, and bathrooms.

Their four children occupied individual bedrooms nearby, and their oldest son Watson's adjoined a separate sitting room. In addition to beds, the family's spacious private rooms were decorated with floral wallpapers, filled with armchairs, divans, writing and dressing tables, armoires, and bookshelves, and personalized with framed photographs and other mementos. The boys' bedrooms were hung with hunting and coaching prints, Seward Sr.'s with views of his 1896 Yellowstone hunting trip, Lila's with photographs of her children and mother, and her daughter Frederica's with portraits of family members and European nobility. Frederica, the musician in the family, also furnished her bedroom with a grand piano.[20]

On the northern end of the house, a new suite of rooms accommodated the grand style of entertaining in which Seward, Lila, and their peers engaged. Adjoining the first-floor family living spaces was the Colonial Revival–style "corridor hall," which was used as a site for more informal meals, as well as occasional dances, musical soirées, and theatrical skits. In the Neoclassical dining room, the most formal room in the house, the couple would often host rich multicourse dinners and luncheons. One frequent guest described dinner at Shelburne House as "a very formal occasion and very impressive with the many courses that were served by the numerous footmen."[21] The menu for Thanksgiving dinner in 1899, for example, consisted of Cape Cod oysters, oxtail soup, roasted turkey and stuffed roasted pheasant, mushrooms, plum pudding, mincemeat and pumpkin pies, and finally, coffee. The mahogany extension table was decorated for the occasion with a centerpiece of "sheaves of wheat, oats and barley…surrounded by a profuse display of artistically arranged vegetables and fruits of every description" and vases of cut flowers from the estate greenhouses.[22]

The oak-paneled north room, dominated by a huge sandstone fireplace and adorned with hunting trophies, adjoined the dining room. Here male guests could smoke cigars and play billiards.

The north room also often housed an enormous Christmas tree during the holiday season.[23]

On the second and third floors, sixteen guest bedrooms accommodated a large number of visiting family and friends. They were individually decorated and furnished in a variety of popular styles, including Colonial Revival, Empire, and Louis XVI. Like the family bedrooms, the guest rooms were decorated with floral wallpapers and filled with a profusion of furniture and framed pictures.[24]

Extensive service areas supported the needs of Shelburne House's inhabitants. Two pantries adjoining the dining room provided storage for dinner services, serving dishes, and glassware. Housemaids' closets on the second and third floors contained storage space and sinks. A cedar closet served as the main storage area for household linens, and a nearby "brush room" probably served as a space for cleaning and storing clothing. A sewing room provided additional facilities for maintaining clothing, including the employees' uniforms. In the new servants' wing, a large tiled kitchen contained marble wainscoting, built-in storage cabinets, work tables, and an enormous wood-fired stove. The laundry facilities consisted of separate washing, drying, and ironing rooms. Two outbuildings located to the north of the servants' wing, the garbage house and ice house/laundry structures, accommodated additional service needs. The ice house/laundry's cellar stored blocks of ice harvested from Lake Champlain that were destined for the main residence's cold storage areas.[25]

Shelburne House was equipped with the latest domestic technology, offering its inhabitants state-of-the-art living and working conditions. Large plate-glass windows and skylights infused public and service areas with natural light. A semicircular iron and glass conservatory connected to the dining room, erected by the New York City firm Thos. W. Weathered's Sons, provided a soothing backdrop to formal meals. A central heating system distributed heated air from three coal-fed boilers in the basement through wall ducts to grates and radiators in the upper floors. During the summer months, the wall ducts served as a passive ventilation system, bringing cool air in through windows in the basement and circulating it upstairs. Shelburne House was wired for electricity powered by a direct-current "dynamo," or generator, located in a nearby outbuilding. Three hand-operated dumbwaiters transported luggage, wood and ashes, and breakfast trays between floors. Three large walk-in safes secured the family's valuables. Call buttons placed in the family and guest areas notified employees of needs via call boxes located in the service areas. A telegraph station and three telephones kept the house's inhabitants in close contact with other estate departments and the outside world. An insulated "refrigerator room," located in the servants' wing and cooled with blocks of ice, provided cold storage for foodstuffs. The nearby ice house/laundry was equipped with a small elevator to facilitate the transport of large cakes of ice up to the ground level of the outbuilding, from which they traveled across the service court to the servants' wing and through exterior

The library at Shelburne House, by Thomas E. Marr, c. 1900. Shelburne Farms Collections.

hatches leading to the refrigerator room's ice storage compartments. And finally, a total of twenty-three bathrooms for family, guests, and employees were installed throughout the residence.[26]

During Shelburne House's regular May to October season, it housed as many as twenty-five employees, including a butler, two underbutlers, two footmen, a chef, four other kitchen staff members, a housekeeper, four chambermaids, four parlormaids, and three laundresses. Additional personal servants included a valet for Seward, a lady's maid for Lila, and the children's nurses, governesses, and tutors. Seward's secretary also spent time at Shelburne House assisting with his business affairs. When the family moved between residences, one or more railroad horsecars containing their personal belongings, family portraits, silver, and favorite horses and carriages would be sent a few days ahead with an advance staff. Most of the household employees moved with the family, leaving a skeleton crew behind to maintain the dwelling when the Webbs were elsewhere.[27]

While the Webbs were in residence, Shelburne House's guest bedrooms were almost always filled with a close-knit group of relatives and friends. Seward's brothers, Lila's siblings, and their families were frequent guests, often visiting two or three times each year and remaining for weeks at a time. Seward and Lila regularly invited groups of their nieces and nephews and their children's school friends to visit. The couple also hosted frequent weekend house parties for New York society members, including the John Jacob Astors, the Ogden Millses, the Frederic Bronsons, and August and Perry Belmont. Several prominent political figures visited Shelburne House, including President William Howard Taft and Admiral George Dewey. Lila was especially proud of President Theodore Roosevelt's 1902 visit with members of his cabinet, and she recorded the seating arrangement for the formal dinner held in his honor at Shelburne House in her diary.[28]

The Webbs were known as excellent hosts who entertained their guests with intellectual conversation and a wide array of outdoor activities. As one young woman staying at Shelburne House during the 1890s gushed to a friend,

Maids at Shelburne House, c. 1895. Shelburne Farms Collections.

I would give anything if you knew the Webbs and could come up here and have the nice time I am having. I cannot take exception to anything that they do. Perhaps this seems too old a remark for me to make, but I can judge pretty well, & think Mrs. Webb and Frederica are two people of remarkable character... You ought to see Mrs. Webb's Library and the way she can discuss books! And this beautiful place when the sun sets and the lake and the mountains are pink by reflection! It is very beautiful.[29]

Guests at a Shelburne House costume party held in honor of J. Watson Webb's fiftieth birthday, by J. Watson Webb Jr., July 1934. Among those pictured are Electra Havemeyer Webb (rear, eighth from left, wearing white), hostess Lila Webb (center rear, wearing black), and Vanderbilt Webb (center rear, next to Lila on the right). Shelburne Farms Collections.

Another guest, the young Electra Havemeyer, recalled a similar experience when she first visited Shelburne Farms in 1903: "The beauty of Shelburne Farms, Vermont, and Lake Champlain took my breath away. From the minute I arrived I loved the Webbs, the country, and felt I was in dreamland. The experience of traveling in a private [railroad] car and being met with a coach and four was almost too much for me to grasp."[30] Miss Havemeyer would marry Seward and Lila's eldest son, Watson, in 1910.

The October 1905 marriage of the Webbs' daughter, Frederica, to Ralph Pulitzer (1879–1939) was perhaps the crowning social affair held at Shelburne Farms. More than 150 guests witnessed the couple's nuptials at the Trinity Episcopal Church in the village of Shelburne. The bride traveled to and from the church in the family's most elegant vehicle, an enclosed Berlin carriage made by the premier Paris firm of Million et Guiet, which was driven by her brothers Watson and Seward Jr. riding postillion. Following a breakfast reception for 600 held on the Shelburne House lawn, the newly married couple left for their honeymoon on the family yacht. Shelburne House was filled to capacity for the event. Consequently, bachelor family members and friends stayed on board the steamer *Vermont*, anchored in Shelburne Bay, and overflow guests had to make do with unheated rooms at the Van Ness Hotel in Burlington.[31]

53

Aerial view of Saxton's Point, by Fairchild Aerial Surveys, New York, July 1928. Visible are Shelburne House and its formal gardens, the private dock to the south, Elm Tree Swamp to the north, and Orchard Point to the northwest. Shelburne Farms Collections.

Special social events notwithstanding, the Webbs and their guests spent much of their time outdoors in the landscape surrounding Shelburne House. Ten acres of grass lawns dotted with elm trees extended in all directions. A grass tennis court was located near the south porch, and rustic wooden benches and armchairs were placed in shady spots with views of Lake Champlain. On the northwestern end of Saxton's Point overlooking the lake, a one-story shingled tea house, constructed sometime before 1890, was probably used by Lila and her friends for afternoon tea and quiet conversation. At the other end of the point, a small one-story shingled playhouse was built for the Webb children by 1890. Around 1905, after the children had outgrown the playhouse, it was replaced by a gazebo, a one-story octagonal structure used by Seward and his friends for playing poker and shooting skeet. Outside the gazebo, a flagpole flew an American flag high above the surrounding tree line.[32]

CHAPTER 5

FARM AND FOREST

Many people in Vermont who are unacquainted with the plan pursued by the Doctor, labor under the misapprehension that Shelburne Farms is maintained simply as a palatial country home for Dr. Webb and his family. It is much more than that. It is an inspiration and an education to every right minded visitor who passes through the Farms, and all are welcome—every week day—to drive on the roads and view the surroundings. Farmers and others who are interested in stock breeding, or other matters pertaining to farm life, will find Manager Taylor always ready to explain matters under his charge. Dr. Webb has earned a high standing in the esteem of Vermont farmers for the generous interest he has manifested in improving the prosperity of Vermont, especially along the lines of better roads and better stock.

— BURLINGTON (VT) FARMER ADVOCATE, 1895[1]

AT THE TURN OF THE TWENTIETH CENTURY, Shelburne Farms was perhaps best known as a model farm. Like many of their peers, Seward and Lila Webb devoted a large portion of their estate and resources to experimenting with the latest agricultural technology and scientific practices. In ideal terms, model farms operated under a "trickle-down" theory: those who could afford to develop and test new approaches would disseminate their results to a broader audience through correspondence with professionals in the field, through the press, and through local word of mouth. By doing so, they would eventually assist in improving production and increasing profits for everyday farmers. Meanwhile, model farm owners would provide their own tables with choice farm products.

Model farming had its origins in eighteenth-century Great Britain, where landed gentlemen established or improved the farms on their country estates "not just to provide for [their] own households and to raise crops for profit, but also as a model to demonstrate new methods and techniques."[2] In the late nineteenth and early twentieth centuries, American model farms were part of a larger "scientific farming" movement. Advocates asserted that a focus on technology and biological sciences would increase farmers' prosperity after decades of soil depletion and increased competition from the Midwest and the Great Plains. In Vermont, "farm experts were unanimous in their view that science would return Vermont to the good old days of soil fertility and the rural prosperity it had brought to their grandparents' generation."[3]

Seward Webb was a passionate proponent of the benefits of scientific farm-

The Farm Barn, by Thomas E. Marr, c. 1900. Shelburne Farms Collections.

Right: The Farm Barn under construction, 1888. Shelburne Farms Collections.

ing, and he wanted Shelburne Farms to make its mark upon local and national agricultural practices. To do so, he created one of the largest and most complex model farm operations in the country, experimenting with a wide array of products and techniques on a huge scale. The Webbs erected magnificent farm buildings equipped with the latest technological and sanitary features; bred prized strains of livestock; produced high-quality crops from fields enhanced by state-of-the-art drainage systems; and created efficient and detailed management and record-keeping systems. Intrigued by both the promise of future benefits to everyday farmers and the magnitude of Seward's ambition, journalists published numerous reports of his agricultural activities in many local and national publications, among them the *Burlington Free Press, Boston Herald, New York Times, Frank Leslie's Popular Monthly, Country Life in America,* and *New England Magazine*.

Farm Barn

Work on the agricultural components of Shelburne Farms began concurrently with the design and construction of Shelburne House. In June 1887, the *New York Daily Graphic* featured architect Robert Robertson's first design for an estate farm building, a "Farm Barn and Stables," alongside his first plan for the Webbs' permanent residence. The Farm Barn plan featured a four-sided,

Queen Anne–style clapboard structure with half-timbering, roofs punctuated by eyebrow windows, and a central courtyard. A four-story main block surmounted by a cupola covered two arched entrances that opened onto the courtyard. Two-story wings completed the other three sides of the courtyard.[4]

Construction started on the Farm Barn just before Seward and Lila moved into Shelburne House in May 1888. By some accounts, the couple had been unable to convince a landowner to sell the land containing the favored site for their Farm Barn at the eastern base of Lone Tree Hill, so construction began on an alternative site nearby. However, the landowner relented and sold the parcel soon thereafter, and the incomplete structure was disassembled, moved to the favored location, and then completed. The story is plausible, as the Webbs' 1886 and 1887 purchases surrounded one missing chunk of land encompassing that site, a 104-acre parcel that was acquired from aging widow Mary Holabird and her thirty-eight-year-old daughter, Harriet, the same month that construction began.[5]

It is unclear exactly why the Holabirds might have refused the Webbs' early overtures to sell their land. They had relied on hired labor to manage their farm after Mary's husband, Cassius, died in 1878, but they appear to have been able to make a decent living. Whatever the case, their reluctance proved profitable, as Seward and Lila paid $20,000 for the property only eight years after it was valued at $6,000 in the 1880 federal agricultural census. The deed of sale granted the Holabirds permission to occupy their former property for the spring and summer of 1888. Their farmhouse, which stood just a few hundred feet from the Webbs' new Farm Barn, would soon be converted into employee housing.[6]

In its final form and location, the Farm Barn was built into the lower flanks of Lone Tree Hill,

oriented to the east with the cleared midsection of the hill directly behind it. The first sections of the building, the four-story main block and its two flanking two-story side ells, were probably completed in the winter of 1888–89. The barn's design had evolved somewhat from the rendering published in the *New York Daily Graphic* in 1887. While the structure retained its Queen Anne architectural style and overall layout surrounding a central courtyard, local stone quarried from the property and wood shingles were substituted for the clapboard sheathing seen in the rendering. The main block featured a redstone foundation, shingled second and third stories, and a hipped roof enclosing gables ornamented with half-timbering. A cupola crowned by a copper weathervane in the shape of a serpent stood atop the main block, and two small ventilators flanked the cupola. A four-sided clock was installed in the cupola and a corresponding bell in the southern ventilator by November 1888. The bell was the result of a wager won by Seward Webb, a loyal Republican, over the presidential election of 1888 and was engraved, "This bell was hung in commemoration of the great republican victory in the election of Gen. Benjamin Harrison, Nov. 6, 1888, and was paid for by a disappointed democrat."[7]

The Farm Barn was completed in 1890 with the addition of two wings and a

The courtyard of the Farm Barn, by Thomas E. Marr, c. 1900. Shelburne Farms Collections.

redstone retaining wall, which together surrounded the north, east, and south sides of the building's central courtyard. The wings, topped by conical turrets, were clad in a combination of redstone, shingles, and half-timbering and contained both enclosed workspaces and open storage sheds.[8]

In its final form, the Farm Barn was a massive building that entirely suited Seward's ambitious plans for his model farm. The main block measured approximately 400 by 50 feet, and the courtyard enclosed by the structure was about 400 by 260 feet. The 1893 edition of *Shelburne Farms Stud*, a catalogue of Seward's horses, boasted, "This farm barn is undoubtedly the most gigantic structure of its kind ever erected on any estate, and should be seen by every one interested in the construction of buildings of a like nature."[9]

Designed to serve as the hub of the estate's agricultural operations, the Farm Barn was a multipurpose structure. The ground floor of the main block contained stables for the seventy to eighty work mules used to pull farm vehicles, with haylofts and granaries capable of accommodating 1,500 tons of crops above. Storage areas for crop planting and harvesting equipment, as well as the devices used to build and maintain the estate's road system, were located on the second level of the main block (which was at ground level in the rear of the building, as the barn was built into a hillside) and in open shed areas in the wings.[10]

The Farm Barn was equipped with the latest agricultural and technological innovations. Steam heat and gas lighting were installed throughout the structure, the steam produced by coal-fed boilers in the northern wing and the gas stored in an underground tank in the courtyard. Indoor plumbing and changing areas were provided for farm employees. Steam-driven hayforks moved hay into the loft storage areas. Sick mules were housed apart from the main stable area in two open stalls. The north wing contained a horse-drawn hose carriage to assist in fighting fires and a hand-operated elevator that facilitated the movement of large items into the loft of the paint shop, where they were hoisted after painting to dry out of the way. In the south wing, a lift allowed vehicle bodies to be removed from their undercarriages and interchanged or stored separately.[11]

The Farm Barn's most elaborate technological feature was perhaps a steam-driven elevator system that transported grain to a storage area on one of the upper floors of the main block. Freshly harvested grain was shoveled from farm wagons into a chute leading to a mechanically driven sifting screen. The screen deposited the grain into a series of buckets attached to a vertical chain conveyor system, which transported it three stories up to a large trough. From the trough, blades pushed the grain onto a horizontal conveyor until it reached a chute leading to one of six tin-lined storage bins.[12]

The extensive agricultural activities were managed from the estate office, which was located in the north wing of the Farm Barn after about 1890. Farm manager Archibald Taylor and his successor, Edward F. Gebhardt (1858–1942), who served as assistant manager from 1897 until Taylor's retirement in 1908, supervised a staff of up to six clerks. They kept meticulous financial accounts of livestock, crop, produce, and lumber inventories; payroll records; and weather diaries. The clerks maintained a detailed accounting system that tracked profits and expenditures from outside individuals and businesses as well as credits and debits for each farm department. When hay was harvested from the fields, for example, the account for each particular plot would be credited for the quantity produced and the various departments that received the hay for their livestock would be debited for the quantity consumed. Farm tool inventories kept track of the equipment that employees checked out from the building's "tool room" to complete their work. Weather conditions recorded three times a day noted the temperature, precipitation, and the type of cloud cover. In 1895, a reporter for the Burlington *Farmer Advocate* marveled at the office and the records its employees maintained:

In this office, reports are received from the heads of each department, showing in detail all that has transpired within their jurisdiction. Dr. Webb's system of running the farms is just as accurate and complete as running a railroad. The cost and expenditure of each department is kept in detail. Full records of all live stock, showing even transfers from one barn to another, or to pasture are kept.[13]

Several features in the Farm Barn office facilitated the work of the farm manager and his assistants. The estate's primary telephone switchboard was located in one corner, from which an operator answered calls, took messages, and forwarded callers to telephones in other estate buildings. The office also contained a telegraph station, a time clock for the building's night watchman, and a water gauge that monitored and recorded water levels in the estate reservoir. The employee payroll was distributed from a counter inside the office, which was outfitted with metal grilles like a bank teller's station.[14]

Field Crops

The Farm Barn served as the primary storage site for the large quantities of field crops that Shelburne Farms produced each year, including barley, corn, corn fodder, hay, oats, potatoes, rye, and wheat. Seward Webb also experimented with growing buckwheat, cabbage, carrots, and mangelwurzel, and producing bran, barley meal, and oatmeal. In 1902, an excellent harvest produced 2,500 tons of hay, "eighty-two tons of mangelwurzel, nine hundred and eighty-four bushels of carrots, six hundred and twenty bushels of turnips and six hundred and ten heads of cabbage, besides a considerable amount of corn fodder and grain."[15] In addition to the primary crop storage areas located in the upper floors of the main block of the Farm Barn, open-air, roofed structures called hay barracks were constructed in the fields as supplemental storage sites. Most of the annual crop yields were consumed by the Webb family and their farm livestock, but small quantities were sold when extra was available. However, because of the large number of farm animals, additional grain supplies were often purchased to supplement those grown at Shelburne Farms.[16]

Throughout the 1880s and 1890s, as land was purchased for Shelburne Farms, ceramic drainage tiles were installed in many fields in order to improve their productivity and versatility. Placed in channels on beds of pebbles from the nearby lakeshore, the earthenware tile system used gravity to draw water away from moist areas toward drainage ditches on the field boundaries. The largest farm drainage project likely occurred in the summer and fall of 1889, when fifty Swedish immigrants living in New York City were hired to install drains in the existing fields and alongside the developing road system. More than 22,700 tiles between one and two feet in length were purchased for the work, creating a system that stretched for more than four miles.[17]

Seward Webb was intimately familiar with the estate farmland and its potential for various crops. In 1911, he wrote Gebhardt to suggest that the Farm consult with the University of Vermont's College of Agriculture in the planting of test patches of alfalfa in the northwestern part of the estate:

There is a side hill [near the] home fence just south of Bay View that is a little wet & on the flat near the fence it was always hard to seed down. I would like to try Alfalfa there. I want to try 8 places this year not over 200 feet square each one & I do not want any thing to interfere with it. Can't you get the Agri. Coll. of the U. of V. to pick out 8 places also to make an analysis of the soil & see what chemicals it needs & pay them for doing it so that we will not be bothered about it.[18]

Teamsters loading hay, attributed to Dr. W. Seward Webb, c. 1890. Shelburne Farms Collections.

The estate fields were tilled with teams of mules and, later, horses through at least the 1920s. As Gebhardt noted in 1911, the tractors available in the early twentieth century were not yet powerful enough: "Tractors I have always intended to try but those made for farming all seem too light in power…I have been looking for development in this."[19]

Orchards

In addition to field crops, Shelburne Farms contained orchards producing apples in large quantities, as well as smaller amounts of other fruits. The area was well suited for apple cultivation, and the land Seward and Lila had purchased for Shelburne Farms contained numerous existing orchards. By 1900, the estate contained approximately 6,000 apple trees. Seward's inventory of modern agricultural equipment included a pesticide pumping machine, in which horsepower was used to build up 100 to 150 psi of pressure to produce a high-volume spray.[20]

Shelburne Farms produced as many as 5,000 barrels of apples, including Spies, Greenings, Baldwins, and smaller quantities of Kings, Russets, Blue Pearmains, Spitzenburgs, and Tollman Sweets. Barrels were regularly sent to the Webbs' residences and to family, friends, and employees as gifts. Shelburne Farms apples were well known for their quality, and merchants from the New York, Chicago, and Philadelphia areas wrote successive farm managers Taylor and Gebhardt requesting to buy them. In 1906, the estate's fruit crop netted $4,355.[21]

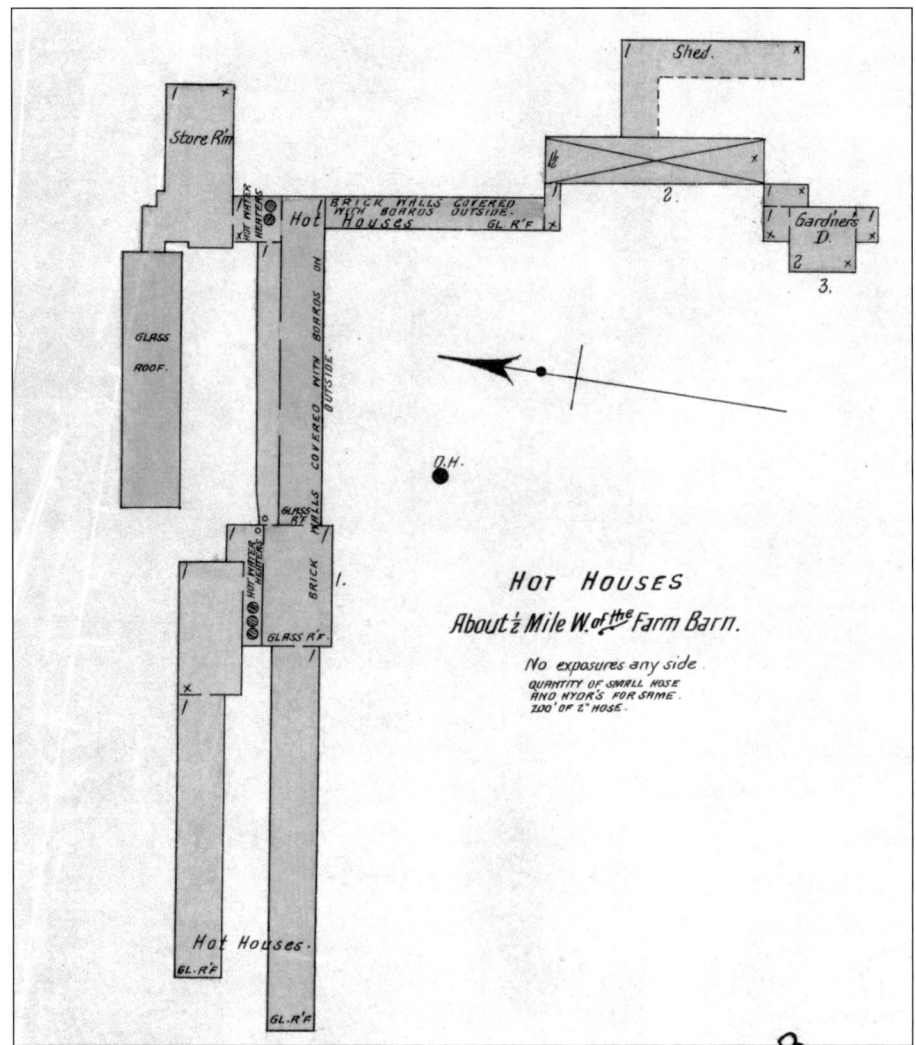

"Hot Houses" at Shelburne Farms, detail of the *Sanborn Fire Insurance Map* of Burlington, Vermont, 1906. Special Collections Department, Bailey/Howe Library, University of Vermont.

Gardener Alexander Graham at work, c. 1900. Shelburne Farms Collections.

Greenhouses

The estate's greenhouse and vegetable garden complex, located west of Lone Tree Hill on former Comstock land, was one of the largest and most productive farm departments at Shelburne Farms. Constructed between 1889 and 1906, the L-shaped greenhouse structures encompassed approximately 25,000 square feet. At least some of the interconnected, steam-heated units were designed by the New York City firm Hitchings & Co. Roughly triangular in profile, the structures possessed glass walls and roofs supported by iron frames resting on brick foundations. Inside, the greenhouses contained packed earthen floors, exposed bundles of piping for steam heat, and plank walkways leading past raised wooden planting beds. Windows for ventilation were located directly below the roof peaks and operated by hand cranks.[22]

The Shelburne Farms vegetable garden and greenhouses were considered "among the best in the country."[23] The estate produced artichokes, asparagus, melons, mushrooms, violets, gardenias, calla lilies, lilies of the valley, and chrysanthemums, among other plants. Individual greenhouse structures, such as the "Grapery," the "Palm House," the "Fern House," and the "Rose House," were devoted to particular items grown in large quantities. In 1899, the *New York Sun* noted that "a specialty is made of English violets and gardenias, which are raised on a more extensive scale than at any other private place in the United States."[24] The *Albany Argus* provided readers with additional detail on the contents of the greenhouses:

> *The extensive greenhouse, costing $20,000, contains ornamental Alamandas from East Indias, palms from Brazil and East Indies, with fine specimens of Ericas, Kentias and Latanias. The greatest space is given to gardenias, carnations, violets and roses, which are raised in enormous quantities and shipped by the thousands to New York three or four times a week when the family is in town.*[25]

The items grown in the vegetable garden and greenhouses were produced primarily for the Webb family's use and enjoyment. Garden plants and flowers were cultivated in the greenhouses during the winter and then transplanted or set out in pots in the formal gardens at Shelburne House when the weather was temperate. Masses of potted palms decorated the interiors of Shelburne House and 680 Fifth Avenue, and Lila wrote detailed annual notices of the number of palms that were required at each residence and where they were to stand. Fresh fruits and vegetables were sent regularly to the family's current residence. At times, the Webbs themselves were amazed at the vast quantities their greenhouses produced. In 1908, an abundance of mushrooms arriving daily in New York led Lila to request that the shipments be curtailed: "Enough have come down to feed 30 people a day, & I have been tired trying to think of people to send them to."[26]

Staggering numbers of some flower varieties—namely, violets, hyacinths, narcissus, roses, carnations, gardenias, and lilies of the valley—were grown in the greenhouses and shipped regularly to 680 Fifth Avenue to decorate the townhouse for the winter. As the 1893 edition of *Shelburne Farms Stud* noted, "No less than a thousand roses of the best varieties, and the same number of violets, are, during the season, shipped every week to New York."[27] Apparently, fewer numbers of flowers than usual were cultivated in 1910, as Lila wrote to Gebhardt, "We are pretty low down at the green house anyway now—900 violet plants, 450 roses, 750 carnations & only 50 gardenias. It will do."[28]

The estate's head gardener was responsible for sending flowers to various locations daily, which often meant packing and loading blooms on the Shelburne Farms railroad car that traveled to New York nightly. While in New York, Lila wrote Gebhardt frequently to request flowers to decorate the tables for her dinner parties and drawing rooms for her balls. A January 1906 letter to Gebhardt contained the following request:

> *Will you tell [head gardener Patrick] Fay, that I have dinners of 20 each here next Tuesday & Thursday nights the 16th & 18th, so send flowers Monday & Wednesday nights, & send each time 20 small bunches of violets for the finger bowls. If he has enough white roses, carnations & lilies of the valley to make the table all white for the Thursday night dinner, it would be pretty.*[29]

Boxes of flowers were regularly sent to friends, family members, and favored employees as gifts, and flowers were donated to decorate or be sold at charitable events in the New York City and Shelburne areas, such as the annual "sociable" of the Girls' Friendly Society in Burlington. Lila took special pleasure in growing lilies to decorate the Trinity Episcopal Church in Shelburne for Easter every year. In April 1913, as many as 4,440 blooms were sent daily from the greenhouses to 680 Fifth Avenue, Shelburne House, the Shelburne House gardens, Trinity Church, the Webbs' sons Watson and Seward Jr. and their families, Lila's sister Margaret Shepard, and three of Margaret's friends. The Webbs' Fifth Avenue townhouse alone received between 707 and 1,557 blooms daily, while Trinity Church received a single shipment of 694 for Easter on April 1.[30]

Livestock

In addition to field crops and greenhouse produce, the model farm at Shelburne Farms was renowned for its livestock. At the turn of the twentieth century, the stock farm consisted of dairy and beef cattle, pigs, sheep, poultry, game birds, and horses. To establish the stock farm, Seward transferred animals from his former estate, Oakledge, purchased additional respected strains and breeds, and then embarked upon breeding programs designed to gradually improve the quality of the livestock and its products even further. As the *New York Times* reported in 1888,

> *This great farm of Dr. Webb's will be remarkable not only for its fine buildings and its complete system of equipment but for its fine stock. There is already a splendid herd of 50 Jersey cows, 100 of the choicest Southdown sheep, several hundred of select breeds of fowls, 150 horses, 30 of which are fine brood mares and 3 stallions. Dr. Webb's stock is all of the finest strains and his purchases are all made with the best judgement. His farm in Shelburne will eventually be one of the greatest centres in the country for pure blooded stock.*[31]

Little is known about the "Steer Farm," which presumably produced beef for the Webb family and high-ranking employees. One of Robertson's early designs for the Farm Barn called for the structure to contain a "Steer Stable" in the northern ell connected to the main block, but there is no evidence that cattle were ever housed there.[32]

The Shelburne Farms dairy was probably a much more extensive operation. It primarily contained purebred Jersey cattle, as well as additional numbers of Holsteins and Durhams by 1889. Light brown animals known for the high butterfat content of their milk, Jersey cattle were just beginning to be introduced to Vermont farmers in the 1880s. At Shelburne Farms, dairy herd numbers averaged about eighty cows and one to three bulls. Seward published a sale *Catalogue of the Shelburne Farm's Herd* in the late 1880s, which listed twenty-seven bulls and cows, their ages, pedigrees, milk yields, prizes won, and number of offspring. One cow, Cherry Budd, was described as a "very handsome and a grand young cow. Won Second Prize at New York State Fair, 1882. Gave for owner, her first year in milk, 4,577 lbs. of very rich milk showing 23 per cent. cream, on ordinary feed, without any forcing."[33]

Between 1889 and 1894, the Shelburne Farms dairy occupied three primary buildings: a barn probably used to stable the cattle, a hay barn, and a house probably occupied by dairy employees. These were likely structures built for one or more of the farms predating Shelburne Farms and then altered and enlarged for the estate dairy. The structures were demolished in 1894, when the dairy moved into a new Robertson-designed barn located on former Tracy family land in the southern portion of the property. Part of a complex devoted to the estate stock farm, the two-story shingled "Cattle Barn" had originally been constructed in about 1890 for horses. When converted to a dairy barn, the horse stalls and their exterior doors were removed and replaced by sections of stanchions and cattle stalls flanking a central aisle to accommodate one hundred milking cows, bulls, and calves. The second floor of the barn stored hay and grain. A year after the dairy had moved to its new facility, the *Burlington Farmer Advocate* reported,

The cattle barn is also an interesting feature of the farms, and it would be an object lesson of health and comfort to all our farmers, to see the arrangement of the barn... The barn is light, airy, high ceiling[ed], well ventilated and kept as sweet and clean as a meadow lot in June.[34]

By 1902, a "Dairyman's Cottage" and creamery building were constructed just behind the cattle barn, which came to be known as the dairy barn. The creamery was built according to the most modern specifications. Its interior was finished with white enamel paint, presumably because of its sanitary qualities, and it contained state-of-the-art butter-making equipment, including a milk separator able to process 1,300 pounds of milk per day. Shelburne Farms' first milking machine was installed in the dairy barn by 1917.[35]

The dairy produced milk, cream, buttermilk, and butter for the Webb family, favored estate employees, and dogs at the estate kennel, and for sale to the railroad industry and other businesses. Large quantities of dairy products were sent daily to the Webb residences, and small amounts of milk and cream were often packed and shipped especially for Seward's personal consumption. Once the Webb children had married and established separate households, quantities were shipped to them as well. The house employees, most often butler Walter Woodgate, were responsible for notifying the dairy of changes to the Webbs' regular shipments, the quantities of which fluctuated with the number of people staying at each residence and the dinner and luncheon parties planned by Lila. In September 1913, while Seward and Lila were living at Shelburne House, between 23 and 42 quarts of milk, several quarts of cream, 8 quarts of buttermilk, and 4 to 14 pounds of butter were sent up daily from the dairy.[36]

The creamery produced as much as 400 pounds of butter each week, which was packaged in two-pound portions stamped with the estate's signature sheaf of wheat. The butter was well known for its high quality and, as noted by the *Albany Journal,* commanded unusually high sale prices:

> *The surplus butter product of the Webb dairy...is disposed of to the Vanderbilts for use on their dining cars, and it is sold to them for precisely the price that is paid for firkin butter though prominent caterers have offered double prices for all that they could obtain. Butter from Dr. Webb's famous farm is classed with the 'diamond-edged' variety and retails at $1 per pound.* [37]

Among the commercial customers purchasing butter from Shelburne Farms were, as might be expected, two Vanderbilt family railroad holdings: the Wagner Palace Car Company and the New York Central and Hudson River Railroad. Farm records indicate that the latter purchased eighty boxes of butter a week between April 1913 and October 1918.[38]

The "Piggery" was located a short distance away from the new dairy barn. Constructed between about 1897 and 1901, and probably designed by Robertson, the piggery was a 30-foot by 90-foot, two-story, shingle style structure with a brick foundation, shingled walls and roof, and large dormers providing plenty of interior light. Wooden pens were built along the side of the building adjoining a larger fenced yard. A reporter for *Country Life in America* praised the piggery, calling it "a model of its kind. The building is in keeping with the

The Piggery, c. 1903, by Barker Brothers Studios, Burlington, Vermont. Shelburne Farms Collections.

others on the place in exterior style, and the interior is finished with hard pine, cement floors and iron troughs and fixtures."[39]

The pigs were raised for the Webb family's and estate employees' dinner tables and for sale to the general market. Eighteen ninety-nine was a busy year, as "two hundred pigs were sold, averaging from two hundred and fifty to three hundred pounds in weight, and bringing one-half cent per pound more than the ruling market prices, because of the superior conditions under which they are kept."[40] The pigs were fed corn on the cob, cornmeal, barley, bran, hay, and the swill left over from processing dairy products.[41]

The "Sheep and Poultry Farm" was another highlight of Shelburne Farms' model farm. By 1890, the department occupied a complex of buildings near the main house: three barns, a hen house, a house for department employees, and an ice house. By 1900, the department had moved to several adjoining buildings in the stock farm complex in the southern part of the property, including the Julius Tracy family's barn, a large two-story U-shaped structure. A "Sheperd's Cottage" designed by Robertson stood nearby.[42]

Frederica Webb with a flock of sheep at the Tracy Barn, by Thomas E. Marr, c. 1900. Shelburne Farms Collections.

The sheep farm's stock consisted of three British breeds: Southdowns, Hampshiredowns, and Shropshires. At the turn of the twentieth century, the sheep flock usually numbered between 100 and 200 head. The sheep were primarily raised for meat, and both lamb and mutton were sent in large quantities to the Webb residences. Seward was known to have donated male lambs from his flock to area farmers to improve their stock.[43]

A long, low-slung one-story barn adjoining the Tracy Barn to the south, originally designed by Robertson for horses, was converted into a poultry barn around 1900, at about the same time that the sheep farm was moved to the area. *Country Life in America* reported in 1903 that the poultry barn was equipped with the latest technological innovations:

> *Another feature of the place is the poultry department. Here hot-water incubators are used and the brooders, all arranged with running water, are heated by a general hot-water plant in the cellar. Any number of brooders can be connected so that separate or long runs can be given at will. Inside winter yards are also provided, and the entire plant is arranged so that every part is easily accessible for cleansing purposes.*[44]

A large variety of poultry were raised at Shelburne Farms, including chickens, geese, ducks, turkeys, and pigeons. White and brown Leghorn chickens predominated, accounting for as many as 557 out of a total of 710 birds in 1913. Originally from Italy, Leghorns were prolific egg producers.[45]

The poultry department produced both fresh eggs and meat. In 1914, as many as sixty dozen eggs were produced each week, of which twenty dozen were sent to the Webbs' current residence. Seward was particular about the quality and freshness of these eggs. He telephoned Gebhardt in 1910 to request that a certain number of eggs less than forty-eight hours old be included in the regular house shipments for his personal consumption. Three years later, Seward's personal secretary, Graham Kerr, wrote Gebhardt to relay a request for "six fresh eggs, smallest from White Leghorn Pullets and send to him [Seward] twice a week, marking date on same."[46]

Seward apparently enjoyed raising unusual types of poultry for agricultural fairs. His grandson J. Watson Webb Jr. remembered his grandfather's fondness for his poultry: "When I was a boy I remember very well going down with Grandfather Webb to see all his prize chickens and prize hens…That was a great hobby of his…He showed them…There were all kinds of exotic roosters and chickens."[47] A one-and-a-half-story hen house, probably designed by Robertson, was constructed at Quaker Smith Point to house Seward's special poultry. Sheathed in clapboards, the building featured large double-hung windows with chicken wire placed on the interior so they could be opened for ventilation without fear of the birds getting loose or predators entering the area.[48]

Pheasantry

Seward was also extremely interested in raising game birds, namely, pheasants. He established a "Pheasantry" about 1891, imported large quantities of eggs from England on several occasions, purchased additional adult birds, and employed a gamekeeper with one or more assistants to raise the birds. The imported pheasants were hatched under chickens and, when grown, released into the estate fields and woods to forage. The gamekeeper called the birds with a whistle four times a day to feed them supplemental grains. The main pheasantry building was located north of the Farm Barn on the former Ezekiel Tracy farm. Likely designed by Robertson, the one-and-a-half-story barn possessed an adjoining fenced yard. The gamekeeper occupied an L-shaped, two-story farmhouse known as the pheasantry cottage, possibly the former Tracy family residence.[49]

Pheasant hunters at Shelburne House, c. 1890. Shelburne Farms Collections.

An avid hunter, Seward invited guests to join him at his annual fall pheasant shoots, which regularly killed several hundred, and as many as 1,300 or more, birds each season. Like other farm products, pheasants bagged during the shoots were sent to the Webb residences and to family members and friends as gifts. Seward kept close track of the results of each year's shoots and gave his family and guests permission to bag a certain number of birds per shoot. He personally wrote Gebhardt on occasion to inform him where birds should be shipped.[50]

Seward saw his pheasantry operation as not only providing birds for sport but also increasing the numbers of a game bird that was rapidly disappearing from the area. As he wrote in a 1900 letter to the editor of the *New York Tribune*,

> *For the last eight years I have been raising each year from 700 to 1,000 pheasants in Vermont. I have not confined them, but have allowed them to roam over the whole western portion of the State. The work I have been doing is regarded by the Vermont game officials as of great public importance, and is more extensive than that done by many of the State Commissions and organizations.*[51]

When released from the pheasantry, the birds quickly dispersed throughout the local area. During the 1890s, the estate's stock was replenished by importing eggs from England as well as trapping birds on the estate, breeding them in the pheasantry to obtain new eggs, and then setting them free.[52]

SHELBURNE FARMS STUD

Despite the large numbers of cattle, pigs, sheep, poultry, and pheasants raised at Shelburne Farms, the horse breeding operation was by far the most extensive component of the estate's stock farm. Seward intended Shelburne Farms to be one of the largest and most important horse farms in the country. Throughout the late 1880s and the 1890s, he threw his energies into purchasing promising stallions and mares; breeding them; raising and training their offspring; and showing them. A certain number were sold each year at prominent horse sales.

By 1888, Seward advertised the services of his prize stallions at his "Shelburne Farms Stud" and boasted of providing the best accommodations to mares shipped to the estate for breeding. As the *Spirit of the Times* noted in April of that year, "The Shelburne Farms Stud is furnished with thoroughbred, trotting-bred, French coaching and Percheron stallions…Mares sent to any of the Shelburne stallions will be boarded at $3 per week."[53] In 1891 and 1893, Seward published catalogues describing his horse stock; the 1893 publication was titled *Shelburne Farms Stud: Of English Hackneys, Harness and Saddle Horses, Ponies and Trotters*. The catalogues listed the estate's best stallions and horses, their lineages and offspring, prizes won at major horse shows, and prices for their breeding services. The program attracted customers from across the United States and as far away as Warsaw.[54]

Right: The Breeding Barn, by Thomas E. Marr, c. 1900. Shelburne Farms Collections.

W. Seward Webb's prize Hackney, Matchless of Londesboro, as pictured in *Shelburne Farms Stud*, 1893. Shelburne Farms Collections.

In 1889, the Shelburne Farms Stud was reported to number 107 horses, including "trotters, thoroughbreds, Percherons, Clyde[sdales], French coachers, Mustangs, Shetlands and Russian ponies."[55] By 1891, the horse farm consisted of an astonishing 219 horses: 30 Hackneys, 39 trotting horses, 106 carriage horses, 40 ponies, and 4 other horses. These numbers did not include the horses in the Webb family's private stable, considered part of the separate "Coach Barn" department. The numbers of horses at the Shelburne Farms Stud kept increasing through the mid-1890s. In 1892, a family friend responded to a letter from Lila reporting her husband's latest purchases, saying, "I did smile at Seward's buying 27 more horses."[56]

While the horse farm included several breeds, Seward specialized in English Hackneys, purchasing a foundation stock of thirty-five mares and five stallions from British gentleman breeder William Bourdett-Coutts' Brookfield Stud in 1890. Webb bred his Hackneys with Thoroughbreds, Cleveland Bays, French coaching horses, and other breeds. By the mid-1890s, he was considered "the most successful amateur hackney breeder on this [the North American] continent."[57]

English Hackneys, which were first bred during the eighteenth and nineteenth centuries for both carriage pulling and riding purposes, possessed the traits of versatility, endurance for long-distance traveling, and a pleasing appearance in harness. Not to be confused with the now-derogatory term for an aged or infirm horse, Hackneys were well known and sought after at the turn of the twentieth century. Their striking high-stepping action made them extremely popular for use as carriage horses. As the *Independent* of Honesdale, Pennsylvania noted in 1894,

> *For those who want a general purpose horse in the way of riding, driving and light hauling, the present day racing trotter is no good. Thousands of people believe they have found the general purpose horse that is needed in the hackney, and the hackney boom is therefore on…The minute a hackney begins to go there is something in his splendid style and gait that draws every eye. Then as he goes faster and faster, dashing around the ring and making his long hind legs jump, the whole crowd at a horse show breaks into cheers. He is the showiest horse in existence.*[58]

Seward's prize horse, the so-called "King of the Harem" at Shelburne Farms, was the Hackney stallion Matchless of Londesboro.[59] Purchased in 1891 from a Virginia gentleman who had imported the stallion from England, Matchless was a chestnut horse who stood 15.3 hands tall. He was a "superb animal, allowed by all good judges to be one of the best specimens of his breed, [who] presents a combination of all the peculiar points characteristic of a perfect Hackney sire."[60] Matchless swept the prizes in almost every horse show in which he was entered, garnering at least twenty-five first prizes and five second prizes in the first ten years of his life. He was featured regularly in both trade media and the general press.[61]

Seward's aim was not only to offer breeding services to his peers but also to fulfill a greater public good by providing stud services to local farmers, thereby improving their horse stock. As he wrote in an 1894 letter to the editor published in the trade publication *Rider & Driver*, "I believe that the Hackney sire cross on native mares will undoubtedly elevate to greater usefulness the driving stock of the country."[62] He strongly believed that the quality of local horses, namely Vermont's native Morgans, had declined over the course of the nineteenth century, and his Hackney crossbreeds would infuse new life and strength into them. Seward put forth his opinion in his 1893 preface to *Shelburne Farms Stud*:

> *Being naturally very much interested in everything that affects the welfare of the State [of Vermont], it became my earnest desire… to exert an influence for the benefit of the horse-breeding industry, which appeared to me to have declined in recent years…The farmer now has on his place a pair of light weedy-looking nags that will trot you, in a light buggy, quite speedily to the station. But they cannot go in any race, they cannot pull a heavy load, they cannot even be used for what may be termed medium-weight draught or express work, nor are they serviceable in the work of the farm…What I desire to do at Shelburne Farms is to bring back to the State of Vermont the old type of draught-horse…By taking a Vermont mare, of light draught, and breeding it to a Hackney stallion you will get a horse which will travel with some style, and perhaps some action, from ten to fourteen miles an hour in front of a light wagon carrying a couple of men. After accomplishing its journey from the farm to the depot and back again, it can be taken out of the wagon, and, with a horse alongside of it, can be put to farm work proper.*[63]

In the hopes of benefiting local farmers, Seward offered breeding services at low cost and placed some of his imported horses up for sale at a fraction of the prices he had paid for them. He also donated a Hackney stallion to the town of Middlebury, Vermont, and a French coaching horse to the city of Rutland, Vermont, with the understanding that their breeding services would be provided to local citizens for only $2 or $3 rather than the $50 to $200 he charged to the general market.⁶⁴

In order to support Seward's sizable horse undertaking, a large complex of "breeding barns" was constructed in the southern portion of Shelburne Farms on the former properties of the Tracy, Morehouse, and Comstock families. Completed in 1891, a year after Seward had imported his foundation stock of Hackneys from England, the C-shaped complex consisted of 75,000 square feet of space in a group of horse barns and other support structures surrounding a central paddock. The complex contained a total of 150 box stalls and 70 standing stalls for the horses.⁶⁵

The centerpiece of the horse farm was an enormous shingle style building designed by Robert Robertson, built between 1889 and 1891, and measuring 418 feet long by 107 feet wide. It was variously referred to as the "Ring Barn," "Exercising Barn," or "Breeding Barn." The two-story, shingled structure featured large dormers, a cupola, and an arched entrance leading to a vast open interior with a horse ring surrounded by ninety-six finely finished box stalls.

The interior of the Breeding Barn, c. 1893–94, by Barker Brothers Studios, Burlington, Vermont. Shelburne Farms Collections.

The second floor contained open haylofts and an observation gallery overlooking the exercising ring. An annex added in 1890–91 to the rear of the structure contained additional box stalls, washing areas, tack rooms, and storage spaces for the vehicles used to break, train, and exercise the horses. The Breeding Barn, as it came to be known, housed the Shelburne Farm Stud's champion stallions. Mares, yearlings, and foals were also boarded there during the winter months.[66]

Facing the Breeding Barn across the main paddock stood another horse barn probably designed by Robertson that contained over forty box stalls. The two-story shingled structure, which later became the dairy barn, was used "during July and August for housing, in the daytime, the mares turned out during the night to graze."[67]

Several connecting buildings stood perpendicular to the Breeding Barn. The former Lee and Julius Tracy family barn, a two-story, U-shaped nineteenth-century structure with additions completed for Shelburne Farms, stood to the north of another barn and a series of long shed-like structures likely designed by Robertson. The Tracy Barn contained box stalls for expectant mares, a horse infirmary for sick animals, and grooms' rooms in its upper levels. The structures extending from the Tracy Barn housed additional horses, including the French coaching horses and ponies. The nearby Tracy House, a nineteenth-century farmhouse formerly occupied by the Julius Tracy family, served as the residence for the stud groom. Two additional "colt sheds," constructed between about 1900 and 1906, and a series of fenced paddocks were located behind the Breeding Barn.[68]

The entire complex of horse barns featured the latest and best agricultural systems and technology. The 1891 edition of the *Shelburne Farms Stud* catalogue informed potential clients that the barns were "well aired and lighted and furnished with all necessary conveniences to assure health, comfort and cleanliness. The Stud is in the charge of a competent groom of long experience, assisted by a corps of able assistants, and mares sent from a distance are assured careful attention."[69] At the height of the operation, a veterinarian inspected each horse daily. In addition to containing deep layers of straw bedding, many stalls were equipped with interior windows and Dutch doors, which allowed their inhabitants to look out into the barns.[70]

The Breeding Barn was especially state-of-the-art. An electric lighting and steam heating plant constructed behind the building by 1891 provided the structure's illumination. The Breeding Barn itself was constructed with an innovative metal truss support system that spanned the width of the building below the roof, providing over 26,000 square feet of open interior floor space unbroken by support columns. The structural system provided enough open space on the ground level for the indoor exercising ring, which in turn allowed the horses to be comfortably exercised and trained in all weather conditions, winter and summer. The materials used for the ground floor of the Breeding Barn provided a high-quality surface for the horses, and a special enclosed training ring allowed young animals to be broken quickly and safely. As the *Albany Argus* reported in 1895,

> *The floor of the stalls is the ground; the ring floor is also earth, with a layer of sand and clay, topped off with tan-bark, making an ideal exercising ring summer and winter. Near one end of the ring is a smaller one inclosed in high board walls, padded on the inside, soft flooring several feet deep, where the colts are taken for first lessons in breaking. No matter how much they plunge or throw themselves, the possibility of hurting themselves is reduced to the minimum. Usually one lesson in the breaking ring is sufficient.*[71]

Left: Several barns in the Breeding Barn complex, c. 1893. The Tracy Barn stands to the right. Shelburne Farms Collections.

Forest

Seward and Lila had decided against planting the full-fledged Vermont Arboretum proposed by Frederick Law Olmsted. However, throughout the late 1880s and the 1890s, the Webbs continued to develop woodland areas that reflected the landscape architect's influence and heightened the aesthetic appeal of the landscape rather than improving its value as productive forestland. Archibald Taylor supervised extensive forestry operations that gradually transformed the estate, creating a pastoral landscape that reduced the dramatic visual impact of wide open fields through the use of borders and islands of trees. Between 1887 and 1900, 20,000 to 155,000 trees were planted annually along roadsides and in fields, including "white and Colorado spruces, ten different varieties of pines, maples, elms, birches and oaks."[72]

It is possible that Gifford Pinchot (1865–1946) informally advised Seward

Webb and Archibald Taylor on the forestry operations at Shelburne Farms, although no written documentation has been discovered. A graduate of L'École Nationale Forestière in Nancy, France, and the first head of the United States Forest Service, Pinchot was an early conservationist who advocated selective harvesting and replanting rather than clear-cutting. His career had been launched just after he had graduated from forestry school when Olmsted secured for him the position of superintendent of forests at Biltmore, Lila's brother George Vanderbilt's estate.[73]

While at Biltmore in the 1890s, Pinchot visited Shelburne Farms several times to consult with Seward on the forests at Nehasane Park, the 250,000-acre Adirondack estate that Seward had recently acquired as a private hunting preserve. Working closely with Seward, Pinchot prepared a forestry plan for Nehasane to improve its value for both timber production and sheltering game animals. He published a book detailing his work in 1898. Pinchot thanked Seward in the book's preface, stating, "I wish to express…my high sense of the public spirit and practical wisdom which led Dr. Webb to sustain the investigation whose results are now published and to approve and apply the plans of work which it has produced."[74]

At Shelburne Farms, Archibald Taylor supervised the forestry department, whose employees were responsible for scouting and purchasing tree stock, raising young stock, planting and transplanting trees, and watering, pruning, and otherwise maintaining them. The estate nursery adjoined the greenhouse complex in the center of the property. Founded in 1887 to propagate trees for Olmsted's arboretum project, the nursery contained 100,000 saplings by 1896, including white pine, Norway spruce, Colorado blue spruce, Black Hills spruce, cypress, tamarack, elms, and maples.[75]

At the turn of the twentieth century—the height of the forestry activities at Shelburne Farms—Taylor made at least two trips to evergreen nurseries in the Midwest to purchase prime specimens. They were destined for a series of new plantations, large stands of trees planted in close proximity to each other. In 1900, Taylor purchased more than 116,000 15-inch to 48-inch white pine and Scotch pine saplings, which arrived by the railroad carload from Dundee Nurseries in Dundee, Illinois, among other locations.[76]

Soon after the saplings had arrived from Illinois, a planting push established 155,000 pine trees in a month. Taylor hired about 400 workers to plant saplings in the estate nursery and in twenty-four new plantations inside or bordering existing forest lands and fields throughout the property. The plantations contained Norway spruce, white pine, and Scotch pine trees edged by "flowering shrubs, such as snowdrops, honeysuckles, elders, etc."[77] The *Boston Morning Herald* considered the work to be "probably the largest undertaking of its kind ever handled in this country."[78]

A total of fifty-five evergreen plantations covering approximately one-half acre to eight acres each were planted throughout the property, greatly influencing the character of the estate landscape. Shaped in organic forms conforming to the topography, they masked and softened natural changes in grade and provided visual contrast and physical boundary lines. The plantations contributed to the viewer's sense of depth in the landscape, visually extending fields into the distance. As E. F. Gebhardt wrote to Lila, the plantations possessed a distinctive beauty heightened when in contrast with snow-covered fields during the winter:

> *The grounds are beautifully covered with snow, and the woods loaded with frost, and this, adding the dark green of the evergreen plantations, is particularly effective during the clear bright moonlight nights we are now having. The steam clouds from the lake cause passing shadows constantly moving and all objects are reproduced in deeper shadows making the scenery quite charming.*[79]

Shelburne Farms, looking northwest, with a young evergreen plantation in the foreground and Valley View and the Farm Barn in the distance, by Thomas E. Marr, c. 1900. Shelburne Farms Collections.

At the turn of the twentieth century, the forestry department's other main project was to purchase and transplant mature maples and elms as specimen trees lining the estate's primary drives and standing in open fields. Taylor advertised the estate's need for mature trees among landowners in the local area and personally selected ones to transplant to the property's roadsides, lawns, and fields. Maples and elms as tall as seventy-five feet were transplanted to the Shelburne House lawn, the two newly developed entrances to the property, the edges of the sea walls, and the areas surrounding the greenhouses, among other locations.[80]

The transplanted trees transformed the character of the landscape where they were placed, masking the bareness and newness of the freshly graded fields, lawns, and road system. Elms and maples planted along the main drives created graceful allées, tunnels of green during the spring and summer months. At Shelburne House, mature elms planted on the lawn rose above the three-story roof, providing an elegant canopy that shaded and granted a sense

of age to the building. Elm Tree Swamp, an area east of the Shelburne House lawn, was planted with more than fifteen elms, creating a park-like character of widely spaced trees growing amidst the grass.

By the 1890s, Seward Webb, with the assistance of Farm Manager Taylor and dozens of other estate employees, had fully developed his model farm at Shelburne Farms. The scale and variety of the operation—indeed, its very nature as a model farm—was made possible by Seward and Lila's independent wealth. The project was not a business designed to generate profits but rather an enormous experiment in the latest agricultural innovations, which would hopefully benefit others in Vermont and beyond. In the meantime, the farm provided the Webb family, their guests, and their friends with choice agricultural products and enjoyable country pursuits.

Elm Tree Swamp, by Thomas E. Marr, c. 1900. Shelburne Farms Collections.

Chapter 6
THE ESTATE

The Shelburne Farm estate comprises nearly four thousand acres…and contain within its borders all those natural advantages so necessary to the full enjoyment of out-door life by the family and friends of a wealthy country gentleman.

— A. H. Godfrey, *Rider and Driver*, 1892[1]

The Webb family's personal interests were wide-ranging, and Shelburne Farms encompassed them all. In addition to a country residence and a large model farm, the estate featured extensive formal gardens and stables, a private golf links, a guest house, and a collection of boats and yachts. The Webbs' activities spilled over beyond their estate's official boundaries into the village of Shelburne, where they assumed responsibility for the local train station and Episcopal church.

Country Pursuits

Formal Gardens

The focal point of the Shelburne House grounds was the formal gardens overlooking Lake Champlain along the western and northern cliffs of Saxton's Point. Elements of the first garden, a parterre, were in place by 1890. In its final form, the parterre featured an oval center with a sundial surrounded by rectangular, triangular, and diamond-shaped beds planted with annuals and perennials. Grassy walks were laid between the beds, and the garden borders were defined by potted bay trees, shagbark hickory trees, cedar and boxwood hedges, and rustic wooden fences.[2]

The designer of the parterre garden is unknown. However, Lila Webb was intimately involved with the design, layout, and planting of the formal gardens by 1904. In his correspondence with his wife, Seward referred to them as "your garden."[3] Lila herself wrote in 1910, "I am busy with my garden plan for planting this spring, and hope soon to have it completed."[4]

Lila proposed and implemented a more informal "Wild Garden" extending along the cliffs to the north. It featured meandering paths through wooded areas filled with forsythia, lilacs, azaleas, honeysuckle, rhododendrons, spirea,

The formal gardens at Shelburne House, by Louis L. McAllister, c. 1920. Shelburne Farms Collections.

and carpets of ferns, daffodils, tulips, and lilies of the valley. Here Lila also experimented with a rock garden called the "Rockery." A large circular fountain imported to the United States by architect and interior designer Stanford White, purchased in New York for the wild garden, was surrounded by lilies and irises. At the northern end of the wild garden, overlooking the lake, stood a small open-air gazebo called the "Summer House," which was overhung with crimson rambler roses and other climbing plants.[5]

From about 1905 to 1915, Lila gathered ideas for further garden expansions and alterations during travels in Italy, France, Spain, England, and the western United States. During a two-month motoring trip in Italy in 1907, she absorbed the Italianate style of gardens and spent time sightseeing and shopping for statuary with William Appleton Potter, Robert Robertson's former architectural partner. In addition to her travels, she also drew influence from contemporary publications purchased for her extensive library, including Charles Platt's *Italian Gardens* (1894), Edith Wharton's *Italian Villas and their Gardens* (1904), Charles Latham's *The Gardens of Italy* (1905), and Gertrude Jekyll's *Wall & Water Gardens* (1901).[6]

Lila directed the expansion and rebuilding of her formal gardens in the Italianate style from 1909 to 1915. The end result featured a progression of garden rooms sited on terraced levels and bordered by low brick walls. Between 1909 and 1911, a terraced stairway connecting the north porch of Shelburne House to the existing garden areas was constructed, and each stair level was ornamented with a series of Spanish stone figures, purchased by Lila in Venice in 1911. The following year, the old parterre garden was abandoned. Some parterre plantings and the center sundial were moved to a new section north of the terraced walkway, which contained a semicircular pergola and oval reflecting pool. The parterre was replaced in 1913–14 by a central court flanked by a rose garden, a lily pool, and a grand allée, a long aisle flanked by wide beds of perennials and annuals. The lily pool, which was filled with goldfish and bordered by irises, stood within a semicircular lawn enclosed by a balustrade framing panoramic views of Lake Champlain and the Adirondack Mountains. Potted bay trees placed at regular intervals ornamented the balustrade. The final major garden element was in place by the late 1920s, when another pergola for climbing roses was added to the rose garden.[7]

Throughout the garden planning and planting process, Webb employee E. F. Gebhardt served as Lila's sounding board, confidant, and garden assistant. Born in Utica, New York, Gebhardt worked for Seward Webb's Wagner Palace Car Company for a number of years before coming to Shelburne Farms in 1890. Within seven years of his arrival on the estate, he became Archibald Taylor's assistant manager. He succeeded Taylor as farm manager in 1908. Gebhardt played a significant role in developing and maintaining Lila's vision for the Shelburne House gardens. As Lila wrote in 1911, "Mr. G. & I are hard at work over the garden, every morning from 8.30–10.30 we go over the plans & talk shop, or rather garden."[8] They exchanged ideas and annotated each other's garden sketches, and Gebhardt obtained measurements and cost estimates and delegated Lila's planting requests. In Rome, in March 1907, she wrote Gebhardt describing her current thoughts on the Shelburne House garden, jumping from subject to subject in her excitement:

> *I must tell you that our wild garden at Shelburne, I think, competes well with any of the celebrated wild bits in the Italian gardens I have seen, including Sicily. Now that we have removed the little boy fountain, can anything be done to make that ground good soil for a lot of irises, & add more to those already there, or would something else suit the place better? I think Horsford's [of Horsford's Nursery, in nearby Charlotte] advice would be good to take, & it might be well to get some more hardy things from him this spring. I am going with Mr. [William] Potter one day this week to look up old marbles here. In spite of everything we have seen, we are still more than ever content with Shelburne, and it is very difficult to beat the views we have there.*[9]

Lila was absorbed by her garden work, regularly spending whole mornings and afternoons working in the wild garden. While she delegated most of the construction, planting, and maintenance work to a staff of gardeners, she did dig and prune herself on occasion. On August 30, 1904, she wrote, "Another fine day. Up early & worked in the garden until noon. Seward Jr. helped me chopping down trees."[10] Another letter to Gebhardt, from June 1908, noted that "There are some branches to be removed from paths in the Wild Garden, where I have done some cutting…You may notice I have marked some."[11]

When completed, the formal gardens encompassed approximately three acres. Lila was proud of her gardens, and in 1915, she engaged the distinguished photographers August and Louis Lumière to produce hand-colored autochromes of them. Her gardens were also featured in contemporary articles published in *Country Life in America* and *Arts and Decoration*. Popular with guests and well known in the community, the formal gardens were opened to the public one or two days each year. On July 23, 1926, Lila noted that "more than 350 people came to see the garden this afternoon in response to our invitation issued through the newspaper. It looks very well. The lilies are superb." The next day, more than 500 people visited.[12]

Golf Links

The Webb family and their guests also spent a great deal of time on the golf links, constructed on former Saxton and Nash family farmland to the north and east of Shelburne House. Seward and Lila may have been introduced to the sport by their architect and friend Robert Robertson, who served as vice president of St. Andrew's Golf Club in Yonkers, New York, and designed that organization's clubhouse. At Shelburne Farms, a preliminary course called a "Golf Court" was constructed by 1894. The following year, Seward met well-known Scottish golfer and course designer Willie Park Jr. (1864–1925) at St. Andrew's. The *Edinburgh Evening Dispatch* later reported that "on the Doctor's invitation [Park] stayed three days at the family residence at Shelburne…During this visit also he gave lessons in the game and found the Doctor, Mrs. Webb, and her daughter apt pupils."[13]

Park designed a nine-hole links course at Shelburne Farms with a par of thirty-seven strokes, his first course commission in the United States. Farm Manager Archibald Taylor, Gebhardt's predecessor, likely oversaw its construction. When complete, the so-called "Shelburne Farms Links" extended from the eastern side of Shelburne House to the northwest, and then up to the fields of Orchard Point overlooking Lake Champlain. Like many golf links, the Shelburne Farms course was characterized by relatively rough terrain and windy conditions caused by its lakeshore location. Golfers played the course in a loop.[14]

Golf clubs and other sporting equipment were stored in the golf room at Shelburne House, a small space added to the dwelling during the renovations occurring in the mid-1890s. The room was

Lila Webb and her brother-in-law G. Creighton Webb at the first tee of the Shelburne Farms Links, c. 1900. Shelburne Farms Collections.

equipped with large wooden, glass-front storage cabinets, and an exterior door led directly from the space to the course's first tee.[15]

The sport of golf was just becoming popular among Seward and Lila's peers when they constructed the Shelburne Farms Links. The United States Golfing Association hosted its first amateur competition in Newport in 1885. Only a few private courses existed in the United States; in an 1894 article titled "Golf Is Fashionable," the *New York Press* named three others in addition to the links at Shelburne Farms. The Webbs' was one of the earliest private courses in the country, and possibly one of the best. The *New York Sun* stated that "there are no finer golf links in the country than those of Shelburne Farms."[16]

Considered "one of the best women golfers in the United States," Lila was an especially avid and competitive player.[17] She often golfed several rounds at a time and day after day in any weather, as long as the course was free from snow drifts and high water. In September 1907, she noted, "Rainy day. Played golf this afternoon & got soaked."[18] During a spell of wintry weather one year, she reported to her son Vanderbilt that "there was too much snow on the links for golf, altho' we did manage to work out 9 holes, by going over the first & last ones several times."[19] When away from Shelburne, Lila peppered Gebhardt with requests for information on the current golfing conditions and particular suggestions for maintaining the links. As she wrote in early May 1910 from Colorado Springs: "I hope you will put in as much early work as possible on the golf links, as we are anxious to use them at once, & very constantly through the summer."[20]

Lila meticulously recorded the members of her foursomes, the winners and losers, and the scores in her diaries. On November 1, 1907, she proudly recorded, "Played nine holes of golf this afternoon with Geo. Bird, & made best score I have ever made on these links. 5.8.8.6.5.9.6.5.7=59. Quite delighted."[21] Lila's three sons, Watson, Seward Jr., and Vanderbilt, often golfed with her, as did the family butler Walter Woodgate, who was an excellent player himself. Many regular guests were also frequent participants. Ruth Wales du Pont, a guest at Shelburne House with her husband, Henry Francis du Pont, in 1917 wrote to her mother, "We had such a good time at the Webbs I fear it will take him [Mr. du Pont] a good while to settle down again. He loved the golf course where you walked to the first tee from the front door."[22]

Golfers in front of Shelburne House, by J. Watson Webb Jr., July 1934. Shelburne Farms Collections.

Orchard House

The second hole of the golf links was situated near a farmhouse occupied by members of the Nash family for almost eighty years before it was acquired by the Webbs in 1886. Standing high up on Orchard Point to the north of Shelburne House, the two-story brick Greek Revival dwelling possessed a wraparound porch and large, square, two-story clapboard addition. Known to the Webb family as "Orchard House," the farmhouse accommodated the family while renovations were underway at Shelburne House and then hosted their overflow or long-term guests. After the Webb children were married, they and their families often stayed at Orchard House, which afforded them more privacy than the "Big House."[23]

Yachting

Seward and Lila were passionate boaters. Their collection of vessels included a catamaran; the *Missisquoi*, a sixty-foot steam launch (a steamboat powered by a coal-fired boiler); and, most notably, a succession of three steam yachts: *Sappho, Elfrida I,* and *Elfrida II*. The Webbs purchased their first steam yacht, the *Sappho,* in 1886 while the family was still living at Oakledge. Originally built in 1879 in Brooklyn and lengthened two years later, the ninety-three-foot wooden *Sappho* would "steam all day without urging, twelve and a half miles and hour."[24] After acquiring the *Sappho,* Seward invested $23,000 in installing a new engine and other mechanical systems and replacing the decking, sails, awnings, pilothouse, and interior upholstery, among other items. An eight-man crew ran the yacht, which accommodated seven people. The Webbs sold the *Sappho* in 1889, soon after they ordered the *Elfrida I*.[25]

Commissioned from the Harlan and Hollingsworth Company of Wilmington, Delaware, for approximately $100,000, the *Elfrida I* was named for Lila (Eliza) and Frederica. The 112-foot yacht featured the most modern technology available, including a steel hull; a detachable bow and stern, which facilitated the vessel's travels through locks (primarily the locks above and below Lake Champlain); a 150-horsepower engine; and a dynamo that powered fifty electric lights and an electric searchlight. The yacht also contained a living area and three staterooms finished in mahogany and oxidized silver, as well as a bathroom with a marble mosaic floor and onyx fixtures. Launched in April 1889, the *Elfrida I* aroused great interest when it arrived in Shelburne that summer.[26]

Just before the Spanish–American War broke out in 1898, Seward sold the *Elfrida I* to the United States Navy at low cost for use as a gunboat. After the war's close in 1899, the navy refused his offer to repurchase the vessel and instead used it for patrolling the country's eastern seaboard through 1918.[27]

To replace the *Elfrida I*, the Webbs commissioned a new steam yacht from the Gas Engine and Power Company and the Charles L. Seabury Co. of Morris Heights, New York. A larger version of its predecessor, the *Elfrida II* was a 141-foot vessel with a steel hull, a detachable bow and stern, and schooner rigging. Its coal-fired twin engines produced a top speed of eighteen miles per hour. Outfitted with electric lights, bronze propellers and valves, and mahogany deckhouses, hatches, and skylights, the *Elfrida II* contained a "saloon," a sitting room, a dining room, five staterooms, and four bathrooms for the family and their guests. Its deck housed four smaller boats, including a thirty-foot naphtha launch, a power boat that ran on naphtha, a petroleum-based fuel. The yacht required a seven- to twelve-member crew.[28]

The Webbs were avid sailors. Seward was an active member of New York Yacht Club and a founding member and commodore of the Lake Champlain Yacht Club, established in 1887. He frequently entered vessels in the latter organization's annual regatta and participated in unofficial yet competitive yachting races with a fellow club member, Major W. Boerum Wetmore, on the lake.[29]

During the June to October yachting season,

The *Elfrida II* docked at the home wharf, by Thomas E. Marr, c. 1902. Shelburne Farms Collections.

Seward and Lila regularly took afternoon and evening pleasure cruises with their children and guests around Lake Champlain. They would often sail or steam to Burlington to attend social events or travel across the lake to points along the New York coast to pick up or drop off house guests. Captain E. W. Blodgett recorded a day of "Cruising on Lake Champlain" in the *Elfrida I*'s ship's log on June 18, 1893:

> *Day opens fine clear & warm. Crew preparing ship for days run. Fires lighted at 9:30. Left home wharf at 11:15 and landed at House at 11:45. Dr. & Mrs. Webb & guests aboard. Left at 12:50 & run south as far as Coals Bay then swung passing close to Barbers P^t. & close in Westport and followed Mountain close to Split Rock then direct to House wharf. Guests went ashore then we went to Harbor arriving at 5 P.M. Days run 42 miles. This ends this day.*[30]

In August 1899, the Webbs took President William McKinley, Vice President Garrett Hobart, and Secretary of War Elihu Root on pleasure cruises on the *Elfrida II* for several days. Vice President Theodore Roosevelt was aboard the *Elfrida II* in September 1901 when he was traveling through Vermont on a speaking tour. While in Isle La Motte, on the northwest end of the lake, Roosevelt learned that President McKinley had been shot in Buffalo, and the *Elfrida II* sped Roosevelt to Burlington so he could catch a train to Buffalo to see McKinley.[31]

As Captain Blodgett noted in his logs, vessels would pull into the "House Wharf" or "Home Wharf" to load and unload passengers. The home wharf was located at what became known as "Dock Bay," directly to the south of Shelburne House. The first version of the home wharf, a dock and boathouse complex consisting of a covered shed and wooden dock with a large triangular terminus, was constructed by February 1889. An extension of the 1889 structure, including a small one-story boathouse building, was in place within the next three years.[32]

The Webbs modified the Dock Bay complex again about 1901–02, after they acquired the *Elfrida II*, in order to accommodate the larger vessel. The bay was dredged to a depth of approximately twenty feet to create a deeper harbor, and a stone retaining wall, the south seawall, was built in a semicircle along the edge of the bay. A massive 250-foot T-shaped wooden dock was constructed, extending into Dock Bay. Finally, a new wooden boathouse housing yachting equipment, smaller sailing vessels, and rowboats was erected adjoining the dock.[33]

Coaching

Skilled equestrians, the Webbs relied upon horse-drawn vehicles for regular transportation as well as pleasure rides and drives. The family's two successive coach barns, which housed their personal carriage horses, riding horses, and coaching equipment, were located near Dock Bay to the south of Shelburne House. When the Webbs moved into Shelburne House in 1888, they converted a complex of existing barns and outbuildings remaining from Horace and Martha Saxton's former farm into a stable. The complex was renovated and expanded at least twice by the turn of the twentieth century, including modifications made in 1890 and 1891 following plans by Robertson. In its final form, the first Coach Barn complex consisted of a group of two- and three-story clapboarded and shingled wooden structures surrounding a central courtyard. An arched entranceway, opposite a central three-story barn with a cupola, provided access to the courtyard. Across the road from the Coach Barn complex, the former Saxton family farmhouse served as the head coachman's dwelling.[34]

The first Coach Barn and coachman's house were demolished by the end of 1902, soon after new facilities were constructed to the south of Dock Bay. The last structures documented to be designed by Robertson for Shelburne Farms, the new Coach Barn and coachman's house featured a Queen Anne architectural style that visually related them with Shelburne House. The brick structures possessed decorative stucco, half-timbering, ornamented brick chimneys, eyebrow windows, and a series of roof dormers punctuating pitched slate roofs.[35]

The new Coach Barn was remarkably similar to its predecessor in form and function. A four-sided, two-story structure, it featured a central courtyard accessed by an arched entranceway. The building housed the family's horse-drawn carriages and sleighs, carriage and riding horses, stable employees, and later, a growing collection of automobiles. A pair of iron gates designed by Robertson ornamented the Coach Barn's arched entrance. Horses, carriages, and automobiles could easily be readied for use in the large, square courtyard, which provided convenient access to each side of the building through double doors. Open sheds for storing vehicles and equipment were located on the north side of the structure. The east and west sides con-

The Coach Barn and coachman's house designed by Robert Robertson, c. 1902. Shelburne Farms Collections.

Horse stalls in the Coach Barn, by Thomas E. Marr, c. 1902. Shelburne Farms Collections.

tained stalls accommodating up to thirty-eight horses, rooms for storing feed and blankets, a tack cleaning room, and a boiler room. On the south side, a large tack room and two vehicle storage rooms flanked a central brick-floored washroom. The second floor contained additional storage areas for lesser-used and out-of-season vehicles; hay lofts; eight dormitory-style rooms for grooms, chauffeurs, stable boys, and mechanics; and a common living area and bathroom. The stalls, tack room, first-floor carriage storage areas, and employee living spaces were all handsomely finished in vertical tongue-and-groove woodwork.[36]

The new Coach Barn featured the latest in stable technology and conveniences. The entire building was wired for electricity when constructed. The barn's steam radiators, heated by twin coal-fired boilers, were mounted high on the walls to provide a comfortable indoor climate without coming in direct contact with carriages or horses or drying out leather tack. A telephone allowed for the instant receipt of horse and carriage orders by Shelburne House occupants, family, and guests arriving at the nearby railroad depot in Shelburne Village. The floors in the stall areas were paved with bricks in the shape of cobblestones to reduce the possibility that the horses would slip. Drains in each stall connected with the building's septic system. A passive ventilation system exhausted warm air and odors from the stall areas up through hay chutes and out from the building's three cupolas. The courtyard and washroom contained built-in drains to collect rain and wastewater, and moveable metal blanket racks in the washroom could be placed against the walls when not in use. In 1905, three years after the building was completed, a hand-operated platform freight elevator was installed in the center of the washroom ceiling in order to move vehicles between the first and second-floor storage areas.[37]

In 1900, the Coach Barn housed twenty-three horses: fourteen carriage horses, including a four-in-hand team; six saddle horses; a horse to pull the farm baggage wagon; and two ponies for the children. The Webbs possessed more than thirty carriages and sleighs, enough for every occasion and number of passengers. A May 1912 letter from Lila to Gebhardt describes the range of vehicles that were called upon on a busy day when the family and their employees were moving from New York to Shelburne for the season:

> *Will you tell [head coachman] Harry Wetson to have a single buckboard meet the early train Tuesday morning May 7th to take over a kitchen maid, who will be the only servant on the sleeper. Also tell him to have a six seater at station at 7 A.M. for other servants on car, & double buckboard at eight o'clock for me. Will you also have Farm baggage wagon at station at 7 A.M.*[38]

The Coach Barn tack room contained enough tack to outfit all twenty-three horses and thirty-plus vehicles, a total of "fifty-two sides of harness, together with many saddles and bridles."[39]

During Seward and Lila's tenure at Shelburne Farms, the Coach Barn department employed as many as seven coachmen, grooms, stable boys, chauffeurs, and garage assistants. They lived on the second floor of the new Coach Barn and in the new coachman's house. On occasion, stable employees' families also lived with them in the Coach Barn's dormitory-style rooms. The

Right: A carriage drive at Shelburne Farms, by Thomas E. Marr, c. 1900. Shelburne Farms Collections.

coachman's house, a two-and-a-half-story brick building constructed in a cruciform shape, contained nine bedrooms—ample room for the head coachman and his family, visiting coachmen and chauffeurs, and dining space for the stable hands who lived in the Coach Barn.[40]

The Webbs enjoyed daily carriage drives on the Shelburne Farms estate and in the local area, often taking their guests, children, and, later, grandchildren out driving for pleasure and to tour the estate. By 1903, the property contained over twenty miles of interior roads, many of them designed for recreational carriage driving. The drives meandered throughout the property: up Lone Tree Hill, through wooded sections with overhanging tree canopies and carpets of leaves and evergreen needles, beside fields and pastures, and skirting the lakeshore from the southernmost part of the estate up to the tip of Shelburne Point.[41]

When President Theodore Roosevelt visited Shelburne Farms in August 1902 with several members of his cabinet, Seward and Lila took them on a carriage drive through the estate before their formal dinner. Lila wrote, "We took a drive about the place…Seward taking the President in his buckboard, and [Treasury] Secy. Shaw going with me in mine, the others following in the vis-à-vis."[42]

By far the highlight of the Webbs' carriage driving activities was the June 1894 trip of the New York Coaching Club from New York to Shelburne Farms, which covered 318 miles over four days. Eight club members took turns driving the club's four-in-hand coach. The trip involved twenty

teams of horses, forty-two grooms, and an average of ten team changes per day. Substitute teams were sent ahead in railroad horse cars to prearranged meeting points. One historian has called the trip the Coaching Club's "greatest undertaking and a masterpiece of timing and arrangement, achieving an average of eighty miles a day over some of the most beautiful, and most challenging, countryside in America."[43]

The entire Webb family was skilled at equestrian activities. While they employed a coachman, they were all accustomed to driving themselves. As they had at Oakledge, Seward and Lila placed a strong emphasis upon teaching their children to ride and drive. They all learned to drive difficult team arrangements, including the tandem and the four-in-hand, at early ages.[44]

The Webbs acquired their earliest documented automobile in 1899, almost as soon as the machines were available. That year, Seward applied for and received membership in the fledgling Automobile Club of America and participated in the organization's annual parade in New York. By 1902, family members drove and stored automobiles at Shelburne. By the 1910s and 1920s, the family relied equally upon automobiles and horse-drawn vehicles, using automobiles for long-distance day trips and carriages for shorter, more recreational trips. The Webbs' guests also motored to Shelburne on occasion. During their tenure, Seward and Lila possessed up to seven automobiles at a time—more than one for each member of their family—including vehicles made by the Oldsmobile, Mercedes, Cadillac, Simplex, Amplex, and Packard companies.[45]

During the first decades of the twentieth century, poor road conditions, frequent mechanical problems, a few fender-benders, and a short summer driving season made automobiles a luxury and carriages and sleighs a necessity. A trip by automobile to Shelburne from Bellows Falls, Vermont, approximately 130 miles to the southeast, took Lila eight-and-a-half to nine-and-a-half hours in 1907. When the roads were in decent condition, the Webbs apparently enjoyed motoring at top speeds. Seward and Lila were stopped for speeding at least once, in 1906: "Seward & I started [from New York City] at 11.45 for White Plains in the auto got arrested at Woodlawn for going too fast, & had to go bail $100.00 for the machine."[46]

By 1914, the west wing of the Coach Barn was converted to an automobile garage for storage and repairs. The existing horse stalls were removed and a section of the floor excavated so mechanics could work underneath vehicles. A vehicle lift was also installed to facilitate repairs and maintenance.[47]

Connections With Shelburne Village

Shelburne Depot

Like many American country estates at the turn of the twentieth century, Shelburne Farms possessed direct access to a local railroad station. Such access was essential considering the frequent arrivals and departures of the Webbs, their guests, and their employees; the large volume of produce shipped from the estate to New York and other destinations; the constant movement of horses, carriages, and other personal possessions between the Webbs' homes; the steady arrival of railroad carloads of goods ordered in large quantities for the estate; and Seward's pressing business correspondence, which necessitated frequent and timely mail delivery. In the Webbs' case, rather than relying on a small, private train siding, at which trains would stop when requested, they assumed control of a public rail station. In 1888, two years after establishing Shelburne Farms, Seward and Lila purchased the Central Vermont Railroad's Shelburne Depot, located on a two-acre plot in the village of Shelburne within a mile of the estate's south gate. For the next sixty-four years, the Webb family owned the depot and allowed the Central Vermont and Rutland Railroads to schedule public stops at the station. By privately owning the site,

The Shelburne Depot, c. 1900. Shelburne Farms Collections.

the Webbs controlled the appearance, use, and staffing of the structure and its surrounding rail yards and outbuildings, using them as much as needed for their own substantial transport needs.[48]

Soon after purchasing the station, the Webbs commissioned Robertson to design a larger shingle style building to replace the original structure built by the Central Vermont Railroad. The new Shelburne Depot, a two-story structure with clapboard sheathing, a broad overhanging roof, and a central cupola, was completed by January 1889. It was surrounded by a raised concrete platform, and a circular drive led up to a porte-cochère (a roofed entryway to protect passengers leaving carriages) in the rear of the building.

A series of three parallel railroad tracks ran in front of the depot, separating the building from a fenced cattle yard, a railroad car shed, and a freight house constructed by 1908. The car shed and freight house were designed by Robertson and strongly resembled his Breeding Barn and other structures in the estate stock farm complex.

Shelburne Depot served local passengers riding on the Central Vermont and Rutland Railroads as well as the Webb family, their guests, and employees. While Seward and Lila were living in New York during the winter months, a railroad car for horses and freight, such as boxes of flowers, cartons of eggs, barrels of apples and potatoes, and personal belongings sent ahead or left behind, ran overnight each day between the depot and the city. The car was probably sidelined in the car shed between runs, and items being shipped were likely loaded from and unloaded into the freight house.

The Webbs themselves regularly traveled on one or more private railway cars made available for their use while Seward was employed by the railroad industry. Depending upon the destination or urgency of travel, the private cars were either attached to trains running their regular schedules or hitched

The crew of the Webbs' private railroad car, the *Ellsmere*, 1900. Shelburne Farms Collections.

View of the *Ellsmere* at Nehasane, 1901. Shelburne Farms Collections.

to an engine to form a "special." The Webbs' favorite railcar was the *Ellsmere*, a custom-built, luxuriously fitted Wagner Palace Car Company car constructed in 1888, which they later purchased for their sole use.

When returning to Shelburne aboard the *Ellsmere* or another private car, the Webbs would often travel overnight and arrive in the early morning. Their car would be sidelined on a track reserved for their use adjoining the depot so they could stay aboard undisturbed until they awoke. They would then disembark into a waiting carriage for the short trip to Shelburne House.[49]

Trinity Church

The Trinity Episcopal Church stood a short distance away from the Shelburne Depot in the village of Shelburne. Devout Episcopalians, Seward and Lila began to attend Trinity Church in 1886, the year they established Shelburne Farms. They soon became active patrons of the parish. Seward served as junior warden for approximately twenty years. Designed by Robertson's former partner William Appleton Potter and completed just before the Webbs became parishioners, the Trinity chapel was a small, one-story Gothic Revival redstone structure. Lila Webb enlisted Potter to enlarge the building with a new porte-cochère, bell tower, and deeper chancel section, and she commissioned prominent New York City artist Louis Comfort Tiffany to design stained glass windows and stenciled wall decorations. The Webbs also funded the construction of a nearby rectory building, as well as horse sheds to shelter parishioners' carriages and horses at the rear of the church.[50]

In 1898, the Webbs financed a parish hall addition to the chapel in memory of Lila's mother, Maria Louisa Vanderbilt. The parish hall contained a kitchen and a large gathering space for Sunday school classes and services during extremely cold weather. Tiffany & Co. was again commissioned to paint the structure's wall decorations. In August 1898 the *Burlington Daily News* reported that the parish hall was well received by the local community: "Mrs. Webb has again endeared herself to the people of Shelburne, by the location of such a beautiful memorial to the memory of one so near and dear to her. That the people recognize this tribute, is beyond question and it will long be cherished by them."[51]

The Webbs sustained the Trinity parish from 1886 through the 1930s. They paid large portions of the rectors' salaries, sent Shelburne Farms employees to maintain the church buildings and lawns, and funded improvements such as new heating and electric lighting systems. By 1903, they donated as much as $2,700 a year, and in the early 1930s, Lila sent $250 to $300 per month. The parish and its activities were dear to their hearts. In 1929, Lila paid for the rectory to be rebuilt in memory of Seward, who had passed away in 1926. Upon her own death in 1936, Lila bequeathed $50,000 to establish an endowment fund for the parish. Shortly thereafter, Lila's children installed a memorial stained glass window in the chapel in her honor.[52]

Trinity Church, by Thomas E. Marr, c. 1900. Shelburne Farms Collections.

Chapter 7
INFRASTRUCTURE

You arrive at the Shelburne Farm station…and if you are expected a carriage is waiting and you are speedily whirling up an excellent road towards the house. The road must have cost a small fortune in itself, as it has been entirely macadamized…and rings as hard and true as if it was one of the famous old coaching roads of England.

— C. S. Pelham-Clinton, *Buffalo (NY) News*, 1895[1]

During the development of the Shelburne Farms estate, extensive infrastructure systems were created to service and connect all aspects of the property. In fact, construction began on the road, water, electric, telephone, and telegraph systems almost immediately after Seward and Lila Webb began to purchase land for their estate in 1886. The systems incorporated many advancements in power, mechanics, communication, and transportation technology, allowing the family, their guests, and their employees to enjoy the latest conveniences of the time.

Road System

Shelburne Farms' most extensive and complex infrastructure system may have been its roads. Frederick Law Olmsted had included a new series of primary and secondary drives in his landscape plan. After he and his firm ceased working on the project, farm manager Archibald Taylor carried on with the designs for the road system according to Olmsted's general concepts. Taylor and his successor, E. F. Gebhardt, coordinated the construction process, building new roads and closing and planting over many of the existing public roads and farm lanes. By 1889, the primary and secondary drives covered fourteen miles, and a total of twenty miles of roads had been laid by about 1910.[2]

The old public roads had served the primarily functional purpose of carrying travelers to and from Shelburne's Harbor Road, at the eastern boundary of the new estate, by the most convenient routes possible. In contrast, the new estate road system was meant to be both functional *and* aesthetically pleasing. Consciously designed with travelers' experience of the landscape in mind, the roads flowed through the property in gently curvilinear lines. Like the "parkways" that Olmsted had designed for many of his public park commissions,

the drives skirted the edges of fields and woodlands, provided glimpses of the estate buildings, the lake, and the mountains to heighten the anticipation of wide vistas, and met in triangular junctions rather than at right angles. As a reporter commented in 1901, the roads were planned "so as to make them conform to the natural beauties of the country. The effect of this is very pleasing, for at every bend or turn in the road one is confronted with a new picture, each more beautiful than the last."[3]

The new road system incorporated some segments of the existing public roads, private driveways, and lanes leading to and within individual farm parcels. However, most of the older roads were abandoned and planted over in favor of new drives. The purchase agreements that Seward and Lila signed with landowners often included clauses allowing new roads to be constructed as soon as they possessed title to a parcel, even if the landowners retained occupancy for a few months longer. As Shelburne Farms grew, Seward petitioned the town's selectboard to close to the public many of the roads that lay within his property, eventually creating a private preserve within the gates. In at least one case, Seward negotiated with a neighbor to allow new public roads to be built on the neighbor's property so he could discontinue others within the Shelburne Farms boundaries.[4]

More than a foot deep, the roads consisted of coarse bedding stone with finer finish materials laid on top to form the surface. They were flanked by drainage ditches connected to stone and ceramic tile culverts, which also served as the outlets for the tile drainage systems in the farm fields. Stone seawalls protected three sections of road where they skirted the shores of Lake Champlain. The first structure stood at the edge of the secondary drive running north along Lemrise Bay. The other two, known as the "North Seawall" and the "South Seawall," were built to protect the primary drive near Shelburne House.[5]

The primary drives were surfaced in a macadam mixture of gray stone purchased from upstate New York and redstone that was quarried and prepared on the estate. The quarry, located near Shelburne Bay in the easternmost portion of the property, was adjoined by a coal-fired "Stone Crusher." Housed in a series of connected one-, two-, and three-story clapboard structures constructed in the summer and fall of 1889, the stone crusher reduced large pieces of stone into several grades of gravel for the roads. Once crushed, the redstone was transported to the new roadbeds, mixed with the gray stone and a binding material, and spread by a coal-fired "road roller" machine. Two successive road rollers, one weighing five tons and the other ten tons, were housed in one of the open sheds at the Farm Barn when not in use. The machines were state-of-the-art, and Seward occasionally lent them to municipalities like the city of Rutland in the southern part of the state.[6]

Even with the road roller machines, road construction was back-breaking work. The majority of the roadbeds and ditches were dug out by laborers wielding shovels. After the redstone was quarried, workers hauled it to the

Left: A drive through "Church Woods," near the Farm Barn, c. 1900. Shelburne Farms Collections.

Dennis Hurley

The Stone Crusher

stone crusher and then shoveled the crushed stone into farm wagons to be transported to the roads and shoveled out again. Between August 1889 and January 1890, at the height of the construction of the primary road system, a staggering 2,444 wagonloads of crushed stone left the crusher to surface the roads.[7]

Roadside landscaping enhanced both the primary and secondary drives on the estate. Many roadsides were planted with formal allées of specimen trees, mostly American elms, which provided canopies of foliage when grown. The triangular islands created at each junction of the primary roads were planted with small groupings of flowering shrubs, evergreens, or deciduous trees. While sod edging formed a crisp, tailored boundary between many roads and their surrounding landscape, forest undergrowth was allowed to grow close to the edges of the drives in wooded areas, thus heightening the sense of lushness and wildness. Fallen leaves and other plant debris were carefully removed from the primary drives to maintain clean-swept road surfaces but left in place on secondary roads, creating a picturesque litter to soften the roads' appearance and to crunch under horses' hooves and carriage wheels.[8]

While the estate's primary and secondary roads were legally private, members of the public were invited to drive on them for recreational purposes six days a week. Some local residents and visiting tourists took advantage of the public access, stopping off at the various farm buildings to tour the facilities. Visitors could travel throughout the property; only the driveway leading to Shelburne House was closed to the public. In 1891, *Boston Home Journal* reporter Lillian Wright waxed eloquent about the estate's roads, writing,

> *The numerous drives are perfectly charming, broad and smooth, winding about in delightful unexpected curves through the open, over the upland, then close to the water's edge. Much has been written about Lover's Lane [a tract running along Lake Champlain by the Coach Barn],… the narrow roadway close to rocks upon which the waves beat harshly, the thick pine archway overhead shutting out the light, the oppressive fragrance of ferns and orchids, devoid of life but for toads and adders, and absolute silence but for the water, the wind-swept pines and an occasional faraway shriek of a solitary heron.*[9]

Entrance Gates

To reach the core of the property, travelers passed through one of two main entrances. The "South Gate," built in 1896, served as the primary entrance for vehicles entering the property from the village of Shelburne to the south; the "North Gate," built in 1899, provided the most convenient access point for vehicles coming from the Burlington area north of the estate. Constructed following very similar designs, the gates consisted of redstone walls and posts

Left, top: Estate employee Dennis Hurley on the road roller, c. 1893. Shelburne Farms Collections.

Left, bottom: The estate stone crusher, c. 1893. Shelburne Farms Collections.

The South Gate, by Thomas E. Marr, c. 1900. Shelburne Farms Collections.

with gray limestone capstones and double wrought-iron gates. The structures were planted with climbing ivy, which almost completely covered them by 1910. Single evergreens stood in the midst of the clipped lawns flanking the approaches to the gates.[10]

Water System

Work commenced on an extensive water system for the property in 1886, even before construction had begun on the first estate buildings. By 1889, the system consisted of eight miles of cast-iron underground pipes reaching throughout the property. Water was drawn from Lake Champlain in the bay to the south of Shelburne House, where the home dock was located. The location of the intake pipe, which extended a half-mile out from the shore and was suspended about a foot above the lake bottom in a wooden crib, ensured that the water was as pure and free from sediment as possible. The intake led to the "Pump House," a square, one-story clapboard structure, possibly designed by Robert

Robertson, constructed by 1890 near the old Coach House and Coach Barn. Dual coal-fed, steam-powered pumps in the pump house drew water in through the intake pipe at a rate of 12,000 gallons per hour and propelled it through the western portion of the estate through two branches of pipes. One branch led up the hill to Shelburne House, the annex, and the gardens, and the other led to a reservoir located on the eastern side of Lone Tree Hill. From the reservoir, water traveled downhill by gravity to the Farm Barn, the gatehouses, and the Breeding Barn and stock farm complex, among other estate buildings.[11]

The first version of the reservoir, completed by 1889, consisted of a structure 100 by 20 by 10 feet with a capacity of 120,000 gallons. But as Shelburne Farms grew, the reservoir proved increasingly unable to accommodate the demand for water in the eastern and southern sections of the estate. By 1899, it had been rebuilt at a slightly higher elevation and enlarged to a capacity of 240,000 gallons. The new reservoir was "entirely underground, arched over, entirely closed and planted on the top."[12]

The estate water system ensured a steady supply throughout the property, essential for both everyday operations and emergencies. A series of hydrants and fire hoses in and near the major buildings provided water outlets in case of fire. They were put to the test in October 1888, when a small fire started in the recently completed Shelburne House. As the *Burlington Free Press* noted,

Fire was discovered in Dr. W. Seward Webb's residence yesterday morning, but it was soon extinguished. The fire caught around one of the fire-places and had got well under way when seen. The entire chimney had to be torn down to put out the fire, and considerable damage was done by water. The system of water works which Dr. Webb has recently placed on Shelburne Farms showed their worth at this time, as he has been careful to have hydrants, with hose attached, placed at convenient points…and what might have been a large fire was prevented by having plenty of water on hand.[13]

Lighting and Heating Systems

Coal served as Shelburne Farms' primary source of power for lighting and heating systems. The fuel was used to heat every major estate building, including Shelburne House, the Farm Barn, the Coach Barn, the Breeding Barn, and the greenhouses. In fact, Shelburne House contained three steam boilers, and the Coach Barn contained two: one for everyday use; a backup for times when the regular boiler needed repairs or for periods of high demand; and, in the case of Shelburne House, a small unit dedicated to heating Seward's bedroom, added after he began to experience health problems. By 1890, a coal-powered "Electric Lighting and Steam Heating Plant" had been built in the southern portion of the property, probably to service some of the new structures used for the stock farm.[14]

When first constructed, the Farm Barn was initially lit with gas. Electric lighting was introduced

Vanderbilt Webb leaning on a fire hydrant near Shelburne House, c. 1895. Shelburne Farms Collections.

to Shelburne Farms by about 1892, when one or more electric dynamos were installed in the steam heating plant near the Breeding Barn. The lighting system in Shelburne House was updated in or before 1893, when a direct current dynamo was installed in the nearby pump house building and electric lines were run underground to the residence. As *Shelburne Farms Stud* boasted in 1893, "in the matter of illumination every department is provided for."[15]

The Webb family, their guests, and their employees enjoyed lighting technologies that were then available to only a small segment of the American population. By the turn of the twentieth century, many cities contained gas plants providing illumination to homes and businesses. However, electricity was not available as a municipal service to residents of the town of Shelburne until the late 1930s or early 1940s. Only the wealthiest could afford the exorbitant cost of constructing and maintaining private gas and electric lighting plants. Historian Merrit Ierley notes that, in the mid-nineteenth century, private gas plants designed for small, single-family houses cost about $350 to build, not including the price of purchasing the gas itself. Seward and Lila spent almost $17,000 between 1890 and 1892 to build their gas, heat, and lighting plants at Shelburne Farms.[16]

Shelburne Farms consumed enormous amounts of coal in order to heat and light the major estate structures and to power the hay and grain elevators, water pumps, and other steam-powered equipment. For example, about 140,000 pounds of coal was unloaded at the greenhouses between October and December, 1890. During that winter of 1890–91, the steam heating plant near the Breeding Barn required 2,000 to 6,000 pounds of coal daily. In August 1902, Gebhardt estimated that the entire estate would need 150,000 to 175,000 tons of coal for the upcoming winter. In contrast, Ierley has estimated that "an average house" in the United States during the 1920s consumed "up to 30 tons during the heating season."[17] The Webbs preferred high-quality egg coal, which minimized smoke and odors. Stove, or "soft coal," less expensive but more polluting, was probably used for equipment and estate structures at a distance from the main house.[18]

Coal destined for Shelburne Farms was probably shipped by boat, unloaded, and stored in bulk at a group of coal docks and sheds located at or near the mouth of the LaPlatte River and Shelburne Bay on the eastern side of the property. From the storage sheds, estate employees transported the fuel by the wagonload to various boilers and pieces of equipment and then shoveled it into storage bins.[19]

Communication Systems

The estate's telegraph and telephone lines provided instant communication within the property as well as with the outside world. Serviced by the New England Telephone and Telegraph Company, the first lines were laid in the late 1880s and early 1890s. When the system was completed in about 1900, telephones were available in twenty sites around the estate, including the farm office, the farm manager's residence, the sheep and poultry farm, the dairy, the Breeding Barn, the stud groom's house, the greenhouses, the electric lighting plant, the Farm Barn boarding house, the Coach Barn, Shelburne Depot, the North Gate, Orchard House, Shelburne House, and the dock at Quaker Smith Point. Shelburne House contained three telephone lines to accommodate the Webb family's personal needs as well as Seward's business communications. In 1900, a local newspaper called the telephones "the most extensive private telephone system in the state."[20]

In addition to telephones, telegraph service was extended from the railroad depot to Shelburne House in 1891 and to the farm office by 1893. In 1893, *Shelburne Farms Stud* noted that "the electric telegraph is also much used, taking advantage of the Western Union wires which are available at Shelburne Station."[21]

The main drive running past the north seawall, with a telephone pole alongside the road, by Thomas E. Marr, c. 1900. Shelburne Farms Collections.

The Webbs and their employees used the estate's communication services, especially the telegraph system, constantly for both mundane and extraordinary business. Seward and Lila and their children telegraphed the farm office to answer urgent questions, inform staff of their travel plans, direct their mail to be sent to specific addresses, request that specific employees, vehicles, and/or horses be sent to meet them at various locations, or trace missing packages. Butler Walter Woodgate telegraphed to request changes in the quantities of farm products being shipped for the family's consumption in New York and other sites. Seward and Lila sent and received invitations, messages of congratulations, birthday and anniversary wishes, and updates on ill relatives by telegraph. Guests telegraphed Shelburne House to inform the Webbs of the train on which they would be arriving. While considering a run for Vermont governor in 1902, Seward wired Gebhardt to request that he send him daily political updates by telegraph. On several occasions, Seward sent confidential telegraph messages, presumably about his business and political affairs, in code to Gebhardt.[22]

Shelburne Farms' roads, water, communication, lighting, and heating systems were an early and essential component of the property. Like those of many American country estates of the era, these infrastructure systems featured the latest and best technology of the late nineteenth and early twentieth centuries, and were designed to be aesthetically pleasing whenever possible. Privately funded and maintained, they provided comforts and conveniences unavailable in many American municipalities for another generation or two. Shelburne Farms' infrastructure systems were further examples of its status as a model farm, with features which farmers and other everyday Americans could aspire to possess.

Chapter 8
EMPLOYEES

Employees are requested to bear in mind that they are engaged to assist in maintaining and beautifying the home of their employer and that their every act should be in harmony with such results. Keep the place neat and tidy is what we are all here for and each man should join with the management in striving for the principal results we are paid for.

— Archibald Taylor, December 1890[1]

Shelburne Farms was an enormous undertaking that required scores of workers to build and keep it in a constant state of near perfection. At the turn of the twentieth century, the estate employed an average of about 150 and as many as 520 men and women at one time, including teamsters, herdsmen, gardeners, clerks, laborers, carpenters, blacksmiths, grooms, coachmen, chauffeurs, housemaids, gamekeepers, engineers, and sailors, among others. A core number of salaried staff members worked year-round, and an additional number of day laborers were paid hourly wages for seasonal work, such as planting, harvesting, and special construction projects. Each year, the number of employees and amount of work activity increased substantially during the late spring, summer, and autumn, when the Webb family was in residence and the farm operations were at their height.[2]

Positions at Shelburne Farms, as at many country estates of the late nineteenth and early twentieth centuries, were highly sought after. Most Webb family employees worked long hours at jobs that required a great deal of physical labor. In return, they received good compensation and benefits compared to the average agricultural, domestic, and office workers in Vermont and the United States. Additionally, due to the Webbs' affluence, high standard of living, and disinterest in turning a profit from their estate, many of their employees—although not all—were probably more insulated from local and national economic downturns than they may have been with other, less wealthy employers or as self-employed farmers, for example.

Moreover, Seward and Lila Webb were kind and benevolent employers, at least according to the standards of their time. In the absence of a number of labor laws that would be enacted over the course of the twentieth century, they made a personal choice to offer extra benefits to their employees, especially to those workers whom they felt met their high standards for professionalism and loyalty. They also offered respect, and in some cases even personal friendship, in exchange for their employees' hard work and devotion.

Work Schedules

Depending on the season and their responsibilities, most estate employees worked nine- or ten-hour days, Monday through Friday, and half days on Saturdays. Those at Shelburne House probably worked even longer hours, receiving only a half day off on Sundays. Everyone in the family's employ was expected to work overtime when necessary, such as for crop harvesting, large house parties, or late-night flower shipments to New York. Farm workers were regularly assigned rotating schedules for necessary work performed on Sundays and holidays, including milking, feeding, and watering livestock. Many employees' starting and quitting times fluctuated throughout the year, following the change in seasons, daylight hours, and the Webb family's schedule. In April 1891, for example, estate employees were assigned a new spring schedule: Farm Barn employees would work from 7 a.m. to 6 p.m.; those at the dairy, tree nursery, and Breeding Barn complex would work from 7:10 a.m. to 5:50 p.m.; greenhouse and pheasantry employees would work from 7:15 a.m. to 5:45 p.m.; those near Shelburne House or Orchard House would work from 7:20 a.m. to 5:40 p.m.; and employees of the sheep and steer farms would work from 7:25 a.m. to 5:35 p.m.[3]

A Multinational Staff

Shelburne Farms attracted workers from the local area and from long distances. Successive farm managers Archibald Taylor, E. F. Gebhardt, and Frank Kendzior received many letters from farmers, gardeners, grooms, clerks, and others asking if work was available on the property. In August 1902, Stanley Johnson of Moira, New York, sent a postcard inquiring, "Have you all the help you want

for this fall and winter. Would you like a first class teamster good references if needed. Will you please answer as you get this. If you do not need help if you should know of any one that does please let me know and oblige."[4] That same month, Englishman W. E. Lay provided a detailed description of his well-rounded abilities and qualifications:

Having only arrived in this country a few weeks ago, I am now on the look out for a good job, & am writing to ask if you have any opening, or happen to know of one you can offer me. I am 30 years of age, Height 5 feet 8½ ins., Single, of good cababilities, willing & strictly temperate, also of good habits, I came from Berkshire, England, & my Father being a large farmer in that country. I am fairly well up among stock in general, & very fond of Horses, & I may say

Left: Breeding Barn employees, including stud groom William West (seated), c. 1900. Shelburne Farms Collections.

Right: Employees sawing wood at the Farm Barn, c. 1900. Shelburne Farms Collections.

am used to riding & driving, I came to this country of my own free will, to see what the country is like, & to try & improve my circumstances if I can.[5]

Many of the employees with managerial duties and/or specialized skills were born outside of the United States, including Walter Woodgate, the Webbs' English butler; Patrick Fay, a native of Ireland and the first person to serve as head gardener; Scotsmen Archibald Taylor, the estate's first farm manager, and Alexander Graham, Fay's successor as head gardener; and Canadian Tuffield Kinville, who also worked in the garden department. Woodgate (1874–1967) married Ellen Chorlette (1875–1976), an Englishwoman who joined the Webb household as a maid. Mrs. Woodgate later became the family's head housekeeper. In addition to the Woodgates, a number of others born in Great Britain worked at Shelburne Farms, including stud groom William H. Hopkins and his cousin, William Street. Lila hired her chauffeur of 1907–08, Sartori, when he asked to return to the United States with her after her 1907 motoring trip in Italy. The estate drainage system was largely constructed by a group of fifty Swedish-born men who were recruited from New York City, and Italian immigrants were hired to help with harvesting at least once.[6]

Supervision

Successive farm managers Taylor, Gebhardt, and Kendzior, the superintendents of the property, oversaw all of the employees save those at Shelburne House, who were supervised by Woodgate. Taylor, Gebhardt, Kendzior, and Woodgate communicated directly with the Webb family about any estate employee matters. They served as advocates for employee issues, such as the upkeep of their housing, and they disseminated information from the Webbs to their workers, including scheduling changes, notices of paid holidays, and rules and regulations, via "general orders" distributed to department heads. Smoking, drinking, racing teams of horses, and speeding through the property on bicycles or, later, automobiles, were not tolerated. In 1925, then Farm Manager Kendzior complained about one speeding employee: "will you please instruct Noonan to observe the 15 mile per hour rule when driving on the Estate, also that when he meets a drove of our cattle as he did this morning not to go at 25 miles per hour straight through the middle of them."[7]

Compensation

At the turn of the twentieth century, estate employees' compensation was at least equal to, and as much as quadruple, the average paid in the state of Vermont for comparable positions. Depending upon the position and workers' experience and skill level, most day laborers received about $1.00 to $1.50 per

The crew of the *Elfrida II*, c. 1905. Shelburne Farms Collections.

Estate employees lined up in front of the farm office on pay day, c. 1893. Shelburne Farms Collections.

day, and most salaried employees received monthly salaries between $10 and $75. The pay for most office clerks ranged between $30 and $50 per month; most farm teamsters, grooms, gardeners, dairymen, and yacht crewmen received about $35 per month; and most housemaids received about $20 per month. In comparison, a local employment agency advertised salaries of $4 and $5 per month for chambermaids and housekeepers between 1910 and 1920. Department heads, including the butler, the yacht captain, the dairy herdsman, the stud groom, and the head farmer, were paid about $100 per month. Finally, Farm Managers Taylor and Gebhardt received a monthly salary of $200 for their work superintending the estate.[8]

Holidays

Salaried farm employees received several regular paid holidays: New Year's Day, Independence Day, Thanksgiving, Christmas, and, by 1912, Labor Day. Gebhardt was conscious of the importance of holidays to estate employees and, at the same time, the hardships that holidays might cause day laborers, who would not be paid for their time off. As he wrote Lila in 1913, a year after the Labor Day holiday had been observed for the first time,

I find we did observe Labor Day last year… and I think it very advisable that we do so again. I think the day fully important as some others we recognize and one that comes very near the men themselves and an observance of their day should be wholesome. Last year I allowed any of the day men to work that wanted to work and not lose their time. The monthly men of course get their time.[9]

In addition to regular holidays, employees were provided half- or full-day paid time off for special occasions, such as a national memorial day observed following President William McKinley's 1901 assassination, and the Webbs' oldest son Watson's twenty-first birthday in 1905. Seward, a staunch Republican, directed Taylor to give estate workers a half-day holiday in 1896 to attend a Republican political gathering whether or not they were members of the party. Registered voters were regularly allowed paid time off to participate in general elections and attend the local Shelburne town meeting day. And when Watson was married in 1910, estate workers were served a luncheon, provided with cigars, and given half a day's holiday.[10]

Perquisites

Many Webb family employees also received housing, which was incorporated into each major section of the estate as it was developed. As early as February 1889, the property contained "two cottages, three tenement-houses, [and] a boarding-house to accommodate sixty men."[11]

Housing for single or lower-ranking employees was generally laid out in a dormitory style, with single- or double-occupancy rooms located near common living and dining spaces. The Farm Barn boarding houses, coachman's house, Coach Barn, Breeding Barn, Tracy Barn, Shelburne House, and the "Potting House" at the greenhouse complex were all outfitted with dormitory-style rooms. The bedrooms were small, and while most often occupied by bachelors, were sometimes assigned to employees with families. Workers living in these rooms were given access to nearby "reading rooms," presumably equipped with books, magazines, and other recreational diversions.[12]

Employees who lived in the estate's dormitory-style housing often received board as well. For example, the coachman's wife was paid for serving meals to stable staff and visiting coachmen and chauffeurs. In 1915, Gebhardt detailed the provisions they received. For breakfast, Mrs. Harry Wetson served cereal, bacon, and eggs six days a week, and hash one day a week, bread or rolls, and coffee. For noon dinner, she served a roast five days a week, steak two days a week, potatoes, two kinds of vegetables, and a dessert. For evening supper, she served "cold meats or steak, hashed potatoes, rolls, tea, and sweets." Gebhardt concluded that the food was "perfectly satisfactory" and in fact often generous, as "they always serve two eggs for breakfast and a third one has never been refused."[13]

At least nineteen single-family houses on the property were occupied by employees and their families, including a number of farmhouses that predated the estate. Several of the preexisting dwellings were occupied by employees in the 1880s and 1890s and then demolished after new replacements had been constructed.[14]

Robert Robertson designed at least fourteen of the employee cottages at Shelburne Farms. In addition to the 1901–02 brick coachman's house, thirteen cottages were built on several sites following a common shingle style plan. These one-and-a-half-story square buildings featured shingled walls and roofs, recessed porches, and cantilevered second stories. On the interior, they contained kitchen and parlor spaces with four bedrooms above. In 1890, nearby Essex, Vermont, builder O. S. Nichols constructed six cottages, and an additional seven more were built by about 1900. Eight of the cottages were sited in a small group at the southern end of the property, to the east of the stock farm complex.

Four of the eight tenant cottages

Employee cottages designed by Robert Robertson, c. 1893. Shelburne Farms Collections.

Another was located to the south of the new Coach Barn, near Orchard Cove. A cottage adjoining the greenhouses was used by the head gardener and his family. And three more cottages, located near Shelburne Depot, were occupied by estate employees with railroad duties.[15]

The estate also included two other structures constructed to benefit estate employees and their families: a chapel and a schoolhouse. The 1890 schoolhouse, near the cluster of houses at the southern end of the property, resembled Robertson's cottage plan. Probably meant to replace the three nineteenth-century schoolhouses within the property that were demolished soon after Shelburne Farms was established, the building was in use until about 1906. It was sold and moved to the center of Shelburne Village in 1923. The chapel, a small, single-story structure sheathed in clapboards, was located in the northern section of the property near the pheasantry. Constructed in 1888–89, the chapel was intended to serve the large number of Roman Catholic estate employees, but it was destroyed by fire just after it was completed. A second chapel constructed on the same site served employees until the local parish built the St. Catherine of Siena church in the center of Shelburne Village in 1895. The Webbs then organized transportation to religious services at St. Catherine's, as they did for Episcopalian employees attending Shelburne's Trinity Church. The chapel at Shelburne Farms was later given to St. Catherine's and moved to a location adjoining the church to serve as a parish hall.[16]

The Boarding House Cottage (in the woods south of The Farm Barn)

The Holabird family house, when it served as the Boarding House Cottage, c. 1893. Shelburne Farms Collections.

Seward and Lila showed their appreciation for estate employees by hosting them and their families at annual social events for Independence Day and Christmas. On July 4, 1905, for example, Lila noted in her diary, "Fete for all the people on the place, and the servants in the house and stable from 5.30–10 this evening. Dancing in a tent on the lawn, and fireworks."[17] The Webbs' 1897 Christmas celebration, held in the Breeding Barn for more than 100 guests, was an extravagant affair. One room was decorated with a large Christmas tree and thirty smaller trees; a boys' choir from New York City sang carols; games of tag and football and a piñata were organized for the children; six-year-old Vanderbilt Webb read from "'Twas the Night Before Christmas"; and dancing followed a banquet. As she did every year, Lila purchased individual presents for each employee and child on the estate. The *Baltimore Sun* reported that "Not a soul was forgotten. The thirty-five employes who were given gold watches could hardly keep them in their pockets, and those who received fur coats and caps, gloves and other things were no less happy."[18]

During their summers at Shelburne Farms, the Webbs occasionally invited their employees to take an afternoon or evening sail. On two consecutive days in August 1906, for example, the yacht was made available to employees and their families. When the house and stable workers were given the evening of August 4 off to sail on the yacht, Lila noted that she and her family fended for themselves at Shelburne House: "All the house servants & people from stable went on yacht from 6.30–10. We had cold dinner & washed up afterward."[19]

Employer–Employee Relationships

Seward and Lila took a genuine interest in their employees and their families. Lila often visited the employees' wives and children, took them on outings, and invited them to lunch and dinner on occasion. She sent packages of magazines to be distributed to the employee reading rooms. Those injured on the job were often provided with health care services, retained on the payroll, and allowed to remain in employee housing when a disability forced them to cease work. Worker's compensation insurance was carried personally by members of the Webb family and by Shelburne Farms by 1931. Lila often asked for news on the progress of ill or injured employees in her letters to Gebhardt, and she attended the funerals of those who passed away. When Gebhardt's own daughter fell ill and remained near death for weeks in about 1910, Lila constantly inquired after her. As she wrote in one letter to Gebhardt,

Thank you for your letter of last week, but the news it contained was most distressing, and I waited anxiously until Dr. Webb returned from Shelburne yesterday with more encouraging accounts, and a little hope. I cannot help thinking daily that your daughter will still be spared to you, but the strain

The Wickson children, whose father worked at the estate's sheep and poultry farm, c. 1895. Shelburne Farms Collections.

Portrait of a footman with linens at a picnic, c. 1905. Shelburne Farms Collections.

is something that no one can ever appreciate, excepting those who had to endure such a trial as you have. It is wonderful how strength seems to be given to meet such sorrow and suffering. I do hope and pray that the clouds may soon lift permanently for you and your wife, who have had such a sad winter.[20]

The Webbs expected their employees to perform their responsibilities well and to be prompt, courteous, and trustworthy. Those who fulfilled their expectations were respected and well rewarded, and those who did not were asked to leave in short order. Lila wrote Gebhardt in 1907 to tell him of her displeasure with Sartori, her Italian chauffeur, and request that the farm manager communicate her feelings to him:

I am a little weary of Sartori's complaints about Vermont roads, & he knew perfectly well what he was coming to when he insisted upon returning with us to America. He can now make the best of it to obey orders, or else I can get someone who will…I have no notion whatever of allowing Sartori to run me as well as the auto, so you may convey as much of this to him as you see fit.[21]

Sartori left Lila's employ soon thereafter, although it is unclear whether he was fired or left of his own accord. Despite her frustration with him, Lila went to bid him and his wife goodbye in person and presented them with photographs of herself and other family members as keepsakes.[22]

J. Watson and Electra Webb (front row), with a group of long-serving family employees, by J. Watson Webb Jr., July 1934. In the back row are (from left): former teamster Edward "Eddie" McGee, former *Ellsmere* crew leader Andrew Jones, former stud groom William West, former teamster Robert Ockert, and former gardener F. "Dad" Benson. Shelburne Farms Collections.

Loyal employees who worked for the family for years were acknowledged and well rewarded for their service. The Webbs granted $250 bonuses to several staff members in appreciation for thirty years of service. In November 1921, the couple held two dinners for sixty people at Shelburne House to honor their longest-serving employees. A 1904 letter Seward wrote to Archibald Taylor, then seventy-eight years of age and ailing, reveals his respect and gratitude for Taylor's long years of service as farm manager. Rather than firing Taylor when his job became too much for him, Seward offered him an honorary role:

My dear Mr. Taylor, I realize fully that you cannot at present give the time and attention to Shelburne Farms that you could some four or five years ago, and furthermore I do not wish you to do so. I realize the valuable services you have rendered me in the past and I want you to continue as Manager of Shelburne Farms right along and to sign checks, etc., the same as you have done heretofore...I want commencing this year to give you a salary of $1,000 a year and I want you to come down just when you feel like it, and to feel that you have a perfect right should you feel so disposed to stay away not only one week at a time, but two or three weeks at a time, and I don't want you to feel the necessity of coming down in bitter cold weather, neither do I wish you to come down so early in the morning...I also think it would be of great service to you if you could take a vacation during the blustering winter weather, of February and March, and take a trip south into a warmer climate...Nobody except Mr. Cornell, my confidential Secretary, Mr. Gebhardt and myself will know about this change, and as I said above I wish the public and all to feel that you are still and will be still the manager of Shelburne Farms in every sense...I hope you will accept this in the kindly and friendly spirit that I write it because as I said above I appreciate most thoroughly your past services.[23]

Lila forged especially close and personal ties with several loyal employees. When gardener Tuffield Kinville died in January 1925, Lila wrote, "Greatly distressed to hear of Kinville's death in hospital in Burlington, after an operation. Will miss him *very* much."[24] After Seward's death, she honored his former personal secretary, Graham Kerr, by giving him $15,000 "in recognition of the many services rendered to Dr. Webb covering a long period of years."[25] As she wrote Kerr, "I know that Dr. W. was fully appreciative of these services, and my personal gratitude and thanks accompany this check."[26] In addition, she continued to employ Kerr as a secretary and to house him and his wife during the remainder of her lifetime, and she asked her children to do the same after her death.[27]

Lila was probably closest to her butler, Walter Woodgate, who provided her with loyal and caring service for over thirty years. She often asked him join her and her close friends for games of golf and bridge and to eat dinner with her when she was

Ellen and Walter Woodgate in the Shelburne House gardens, by J. Watson Webb Jr., c. 1950–60. Shelburne Farms Collections.

115

alone, and she solicited his advice on family matters on occasion. Woodgate reciprocated her respect and friendship. In 1935, when she was recovering in Florida from a grave illness, during which she had been incommunicado for months, he wrote from New York that he had "received your two letters, was thankful & excited to see your handwriting again and just had to celebrate. Hope you will soon regain your strength."[28] Woodgate was with Lila when she died at Shelburne House in 1936. In accordance with her wishes, he received a trust fund worth over $25,000 upon her death. Although they both retired after Lila passed away, Mr. and Mrs. Woodgate were welcomed by her children at Shelburne Farms as their guests, and the couple returned to their quarters in the annex next to Shelburne House each summer through the 1950s.[29]

Chapter 9

TRIALS

*She's seen our days of gladness,
As they sped swiftly by,
She's watched our hours of sadness,
In silent sympathy.*

— Lila Osgood Webb, "Christmas Greeting 1922"[1]

The Shelburne Farms envisioned by Seward and Lila Webb was astonishingly enormous and complex. While most of their peers chose one or two interests to focus upon at their country estates, such as golfing or dairy farming, the Webbs embraced an ambitious array of activities on a scale that was perhaps unmatched by any other country estate in the nation. During the first flush of acquisition and construction at Shelburne Farms in the 1880s and 1890s, everything seemed possible. However, as the nineteenth century waned and the twentieth century began, Seward and Lila found it difficult to continue to build and maintain their property in the impressive scope they had intended. Had the Webbs planned Shelburne Farms on a smaller scale, it might have survived the difficulties that the family experienced from the 1890s to the 1920s more or less unscathed. However, the depth and breadth of the activity they had initially envisioned soon became unsustainable.

During the mid- to late 1880s, Seward and Lila focused primarily upon developing Shelburne Farms. To be sure, they also devoted a great deal of time to their active social life, Fifth Avenue townhouse, and prolonged travels in the American West and Europe, among other diversions. But their new estate, Shelburne Farms, and the myriad plans and decisions associated with it, absorbed their energies. However, by the early 1890s, other projects and concerns began to divert their attention.

Seward's Business Affairs

Seward Webb was a tremendously busy man. In addition to serving as president of the Wagner Palace Car Company from 1885 to 1899, he was a member of the board of directors for numerous Vanderbilt railroad companies from the 1880s to the 1920s. These included the New York Central Railroad, Fulton Chain Railroad Company, Fulton Navigation Company, Raquette Lake Transportation Company, Lake Shore and Michigan Southern Railroad, Central Vermont Railroad, and Rutland Railroad, among others. He also served as president of the Rutland Railroad from 1902 to 1905.[2]

Along with his railroad activities, Seward was an active member of the American Hackney Horse Society, and he served on the boards of the University of Vermont and the National Life Insurance Company, based in Montpelier, Vermont. He wrote an account of his family's railroad voyage to the American West, *California and Alaska and Over the Canadian Pacific Railway,* published in a lavishly illustrated edition in 1890 by Putnam's Knickerbocker Press, and coordinated the publication of a limited-edition three-volume set of his grandfather's correspondence, *Correspondence and Journals of Samuel Blachley Webb.* As one of his railroad employees stated after his death, Seward

> *put the utmost energy into everything he undertook. He followed the old trackman's motto, "Crowd your work or your work will crowd you." To be on his staff was like belonging to a fire department—the calls were sudden and frequent, and always interesting. Major [Edward] Burns used to say, "He has a dozen irons in the fire, and they're all red hot."*[3]

Seward was engrossed in his work for the Vanderbilt family railroad interests by the early 1890s. Appointed president of the Wagner Company in 1885, he quickly demonstrated his business acumen by reinvigorating the languishing firm in approximately five years. Under his direction, the company's railroad cars were refurbished and customer service was significantly improved. Seward was lauded for his efforts to make railroad travel more comfortable. An 1887 editorial in the *New York Truth* exclaimed,

> *The continued improvement in the service of the Wagner Palace Car Company since its management passed into the hands of Dr. Webb is noticed by all people who travel much. It is only a little while since the service on these cars was a bye-word. The cars were dirty, the conductors careless, and the porters objectionable. Now this is all changed, and in the place of dirty cars are a number of new ones which, for elegance and comfort, cannot be surpassed anywhere, while the service itself is on a par with that of the leading hotels in the country. For all this I think Dr. Webb is deserving of a good deal of praise.*[4]

Seward remained president of the Wagner Company until 1899, when it was acquired by the Pullman Company, a move that benefited both the latter and the Vanderbilt family railroad conglomerate. In exchange for stepping down as president, Seward became a member of Pullman's board of directors.[5]

The Adirondack and Saint Lawrence Railroad

Once the Wagner Palace Car Company was stabilized, Seward set his sights on even greater railroad undertakings. Between 1891 and 1892, while still leading the Wagner Company, he purchased as many as 250,000 acres in New York State's Herkimer and Hamilton Counties and constructed the Adirondack and St. Lawrence Railroad, which extended from Herkimer to Malone. The new line was intended to provide the Vanderbilt-controlled railroad companies with direct access to Montreal, Canada, circumventing the competing Delaware and Hudson Canal Company's route to the city through Vermont. With this ambitious venture,

W. Seward Webb at his desk in his New York office, c. 1890. Shelburne Farms Collections.

A dining room car constructed by the Wagner Palace Car Company, published in the *New York Daily Graphic*, December 1887. Shelburne Farms Collections.

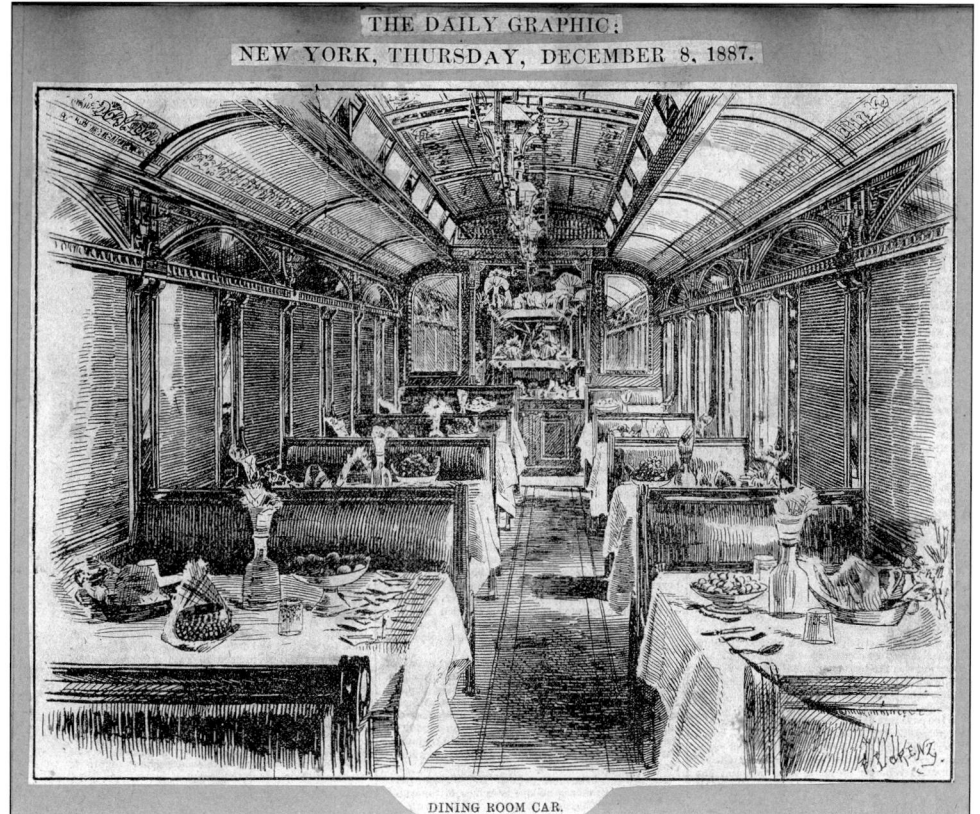

W. Seward Webb (far right) at Nehasane station with his son Seward Jr. (second from left), and three railroad employees, c. 1905. Shelburne Farms Collections.

Seward hoped to enhance his public standing as an adept businessman and pave the way for a possible bid for political office.[6]

However, the Adirondack and St. Lawrence project proved difficult from the start. Seward was dogged by delays and by protests that constructing pieces of the line on rights-of-way over state land would ruin the newly formed Adirondack Park by destroying pristine wilderness. During the contentious legal and public relations campaign about the park lands, Seward was portrayed as a greedy land-grabber in such sources as the *Buffalo Enquirer*, which titled an article about the affair "Webb Wants The Earth."[7]

In addition, Seward was lambasted in the press for allegedly mistreating the workers employed to build the railroad, who were mostly Italian- and African-Americans. In December 1891, articles entitled "Slaves on Webb's Road" and "Treated Like Slaves" published in the *New York World* and the *Standard* of Syracuse, New York, accused him of underpaying the laborers, inflating prices at the company store to keep them in debt, failing to provide them with decent shelter and food during the harsh Adirondack winter, cruelly overworking them, and therefore "murdering" them.[8]

It is unclear to what extent the allegations were true. Other articles supporting Seward contested the accusations and ascribed the issues to racial, ethnic, and class tensions between individual workers and contractors. At least one employee blamed his mistreatment on a contractor rather than Seward's actions or policies. In Seward's later life, as his daughter-in-law Aileen Webb recalled, he was remembered fondly by many of the railroad workers with whom he had come in contact:

> *He was a very attractive man, undoubtedly, was tall good looking with a very affable manner. I say that because we never traveled in a Pullman car, or anywhere where Dr. Webb had been known, that the porters or conductors wouldn't come up and say oh how's the doctor. We remember the doctor, he was such a wonderful person. And [he] obviously made an impression not because of his wealth or position but because of his personality.*[9]

In 1932, after Seward's death, Lila financed the publication of a book detailing the construction of the Adirondack and St. Lawrence. Written by Charles Burnett, a loyal employee who had served as a purchasing agent for the company, *Conquering the Wilderness: The Building of the Adirondack & St. Lawrence Railroad by William Seward Webb* was probably commissioned in large part to vindicate Seward. The limited edition was sent to "friends and relatives of Dr. Webb, and also all officers or employees of the railroad during construction."[10]

Despite the challenges, the Adirondack and St. Lawrence Railroad was completed in 1892. Seward remained president of the company until 1905, when it was purchased by the Vanderbilt flagship, the New York Central Railroad.[11]

Nehasane Park

Meanwhile, the Webbs were also planning another new estate for their family. Seward reserved approximately 150,000 acres of the land he had purchased for the Adirondack and St. Lawrence Railroad for a private hunting preserve located near Long Lake, New York. Ne-Ha-Sa-Ne—or Nehasane—Park was named for a Native American term translated at the time as "beaver crossing

Forest Lodge at Nehasane, c. 1900. Shelburne Farms Collections.

river on log."[12] The estate encompassed a 9,000-acre fenced game park, a small farm, and extensive forestry operations, on which Seward worked with forester Gifford Pinchot. The Webb family stayed at Nehasane for long weekends and periods of one or two weeks throughout the year at a shingle style lodge complex designed by Robert Robertson. Built in 1892–93, Nehasane's Forest Lodge stood on the site of a former hotel overlooking Smith's Lake, which the Webbs renamed Lake Lila. A series of twelve cabins providing additional accommodations for family, guests, and employees stretched out along the lakeshore near the lodge. The main residential complex also included a large stable and a boathouse.[13]

Politics

In addition to his business concerns, and the design and construction of the family's new Adirondack estate, Seward's growing political aspirations also absorbed a great deal of his time. By the late 1880s, he began to position himself for the Republican nomination for governor of Vermont. He and his wife changed their legal residences from the state of New York to Vermont in about 1890. At Shelburne Farms, Seward demonstrated his political allegiance by lighting celebratory bonfires on the top of Lone Tree Hill after election days in which Republicans prevailed. After the election of Republican Benjamin Harrison as president of the United States in 1888, Seward commemorated the victory by sending 200 men to participate in a parade in Burlington and installing a bell in the cupola of the Farm Barn at Shelburne Farms.[14]

The Republican Party ruled Vermont politics throughout the late nineteenth and early twentieth centuries, habitually sweeping state elections. Seward was assured an excellent chance of winning an office if he attained the support of Vermont's Republican political leaders. In order to increase his public stature, Seward engaged in as many state political and military affairs, and influen-

W. Seward Webb in his Vermont militia uniform, by L. Alman & Co., New York, c. 1888. Shelburne Farms Collections.

tial organizations, as possible. In 1887, he and Lila hosted President Grover Cleveland on board their private railroad car during the latter's trip to Vermont and the Adirondacks. Seward was appointed inspector-general of rifle practice for the Vermont militia and named an honorary colonel in 1888. He served as secretary, and then president, of the Vermont chapter of the newly formed Sons of the American Revolution. The Webbs joined Vermont governor John McCullough during President Harrison's 1891 visit to the state. In 1892, Seward led a fundraising campaign to build what became Fort Ethan Allen in Colchester, Vermont, for the Vermont militia. The fort was a pet project of Redfield Proctor, a former secretary of war whom President Harrison had appointed to the United States Senate to represent Vermont. Seward accompanied Vermont-born Admiral George Dewey, a hero of the Spanish-American War, on his triumphal tour of the state in 1899. Seward and Lila entertained Vice President Theodore Roosevelt during his 1901 speaking tour of Vermont. During the early 1900s, the Webbs socialized with President Roosevelt and several Cabinet members, Supreme Court justices, and United States Senators. Additionally, in 1902, Seward shipped crates of live pheasants from Shelburne Farms to local Vermont political leaders.[15]

Just before the Spanish–American War began in 1898, Seward contributed to the war effort by selling his yacht the *Elfrida I* to the United States Navy at low cost for use as a patrol boat. While numerous wealthy individuals responded to the navy's appeal for private vessels, Seward's gesture was seen by many as extremely generous and patriotic. The *Troy Times* stated that "in case of hostilities [the *Elfrida*] would be a valuable addition to the nation's fleet of war craft. Dr. Webb's generous proposition shows how fully he appreciates his country and how ready he is to give it aid in time of need."[16] Seward also received an anonymous letter signed by a "Patriotic Proletariat" stating his appreciation:

> *I cannot refrain from expressing the high opinion which I, and thousands of others, entertain of your noble action in offering your boat to the government. Your conduct is all the more refreshing when contrasted with that of others who endeavor to avail themselves of the opportunity and demand exorbitant prices for their craft.*[17]

After the war's close in 1899, the navy refused Seward's offer to repurchase the *Elfrida I*. The vessel was owned by the navy and used to patrol the eastern seaboard until 1918. However, the navy demonstrated its gratitude when Admiral Dewey visited Shelburne Farms in October 1899.[18]

Seward's political philosophy appears to have been a conservative one, centered upon the doctrine of noblesse oblige and the "trickle-down" approach. He sought to appeal to the working classes by serving as a champion for the welfare of the public. In 1896, he was quoted in the *New York World* as stating,

> *It is time the rich, who have leisure for such work, took a hand in the fight. Not so much to protect themselves, for in any case they would not be the worst sufferers, but to show their patriotism by helping to look after the interests of the men whom they employ— the men upon whose prosperity and cooperation depends the success of their own enterprise.*[19]

By 1896, and for almost a decade following, Seward was often rumored to be a candidate for governor of the state of Vermont. In the late 1890s, he successfully ran for state representative for the town of Shelburne and served one term from 1896 to 1897. At that time, his political progression was

Admiral George Dewey and Frederica Webb on the South Porch at Shelburne House, October 1899. Shelburne Farms Collections.

predicted to be state representative, speaker of the Vermont House of Representatives, then governor of Vermont.[20]

Seward also considered serving in politics on the national level. He was rumored to be a candidate for secretary of war under President McKinley in 1897, explored a campaign to become Senator Proctor's successor in 1899, and served as a state delegate to the 1904 Republican National Convention in Chicago. He continued his public and behind-the-scenes political efforts until about 1905.[21]

Shelburne Farms' farm manager E. F. Gebhardt served as Seward's local political advisor and campaign manager of sorts, and spent a great deal of time working on his political affairs. Gebhardt wrote Lila in 1902 to apologize for neglecting some of her requests, stating, "Dr. Webb's directions to me were to abandon everything for politics, as he put it."[22] In 1905, Gebhardt wrote to Lila to report that her husband still possessed strong support in the state for a gubernatorial campaign: "Half the state appears to have their ear on the ground waiting to hear from him. I cannot move off the farm without bushels of inquiries as to whether he will make the run for governor or not."[23]

Yet Seward's political aspirations never crystallized. His background as a New Yorker, member of the Vanderbilt family, and railroad magnate both assisted and hindered him. Although Vermont had a history of electing railroad presidents as governors (Edward Smith, the president of the Central Vermont Railroad, was elected governor in 1898), public opinion was divided about Seward's suitability for the position. The *Burlington Free Press* came out in favor of a possible gubernatorial run in 1898, stating, "Webb would make an ideal candidate and a governor that would lend dignity to the office and honor to the State."[24] The Hartford, Connecticut, *Courant* spoke for his opposition: "If a mere Vanderbilt millionaire sets in to carry Vermont, we very much doubt if Vermont will carry him. The notion that a rich young man can lay down a pocketbook and take up a governorship in exchange for it isn't popular just now nor is it likely ever to be in New England."[25]

Seward confronted a growing divide between two factions in the Vermont Republican Party—and in Vermont society in general. As historian Paul Searls has related, Seward's background and political leanings resonated with one contingent of the party, which was mostly composed of the professional, middle-class, and more affluent residents of Vermont's villages and cities. They tended to espouse modernity and reform and were receptive to the influences of urban and industrial America that Seward represented. Seward's political activities, as well as his efforts to improve agriculture in the state, had allied him with the Vermonters of this "downhill" contingent, who had dominated Republican politics for some time. However, Seward's stance was in opposition to the "uphill" faction of the party, which drew heavily from the farming communities of the more isolated, rural hill towns. Those of the uphill persuasion tended to be heavily rooted in tradition and skeptical of the influences of modern society. While the downhill contingent accepted Seward as a Vermonter, the uphill faction saw him as an outsider and a possible threat to the continuity of their way of life.[26]

Unfortunately for Seward, the divide between uphill and downhill came to a head during the 1902 gubernatorial race, his strongest political push. A growing protest against the downhill domination of the party, and their perceived tactics of determining candidates among themselves from behind closed doors, led the party leaders whom Seward had so carefully cultivated to urge him to withdraw from the race, which he did in the spring of 1902. Searls writes, "Webb's candidacy became a hapless victim of overflowing uphill discontent" in the 1902 gubernatorial race: "Although Webb was considered early on the heavyweight in the race, by March 1902 his candidacy was enormously unpopular, especially in rural sections of the state."[27]

Seward's decision to withdraw from the 1902

gubernatorial campaign saved him the embarrassment of a sizable loss on election day. His decision may also have been influenced by the fact that he did not relish a scrappy political campaign. He preferred to be the sole Republican candidate and had refused to enter a race at least once before when it threatened to become divisive. In a 1910 letter to their son Vanderbilt, Lila related an account of her husband's decision not to run for governor in 1891 because of the direct appeal of another candidate's wife:

> *Papa did a nice thing for Mr. [Edward C.] Smith years ago, & by doing it, lost his sure chance of being governor of Vermont. He was too unselfish, as I told him at the time...A large party wanted him to run for governor of Vt. & many people felt he would get it, & I know he would have. Mr. Smith's Father, Gregory Smith, Pres. of the Cent. Vt. R.R. [Central Vermont Railroad] had been governor, & E. C. Smith was to run for it also. Mrs. [Edward] Smith, knowing Papa's popularity in the State & that his chances would be greater than her husband's, came personally & asked Papa not to run. He gave it up, altho I wanted him to fight it out squarely, & I think he made a mistake to give it up. He was placed in a difficult position, as he is a gentleman through & through, & hated to refuse a woman her request.*[28]

Seward's reluctance to stir up a political fight probably also influenced his decision not to run in the 1905 governor's race. As Gebhardt wrote to Lila regarding her husband's gubernatorial chances, "I will say now and again that Dr. Webb can win out this time but he will have to enter an action stirring contest. Many of his friends fear he would not do this...I appreciate that Dr. Webb will be somewhat adverse to entering into a contest. He seems to think it undignified."[29]

Seward's lack of success in state and national politics was a source of great disappointment to him and his family. In 1907, two years after the last rumors about his gubernatorial chances had subsided, Lila wrote Gebhardt that she had "never ceased to wish that Dr. Webb might be governor of Vermont, but he never speaks of it, nor does he care to have me do so."[30]

Financial Problems

The Webb family's financial affairs, increasingly complicated and constraining by the 1890s, also consumed much of Seward's time. In the early years of their marriage, the couple's significant financial resources sustained their active, lavish lifestyle and costly building projects, including expensive yachts, prolonged travels in the American West and Europe, the Shelburne Farms estate, their Fifth Avenue townhouse, and participation in New York social events. In the 1880s, after the death of Lila's father led to an inheritance of $10 million, the Webbs' finances seemed to be limitless. In 1889, the *New York Journal* reported that Seward spent $500,000 per year. By 1894, with Seward's Wagner Palace Car Company salary and an inheritance received from his mother in 1890, the Webbs were jointly estimated to be worth a staggering $30 million, with an annual income of $1,500,000.[31]

Yet despite their wealth, the Webbs soon found themselves plagued by financial problems. The first sign of difficulties surfaced in the early to mid-1890s, when Seward's business activities began to tie up and drain their funds. Throughout the 1880s and 1890s, while serving as president of both the Wagner Palace Car Company and the Adirondack and St. Lawrence Railroad, Seward retained the Wall Street stock business he had launched in order to impress Lila's father. He had formed W. S. Webb & Company with his brother H. Walter Webb around 1883. About four years later, the company became Webb, Prall & Co. when the brothers added two new partners: a third sibling, Frank Edgerton Webb, and John H. Prall.[32]

Because of Seward's consuming work for the Vanderbilt railroad interests, he was probably only nominally involved with managing the stock business. However, he was obligated to assist the company and its active partners when they faced financial crises. The business experienced deep financial losses as a result of poor management decisions made in the aftermath of the Panic of 1893, a stock market crash that caused "the worst economic collapse the nation…experienced before the Great Depression."[33] Frank Webb faced personal ruin, and another Webb brother, J. Louis, lost most of the money he had placed with the firm to be invested. In December 1895, Walter Webb wrote to Seward to apprise him of the situation.

I have very bad news for you. Frank's affairs are in deplorable condition…They have lost everything, and will have debt amounting I fear to over $300,000…They were carrying on their own accounts about 6000 shares of the darndest trash in Wall St…Poor Louis has most of his things involved…the nature of their doings are such that I fear…we will have to pay up in order to keep it quiet.[34]

Two years later, Frank appealed to Seward for additional funds to pay off his personal debts, this time requesting him to ask Lila to loan him money from her Vanderbilt trust in order to "save me and mine from ruin and disgrace."[35] No record of the Webbs' response to this request has yet surfaced, but it seems likely that the couple did indeed bail him out, as they had previously done.

Seward and Lila's personal funds were also tied up with Seward's other business ventures. The Adirondack and St. Lawrence Railroad experienced serious cost overruns from the start, and some of these were personally absorbed by the Webbs. For example, Seward apparently covered a $147,000 debt owed by a bankrupt contractor with his own money.[36]

After the construction of the Adirondack and St. Lawrence, Seward became involved with several additional railroad companies, among them the Rutland Railroad in Vermont. In 1904, two years into his stint as president of the Rutland Railroad, he told Gebhardt that a substantial amount of his funds were tied up in company stock:

Regarding our conversation this morning as to expenditures for the coming year. As I told you, and as you are well aware I am carrying a very large amount of Rutland stock and I do not care to realize on it or part with it at present prices, and of course it is not paying me any dividend, but is costing me quite a large amount of money to carry, consequently I am going to make quite a reduction in my personal and farm expenses for the next year or so.[37]

Even more devastating was the fallout from Seward's failed deal with business associate Alfred Meyer. Both served on the board of directors of the Cape Breton Railway and were involved with the Dominion Securities Company, which managed the construction of the Cape Breton. Seward was president and Meyer was treasurer. In 1901 and 1902, the two men struck a personal deal, and Meyer obtained bank loans to purchase almost $4 million of stock in the Cape Breton, the Rutland, the Adirondack and St. Lawrence, and other companies from Seward. When Meyer went bankrupt, Seward was forced to pay off the loans in order to counter claims that he and Meyer had been conspiring to defraud the banks. Lila's brother William K. Vanderbilt stepped in to assist with a $3,375,000 loan to Seward.[38]

Shortly thereafter, the Dominion Securities Company went bankrupt, and because of their personal business dealings, Seward and Meyer were accused of falsely inflating the stock values of the Dominion, the Cape Breton, and other companies in which they were involved together and misrepresenting those values to the public. In 1902, the *Tammany Times* went so far as to accuse Seward of conspiring with Meyer to inflate stock values in order to increase his public standing and his chances of winning the governor's race in Vermont. A series of lawsuits followed, in which Seward was sued by Meyer's creditors, by Meyer himself, who claimed that he too had been cheated by Seward and had purchased stock at falsely inflated prices, and by Henry Sprague, one of Meyer's business associates. To make matters more complicated, Sprague also sued Meyer.[39]

Seward publicly denied all price-inflation accusations, claiming that his intentions had always been honest. However, the matter smacked of wrongdoing, and Seward faced a great deal of negative publicity. The media pounced on the juicy story of the millions allegedly dishonestly made and lost by a wealthy society man and member of the Vanderbilt family. Privately, Seward felt "blackmailed."[40] In a confidential, anxiously scribbled note to Gebhardt describing Sprague's suit against Meyer, he wrote:

> *Sprage & Meyer have fallen out & each sueing each other it is a case of dog eat dog when thieves fall out & both sides want to subpoena me & I don't intend to have them do it as it will be a long drawn out affair & they both hate me &…they are liable to ask some nasty questions to embarass me, questions they know are not true & I do not want to go on the stand & have my name in the papers.*[41]

Seward sought to keep a low profile by settling as much as possible out of court. He bought back at a loss some of the stock he had sold to Meyer

"Construction Engine No. 1," used in the building of the Cape Breton Railway, c. 1900. Shelburne Farms Collections.

and took out additional loans in order to settle the claims with Meyer's creditors and prop up the failing Dominion Securities Company. As the lawsuits dragged on, he tried to avoid subpoenas, spending a great deal of time in Europe. He traveled back to New York clandestinely at least once, writing to Gebhardt a hurried, undated note: "I am in N.Y. [secretly] for a few days on account of trying to avoid a sub[poena]. To appear as a witness against Meyers. *No one knows* I am here except [Karl] *Heine* [Webb's personal secretary] so do not telegraph or write me here." A postscript stated: "When I say no one knows I am here I mean it. *No one.* I came in after dark if anyone should call & ask for me the servant will say I am south yet."[42]

It is unclear how culpable Seward really was in the Meyer stock debacle. Certainly his and Meyer's personal stock deals would be considered a conflict of interest today. Whatever the case, the state of affairs caused much anxiety and consumed a great deal of Seward's time and available funds. The lawsuits dragged on until 1915, when Seward received at least partial vindication after the New York State Supreme Court ruled on appeal that Henry Sprague's lawsuit against him was unfounded and that Sprague and Meyer's business plans were "illegal and immoral."[43]

Compounding the financial losses from Seward's business ventures was the volatile nature of the stock market during the 1890s and early 1900s. Seward and Lila were primarily supported by the income they received from invested funds. While the principal of Lila's Vanderbilt inheritance was placed in relatively secure New York City bonds and real estate, some of the couple's other funds were invested in higher-risk stocks. At times the Webbs did quite well in the stock market. However, they were seriously affected by a series of financial panics and economic depressions from the 1890s to the 1920s, including the disastrous Panic of 1893. Seward wrote Gebhardt in one confidential letter, "I lost a great deal in the last two panics & it will take time to pull out."[44] In fact, Seward's losses were significant enough that he felt the need to boast to his wife when his finances were doing well. As he wrote in an undated letter,

> *I have been* more *than fortunate in the past two years in fact to be honest I have made more than 2 and a ½ million…It has been by hard work & not by idleness…I deliberately bought some stock & sold it…& I put ½ the money in a new bank a/c [account] for that purpose. Strange as it may seem I have not made one single loss in the stock market for over 3 years & never will for I buy only the good stock…I tell you all this so you need not worry about money.*"[45]

Despite Seward's assurances, the family's assets were probably seriously depleted by the first or second decade of the twentieth century. The $5 million principal of Lila's trust remained mostly intact, but other Webb finances were in disarray, with funds tied up in poorly performing railroad stock, business debts, and lawsuits. Despite it all, Seward continued to speculate on Wall Street. He mortgaged Nehasane Park and used his wife's trust as collateral for his loans, involving the funds in potentially precarious deals.[46]

Health Problems

Seward's growing health problems only added to the family's troubles. The first documented signs of his illnesses appeared in 1879, when he was only twenty-eight years old and still courting Lila. Forbidden to see or correspond with her, Seward wrote of repeatedly suffering from "worry and neuralgia" so debilitating that it caused insomnia and necessitated taking laudanum, a mixture of opium and alcohol then popular as a source of relief from pain, anxiety, and sleeplessness.[47]

By the late 1890s, a series of crippling physical ailments began to seriously impact Seward's life and curtail his professional and social activi-

W. Seward Webb and a family dog at Forest Lodge, Nehasane, by Thomas E. Marr, c. 1900. Shelburne Farms Collections.

ties. He suffered from headaches, bronchitis, gout, rheumatism, kidney problems, intestinal trouble, insomnia, ulcers on his gums, sciatica, lumbago, and unspecified skin issues. In 1898, his son Watson wrote to Lila, "Papa has a bad headache and can't get up or even talk to me he is so sick."[48] In 1900, Seward was ill for a period of several months with what the press described as "inflammatory rheumatism" and "gout."[49] In 1901, he took to his bed with recurring headaches at least twice. In January 1903, Seward slipped and fell on the ice outside 680 Fifth Avenue and was laid up for much of the rest of that year and the following, suffering from the fall, the gout, and the other ailments that they triggered. In March 1904, 300 gallons of "Walton's Oxygen Compound," prescribed for respiratory problems such as "Pneumonia, Heart Failure and Spasmodic Asthma" and other afflictions, including bronchitis and anemia, were purchased for him.[50]

As the years went on, Seward began a cycle of periods of poor health followed by partial recovery, becoming more and more of an invalid. His chronic health problems developed as he entered middle age, while he was deeply involved with his railroad ventures, and as his financial problems grew. The gout and rheumatism were probably at least partly genetic, as several relatives, including his father, brother, and son Vanderbilt, also experienced stiff, swollen, and painful joints that were diagnosed as gout and/or rheumatism. Seward's other health problems, such as his headaches and back pain, may have resulted from stress and overwork. In 1910, he wrote that once he finished "cleaning up old debt" from his business concerns, he would "have no more money troubles or worry which has truly made me ill."[51]

By the turn of the twentieth century, Seward's physical ailments were compounded by a growing addiction to morphine. In a letter to Lila written some years later about his problems with morphine, he noted that he had "been ill," i.e., addicted, since 1898.[52] He was most likely given morphine injections starting in the mid-1890s to combat the pain he felt from his debilitating illnesses. While quite addictive, morphine was one of the only drugs known to be an effective painkiller during the nineteenth century. It had long been prescribed for a wide range of afflictions, including neuralgia, headaches, insomnia, rheumatism, and "chronic respiratory diseases (asthma, bronchitis, tuberculosis) or infectious diseases of long duration."[53] In 1872, a British physician published a treatise in which he put forth morphine as an ideal treatment for back pain.[54]

The addiction haunted Seward until his death in 1926. He attempted to wean himself of the drug repeatedly over the years, but he always found himself slipping back into addiction. A medical doctor in his own right, Seward probably knew about the addictive qualities of the drug and the difficulty of recovering from a dependence on it, which were widely understood by medical authorities in the late nineteenth century. He occasionally treated himself. However, he was more often attended by other physicians, at least eight different individuals during the course of his illnesses.[55]

The physiological effects of the morphine and numerous attempts to fight off addiction probably weakened Seward and led in part to additional health problems. Withdrawal symptoms for morphine addiction often included intestinal upset, which may explain his digestive ailments. Paradoxically, morphine was sometimes prescribed to ease Seward's discomfort from his physical illnesses even while he was attempting to wean himself from the drug, causing him to relapse. In 1912, he wrote to his wife that his latest effort to beat his addiction had failed because a doctor had prescribed it to him to counteract his health problems:

> *I called up Dr. Stoddard in the [Shelburne] Village & told him how I felt, & had been feeling although I had not taken any Morphine. He said nothing will do you any good to pull yourself up but take a good dose of Morphine. I said a ¼ of a grain he said no no one grain I said can't I do any thing else & he said no. I told him I had only taken two Small doses since the middle of June… & said my God Doctor I have been working all Summer to get off the stuff. He said was nothing else would do any good… Soon after I took it, it helped me some. but not enough. I told Dr. Markoe about it & he said I should have taken a larger dose 2 or 3 grs. & taken it entire & [I] would have been alright.[56]*

Seward was far from alone in his addiction. Scholars have estimated that at the turn of the twentieth century, between 313,000 and one million Americans were addicted to morphine and other opiates, such as heroin. During the second half of the nineteenth century, the majority of American morphine addicts were middle-aged Caucasian members of the middle and upper classes—those who were able to afford to pay a physician to treat them with morphine for the chronic ailments that they were developing as they grew older. Doctors themselves were prone to self-medication. Medical studies conducted between 1899 and 1913 estimated that between 6 percent and 23 percent of American doctors were addicted to morphine. The prevalence of physician dependence on morphine had entered the public consciousness by 1907, when Edith Wharton published *The Fruit of the Tree*, a novel about a promising young doctor who deteriorates into physical and moral depravity after he becomes dependent upon morphine. As one historian has noted,

> *Among male addicts the leading occupation was unquestionably that of physician… The widespread use of opium and morphine as tranquillizing and somniferous agents helps explain why so many physicians and other health professionals became addicted. Long and irregular hours, stiff competition, and constant pressure from impatient patients sorely tempted the physician to treat his headache or insomnia with morphine, a drug he knew to be quick, effective, and readily available.[57]*

To be sure, Seward had ceased to practice medicine by 1879, years before his addiction became apparent. However, his new lines of work, financial troubles, and competing interests certainly brought with them similar kinds of "long and irregular hours, stiff competition, and constant pressure."

While undergoing "cures" for his morphine addiction and recovering from his latest physical ailments, Seward spent long periods sequestered with an attending physician and/or valet and footmen at Nehasane, in Europe, in Florida, and, at least once, in Cuba. Even when staying in the same residence as his wife and children, he often lived

W. Seward and Lila Webb with their grandson, J. Watson Webb Jr., on the porch at Forest Lodge, c. 1925. Shelburne Farms Collections.

and ate alone in his own suite of rooms. His various treatments required "perpetual solitary confinement" in order to keep him away from temptations, allow him to undergo withdrawal symptoms privately to avoid alarming or embarrassing his family and friends, and then recover.[58] Tellingly, Seward did not attend President William Howard Taft when he visited Shelburne Farms in 1909. Neither Seward nor his family admitted his addiction publicly during his lifetime. The rumors about his health problems that circulated in the family's social circles and in the press were either flatly denied, or his ongoing phalanx of physical ailments was emphasized to draw attention away from the addiction.[59]

Seward's illnesses, business problems, and financial troubles were all intertwined, each one affecting and/or fueling the others. For instance, Seward's illnesses affected his chances for being elected governor of Vermont. In April 1905, Gebhardt wrote to Lila:

Others fear his health might not permit it [a run for governor]. This latter condition springs from the fact that Dr. Webb has had Dr. Bingham in such close attendance for so long a time, the impression has gained currency, his health was much impaired. I hope I am not transgressing but I know, or at least expect you will be consulted in these matters. Or I might better say an effort will be made to consult you in relation to

Dr. Webb's health. There are some friends who are very earnest in Dr. Webb's behalf, that will not enter a contest unless they are assured he will, to use a common phrase, "stick." These same friends do not wish to encourage Dr. Webb to accept if there is the remotest possibility that the annoyance of a campaign would be a burden.[60]

As the years went on, Seward became progressively less able to function in the life he had previously enjoyed. It was a lonely existence, one that increasingly isolated him from his work, his family, and his friends. By about 1905, it was becoming clear to him and his family that the addiction and its related health problems were likely to stay with him for the rest of his life. Significantly, 1905 was also about the time in which Seward withdrew from active business pursuits and his last political interests. By about 1910, he had ceased active management of the Shelburne Farms estate. But he would live and struggle on with his afflictions for another sixteen years.

Chapter 10
TRANSITIONS

I want to further impress on you to try and keep the expenses down on Shelburne farms to [the] lowest possible point.
— Seward Webb to E. F. Gebhardt, July 1903

I certainly love this place, & would give a lot to live here most of the year.
— J. Watson Webb, July 1913[1]

With Seward and Lila Webb's attention diverted by business and political affairs, their new Adirondack property, and Seward's growing health concerns, Shelburne Farms was no longer their primary focus. Financial problems forced them to review their annual expenditures more critically. By the turn of the twentieth century, the couple had abandoned many aspects of their ambitious vision for Shelburne Farms and dramatically reduced its size and scope. Although it remained one of the largest and most well-known country estates in the nation, the heady sense of optimism and prosperity that had characterized the property's earliest years was gradually replaced by stasis and decline. By 1930, Shelburne Farms had changed immeasurably.

Estate Reductions

The Shelburne Farms estate was not designed to be a profitable operation, and it probably never was. The Webbs supported it with large outlays of cash, seeing little to no financial return on their enormous investments in land, estate buildings, landscaping, and model farm activities. While several estate departments, such as the dairy, brought in some income, the overall expenses far outweighed the profits. As the family's financial problems grew, Seward and Lila were forced to determine which of their many expensive pursuits were to be continued, and at what price. Shelburne Farms was one of the largest drains on their income, and although the couple had no intention of selling it, the estate was a logical place to look to reduce expenses.

Major reductions in the size and scope of Shelburne Farms started as early as 1894 and continued through the 1910s. By the first decade of the twentieth century, farm manager E. F. Gebhardt received regular directions from the

Webbs to cut costs. Between 1903 and 1908, over $30,000 was trimmed from the estate's annual budget. In 1903, a large number of employees were laid off, and several departmental budgets were cut back. Gebhardt wrote to Seward in March of that year to report: "We have been running with a very small force for the past few weeks…You see we are doing our best to keep within limit."[2] But three months later, Seward requested additional cuts: "I want to further impress on you to try and keep the expenses down on Shelburne farms to [the] lowest possible point until I can return and arrange about money matters."[3] Starting in 1904, the Coach Barn was closed during the off-season, its horses and tack were moved to the Breeding Barn for the winter, and some Coach Barn employees were laid off. In 1907, Gebhardt stated that "Dr. Webb directed that we cut everything."[4] In order to offset some of their costs, the Webbs leased some estate lands in the northern portion of their property to local farmers by 1908 and continued to do so into the 1930s. In 1911, the dairy was reduced to a quarter of its previous size. The following year, Seward sold all of the Hampshiredown sheep in his flock. Also in 1912, after a series of gradual reductions, the Coach Barn staff was decreased to three men from a maximum of about seven. By 1914, Seward had also directed Gebhardt to sell all but the white leghorns from the poultry farm. Every estate department had been affected by the economizing measures by about 1915.[5]

The costliest departments were the most affected by the reductions. Beset with difficulties since its establishment in the early 1890s, the pheasantry department had never been profitable. Its annual budget consumed approximately $1,500 to $5,500 between 1900 and 1905, the latter amount being more than double the top salary received by Gebhardt, the highest-paid farm employee. As Seward's health declined and he became increasingly unable to participate in the annual pheasant shoots he had once enjoyed, the department's costs probably seemed less worthwhile. The pheasantry's staff and budget were substantially reduced starting in 1903, and the department was completely eliminated four years later.[6]

The Shelburne Farms Stud experienced the most significant cuts. Not only was the enormously ambitious horse breeding project extremely costly, but it had also failed to live up to Seward's dreams of success. Reflecting upon the operation in 1915, Gebhardt stated that Shelburne Farms "never could raise [horses] profitably."[7] The few gentlemen who patronized the service did not bring in much revenue, and the number of those who did pay in full was rather small, as personal friends, relatives, and business associates were often given complimentary services or reduced rates. In 1905, Gebhardt reported to Seward's eldest son, Watson, that "outside parties" were charged twenty-five dollars a year in breeding fees, but the Shelburne Farms Stud had "not had over one or two a year."[8] Unfortunately, Seward had established his business just as the newly invented automobile was beginning to attract the traveling and sporting interests of his peers and draw them away from horses and horse breeding. In 1911, Gebhardt noted, "the horse business is largely a pastime."[9]

Although local farmers would continue to rely upon horses for agriculture and transportation for several decades to come, Seward's efforts to offer stud services to them at reduced or complimentary rates were never very popular. He was likely perceived as a wealthy outsider attempting to tell the locals what was best for them, a tactic that was probably especially irritating to farmers belonging to the uphill contingent of Vermont society. They found comfort in tradition and, although not diametrically opposed to improvements in agricultural practices and technology, were often skeptical of change that they felt was being imposed on them. Seward certainly had not minced words in his 1893 catalogue, *Shelburne Farms Stud*, in which he described the local horses as "light weedy-looking nags" that had degenerated over the course of the nineteenth century.[10] His statements conveniently ignored Vermonters' long attachment to the Morgan horse breed, which was known for its stamina and attractive appearance. He also insinuated that the farmers themselves were only interested in breeding horses for frivolous racing activities rather than practical needs.[11]

As Seward's financial and health problems mounted, he was increasingly unable to devote time and funds to salvaging the horse breeding operation. In 1911, Watson noted, "You see it was foolish to keep on with the remnant of hackneys we had left, Father being always sick & having lost interest."[12] The Shelburne Farms Stud was the model farm's greatest failure.

Thus, when it came time to cut costs, the Stud witnessed the earliest and most dramatic reductions of any estate department. The auxiliary barns near the Breeding Barn, originally designed for horses, were converted to house sheep, poultry, and cattle by 1894. A large portion of the horse stock was sold at auction in the late 1890s and early 1900s. Seward's prize Matchless of Londesboro was auctioned for $12,000 in February 1897. Gebhardt characterized a 1903 auction, which netted over $7,000, as a "complete…cleaning out."[13] Financial pressures apparently forced Seward to sell poor-quality and very young horses in addition to prize animals in order to recoup some of his costs, and the mixed character of these public sales damaged the reputation of the Shelburne Farms Stud. In 1910, Watson remarked to Gebhardt that "the name we once had for good horses…was destroyed by sales of bad ones at different times lately."[14]

In some ways, the drastic reductions to the model farm's size and scope may have succeeded in creating a more efficient operation. In 1903, Gebhardt advised Seward to consolidate control of the estate finances within the main farm office, thus giving department heads less opportunity to "run everything on gilt edge lines regardless of expense."[15] He continued, "In the past I have always felt as though I were fighting you on expense, with scores of people on and off the place lying awake nights wondering how they could help you spend your money."[16]

However, by the 1910s, the repeated economizing measures began to cut to the heart of the operation, and Gebhardt struggled to comply with Seward's wishes and maintain the estate as best he could. He wrote, "I am of course awful sorry to hear of the conditions…I am taking immediate action and stopping all unnecessary work, but the laying off of four is a very trying duty to me."[17] Buildings and infrastructure began to suffer from deferred maintenance, outdated equipment was not replaced, and the scale of the farm operations shrank dramatically. By 1910, what was once a cutting-edge model farm had started to slip into decline.

Lifestyle Changes

By the 1890s, the Webbs' personal worth had declined from its height of 1885, the year Lila received her inheritance. Although they remained exceedingly wealthy for their time, they began to make some efforts to prioritize their personal expenses. It is likely that an awareness of their less certain financial future contributed to their 1894 decision to renovate and expand Shelburne House rather than build a more elaborate dwelling.[18]

By 1903, the Webbs were also considering sacrificing one of their most expensive passions: the *Elfrida II*. They weighed the enormous annual expenditures required to outfit, maintain, and staff the yacht against the pleasures they and their guests derived from it. They left the *Elfrida* dry-docked for entire seasons, operated it for shorter periods in other years, and chartered it out for several seasons. As the yacht aged, its annual maintenance expenses ballooned, and its market appeal decreased. Matters were only made worse when the *Elfrida* suffered an accident in 1910, requiring a return to its shipwrights for expensive repairs. Soon after the accident, the Webbs began concerted efforts to locate a buyer for the yacht. Gebhardt offered it to the United States Navy for $50,000, estimated to be half of its market value, but he was refused. In 1912, after further efforts to sell it had failed, the *Elfrida* was taken completely out of commission. After six years of dry-dock, the yacht had accumulated serious deferred maintenance. It was probably a 1918 tax levied against pleasure yachts that finally prompted the Webbs to offer the *Elfrida* for sale at a price guaranteed to take it off their hands, and it was purchased the following year by a wealthy gentleman.[19]

Several years later, in 1921, Seward and Lila sold their private railcar, the *Ellsmere*, at a substantial loss. With Seward's retirement from active railroad concerns and his poor health, the couple's days of extensive rail travel had ended, and it was probably difficult to justify the expense of maintaining and staffing a private car.[20]

The Webbs also entertained plans to place Oakledge Farm, their first country estate, on the market. After moving to Shelburne Farms in 1888, they had used the Burlington property only occasionally. In 1891, they had hired a local real estate developer to prepare a plan to subdivide the property, but the project never came to fruition. Instead, the Webbs boarded up the main house and rented the farm. By 1913, they had decided to sell the estate. However, after two years, they removed the property from the market in favor of renting it again. It is unclear whether they had second thoughts about selling the estate or were unable to find a purchaser at the price they named.[21]

The most significant casualty of Seward and Lila's efforts to reduce their personal expenses was their townhouse in New York City, 680 Fifth Avenue. After much soul-searching during the winter of 1912, the Webbs placed the house on the market. Encroaching commercial development was changing the character of the neighborhood, and the townhouse's large household and aging structure were extremely costly to maintain. In addition to regular expenses, a serious fire in 1905 caused considerable damage and required extensive repairs and refurbishment. And as Seward grew increasingly incapacitated and the couple's discretionary funds decreased, they no longer needed a large townhouse for the extravagant dinner parties and receptions they had once hosted, and the cash to be realized from its sale was probably welcome.[22]

In February 1913, the Webbs signed an agreement to sell the property for approximately $1 million to John D. Rockefeller Jr. The decision to sell a house in which they had lived for more than twenty-seven years proved to be emotionally wrenching for both Seward and Lila, especially when they discovered that Rockefeller intended to demolish the residence in order to free the site for commercial uses. To make matters worse, another serious fire damaged the townhouse just before the Webbs departed. While there were no personal injuries, the fire caused extensive damage. When the townhouse changed hands in May 1913, Lila wrote in her diary, "I feel quite lost."[23]

Although the couple's new city residence likely saved them a significant amount of money compared to 680 Fifth Avenue, it was only slightly less luxurious. They leased a two-story, custom-designed apartment overlooking Central Park on the 11th and 12th floors of 903 Park Avenue at 79th Street, moving in during the month of October 1913. But still, it did not hold the same emotional attachment as 680 or Shelburne Farms did. As Lila wrote to Vanderbilt describing the new residence, "Our panoramic view is something quite wonderful, but there is nothing 'old fashioned' or 'quaint' about it. It suits N.Y. & the 20th century that is all there is to be said about it. Shelburne is our 'home.'"[24]

Management Transitions

As Seward's health problems grew, the responsibility of overseeing Shelburne Farms fell to Lila. Gebhardt continued to consult with Seward and keep him informed of estate activities, but Lila assumed the role of primary advisor from the early 1900s to the 1930s. By February 1904, she was reviewing the accounts and approving the monthly Shelburne House payroll. By 1913, she signed all of the checks that sustained the estate. By 1924, Frank Kendzior, Gebhardt's successor as farm manager, would note the complete transfer of oversight in a letter to the American Jersey Cattle Club: "In view of your rules and the fact that Dr. Webb is a member of your club would you be willing to transfer his membership to his wife Mrs. L. O. Webb. Dr. Webb was the founder of this Estate but owing to advanced years and failing health he has now ceased all interest in it."[25]

Gebhardt, who served as farm manager from the early 1900s until 1922, guided Shelburne Farms through a critical transition period. Although the Webbs had relied heavily upon him since the 1890s, he was indispensable to them by about 1905. As Seward withdrew from an active management role, Gebhardt assumed even greater responsibility for the day-to-day managerial and financial decisions, which only grew more challenging as time went on. He kept Lila informed of the latest developments and taught her how to understand the estate's financial statements. With Gebhardt's guidance, Lila proved to be an active and capable manager of the Shelburne Farms estate, keeping a very close eye on expenditures and departmental activities. She maintained constant contact with Gebhardt and regularly made the rounds of the various estate departments.[26]

Watson Webb began to assist with the management of his parents' properties in about 1906. Over the next thirty years, Watson would advise them on many of the family's affairs. Unlike Seward and Lila's daughter Frederica, who was newly married and starting a family of her own, and their younger sons Seward and Vanderbilt, who were still in their teenage years, Watson was in his early twenties and close to completing his undergraduate degree at Yale University. Of all the Webb children, Watson had demonstrated the strongest preferences for

J. Watson Webb, by Alman & Co., New York, c. 1900–02. Shelburne Farms Collections.

agriculture and outdoor sporting activities from a young age. Throughout his life, he often expressed frustration and boredom with the social and business affairs of New York, and he found physical and spiritual renewal at Shelburne and Nehasane through the rigors of country life, including horses, fox and deer hunting, and agricultural labor. As he wrote in 1913, "Hated like anything to come to town [New York City]. I certainly would like to spend all my time in the country."[27]

While away from home at school during his adolescent and young adult years, Watson yearned for news of Shelburne. A letter he wrote to Gebhardt in March 1905, while a sophomore at Yale, demonstrates his keen interest in estate matters: "Has [stud groom William H.] Hopkins gotten back yet [from a horse buying trip in England]? I should like to know, also all the other news about the place. How are the new hounds and horses doing…Has the snow left yet and how is the weather generally?... Please let me know all the news."[28] In 1910, he wrote Gebhardt from Chicago, "I wish I could be home to see the farm."[29]

Watson's developing passions for horses and hunting strengthened his ties to Shelburne Farms. Although his parents practiced increasing economy in their personal and farm activities, they indulged Watson's interests in these areas. He started foxhunting on the property and the local vicinity with a pack of beagles in 1902 and began to use harriers, a smaller, specialized breed of foxhound that was accompanied in the hunt on foot, the following year. In 1904, Seward purchased six couples of English foxhounds for his son, noting, "With this new stock he should, in a short time, have a first class pack."[30] Seward's gift effectively established the Shelburne Foxhounds and the Shelburne Hunt, traditions that would continue for over fifty years.

Watson Webb also took up competitive polo in 1904, playing on Yale's team and holding informal games at the indoor exercising ring in the Breeding

J. Watson Webb with polo ponies, outside of the Breeding Barn, c. 1905. Shelburne Farms Collections.

Barn with his college friends and younger brother Vanderbilt. Watson's son Samuel later recounted, "The large hackney barn at Shelburne with tanbark floor and corral was…large enough to play indoor polo. It was only natural that Father…began with stick and ball on homebred horses which were too small to make hunters."[31]

Watson worked to revive the Shelburne Farms Stud and transform it into a more financially sustainable operation. By 1906, he began to play an active role in managing the Breeding Barn and the remnants of the Stud. That year, he informed Gebhardt that his father "*says* now I shall have absolute say in the B.B. [Breeding Barn] & I would like to start off with the acc'ts [accounts], valuation of stocks etc. on Jan 1st & see the yearly losses as soon as you can give them to me, as far back as possible."[32] For the next six years, he worked on his parents' behalf to purchase and sell horses, manage the department's accounts, supervise Breeding Barn employees, and acquire new tack and other equipment for the Breeding and Coach Barns. Stud groom William Henry Hopkins advised Breeding Barn workers seeking promotions to approach Watson, and Gebhardt requested the younger Webb's guidance regarding the disposition of individual horses between departments. By 1907, Watson was receiving bimonthly reports about Breeding Barn activities from Gebhardt: "I want such news as what was sold, foaled, or anything going on with the hounds, farmers, etc. Of course you know that I like to hear about the rest of the farm as well."[33] In 1911, Seward and Lila gave their son title to almost all of the remaining horses in the Breeding Barn.[34]

Under Watson's direction, Hackneys were phased out of the Shelburne Farms Stud operation in favor of other breeds. As Watson wrote Gebhardt in 1908, "It seems to me Hackneys can never be a success in our country, for farmers will never take to them, and [trotting] bred carriage horses are better for our use & apt to bring more money."[35] However, Gebhardt cautioned Watson that trotters were still not a foolproof source of profit, and that the Stud was likely to remain a losing proposition:

There is no question but what a trotting bred stallion would appeal more readily to the local farmers. As for making any money on one though I think it is only a question as to which breed will bring you the smallest loss…If you go into trotters try and get a stallion with a reputation, or one you can get a reputation for. You might possibly turn a dollar, but the probabilities are that you will have to be content with the sport you get out of it.[36]

By 1911, Watson had decided against trotters in favor of polo ponies and hunters for foxhunting, a determination that would shape his horse operation for the next fifty years. He marketed the new horse business in part by appealing to his father's peers. As he wrote James Appleton,

You would be doing me a great favor if you would mention to some of your friends— men or women—looking for horses that we have others at Shelburne and while our horses may not be as good types as Colt's any I sell as hunters I will guarantee can jump (they are started as yearlings) and gallop fast enough to go with any drag hounds, and also will be well worth their price…[A]s it is necessary for manure for the place etc. to keep a good many horses at Shelburne, I started to try & breed hunters. Now we have Alan-a-Dale acknowledged about the best hunter stallion in this country and some good hunter & clean brood mares and we raise about 8 or 10 colts each year, which gives us a lot of fun schooling.[37]

In addition to managing the Shelburne Farms Stud, Watson showed interest in almost every aspect of the estate's operations. He researched agricultural techniques and equipment, corresponded with other gentleman farmers, and peppered Gebhardt with questions. In addition, he took it upon himself to review departmental accounts and look for additional ways to help his parents economize in the face of mounting financial pressures. "On looking again today over the question of waste of hay in the stacks in BB [Breeding Barn] yards I find as before that there *is* considerable waste on all stacks in the west yard."[38] And later, "Can you give me some idea as to the amount of coal burned per month at the Big House [Shelburne House] in October–December and February. I find we are burning a terrific amount."[39]

Property Divisions

By 1909, Seward and Lila had begun to think about the future of Shelburne Farms and assess their own ability to continue to oversee and support the estate. Seward's health had declined considerably; by the early 1910s, he possessed at best only brief periods of physical and mental vigor. The Shelburne Farms estate was thirty years old, and its aging buildings and infrastructure were becoming more and more of a financial and managerial burden.

In addition, there were no signs that the Webbs' annual income would ever rebound. By 1912, it was apparent that the Sixteenth Amendment to the United States Constitution would soon be ratified, clearing the way for Congress to enact a permanent income tax. A tax bill signed into law in October 1913 took effect in 1914. In 1916, the income tax was followed by a permanent estate tax.[40]

During this period, the Webbs completed two major property transactions involving Shelburne Farms, and they contemplated further measures. In 1909, Seward officially deeded the whole of the estate to Lila, a transfer that was probably due to his failing health and her increasing management role. In addition, by the early 1910s, the Webbs conceived the idea to give each of their three sons a section of outlying estate property, reserving the core land and buildings for themselves for the rest of their lives. Their sons, in their early to late twenties, were all in the process of launching their professional careers and starting their own families.[41]

The couple had three main objectives in deeding the outlying areas of the estate to their sons. Seward and Lila wanted to make room for them to develop their own country residences in the hopes that they would choose to spend more time close to their parents at Shelburne Farms. Additionally, by making these decisions while they were still living, the elder Webbs would gain the peace of mind that the transactions were settled as they wished them to be and that their children would avoid substantial estate taxes.[42]

Each parcel considered for subdivision encompassed approximately 700 acres containing a house that could be converted into a suitable country residence. The first consisted of the property to the south of the Farm Barn, in-

Right: The Webb family on the North Porch at Shelburne House, c. 1917. From left: Vanderbilt, Frederica, Lila, Aileen (Osborn), Ralph Pulitzer, Electra (Havemeyer), Gertrude (Gaynor), J. Watson, W. Seward Jr., and W. Seward. Shelburne Farms Collections.

cluding the Breeding Barn, Quaker Smith Point, and the Comstock family's nineteenth-century brick farmhouse. The second consisted of the estate lands to the north of Shelburne House along Orchard Point, including Orchard House, the Nash family's nineteenth-century farmhouse, which had previously been used by the Webbs as a guesthouse. The third consisted of the property to the east of the estate's main gates, including Bay View, a nineteenth-century farmhouse overlooking Shelburne Bay, previously owned by the Rogers family.

Seward and Lila apparently gave Watson, as their eldest son, his choice of the three parcels. Discussions with Watson were underway by January 1910, shortly before he established a lifelong career in the insurance business and one month before he married Electra Havemeyer.

The youngest daughter of Louisine and Henry Osborne Havemeyer, the president of the American Sugar Refining Company, Electra (1888–1960) belonged to the same social circles as the Webbs. She had in fact visited Shelburne Farms several times before she married Watson. A superb equestrienne, Electra shared her husband's passion for foxhunting. Several months after their marriage in February 1910, the couple settled in Chicago. They moved to New York City in 1912, when Watson began work at the Manhattan insurance firm Marsh & McLennan. Watson and Electra occupied a series of country residences on Long Island starting in 1911. In 1921, they established the estate that they would own into the 1950s in the town of Westbury, New York, enlarging an existing farmhouse to create a country residence. The Westbury property included a stable for Watson's polo ponies, and a small farm containing cattle, sheep, and chickens that supplied the family with fresh agricultural products. After 1914, the year that Electra received a family inheritance of $4 million, the couple also maintained a townhouse in Manhattan. Watson went on to join Vander Poel, Pausner & Webb as a partner in 1929, and he subsequently established his own insurance firm, Webb & Lynch, in 1933. By 1922, Watson and Electra had five children: Electra, Samuel Blachley (named in honor of Watson's great-grandfather), Lila Vanderbilt, James Watson Jr., and Harry Havemeyer.[43]

At Shelburne Farms in January 1910, Watson and Electra "looked over The Orchards and the Little Red Brick House [the Comstock house]. She preferred the latter and so do I."[44] He was also charmed by Bay View ("Went through Bay View… Wonder if it could be moved. It's a bully house"), but he and his wife eventually settled upon the portion of the property containing the Comstock house and Breeding Barn complex as their inheritance.[45] Watson's selection of this section was an appropriate one considering his passion for horses and ongoing role as manager of the Shelburne Farms Stud. He began to make plans for developing his own country estate and farm on the parcel in mid-1912, and the official deed of gift transferring ownership from parents to son was signed in April 1913. Although Watson and Electra would make New York their primary residence for most of their lives, Southern Acres Farm, as it would be called, remained the center of Watson's life until his death in 1960.[46]

Property transfer discussions between the elder Webbs and their two younger sons, Seward Jr. and Vanderbilt, continued through the late 1910s as the two brothers established their own families and careers. After graduating from Yale in 1909, Seward Jr. worked for J. P. Morgan Company for two years, served as a partner in the Wall Street firm Grier, Crane and Webb from 1912 to 1917, and then entered the real estate development business as a partner in the New York–based company Webb and Knapp in 1919. He married Gertrude Gaynor (1888–1972), daughter of New York City Mayor William Gaynor, in 1911. By 1930, Seward and Gertrude had five children: William Seward III, Frederica, Jacob Louis, Gertrude, and William J. Gaynor Webb.[47]

Vanderbilt married Aileen Osborn (1892–1979), the daughter of New York lawyer and philanthropist William Church Osborn, in 1912. Vanderbilt completed his studies at Yale in the spring of 1912, and the young couple lived in Oxford, England, during the 1912–13 school year, while he studied law at Balliol College as a Rhodes Scholar. They returned to the United States in 1914, where Vanderbilt attended Harvard Law School, edited the *Harvard Law Review*, and sat for the New York State Bar. He started his career as a clerk at a New York City law firm and later served as a partner in several succeeding practices. By 1915, Vanderbilt and Aileen were settled in a brownstone at 66 East 79th Street. Aileen's parents gave the couple more than 500 acres in her hometown of Garrison-on-Hudson, New York, as a wedding present, and there they developed a country estate called Whippoorwill Farm, at which they spent weekends and holidays. Whippoorwill Farm contained a large residence, extensive formal gardens, and a small farm with several dairy cattle. The Vanderbilt Webbs had four children: Derick (named in honor of his grandmother's brother Frederick Vanderbilt), William Osborn (named in honor of Aileen's father), Barbara, and Richard Humphrey. A fifth child, Alexander Stewart (named in honor of his grandfather's brother Alexander Stewart Webb), died in infancy.[48]

Between about 1914 and 1917, Seward Sr. and Lila decided to give Vanderbilt the Orchard House property and Seward Jr. the Bay View property. During the early 1910s, Vanderbilt and Aileen occupied Orchard House during several extended visits to Shelburne, made some renovations to the dwelling, planted a large kitchen garden, and kept chickens. Aileen later remembered, "Our real life during [Vanderbilt's] law school years was spent in The Orchards in Shelburne during the summers."[49] From these experiences at Shelburne, Aileen stated, "Van got bitten by a farming bug."[50] However,

The Comstock/McNeil family house, which later became the Brick House, c. 1910. Shelburne Museum.

The Nash family house, known as Orchard House or The Orchards, c. 1900. Shelburne Farms Collections.

his budding passion for agriculture would not result in direct and lasting ties to the farming operation at Shelburne Farms for some years to come.[51]

Both Vanderbilt and Seward Jr. left to fight in World War I in about 1918, and while away they reconsidered their parents' arrangements to give them sections of the Shelburne Farms estate. Seward and Gertrude began to think seriously of living in Shelburne year-round after he returned to civilian life, and in 1919 he wrote Vanderbilt to request a swap of their intended properties:

Dear Van, I am writing to ask if you would consider trading places at Shelburne, and please be perfectly frank in giving me your answer. Would you be willing to take the North End & Bay View House in place

Bay View, c. 1910. Shelburne Farms Collections.

of the Orchards, my paying say $3,000 or a sum that would cover the money you have put in the Orchard place. As we intend to live here permanently from now on I would like to be nearer the big house [Shelburne House] than Bay View is. Please let me know as soon as you have come to a decision, as if you are agreeable I would start improvements this Autumn.[52]

This plan suited Vanderbilt, who, though passionate about Shelburne Farms, felt that he could not devote enough time and attention to either parcel for at least ten years because of their distance from his growing professional concerns in New York. He accepted Seward's offer, and Seward soon began to make plans to redecorate Orchard House in anticipation of making it a permanent residence for himself and his family.[53]

However, the brothers' plans for the two properties remained unresolved. Neither Seward nor Vanderbilt ended up making Shelburne a permanent country residence after World War I ended, due at least in part to the demands of their careers, which kept them tied closely to New York. Vanderbilt and Aileen's decision may also have been partly a result of their fondness for Whippoorwill Farm.[54]

As a result, throughout the next twenty years, Orchard House and Bay View remained mostly uninhabited, used only occasionally as guesthouses before deferred maintenance made them unfit for occupancy. The fields surrounding Bay View were often rented to local farmers to grow hay and pasture cattle. In the early 1920s, Seward Sr. converted the outbuildings at Orchard House into henhouses for a small poultry farm containing chickens, geese, and ducks.[55]

Seward and Lila's daughter Frederica was apparently not included in the plans to divide up the outlying acreage at Shelburne Farms, possibly because of traditional assumptions regarding the inheritance of property by male heirs only. In addition, by the 1920s, Frederica was rooted elsewhere. She had married Ralph Pulitzer (1879–1939) in 1905, and they had two sons by 1911: Ralph Jr. and Seward. Ralph Sr. worked as publisher of his father Joseph Pulitzer's newspaper the *New York World* and as vice president of the family's Press Publishing Company. The young couple established a country estate named Kiluna Farm in Manhassett, Long Island, overlooking Manhassett Bay and Long Island Sound.[56]

Frederica did not obtain a share in the family's property until 1921, when she received Oakledge Farm, which had remained underutilized and unoccupied since her parents had attempted to sell it in the mid-1910s. Even then, the transaction was a purchase rather than a gift and was probably related to the unsettled state of her personal affairs. Frederica had recently separated from her husband, and the purchase would have provided her with a residence of her own should she have required one. However, it does not appear that she ever made Oakledge a seasonal or main residence, and her ownership of the property was very short-lived, lasting until just after her divorce and remarriage to Cyril Hamlen Jones (1893–1972) in 1924.[57]

A native of England, Cyril received undergraduate and law degrees from Harvard University. After serving in the United States Navy during the First World War, he was hired by the Pulitzers to be a tutor for their sons. After their marriage, Frederica and Cyril settled in Hyde Park, Massachusetts, where Cyril taught mathematics and Latin at the nearby Milton Academy, a private boys' school.

He later became director of admissions and then headmaster of the academy, retiring in 1947.[58]

Southern Acres

Of the four Webb children, only Watson would settle in Shelburne during Seward and Lila's lifetime. Watson and Electra began planning their new country estate in earnest as early as July 1912, almost a year before his parents legally transferred the property to them. On July 6, 1912, Watson noted in his diary, "Rode with E[lectra] & planned out all about our new place. The idea is fine & I do hope it goes through. We'll fix over the little brick house at once."[59] Throughout the summer of 1912, the couple developed their initial plans for Southern Acres Farm, riding and driving over the property, reviewing boundary and fence lines, counting the apple trees, thinking about the staff they would hire, making arrangements to repair the existing estate structures, and discussing the modifications they would make to the "little brick house" that would become their country residence in Shelburne.[60]

The Brick House

One of Watson and Electra's first priorities was renovating and expanding the Comstock family farmhouse into a new country home that they would name the "Brick House." Constructed between 1844 and 1845, the house and surrounding 140 acres had been acquired by Seward and Lila Webb from William and Lucia (Comstock) McNeil in 1889. Although most of the accompanying farm buildings purchased for Shelburne Farms had been reused or demolished during the development of the estate, the Comstock house, once a comfortable dwelling, had been left empty and neglected. Watson had expressed interest in the deteriorating house as early as 1908, when he was twenty-four years old: "Went over brick house with Mr. G.[ebhardt]. Amazing fireplaces etc."[61] He subsequently volunteered $500 of his own funds to stabilize the structure, which included foundation and grading work and the construction of shutters to protect the windows and interiors. Years later, Electra recalled visiting the derelict house with her new husband:

> *He took me up to a little pink brick farmhouse. He said, 'Don't you think this is a lovely old house?' I must say I did not know what to answer. It looked in poor repair; the windows were boarded up and I don't believe until that minute I had ever thought of a house as anything but a place to live in. Then he went on to tell me to look at the lovely proportions, told me of the history attached to it and then lastly said, 'I used my allowance to board up the windows so it would not go to pieces.'*[62]

In July 1912, the Watson Webbs engaged young New York architect Eliot B. Cross (1884–1949) of Cross & Cross to renovate the Brick House. A Groton School classmate and close friend of Watson's, Cross had been a guest of Watson's parents at Shelburne House numerous times. The architect would go on to design a number of Colonial Revival and Tudor Revival country houses for the new generation of New York's elite, mostly on Long Island, and would later work with Watson's brother Seward on real estate ventures in the New York area. At Southern Acres, Cross worked with the Burlington-based contractors Kieslich and Company and A. I. Lawrence to renovate the existing structure and construct a large addition. As Shelburne Farms Curator Julie Eldridge Edwards has noted, "The new floor plan for The Brick House included a large living room, dining room, kitchen, pantry, a small den, eight bedrooms, a dressing room, and a servants' quarters on two levels. Porches were added to the southern and eastern sides of the house."[63] Seward and Lila gave Watson and Electra a number of items removed from 680 Fifth Avenue just before its sale in 1913, including woodwork and service equipment, for the Brick House. Construction began on April 15, 1913, and when the family moved into the dwelling on October 5 of that year, Watson proudly noted in his diary, "Our first day in a house of our own."[64]

In 1919, Watson and Electra employed Cross & Cross to modify and enlarge the Brick House again, constructing a large addition to the north end of the dwelling. The new wing contained a new entrance hall and front door as well as additional formal and informal living spaces, guest bedrooms and bathrooms, and expanded service areas.[65]

Based primarily in New York City and Long Island from the 1910s through the 1940s, Watson and Electra followed a regular schedule each year that revolved around their preferred sporting activities: winter quail hunting in North and South Carolina, fishing at Nehasane in the spring, polo on Long Island during the summer, foxhunting at Shelburne in the autumn, and a return to Nehasane in the late fall for deer hunting. They resided at the Brick House for a month or two during the foxhunting season and often made additional visits for the Easter and Christmas holidays and other occasions. Watson returned regularly by himself throughout the year for brief stays in order to oversee the management of the Southern Acres estate.[66]

Electra decorated the Brick House in an eclectic and informal style befitting a residence used primarily as a hunting lodge in the country, although quite in contrast with her in-laws' late Victorian interiors at Shelburne House. A journalist described the Brick House in 1928:

> *Its brick walls with white wood trim lend it an air of comfortable stability to match that of the country of which it is a part. Its low, rambling design bespeaks the charm which its interior confirms, for there is none of the formal austerity which so often afflicts "manor houses." The rules of the American colonial period have dictated the furnishings throughout, and each appointment of utility*

or decoration bears the unmistakable stamp of its origin. As might be expected, there is a noticeable emphasis on sport in the details of decoration. Many hunting prints color the walls, and the trophies of the chase lend their interest to the living rooms.[67]

A collector of American decorative arts objects since her childhood, Electra filled the Brick House with prints, wallpapers, quilts, hooked rugs, ceramics, pewter, glass, furniture, architectural elements, dolls and dollhouses, and other items. For almost fifty years, the Brick House would prove to be an ideal showcase and testing ground for decorative ensembles of her collections.[68]

In fact, by the mid-1910s, Electra's passion and growing confidence in her collecting led her to consider establishing a museum in the Shelburne area. She later recounted speaking with Watson about renovating a farmhouse on an outlying area of the Shelburne Farms property, known as the Captain White house, to serve as a museum building:

One day while hunting on Shelburne Farms I asked my husband couldn't we ask Dr. and Mrs. Webb for an [another] old brick house, which had been deserted for many years. This house was on the road to the Harbor and I suggested it would be fun to make it into a museum. He thought it would not be practicable—too far out of the way. Nevertheless I thought of it more and more and went down through it several times and it was a lovely old place. I realized it was too far out of the way and time drifted on.[69]

Electra's interest in establishing a museum would come to fruition in the 1940s, when she founded the Shelburne Museum on a separate piece of property in the center of Shelburne. Here she would use many of the display and design concepts she had developed at the Brick House.

Southern Acres Farm

Watson threw himself enthusiastically into developing Southern Acres Farm, establishing a smaller version of his parents' model farm. He focused on beef cattle, sheep, pigs, chickens, horses, and foxhounds, and he raised oats and alfalfa to feed his livestock.[70]

One of Watson's first priorities was to establish a herd of Hereford beef and Jersey dairy cattle. Originally from Herefordshire, England, Herefords had proven themselves to be well suited to New England by the mid-1910s. They were known to be hardy enough to survive Vermont's long winters without much stress and to produce high-quality, marbled beef.[71]

Watson began to assemble his dairy stock by the spring of 1914, when he purchased a number of Jersey heifers in Shelbyville, Kentucky. He hired

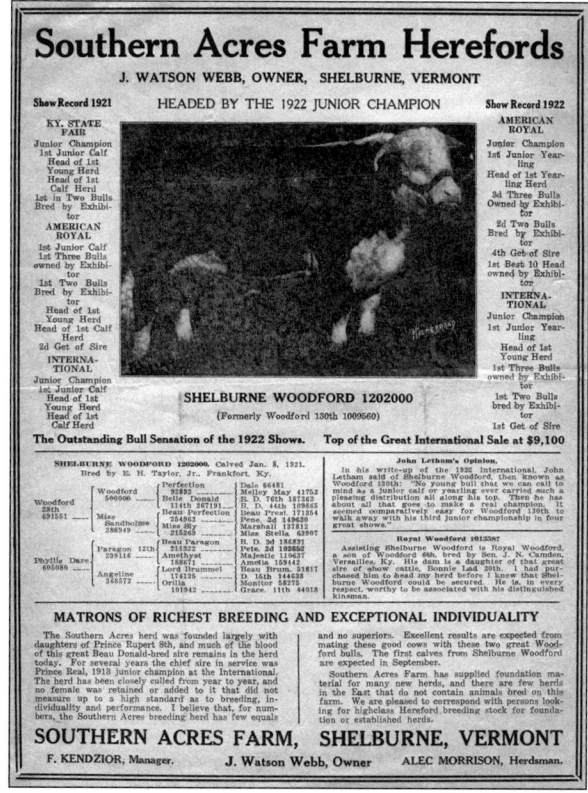

An advertisement for Southern Acres Farm, published in the *Hereford Journal*, 1923. Shelburne Farms Collections.

Alexander "Alec" Morrison (1883–1965) to oversee the operation, sending him as far as Syracuse, New York, and Pittsburgh, Pennsylvania, to examine and purchase cattle.[72]

Watson's beef and dairy herds began to garner prizes in agricultural fairs within a year after their establishment. In 1916, photographs of Watson's Herefords appeared in the *Hereford Journal*. However, Watson eventually ceased his dairy operation to concentrate on beef cattle. By 1928, the Southern Acres Farm beef herd numbered approximately eighty.[73]

Watson focused most of his energies on raising polo ponies, horses for hunting, and hounds for foxhunting. By 1916, he had amassed almost fifty horses and won several prizes in competitions. The previous year, Watson sold eight horses for a total of $8,300. It is unlikely, however, that his horse breeding activities generated an overall profit.[74]

Watson was most passionate about his hounds. As he wrote in 1933, "Guess I am nuts on fox hunting & always will be."[75] After acquiring Southern Acres, Watson expanded his foxhunting activities, working with his head groom William Hopkins and huntsman Fred Ingleson to develop the kennels and stage the Shelburne Hunt each autumn. He developed a champion pack of foxhounds, bred to scent and chase foxes, and terriers, bred to dig out the animals, importing prized hounds from England and Pennsylvania in 1910, 1914, and 1915 to introduce new bloodlines and strengthen the pack.[76]

In the 1910s and 1920s, the "Shelburne Foxhounds" averaged between twenty and thirty pairs, enough for Watson to sell off extra hounds to his peers. In a 1927 article in *The Sportsman*, Watson informed readers (potential clients all) that the dogs were skilled hunters and good domestic pets as well: "I find in these dogs as much individuality and personality as in any breed I have ever seen… They are primarily one-person dogs, intelligent, faithful, game, hardy, and—above all—wonderfully kind to children."[77]

Watson and his staff took the hounds out regularly each year during the August to November hunting season, starting at two or three days a week and then increasing to up to seven days a week after the First World War. During the early years, the hunt schedule was limited by Watson's school and work responsibilities, his leave of absence while abroad fighting in World War I, and the decline of wild foxes in the area.[78]

During the early 1910s, the lack of foxes caused Watson to seriously consider disbanding the Shelburne Hunt and cease breeding hounds. He decided to solve the problem by raising his own foxes and setting them out each autumn in anticipation of the hunt. He built fox pens in the Breeding Barn and hired a local man to care for them.[79]

Watson recorded the results of the day's hunt in great detail in his diaries, noting the ground covered and the performance of his hounds as well as the foxes cornered and bagged. October 27, 1928, was,

A red letter day found Rocky cove south to Bymton's swamp but not straight then East to nearly Blue woods, right & south to E. Charlotte road, back N & East to 42 mile at Cleast beyond Hinesburg-Bur[lington] Road in the foothills where we got hounds. With them most of the way…All but 3 couples up. 12½ out—10½ miles at least a good hour hardly any checks. A grand hunt.[80]

The Shelburne Hunt ranged over miles of farmland and forest on Southern Acres, Shelburne Farms, and adjoining properties as far afield as the neighboring towns of South Burlington, Williston, St. George, Charlotte, Hinesburg, Starksboro, and Ferrisburg. Watson requested permission from his neighbors to hunt over their property, hosting an annual luncheon or dinner in their honor and offering the services of a draft horse on occasion as a gesture of thanks.[81]

However, many of his neighbors did not look

favorably upon the Shelburne Hunt, which had a reputation for trampling crops and leaving pasture gates open as it passed through. The Shelburne Farms main estate was no exception. In September 1928, then farm manager Frank Kendzior wrote Watson to complain:

> *I beg to report that when hounds were out hunting yesterday morning (11th) considerable damage was done. On Lone Tree the post and rails fence was broken in three places and a cow, close to calving, made her way out and I could not find her until this morning. She had calved and has not cleaned. Between the Pheasantry and North Pastures three gates were left open and the cattle all mixed up. One gate was lifted from its hinges and thrown on the ground. The standing corn in the north and in front of the Farm Barn has been ridden through and hounds have knocked a considerable quantity of it down. I know it is not your wish that this should occur and you will I am sure agree that it is most disheartening for me. Is it possible to delay hunting a little longer so as to avoid knocking down the standing corn and in order to leave the cattle in the North quiet.*[82]

Watson responded with an apology, noting that he had reprimanded his hunt employees. He offered to reimburse Kendzior for the costs of chasing down the loose cattle and to have the fences repaired. By the 1930s, Watson and his employees rode the course after each hunt to review for possible damage.[83]

Although many of his neighbors were not especially fond of the Shelburne Hunt, Watson earned respect among his peers. The Shelburne Foxhounds swept prizes at prominent hound shows in the eastern United States and England by 1914. That year, Watson noted that his hounds had won "2-1st, 2-2nds, & 4 3rd at the Boston Dog Show which was pretty good."[84] They also consistently placed well at the annual Riding Club Hound Show in New York. The year 1935 was an especially good one at the latter event: "Hound Show…We did wonderfully well all day…Out of 15 classes we won 12 firsts, which included the two championships, 4 2nds (met'g one Reserve Champ) & 4 3rds."[85] Watson himself became one of the longest-serving Masters of Foxhounds in the United States and was president of the Masters of Foxhounds Association from 1948 to 1954.[86]

With the acquisition of Southern Acres Farm, Watson acquired a large stock of buildings that remained well suited for his purposes. He reused the existing barns and employee houses on the property, making a few renovations and additions where necessary. Watson modified and expanded the nineteenth-century farm complex at Quaker Smith Point, which consisted primarily of structures built for the Smith family farm, to house his cattle, sheep, pigs, and at least some of the employees who tended them. He constructed at least one new silo and a new sheep fold on the Point as well.[87]

The Breeding Barn became the headquarters of the Southern Acres Farm operations, housing Watson's horses, fox pens, and, later, beef cattle. Watson updated the structure for his needs, adding a training corral in the barn's open interior, cutting new exterior doors leading from individual stalls to outdoor paddocks, installing electricity, and creating a garage area inside the barn for his own automobile. He installed a conveyor belt system to efficiently remove manure from the horse stalls, and a grain crusher to prepare oats grown on Southern Acres for feed. On the exterior, Watson planted jumping hedges to train his hunters and straightened the entrance drive to the building, planting elms to create a formal allée. He also renovated a section of the barn to house his beef cattle, which he moved from Quaker Smith Point by 1928. That same year, thirty-seven years after its construction, the Breeding Barn was still reputed

to possess "the largest privately owned indoor ring in America."[88]

It is unclear exactly where the kennels were located before Southern Acres Farm was established. In 1912, Watson moved an existing kennels building to a site near the Breeding Barn, and in 1928, he constructed a new structure behind the Breeding Barn. The new kennels, and the series of outdoor pens that adjoined the building, provided state-of-the-art accommodations for the Shelburne hounds and the employee who cared for them.[89]

Although Southern Acres Farm was considered a separate entity from Shelburne Farms from the time of its official establishment in 1913, the two estates and their managers maintained a very close relationship throughout the 1910s and 1920s. Watson relied heavily upon Gebhardt's experience and consulted him frequently about many aspects of estate management. The latter was indispensable in the remodeling of the Brick House and the construction of the new kennels, serving as Watson's local contact while he was in New York, meeting with potential contractors, and ensuring that the work was proceeding smoothly. Gebhardt was also consulted about such issues as the hiring of a farm manager and other new employees, the purchase of new livestock, the expansion of the Shelburne

The kennels at Southern Acres Farm, by J. Watson Webb Jr., July 1934. Shelburne Farms Collections.

Farms water and telephone infrastructure to the Brick House, and accounting paperwork. Watson met frequently with Gebhardt, including "a long talk with EFG about everything" in September 1912.[90]

Throughout the 1910s and 1920s, Shelburne Farms served as a kind of parent organization for Southern Acres. The younger estate purchased multiple items from Shelburne Farms, such as electricity, water, and telephone service; stores of ice and coal; and quantities of milk. Shelburne Farms conducted all of Southern Acres' accounting and billing. Watson often borrowed resources from Shelburne Farms, including employees, tools, equipment, and work horses. A January 1926 letter from Shelburne Farms' farm manager Frank Kendzior to John Earley, a Southern Acres employee, provides an example of the range of items that Southern Acres received from Shelburne Farms:

For the purpose of account please to let me know;

(1) How many tons of hay you baled recently with our baler
(2) How much ice was fetched from the Dairy to the Brick House last fall
(3) How many days you used the corn husker.

…If Mr. [Watson] Webb wants any coke or soft coal, please to let me know at once as we expect a car [load] of each this week…We will cut ice for Southern Acres, weather permitting, commencing Monday.[91]

Left: The Breeding Barn, by J. Watson Webb Jr., July 1934. Shelburne Farms Collections.

When he founded Southern Acres Farm, Watson modeled its organizational structure upon the system that his father developed at Shelburne Farms in the 1880s. He established separate departments for the farm, horse breeding, kennels, and Brick House operations, and he hired R. S. Towers to serve as his first farm manager.[92]

Stud groom W. H. Hopkins (1867–1930) proved to be the heart of the Southern Acres Farm operations. An Englishman, Hopkins had served as "whipper-in" at the North Cotswald Hunt, in charge of controlling the hounds during the hunt, and foreman of the W. J. Smith Cadogan Riding School before immigrating to the United States. He was one of the Webb family's most loyal employees and valued friends, starting as a groom in the Breeding Barn in about 1902, when Watson was eighteen years old, and working as head stud groom from 1906 until 1930. Hopkins oversaw the transition from Hackneys to polo ponies and hunters and established the Shelburne Foxhounds and Shelburne Hunt. In a 1955 letter, Watson described the significant influence that Hopkins had made on his life:

Hopkins really taught me to ride and we rode and schooled miles together. He schooled many home-bred hunters and later polo ponies which I bred too. He was schooling a four year old pony when he dropped dead and we found him. I should never have been a top polo player without his guidance…[H]e was really a remarkable horseman and there never will be another like him. We were very close and I was sole executor of his Estate. It was like losing a valued friend when he died, and I have never had a really good stud groom since.[93]

Watson himself thrived on his work at Southern Acres Farm and was involved with every detail of the operations. In addition to directing the management of the estate, he enjoyed actively working alongside his employees when he could spare the time from his insurance work and busy competitive polo schedule. Over the years, he built and repaired fences, sheep folds, and fox pens; cleared brush, chopped wood, and cut lawns; removed stones from fields; and watered trees, harvested hay, and exercised horses. On July 17, 1916, for example, he recorded his activities as follows:

Up at 6 & bk [breakfast] 6.30. To Bb [Breeding Barn] with E.[Electra] & she rode. I went around with RST [Farm Manager Towers] over east fields. Too wet yet to work so will lie idle this year. Worked on road… to BB to see Hopkins, cut burdock with RST & loaded stone from field. P.M. Fishing with kids till 4 drove to BB. Saw Horsford again to talk over putting out foxes & then picked up more stone.[94]

Stud groom William H. Hopkins with Shelburne foxhounds, by L. Stanger, New York, 1919. Shelburne Farms Collections, Gift of Kitty Webb Harris.

J. Watson Webb and W.H. Hopkins during a fox hunt, c. 1920. Shelburne Farms Collections.

Watson very clearly preferred Southern Acres to his residences elsewhere. As he wrote in 1913, "I certainly love this place, & would give a lot to live here most of the year."[95] However, Southern Acres was not profitable, and Watson felt obligated to continue his insurance work to maintain it. According to his grandson, Samuel B. Webb Jr., Watson's wife Electra paid for the expenses related to the couple's Manhattan townhouse and successive Long Island estates from the income she received from her invested inheritance, and Watson devoted his own investments and insurance profits to Southern Acres. In 1916, he noted, "Wish I could find some way to make money out of farming. It would then be considered 'worthy' I suppose. Do not like office work."[96] As time went on, he grew less and less happy with his life and work in New York. In 1933, just after returning from the fall foxhunting season at Southern Acres, he wrote,

> *New York & God how I hate it & always will. How much I have missed by not trying to work somewhere that will take me to the country often. What a contrast to the delight of yesterday [at Shelburne]. The pleasure of it all. Perhaps the contrast makes it all the more worth while. I was never born to be a city guy or a business man.*[97]

Watson and Electra would not move permanently to Southern Acres until the early 1950s, when he ceased full-time work in the insurance business.[98]

World War I

The war that erupted in August 1914 had a significant impact upon the Webb family, Shelburne Farms, and Southern Acres. Frederica, her first husband Ralph, and their son Ralph Jr. were trapped in Germany for two weeks when the war began, and they experienced a harrowing journey out of Europe and back to the United States. After the United States entered the war in 1917, all three of Seward and Lila's sons enlisted and were posted overseas. Watson was a captain in the 351st Field Artillery division of the army and saw action in France in 1918. Seward Jr. became a naval lieutenant, serving on the mine-laying ship *Roanoke* in the North Sea in 1918 and early 1919. Vanderbilt was an army captain and judge advocate, fought on the front lines in France in late 1917 and 1918, and attended the Paris Peace Conference in December 1918.[99]

On the home front, Lila Webb became a member of the Vermont contingent of the Committee on Convalescent Hospitals, a part of the Women's Section of the Navy League that sought to locate buildings suitable for use as hospitals for wounded servicemen should they become necessary. In 1916, she offered Shelburne House as a possible convalescent hospital, but nothing came of her proposal. A year later, Lila created a "Red Cross Workroom" stocked with sewing and knitting machines at Shelburne House and invited female family members, guests, estate employees, and their families to help her to prepare clothing and bandages for American soldiers serving in the war. An unidentified writer captured the scene:

> *Here were the bandages being rolled by mechanical means and dressings by hand, an operator at a hand knitting machine turning out socks at the rate of a pair every hour and in other parts of the room sweaters, helmets, scarves and wristlets were rapidly taking form...Three afternoons a week are given over to this work for which the materials are supplied, and prepared in advance by Mrs. Webb, who in order to qualify herself properly for this undertaking has taken a special course of training.*[100]

The war and its attendant increases in personal income taxes and inflation had an impact on Seward and Lila's finances. Moreover, it seemed extravagant to maintain their personal standard of living at prewar levels in light of the hardship the country was facing. To economize, the couple changed the living patterns they had adhered to since their marriage in 1882, closing Shelburne House earlier than usual in the 1917 and 1918 seasons. On December 25, 1917, Lila noted: "First Christmas in N.Y. in 21 years. On account of the war, had to leave Shelburne."[101]

Lila also altered the family menus to conform with ongoing food rations. She researched freeze-dried products and proudly reported to Gebhardt in 1918 that "We are keeping *well* within our allowance of half a pound of sugar a week, per capita, & 3 lbs. flour."[102]

Many of Shelburne Farms' and Southern Acres' employees left to fight overseas, and it became increasingly difficult to find and keep workers. As Gebhardt wrote to Seward Jr. in February 1918, "We expect pretty hard picking for help this coming season but we are all agreeing to do our best to back up the army. I thought two years ago I was getting too old to work but I am working as hard to-day as I ever did and really seem to be coming back."[103] Indeed, Gebhardt's work as the local county food administrator and district chairman for the National Council of Defense gave him "but a short time each day to spend at the farm office."[104]

On the main Shelburne Farms estate, Gebhardt

Red Cross volunteers on the dining room terrace at Shelburne House, 1918. Shelburne Farms Collections.

altered the production and sale of agricultural products to meet the country's wartime demands. In April 1918, Gebhardt informed Lila that he had responded to a call for wheat by selling the estate's stores, writing, "Owing to the great need of our allies for wheat, we feel obligated to dispose of the wheat we have from last year's harvest at once. Our quantity is not a large one—about 200 bushels but this in the local market will release that quantity for shipment abroad."[105]

In January 1918, growing inflation and fuel shortages caused Lila to decide to reduce the staff levels and budgets of the Shelburne Farms greenhouses and gardens. She announced the news in a letter to Gebhardt:

My dear Mr. Gebhardt, With conditions as they are, and even should peace come during the present year, it will take us so many years to readjust ourselves, I feel that I must do something more in reference to our garden and greenhouse conditions. I do not think that we should any longer retain two heads in this department, at the prices we are paying. There should be one head, well paid, in charge of greenhouses, house garden, & golf links, & general care of house grounds. If the war continues through another winter, more glass will have to be given up, even if this means confining ourselves entirely to what can be grown in summer…No flowers are used here any longer on dinner tables, excepting in cases where people have glass houses near New York.[106]

Accordingly, Gebhardt oversaw the renovation of the heating system at the greenhouses. He reported, "We have just spent a hundred dollars arranging our heat at the Greenhouse so that certain ranges could be cut off for the conservation of coal, and coal may be difficult to get before the winter is over."[107]

The First World War also brought illness to the Webbs and Shelburne Farms, specifically the influenza epidemic that erupted worldwide in 1918 and 1919. The 1918–19 strain of the flu was particularly contagious, fast-acting, and deadly. In addition to infecting many infants and elderly people, the strain targeted healthy young adults. By the end of the epidemic, influenza had killed an estimated 675,000 Americans out of a total population of 105 to 110 million people.[108]

The Webb family experienced tragedy firsthand in early January 1919, when Vanderbilt's two-year-old daughter, Barbara, fell ill and his newborn son, Alexander, died of influenza. Away attending the peace talks in Paris, Vanderbilt never saw his young son. While Barbara did recover, the Shelburne Farms estate was also hit with influenza in early 1919, affecting at least some of its remaining staff members as well as several family members of employees. Gebhardt wrote Lila, "We had seven new cases in Shelburne last week. It is too early to say how serious they may become. The condition of the little boy at the dairy still continues to fluctuate from day to day."[109] The "little boy at the dairy" was the son of dairy herdsman Howard Vosburgh, who had died of influenza less than a month previously at the age of thirty-seven. His wife predeceased him by a week, succumbing to the virus shortly after giving birth to their sixth child. The orphaned Vosburgh boy about whom Lila and Gebhardt had corresponded survived, along with all of his siblings, ages nine years to newborn. The children were all transferred to the care of their grandmother. The Webbs paid for the Vosburgh family's medical care throughout their illness, including doctor's bills, prescriptions, and the twenty-four-hour attendance of a professional nurse.[110]

CHAPTER 11

INCORPORATION

Then cheer the corporation,
With one hundred hearty cheers,
That the coming generation,
May carry on for years!

— LILA OSGOOD WEBB, "CHRISTMAS GREETING 1922"[1]

SHELBURNE FARMS CORPORATION

After the First World War, the Webb family revisited the question of the future of Shelburne Farms. While the disposition of a large portion of the property had been settled with the establishment of Watson's Southern Acres Farm, the prospects for the rest of the estate remained undetermined. Despite the budgetary reductions imposed in the previous fifteen years, Shelburne Farms' financial needs remained a concern. Seward and Lila were aging, and Gebhardt was contemplating retirement. Rather than sell their beloved property, the Webbs developed a plan for the farm operations to become more financially self-sufficient and for the second generation of the family to assume more responsibility for the estate.

Between early 1921 and mid-1922, the major stakeholders in the estate—parents, children, and Gebhardt—discussed a plan to transfer ownership and management of the farm and forest areas of the estate to a new corporation owned jointly by the senior Webbs and their three sons. A January 1921 letter Lila wrote to Watson introduced the idea:

> *Why could a much larger thing, (a company) not be made of it [the property] now. The company to include Seward & Van & Mr. Gebhardt with you…To take over all our cows, bulls, dairy, sheep & chickens, & make a co-operative farm. Our share in this (Papa's and mine) would be the gift of all the stock, with certain reserved privileges, to you, Seward & Van, & the gift to Seward & Van of the rest of our property…To these acres, you could add a share of your farm, already given to you by us…Our stock & land are valuable enough assets to make our share in this scheme worth consideration, altho' the plan has* just *come to me, my*

mind is very busy these days with pros & cons, I want you to consider it carefully, & to talk it over with Van to whom I think it would appeal strongly & should Seward not wish to go in with it it could be decided now, & he could receive in equivalent his share of stock, and land outside our fence, & would still have a piece of property inside [the] fence if he wants it. The Bay View house could work in this scheme also.[2]

The creation of a jointly owned company ensured that the three Webb sons could retain an interest in Shelburne Farms, part of their future inheritance, without the burden of full ownership and management at a time when they were busy with their own families, professional careers, and residences elsewhere.

Shelburne Farms Corporation was formally established in April 1922. Two months later, Seward and Lila transferred ownership of the main portion of their estate, comprised of 2,710 acres and all of the buildings, tools, equipment, and livestock contained within, to the new entity. They retained ownership of 300 acres of parkland, the so-called "Home Estate," along with a few additional acres in Shelburne Village proper. Four hundred shares in the new corporation were divided among Lila and her three sons. Lila's 200 shares ensured that she retained a large stake in the farm operations for the remainder of her life. Seward Jr. and Vanderbilt each received eighty shares, and Watson received a smaller allotment of forty shares, presumably because he had already been granted a considerable portion of the family property. Just as Frederica did not receive a substantial portion of the estate property for her own use during this period of time, she was not included in this initial allocation of shares in the corporation.[3]

While Lila was named president and all three sons were named directors of the corporation, Watson would in practice assume the lion's share of the responsibility for overseeing the company's activities and finances. By 1931, he would be elected vice president. With his passion for agricultural activities and his close proximity at Southern Acres, Watson was perhaps the best equipped and the most interested in active involvement in the operations of Shelburne Farms Corporation. Seward Jr. demonstrated little interest in the corporation and would eventually bow out of its management. Vanderbilt, on the other hand, kept himself abreast of and weighed in on the latest developments, mostly by frequent communication with Watson.[4]

Shelburne Farms Corporation was very much a family affair. According to an agreement completed in June 1922, shareholders were required to give notice of their intent to sell stock. If they intended to sell or bequeath stock to anyone outside of the family, they were obliged to offer immediate family members the right of first refusal.[5]

The establishment of Shelburne Farms Corporation marked the changing of the guard in more ways than one. In 1922, Gebhardt formally retired as farm manager, a position he had held officially since 1908 and in reality since several years earlier. He had contemplated retirement for some time, and the transition to the corporation likely proved a convenient and appropriate moment to step down. Lila found Gebhardt's retirement and her own decreasing role in Shelburne Farms to be bittersweet. As she wrote to Gebhardt,

We have worked together so long, & have given so many hours of thought to Shelburne Farms with its many problems, it seems hard to more or less turn over the greater part of it to a younger management, but I have felt for some time that if this were not brought about soon, interest would not be maintained there & from love of Shelburne Farms I wanted it to go on if possible, even though in a modified form. You have been so closely identified with all its interests, and have done so much to help work out problems & hold things together, I know you must feel the break as I do...I can never forget our years of work together, and hope that through the year of 1923 we may still have matters to discuss, and suggestions to offer, that may be of assistance to the Corporation.[6]

Gebhardt retired to Burlington, where he was occasionally called upon to consult on such matters as past real estate transactions and changes to the formal gardens. He died in 1942, at the age of eighty-three.[7]

Reorganization

The Webbs selected Englishman Frank F. Kendzior as the new manager of Shelburne Farms Corporation. He began work in January 1923.[8]

Kendzior assumed a tremendous challenge: to guide an unprofitable, forty-year-old operation based upon late-nineteenth-century ideals in transition to a modern, self-sufficient business. When Kendzior took stock of the property, he found a vast group of aging structures; inefficient activities and systems; and outdated tools and equipment. Despite Gebhardt's best efforts, the estate had suffered from years of reductions in staff and funding. In Kendzior's eyes, Shelburne Farms had stagnated. He diagnosed the situation as

a very wrong policy of management spread over many years back during which buildings, land, all equipment and live stock were allowed to reach the lowest possible condition of efficiency, instead of Maintaining them in working order at a reasonable annual expenditure. This [requires] today a heavy outlay in order to bring the Estate back into a proper working condition.[9]

In many ways, Seward and Lila's estate was no longer a model of modern agriculture, and it would take what Kendzior termed "a complete reorganization" to make it meet the Webbs' goals for modernization and financial self-sufficiency.[10] Over the next thirteen years, he labored to update farming equipment and structures, streamline systems, eliminate unprofitable areas of operation, and develop new, promising ventures.

One of Kendzior's first orders of business was to identify the estate activities that provided current or future sources of income for the property and phase out those that were unprofitable or peripheral to the operation. He started by reviewing employee positions for overlap, eliminating the estate's independent telegraph service and internal telegraph stations, and laying off the telegraph operator. The farm's remaining Southdown sheep were sold to a farmer in Lexington, Kentucky, in 1923. That same year, most of the approximately 230 birds left in the poultry department were also sold. The remaining birds were transferred from the corporation to the personal oversight of Seward Sr., who continued to pursue his interest in raising poultry despite his ongoing illnesses. Seward established a small poultry operation in one of the barns at the vacant Orchard House with the intent of supplying his family's personal needs for eggs and chickens during their residence and selling any surplus. Also, in 1922 and 1923, Kendzior auctioned off extra livestock and broken-down and outdated farm equipment. He continued to sell additional items from time to time throughout the remainder of the 1920s.[11]

Kendzior also tried to rent unused equipment to other companies, but he met with mixed results. The Vermont State Highway Board was less than pleased with the condition of the corporation's steam-driven road roller, which they rented for the spring and summer of 1924 for road work in Windsor and Danville. Kendzior fared slightly better with the estate's stone crusher, which he rented to local contractors Frissell & Snyder for road maintenance in the summer of 1926. But by 1930, the stone crusher was no longer profitable and was in a sad state of disrepair. One engineer who was asked to inspect the structure and its equipment found "that there is no possible salvage except what you may be able to realize on the metal for junk, as it is obsolete and the building itself is of little or no value when converted into salvage lumber."[12] Kendzior sold the crusher soon thereafter, and the building was dismantled for scrap lumber.[13]

The gradual elimination of unprofitable farm operations and outdated equipment was only the beginning for Kendzior. He also needed to slow the ongoing deterioration of the farm's buildings and infrastructure before they, too, became unusable. As Watson noted, "Everything had run down & there were lots of repairs to be made."[14] Soon after he was hired, Kendzior embarked on a program to "gradually put all buildings into good order and use."[15] It was a daunting undertaking. The vast majority of the estate's building stock and infrastructure was more than thirty years old, and their capital needs were extensive.

Throughout the 1920s and early 1930s, one of Kendzior's most pressing tasks was reroofing most of the structures on the property, including barns, outbuildings, hay barracks, and employee housing. In 1923, Kendzior contracted with the Anaconda Roofing Company to reroof the Farm Barn and dairy barn with zinc shingles. Unfortunately, the zinc material proved to be defective, and the farm manager spent much of the rest of the decade dealing with ongoing roof leaks and repairs. It would not be until 1932, nine years after the defective shingles had been installed, that the shingle manufacturer agreed to pay for the complete re-roofing of the buildings in copper.[16]

During the 1920s and 1930s, Kendzior also oversaw improvements to employee housing occupied by both those working for Shelburne Farms Corporation and those employed directly by Seward and Lila. In addition to basic maintenance, such as exterior and interior painting, most of the buildings required new heating systems to replace the original thirty- and forty-year-old coal-fired steam boilers.[17]

During the late nineteenth century, when most of the estate's employee dwellings had been constructed, modern amenities such as electricity, indoor plumbing, water heaters, and electric cooking stoves were not considered essential for staff housing. However, in the ensuing years, employees had come to expect them. Kendzior was conscious that such amenities could help him to attract and retain valuable workers, and he gradually made improvements throughout the 1920s. In 1925, for instance, the farm manager informed Lila, "I think that I have found a suitable man for the Golf Course. His name is J. E. Torok, age 28, married with two young children…Torok asks for a bath and inside toilet to be fixed in his house, before next Winter."[18]

Kendzior faced similar challenges maintaining the estate's infrastructure, including telephone and power lines, roads, and field drainage systems. In 1925, Kendzior reported that "the telephone lines need extensive repairs—many poles and lines are down and need renewal."[19] The extensive network of pasture fencing constructed in the late nineteenth century was failing, and every year funds and labor were required to replace deteriorated sections. The original water system also needed significant repairs and improvements. Just after starting work at Shelburne Farms in 1923, Kendzior replaced the pump and motor system that drew water for Shelburne Farms and Southern Acres from Lake Champlain. Nonetheless, he remained concerned about the system, which lacked backup equipment:

Many times has the question of the water supply to this Estate been discussed but nothing definite has ever been done and I suggest that the grave risk which is daily being run is not fully realized. The whole water supply is dependent upon the proper and daily working of one pump and one motor only. If anything goes wrong with either or both, the result, especially in winter would be very serious.[20]

The Farm Barn, by Henry A. Strohmeyer, c. 1920. Shelburne Farms Collections.

In addition, by the early 1930s, the demand for water from Shelburne Farms Corporation's dairy, and the kennels and Breeding Barn complex of Southern Acres Farm, had outgrown the system's capacity. After debating options for several years, including the construction of a new, independent water system for Southern Acres Farm, Watson and Kendzior decided to dig up and replace the original water pipes leading from the main reservoir behind the Farm Barn with larger ones. Southern Acres and the corporation shared the expense, and the work was completed in 1934.[21]

With the enormous amount of money needed to keep the estate's buildings and infrastructure in working condition, Lila, Watson, Vanderbilt, and Kendzior were forced to delay certain projects and even sacrifice some outlying structures. Undermaintained for years, Bay View was in such poor condition by 1925 that Kendzior was forced to refuse a request to rent the building. Along with major roof leaks and other concerns, Bay View lacked a reliable, year-round water supply. In the late 1920s and early 1930s, Kendzior managed to keep the building's envelope intact, but by 1932, the house was no longer habitable even during the summer months, and it was boarded up and left unoccupied. The dwelling would remain vacant and dilapidated into the next decade.[22]

The farm manager faced similar concerns with an outlying parcel on Shelburne Point which included the Captain White house, another dwelling that, like Bay View, predated the establishment of Shelburne Farms. The property had been rented to tenant farmers for a number of years, but by 1929 it was in a deplorable condition. Kendzior reported to Watson that the current tenant, a dairy farmer, had been forced to stop selling milk in Burlington because the barns were no longer in good repair or in compliance with city ordinances requiring a separate milk room for the storage of dairy products in cool and sanitary conditions. The farm manager suggested extensive improvements be undertaken in order to return the property to a marketable condition.[23]

In spite of this, Watson declined Kendzior's proposal, preferring not to invest any funds in the property:

> *It has been proven for a long time at Shelburne, and nothing in recent years has changed the axiom, that the more extensively one engages in farming activities, the greater the loss. Therefore we cannot recommend any more expenditure even to preserve property of doubtful value… None of the family would want a hotel on the point. If a reliable tenant known to some member of the family should appear, the White House could be fixed up…Our decision therefore is to lease the property for pasture for what it will bring…If less than $100.00, it is much better idle…Secure a tenant (no rent) for the White House as it is with the understanding he is to watch trespassers to some extent and report. Failing that, to board up the White House tight as Bay View is, in order to preserve it as much as possible.*[24]

Yet Bay View, the Captain White house, and their outbuildings fared better than other structures on the Shelburne Farms estate, including the defunct pheasantry and the employee boarding house adjacent to the Farm Barn. In 1925, Kendzior reported to Vanderbilt Webb that the pheasantry was "going to ruin."[25] In 1928, the house and barn were sold and removed from Shelburne Farms. The boarding house near the Farm Barn was taken down three years later. It is unclear if the structures were salvaged and rebuilt elsewhere or dismantled for scrap lumber.[26]

Farm Income

Soon after he was hired, Kendzior proposed four main methods of generating income for the corporation: the sale of surplus farm products, the sale of fluid milk from an expanded dairy, raising Hereford steers, and livestock dealing. During his tenure from 1922 to 1935, he experimented with all four methods.

Kendzior's efforts to sell surplus farm products were somewhat successful. Throughout the 1920s and 1930s, the corporation sold large quantities of hay and smaller amounts of ice, sawdust, potatoes, and apples to farmers and wholesale dealers in Vermont, southern New England, and Long Island. The Lyman Farm in Middlefield, Connecticut, purchased 22,115 pounds of hay in 1924 and a comparable amount in 1925. In 1929, the corporation sold a significant amount of apples to a fruit and produce wholesaler in Burlington, including over 35,000 pounds of cider apples and 58 barrels of Greenings.[27]

However, depressed prices for farm products, rising labor costs, and declines in productivity hurt Kendzior's plans. As he reported in 1924,

"Hay is finished and is only half a crop due to a bad season and the fact of so much land being grown out and requiring ploughing…Amount of wages paid shows a decrease over 1923 but are still too high in view of the lack of income from the farm which I trust will improve in time, when [the] cow business is established and land worked round to yield crops."[28] Additionally, as the decade continued, Kendzior required more and more of the field crops he produced to feed the large numbers of livestock he began to purchase for the other profit-generating ventures, leaving less to sell as cash crops.

In the early 1920s, Kendzior experimented with importing and raising Hereford steers for the beef market. In January 1923, he wrote, "It is our intention to feed steers on these farms in the future, our plan being to buy in early May, steers aged from 13 to 16 months, put them on the early grass and finish before fall on corn and Soy beans."[29] That year, Kendzior purchased 50 head from New Mexico, with the goal of gradually increasing the operation each year to reach 500 head. However, there is no evidence that the project was continued beyond this initial importation, as Kendzior found that it was indeed difficult to make a profit at the venture. As Watson wrote him in February 1924, "Re steers. I think we have proved conclusively there is nothing in buying them in the West. They cost $40.00 in the [western cattle] yards, & we have sold the best for $43.00 net; =6% interest is about 200, and $100 won't begin to cover the other costs, pasture alone per head was worth $500 to $700."[30]

Kendzior also tried dealing in farm livestock. He expressed his ambitions in 1923: "It will take time but I hope gradually to build up a big business here of supplying horses, cows, pigs, and lambs to people who know they will get good value for their money."[31] After experimenting with selling sheep and horses imported from the western United States in 1923 and 1924, the farm manager changed his focus to Guernsey, Jersey, Ayrshire, and Shorthorn dairy cattle. He explained his plans in a letter to the Vermont Commissioner of Agriculture:

> [W]e have a large number of very fine cows, which…we are prepared to sell at any time either singly or by carload. Every animal which comes on to these farms is tested [for tuberculosis] and is sold subject to test. Our object in time is to turn over at least 1000 cows every year all tested and straight. We believe that sometimes you receive enquiries from prospective buyers asking where good cows may be bought and we should esteem it an enormous favor if you would refer these enquiries to us. We believe that by selling good tested animals only and giving a straight deal every time a large business can be created on these farms.[32]

Between 1923 and the early 1930s, Kendzior purchased cows from Vermont, western New York, and the Canadian provinces of Quebec and Nova Scotia and sold them to farmers in New England, upstate New York, Long Island, and New Jersey. He contracted with several individuals in the regions where he purchased the livestock to seek out cows in their vicinity, make purchases on his behalf, temporarily house and feed the animals while awaiting the results of veterinary tests, and ship them either to Shelburne Farms or directly to their buyers. As he wrote to a farmer in Cambridge, Vermont, "I want cows of all breeds except Holstein, must be big, good mouths, handle big calves, and straight. They must be bought subject to test. We could if you agree make your farm a depot where cows could be delivered by the sellers, tested and paid for after passing."[33]

In order to handle the projected 1,000 extra cattle passing through the estate each year, Kendzior received permission to repair existing fences and to fence in additional pastureland; make alterations to the Tracy Barn, formerly a sheep barn, to allow it to accommodate cattle; and build a large stockyard at the Shelburne Depot. In 1924, a year after the estate's remaining sheep were sold, stanchions, running water, and electric lights were installed at the Tracy Barn in order to convert it to a modern facility for housing cows. In 1925, Kendzior reported that a total of 650 acres of pastureland would be fenced in.[34]

At first, it seemed as if the dairy cattle dealing business might succeed. Farmers in New England and its adjoining states were increasingly specializing in supplying perishable dairy products to consumers in the region's urban centers, a market in which they could effectively compete with their western counterparts. During the early to mid-twentieth century, Vermont farmers produced more fluid milk, cream, butter, and cheese than any other state in New England. By the end of 1923, Kendzior had sold over 300 cows, profiting more than $1,500. The following April he reported that "the demand for Guernseys is enormous."[35]

Nevertheless, the farm manager encountered difficulties almost immediately. The vagaries of the market meant constant fluctuations in demand for dairy cattle and, at times, slim profit margins. In September 1924, he wrote to a potential seller, "At present owing to the entire absence of a satisfactory market for dairy cows we are unable to buy any more but should this condition alter we would be glad to have a look at your animals."[36]

Another concern was the ability of his customers to pay for their purchases. Kendzior established a close relationship with The Lyman Farm in Middlefield, Connecticut, selling them several loads of cattle, as well as hay, in 1925. Yet it took multiple appeals to the proprietors to receive full payment. As Kendzior wrote in March 1925, "We have anxiously looked for your cheque $777.92 due March 2nd last, and shall be glad please to receive it as its absence is causing a slight financial panic at our bank."[37] And again in May: "We are anxious please to receive a cheque for the last load of cows. We wish to reinvest this money but cannot do so until we receive it, and are greatly handicapped by its absence. Kindly oblige."[38]

Kendzior's greatest challenge was perhaps his constant need for large sums of cash to purchase cattle in order to keep up with the demand when it was strong. In 1923, he requested permission from Watson to establish a line of credit with a local bank in the amount of $15,000, noting, "I have been greatly handicapped…not being able to buy cows as the trade demanded, and when I saw them…I am confident that by this means a substantial profit can be made next year from cattle dealing."[39] It is unlikely that this request was approved, as Kendzior was still appealing for funds in February 1924.[40]

While at times the cattle dealing business did generate some profit for the corporation, the challenges and lean times made it difficult for Kendzior to maintain the operation on a large scale. He continued to deal in cattle on a more limited basis into the late 1920s.[41]

The Dairy

An improved and modernized dairy would prove to be the most reliable source of income for the Shelburne Farms Corporation. Soon after he was hired, Kendzior visited several prominent facilities in southern New England and New York to gather ideas. After his return, he presented Watson and Vanderbilt with a plan to improve and expand Shelburne Farms' dairy by building a new barn as well as renovating the existing one. While he was not able to convince the brothers of the need for a new barn, he did receive $10,000 to purchase new cows and embark upon major renovations to the existing barn immediately. By January 1924, the newly improved dairy contained 110 cows and employed four workers.[42]

For the next three years, the corporation sent its milk and cream to the Shelburne Cooperative Creamery, which possessed some 300 local members and sold dairy products to the Boston area. In doing so, Shelburne Farms was participating in a regional trend: In the 1920s, Vermont farmers were

Shelburne Farms dairy cattle grazing near the dairy barn, c. 1920–40. Shelburne Farms Collections.

the largest suppliers of fluid milk and cream to the Boston metropolitan market.[43]

As a member of the Shelburne Cooperative Creamery, the dairy was subject to the health regulations of Boston and its surrounding towns. Milk inspectors from the area paid visits to the estate in 1925 and 1926, and required additional modifications to the corporation's milking methods and dairy structures. In 1925, H. E. Bowman, an inspector in the Department of Milk Inspection in Somerville, Massachusetts, wrote Kendzior to inform him of the results of a recent assessment:

After analyzing score of your dairy made by Mr. Clark of Boston the following changes should be made to comply with "Grade A" regulations...You will note that in Regulation #2 that milk shall be drawn from udders that are thoroughly cleaned by a milker with clean dry hands, into a small top pail; also that milk shall be immediately removed from stable and strained and scored in milk house. I also note that stable should be cleaned and whitewashed. Kindly notify me when these changes have been completed.[44]

In 1926, Kendzior noted an additional requirement: "the Boston Health Authority who controls our milk requires a milk house to be built adjoining the dairy barn in which to cool our milk."[45] A new milk house, containing a tank to keep the milk cool in the summer and a wood stove to keep it from freezing in the winter, was added to the dairy barn shortly thereafter.[46]

In 1927, Kendzior ended the corporation's relationship with the Shelburne Cooperative Creamery and signed a contract with Burlington-based retailer Laughton Edward Brigham to supply thirty 40-quart cans of milk daily. He explained his hopes to obtain a higher price for his milk by doing business with Brigham in a letter to Watson:

The looked-for benefit to the Corporation depends entirely on the Burlington retail price of milk, and I am distinctly of the opinion that this will rise rather than fall, as my information is to the effect that within the current year a city ordinance will be passed allowing only pasteurized milk or milk from State tested herds to be sold in Burlington—such a rule would force up the price of milk and benefit us...Our milk is now of very high quality—bacteria is down to 5,000—certified need not be below 10,000—and butter fat averages about 4%. It will be struggle to supply a regular 30 cans (1,200 quarts) every day but I am confident that we can do it.[47]

Shelburne Farms sold milk and cream to Brigham through the late 1930s. In 1932, at Brigham's request, the corporation increased production to thirty-five cans per day by purchasing additional cows. Within the next four years, the dairy contained 135 to 140 head.[48]

Kendzior was faced with the challenge of modernizing the dairy operations to meet evolving standards for animal husbandry and the storage and handling of fluid milk. In the late nineteenth

The Shelburne Farms dairy, with its milk house addition, by J. Watson Webb Jr., July 1934. Shelburne Farms Collections.

and early twentieth centuries, an increasing understanding of the links between barn sanitation, cattle diseases, and consumer health risks led to a nationwide series of new dairy programs and regulations. In the 1920s, numerous modifications were made to Shelburne Farms' forty-year-old dairy barn and its surrounding outbuildings to keep them in working order, update systems and equipment, accommodate expanding milking operations, and comply with sanitation standards. These improvements included the milk house; the installation of an additional silo adjacent to the barn for feed storage; a clipping machine, which was used to groom the cows and ran on a track above the stanchions; and a new milking machine able to accommodate eight cows at a time.[49]

The milking machine was apparently a success, as Kendzior wrote a letter to the editor of the London-based *The Field* in March 1926, extolling the virtues of the system:

As a possible means of assisting farmers in England to reduce the cost of production and to improve the cleanliness & bacteria content of their milk I earnestly recommend to their attention the use of a milking machine. In the United States with the cheapest labour costing 15/– per day and milk selling at 1/– per gallon wholesale the use of such a machine is essential and almost universal in both pedigree and grade herds, and from personal experience I am certain that most of the prejudice existing against it in England is entirely without foundation. There are many well known and equally efficient designs but in use all are governed by one rule—supreme cleanliness.[50]

During his tenure at Shelburne Farms from 1923 to 1935, Kendzior completed several other improvements to the dairy barn complex, including the installation of brick flooring, the overhauling of the main building's manure gutters and drainage system, renovations adding space for fourteen more cows in the main barn, and the purchase of another silo for the calf barn.[51]

In Kendzior's mind, the condition of the dairy barn was all-important. He subscribed to the theory that silage and grains were more nutritious than fresh pasture grasses for most of the year, and therefore cows would produce more milk if they were kept indoors tied to stanchions in all but the peak growing months of late spring and early summer. As he wrote to Lila,

I am convinced that the idea of pasture for dairy cows in Vermont is a mistaken one as there are seldom more than six weeks in every year when cows can obtain any feed from the pastures, after that they become only exercising grounds. I therefore propose in future to grow more of such crops as alfalfa, peas and oats, and millet and to feed them to the cows in the barns and to greatly reduce the so called pasture land.[52]

Yet despite the major capital improvements Kendzior made to the Shelburne Farms dairy barns, the herd remained susceptible to outbreaks of diseases common for the time, such as bovine tuberculosis. At least two such incidents occurred during the manager's tenure. The more serious of the two was the discovery of brucellosis at Shelburne Farms during a statewide epidemic in 1933 and 1934. Also known as Bang's Disease, brucellosis is commonly found in domestic and farm animals and is communicable to humans, where it often causes influenza-like symptoms. Kendzior explained its impact upon cattle to Lila in 1934: "This disease which is prevalent throughout the world is a germ which is taken in through the mouth of the animal thence attacking the unborn calf and causing premature birth. The calf is usually born dead and the cow more or less rendered useless. The… losses to stock owners are enormous."[53] Indeed, the discovery of the disease at Shelburne Farms resulted in the compulsory sale for slaughter of infected animals and a great deal of lost revenue. Kendzior continued,

In the first nine months of this year losses from Bang's disease were approximately $1,000.00 and in 1933 about $2,000.00 resulting from the forced sale of 65 cows which had aborted. To give an idea of the prevalence of this disease the Vermont Department of Agriculture estimate that 60% of all the cattle in the State will be slaughtered before it is cleaned up. These are the known cash losses to which must be added the loss of milk which has been proved to be as high as 28.05% in an infected herd, loss of calves, loss from non-breeders and other causes. In June, 1934, an ordinance was passed by the Burlington Board of Alderman to the effect that Baby Milk must be produced from Bang's disease free cows and since Mr. Brigham (our milk distributor) sells between six and seven hundred quarts of our milk under the Baby Milk label I considered that we had no choice but to test our cows and comply with the ordinance or lose our trade, and go out of the dairy business. The question of finance then arose and Mr. Brigham offered to lend us $5,000.00 free of interest for five years. The advantage to him would be that he would receive the milk his trade demands and we in turn *would greatly enhance the value of our herd by eliminating the disease. By testing now we would also make sure of the Federal aid…On October 8th the Federal Veterinary surgeons took blood samples of 192 cows and condemned 83. These by law must be slaughtered…I estimate that we shall lose in all 100 head for which we shall received about $4,500.00. The cost of replacement will be approximately $7,500.00 leaving a debit balance of $3,000.00.*[54]

With the loan from Brigham, Kendzior was able to pay for the testing and replenish his dairy herd. In the end, the situation did have some positive effect, as Brigham was then able to make the following advertisement:

This is our new CREAM, please note its excellent qualities—there is none better on the market. All our milk and cream comes from Shelburne Farms where the cows are all certified by the Vermont State Department of Agriculture as free from Tuberculosis and Bang's disease. This is the only farm producing milk and cream for the Burlington market which can make this claim.[55]

An Ongoing Struggle

Kendzior's task of maintaining and improving the aging estate while also making it more profitable and less dependent upon the Webb family ultimately proved to be too great a challenge for him. A letter from Kendzior written to the estate auditor in April 1926 illustrates the scope of his challenge:

Thank you for your long letter of the 22nd, with the careful and detail[ed] explanation of the accounts for the past year. May I please make one remark? "Loss on Farming $16,398.11." I think it is scarcely correctly described and covers a point which I always am trying to explain to the owners of this property, and find it difficult to substantiate by figures. Firstly to call the property a 'Farm' is incorrect—it is an 'Estate,' and the figure $16,398.11 really includes loss on farming…upkeep of roads, repairs and alterations to buildings, roofs and fences, trimming of trees, cleaning ditches, upkeep of farm implements and harness, and lastly, but a very large item, improved agricultural value of the land…Most of these items I maintain were much neglected for many years past and the fact that they are now being done accounts in a large measure for our bad financial position—to carry on and at the same time improve the Estate I assure you is a very hard struggle.[56]

Although the dairy operation proved to be a success for the most part, the income it provided could not completely sustain the estate as a whole. Other sources of profit, including sales of hay and other farm products, provided occasional but unreliable income. And the Hereford steer and cattle dealing operations were decidedly unsuccessful.

In the early to mid-1920s, Lila Webb loaned the corporation more than $60,000 from her personal investments to eliminate the backlog of deferred maintenance and pay for additional capital improvements that would, it was hoped, allow Shelburne Farms to become self-supporting. But her loan was quickly exhausted, and Lila continued to contribute between $15,000 and $20,000 in additional funds each year. Even that was ultimately insufficient, and by the mid-1920s, Kendzior received the Webb family's reluctant permission to borrow from at least one local bank in order to cover disparities between income and expenses. To make matters worse, the farm manager found it difficult to pay down the loans as quickly as he had optimistically promised. Annual deficits became the norm, and the Webbs began to balk at his constant requests for additional funds. Vanderbilt wrote the farm manager in October 1927 to inform him of the family position on the matter:

> It is, of course, quite clear from the figures that there will be a substantial deficit on November 1st which will have to be met. We anticipated...that there would be a deficit this autumn on account of the large sums which you were expending for new equipment, in spite of your own continued hope that all this new equipment would be in some way be paid for out of income... In spite of our not liking to face the present deficit, we have talked the matter over with Mrs. Webb and she is willing to advance an additional $5,000...The important question to my mind is as to the future...I still am unable to believe...that it is not possible to obtain ... satisfactory results for her at some fixed outside limit in respect to her annual contributions to Farm deficits, which we had hoped would be set at $15,000.00. Instead of this, however, she has, after loaning the sum of $61,140.00 of all the capital improvements which we thought would be required to put the property in good running condition, contributed $20,000 toward the deficit for the year ending March 31, 1926, and $17,500 toward the deficit for the year ending March 31, 1927, and now will have again contributed at least $20,000 toward the deficit for the year ending March 31, 1928. Moreover, these contributions on her part will not actually cover the aggregate of the operating deficits for these three years.[57]

Over the years, the Webbs repeatedly expressed their desire to keep their annual contribution to $15,000 or less and warned Kendzior that they would consider ceasing the farm operations if he was unable to reduce their expenses. As Vanderbilt wrote to Kendzior in June 1925:

> I am afraid that it is going to be absolutely impossible for us to go on running the farm even for a few years at an annual operating deficit substantially in excess of $15,000, in the hope that by so doing the place will be so greatly improved in its productivity as to permit ultimately of the reduction of the annual deficit below $15,000. The chance of realizing this hope seems too remote to justify the outlay. In the meantime, I recognize the fact that the farm looks in far better shape and it is a real pleasure to all of us to see it so, but I am afraid that this is a luxury which under the circumstances cannot be afforded.[58]

Since the Webbs were insistent upon reducing their annual subsidy of the corporation, Kendzior frequently proposed to offset growing deficits by selling or developing outlying sections of the estate property on Shelburne Point, most of which had been leased to tenant farmers since at least the early 1920s. In 1925, for instance, Kendzior suggested that the Webbs

> sell all property North of the Crusher and bounded on the West by the road to the Harbour...I consider that there is a distinct demand for camp sites and this land includes some very attractive ones. If properly handled it should be possible to sell all this land. Some such scheme as this would reduce overhead charges and responsibilities and enable you to concentrate on a reduced area.[59]

The Webb family had entertained the idea of selling some of their property in the past, primarily outlying lands beyond the main gates, and they continued to do so. In fact, Seward and Lila had sold a small parcel of forty-six acres on Shelburne Point in 1910, with the stipulation that the purchasers use the property only as a private residence and grant members of the Webb family first right of refusal should they wish to sell in the future. Comments that Lila made to Kendzior made it clear that the family would even consider subdividing the property within the gates if necessary. However, they would contemplate doing so only under very strict conditions: in cases of severe financial hardship and/or in ways that ensured the property would remain as unchanged as possible. Ultimately, only two small additional parcels on Shelburne Point left the Webb family's ownership during the tenure of the Shelburne Farms Corporation. They were sold to the Champlain Transportation Company in 1932 in exchange for the deed to an existing right-of-way that the Transportation Company held within the Shelburne Farms boundaries.[60]

The Great Depression

The onset of the Great Depression in 1929 only made the Shelburne Farms Corporation's financial situation worse. Kendzior's profit margin became even more slight, and the Webbs felt themselves increasingly unable to contribute substantial funds to sustain the corporation. The first sign of impending trouble appeared in February 1930, when Burlington dealer L. E. Brigham was forced to reduce his payments for Shelburne Farms milk in order to remain in business. David Tower, the corporation's second in charge, reported to Kendzior: "The milk is just over 30 cans per day now, but Mr. Brigham had to cut his price to 12 cents on February 1st, the other milk dealers were coming on to his route and offering their milk to his customers for 12 c., he lost a few customers and thought it best to cut his to 12 cents in order to hold the others."[61] In the next three years, the retail price would drop two more cents, reducing the wholesale price that the corporation received to four cents per quart. Although this was certainly a better price than the two cents per quart that many other farmers in the area were receiving, the reduction translated into a significant decline in the corporation's monthly earnings. In 1931, Kendzior reported to Watson that he expected milk sales to earn $4,000 less than in the previous year. To make matters worse, he was doubtful that he would be able to rent many of the outlying lands that had been leased to tenant farmers, an additional loss of more than $1,300 in annual income. As a result, Kendzior was forced to enact a ten percent wage reduction for all corporation employees, including himself, by July 1931.[62]

Although they experienced some losses, the Webb family managed to weather the Great Depression well compared to the many Americans who became destitute. Because much of Lila's trust was invested in real estate and city bonds, her income was mostly protected from the dramatic losses in the stock market. She did, however, cut costs by reducing her own staff's wages by ten percent and occupying only a small portion of Shelburne House when in residence. Her sons Watson and Seward fared less well. Seward suffered the most serious losses. In 1932, he and his wife, Gertrude, were obliged to rent their house in Long Island and lay off their staff. They spent summers as Lila's guests at Shelburne House through at least 1935. Watson lost all of his investments, and his wife Electra's holdings were also affected. Their changed circumstances would require Watson to postpone his retirement, a fact that greatly disappointed him. But Electra was grateful for all that they still had. As she wrote to Lila in 1932,

> *We cut all our help Mar. 1st but not according to percent as that seemed unfair. The high priced ones have to come down more... Not a complaint from any one... My own income last year was ¼ of what it was before. Heavens knows if we will have enough next year to keep up as we have. Well the apartment goes first, we have decided on that. I don't care as long as we can stay happy and well.*[63]

Lila Webb remained cognizant of the difficulties that Americans with fewer means were encountering, and for several years she subsidized the corporation's provision of year-round work to otherwise seasonal employees and also employed destitute men with families. This, of course, provided the corporation with an increased labor pool and allowed Kendzior to complete additional work with no added expense. It also removed some unemployed men from the care of the town of Shelburne. Indeed, Kendzior was bombarded with inquiries for employment from all over the state of Vermont, upstate New York, New Hampshire, Massachusetts, and as far afield as southeastern Pennsylvania. From 1931 to 1934, the farm manager employed up to fifteen destitute men at a time, paying them to repair fences, trim trees, chop wood, maintain farm equipment, and dismantle the boarding house adjacent to the Farm Barn, among other tasks. Lila also provided housing to at least two families at Shelburne House during the winter of 1932, when the servants' wing was unoccupied. Although some who inquired were turned away because they did not meet Lila's qualifications that they have families to support and be completely destitute, her financial assistance made a huge difference in many lives. In 1933, Kendzior reported that "so far no married man has been a charge to Shelburne this winter. A contrast to Burlington which is today supporting 745 families."[64]

The ongoing depression forced the Webb family to review their annual financial support for Shelburne Farms Corporation even more critically. In 1931, Watson wrote Kendzior to advise him to scale down his ambitions for the business:

I cannot agree with you at all that Mrs. Webb, Sr. or ourselves want to enlarge in any way the farming activities of Shelburne Farms Corporation. It has been conclusively proven over a period of 40 years that the larger the operations are the greater the cost and the net loss is, and if any changes are made, it will be rather in the form of a reduction and working less land, etc. than enlarging the present plant.[65]

By 1933, Watson's forecast for the future of the corporation was more pessimistic:

Just a line to tell you I think you made a very good showing in the financial position of the Corp'n over last year. I hope we can continue. We all have such drains now on income we must do everything possible to lighten Mrs. W's [Lila's] load, for it might end in just about closing down everything up there on the farm, unless things improve. I like to be hopeful, we all do, but I can see no real improvement yet, and we have a lot of difficulties to handle.[66]

Both Kendzior and the Webb family painted the picture in increasingly dire terms. In February 1933, Kendzior requested permission to purchase a Frigidaire unit for the dairy barn in order to comply with a new Burlington City Ordinance requiring mechanical cooling systems for fluid milk storage. Such systems were considered to be more reliable and sanitary than local ice, the traditional method used. Vanderbilt refused Kendzior's request:

In view of the doubt in times like this as to the future of all farming operations at Shelburne, I cannot see that we would be justified in approving this expenditure on Mrs. Webb's behalf if, as it seems to me must be the case, it can be avoided or at least postponed until another year when we will know more about the future of the milk business…In any event, neither Mr. Watson Webb nor I feel that we would be prepared to recommend the expenditure which you have suggested without taking the matter up with Mrs. Webb and frankly facing with her again at this time the alternative, which as you know we have frequently considered in the past, of practically abandoning farming operations entirely.[67]

Kendzior replied that if the City of Burlington barred the corporation's milk because it was not cooled mechanically, he felt that the business would go under and they would have no choice but to "abandon the whole Estate."[68] He wrote to Vanderbilt,

I claim that it is impossible to cease farming operations without abandoning the whole Estate—there is no halfway measure. Cattle would be given away, they would not sell at auction as no one has any money to pay for them with and there are practically no buyers. The same applies to horses and implements, and the whole of Shelburne would be out of work, "on the Town," with resulting enormous increased taxes. They may all become necessary, it is not for me to say, but I think the ultimate loss would be far greater from a policy of abandoning everything than from carrying, making as much and as good quality milk as possible at the least possible cost.[69]

It is unclear whether Kendzior was ultimately authorized to purchase the Frigidaire unit.

Managerial Tensions

By the mid-1930s, the Webb family was frustrated with what they perceived to be Kendzior's lack of fiscal responsibility. Most of his experiments aimed at generating additional income had failed. His repeated promises that the corporation would be able to pull itself out of debt never seemed to develop results, and he continued to request additional funds year after year. As he stated in 1926,

"lack of income is and always will be our main difficulty and with but a little more money I could increase this very materially."[70] The following year he complained to Watson, "I do the best possible for the Corporation. I am always so short of money with which to carry out your wishes and instructions…I feel discouraged with my apparent failure and lack of success in general."[71] By the end of 1934, Watson had lost confidence in Kendzior and resigned as treasurer of the corporation.[72]

On the other hand, Kendzior had been charged with an almost impossible task: to take an aging and undermaintained estate property and turn it into a self-supporting business, preferably within only a few years. This would have been a challenge in the best of times, but Kendzior encountered numerous unforeseen difficulties, including the disease outbreaks that forced him to slaughter many dairy cattle and quarantine the corporation's milk; new, stricter sanitary standards for dairying that required significant capital improvements to stay in business; economic depression; and other issues such as a series of unexplained fires that damaged several estate buildings in 1930. As the farm manager noted in 1926, "to carry on and at the same time improve the Estate I assure you is a very hard struggle."[73]

Moreover, the Webbs did not always recognize Kendzior's challenges. For instance, Seward and Lila often requested the assistance of corporation staff to complete projects on the Home Estate at the busiest times of year. In October 1924, Kendzior wrote to Lila,

As per your order I am sending a man to roll the Golf Course tomorrow—he must come off ploughing as we are filling silos tomorrow and all next week using every available man. We are at a very critical time owing to the late season and I would ask to be allowed to point out that the Golf Course and Gardens with ten men and a team are staffed, as to numbers of men, exactly like the Farms, and yet we constantly have to keep the Golf Course, always at a very busy time...Dr. Webb tonight orders a team and a man to draw manure. Can this work be postponed please? We have silos to fill, potatoes to dig, apples to pick and all the fall ploughing and if men are now to be called away from the very limited farm staff, I simply cannot carry on.[74]

Likewise, in June 1925, Lila wrote Kendzior a polite reprimand, stating that she and her husband had engaged a carpenter in Burlington to work on Shelburne House "as we find we cannot depend on the Corporation."[75] Kendzior replied,

I am very sorry indeed to think that Dr. Webb and yourself can no longer depend on the Corporation as I have always tried to carry out your wishes at the very earliest possible moment with the very limited staff at my command. May I point out that from the 2nd of May inclusive to date Joe Wetmore and F. Gosselin have worked entirely on your personal work with the sole exception of six hours when they were employed on really necessary farm work. All other work here has stood postponed.[76]

Kendzior found himself in an even more challenging situation when it came to Watson Webb and Southern Acres Farm. Watson was in many ways Kendzior's supervisor, yet the former's management of Southern Acres was sometimes at odds with the interests of the corporation. Southern Acres depended greatly on Shelburne Farms, an arrangement that rankled Kendzior at times. In 1923, he observed to Watson, "If it was not for the constant assistance of men, horses, harness, and tools from [Shelburne Farms] you could not carry on."[77] He complained that tools and equipment were returned late or in disrepair, that Watson was reluctant to reciprocate in the loaning of his staff for Shelburne Farms projects, and that in general the relationship burdened Shelburne Farms with extra work.[78]

The close proximity of the two estates' most important operations, the corporation's dairy business and Southern Acres' kennels and the Shelburne Hunt, caused additional tensions. Kendzior's 1928 complaints of damage done to crops and cattle by the Shelburne Hunt have already been described. By 1935, his frustrations had escalated:

I have repeatedly asked [Huntsman Fred] Ingleson to keep hounds away from the Dairy Barn, Creamery, and pastures but he does not do so nor does he seem to realize the risk of infection and how unsanitary and unpleasant it is when hounds empty themselves on and around the door steps of these buildings and even jump on the truck carrying the milking machine pails and strainers. Also if Morgan's terriers could be controlled I would be grateful, they chase the cows and have made a habit of searching the manure heaps thus spreading infection. I consider myself to be personally responsible for making a success of the Bang's disease eradication plan...Unless every precaution and care (none is too small or trivial), is taken to prevent the spread of disease all our money and efforts are thrown away.[79]

To Watson, Kendzior's claims pointed to the manager's opposition to the decades-old Shelburne Hunt:

Ever since you have been at Shelburne you have, in spite of our requests, wired up the fences and gates to an unnecessary height and made it as difficult as possible for me and my family and guests to enjoy the sport...Are the hounds to be kept off Corporation land or not? They cannot hunt without crossing pastures...It would seem to me that a sport which gives pleasure to a great many of Mrs. Webb's descendants and guests, and occupation to a number of people, should have precedence over the Dairy which gives pleasure to none of her family and has cost her a lot of money… Please discuss this entire question with Mr. V. Webb at the first opportunity, as your attitude in the future towards my entire establishment must be settled once and for all before long.[80]

The conflict would end badly for Kendzior. His complaints were the last straw for Watson, who had disliked the manager for years and even suspected him of embezzling funds. In the summer of 1935, Kendzior was asked to leave the corporation's employ; his second-in-command, David Tower, became farm manager on September 1, 1935. Kendzior received $2,500 in severance pay, and he left Shelburne for South Africa, where he started a new business.[81]

The 1920s and early 1930s had been a time of great transition, and at times great turbulence, for the Webbs and for Shelburne Farms. Yet despite their constant concerns that they might have to abandon the farming operation, the Webbs and their staff had managed to hold the estate together. The building stock and infrastructure had been stabilized for the most part, and in some cases they were modernized to twentieth-century agricultural standards.

The Home Estate

After the Webb family established Shelburne Farms Corporation in 1922, Seward and Lila's personal property at Shelburne Farms consisted of 300 acres at the edge of Lake Champlain, which encompassed Shelburne House and the Coach Barn. Lila faced challenges and decisions similar to Kendzior's when it came to the Home Estate: the buildings were aging, their boilers and roofs were failing, and staffing costs continued to increase. In addition, while still enormously wealthy for their time, the elder Webbs' assets and lifestyle had changed considerably since the establishment of Shelburne Farms in the 1880s. The couple simply did not need to use all of their property, nor could they afford to maintain it in the style they had originally intended while also sustaining their other residences. They no longer entertained on a lavish scale, and their children all possessed their own homes elsewhere. As the couple aged, and Seward became increasingly ill, Lila began to allocate their personal funds differently, including paying for increasing amounts of time in Florida.

During the 1920s and early to mid-1930s, Lila scrutinized her Shelburne Farms property for areas of possible economy. She chose not to fully open Shelburne House during several seasons. By 1925, Seward's illness prevented him from overseeing the small poultry operation he had established at Orchard House, and the chicken coops were dismantled and sold within the next several years. By the late 1920s, Lila had also decided to dispose of the remaining horses at the Coach Barn. The Webb grandchildren had outgrown the ponies kept for them, and neither she nor Seward required driving teams any longer.[82]

During the 1920s and 1930s, Lila also reduced the budgets of the greenhouse and formal garden departments. With a smaller household and less entertaining, she no longer required vast quantities of flowers and vegetables. While already greatly decreased in size from their heyday, the gardens and greenhouses still required significant funds and employed approximately ten gardeners in the early 1920s. Over the next fifteen years, Lila gradually curtailed her use of potted palms and other plants in her residences, introduced more hardy species to the formal gardens at Shelburne Farms, and decreased the quantities of exotic fruits and vegetables raised. In the fall of 1927, when the exotic potted bay trees that had long framed the view of Lake Champlain from the lowest level of the gardens died as the result of an early frost, Lila replaced them with hardier yews.[83]

Lila also reduced the number of gardeners and greenhouses on the estate. She decreased her garden and golf links staff to a total of nine for the 1926 season. In 1930 and 1931, after the onset of the Great Depression, she reduced the staff to eight, and then six, and halved the size of the vegetable garden. Although these last measures significantly reduced Lila's Home Estate expenses, her concurrent subsidy of the corporation's employment of destitute men most likely offset the savings.[84]

Kendzior began negotiating to sell unused and undermaintained greenhouse structures on Lila's behalf as early as 1923. Four greenhouses, along with their requisite boilers and heating pipes, were sold in 1927. At that time, the remaining contents of the palm house were also offered for sale.[85]

Like Kendzior, Lila found that the aging buildings and landscape features

The Shelburne House gardens, by J. Watson Webb Jr., c. 1930. Shelburne Farms Collections.

Gardeners at work in the Shelburne House gardens, c. 1920–40. Shelburne Farms Collections.

on the Home Estate required considerable and constant investments to keep them in good condition. The annual cost to open Shelburne House and restore it to working order for the season increased every year. In the late 1920s, some of the brick walls in the formal gardens collapsed and required extensive rebuilding; other garden walls needed re-pointing to avoid failure; the mowing machines for the golf links were beyond repair and had to be replaced; the irrigation system that nourished the greens no longer functioned; and the annex roof leaked. In the early 1930s, the original boilers in the remaining greenhouses, Shelburne House, annex, and coachman's house failed, one after another, necessitating replacements. In addition, the roof and gutters on the Coach Barn, Shelburne House, and the annex required extensive repairs in 1929, 1931, and 1935, respectively.[86]

The End of an Era

The illnesses and deaths of both Seward and Lila Webb would represent perhaps the greatest of all the changes to occur at Shelburne Farms during the 1920s and 1930s.

After decades of poor health and addiction, Seward Webb died on October 29, 1926, at Shelburne House. He had been very ill and bedridden for months before his death, but the end came somewhat unexpectedly. Lila recorded the day in her diary: "Up until 4 this a.m. with Seward… Seward passed away at 4.20 P.M. painlessly & peacefully. I feel utterly heart-broken."[87] He was interred in the Webb family plot at Woodlawn Cemetery in Bronx, New York. A boulder from Nehasane marked his grave.[88]

Although Seward had been ill for years, Lila was devastated by her husband's death. She recorded her feelings in her diary. October 30: "I cannot realize my dear husband has really gone." November 1: "Oh, how I shall miss him!" November 3: "Life seems hard to take up again." December 14: "Lonely!!!"[89] It was more than a year before she began to recover emotionally. During the winter of 1927, her longtime butler and friend Walter Woodgate informed the staff at Shelburne Farms: "We have had a good season here [in Florida], Mrs. Webb [is] beginning to look more happy & I hope will soon get over her trouble."[90]

After Seward's death, Lila followed an annual pattern of spending the winter in Florida, most of each summer and autumn at Shelburne House, and a month at Nehasane during the warmer months, stopping in New York in between seasons. For the first few years of her widowhood, she remained quite active, embarking on motoring trips to Canada with close friends and making an extended trip abroad in 1930.[91]

Miradero, Lila Webb's house in Delray Beach, Florida, c. 1933–40. Shelburne Farms Collections.

Lila used some of her remaining personal funds to construct two smaller residences of her own: a cottage on the Nehasane property, built in about 1926, and an oceanfront residence in Delray Beach, Florida, constructed between 1931 and 1933. A four-bedroom, shingle-style residence, "Fern Lodge" was located a short distance from Nehasane's main lodge on Lake Lila. It provided Lila with a peaceful haven away from the hubbub of her vacationing children and grandchildren while still allowing her to remain in close contact with them when she was in residence, typically for a month to six weeks in the late summer. The Florida house, named "Miradero del Mar" ("Watch Tower of the Sea"), became Lila's winter retreat.[92]

Yet as the years went on, Lila had begun to experience health problems of her own that eventually circumscribed her life. Her hearing had begun to fail years earlier, while she was in her forties. It is unclear if she ever became completely deaf, but her hearing loss became progressively more serious as she aged. It was possibly genetic, as her mother had also lost her hearing at about the same age. Lila made her first known reference to her hearing problems in 1906. Her daughter-in-law Aileen, who married Vanderbilt in 1912, noted that "by the time I knew her she was very deaf."[93] Over the years, Lila consulted numerous doctors in the United States and abroad, underwent several procedures that provided some temporary improvement, and resorted to using a number of instruments designed to magnify sounds, such as ear trumpets and hearing aids. In 1913, she found herself at a loss when several trumpets were destroyed in the fire at 680 Fifth Avenue. By 1925, she was unable to use the telephone.[94]

As a result of her hearing loss, Lila increasingly limited her social activities, especially with those whom she did not know well. She often felt frustrated by her inability to communicate. As she wrote in her diary in October 1931, "Florence [Twombly, Lila's sister], Ruth [Bird, one of Lila's best friends] & I alone for dinner. Felt my deafness more keenly than ever."[95]

By the late 1920s, when Lila was in her late sixties, her physical ailments were increasingly serious. She tired easily and pushed herself to the point of collapse at times, requiring days of bed rest to recover her energy. Heavy colds took weeks to shake off. More seriously, Lila developed diabetes, high blood pressure, and heart trouble.[96]

In January 1935, she began a long decline after fainting during a church service in Florida. Lila remained bedridden and too ill to write for almost two months. For the next year and a half, she struggled to recover her former strength and experienced long periods of illness followed by ever-shorter stretches of recovery. As she wrote in June 1935, "I do not seem to pick up at all. Even the lilacs do not rouse me."[97] Her children began to limit her contact with the outside world to keep her from overexertion.

As a result, Lila began to relinquish active oversight of Shelburne Farms. In March 1935, Vanderbilt wrote Kendzior to inform him that she would be unable to answer a question related to the management of the estate:

Although, as you have probably heard, my Mother is very much better...I certainly do not feel that I can write to her about the matter referred to in your letter, and I am quite sure that I would not even wish to discuss such a proposal with her at this time...

Lila Webb, 1931. Shelburne Farms Collections.

knowing how ill she has been and how important it is not to have her worried about questions of this sort for some little time to come.[98]

The end came in July 1936, just after Lila had insisted upon hosting her granddaughter Frederica's wedding at Shelburne House. As Frederica's cousin J. Watson Webb Jr. later recounted,

Grandmother really extended herself for this wedding. She wanted it to be special because here was another Frederica Vanderbilt Webb getting married in Shelburne House, and she absolutely exhausted herself. The wedding was the first few days in July and when the wedding was over, she was just absolutely done in and she walked upstairs, so Woodgate told me later on, and she said, 'Woodgate, I'm so tired, I don't think I ever want to come downstairs again.' She never did. She died…from exhaustion and the complication of diabetes.[99]

After a memorial service at Trinity Church in Shelburne on July 14, 1936, Lila was buried in Woodlawn Cemetery, next to her husband.[100]

For Shelburne Farms, it was the end of an era. Many estate employees felt Lila's death keenly, including longtime head gardener Alexander Graham, whom Watson reported was "quite broken up."[101] As Kendzior had once stated, "I have never known anyone in my life who so completely won the admiration, respect and affection of all with whom she came in contact, as Mrs. Webb."[102] Watson himself cut to the heart of the matter when he wrote, "Dear old Shelburne can never be the same."[103]

CHAPTER 12

THE NEXT GENERATION

The entire place has been gradually transformed during the past few years from an old-fashioned "estate" to a really producing farm, with a good sized dairy, a beef herd of about 300 breeding cows, and a comfortable and productive flock of sheep. Our oldest son has made the running of the farm his job, and is certainly getting a fine life out of it, if not yet a "living"! I often envy him.

— VANDERBILT WEBB TO HENRY FRANCIS DU PONT, JUNE 27, 1947[1]

AFTER LILA WEBB'S DEATH IN JULY 1936, THE NEXT GENERATIONS of the Webb family assumed full ownership and responsibility for Shelburne Farms and Southern Acres. Seward and Lila's children and grandchildren possessed different perspectives about the estates and about their role in the family and the community at large. The years leading up to the Second World War brought new directions for the family properties, modern agricultural innovations, and new challenges and hardships. Through it all, family members endeavored to keep the properties within family ownership and to maintain them as productive farmland.

Despite the financial pressures she had experienced during the latter part of her life, Lila was a very wealthy woman when she died. Her net worth had been somewhat reduced since 1885 when she received her $10 million inheritance, as she had used a significant amount over the years in order to build her residences and estates; fund her family's luxurious lifestyle; and offset some of her husband's financial difficulties. Some of the income from her assets had also been diverted by the institution of income taxes; the maintenance of the aging buildings on the Home Estate portion of Shelburne Farms; and the outlays required by the Shelburne Farms Corporation. However, in the end, she left a large legacy for her descendents. Lila's estate was valued at more than $7,380,000, including approximately $5,730,000 in the trust created for her by her father, William Henry Vanderbilt, and $1,650,000 in stocks, bonds, real estate, and personal property.[2]

Lila's four children, Frederica, Watson, Seward Jr., and Vanderbilt, were the major beneficiaries of her estate. According to the terms established by Lila's father, her trust dissolved upon her death, and its proceeds were divided among her children. Lila also bequeathed her majority shares in Shelburne Farms Corporation to her children, appointing them the sole shareholders in the family company. She gave the corporation all of her remaining property in Vermont, thus making the company the official owner of the Home Estate, which included Shelburne House and the Coach Barn. As residual legatees of Lila's estate, her children also received equal interest in her other property, including stocks, bonds, her Florida residence, and her shares in Nehasane Park Association, the family-run entity that officially owned their Adirondack estate.³

Over the next three years, Watson and Vanderbilt served as the executors of Lila's estate and disbursed her assets. During this period, the four Webb siblings held a series of discussions about the components of Lila's property to determine whether and how they would manage it. Although the demands of their individual lives kept them tied to their own primary residences elsewhere, all of the children agreed that at least Shelburne Farms and Nehasane should be kept within the family and maintained in their current forms for the foreseeable future. Vanderbilt took the lead role as executor, coordinated his siblings' discussions, and led them to this consensus. In a 1952 letter to his uncle, Watson's son Samuel expressed the appreciation his branch of the family felt for Vanderbilt's actions during this period: "[W]e haven't forgotten how you stepped into the breach after Grandmother died and kept the property together."⁴

While the Webb siblings agreed that the two family estates should remain intact, they did not all wish to assume equal financial and managerial responsibility for the properties. Frederica and Vanderbilt both desired to be actively involved with Shelburne Farms and were willing to undertake the oversight of the estate's agricultural operations. They were also interested in living in Shelburne on a seasonal basis.

Vanderbilt's attachment to Shelburne Farms had grown since the late 1910s, when he had declined to assume ownership of a portion of the estate. By the mid 1930s, his professional responsibilities were even more consuming than they had been

at the start of his law career twenty years earlier; however, he "had tremendous emotional ties to Shelburne Farms…and he became more and more interested in farming as he got older."⁵ Vanderbilt felt strongly that the property should remain in agricultural use. He also believed that the costs of maintaining the estate were counterbalanced by the benefits it provided by employing a number of local residents. Several years later, he wrote, "I feel that the money [for Shelburne Farms] is well spent, its chief function being to keep up a payroll of about $24,000 a year at a better rate than could be earned by those involved, provided they want to stay in farming, and to produce a pretty substantial quantity of food."⁶

In addition to his personal attachment to Shelburne Farms and loyalty to its employees, Vanderbilt wished to maintain ownership in Shelburne Farms for the sake of his eldest son, Derick (1913–84). Derick possessed a keen interest in agriculture and had started working on the Farm just before Lila's death. He became the estate's farm manager in 1938. By the time Lila's estate was settled in the summer of 1939, it was becoming apparent that Derick would make the Farm his career. As Vanderbilt wrote to a friend in 1938, "He has just about made up his mind that he wants to spend his life in some kind of farming activity in this part of the country, and with our substantial property in Vermont which we all wish to continue to hold, the logical thing would seem to be to work him into its management."[7]

Watson's and Seward Jr.'s different personal interests and financial circumstances led them to prefer to receive other segments of Lila's property. Watson, already ensconced at the Brick House and busy managing Southern Acres, was less inclined to maintain his ownership in Shelburne Farms or his shares in the corporation. Vanderbilt wrote that Watson felt that "he already has sufficient responsibilities and property at Shelburne."[8] Yet as a consummate outdoorsman, Watson felt a keen attachment to Nehasane. Seward's finances had not rebounded after his losses in the stock market crash of 1929. He possessed fewer means to maintain either Shelburne Farms or Nehasane and less interest in doing so than his siblings.[9]

Complicating the matter was the question of what to do with Shelburne House. Lila's children considered the dwelling somewhat of a liability rather than an asset. As Vanderbilt wrote, "its ultimate use or disposition have presented a serious problem which has been the subject of continuous consideration."[10]

The enormous, complicated, and aging building demanded constant maintenance. A large staff was required to keep the residence clean and running smoothly, and its roofs, boilers, and plumbing systems were aging. As early as 1916, Lila herself had noted that Shelburne House was not "equipped with modern conveniences."[11] Additionally, the building's design and aesthetics appeared increasingly old-fashioned in the advent of modernist design sensibilities and changing American attitudes toward lavish expressions of wealth. Shelburne House was becoming a relic of an earlier time.

As the children discussed the fate of Shelburne House in the late 1930s, they briefly revived the idea, first proposed in the early 1920s, of converting the dwelling into an income-producing inn or club. They quickly found, however, that it was impractical to either undertake the work themselves or find an individual who would be interested in purchasing the residence at a reasonable price in order to do so. In 1939, Vanderbilt wrote, "The house itself is an unusually large dwelling built over forty years ago, for which there is absolutely no demand at the present time, and it is not so laid out that it could be used as an inn or hotel without substantial reconstruction, including the installation of new plumbing and heating throughout."[12]

Of the four children, only Vanderbilt was willing to "assume [the] burden of [the] big house."[13] Watson already owned large country residences at South-

Left: Vanderbilt Webb at Shelburne Farms, c. 1945. Shelburne Farms Collections.

ern Acres and Westbury, Frederica was interested in building a new house of her own design in Shelburne, and Seward did not wish to incur any additional financial responsibilities.[14]

Thus, during the three years that followed Lila's death in 1936, the siblings decided to divide their inherited holdings rather than to continue joint ownership. They came to a mutual consensus to buy and exchange each others' interests in the various components of their mother's property in ways that met with their own needs and ensured an equitable distribution of the assets. The disposition occurred in the summer and fall of 1939, just after Lila's estate was officially settled.

In the end, Frederica and Vanderbilt became joint owners of all of Shelburne Farms. The siblings dissolved the corporation and transferred its assets to Frederica and Vanderbilt, who then divided the Shelburne Farms property between themselves. Vanderbilt received 1,400 acres encompassing the main portion of the estate, including the dairy barn, Farm Barn, Coach Barn, and Shelburne House and its contents. Frederica obtained 1,045 acres in the northern and eastern sections of the estate, including lands on Shelburne Point and Shelburne Bay, Bay View House, and the former Collamer, Ezekiel Tracy, and Edgar Nash farms. The two retained joint ownership of the estate's livestock and equipment. Of the other family properties, Watson acquired Nehasane, and Seward received the house in Florida.[15]

Shelburne Farms: A Family Partnership, 1939–1949

Between 1939 and 1949, Frederica and Vanderbilt shared ownership responsibilities and contributed equal amounts to the financial upkeep of Shelburne Farms. Frederica received detailed operational information, conferred frequently with Shelburne Farms employee David Tower and Vanderbilt's son Derick, and trusted her brother's opinions and insights as he assumed the lead management role for the property and agricultural operations.[16]

A Vermont native, Tower (1879–1966) spent more than fifty years at Shelburne Farms. After working as an office clerk and telephone operator on the estate, he served as second in command under former Farm Manager Frank Kendzior. When Kendzior left the estate in 1935, Tower was promoted to farm manager, a position that he held until 1938, when Derick Webb assumed a leadership role after completing his education. From 1938 until his retirement some twenty years later, when he was in his seventies, Tower remained on staff as Derick's bookkeeper and all-around right-hand man. A trusted employee, loyal friend of the Webb family, and well-respected manager, he would work with Derick to implement many of the family partners' agricultural projects at Shelburne Farms.[17]

Derick had possessed an interest in agriculture from an early age. As an adolescent, he had thrived during several vacations his family took on dude

Shelburne Farms employees and Webb family members with Frederica (Webb) Jones (center rear), Vanderbilt Webb (center rear), and Derick Webb (second row, sixth from right) in front of the Farm Barn, c. 1940. Shelburne Farms Collections.

ranches in the western United States. Following the Webb family academic tradition, he studied at Yale University after graduating from Groton School in 1931, expecting to follow in his father's footsteps and enter the law profession. However, in the fall of 1934, at the start of his senior year at Yale, Derick suffered a detached retina in his right eye after being accidentally hit by a tennis ball. His retina trouble required prolonged hospitalization, surgery, and a long recuperation, forcing him to withdraw from Yale and finish his degree by correspondence. He never regained sight in his injured eye and eventually developed problems with his other eye as well. Physicians advised outdoor activity in lieu of regular office work, and Derick abandoned his hopes of a law career.[18]

After his eye was stabilized in early 1935, Derick began to explore farming and ranch work to determine whether his interests could result in a lifelong career, and to recover his physical strength. His parents encouraged him. During 1935 and 1936, Vanderbilt and Aileen financially supported Derick while he held several unpaid and low-paying entry-level positions, jobs he could obtain with little or no experience during the ongoing national economic depression. Derick wanted to learn about self-sustaining commercial farm operations. As he wrote to his parents,

> I believe it will be fairly difficult to get a job on a really commercial outfit such as I have contacted so far because they want either experienced hands or men who have done plenty of hard work. However, it would be more interesting and of more value to me if I could get doing something on that kind of place, rather than on some fancy layout.[19]

Vanderbilt and Aileen connected Derick with family friend James McClure, who led the Farmers' Federation Inc. in Asheville, North Carolina, an organization that developed cooperative ventures for local farmers and found outside markets for their products. Derick worked for the Farmers' Federation for several months in 1935 and then traveled to California to learn more about horse and cattle ranches and obtain more experience as a laborer. He worked for two ranches in the state from late 1935 to mid-1936. At the Rancho Santa Rita in Templeton, he was responsible for feeding beef and dairy cows, cleaning out the horse barn, and performing other duties as needed. It was a valuable experience for him. As he wrote to Aileen in March of 1936,

> I could have learned about all this kind of thing, and done it at home [Garrison, New York] or at Shelburne. However, seeing a different part of the country, and getting a slant on how things are done out here is very interesting. I had lunch…with a Mr. Ledbetter…He said that it did no harm at all, rather a lot of good, to spend a little time wielding a shovel with men who spend their lives at that sort of thing. That's true, all right.[20]

Although Derick had received his start in the agricultural world by means of his parents' connections, he quickly proved his own worth through hard work and initiative, earning the respect of his employers and proving that he possessed an aptitude for the field.[21]

By the spring of 1936, Derick had determined to make farming his career and applied for a one-year course of study at Cornell University's Agricultural College during the 1936–37 school year. He spent the summer of 1936 at Shelburne Farms milking cows, cleaning the dairy barn, and assisting with the hay and grain harvests, later recalling, "I think I was the first Webb ever to have worked on the Farm per se…I was one of the day crew for extra summer help."[22]

At Cornell, Derick studied livestock feeding, judging, and showing; farm records and accounts; agronomy; animal husbandry; and agricultural economics and farm management. This well-rounded program prepared him well for his future role as a farm manager. After graduation, he returned to work at the Farmers' Federation in Asheville for several months. However, by the beginning of 1938, he had resolved to return to Shelburne to work for his father and aunt.[23]

At Shelburne Farms, Derick was charged with continuing efforts to transform the former model farm into a self-sustaining operation weaned from the Webb family's financial support. Since the mid-1920s, the estate's primary source of income had consisted of proceeds from the sale of fluid milk. When Derick began work for the Farm in 1936, the dairy herd consisted of 135 to 140 milking cows, plus additional dry cows and heifers, producing approximately 1,400 quarts of milk per day for sale to the local Burlington market.[24]

However, by the late 1930s, Shelburne Farms' income from its milk was becoming increasingly unreliable. Because the retail price of milk fluctuated according to supply and demand, the Farm's income depended upon maintaining a profitable relationship with a milk distributor, one who would also reliably meet contractual obligations. Shelburne Farms had contracted with local wholesaler L. E. Brigham since 1927, but at times experienced trouble receiving timely payment from him. Yet, as Tower wrote to Vanderbilt in 1938, the other local distributors were in all probability no better: "In spite of the fact that Mr. Brigham has not paid us as he agreed, I think, probably we will get more out of the milk by selling to him than we would get elsewhere…The other concerns…where we might sell our milk, are all financially unsound, and if we should sell to them and lose payment for the milk for a month or six weeks, it would more than offset any better price we might be able to get from them."[25]

Moreover, despite Kendzior's and Tower's best efforts, serious diseases were still a risk to the Farm's dairy cows. Strict health regulations required that the milk from infected cows be discarded rather than sold, and that the infected animals themselves be slaughtered. From 1936 to 1939, the Shelburne Farms dairy herd experienced several outbreaks of Bang's disease and mastitis, an infection of the udder. As a result, the Farm was not always able to meet the milk quotas specified in the contract with its distributor, which prompted daily penalties. Tower was forced to purchase milk from other local farmers on occasion to fulfill the contracted quota with Brigham. Further, with the gradual loss of milking cows from disease, the daily quota the Farm was able to commit to dropped from a high of 1,400 quarts in 1935, to 1,000 quarts in 1938, to 600 quarts in 1940. The Farm's income plummeted accordingly; by 1939, the operation was losing $2,000 a month.[26]

By September 1938, the situation was serious enough that Vanderbilt began to express some doubts as to the long-term future of Shelburne Farms' dairy operation. As he wrote to Tower, "It begins to look as if the question of our continuing in the milk business was being decided for us by other factors, and as if we would soon be out of it entirely."[27] An expansion of the dairy herd, or even replacing the cattle that had succumbed to disease, was a risky proposition. Later that month, Vanderbilt wrote again to Tower:

The only feeling which I have, unless I can be persuaded to the contrary, is that it will be very unwise for us to enter into any contract which will commit us to the purchase of additional milking cows. I am still convinced, particularly in view of recent events, that it would be much wiser to use any funds which might be used for this purpose for the purchase of other stock which will not involve us to such a large extent in such a complicated business as the milk production business.[28]

As a result, Vanderbilt, Derick, and Frederica began to explore options for other livestock ventures that would diversify their operations and augment the Farm's income. In 1938, Derick and Vanderbilt conferred with the agricultural faculty at Cornell and with Vanderbilt's close friend Richard Robbins, who owned large cattle ranches in Kansas and Oklahoma, to determine the most prudent course of action for introducing additional livestock to Shelburne Farms. Watson, who had years of experience raising beef cattle and other stock at Southern Acres, also weighed in.[29]

Shelburne Farms was blessed with two underutilized assets that made the introduction of additional livestock possible. First, the estate encompassed a large acreage of fertile crop- and pasturelands that already produced, or could produce, the extra feed the animals would require. Much of this acreage had been rented to other farmers in recent years. Second, Shelburne Farms also contained some available barn space, which had remained vacant or underused since the early 1900s. The Webbs hoped that additional livestock would prove to be less labor-intensive and more profitable than simply growing surplus crops for sale. Vanderbilt reported to his friend Robbins in

September 1938: "As a result of a number of conferences which we have had during the summer with the Cornell experts, and a good deal of independent thought on our own part, we have…determined to acquire the necessary additional stock for disposing of our surplus hay, grain, ensilage, and pasturage, without getting deeper into the milk business."[30]

During the late 1930s and early 1940s, the family partners would add beef cattle, sheep, hogs, and chickens to the Shelburne Farms operations. Ironically, their actions would lead the Farm back to several ventures with which previous leaders had experimented. Under the guidance of Vanderbilt, Frederica, Derick, and David Tower, these ventures would prove to be relatively successful, although still not successful enough to make the Farm completely self-sufficient.

Beef Cattle

At least one local agricultural expert recommended beef cattle as a profitable venture for farmers with a surplus of fertile land: "On a farm on which all the roughage and pasturage are not being utilized, the owner may well consider whether he would realize greater returns by…raising beef cattle or other roughage-consuming livestock as a sideline or as the main business."[31] By the fall of 1938, the Webbs had decided to invest in two breeds of beef cattle: Aberdeen Angus and Herefords. Originally from Scotland, the black Aberdeen Angus breed was first imported into the western United States in the 1870s and had arrived in the eastern part of the country by the early twentieth century. It was understood to be one of the best for beef production, producing a comparatively large quantity of high-quality, marbled meat per animal and also hardy enough to withstand Vermont's harsh winters without significant weight loss and stress. Watson's ongoing Hereford beef operation at Southern Acres Farm was proof that the Hereford breed would also do well.[32]

Upon the recommendation of a Cornell professor, Shelburne Farms' first group of seven registered Angus cows and heifers was acquired from a farm in upstate New York in September 1938. By the following spring, Shelburne Farms had purchased an additional fifty-six Angus from farms and ranches in upstate New York, northern Vermont, and Nebraska. With this initial group, the family partners established a starter herd from which they would sell the excess young stock each fall.[33]

In September and October 1938, Derick traveled to farms in eleven western and midwestern states to research beef cattle operations and look for sources for future purchases of Angus and Herefords. He spent a great deal of his time visiting his father's friend Richard Robbins's ranches in Kansas and Oklahoma. With Robbins's guidance, Derick arranged for the purchase of forty-three castrated male Hereford calves in New Mexico. These steer calves would be fattened for market and sold the following autumn.[34]

In October 1939, Derick purchased about one hundred Hereford heifers

Right: The Farm Barn, with cattle pens and silos in the courtyard, c. 1945. Shelburne Farms Collections.

from Richard Robbins to establish a breeding herd of Herefords at Shelburne Farms. The following spring, he acquired two Hereford bulls from Watson. However, Derick eventually found his Angus cattle to be more profitable and phased out Herefords in the late 1940s or early 1950s.[35]

From 1938 to 1951, Derick managed a beef herd that averaged 200 to 250 animals. The cattle grazed on estate pastures during the summers and consumed Farm-produced corn silage, grains, ground soybeans, and alfalfa hay during the winters. Employees Clifford Bessette (1908–97) and William Darcy Patterson (1895–1978) oversaw the daily care and feeding of the animals, and the Farm's teamsters were responsible for hauling manure as well as the supplemental feed brought out to the animals in pasture during the early spring and late fall.[36]

During the winter, the cattle were stabled in several locations around the property. The Farm Barn served as the hub of the beef cattle operation. Between 1938 and 1941, the former mule stall area in the lowest level of the main block was transformed into the main cattle stable. Over the next few years, additional areas in the ells were also converted into cattle stables, and a large shed structure was built just to the south of the Farm Barn. The upper third of the barn's courtyard, as well as the area adjoining the new shed, was fenced in to provide outdoor cattle yards. In succeeding years, the burgeoning herd briefly required the creation of auxiliary stable areas in the Tracy Barn and the Coach Barn.[37]

The converted stables required some building alterations over the years. As Derick later stated, he "tore out the front of the horse [mule] stalls in the Farm Barns, and built a cat walk above to help feed" the cattle.[38] The elevated walkway ran the length of the former stall area above newly constructed feed racks and was connected via chutes with the hay lofts on the upper levels of the Farm Barn. Employees could efficiently transfer bales of hay from the lofts into the feed racks, which could be accessed simultaneously by a number of animals. In addition, the original floors were removed from the north and south ell sections of the Farm Barn, and a door was cut in the north ell to provide the cattle with access to the outdoor pens. At the Coach Barn, a small doorway was cut into the large main entrance door to give the cattle access to the courtyard, which was used as another outdoor pen.[39]

During the years of the model farm and Shelburne Farms Corporation, the beef cattle operations on the property had lasted only a short while. However, the reintroduction of beef cattle under the management of Derick, Vanderbilt, and Frederica proved to be quite successful. By 1940, two years after acquiring beef cattle, Derick would report:

> We are not disappointed with the way the steers have performed. In our particular case, the steers mean just so much more income without adding anyone to the payroll or turning over any more ground than previously. Instead of selling surplus hay, carrying over surplus silage, or growing less grain (or carrying over surplus), we are just marketing it through the steers and getting a lot of it back on the land in the form of manure.[40]

Starting in 1940, Shelburne Farms established ongoing relationships with two Pennsylvania farmers who acquired most, if not all, of the Farm's annual crop of young stock. Derick sold excess Hereford heifers to farmers in Maine, New Hampshire, and Vermont. A few additional animals were purchased by Farm employees for their own consumption. A letter from one buyer, written in 1945, attests to the success of the program:

> I wanted to report to you long ago regarding the progress we have made with your feeder calves. They have all done very nicely this winter and Spring, they made very satisfactory gains and as a matter of fact we have slaughtered some and they all hung up choice carcasses…I have been wondering how your calf crop has been this Spring and I surely hope that you will give me first consideration when you are ready to dispose of them.[41]

Sheep, Hogs, and Chickens

It would take two or more years for Vanderbilt, Frederica, and Derick to receive a return on their initial investment in beef cattle. In the meantime, they decided to reintroduce sheep, hogs, and chickens to create additional sources of revenue. In the spring of 1940, Derick traveled to Ithaca, New York, to make the first purchases, which included twenty-three ewes, one ram, three young female hogs, and two boar hogs. The newly acquired sheep, a cross between the Dorset and Merino breeds, could produce both excellent lamb meat and wool. However, by 1943, the family partners had decided to focus on Shropshires, one of the breeds that Seward Webb Sr. had acquired for his model farm.[42]

The group of red Duroc Jersey hogs purchased in Ithaca established a herd from which the excess young stock was sold for pork. An American breed, Duroc females were known to produce a relatively high number of litters over their longer life spans, and their offspring tended to generate high-quality meat. The initial group of hogs soon yielded approximately 100 to 150 animals annually. After a brief hiatus in hog production during the Second World War, Derick introduced Hampshire hogs, a breed known for its hardiness and lean meat, in the late 1940s.[43]

Derick had high hopes for both the sheep and hog ventures. As he wrote Richard Robbins in 1940, "I do not like sheep as well as cattle, but I am inclined to believe that they might be more profitable in many instances…We are also going in to hogs…It would not surprise me were this to turn out to be the best market for our Farm."[44]

Shelburne Farms sold the pork, lamb, and wool locally. In the 1940s, the Farm found a market for its hogs with local farmers, a Burlington-based meat processor, and its own employees. From the late 1940s to the early 1960s, Verret's, a grocery store in Burlington, purchased much of Shelburne Farms' pork and lamb. The Farm's annual crop of spring lamb was especially popular among local residents.[45]

In 1942, the family partners further diversified their operations by establishing a flock of Hall Cross chickens to produce eggs and meat for the local market. David Tower consulted with both a poultry specialist at the University of Vermont and with R. S. Towers, the Southern Acres Farm employee responsible for Watson's small chicken operation. An initial flock of 500 chicks was purchased in early 1942 and another 500 acquired the following year. Between the early 1940s and late 1960s, employees Hector Beaudin (c. 1886–c. 1965) and John Boisvert (1911–94) maintained a flock averaging from 500 to 750 birds.[46]

With the acquisition of significant numbers of new livestock came the need for appropriate accommodations for them all. The farm buildings devoted to sheep, pigs, and poultry during Shelburne Farms' early years were no longer available to house the family partners' new stock. Watson now owned the former poultry barns at Quaker Smith Point and the Breeding Barn complex as part of his Southern Acres Farm, and he would acquire the Tracy Barn, once used for housing sheep, from Vanderbilt in 1944. The original piggery, owned by Vanderbilt, was dismantled by 1949.[47]

Therefore, Derick converted other underused barn spaces into appropriate housing for the new herds and flocks. Already the headquarters of the Angus and Hereford beef cattle, the Farm Barn also became the site of the new poultry operation. In 1942, when the chickens first arrived, the former paint and varnish rooms in the north wing of the building were converted into a new facility. Tower supervised the construction of coops and manure pits and the replacement of the original windows with others that provided better ventilation. The rooms' steam radiators were reconnected to the building's heating system to ensure that the fragile young chicks would stay warm. Later, the chickens were moved to the south wing of the Farm Barn, where a trap door was cut in the floor of one of the rooms so the manure could be easily shoveled into the bed of a truck below. In 1959, a new slaughtering facility to dispatch lambs and hogs was established in the south ell of the Farm Barn, and a cooler was installed to safely store the Farm's fresh meat.[48]

Crops

During the 1930s and 1940s, Vanderbilt, Frederica, and Derick supported their livestock with approximately 800 acres of pasturelands and 500 to 700 acres of croplands, which were planted with a variety of grasses and grains. In years of surplus, the family partners sold excess timothy, clover, and alfalfa hay to buyers in Vermont and Massachusetts. As their livestock holdings increased, and when their own harvest was light, they purchased some supplemental hay and grain. Derick later recalled, "I remember the whole of Main Drive [pasture] being in oats and barley…After the grain, you would rotate the alfalfa. Normal rotation would be six years: a year of corn, a year of oats, four years of hay and then you would plough up the hay and plant the corn. The grain was ground here at the Farm Barn."[49] Shelburne Farms also raised soybeans, squash, and carrots, the latter for the farm horses. Once harvested, the crops were stored in various sites around the property.[50]

Shelburne Farms participated in the Agricultural Conservation Program organized by the United States Department of Agriculture during the 1930s and 1940s. The program provided financial incentives to improve the quality of farm acreage by subsidizing the purchase of fertilizers and discouraging the planting of crops that exhausted soil productivity. Through the program, Derick

received superphosphate fertilizer, which he applied to the Farm's crop- and pasturelands.[51]

Continuing a trend that dated to the 1920s, Shelburne Farms relied on a combination of farm horses, tractors, and trucks to cultivate the land through the mid-1940s. Derick recalled harvesting grain using horse-drawn equipment in 1936:

That reminds me of one of the other jobs I had that summer of 1936, and that was stooking or shocking the grain. It was all cut by a teamster who drove three horses ahead of a reaper and binder. It was cut and bound in bundles which were scattered all over the ground. You had to go and set those bundles up, six in a pile so that the wind could blow through the 'tunnel.'[52]

In 1937, Tower reported that the Farm owned six teams of horses. However, with the exception of a brief hiatus taken during the Second World War, the family partners invested more and more in mechanized equipment. As tractors and trucks became more powerful and reliable, the benefits of using teams of horses to pull farm equipment and wagons decreased. Although motorized farm vehicles required a larger capital investment, they proved to be more efficient in terms of labor costs and required less outlay for maintenance than horses. Unlike horses, which required regular exercise, vehicles could be placed in storage for months at a time when not needed. By the start of the Second World War, Derick kept only a few work horses on the Farm, mostly to perform tasks that could not be done well with vehicles, such as rounding up cattle in the fields and logging trees in the winter. He would completely phase out horses by the mid-1940s.[53]

Farm Management

As a result of their new enterprises, and the able management team of Derick Webb and David Tower, the family partners were able to slightly improve Shelburne Farms' financial situation from its worst performances of the 1920s and early 1930s. However, the property remained very much a family estate and, by the mid-1940s, was only slightly closer to the long-term goal of self-sufficiency.

Left: Haying at Shelburne Farms, c. 1950. Shelburne Farms Collections.

In the mid to late 1930s, although Shelburne Farms was still receiving up to $20,000 a year from the Webb family, decreased dairy revenue obligated Tower to borrow several thousand additional dollars from a local bank to cover payroll and other regular expenses. During this time, in order to improve the Farm's financial standing, allow it to pay off some bank loans, and pay for the initial purchase of beef cattle, Vanderbilt borrowed $15,000 in his own name and lent the cash to the Farm.[54]

The operation began to show limited financial improvement by 1944, after several years of heavy monetary support from Vanderbilt and Frederica while the new livestock concerns were established. That year, Vanderbilt and Frederica contributed at least $11,000 to Shelburne Farms. Although this amount represented a decrease of several thousand dollars from the poorest years of the 1930s, it was still a large financial commitment. In November, 1944, Vanderbilt offered to buy out Frederica's interests to relieve her of the financial and managerial burden of the property: "As you know, I am always somewhat concerned as to whether you really want to continue going along with the farm in this way on a fifty-fifty basis, and as you also know I am entirely willing to assume the necessary expense myself, if you would prefer it this way, as I feel that the money is well spent."[55]

Vanderbilt saw his financial support for Shelburne Farms as a worthy public service, much like his parents had viewed their model farm activities. Frederica apparently agreed, as she declined Vanderbilt's offer, and their joint partnership continued until her death in 1949. However, in 1946, she sold Vanderbilt more than 400 acres of her Shelburne Farms holdings, a transaction that may well have been completed in order to reduce her level of direct responsibility and tax burden.[56]

During the eighteen years Derick spent working for his father and aunt at Shelburne Farms, he proved himself to be a capable farm manager, able to juggle the various agricultural operations, improve the Farm's financial health, and win the respect of those in his employ. He remained in constant touch with all of the Farm's activities and labored alongside his employees every day. In May 1941, he wrote to Vanderbilt,

> *Dear Father, It's 9:15 PM, & has been a good busy day. Thought you would be amused and interested to hear briefly what can be missed on a Sunday in spring—and what can happen on a Monday—*
> *Sunday—1 new Angus calf*
>   *14 more pigs*
> *Monday—Started harrowing at 4 AM*
>   *Finished planting 20 acres corn 9 PM*
>   *2 more Angus calves*
>   *3 more Hereford calves*
> *Plus miscellaneous…P.S. I think I'll sleep tonight!*[57]

Derick's son Marshall later recalled that his father "was just as much of a farm hand as any of the other men, milking several times a week and operating equipment on a daily basis. He didn't lose the smell of manure until he went into the [state] legislature in the late 50's."[58]

Derick thrived at Shelburne Farms, and he had decided to make a career of his work on the property by 1942. He wrote his father in September of that year: "In regard to the work here, I'd like to take this opportunity of saying that regardless of the ties of family, inheritance, etc., it's a lot of fun and darn satisfying to work for you."[59] His parents felt similarly. In 1947, Aileen wrote Derick, "It makes us so happy to have you at Shelburne and to know such a beautiful place will be carried on. It is almost an anachronism in this day and age, but it needn't be feudal in character and if it can be developed in an increasingly cooperative way it should continue to flourish & expand."[60]

The Home Estate: Residence of Vanderbilt and Aileen Webb

After Lila Webb's death in 1936, Vanderbilt acquired ownership of the Home Estate section of Shelburne Farms. He assumed full responsibility for Shelburne House, the formal gardens, the golf links, and the greenhouses in 1939.

Shelburne House

Between 1938 and 1956, Vanderbilt, his wife Aileen, and members of their family spent a portion of each summer in residence at Shelburne House. Aileen often stayed during the months of June, July, and August, and Vanderbilt typically spent his month-long vacation there and commuted up from New York on other summer weekends. They welcomed Lila's former butler, Walter Woodgate, and his wife, Ellen, who, though officially retired, spent their summers living in their old quarters in the annex building through the 1950s.[61]

Vanderbilt and Aileen cherished their time at Shelburne. Aileen recalled, "Shelburne seemed like a beautiful Shangri-la of our own. One could never tire of its beauty, no matter how long one lived."[62]

Although their personal wealth did not reach the heights Seward and Lila had enjoyed, the Vanderbilt Webbs were quite affluent. In addition to Vanderbilt's law income and the inheritance he received from Lila, Aileen possessed a substantial trust provided by her aunt. However, compared to their parents, Vanderbilt and Aileen led a relatively informal life. They divided their time among three residences and employed a butler and several other domestic employees, but they eschewed many of the extravagances that Vanderbilt especially had experienced as a child and young adult. In 1977, toward the end of her life, Aileen reflected, "Van took his family's way of life for granted, but saw as he grew older the false premises on which it had thrived. We, ourselves, always lived comfortably, and nowadays although it would be called luxuriously, to our families' eyes we were living most circumspectly."[63]

Vanderbilt and Aileen chose not to spend substantial sums on Shelburne House. The few changes they made were designed to facilitate use of the house during the summer season only and consolidate their living and service areas into a smaller portion of the building. In 1977, Aileen stated,

The house has changed extraordinarily little…The hall is still as it was; the library still beautiful; and the big dining-room, magnificent. The only real change Van and I effected when we moved in after Mrs. [Lila] Webb's death was that we turned the corridor hall area into a lovely dining-room with family portraits and furniture against blue and white walls. During the 14 summers we ran the house I did over a bedroom a year, and now the house has a somewhat genteel and faded look, but is still livable and lovely. Dr. Webb's workrooms and study became the kitchen and pantry.[64]

As part of her transformation of the corridor hall space into a dining room, Aileen had the decorative dentils removed from the room's coffered ceiling in an effort to modernize the appearance of the space. Seward Webb Sr.'s former office and personal storage area on the first floor were converted into a new kitchen and pantry space in 1939. This renovation provided the family with much-needed modern kitchen equipment. It also resulted in a more efficient use of service spaces by their household staff, which represented a significantly smaller force than Seward and Lila had employed.[65]

Vanderbilt and Aileen removed one major original component of Shelburne House: the iron and glass conservatory attached to the dining room, which had been built to display potted palms and other exotic plants in the Victorian style. Always expensive to maintain, the structure had suffered repeated damage over the years during the region's severe winters. David Tower described the situation in November 1936: "I would also suggest that we purchase a canvas to be put over the wire screen of the conservatory roof, to prevent snow falling through the screen and breaking windows, and then melting and the water running into the dining room, which has always happened every winter."[66] The structure was dismantled during the winter of 1941 or spring of 1942, and the opening leading from the dining room into the former conservatory was subsequently filled in with brick and sheetrock.[67]

With their smaller domestic staff and new kitchen facilities, Vanderbilt and Aileen also chose not to invest in maintaining the servants' wing or the several service outbuildings that stood nearby. After deeming a contractor's estimate to demolish the servants' wing too expensive, they left the structure standing but chose not to maintain it. The garbage house was dismantled in the spring of 1942, and the nearby laundry/icehouse structure was allowed to deteriorate. Over the next twenty years, between the early 1940s and the early 1960s, the servants' wing and outbuildings would fall into serious disrepair.[68]

Greenhouses, Golf Links, and Formal Gardens

Even before Lila's estate had been settled and the Home Estate section of Shelburne Farms formally deeded to Vanderbilt, the four Webb siblings had concluded that the greenhouses were an extravagance none of them could afford. Family members staying at Shelburne Farms and Southern Acres Farm required significantly less fresh produce than had previously been raised, and the costs of shipping items to Webbs located elsewhere were prohibitive. As Watson noted in 1937, most of the fruits and vegetables they consumed could "be bought more cheaply than raised" on the Farm.[69] In addition, many of the flower varieties raised in previous years did not meet the tastes of the current generation.

However, the siblings felt some loyalty toward aging head gardener Alexander Graham (1864–1944), who had been employed by the family since 1895. Watson wrote, "Were it not for Graham all of us agree we would close the garden entirely, with possibly some one to look after grapes when needed, & a few melons."[70] After Lila Webb's death, the remaining flowers and produce planted at the greenhouses for the 1936 season were sold to the local market as a way to dispose of them. At the end of 1938, the family decided to discontinue the growing of all flowers, fruits, and vegetables in the greenhouses and its adjoining outdoor garden plots. Graham was given a pension of $75 a month and the use of the gardener's cottage, with heat and electricity included, for the rest of his life. He died six years later, at the age of eighty, having spent forty-three years working at Shelburne Farms. David Tower was charged with selling the remaining greenhouse structures, which were purchased by a Shelburne nursery in 1940 for $100.[71]

Unlike the greenhouse operation, the fate of the formal gardens and golf links was left to Vanderbilt and Aileen. At least initially, they decided to maintain both. The links continued to be enjoyed each summer by the couple, their children, Woodgate, Watson, and other family members. A new tractor with a power mower attachment, purchased for the course shortly before Lila died, kept the course in excellent playing condition while decreasing labor needs.[72]

A passionate gardener, Aileen happily oversaw the Shelburne House gardens. During the 1940s and 1950s, she continued efforts begun in the 1920s to make the garden plantings hardier and less labor-intensive. She also adjusted Lila's planting schemes to meet her own tastes. Aileen replaced some of the perennials and annuals in the grande allée and rose garden sections with yew hedges and hostas, among other plants, and she introduced roses to a former lawn area near the peony bed.[73]

In addition to her gardening skills, Aileen was also a painter, wood sculptor, and potter. Each summer, she used two outbuildings near Shelburne House as studios. She converted the original teahouse, located on the northeastern boundary of Saxton's Point, into a painting studio that she called "Waveledge." In the 1940s, she also used an existing small one-story building, located just behind the annex structure, as a pottery studio.[74]

An early advocate for American crafts, Aileen founded Putnam County Products in 1932 to give impoverished women in the Garrison, New York, area a venue to sell their sewing, quilting, hooked rugs, and other crafts. In the late 1930s, Aileen hosted a gathering of crafts advocates at Shelburne House, during which "the first national organization of United States craftsmen was formed under the name of the Handcraft Cooperative League of America."[75] She would go on to found the American Craft Council, the School of American Craftsmen, the American Craft Museum, and the World Crafts Council. She served as chairman of the American Craft Council's board of trustees from 1958 to 1976.[76]

Frederica Jones at Sled Runner Point, 1939–1948

When Lila Webb's Shelburne Farms property was divided among her four children in 1939, Frederica received approximately 1,000 acres of land on Shelburne Point to the north and east of the core estate. Frederica's new holdings included the Bay View farmhouse and a smaller, nearby dwelling called Bay View Cottage. Once envisioned as a possible seasonal residence for Vanderbilt or Seward Jr., the main Bay View House was then in severe disrepair.

Frederica's decision to obtain this section of the estate likely resulted from her desire to build her own seasonal residence on a piece of the property known as Sled Runner Point. In fact, she and her second husband, Cyril Jones, had conceived the idea of constructing a house there by early 1938, more than a year before they were officially deeded the land.

A promontory jutting into the bay on the eastern side of Shelburne Point, Sled Runner Point had been purchased by Seward and Lila Webb from the Collamer family in 1899. The Joneses commissioned architect Frederick Rhinelander King of the New York City firm Wyeth & King to design their new house, a rambling brick structure with French style accents. The Webb family's regular local contractor of the time, Charles Congdon of Burlington, constructed the residence. To keep track of the work, the Joneses lived in a section of Shelburne House in the summer of 1938. They moved in to their new home in the autumn, and the house's finishing touches were completed by the fall of 1939. The following year, Frederica and Cyril built a two-bedroom guest cottage nearby.[77]

Between 1939 and 1948, the Joneses spent several weeks to several months in residence each spring and summer on Sled Runner Point. They hired John Botala Sr. (1898–1947) to maintain the grounds and look after their property each season, sharing employment of him with Shelburne Farms.

Cyril and Frederica (Webb) Jones, winter of 1940–41. Shelburne Farms Collections.

After the Joneses departed for their main residence in Massachusetts each fall, Botala returned to work for the Farm until the Joneses returned the following spring or summer. Botala, his wife, and their eight children occupied Bay View Cottage.[78]

Over the years, Frederica substantially reduced her land holdings in Shelburne. With the blessing of her siblings, she sold a ninety-four-acre parcel in the northern section of Shelburne Point in 1940. The parcel, which included the then dilapidated Captain White house, was purchased by Archibald and Mary Brown, family friends of Vanderbilt and Aileen's from Maryland. Mrs. Brown's sister would later become Derick's wife. Following the precedent established by her parents when they sold a small adjoining piece of Shelburne Point property in 1910, Frederica stipulated that the Browns could use their property only as a private residence. This ensured that the character of Shelburne Point would change little despite a transfer of ownership outside the Webb family. Additionally, Frederica sold 400 acres on the southern boundary of her lands to her brother Vanderbilt, the adjoining landowner, in 1946.[79]

Southern Acres

Through the 1930s and 1940s, the main Shelburne Farms estate experienced a number of changes. At Southern Acres, however, the same time period was largely one of continuity. Watson and Electra continued to divide their time among their homes in New York City, Long Island, and Southern Acres, spending additional time at Nehasane once Watson was officially deeded the Adirondack estate in 1939. Watson shuttled constantly between the properties, traveling up to Shelburne or Nehasane for most weekends.

Southern Acres Farm

At Southern Acres, Watson continued his ventures in beef cattle, sheep, chickens, hunters, and foxhounds into the 1950s. Despite occasional problems with distemper outbreaks and fox shortages, his foxhounds and terriers continued to garner prizes at competitions such as the Bryn Mawr Dog Show and the Hound Show at Madison Square Garden, and his dogs were sought after by buyers in Massachusetts, Virginia, Colorado, Long Island, Kansas, and Canada. Watson also sold several hounds to the venerable Pau Hunt in France from 1919 to 1940. In 1952, a former Long Island huntsman who had purchased a number of dogs from Watson wrote: "All the years I was Huntsman it was the Shelburne hounds blood that won on the

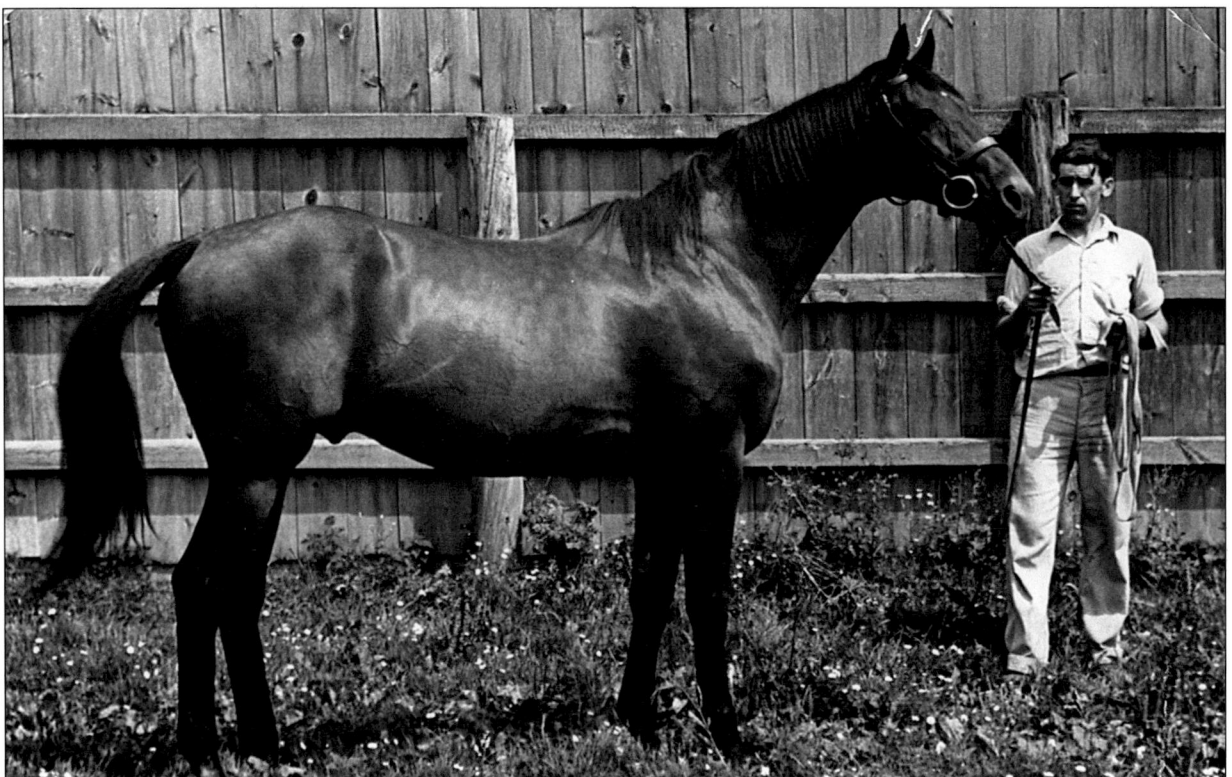

Southern Acres Farm's Star of Gold, c. 1950. Shelburne Farms Collections.

bench and in the field…and I owe you all the praise for my success, as the first real hounds we had…came from you."[80]

With the exception of a short hiatus taken during the Second World War, Watson continued to stage the Shelburne Hunt each fall. His wife, Electra, their children, in-laws, and other Webb relatives joined him at times. However, as the 1930s and 1940s progressed, the frequency of the fox hunts dwindled. Watson was sometimes compelled to return to New York during the hunting season to attend to his insurance business, and of his children, nephews, and nieces, only his son Harry (1922–75) showed a strong interest in hunting. In fact, in 1941, Watson wrote, "Were it not for Harry I'd definitely give it up."[81]

During the 1930s and 1940s, Watson's Hereford beef cattle herd was his main source of agricultural income. Like the family partners at Shelburne Farms, Watson sold the excess young stock from his breeding herd each year and occasionally imported feeder steers from the western United States. He also found a local market for his young bulls, which were purchased by other breeders to augment their stock. On Watson's behalf, herdsman Alec Morrison often traveled west to purchase cattle, met with prospective buyers at Southern Acres, and accompanied animals to cattle shows to be sold.[82]

Like Vanderbilt and Frederica at Shelburne Farms, Watson contributed large sums to support Southern Acres financially each year. He considered his estate a private affair rather than a strictly commercial one, and he had no real plans to transform Southern Acres into a self-sufficient operation. Watson's portion of the shared inheritance from his mother's estate made him an extremely wealthy man, and he could well afford to support the farm in a manner of his choosing despite an increasingly unpredictable income stream from his insurance business. Southern Acres remained a source of intense personal pleasure to Watson, an outlet for his passion for agriculture and a refuge away from his career and the city life it entailed. Little made him happier than training hunters, fox hunting, and working on farm repairs with the assistance of George Edward "Eddie" Steen (1904–79), one of his longtime employees.[83]

However, like his brother and sister, Watson continued to weigh the costs of the venture against its benefits. He expressed concern from time to time about the estate's limited income and its mounting financial requirements as a result of increasing employee and capital expenses. However, as long as Southern Acres remained a source of personal pleasure, and a home that he and his family enjoyed, he felt that its costs were by and large worth the effort. In fact, when Watson found himself stretched thin between his responsibilities in New York, Long Island, the Adirondacks, and Shelburne, he chose to trim expenses at Westbury, his least favorite estate, rather than Southern Acres. As time went on, Watson spent less and less time at Westbury and eventually persuaded Electra to sell the property. In the late 1930s, they gave some acreage at Westbury to their daughters, Electra and Lila, and sold an additional parcel to their niece Frederica, daughter of Seward Jr. Watson closed the Westbury stables in 1943.[84]

At the same time that Watson and Electra were reducing the size and scope of their Westbury estate in Long Island, they were increasing their property in Shelburne. In 1932, they acquired 400 acres of adjoining farmland to the south. And in 1944, they purchased a small parcel of land containing the Tracy Barn from Vanderbilt, thus adding to Watson's holdings in the area of the Breeding Barn complex and simplifying the boundary line between Shelburne Farms and Southern Acres Farm in that area of the property.[85]

Bostwick Farm and Quaker Smith Point

In the early to mid-1930s, Watson and Electra began to consider making provisions for their children at Southern Acres. In fact, they may have acquired the 400 acres of property in 1932 at least in part for their eldest daughter, Electra (1910–82), who married Dunbar Bostwick (1908–2006) in June of that year. As a wedding present, the elder Webbs gave Electra and Dunbar 18 of the 400 acres, which consisted of the former Fletcher family farm located just south of Southern Acres on the shores of Lake Champlain. Watson renovated the farmhouse on the property, installed a new water system, and added a stable building for his daughter and son-in-law.[86]

Over the next fifteen years, the Bostwicks enlarged their property to more than 400 acres by purchasing adjoining parcels totaling eighty-eight acres from Shelburne Farms and Southern Acres Farm, plus substantial acreage to the south. They raised Vermont Standardbred trotters and Holstein and Hereford cattle on their new estate, first named "South End" and later referred to as "Bostwick Farm." One of their horses, Nibble Hanover, set a world record in a trotting race and was later in great demand for stud services. An aviation enthusiast, Dunbar also cleared an airstrip and built a hangar on the property. After the original Fletcher farmhouse was destroyed by fire in 1950, the Bostwicks built a new residence on the same site. Although the couple divided their time among Shelburne, South Carolina, and New York, they spent substantial periods of time at Bostwick Farm with their growing family, which eventually included four daughters.[87]

In 1935, Watson and Electra gave their eldest son, Sam (1912–88), the use of the main farmhouse at Quaker Smith Point with the understanding that the house and the forty-five acres that surrounded it would eventually become his inherited portion of Southern Acres Farm. Sam married Elizabeth ("Betty") Johnson (1914–90) in June of that year, and the young couple eventually had two children. Although they were based in New York, where Sam worked in his father's insurance business and their children attended school, Sam and Betty returned frequently to the former Smith family farmhouse, which they renovated and expanded. An avid hunter and fisherman, Sam added a "Trophy Room" extension to the house in about 1936 to showcase his and his parents' hunting trophies and constructed a substantial addition to the dwelling in 1947. That same year, Sam acquired from Vanderbilt and Aileen, for $1, an adjoining parcel of sixty-eight acres to the north comprising the western portion of what was known as Windmill Hill. The transaction included the stipulation that Derick and his children possessed right of first refusal on a future sale and could repurchase the parcel for $1 if it was ever offered for sale. Watson continued to use several agricultural buildings on Quaker Smith Point for Southern Acres Farm until he officially deeded the property to Sam in 1949.[88]

Community and Collaboration

The 1939 transfer of Shelburne Farms from the corporation, in which Watson shared interest and responsibility, to the private ownership of Vanderbilt and Frederica brought an end to most of Southern Acres Farm's historic dependence on Shelburne Farms for labor, equipment, and other support. Although the two establishments continued to share a few direct links, such as Watson's purchase of water and electricity from Shelburne Farms and joint

The Smith family house at Quaker Smith Point, c. 1900. It became the residence of Samuel B. Webb Sr. in the 1930s. Shelburne Farms Collections.

road maintenance costs, the two estates existed as primarily separate and independent operations by the late 1930s.

However, the owners and managers of Shelburne Farms, Southern Acres, and Bostwick Farm maintained close contact with one another and fostered a sense of neighborly community and collaboration between the operations. Throughout the 1930s and 1940s, Watson, Vanderbilt, Frederica, Derick, and Dunbar saw each other frequently in Shelburne and New York, gathering for meals, talks, and golf games, meeting at services held at the Trinity Church in Shelburne, racing sail boats against each other on Lake Champlain on Sunday afternoons during the summer, and traveling up and back on the train together.[89]

Their similar ventures in livestock and crops resulted in an amicable sharing of information, resources, and advice. Indeed, the conflicts that existed between Shelburne Farms and Southern Acres Farm during the years of the Shelburne Farms Corporation seem to have been resolved. The owners and managers of Shelburne Farms, Southern Acres, and Bostwick Farm often visited each other's properties to view new livestock additions, building alterations, and the progress of various crops. Throughout the 1930s and 1940s, the three farms bought and sold cattle from each other, and the managers referred potential buyers to each other when they themselves were unable to satisfy inquiries. During the dairy troubles of the late 1930s, Frederica, Vanderbilt, Derick, and Dunbar discussed the possibility of collaborating on dairy contracts to provide each party with additional security in times of lower milk production. Arrangements for any labor and materials that were shared between the operations were completed in a businesslike manner; Watson paid Shelburne Farms to grind grains for his livestock and rented a few pieces of farm equipment from his siblings on occasion. Thus, they were able to "keep the money in the family," as Watson phrased it.[90]

World War II

The Second World War would affect Shelburne Farms and the Webb family to an even greater extent than did the First World War. In the minds of many family members, the agricultural operations at Shelburne Farms and Southern Acres Farm became an even more significant public service, producing large quantities of food to sustain the local population and providing essential jobs to employees who could not join the armed forces, or were not interested in doing so. The property also seemed like an oasis of calm, continuity, and beauty in an increasingly frightening and ugly world. As Seward's wife, Gertrude, wrote to Tower in the midst of the war, "We're all looking forward so happily to another summer at Shelburne. With the whole world in such chaos it seems so peaceful and beautiful there."[91]

The earliest effects of World War II reached Shelburne Farms some time before the United States officially entered the conflict in December 1941. By 1940, Frederica was hosting volunteer gatherings to benefit the Red Cross and the war charity Bundles for Britain, organizing family members, farm employees, and local residents in making clothing for European soldiers and civilians. In 1940, Vanderbilt and Aileen gave permission for the volunteers to use the north room and dining room at Shelburne House for their operation. The following year, the work was moved to Bay View House on Frederica's property, where it remained for the duration of the war. While the aging farmhouse remained unsuitable for regular, year-round occupancy, it served well as a seasonal site for volunteer work.[92]

The war also brought the Seward Webb family back to Shelburne Farms on a seasonal basis. In the spring of 1941, Seward and Gertrude abandoned their plans to travel to South America because of the elevating conflict abroad, and Vanderbilt and Aileen invited them to stay at Shelburne House that summer. During the next five years, the two families would share the house for the summer months. Vanderbilt and Aileen resided in the southern and central portions of the dwelling, and Seward and Gertrude occupied the north wing. Walls with doors were constructed on each floor at the junctures of the two portions of the house, resulting in two distinct households with separate living, sleeping, and service areas.[93]

At some point during the war years, Vanderbilt concluded that it was unlikely that Shelburne House would ever be occupied during the winter, spring, or fall, when heat was needed in the building. The poor condition of the two aging main coal-fired boilers, increasing coal shortages, and restrictions on pleasure travel likely prompted this assessment. As a result, one of the main boilers was removed and donated to the war effort as scrap metal. Although the second boiler and other elements of the heating system remained in place until 1986, the house was never heated again after the early to mid-1940s.[94]

Like numerous Americans, the Webbs and their employees established victory gardens to supply their own fresh vegetables during the war. Shelburne Farms employees were given the opportunity to cultivate their own gardens on the now defunct garden plots adjoining the greenhouses. Seward established a large garden for his family and Vanderbilt's at the base of the Shelburne House lawn, near the ninth hole of the golf links. He grew peas, beans, beets, carrots, sweet corn, spinach, cucumbers, squash, pumpkins, onions, parsley, and radishes, some of which he canned for off-season consumption. Frederica and Cyril grew a similar selection of produce at their garden at Sled Runner Point, which was maintained by their employee John Botala. In addition to his large vegetable garden on Quaker Smith Point, Sam Webb also raised chickens for his family's consumption.[95]

The fear of possible invasion by enemy forces reached even the sanctuary of Shelburne Farms. A lookout station was constructed atop Lone Tree Hill, the highest point in the vicinity, so volunteers could keep watch for a possible air attack. Members of the Webb family, their employees, employees' families, and local residents worked in shifts to staff the station, which consisted of a small shelter containing binoculars and a telephone with which the authorities could be contacted should something suspicious be spotted. The interior of the shelter was papered with images of enemy aircraft to assist volunteers with identifying them. Luckily, the threat never materialized.[96]

Soon after the United States entered the war in late 1941, numerous family members and employees joined the war effort. As Aileen later wrote, "Our life changed radically in short order. There was no question in any of our minds that we must all sacrifice our personal desires for the

W. Seward Webb Jr. gardening, c. 1945. Shelburne Farms Collections.

sake of all."⁹⁷ Several members of the Webb family entered military service, including Vanderbilt and Aileen's three sons, Derick, Richard, and Osborn ("Obbie"); Watson and Electra's sons Sam and Harry and sons-in-law, Dunbar Bostwick and John Wilmerding; and Seward's son Jacob ("Jake") and son-in-law David Gamble. Vanderbilt and Aileen's son-in-law, H. Benson Rockwell, spent a short time building PT boats for the United States Navy in a Rhode Island shipyard. Watson Jr. took a hiatus from editing films at Twentieth Century Fox Film Corporation to work on two films for the Army Signal Corps. Seward Webb III was also involved in producing training films for the military. Watson Sr. himself sought to reactivate his military standing, dormant since the end of the First World War, but he failed the routine physical examination after the discovery of a heart murmur. His wife, Electra, threw herself into war work, leading the Civil Defense Volunteers Office of Information and War Activities Center and then becoming the Director of Blood Donor Development in New York for the Red Cross. Watson Sr. voiced the apprehensions of many when he wrote in his diary in 1942, "It just hurts so, everything one cares about is going, going, going, & soon it will be family in action. I just dread the future now."⁹⁸

Shelburne Farms, Southern Acres Farm, and Bostwick Farm were all deeply affected by labor shortages. Shelburne Farms and Bostwick Farm both lost their managers. In the spring of 1941, before the United States joined the war, Derick worked in Washington, D.C., and New York for the Committee to Defend America by Aiding the Allies, returning to the Farm on weekends. Although his poor eyesight exempted him from the draft, Derick volunteered for service after the United States entered the war. He was first assigned to study Norwegian at the University of Minnesota in preparation for a planned Allied invasion through Norway. From 1942 to 1946, after the Norwegian invasion was cancelled, Derick served in an army military police unit stationed in the United States, Europe, and the Pacific. Meanwhile, Dunbar served in the Army Air Force from 1942 to 1945. He was involved in the planning of the 1944 Allied invasion of Normandy.⁹⁹

Numerous employees of the three operations and their children either enlisted, were drafted, or left for employment at companies directly involved in defense work. David Tower's two sons, Winfield and Arunah, both left to fight. Teamster Wallace Coleman resigned after more than fifteen years at Shelburne Farms to work at Vermont Structural Steel in Burlington, and his son Robert Coleman, who had also worked for the Farm, served in the army. Watson's chauffeur and carpenter Eddie Steen took a leave of absence to train pilots in Burlington. Webb family members understood and appreciated their employees' decisions and supported them whether they left Shelburne or remained there to help with food production. However, as more and more men left, the labor shortages became severe. As Derick wrote to the Shelburne Farms staff soon after the United States entered the war,

*The last thing I want to do is to influence what in the end must be your own decision. Nevertheless my advice is not to forget the importance of your job. Each man here now is helping to produce food. In fact there is quite a lot of food walking around on four legs. I hope we will continue to produce even more. If there are individuals who say that staying on the farm is being a slacker, they are woefully short-sighted. I should like to tell them that their talk does not help anyone.*¹⁰⁰

Amazingly, only two of those connected with Shelburne Farms, Southern Acres, or Bostwick Farm who fought in the war are known to have died in service or sustained serious injuries. Henry Edgarton, a young man who worked at Shelburne Farms during the summer of 1942, was killed in

Derick Webb and his new wife, Elizabeth (Canfield), 1945. Shelburne Farms Collections.

action later that year. And Vanderbilt and Aileen's son Richard was seriously wounded in Italy in 1943.[101]

Only skeleton crews were left behind to maintain the agricultural operations at Shelburne Farms, Southern Acres Farm, and Bostwick Farm. Between 1942 and 1946, Derick was able to return to Shelburne Farms only for brief furloughs. However, he remained in close contact with David Tower, advising him on agricultural affairs via correspondence. Tower temporarily increased his responsibilities to compensate for Derick's absence, becoming the Farm's "General Superintendent," and Vanderbilt also assumed more day-to-day oversight. As Vanderbilt wrote in 1944, "I have been taking a much more active part during the past year in the operation of our farm here, due to the fact that my son, Derick Webb, who usually runs it, has been in the army."[102] Along with two of their close friends, Vanderbilt and Aileen worked in the fields themselves daily for two or three months each summer harvesting hay. They were responsible for mowing, raking, and transporting loads of hay in a horse-drawn wagon and farm trucks.[103]

Tower appealed to the local draft board several times on behalf of Shelburne Farms' employees, arguing that their farm work was an essential war service that should exempt them from military service. At times his arguments were successful, but on other occasions they were not. As a result, the remaining farm employees worked more overtime, and young men attending Cyril Jones's Milton Academy in Massachusetts were hired to help during at least one summer.[104]

With these stopgap measures, Shelburne Farms was able to maintain most of its prewar level of production. Everyone was conscious that their extra efforts would contribute to the success of the Allies in the war. As Derick wrote to Shelburne Farms staff members in 1942, food produced at Shelburne Farms and sold to consumers in Vermont and New England would free up supplies for those serving in the war:

> *Remember that everyone on Shelburne Farms is doing an important war job. Our crops are being turned into milk, meat, and eggs—high-protein foods for men at the front and civilian defense workers at home. Each extra forkful of hay or manure, and each extra bundle of corn or grain, will mean another glass of milk, another piece of steak, or perhaps another slice of bacon for a man at the front. Let's keep things going.*[105]

Southern Acres and Bostwick Farm experienced similar situations. Watson was torn between his insurance work in New York, which had increased as his son Sam and other employees had left the business to serve, and his duties at Southern Acres, where he was also plagued with labor shortages. When his farm manager, Thomas Patterson, left for another position in the spring of 1943, Watson scrambled to find a replacement. He noted in his diary, "Tough on me. Hard to get anyone new these days…Shel[burne] is now a worry instead of a pleasure & rest as it used to be."[106] Watson also performed some additional physical tasks, such as seasonal maintenance on the Brick House and assisting with grain harvesting, to free employees for other work. In the spring of 1944, Watson noted that the Brick House grounds were looking "very shabby. The war & can't be helped."[107]

After Dunbar Bostwick left to fight, Watson also assisted his daughter Electra in overseeing the operations at Bostwick Farm and supervising the Bostwick employees. Watson instructed his Southern Acres staff to "work together and cooperate as much as possible" with their counterparts at Bostwick Farm, which included assisting with harvests and combining errands to save time and gas.[108]

Wartime rations and other restrictions also impacted the Webb family properties in Shelburne. Prohibitions on nonessential travel made it difficult at times for the Webbs to get to Shelburne. Watson postponed trips on occasion, and Vanderbilt resorted to extreme measures to have a car at Shelburne in the summer months. His grandson Marshall Webb later recalled, "Every summer John Boisvert would drive Van's 1940 Buick convertible up from Garrison [New York]. He would save gas coupons in the winter to have enough fuel for the journey, but even so, he had to turn off the motor and coast down every hill to make it to Shelburne."[109]

Tire and gasoline shortages, the rationing of new farm equipment, and the scarcity of spare parts led both Shelburne Farms and Southern Acres Farm to temporarily reduce their reliance on trucks and tractors and increase their use of farm horses once again. Watson spent hours repairing previously retired sets of harnesses so they could be used again. In November 1942, Derick wrote to Tower to inquire if he was "using trucks as little as possible & are all trucks not in use on blocks to save tires?"[110]

Webb family members and farm employees fared better than many in terms of food rationing due to the availability of items raised in Shelburne. In Massachusetts, Frederica and Cyril found it difficult to obtain meat in 1945 and appealed to Tower to supply them with eggs and chicken from Shelburne Farms throughout that year. Even after the war officially ended, Shelburne Farms was able to obtain exemptions from some ongoing commodity rations for its employees by citing its role as a provider of essential food supplies. In July 1946, Tower appealed to the state Office of Price Administration for a continued supply of a greater amount of sugar, stating,

> *Due to the shortage of farm labor for the past few years we have been forced to work our employees overtime during haying and harvest, serving them lunches at 5:00 P.M. Serving lunches to twelve men three or four times a week up to about the first of November and we have been allowed twenty five pounds of sugar each year for these lunches, and would ask please if it will be possible for us to get this same allowance of sugar this harvesting season.*[111]

During the war, Webb family members curtailed several estate activities due to labor shortages, rations, other restrictions, and a desire to reduce personal activities that had begun to feel like extravagances. Watson suspended the Shelburne Hunt from 1943 to 1946, noting that he "had no heart for it."[112] As a result, he reduced the size of his kennels and the number of hunters in his stables. He also laid off at least one staff person.[113]

The golf links near Shelburne House proved to be a more lasting casualty. In the spring of 1942,

Derick and Vanderbilt decided to cease maintaining its greens because of gasoline and labor shortages. The links quickly became overgrown. Watson played the last recorded rounds on the course in May and June, 1942. On June 1st, he reported, "Course very poor & rough."[114] The land was eventually reclaimed as crop- and pastureland by Shelburne Farms.

The end of the war in August 1945 was greeted with celebration in Shelburne. As Watson wrote in his diary, it was "wonderful to think this frightful war is over."[115] He gave all his employees a day off the next day.[116]

CHAPTER 13

THE POSTWAR YEARS

"If you are thinking of a pen stable the Webb Estate comes the closest to being an ideal layout of any I have seen…Certainly here is a farm building layout of modern design that Mr. Webb can well be proud of."

— BYRON E. COLBY, *PROCEEDINGS OF THE NEW YORK FARMERS*, C. 1953[1]

THE POSTWAR YEARS USHERED IN A NEW ERA for Shelburne Farms and Southern Acres, one in which the ownership and management of the Webb properties would be transferred to the third generation of the family. As Seward and Lila Webb's children grew older and began to think about the future of their estates in Shelburne, several of their own children expressed a strong interest in keeping the acreages intact and assuming more responsibility for them. The late 1940s, the 1950s, and the 1960s brought the deaths of all four members of the second generation of the Webb family and modifications to the properties that reflected the abilities and interests of the third generation.

SHELBURNE FARMS

Vanderbilt's son Derick had played an active role in the management of Shelburne Farms for years, and he was a logical choice to succeed his father and aunt as owner of the Farm. Derick's siblings had all established their own careers and families elsewhere. After the Second World War, Osborn (1914–2002) worked for the Central Intelligence Agency in Washington, D.C., and then moved to Palm Beach, Florida, where he became a stockbroker. Richard (b. 1921) settled in Sunapee, New Hampshire, where he established a farm and large forestry enterprise. Their sister, Barbara (1916–91), and her husband, Henry Benson Rockwell (1915–74), were busy raising four children and teaching at two private secondary schools, first the Pomfret School in Connecticut and then the Putney School in southern Vermont.[2]

After returning from military service in 1946, Derick resumed his role as farm manager at Shelburne Farms. During the late 1940s and the 1950s, he effectively took full control of the farm operations as first Frederica and then Vanderbilt experienced failing health and died.

During the 1940s, Frederica and her husband Cyril returned to Sled Runner Point less and less frequently, and for shorter periods of time. Frederica had been afflicted with respiratory, arthritis, and heart problems for a number of years, and her poor health resulted in several hospitalizations and long respites in Tucson, Arizona. After suffering two heart attacks in the summer of 1945, her health deteriorated rapidly. Frederica returned to Shelburne for the last time in the summer of 1948 and passed away in Tucson the following February. She was sixty-six years old.[3]

Frederica bequeathed all of her property in Shelburne to her husband Cyril, who returned to Sled Runner Point periodically through at least 1953. He eventually sold all of the property he and his wife had owned on Shelburne Point, most to other Webb family members. Vanderbilt acquired two parcels south of Sled Runner Point, including Bay View House, in 1952 and 1954 and transferred ownership of them to his son Derick shortly thereafter. In 1953, Watson's son Harry purchased some additional acreage on Shelburne Point. The Sled Runner Point house and guest cottage were acquired by Robert and Jane Patrick, a prominent Burlington couple, in 1953. Cyril retired to Cape Cod, where he died in 1972.[4]

After Frederica's death, Vanderbilt became the sole proprietor of Shelburne Farms' agricultural operations. Derick consulted his father regularly and kept him informed of farm activities, but in practice the younger Webb assumed more and more responsibility and decision-making power. Vanderbilt's law duties continued to consume a great deal of his time. He served as a lead attorney for the Rockefeller family, among other responsibilities. His time was also occupied by trustee work on a number of corporate, government, and nonprofit boards, including the New York Trust Company, Rockefeller Center, the Taconic State Park Commission, the Metropolitan Museum of Art, Colonial Williamsburg, and Groton School. Moreover, Vanderbilt was not in the best of health; he struggled periodically for years with severe sciatica. In the end, however, a heart attack felled him unexpectedly at the age of sixty-five in 1956, only six months after his older brother Seward died in Florida. Vanderbilt bequeathed all of his property in Shelburne to Derick, including 1,800 acres of land, the Shelburne Farms buildings, the contents of Shelburne House, and the Farm's agricultural equipment and livestock. Derick's Shelburne real estate holdings now totaled some 2,000 acres, between his inheritance from his father and the approximately 200 acres of land near Bay View that he had acquired from Cyril Jones in the 1950s. Along with his three siblings, Derick also received a cash inheritance from Vanderbilt's residual estate.[5]

Agricultural Operations

By the 1940s, Webb family members felt that the prospects for the agricultural operations at Shelburne Farms were improving. While the Farm still required significant financial support, Derick, working with Vanderbilt, Frederica, and David Tower, seemed to be making good progress in managing the property as a diversified operation. It was quite a contrast from the 1920s and early 1930s, the years of the Shelburne Farms Corporation, when, in the eyes of many family members, the estate had seemed to founder. Derick possessed several key advantages over his predecessor, Frank Kendzior. First, he had the benefit of timing. The economic impact of the Great Depression had begun to fade, and the worst of the disease outbreaks among the Shelburne Farms dairy herd was over. The second and third generations of the Webb family possessed somewhat simpler private lifestyles and fewer expectations that Farm resources should be expended to maintain them. Derick also reaped the benefit of the years of investments in capital improvements to the farm buildings, fences, and infrastructure that had been completed under Kendzior's watch. Finally, Derick won the full trust, respect, and support of the Webbs, who proved to be perhaps more willing to listen to and support a family member and heir than an individual from outside the family. These factors, plus the strength of Derick's own character and skills, would allow him to succeed at Shelburne Farms where Kendzior had not.

During the 1940s, 1950s, and 1960s, the dairy remained an important component of Shelburne Farms' agricultural operations. Derick sought to improve the quality of the herd as much as possible to increase his net profits, adopting many new innovations in the American dairy industry. First, in addition to incorporating new sanitary regulations as they were instituted, he was receptive to further quality-control suggestions made by government inspectors, such as installing a sink in the milking parlor area of the dairy barn for washing milking equipment. Second, he worked to ensure that the cattle grazed on the best-quality grasses by rotating them between pastures every seven days. Third, he concentrated on building an excellent herd. He initially decreased the number of milking cows to approximately fifty Holsteins and Guernseys, those that were healthy and produced a higher yield. He acquired registered animals with established bloodlines and documented high production and butterfat yields, developing a herd consisting entirely of registered cattle by the early 1960s. He also invested in bulls with proven track records and began experimenting with artificial insemination as early as 1942. Finally, he regularly tested and vaccinated the animals to eradicate bovine tuberculosis and Bang's disease.[6]

In 1946, Derick obtained accreditation for the herd and registered it with the American Dairy Cattle Club. He would later note that the organization "prodded the traditional pure bred dairy associations of this country to recognize production a lot more…Up to that time, you could register a dairy animal as long as it met the color standards; but there were no production standards or requirements."[7]

In 1947, Derick introduced the Brown Swiss breed of dairy cattle to Shelburne Farms. Originally from Switzerland, Brown Swiss had first been imported to New England in the mid-nineteenth century. They were known for their physical hardiness and for producing a good volume of milk with a relatively high butterfat and protein content. That year, Derick purchased the Brown Swiss bull Norman B. of Ethan Allen from the nearby Ethan Allen Farm in South Burlington, and crossed the bull with his existing herd of Holsteins, Guernseys, Jerseys, and Ayrshires. The following year, he began to phase out the four latter breeds in favor of an all–Brown Swiss herd, and he transferred his herd registration to the newly formed Brown Swiss Association. In 1948, he purchased three Brown Swiss heifers, and he acquired a larger group of Brown Swiss six years later. A 1948 letter illustrates his priorities for the new purchases: "We are not interested necessarily in show animals, but would like good, strong, well grown heifers with a good production background—preferably from dams which have averaged 400 lbs of fat or more."[8] In 1962, Derick purchased an additional forty head from well-known Brown Swiss farmer Harold Magnussen (1904–90) of upstate New York, whom he then hired to work as Shelburne Farms' cattle superintendent. The dairy herd was completely comprised of purebred Brown Swiss cattle by 1963.[9]

Derick also studied ways to maximize his return on the dairy by improving the physical layout of the operation. While serviceable, the existing dairy barn was not ideal. Ever since the creation of Southern Acres Farm in 1913, its location on the southern boundary of Shelburne Farms at the Breeding Barn complex had been a handicap, as it was some distance from most of the Shelburne Farms crop- and pasturelands. The fields between the dairy barn and the Farm Barn were the only ones available for pasturing Shelburne Farms' cattle, as they were close enough to the dairy barn to allow the cows to move back and forth to the milking parlor. Teamsters had to travel miles within the property to spread manure on pastures and cropland and transfer hay and silage to the dairy, traversing a steep drive to and from the barn in the process. The long distances and hilly terrain increased labor, equipment, and fuel costs. Derick later recalled,

> *I remember when they hauled manure on sleds in the winter time. Teamsters would leave from the Farm Barn and drive up the Dairy Hill to the Dairy Barn. If they were lucky, they could get out two loads in the morning, and two loads in the afternoon. They'd drive up to the pile that had been taken out of the gutter. All the manure was shoveled onto the sled by hand, and they'd drive out the slippery road to some northern field in the snow and spread it as best they could, either side by hand.*[10]

The dairy barn and its attendant outbuildings were also becoming outmoded. The creamery building was destroyed by fire in 1942, forcing a consolidation of equipment storage and can sterilization to the dairy barn's milk house addition. The dairy barn itself followed the traditional plan of tying cows up at stanchions during the long winter season. Starting in the late 1940s, however, a new theory arose in the dairy industry that free-stall barn structures, called pole barns, which allowed the cows to come and go from indoors to outdoors even in the dead of winter, were healthier, led to production improvements, and saved in labor costs. Derick later remembered,

> *In the winter of 1950 I was reading about the developments in dairying in the agricultural press. The articles were saying, "Get the cows out of*

Derick Webb in front of his pole barn, by Noonan Photography, Burlington, Vermont, c. 1955. Shelburne Farms Collections.

stanchions, get them outdoors. If deer can live outside in the winter, cows can."...The Extension Service at the University of Vermont brought in a young agricultural engineer named Ivan Bigelow from Cornell University to advise many...farmers...Bigelow was interested in this new type of pole barn which didn't need stanchions. You could put it up in no time.[11]

As a result, Derick persuaded his father to construct a pole barn for the dairy on a new location: just south of his house, Orchard House, in the midst of the former golf links. The new site was more centrally located within the Shelburne Farms property and only a five-minute walk away from Derick's house. In 1952, Derick commissioned architect William S. Cowles Jr. to design the structure, which featured low-pitched roofs covering open free-stall shed areas, an attached outdoor yard, a manure pit, and a second-floor office. The new barn could accommodate up to 100 milking cows. Soon after its construction, the structure was described thus: "The layout is in the form of a large 'U' with the feeding area on one side, the loafing area on the other side with the closed end of the 'U' housing the 2 strings of tandem milkers [milking parlor] and the milk room. Inside the 'U' is an open paved lot."[12]

In addition to its innovative design, the pole barn also incorporated new agricultural technology: pit-style milking parlors, bulk milk tanks, and trench silos. The milking parlor contained a central pit that placed dairy employees at chest level with the cows' udders, allowing them to work more efficiently. The stainless steel, refrigerated bulk cooling tanks stored a large volume of milk in sanitary conditions until it was retrieved by a milk hauler, reducing the risk of

The pole barn complex, c. 1955. Shelburne Farms Collections.

spoilage and labor costs involved in trucking milk cans to a local distributor each day. The trench silos were concrete-lined storage pits built into a natural rise in the land approximately one mile to the east of the new dairy. Centrally located in the midst of the Farm's cropland, these silos could be filled and emptied more efficiently than traditional vertical silos, and they accommodated silage with a higher moisture content, allowing hay to be harvested in less than perfect weather conditions. Together, the two new silos accommodated 1,100 tons of silage. Derick also purchased front-end loader tractors to clean the barns of manure more efficiently than hand shoveling.[13]

Derick moved the dairy operation to the pole barn in the summer and fall of 1952. Over the next few years, he constructed a series of support structures and a house nearby for the dairy herdsman and his family. Additionally, Derick built a dwelling called Orchard Cove House on the lakeshore, to the south of the Coach Barn. Designed by William Cowles in 1963 to eventually serve as Derick's own retirement home, the building was first occupied by dairy superintendent Harold Magnussen, who was hired that same year.[14]

Derick's efforts at the dairy began to pay off in the mid-1940s. As Tower wrote to Derick in 1945, "The tester told me…that our average production of milk per cow was the largest of any herd that he tests, even herds where they are feeding as high as 12# of grain per day to some of their cows, the most that any of our cows gets is 8# per day."[15] The more centrally located dairy and its technological innovations reduced labor and equipment costs and stress on the cows. In the early 1950s, an animal husbandry specialist at the University of Vermont wrote a glowing account of his tour of the new dairy facilities, noting, "If you are thinking of a pen stable the Webb Estate comes the closest to being an ideal layout of any I have seen…Certainly here is a farm building layout of modern design that Mr. Webb can well be proud of."[16] By the 1960s, the Brown Swiss herd had acquired a reputation as one of the best in the region. Between 1961 and 1972, buyers flocked to the cattle sales that Derick hosted at the Coach Barn each fall.[17]

From the 1940s to the 1960s, Derick continued to sell Shelburne Farms' milk to local distributors to be retailed to consumers in the Champlain Valley. In the early to mid-1940s, he contracted with White's Dairy Products in Burlington. After the war, he sold milk to the Ethan Allen Creamery in Essex Junction, to Borden in Burlington, and then to Hood in Burlington.[18]

By the late 1950s, the dairy at Shelburne Farms had surpassed the other livestock ventures in terms of its ratio of profits to expenses. As a result, Derick decided to concentrate on dairy cattle for the first time since the 1930s. By the late 1960s, Derick had eliminated his beef cattle, hogs, and chickens. He also ended the sheep operation at about the same time, after longtime employee Darcy Patterson retired. In regard to the beef cattle, Derick later recalled, "We gradually reduced the beef cattle when we put in the new Dairy Barn and found that you could handle so many more dairy cattle for so much less labor

Left: Shelburne Farms' Brown Swiss cattle at the Coach Barn, during one of Derick Webb's cattle sales, by Noonan Photography, Burlington, Vermont, c. 1961–72. Shelburne Farms Collections.

Shelburne Farms employees with Derick and Robert Webb (front row, third and fourth from left), by Noonan Photography, Burlington, Vermont, 1967. Shelburne Farms Collections.

and much less investment…The combination of open housing, bulk tank, trench silo, a new form of dairying, and building up a new purebred herd is the reason we phased out the beef cattle before 1960."[19]

Derick eventually built his Brown Swiss dairy herd to 300 cattle, approximately 170 of them milking at any given time. As the herd size increased, the original pit-style milking parlor in the pole barn, which accommodated eight cows at a time and was equipped with side-opening gates that allowed them to be milked individually, became increasingly inefficient. It was replaced during the 1960s with a herringbone-style parlor that took groups of sixteen cows at a time, eight on each side.[20]

Derick continued to actively oversee the agricultural operations at Shelburne Farms through the early 1980s. In addition, he represented the town of Shelburne in the Vermont State Legislature, first as a member of the House of Representatives in 1955 and 1957 and then later as a state senator from 1966 to 1967. He was active in town politics as a selectman, a member of the planning and zoning commission, and a member of the school board for the local union high school. He also served as chairman of the Republican State Committee, as president of the Vermont Dairy Council, and as a trustee of the University of Vermont.[21]

Derick promoted community use of some sections of his Shelburne Farms land. In 1957, he signed a twenty-year, $1 per year lease with the state of Vermont's Fish and Game Commission to allow public use of the property located at the convergence of the LaPlatte River and Shelburne Bay for fishing, boating, and swimming access. In 1960, he gave a parcel of land at the southeastern end of his property, adjoining Harbor Road, to the town of Shelburne for recreational purposes. The town developed a community outdoor skating rink on the site, and Derick subsequently moved a former garage structure from its original location near the Shelburne House servants' wing next to the rink to be used as a warming hut.[22]

For most of his career, Derick oversaw the agricultural operations at Shelburne Farms with the assistance of David Tower. In 1956, faced with the sudden death of his father, his growing responsibilities in the state legislature, and Tower's recent retirement, Derick hired Herbert Stapleton to serve as his farm manager. An agricultural engineer and former agricultural professor at the University of Massachusetts at Amherst, Stapleton was seeking a farming position where he could more fully implement his ideas for improving crop management and equipment. During his five-year tenure, Stapleton redesigned Shelburne Farms' crop plans and introduced numerous agricultural innovations, including outfitting four-wheel-drive trucks with used balloon tires purchased from the military. The tires allowed employees to drive in muddy conditions to plant and harvest crops and spread manure. Stapleton also introduced the use of liquid nitrogen spread on the fields as a fertilizer. Shelburne Farms benefited from his inventions. These included a self-propelled haying machine that combined the functions of mowing, conditioning the hay so it dried more quickly, and moving it into windrows, as well as custom-designed, front-end loaders for gathering bales of hay in the fields.[23]

The Home Estate

The postwar years brought the Webb family a new perspective toward the Home Estate section of the Shelburne Farms property. Focused on making the agricultural operations more self-sufficient, Vanderbilt and Derick placed less priority on maintaining the original vision for the parkland section as a private residence for the family's personal enjoyment. To them, the demands of the Farm were more important than the vestiges of the private estate. The construction of the pole barn dairy complex in the midst of the parkland landscape made the most impact. Not only was there no way to resurrect the golf links, but each time family members and their guests traveled to and from Shelburne House, they were obligated to drive by the dairy's utilitarian buildings and all of its requisite odors and activities at close range.[24]

In addition, in the 1940s, Derick transformed the Coach Barn into a stable for cattle and sheep and used the surrounding fields, including the Shelburne House lawn, to pasture the animals. After the end of the Second World War, the Coach Barn was emptied of most of the horse-drawn vehicles remaining from Derick's grandparents' time at Shelburne Farms. The carriages had stood in storage inside the building for years, visited only rarely by family members desiring to show them to guests, and by young Webbs and employees' children playing in and around them on rainy days. In 1946, ten years before his death, Vanderbilt offered the carriage collection to his sister-in-law Electra in light of her longtime wish to establish her own museum. Electra eagerly accepted, later noting, "The idea of a Museum had been steadily on my mind and the collection of carriages gave me the excuse I needed."[25] By 1947, she had formed the Shelburne Museum, purchased land in the center of the town for the organization, and constructed a large barn on the property to house the carriages. That year, Electra received twenty-eight Webb vehicles from Vanderbilt for her museum.[26]

While the Coach Barn and former golf links

were converted from their original functions, Shelburne House, its outbuildings, and the surrounding landscape on Saxton's Point continued to be used for the family's enjoyment. After the end of the Second World War, Seward and Gertrude Webb chose to spend their summers in Bar Harbor, Maine, but Vanderbilt and Aileen continued to return to the dwelling each summer with their family. They primarily occupied the southern section of the house, leaving the walls that separated the two components of the house intact.[27]

After Vanderbilt died in 1956, Aileen spent time in Shelburne each summer until her own death in 1979. She lived at Shelburne House until 1960, when she constructed a residence of her own at the northern tip of Saxton's Point. Designed by William Cowles, the same architect who worked on the new pole barn complex, Aileen's summer house was a modern, one-story residence with large windows on all sides.[28]

When Derick returned from the war in 1946, he brought his new bride, Elizabeth Canfield Webb (b. 1924), with him (see photo on page 202). The two had been married in 1944 while Derick was on furlough. The daughter of family friends of Van and Aileen's, Elizabeth had grown up in New York City and on the Canfield family farm in Peekskill, New York, not far from the Webbs' country residence in Garrison. Derick and Elizabeth had reconnected as young adults after Elizabeth's sister and brother-in-law, Mary and Archibald Brown, purchased land on Shelburne Point from Derick's aunt Frederica in 1940.[29]

After the war, Derick and Elizabeth lived first in "Orchard Cottage," a farmhouse near the former Nash family homestead, Orchard House. In 1948, they hired William Cowles to renovate Orchard House in order to accommodate their growing family, which would consist of six children by 1958. Cowles's

Shelburne House, summer 1951. Shelburne Farms Collections.

work at Orchard House included the construction of a large new addition.³⁰

After Aileen built her own summer dwelling in 1960, Derick and Elizabeth moved their family from Orchard House into Shelburne House each summer. They primarily occupied the same sections of the residence that Vanderbilt and Aileen had. The young couple entertained friends frequently at Shelburne House, and they often held reunions for Derick's Yale classmates there. Their children remember their summers at Shelburne House as an idyllic time: "games of hide-and-seek in the Main Hall…home-cooked meals eaten family style…and a pet crow flying through some of the 110 rooms."³¹ Derick and Elizabeth's son Alexander ("Alec") Webb (b. 1952) described the experience as "just like a rambling summer camp where you had loads of fun."³²

Nevertheless, by the 1960s, Shelburne House had begun to exhibit signs of deterioration. Like the other estate buildings, Derick invested only the minimum needed to maintain the dwelling for its current use, focusing on those areas of the house where he and his family spent most of their time. He upgraded the structure's sewage system, which originally channeled waste directly into Lake Champlain, by installing a leach field. He also replumbed key bathrooms with new copper lines, but other bathrooms were closed because of inoperable fixtures. More important, leaking plumbing from a second-floor bathroom, and localized roof leaks, a consequence of missing slates, deteriorated flashing, and gutter failures, resulted in mounting water damage to some areas of the house. The leaks compromised plaster walls and ceilings and caused structural settling as moisture traveled down to sections of the third, the second, and eventually even the first floor. The oak room, a bedroom in the north wing, was closed because of falling plaster and a crumbling chimney. Other unoccupied bedrooms also suffered from water damage. However, Derick and Elizabeth's son Marshall (b. 1948) later recalled, "If it wasn't raining and drawing your attention to all the water problems, everything looked pretty good."³³

In the servants' wing at Shelburne House, habitable quarters were maintained only in the northern end until about 1955, when a dairy herdsman and his family, who had lived there for a period of time, moved into the newly completed herdsman's house at the new dairy complex. The servants' wing structure remained solid into the 1970s, but it was plagued with problems resulting from deferred maintenance, such as roof leaks, moisture infiltration, peeling exterior paint, and deteriorating plaster. In addition, a break in a basement water pipe one winter during the mid-1960s resulted in major flooding. By the time the leak was discovered after approximately two weeks, the basement of the servants' wing was filled with six feet of water, which was running out of the cellar windows. The moisture, and the resulting freezing and thawing of the walls and floors that followed in the unheated building, caused the basement's concrete floors and the stone foundation to heave and the first-floor wood floors to rot. The flood compounded the servants' wing's deterioration, but the structure remained standing.³⁴

Southern Acres

While Derick expanded and modernized Shelburne Farms' agricultural operations during the late 1940s, the 1950s, and the 1960s, Watson sought to maintain the status quo at Southern Acres Farm. After the end of the Second World War, his dream of retiring from the insurance business and making Southern Acres a permanent, year-round residence began to seem like a distinct reality. The establishment of Electra's Shelburne Museum two years later was an additional impetus for the couple to spend more time at Southern Acres. They declared Shelburne as their legal residence in 1949 and sold their Westbury house and most of its surrounding acreage in 1955.³⁵

However, like his siblings, Watson began to ex-

The Breeding Barn complex, by Richard Meek, 1957. Kitty Webb Harris.

perience heart trouble. By the mid-1940s, he had developed congestive heart failure. Much to his dismay, his failing health curtailed active physical work at Southern Acres as well as his usual schedule of hunting trips to the Adirondacks, South Carolina, and abroad. He was forced to spend several long periods of time recuperating away from Shelburne, and when he was able to travel, he was sometimes unable to rally himself to do more than drive around his property.[36]

As Watson's health declined, the expenses of Southern Acres continued to climb, and the challenges of maintaining an estate farm began to seem less worthwhile. As he wrote in 1947, "What a care the farm now is. It worries me & costs so d—d [damned] much too."[37] And again in 1950: "This place now is just too much of care & expense & worry & bound to get worse."[38] In 1951, Watson budgeted $30,000 from his funds for Southern Acres Farm, and in succeeding years he noted that its financial demands only increased. His health problems meant that he derived less and less personal fulfillment from physical activities, and he began to feel that he did not possess the necessary energy to oversee a complex enterprise with a number of employees. Added to these challenges were the usual trials of an agricultural operation, including unusually wet springs that delayed planting, pests that damaged crops, diseases that infected livestock, equipment trouble, and the vagaries of the beef cattle market.[39]

Right: J. Watson Webb with a Shelburne terrier, by Richard Meek, 1957. Kitty Webb Harris.

Watson considered reducing or eliminating certain farm activities, such as the horse breeding operations, but he ultimately decided to cut only the Shelburne Hunt. Watson and his youngest son, Harry, hunted foxes on a limited basis from 1946 through at least the late 1940s. By that time, Watson's health was declining, longtime huntsman Fred Ingleson was nearing retirement, and Harry was occupied with other activities. In addition, neighboring farmers began to replace their rail fences with barbed wire and electric fencing, making it difficult for hunters, horses, and hounds to navigate them safely. As Watson wrote in 1948, "It's impossible to keep any show going…& we must close it. H.[arry] also is busy & does not show enough interest. E[lectra] & I are too old. And so will end a great sport here after nearly 40 years!"[40] The last hunt occurred in about 1949, and Watson sold his final group of eighteen Shelburne foxhounds in 1952. He kept a few terriers but moved them to a new, smaller kennels and dog yard behind the house of Alec Morrison, his retired herdsman.[41]

Watson's children were united in their desire to retain Southern Acres as a family property. However, the selection of a single successor to Watson was not as straightforward as at Shelburne Farms. Watson himself was reluctant to hand over the reins to one or more of his five children, many of whom were preoccupied with their careers, families, and properties elsewhere. Watson Jr. had found success in the California film industry, Dunbar and Electra (Webb) Bostwick owned their own nearby farm, and Lila (Webb) Wilmerding lived primarily in the Boston, Massachusetts, area, with chronic ill health preventing her from taking an active role.[42]

After the end of the Second World War, Harry returned to Southern Acres and established a residence of his own there. In 1947, he married Kate DeForest Jennings (1927–2002). The newlyweds moved into the southern wing of the Brick House, which was partitioned off from the main section of the dwelling to provide them with a separate residence. By 1952, they would have three children of their own. Harry began an independent farming operation with Holstein dairy cattle and work horses on two farms in the neighboring town of Charlotte by the spring of 1948. In 1950, Watson gave him 110 acres on the southern edge of Southern Acres, adjoining Bostwick Farm, on which to build his own residence. The house was completed in 1952. Harry also constructed two barns on his new acreage in Shelburne, which he called High Acres Farm, to house Hereford beef cattle, pleasure horses, and sheep.[43]

Harry retained an apartment in New York City, yet he primarily resided at High Acres Farm. He also owned a significant amount of his aunt Frederica's former acreage on Shelburne Point, and he operated the former Clarence Morgan residence (a property located on Shelburne Point that his grandparents Lila and Seward Webb had sold in 1910) as the Shelburne Harbor Inn from 1959 to 1962.[44]

Although Sam, the eldest son, continued to be actively involved with the family insurance business in New York, he returned to his home on Quaker Smith Point frequently for weekends and vacations. An avid outdoorsman, Sam also spent a great deal of time hunting and fishing at the family's properties at Nehasane and in South Carolina, as well as at sites in Canada and England.[45]

Sam was not as passionate about agriculture as his father, but he valued Southern Acres. He later wrote, "Farming, per se, is not a consuming interest of mine. I think this is a lovely place to live, and…I'd like to keep the property together if possible."[46]

Sam served as the family spokesman in negotiations with Vanderbilt in the 1950s and Derick in the early 1960s over the purchase of additional acreage on the boundary between Shelburne Farms and Southern Acres Farm. In 1961, the old dairy barn, the south gate, and the surrounding 149 acres were transferred from the former to the latter.[47]

Until his death in 1960, Watson Sr. continued to oversee Southern Acres Farm primarily on his own. He passed away in New York early in the year, and his wife, Electra, died several months later. According to the terms of their wills, their property at Southern Acres, including the Brick House and some six hundred acres of land, descended to their sons Sam, Harry, and Watson Jr.[48]

The three brothers all wished to see the estate continue as a private family preserve more for its aesthetic appearance and for the sake of the family tradition than for agriculture alone. As Watson once stated to Sam, "My committment is to maintaining SAF with fences, trees, roads and lands presenting a generally decent appearance."[49] Sam concurred, replying, "I think you have the impression that…I want to farm; that is not so at all. My interest in a cow is the same as yours—NIL. My interest in keeping S.A.F. the show place it is, is also as great as yours."[50] Although Harry possessed more interest in farming for its own sake, he too was likely unwilling to continue to support Southern Acres Farm to the same extent due to its financial requirements.

Since Watson Jr. was the only one of the three brothers who did not already own a house in the area at the time of their parents' death, he purchased his brothers' interests in the Brick House, along with the ten acres immediately surrounding the dwelling, in 1961. He subsequently renovated and redecorated the residence to reflect his own taste. While continuing to work in the film industry in California, Watson served as president of the Shelburne Museum's board of trustees from 1961 to 1977. He divided his time between a house in Los Angeles, a vacation home at Lake Arrowhead, California, and the Brick House. He usually spent May, June, September, October, and one week each winter in Shelburne.[51]

From 1960 to 1975, Sam, Watson Jr., and Harry jointly managed the agricultural lands and buildings of Southern Acres Farm, including the Breeding Barn complex, and evenly divided financial responsibility. However, Sam assumed a

Right: The Watson Webb family in front of the Brick House, c. 1952. From left: Lila (Webb) Wilmerding, Electra (Webb) Bostwick, J. Watson Sr., Sam Sr., Electra, Harry, and J. Watson Jr. Shelburne Museum.

leadership role, overseeing day-to-day farm activities and supervising the farm manager.[52]

Sam, Harry, and Watson continued to employ their father's farm manager, John Brotz (1919–98). An additional three to six employees assisted Brotz with the livestock and crop operations. Under the Webb brothers' direction, Brotz managed Southern Acres Farm for its aesthetic appeal as much, or more than, as an efficient agricultural operation. Fences and crop lines were perfectly straight, the grass under the fences was hand-scythed, and the main interior space in the Breeding Barn was carefully raked on a daily basis. In keeping with the Webb family's longstanding policy of borrowing employees from one place to assist with projects at another, the brothers often shared staff from Southern Acres Farm, the Shelburne Museum, and their own country residences in the area to complete various projects.[53]

In the 1960s, Sam led his brothers in revising the scope and scale of the agricultural operations in an effort to improve Southern Acres Farm's financial viability. Like their father, Sam, Harry, and Watson were willing to make annual contributions to maintain a private family estate. Yet they possessed less disposable income than their parents, and the property's expenses continued to increase over time.[54]

The three brothers disbanded the horse breeding, pig, chicken, and sheep operations and reduced their Hereford cattle stock. The Hereford business, the estate's primary source of agricultural income for many years, proved to be less profitable than similar concerns in the western United States. In an era when many farmers were improving profits by economies of scale, Southern Acres was a much smaller concern than many of its competitors.[55]

In 1962, Sam, Harry, and Watson launched a

new venture that they hoped would improve Southern Acres' financial independence: a steer fattening business similar to the one with which Derick had experimented at Shelburne Farms in the late 1930s. However, like their cousin, they would soon find that the financial challenges of managing agricultural operations on a country estate were increasingly intractable.[56]

CHAPTER 14

TURNING POINTS

If Shelburne Farms can be kept intact for future generations to enjoy, my children and their families will deserve a large share of the credit.

— Derick Webb, 1979[1]

THE LATE TWENTIETH CENTURY WOULD PROVE to be a major turning point for Shelburne Farms and Southern Acres. Despite recurring financial pressures, family members had managed to maintain the heart of their agricultural estates into the 1960s. But the 1960s and 1970s brought redoubled financial challenges, as well as new perspectives about the purpose and social value of the properties. Family members were forced to weigh the private benefits of developing Shelburne Farms and Southern Acres against the community benefits of conserving and sharing them. After years of exploration, discussion, and debate, they succeeded in implementing innovative solutions that took them on an entirely new path toward public access and ownership.

Shelburne Farms: The Challenges of the 1960s

Of all of the owners and managers of Shelburne Farms, Derick Webb came the closest to establishing a self-sufficient agricultural operation. According to Derick, the Farm officially functioned "either on a slight margin of profit or breaking even" from the 1950s to the mid-1960s.[2] To cover the Farm's cash shortfalls in leaner years, Derick relied on his personal funds, derived from his inheritance from his father and three trusts established by his parents. In addition to improving the Farm's bottom line, his actions also allowed him to show a profit at least two out of every five years so he could qualify for an agricultural deduction on his federal income taxes. Derick did draw a small salary from the Farm, but the family funds allowed him a measure of personal financial independence; he did not have to depend on the success of Shelburne Farms to support himself and his family.[3]

Derick's efforts to make the estate more self-sufficient came at the price of the ongoing maintenance of the buildings, infrastructure, and major com-

The main drive at Shelburne Farms, looking west, depicting an allée of elms soon to be lost to Dutch elm disease, by Marshall C. Webb, August 1977. Shelburne Farms Collections.

ponents of the landscape. By 1960, the core Robertson-designed structures at Shelburne Farms were between sixty and seventy years old. Since the 1920s, the Webb family had invested little more than the bare minimum needed to ensure that the buildings and infrastructure remained functional. Many structures, including those required for active farm operations and employee housing, had been allowed to deteriorate. Derick made significant alterations to sections of the Farm Barn and Coach Barn to house his cattle, chickens, and sheep; the livestock and the manure they left behind took their toll. In 1954, Watson visited the Coach Barn and noted, "What a mess it is there."[4] Derick's son Marshall later reflected, "I don't think [my father] thought that any of the buildings would survive many more years. There just wasn't enough money to keep everything up. So it didn't really matter that manure was causing damage at the Farm Barn and Coach Barn."[5]

The estate road system also suffered. In an effort to make the primary roads easier to maintain, Derick invested in asphalt surfacing in the late 1940s or early 1950s. However, after 1960, he possessed limited funds to keep the asphalt in good repair. By the end of the decade, in the midst of the Vietnam War, the main drive was so pocked with potholes that Derick's children referred to it as the "Ho Chi Minh Trail" because, as Marshall remembered, "It looked like B-52's had just carpet-bombed it."[6]

Similarly, Derick chose not to invest in major, ongoing forestry work. He

Right: Derick Webb on his airstrip at Shelburne Farms, by Marshall C. Webb, July 1965. Shelburne Farms Collections.

periodically harvested a small amount of lumber needed for active farm operations, and in the 1950s sold some hardwood with the assistance of a contract forester. Nonetheless, his limited operation was not enough to ensure the woodlands' long-term productivity. In addition, he mowed areas bordering fields and secondary roads less frequently, resulting in the infiltration of invasive species such as buckthorn and Norway maple. Derick later stated, "I just tried to keep the forestland the way it was. I regret now I didn't have more interest in trees. I was so busy with the livestock and machinery and just what was here that I was a little shortsighted."[7]

The arrival of Dutch elm disease in the 1960s was a further blow to the character of the Shelburne Farms landscape. As it did in many places across the country, the disease killed almost all of the hundreds of elms planted in the late nineteenth and early twentieth centuries along the roadways and across fields at the estate. There was little Derick or anyone else could do.[8]

As the 1960s progressed, Derick's ability to maintain an at least nominally self-sufficient farm met with a pressing challenge: dramatic increases in the town property taxes assessed on the approximately 1,850 acres that he owned. During the second half of the twentieth century, the nearby city of Burlington stood at the center of an explosion in economic growth. In Shelburne, the population rose an estimated fifty-six percent, from 1,800 to 3,200, between 1960 and 1967. The result was burgeoning real estate development and an attendant rise in property values. Land on the shores of Lake Champlain, such as that at Shelburne Farms, began to command a premium for potential residential development. The taxes on Derick's land and buildings climbed from approximately $6,200 a year in 1939, to about $23,000 in 1969, to $46,000 in 1975.[9]

Derick feared that his ability to maintain financial self-sufficiency would decline as the value of his property, and thus his property taxes, continued to rise. At the same time, his six children were entering their teens and twenties, and he was funding their tuitions at several private schools

and colleges. A lifelong aviation enthusiast, Derick was also contemplating establishing a local air charter business.[10]

In the 1960s, incentives to conserve agricultural lands, such as tax abatement and conservation easement strategies, were not widely recognized or available in Vermont. Derick perceived that his only option was to deal with his property tax burden privately. However, he felt strongly that as much of the Shelburne Farms property as possible should be preserved as farmland and remain within family hands, and the area that he had already leased to the state for public use remain dedicated to the benefit of the community.[11]

During the mid to late 1960s, Derick began to investigate methods of raising funds from some portion of his property, while preserving the estate's core acreage. He turned his attention to the approximately 575 acres located to the north and east of the estate's gates, including the Bay View area and lands bordering Shelburne Bay and the LaPlatte River. As he later stated, "My feeling was that this was the logical land to develop in order to provide an economic return to properly maintain the inside property [the core area inside the gates]."[12]

In 1967, Derick hired prominent landscape architect Daniel Urban Kiley (1912–2004) to prepare a plan for this outlying acreage. Kiley's proposal featured a combination of land use strategies that would provide Derick with much-needed funds, while at the same time preserving the area dedicated to community use. Two hundred acres bordering Shelburne Bay, the LaPlatte River, and McCabes Brook, including the Shelburne Bay fishing access that Derick had leased to the state, were envisioned as a state park. To the south, on nearby land that Derick had already given to the town of Shelburne for its skating rink, a town sewage treatment plant and community center would be constructed. Bordering these areas were additional sites to be developed: an industrial park located near the sewage treatment plant; a residential neighborhood located in the 135-acre pasture directly east of the estate gates; and a golf course with or without a residential subdivision located on 225 acres in the vicinity of Bay View and the site of the former stone crusher building.[13]

Over the next two years, Derick contemplated several variations of the subdivision plans outlined in Kiley's proposal. According to Gordon Paterson, who served as Derick's administrator and financial advisor from 1969 to 1973, he first investigated options for leasing various parcels. Between 1967 and 1969, Derick approached International Business Machines Corporation (IBM), which had opened a major manufacturing plant in the nearby town of Essex Junction in 1957, regarding the possibility of leasing the company a parcel of land outside the Shelburne Farms gates for use as a private employee recreational area. Together with Paterson, Derick also approached two additional companies about leasing other outlying lands: a Connecticut real estate firm, which was considering the construction of a large residential retirement village, and the Burlington Country Club, for the creation of a satellite golf course facility. Although none of these conversations came to immediate fruition, Derick continued to explore his options.[14]

In 1969 and 1970, Derick held three family meetings to discuss his financial challenges and subdivision plans. He later recalled, "I wanted the children to understand the problem we faced. Shelburne Farms was their inheritance. I felt they had to realize how difficult it was going to be to keep things intact when the only income from the land was through farming."[15] He was joined by his wife, Elizabeth, his mother, Aileen, and his six children: Derick Osborn (who later changed his name to Quentyn) (b. 1946), Marshall (b. 1948), Mary (b. 1950), Alexander (Alec) (b. 1952), Elizabeth (Lisa) (b. 1955), and Robert (b. 1958), who then ranged in age from twenty-three to eleven. Quentyn's wife, Leslie (Davis) (b. 1948), Marshall's fiancée, Emily Wadhams (b. 1948), and Mary's fiancé, David Phillips (b. 1946), were also present. Derick first intro-

The Derick Webb family, by Clyde Smith, c. June 1969. From left to right: (front row) Alec, Lisa, and Robert; (middle row) Derick, Aileen, Elizabeth, and Marshall's fiancée Emily Wadhams; and (back row) Mary's fiancé David Phillips, Mary, Quentyn, and Marshall. Not pictured is Quentyn's wife, Leslie. Shelburne Farms Collections, Gift of the Estate of Killian Webb.

duced the plans at a meeting held on the south porch at Shelburne House in August of 1969. Subsequent meetings were held later that month and in June of 1970. Family members discussed, among other issues, "profitable vs. charitable development, private vs. public recreation, [the] establishment of recreational clubs, and [the] possibility of interested groups."[16]

Derick's children reacted vehemently against his proposal to subdivide portions of the estate. They were united in their desire to conserve the Shelburne Farms land as a single, intact, and agricultural entity. Part of the first generation of the Webb family to grow up living at Shelburne Farms year-round, they had developed a keen appreciation for the property and its value as a working farm. Their family residence, Orchard House, was located only a short walking distance away from the dairy complex, and the siblings had often accompanied and assisted their father with the farm chores. Derick had encouraged his children's interest in farming, assisting his daughter Lisa, for instance, in raising her own chickens, pigs, and horses. Derick's son Alec later explained, "We grew up on a farm in a beautiful place. We had that exposure at a young age."[17] Alec's brother Marshall recalled, "None of us wanted to inherit [Shelburne Farms] and then have to sell half of it to pay the estate taxes…Our souls at an early age became entwined with the spirit of the farm. We wanted it to stay in one piece."[18] Marshall felt so strongly about the subdivision proposal that he thought of it as an "all or nothing" proposition: either the entire estate must be saved, or he would leave Shelburne Farms altogether.[19]

Moreover, the siblings were coming of age during the heady social environment of the 1960s. In the wake of publications such as Aldo Leopold's *Sand County Almanac* (1949), Rachel Carson's *Silent Spring* (1962), Paul Erhlich's *The*

Population Bomb (1968), and Donella Meadows's *The Limits to Growth* (1972), a growing awareness arose nationwide of the value of natural resources and healthy ecological systems, and of the potential devastation that modern society, with its ever-expanding population, could impose on the earth. In the United States, the nascent environmental movement led to, among other events, the passage of the first Clean Air and Water Acts in 1963 and 1972, the establishment of the Environmental Protection Agency in 1970, and the celebration of the first national Earth Day in 1970. Concurrently, the emerging back-to-the-land movement promoted the traditional virtues of rural life, self-sufficiency, agricultural diversity, and decreased reliance on modern technology. Derick's children were passionate about the values espoused by both movements. Alec later stated, "Certainly we were doing the planet in, and felt a place like this should be used for some higher purpose. We were coming out of a concern for the environment. It was more that than trying to preserve the family heritage."[20]

Derick's children and their spouses persuaded him to postpone his subdivision ideas in order to give them time to explore other ways of offsetting Shelburne Farms' tax burden. They hoped to keep the entire property in agricultural use and as a resource for new educational programs. As Alec, Marshall, and Marshall's wife, Emily, wrote in about 1972,

> *The more we thought, the more we realized that the land had to retain its rural, open space quality at all costs. So attention turned…to farming the land more heavily. But other possibilities which would preserve the land were also considered, such as giving or selling the farm to a group like the Nature Conservancy, which would guarantee its preservation, or to the state of Vermont, which would turn it into a public park. These possibilities, however, didn't strike us as being the right things to do at the time.*

> *We thought we should attempt to farm the land more extensively first to see if that was feasible. Then we began to think much more seriously about the future of the world in general, as opposed to the future of the farm alone, and naturally we began to work the two together, looking at the problems which exist today in the world (societal and environmental) and trying to figure out how we could use the farm in order to help solve these problems for the future. This led to the idea of starting educational programs designed to help people rediscover how intimately they are related to nature.*[21]

Thirty-five years later, Marshall reflected, "Without the inspiration derived from the naïve enthusiasm and ignorance of youth, we would never have conceived the idea that we could save the Farm and start programs to help save the planet. Looking back on it now, you can understand how ridiculous the idea must have seemed at first to our father and those of his generation."[22] Alec recalled that Derick's advisors "thought he was nuts" to delay or relinquish developing his land in order to give his children a chance to pursue their vision.[23] Marshall has speculated that Derick may have been willing to let his children carry out their experiments in order to "give us enough rope to hang ourselves"—that is, allowing the siblings to play out their idealistic goals, which seemed unlikely to succeed, because he believed that the value of the property would continue to increase, thereby generating a greater return on any future subdivision.[24]

Whether or not he felt that his children's wishes were realistic, Derick's willingness to postpone subdivision demonstrated a fundamental respect for them. In 1972, two years after the siblings had launched their first educational and agricultural activities, he expressed "surprise at [their] implementation [and] admiration for [their] persistence & patience [and their] ability to follow through under difficult and trying circumstances" and stated that he "couldn't conceive of having done it himself at that age."[25] His initial and ongoing support of his children's vision would be crucial to its eventual success.

Shelburne Farms: Experiments in Agriculture, Education, and Land use, 1970–1984

During the 1970s and early 1980s, Derick's children and their spouses embarked on a two-part approach to achieving their goal of creating a viable alternative plan for Shelburne Farms. Several of them participated in the agricultural operations, hoping to assure the success of their father's ongoing ventures and develop new ones. Others turned to educational programs and potentially profitable enterprises. Some divided their time between the agricultural and educational ventures. The siblings and their spouses developed their enterprises concurrently, and often interdependently. Marshall later reflected, "The private farm business and the nonprofit environmental educational organization had to grow simultaneously because the success of one depended on the success of the other."[26]

Then predominantly in their teens and twenties, the Webb siblings and their spouses all spent some time living and working at the Farm during the fifteen years following the seminal family meetings in 1969 and 1970, coming and going as their education, career opportunities, and other responsibilities allowed. After returning from service in the Vietnam War, Quentyn lived in a makeshift apartment located under the north tower of the Farm Barn from 1968 to 1973. Marshall left his undergraduate studies at Wesleyan University and returned to Shelburne Farms in 1969, and he and his wife, Emily, moved into the Orchard Cove House two years later. Alec returned in 1970 after graduating from Groton School, and five years later, he and his wife, Marilyn (Thompson Leimenstoll) (b. 1946), built a small cottage residence for themselves just northeast of Orchard Point. Mary and her husband, David, lived in Orchard Cottage, near Derick's Orchard House, from 1974 to 1979. Lisa and Robert lived on the Farm year-round during their teenage years and attended the local public high school. From 1974 to 1977, Lisa and her husband, John Roberts (b. 1951), lived in the Valley View farmhouse.[27]

Derick's six children were fortunate enough to each possess a $60,000 inheritance from their grandmother Aileen Webb's brother, Earl Osborn, which they received after they turned twenty-one years of age. During the 1970s, many of the siblings and their growing families relied upon the income and principal of this inheritance to support themselves.[28]

Throughout the 1970s, Derick, his children, their spouses, his first wife, Elizabeth, and later his second wife, Helen ("Rusty")(b. 1926), met regularly to discuss the future of Shelburne Farms, possibilities for the use and potential disposition of the property, and their educational programs and agricultural ventures. It was an extremely difficult process for all of them. Tensions would ebb and flow as family members struggled to find and agree upon methods of saving the property that they all dearly loved. As the family patriarch and legal owner of the estate, Derick retained the power to make final, significant agricultural and land use decisions. However, as Marshall later noted, "All of us, including our spouses, were equally involved when it came to providing input."[29] By 1975, they had developed an informal structure for a "cooperative family business," in which various siblings and in-laws were responsible for different aspects of the operations, such as the dairy, finances, buildings and grounds, and forestry.[30]

By the late 1970s, Marilyn was managing the family's growing educational and public programs, and Alec was overseeing the agricultural operations and land use plans. Alec later recalled that, throughout the 1970s and into the 1980s, both he and Marilyn "lived and breathed" Shelburne

Farms and that "Marilyn bridged family and community interests, providing the leadership needed to establish the nonprofit organization and facilitate the property's transition into public use."[31]

Marilyn's connections to Shelburne Farms were well established by the time she and Alec were married in 1975. She first visited the property as a young girl with her father, Bryson ("Tommy") Thompson, who had briefly worked there as a caddy in the 1930s. One summer day in 1969, Marilyn and her first husband, architect Jerry Leimenstoll, knocked on the front door of Shelburne House to offer their assistance in preserving Shelburne Farms, in response to a rumor that portions of the property were to be developed. While the Webb family politely rebuffed the couple's efforts at first, they would soon find both Marilyn's and Jerry's interest in the property and professional connections to be significant assets in the development of their land use plans and educational activities.[32]

In 1970, while serving on the Shelburne Planning Commission alongside Derick, Jerry arranged a meeting between Derick and Davis Cherington, the Vermont field representative for the Nature Conservancy. This early connection with the nonprofit organization, which was dedicated to the "preservation of the plants, animals, and natural communities that represent the diversity of life on Earth," would later prove to be instrumental in preserving a portion of the Shelburne Farms property.[33]

By the mid-1970s, Marilyn especially emerged as a key player at Shelburne Farms. An interior designer by training, she had been active in a wide range of local education and conservation projects since the late 1960s. She volunteered for the Vermont chapter of the Nature Conservancy and created and led environmental education programs for elementary students and teachers. In addition, Marilyn also cultivated local and state support for local agriculture. Working for local entrepreneur Lyman Wood and his Vermont garden products company, Garden Way Associates, she helped to develop both the "Vermont's Own" product labeling and advertising campaign and the first farmers' market in the area, in Burlington.[34]

Shelburne Farms Resources

Derick and Elizabeth's children and their spouses and friends all helped to establish Shelburne Farms' first educational programs and the nonprofit organization, Shelburne Farms Resources, which sprang from them.

In the summer of 1970, less than a year after the siblings had persuaded their father to postpone his plans for subdivision, Alec launched the group's first educational program. That spring, Alec spent his last semester of Groton School in Burlington completing an internship at a local alternative secondary school, the Shaker Mountain School. Out of this experience grew the idea for a summer camp program for urban and rural youth, which operated from 1970 to 1975. That first year, Alec planned and managed the camp together with his friends Bill Ladd and Philip Kunhardt and one of his teachers from the Shaker Mountain School, Alan Boutilier. The program was designed to instill an awareness of the environment and a love of the land in the participants by having them camp in tents and participate in outdoor activities for several weeks. In its first year, the camp attracted about fifteen children from the Burlington area as well as areas farther afield, including the Bronx, New York, and an isolated fishing village in Labrador. Later, the program added craft projects related to natural and agricultural products, an organic vegetable garden, responsibilities for the care of farm livestock, and participation in the local community farmers' market that Alec's future wife, Marilyn, had helped to establish. The farmers' market provided a crucial source of income for the camp. In about 1974, the program was described as follows in a Shelburne newsletter:

>...15 or more 4th, 5th, and 6th graders focus life for four midsummer weeks closely on the

land…Expenses and campers' scholarships are partly met by a produce booth manned by kids and counselors at the Burlington Farmers' Market. But garden and market mean much more than making ends meet. Working in the earth is seen as a way to become sensitive to nature's cycles, to learn to love the outdoors. Kids live simply, care for ducks and a goat, enjoy land and lake, sleep in tents on a hillside ¼ mile away and eat natural food. The market brings kids, who come from the Baird Center, downtown Burlington, urban New Jersey and suburban Shelburne, into the thick of a more familiar way of life. They get to see how city folk appreciate their country produce, [and] learn that they depend on urban areas to market it.[35]

In 1972, Alec received conscientious objector status after being drafted by the military for service in the Vietnam War. He fulfilled a two-year alternative service requirement by working as the Burlington-area community coordinator for the Arts & Crafts Service of the Vermont Department of Education. With the blessing of his supervisor at the Arts & Crafts Service, D'Ann Fago, he divided his time between projects related to strengthening rural craft enterprises and advocacy work at the state level.[36]

As a result of Alec's new commitments, Marshall, Emily, and their friends Robert and Amy Kinzel assumed management of the summer camp program

Alec Webb operating a windrow turner, by Derick Webb, July 1965. Shelburne Farms Collections.

from 1972 to 1975. Lisa also assisted by sharing responsibilities for meal preparation. In addition, Marshall developed a vision for another, complementary educational venture. While completing his undergraduate degree at the University of Vermont in 1971 and 1972, an assignment for an education class led to his proposal to create a private elementary school featuring a curriculum grounded in the four seasons. The school, which Marshall proposed to manage with Bob Kinzel, would be in session from March to November each year at the Shelburne Farms Coach Barn. Students would learn about nature and the environment by growing their own food, among other projects. Marshall's plan did not come to fruition, in large part because he and his siblings did not possess the funds needed to address the maintenance work and renovations that the Coach Barn would have required in order to house such an institution. However, his vision for an environmental education program oriented toward elementary school students, along with the ongoing summer camp, influenced the mission and goals of several later activities that he and his siblings would develop.[37]

In 1971, during the second season of the summer camp, the Webb siblings provided space at Shelburne Farms for two programs conducted by others whose philosophies were congruent with their own: a crafts program organized by a group of local residents, and professional development workshops for high school teachers on the topic of environmental education, led by Alec's future wife Marilyn. The goal of the teacher workshops was to explore the connections between science, art, and ecology and, as Marilyn described it, "to rediscover, through nature, some pleasures and virtues—such as eating home-grown food—which seemed to have been skirted or ignored by technological society."[38] The programs were held concurrently in and near the historic barn at Bay View, and they set a precedent for future partnerships with like-minded groups, which the Webbs would pursue with enthusiasm into the 1980s and beyond.

In 1972, the siblings' fledgling programs and visions coalesced in the establishment of a nonprofit organization. That summer, Quentyn, Marshall, Emily, Alec, and Lisa formed Shelburne Farms Resources, Inc. (SFR) as an umbrella under which to operate their current programs and develop additional ventures. The organization's articles of association set forth the following purposes:

1. To enable the use of Shelburne Farms' resources to serve human educational needs
2. To enable the maximum realization of the potential of Shelburne Farms' function as an educational resource
3. To educate the public to recognize the wealth in natural, rural resources and to use that wealth for the satisfaction of individual and common human needs
4. To educate the public concerning some of the diverse ways of more fully using and benefiting from natural resource wealth through such means as learning, recreation, food, clothing, color, quiet, hand skills, open spaces, wild life, farmers' markets, recycling of "wastes," transportation, planting, etc.
5. To encourage learning in a contemporary and functioning rural atmosphere through the living example and participation in diverse rural activities and through human organization and activities such as work shops, camps, conferences, schools, square dances, etc.[39]

Shelburne Farms Resources' ambitious, complex mission embraced wide-ranging ideals rooted in the environmental and back-to-the-land movements, including conservation education and environmental stewardship; the fostering of rural arts, crafts, and enterprises; and the promotion of local agriculture and agricultural products. At the heart of their goals was the wish to become a "model to the State of Vermont and the world."[40]

In developing such a diverse and complex mix of programs and activities, Shelburne Farms Resources was largely sailing through uncharted waters. In 1980, SFR's education director, David Barash, researched comparable institutions and programs in the United States. He reported,

> *Shelburne Farms was unique in the literally hundreds of operations that I heard about. Its history, diversity and goals primarily make it so…The whole idea of using a farm as a site for education programs and a tool through which to teach about basic life processes is one that is gaining a lot of ground around the country, though it is still the exception rather than the rule. This is evidenced by the fact that four of the five educational farms I visited in New England are just starting and only one had programs going for several years.*[41]

The six Webb siblings and their spouses all lent their support to SFR, albeit in differing ways and with differing levels of commitment. Quentyn was named the first president of the organization. Alec and Marshall served, respectively, as vice president and treasurer, and Emily held the position of secretary. Lisa and Robert attended early meetings and joined discussions about the goals of the organization. Mary and David joined the board in 1974. Marilyn served as the organization's first employee, responsible for managing programs and fundraising projects starting in 1974, and as president from 1976 to 1988. Quentyn, Marshall, Alec, and Mary and David loaned a total of approximately $10,000 from their own pockets to launch the fledgling nonprofit. SFR's first assets consisted of items purchased for the summer camp, including kitchen equipment, tents, a tractor, and a manure spreader.[42]

The siblings all agreed that no one would be compensated by the organization until it was more firmly established. Webb family members who were officially employed by the organization, including Marshall and Emily, who ran several programs, and Marilyn as manager and then president, did not receive salaries until the late 1970s and early 1980s, respectively.[43]

Although not all Webb family members officially served as directors of the nonprofit, they all contributed to ongoing discussions about the organization's programs and future development. In addition, by 1973, the Webbs also recognized the need to involve individuals from outside the family in order to provide different perspectives and levels of expertise. Over the course of the 1970s, they solicited advice from a number of friends and community members and invited several people to serve as board members. Marilyn recruited many advisors from her professional connections in interior design, conservation, environmental education, and the promotion of local farm products. As Marshall later recalled, Marilyn's "talents and ability to enlist prominent members of the community to join the board were critical to SFR's success."[44]

The early board members included Bob Kinzel, who served as the organization's second president and co-managed the summer camp; local business community leader Pat Robins; retired lawyer and diplomat Lewis Metcalfe Walling; environmentalist, author, and sustainable-business leader Paul Hawken; D'Ann Fago, director of the Vermont Arts & Crafts Service; Lyman Wood, founder of Garden Way Associates; and botany professor and ecologist Hubert ("Hub") Vogelmann. Family friend Hunter Lewis, a founder of Cambridge Associates LLC, a firm offering investment advisory services, played a key advisory role even before he became co-chair of the board in 1984. Local architect Peter Woodside, a former colleague of Marilyn's, prepared schematic plans for several of the organization's programmatic land use proposals.[45]

During the 1970s, those involved with Shelburne Farms Resources all worked together to map a strategy for the organization's future and its relation to both the family's estate property and the surrounding community. The leaders of Shelburne Farms Resources were committed to providing public access to Shelburne Farms through their nonprofit organization's programs, and they believed in using the property as a model to inform the public's understanding of environmental and agricultural issues in the world at large. The envisioned symbiotic relationship between Shelburne Farms and Shelburne Farms Resources was expressed at a board meeting in 1974:

> *Umbrella for projects involving access to the Farm on educational, environmental and agricultural education…[T]o keep land and buildings from being developed—keeping place beautiful and showing others the value of it…Maintenance and use of land and buildings that are here for educational purposes…[T]o aid in a regional and global effort to educate people by showing value of all activities on the farm. Farm would set the example—educating them to solve various problems which the world is facing now…Environmental balance of farm and allowing local people to use it would enrich the community.*[46]

Right: A Shelburne Farms camper selling produce at the Burlington Farmers' Market, by Marshall C. Webb, August 1972. Shelburne Farms Collections.

The partnership model first developed in the early 1970s was equally important. By working with individuals and entities that shared their vision, they could reach a much wider audience than they could manage with their own limited staffing and finances. Additionally, providing buildings and acreage to their partners offered the prospect of earning much-needed income. Over the next thirty years, these key concepts would shape the course of the development of Shelburne Farms Resources, its programs, and, ultimately, the fate of the property itself.[47]

Between 1972 and 1974, Shelburne Farms Resources received Derick's permission to use space in the Farm Barn, Coach Barn, and Shelburne House for its ventures and those of its partners. Large sections of the Farm Barn and Coach Barn, vacated when Derick discontinued his chicken, sheep, and beef cattle operations in the mid- to late 1960s, were immediately available. The opportunity to use Shelburne House for public programs arose in 1974, when Derick and Elizabeth separated and chose not to live there that season. By the following year, after their divorce was finalized and Elizabeth moved away, Derick no longer wanted to use the house as a family residence.[48]

Between about 1973 and 1976, a vision emerged for the three main historic buildings. The Farm Barn would become a center for the offices and activities of the organization's partners, including farm-related enterprises, other nonprofits, craftsmen, and artists. The Coach Barn would be devoted to educational programs such as summer camps, school field trips, teachers' workshops, and classes for adults offered either directly by SFR or by its partners. Shelburne House would serve as a center for cultural programs such as musical performances and art classes. The vision was solidified in 1976,

when Derick donated the three historic buildings to Shelburne Farms Resources, a gesture that illustrated his support for the young organization and allowed for improvements to be made without prompting steep increases in property taxes. He stated, "My intention and hope is to see the buildings restored and used for educational purposes and more specifically to be used for the development of agricultural, educational, and cultural activities and programs directed towards 'restoring, maintaining and enhancing the quality of the rural environment.'"[49]

Shelburne Farms Resources opened Shelburne House to the public for the first time in 1974 and regularly hosted tours, workshops, conferences, and performances each summer at the residence from then on. After readying the building for its first public events in 1974, Marshall and Emily decided to live there to oversee its daily operations, including program management, cooking, and cleaning, which they did for the next four years. By 1980, Shelburne House had developed into a regular seasonal center for cultural programs. Some programs, such as a five-day series of cooking classes held in 1977 in the dwelling's kitchen, were organized and managed by SFR itself. Others consisted of day and overnight residency programs hosted for partner organizations. Day programs included public tours of the house benefiting the Shelburne Bicentennial Committee, meetings of the Northeast Agriculture Association and the University of Vermont's Department of Environmental Studies, dance and music camps for children, and classical and contemporary musical performances organized by the Vermont Symphony Orchestra and the University of Vermont's Lane Series. Overnight residency programs included teacher workshops led by the Vermont Council on the Arts and conferences on such topics as holistic health.[50]

Shelburne Farms Resources established a long-lasting partnership program with the Vermont Mozart Festival at Shelburne House in 1974. A newly formed organization dedicated to seasonal performances in scenic settings around the state, the Festival held its first concerts in the dining room at Shelburne House. The following year, the relationship with SFR grew into an annual three-week summer residency program, during which Festival musicians lived and practiced in the house and held workshops and performances there. Starting in 1975, their concerts were held outdoors to accommodate a larger audience, with musicians performing on the south porch and the audience seated on the surrounding lawn. Over the years, additional performances were also held in the Coach Barn. The Festival's overnight residency program operated through its 1985 season, and the organization continues to hold performances at Shelburne House and the Coach Barn each year.[51]

To raise funds, Shelburne Farms Resources also began offering dinners and overnight accommodations at Shelburne House to the general public when the dwelling was not already devoted to specific events. During several summer weekends in 1979, "for $95 a couple, and somewhat less for an individual, guests [could] spend two days sampling farm-fresh meals, taking guided tours of the property and swimming."[52] These initial offerings would eventually lead board member Paul Hawken to propose converting Shelburne House into an inn.[53]

At the Farm Barn during the mid- to late 1970s, SFR set up an office, developed plans to repair damage from accelerating water infiltration, and offered space to several partnership organizations, small businesses, and local craftspeople. Partners in the 1970s and early 1980s included the Shelburne Spinners, an organization that promoted hand spinning and the sale of wool and woolen goods; weaver Eileen McGrath Rockefeller; boat builder Tom Hill; and woodworkers Bruce Beeken, Tim Downey, and Jeff Parsons. Gardens For All, a non-profit organization dedicated to urban community gardening and led by Marilyn's father, Tommy Thompson, and SFR board member Lyman Wood, rented office space and managed approximately forty community gardening plots in the field just east of the barn. Gardens For All also operated a canning center for local residents on the ground floor of the Farm Barn's north wing. The O'Bread Bakery, an organic sourdough bakery, succeeded the canning center.[54]

By the mid-1970s, Shelburne Farms Resources and its partner programs also began to occupy sections of the Coach Barn. In 1977, the Ethan Allen Child Care Center and the Norris and Ellyn Day Camp, devoted to music, dance, arts, and crafts, both occupied sections of the building on rainy days. The following year, SFR launched its first formal school field trips, which used the former tack room at the Coach Barn as a home base. Elementary school students visited the building and surrounding areas to participate in monthly programs exploring concepts related to agriculture and the natural world. Stephanie Spencer, SFR's volunteer coordinator, and Eileen Rockefeller, who performed public relations and fundraising duties, worked with Marilyn to develop the first school-based educational programs and seasonal activities. With her engaging personality and extensive family contacts, Eileen was able to give the project its first national visibility.[55]

By the early 1980s, staff at Shelburne Farms Resources oversaw an expanded series of environmental educational programs at the Coach Barn benefiting elementary students and teachers. According to David Barash, SFR's first education program director, the mission of the programs was "to contribute to the revitalization of regional agriculture through the teaching of the principles of natural resource conservation…The sounder [an] understanding people have about the natural cycles of agriculture, the better citizens they will be in terms of environmental issues."[56] In 1984, a local reporter described SFR's programs:

A school field trip visiting the Farm Barn weaving studio of Eileen McGrath Rockefeller, by Theo Barash, 1981. Shelburne Farms Collections.

Involving children directly in the world around them, the Environmental Education Program of Shelburne Farms Resources goes beyond the traditional classroom experience. The young scientists become "detectives" as they sleuth for animal tracks, animal food and homes, or woodpecker holes. The kids play "diversity tag," finding different plants in several environments, create a "web of life" with yarn, and join in games like "predator-prey." Through writing and drawing exercises, games, experiments, drama, and other environmentally-oriented activities, the program tries to find the right blend of structure and freedom. Science can be demystified, and the mystery of nature can be left intact.[57]

In 1980, the Coach Barn also became the site of an annual public Harvest Festival. Initiated by board and community members Jack Lazarowski, Margie Holden, and Judy Candido, the annual Festival featured musical performers, hay rides, traditional foods, and other activities. It remains one of the organization's most popular programs.[58]

In addition to utilizing the three major estate buildings, Shelburne Farms Resources received permission from Derick to devote a small portion of his property's acreage to agricultural research conducted by faculty at the University of Vermont. By 1977, members of the university's Plant and Soil Science Department were experimenting with test plots of rye, corn, and hay, including fertilizing them with sewage sludge. Over the next few years, SFR also arranged for the university to grow soybeans, lentils, rice, and black walnut trees, among other trial crops, on the Farm.[59]

In 1979, Shelburne Farms Resources launched the first regular public tours of the property. Organized by Education Director David Barash, groups led by volunteer guides visited the Farm Barn, the Coach Barn, Shelburne House, and the dairy from May to October each year. By 1984, the tours attracted some 5,000 people annually.[60]

During the 1970s and early 1980s, as Shelburne Farms Resources matured, the organization maintained a vibrant complexity. Instead of simplifying their programs over time, family and board members continued to diversify and expand the programs they offered. As Marilyn remarked in 1979,

> [O]ne of the fascinating problems in managing Shelburne Farms Resources is the temptation to channel this place into some particular, existing philosophy. Like the American Folk School, or an Anthroposophical Center which relates to biodynamic farming and Steiner Education. Some people have even suggested that [Shelburne Farms Resources] might be a Zen Center. Of course it's tempting to have S.F.R. become crystal clear and simplified. But I think all of us here resist that kind of institutionalizing, because we have a mix of activities that is unique to this particular place. We're still searching, and we're still fine-tuning.[61]

A British organization with a similar wide-ranging mission, the Dartington Hall Trust of South Devon, proved to be a major influence for Shelburne Farms Resources in the late 1970s and early 1980s. The organization was established in 1925 by a wealthy couple, Leonard and Dorothy Elmhirst, to use an agricultural estate dating to the fourteenth century as a resource for revitalizing rural communities in England. The Elmhirsts and their subsequent managers conserved the estate's farmland, rehabilitated the historic structures, and developed a series of successful educational, cultural, and for-profit ventures, including a school; arts, publishing, and music programs; a glassworks; and farm and forestry operations. Dartington Hall possessed a size and scope similar to that of Shelburne Farms. In 1979, Marilyn and Eileen Rockefeller visited Dartington Hall to research its organizational structure and innovative combination of charitable programs and for-profit ventures. In Marilyn's words, Dartington Hall was "a very good model" for Shelburne Farms Resources.[62]

Twelve years after the establishment of Shelburne Farms Resources in 1972, the organization had grown from a fledgling organization offering a handful of programs based on the periphery of the Shelburne Farms property to an entity touching thousands of individuals through numerous programs and events occurring in the heart of the estate. In 1972, SFR reached approximately twenty students and teachers through the work of four seasonal volunteers. By 1984, SFR reached approximately 25,000 people and employed twenty-five year-round employees, along with an additional five seasonal staff members.[63]

Yet despite its programmatic successes, Shelburne Farms Resources struggled financially throughout the 1970s and early 1980s. Program fees and rents paid by SFR's partners barely covered the costs of the nonprofit's programs. Already having difficulty managing its finances in 1976, the organization acquired a significant additional monetary burden when it accepted Derick's gift of the three enormous and deteriorating estate buildings. Two years previously, Marilyn had characterized the condition of the Farm Barn, Coach Barn, and Shelburne House as quite poor: "Damage in buildings much worse than thought. Incredible rot—ceilings, main beams. Will cost a fortune."[64]

During the 1970s and early 1980s, the nonprofit did its best to maintain the estate buildings using funds from its meager annual operating budget of approximately $70,000 to $80,000. Marshall, who served as the organization's buildings and grounds manager during this time, used some of his inheritance to hire a crew to repaint the exterior trim at

Shelburne House and the Coach Barn, a considerable project. When his funds ran low, he paid part of one painter's wages by bartering his electric guitar. The crew completed a primer coat on most of the two buildings during the summers of 1972, 1973, and 1974 before Marshall's funds were completely depleted. Marshall also removed the livestock manure from the Coach Barn and Farm Barn in an effort to arrest the ongoing deterioration and prepare the spaces for programmatic activities.[65]

The public, educational uses that Shelburne Farms Resources' board members envisioned for Shelburne House, the Farm Barn, and the Coach Barn required millions of dollars in structural work, significant repairs to the roofs, windows, and sheathing, and major systems upgrades to meet modern safety, power, heating, and sanitary standards. During the 1970s and early 1980s, board members and employees set about raising funds to complete these projects. Their appeals were assisted by the addition of Shelburne Farms to the National Register of Historic Places in 1980. Due primarily to the financial support of board member and local philanthropist Lenore ("Norrie") Broughton, who possessed a strong interest in alternative education and social issues, Shelburne Farms Resources raised approximately $50,000 for building preservation work by 1984. At the Farm Barn, the roof was repaired, compromised structural posts and beams were replaced, and interior work was completed in the building's north wing to accommodate the nonprofit's growing group of partners. A new furnace, lighting, and bathrooms were installed in the Coach Barn to facilitate year-round use of the building. And at Shelburne House, plumbing repairs allowed the nonprofit to use additional bedrooms for overnight programs without the fear of more water damage from leaks.[66]

Additional fundraising proved to be extremely challenging. Many members of the local community continued to perceive the organization as the private enterprise of a wealthy family. Some wondered if SFR was merely a tax shelter. Furthermore, potential benefactors were often reluctant to donate to an organization that did not legally own the land on which it conducted its programs. As reported in the minutes of a 1977 board meeting, two recent appeals, one to the National Trust for Historic Preservation and the other to the State of Vermont, had been rejected:

> [The] National Trust turned us down citing confusion over the connection between Shelburne Farms Resources, Shelburne Farms, Shelburne Museum, and Webb Family and any possible inside money available for the project…Marilyn…cited the unenthusiastic response from [Vermont] Governor Snelling who felt that no public $ should go towards a place such as SFR with its history of wealth.[67]

Repairs to the main block of the Farm Barn, by Marshall C. Webb, March 1976. Shelburne Farms Collections.

In 1978, SFR mortgaged the three major estate buildings to fund its ongoing operations. Two years later, the organization had managed to pay off its bank loans but was barely meeting its annual operating costs.[68]

Agricultural and Forestry Operations

At the same time that Derick's children, their friends, and their advisors were developing Shelburne Farms Resources and its growing web of programs and partnerships, many of them also contributed to the property's agricultural operations. At various times during the 1970s, Quentyn, Mary, Lisa, Alec, Marshall, as well as Mary and Lisa's husbands, and family friend Bill Ladd all assisted Derick with his dairy operation, working alongside his five to seven other employees to complete milking, crop harvesting, and other chores. Quentyn worked as Derick's crops production manager from 1968 to 1973, responsible for planting and harvesting as well as maintaining equipment. Lisa's husband, John Roberts, then a recent agricultural school graduate, served as Derick's farm manager from 1974 to 1977. Alec worked as his father's bookkeeper from 1977 to 1979, overseeing the finances for the agricultural operations as well as Derick's personal funds. In 1979, after Lisa and John had left to start their own dairy farm in Cornwall, Vermont, Alec assumed the role of general manager of Shelburne Farms for his father, overseeing Farm employees and finances and administering the daily agricultural operations.[69]

Marshall, meanwhile, managed Shelburne Farms' 600 acres of woodlands. In the early to mid-1970s, he learned to operate a chainsaw by helping longtime Farm employee Tom Bessette to remove hundreds of dead and dying elm trees on the property as they succumbed to Dutch elm disease. He continued to remove the trees as they died into the 1980s. In 1974, he worked with Chittenden County Forester Bill Hall to develop a forestry management plan that would improve the health, future productivity, and earning potential of the woodlands, taking their historic character and importance as wildlife habitat into account. Marshall also hoped to provide recreational opportunities for the general public by means of the logging trails that would be cut for harvesting purposes. In the winter of 1974–75, he harvested 250,000 board feet with the assistance of two contract loggers, and in the following years, he continued to harvest lumber and firewood for commercial sale. He also launched Lone Tree Lumber, a custom milling business operated with a portable sawmill he purchased with his own funds. In 1978, Marshall's efforts resulted in Shelburne Farms' designation as Vermont's Tree Farm of the Year. The following year, Marshall explained his ongoing goals for the forestry operations: "In the future, I see a continuous annual harvest of timber and firewood that would pay the taxes on the woodlands and hopefully generate some profit."[70]

Derick welcomed his children's involvement in the agricultural operations, considering their relationship to be, in his words, a "cooperative endeavor."[71] He turned over management of the daily farm operations to his children starting in 1974, when his son-in-law John Roberts became farm manager, but he continued to be actively involved and responsible for all major agricultural decisions until his death in 1984.[72]

In order to supplement the low salaries they received as Derick's farm employees, several family members and friends developed small-scale, independent agricultural enterprises on the Farm in exchange for little or no rent. Mary and David raised sheep, turkeys, and chickens at Orchard Point from 1974 to 1978, selling lamb to the local Shelburne Supermarket and wool to the Vermont Sheepbreeders Association. In the 1970s, Bill Ladd used a team of horses to produce maple syrup, cultivate corn, and grow wheat for the O'Bread Bakery, which rented space in the Farm Barn. He and his horses also assisted Marshall with logging activities in the winter months. Ladd stabled his team at the Farm Barn and transformed the north tower of the building into a living space. After the summer camp's final season in 1975, Ladd moved to the gardener's cottage with his partner, Cricket Laffin, and assumed management of the camp's commercial organic vegetable garden, which became known as the "market garden." In 1981, Ladd and Laffin were succeeded at the market garden by David and Susan Miskell.[73]

During the 1970s, the Webbs, their friends, and their advisors debated two distinct models for the agricultural operations. Lisa's husband, John, espoused

Marshall C. Webb, April 1981, photographer unknown. Shelburne Farms Collections.

a model based upon more conventional agricultural philosophies of the time. Under his plan, the Webbs would focus on the large-scale production of fluid milk, expand the Brown Swiss dairy from approximately 160 to 500 cows, and build a second dairy complex in the Bay View area of the estate. In doing so, they would fully utilize Shelburne Farms' large land base, capitalize on the latest in farm technology, and make significant investments in new equipment for planting and harvesting feed and bedding crops. His proposal would have kept Shelburne Farms on the path that Derick had commenced in the late 1960s when he decided to focus solely on the dairy operations. Mary, David, Alec, Marilyn, Marshall, and Bill Ladd espoused a smaller-scale, more diversified agricultural approach that required a less significant capital investment—one which, by design or not, reflected the diversity and self-sufficiency of the small farms that existed at Shelburne Farms in the late eighteenth and early nineteenth centuries. Marshall would later characterize their philosophy as "small is beautiful."[74] Under their plan, they would organically produce small grains, fluid milk, meats, and maple syrup, market them directly to local consumers, and minimize soil erosion and potential pollution of Lake Champlain caused by a lack of crop cover and agricultural runoff.[75]

During the 1970s, the Webbs experimented with both philosophies. Derick borrowed approximately $70,000 to purchase dairy equipment, including two Harvestore silos, which were constructed at the pole barn complex to improve the quality and efficiency of Farm-grown feed. In anticipation of a major expansion of the dairy herd, John began to increase hay production and cull underperforming cows to improve the herd's quality. Meanwhile, Mary, David, Marshall, and the Ladds raised sheep and poultry, harvested lumber, tapped maple trees, and grew wheat. By 1979, the group had also launched a conservation-minded crop system. As a local reporter noted, "most of the cows' grain, forage and bedding is grown by ecological measures—composting manure, cover cropping, [and] non-toxic weed control."[76]

Derick eventually concluded that "a massive farm enterprise on a commercial scale" would not earn significantly more than a smaller, more diversified operation after the necessary capital investments and outlays in additional staffing costs were made.[77] As he wrote to his children in 1976, "I am convinced that the present Brown Swiss herd can be maintained on a profitable basis at its present size while at the same time supplementing income by the addition of diversified enterprises."[78]

By 1980, the Webb family had decided not to develop a large-scale commercial dairy to the exclusion of other ventures. However, the differences of opinion led to the dispersal of several family members. Lisa and John left to start their own farm in Cornwall, Vermont, in the spring of 1977, and Mary and David left two years later to pursue other interests. Alec, Marilyn, and Marshall remained and continued to work on developing the agricultural operations without increasing the size of the dairy. In December 1979, they expressed their goals for the Farm:

> *To develop a bio-ecological agricultural system which conserves natural resources and creates a healthful living environment based on an awareness of soil-plant-human inter-relationships. To demonstrate a balance of tradition with new information and ecological health with economic realities. To demonstrate the benefit of developing on a regional basis, strong, functional relationships between population centers and neighboring farmlands. To develop an agricultural system which over a period of time will become* less *and* less *dependent on non-naturally renewable inputs.*[79]

Over the next five years, family members and Farm employees continued efforts to improve soil health and reduce negative environmental impacts caused by their agricultural practices. In addition to their concern for potential pollution and erosion, they also sought to reduce their use of fossil fuels and conserve wildlife habitats. As Alec stated in 1983,

> *Because we have relatively few cows on a relatively big acreage, we're able to use our land less intensively than other dairies do… We rule out poisons: herbicides and pesticides. I think we've used an herbicide once in ten years, and we don't expect to use any again. We use purchased fertilizer on our fields if they need it. But we hope they'll need it less and less as we manage the application of our manure better, and as we move our time-of-harvest up so we're feeding younger, more nourishing hay.*[80]

In 1978 and 1979, family members and Farm employees also moved toward developing a diversified farm operation geared directly to the local market. They added small herds of beef cattle and hogs to Shelburne Farms, selling pork, beef, and veal.[81]

However, their main agricultural focus remained the dairy. In 1979, the family launched a raw milk business, selling unpasteurized fluid milk directly to local retailers. The Webb siblings had been accustomed to drinking raw milk produced at Shelburne Farms since their childhood, when Derick and Elizabeth had installed a cafeteria-style milk dispenser in their dining room at Shelburne House, and family members felt that their milk was healthier and better tasting than commonly available pasteurized and homogenized milk. The raw milk was subject to strict sanitary procedures, including more frequent testing of the cows for diseases. It was packaged in half-gallon containers directly from the bulk tanks in the pole barn and trucked to stores daily. Shelburne Farms was one of only three Vermont dairies to sell raw milk at the time.[82]

Family members also envisioned additional diversification into vegetables, eggs, and other farm products. As Alec stated in 1979,

> *As far as the farming operation goes, we are trying to continue diversification. We're raising beef calves in addition to dairying. We have sheep and pigs, and we use a local slaughter house. We hope that we can begin to distribute our own meat in the future. We have a refrigerated truck which delivers our milk, and we'd like to use that truck to also deliver our meat directly to people's homes…perhaps to eventually open our own store to sell our own products. But the first goal is to get the milk going to full capacity. So far, we've had a 100% favorable response on our local sales of milk…[W]e've got the basis for introducing meat and produce on the local market and a whole range of agriculturally related products.*[83]

Alec and Marilyn hired two new employees to oversee the Farm's new ventures: Gordon ("Buster") Searles, who served as farm manager from 1980 to 1994, and William Clapp, who managed milk packaging and sales and helped with crop production. From 1979 to 1982, Shelburne Farms marketed approximately half of its milk as raw milk and sold the remainder to a local creamery, where it was blended with the milk of other nearby farms. The Webbs planned to eventually utilize all of their milk for their own dairy products, such as yogurt, ice cream, or cheese. They settled on the production of cheddar cheese in about 1980.[84]

In the fall of 1982, while establishing the cheddar cheese operation, Shelburne Farms became mired in local controversy when its raw milk was suspected of causing intestinal illnesses in a dozen of its consumers. The Webbs voluntarily pulled the Farm's milk from store shelves and eventually decided to discontinue the product, although evidence of bacterial contamination was never definitively traced back to the Farm. In doing so, the agricultural operation lost $120,000 worth of annual gross income, a significant source of revenue.[85]

As a result, family members pinned their hopes on their new cheddar cheese venture. Between 1982 and 1984, the Farm's staff studied and perfected methods of producing cheese from Shelburne Farms' raw milk in the tradition of English farmhouse cheddar cheese, in which the dairy herd and cheese making processes were entirely located on one farm. Because the cheese was aged for a minimum of six months before being sold, potential bacterial contamination would not be an issue. The Webb family converted half of the milking parlor at the pole barn into a cheese-making facility and purchased secondhand equipment. Bill Clapp and Marshall Webb, the Farm's first cheese makers, received encouragement and instruction from colleagues involved in commercial cheese making in Vermont, and they attended a course offered by the University of Guelph in Ontario. Clapp also traveled to England, where he witnessed traditional cheese making methods that informed his subsequent refinement of the Shelburne Farms' cheese recipe. The Farm began to sell cheese to gourmet retail outlets in Vermont and the eastern United States in the fall of 1982. Shortly thereafter, the Farm launched a mail-order business and store to sell cheese and other farm products on site in the Farm Barn's north ell, directly below the Farm's administrative offices. However, it would be several years before the new cheese operation began to realize a profit.[86]

In fact, throughout the 1970s and early 1980s, the Webb family's agricultural ventures realized little if any financial return. Derick summarized the challenges that they faced in a 1976 letter to his children:

Bill Clapp making cheese, by Marshall C. Webb, March 1988. Shelburne Farms Collections.

It should be plain to you all by now that the economic well being of the farm prospers or languishes in almost direct proportion to the amount of active involvement by the owners. When I was really involved we were usually on an even keel. When I became otherwise involved there was a gradual deterioration, & since you all have become active there is again good cause for optimism. This is no great revelation & is true for any business. However, it is especially true about farming for many different reasons which all add up to a very low margin of profit. Some of the reasons of which you are becoming aware, I am sure, are the high capital requirements, sharply escalating production costs, lack of skilled & experienced labor, long hours, vagaries of the weather, unpredictable livestock performance, etc. etc.... The rate of return from capital invested in farming is unpredictable at best.[87]

In addition to these factors, the Farm faced several other financial challenges. The energy crisis of the 1970s, sparked by the 1973 oil embargo by the Organization of Petroleum Exporting Countries (OPEC), led to dramatic increases in the cost of fuel. Moreover, the family's ambitious diversification plans required an initial investment of funds and a generous amount of lead time before they began to pay off. By 1979, the Farm was incurring a $50,000 annual deficit. That year, Alec stated, "Financially we're close to the bottom."[88] The following two years produced some improvement, but the 1982 raw milk crisis dashed hopes that the agricultural operations would soon begin to turn a profit.[89]

Financial Sustainability

During the 1970s and early 1980s, family members frequently revisited the question of the long-term use and ownership of the Shelburne Farms estate. The property taxes assessed on the property continued to grow, but Derick's children and children-in-law were consistently unable to fulfill their goal of raising funds through their ventures to offset his tax burden. In addition, Derick turned sixty in 1973, and although he was in good health, the specter of the estate taxes that would be levied when he died began to trouble the family.

Derick's finances were also growing increasingly untenable. He received approximately $80,000 in annual income from his personal trusts, but his property taxes for Shelburne Farms claimed more than half of that amount, the agricultural operations required regular cash infusions, and he was still paying for his younger children's high school and college expenses. In addition, he used $150,000 of his first wife Elizabeth's inheritance to launch an air charter business based at the Burlington airport in 1972. However, in the wake of the 1973 oil embargo and the subsequent decline of the American economy, the cost of aviation fuel dramatically increased, the company's clients curtailed their chartering activities, and the business began to fail.[90]

Between 1970 and 1976, Derick accumulated significant debt. He mortgaged 200 acres of land located outside of the estate gates for approximately $125,000, borrowed $87,000 to cover his property tax expenses, and borrowed more than $70,000 to purchase new farm equipment. He also borrowed $400,000 against his future inheritance from his mother, Aileen, to pay off some of his bank loans, tax obligations, and Shelburne Farms' outstanding debt. Derick and his first wife Elizabeth divorced in 1975, and the terms of their settlement included the repayment of the funds he had used from her inheritance for his air charter business. In 1976, Derick married Helen ("Rusty") Allen. While she was a strong supporter of his children's desire to preserve Shelburne Farms, and she appreciated the financial sacrifices Derick was making in an attempt to do so, she and Derick both wished to build a new home of their own on the property, a project that would require additional funds. That same year, Derick mortgaged the majority of the remaining estate property for $154,000 and realized approximately $20,000 from the sale of a number of valuable furnishings from Shelburne House.[91]

It became imperative that Derick and his family develop a sustainable course of action for Shelburne Farms. Marshall later characterized the financial challenges they were facing as a "guillotine blade waiting to drop."[92] The question of who would become the next owner(s) of Shelburne Farms, and how they would pay the costly estate taxes that would be due, also continued to weigh heavily on family members' minds. Subdivision remained a very real possibility, albeit one everyone wanted to avoid.[93]

As a result, in the 1970s and early 1980s, the Webb family explored a number of land use solutions for Shelburne Farms that they hoped would both solve Derick's financial problems *and* conserve the estate. The first prospects appeared in 1972, when Derick and Alec began to negotiate with the town of Shelburne to reach a property tax stabilization agreement. Following a town reappraisal conducted for property tax purposes, Derick had filed a lawsuit to contest Shelburne's assessment of the value of Shelburne Farms. The court ruled in Derick's favor, finding that his approximately 1,850 acres should be assessed at $1.3 million to reflect its use as agricultural land, instead of the $1.7 million the town's appraiser had selected based on its potential use as a site for residential and/or commercial development. Instead of pursuing an appeal of the decision, the town selectboard agreed to consider a property tax stabilization agreement.[94]

Completed between a municipality and an individual landowner, such agreements strike a balance between generating revenue for a community and burdening owners with heavy taxes. The two parties agree to a compromise value for the property, and the taxes are levied according to that figure. In doing so, communities recognize that the value of the property to its residents may be greater than its maximum financial worth. In 1955, in an effort to provide financial relief to farmers in the state, the Vermont legislature had enacted a law authorizing municipalities to enter into such agreements for agricultural properties. In the early 1970s, however, tax stabilization remained a relatively novel concept in Vermont.[95]

Discussions with the town began in earnest in the spring of 1972, after Shelburne residents voted overwhelmingly in favor of authorizing their selectboard to negotiate a stabilization agreement for Shelburne Farms. Protracted negotiations occurred over the next ten years, as provisions of the agreement were considered and revised in light of the Webb family's developing educational, agricultural, and estate planning goals for the property and Derick's worsening financial situation. Over time, two separate agreements evolved: one stabilizing the property taxes assessed on the three main estate buildings (the Farm Barn, the Coach Barn, and Shelburne House) was finalized in 1975, and another covering the bulk of Derick's land at Shelburne Farms, some 990 acres, followed in 1982.[96]

The earliest versions of the tax stabilization agreement, discussed between 1972 and 1974, incorporated two additional land use strategies that were innovative in their own right. The first strategy consisted of the establishment of permanent development restrictions on the core of the Shelburne Farms estate in the form of a conservation easement, an action authorized under a 1969 state law enacted to encourage land conservation. Such easements were then emerging around the country as an important strategy for protecting land from intensive development. They legally limited the uses of the acreage to which they pertained, resulting in reduced real estate values and decreased property taxes. By donating an easement to the town of Shelburne, Derick could reduce his future property taxes and receive an income tax deduction for the value of his gift.[97]

Along with the donation of a conservation easement on his land inside the estate gates, Derick also offered to give the 575 acres that he owned outside of

Right: A Vermont Mozart Festival performance at Shelburne House, by Marshall C. Webb, c. 1980. Shelburne Farms Collections.

the gates to the town, with the caveat that the land be preserved as open space for public use. This proposal was also appealing to all parties involved, as it would avoid subdivision and provide for permanent public enjoyment of the area, which included the fishing and boating access on Shelburne Bay that Derick had leased to the state in 1957.[98]

In 1974, the two provisions were included in a proposal for a property tax stabilization agreement for Shelburne Farms approved by town voters. However, soon after the vote, Derick delayed final negotiations with the selectboard. His financial situation had worsened since the discussions had commenced, and he probably realized that neither an easement nor a gift of property was feasible in his present circumstances. He needed to reserve the right to mortgage, or even develop, his property if necessary.[99]

In 1973, while the property tax stabilization negotiations were underway, Alec and Marilyn had developed their own proposal for preserving Shelburne Farms that incorporated Derick's children's values and complemented the goals and philosophies of their fledgling nonprofit programs and agricultural ventures. In keeping with their generation's desire to keep the property intact, Alec and Marilyn proposed various ideas "to treat the land as one parcel" so that it could be "held in trust to be preserved for agricultural and educational uses."[100] Just as Seward and Lila Webb had established Shelburne Farms Corporation in the 1920s, Alec and Marilyn sought a way for Derick to transfer

the property to a newly created partnership or corporation that would be responsible for the estate's management, property taxes, and other operating expenses. The income that Derick received from his personal trust, no longer diverted to Shelburne Farms, would then become available for him to use for his living expenses and the repayment of his debt.[101]

Alec and Marilyn's land use plan utilized the traditional British concept of leaseholds, which would allow them to keep the property intact and retain control over its fate. Alec and Marilyn proposed that, once established, the partnership or corporation would own the entire Shelburne Farms property and create inholdings as necessary for family members' private residences and other limited development rather than subdivide separate parcels. As Alec wrote in a letter to his family in 1976,

> *All land and common property assets held in trust to be preserved for agricultural and educational uses. All income from above to be used for property operating and maintenance expenses (debt, taxes, labor, etc.). All structures on the land to have a consistent "lease" relationship to the land whether privately constructed and owned, privately purchased, privately leased, gifted, willed, sold etc. in order to maintain the integrity of the property as a whole and to maintain consistent market values and property taxation. A land use plan defining appropriate land uses indicating: natural areas to be preserved, agricultural and farm homestead area, residential area. A clear decision making and operating structure (as clearly defined as a conventional corporate structure).*[102]

The proposed plan hinged on the siblings' willingness to give up their individual inheritance rights to the property in favor of preserving it as a whole. They were unanimous in their support. In 1976, Alec reflected that the conservation of the Shelburne Farms property "was more valuable than inheriting any amount of money."[103] Two years later, Marilyn stated, "This is an unusual family. The Webb children don't think of themselves as heirs. We like living and working on the farm, share the same ideas about it and make our decisions jointly."[104]

Alec and Marilyn held fast to their wish to avoid any development whatsoever, but they felt that if subdivision was the only alternative, it should avoid following typical patterns of suburban growth. Under their proposal, the new ownership entity would raise funds to support and conserve Shelburne Farms by creating a limited residential development in a carefully selected site on the property. The strict land use restrictions they envisioned were in marked contrast to the town of Shelburne's zoning regulations of the 1970s, in which the whole of Shelburne Farms was zoned for subdivisions of five-acre lots. Alec and Marilyn envisioned a cluster of houses surrounded by the Farm's agricultural fields, a land use scheme common in rural areas of Europe. As Alec explained, this concept would "creat[e] over a period of years a concentrated village. If we think ahead 200 years and several more generations we can visualize a clustered European type village in the midst of farmed, wooded, and open land dotted with farm homesteads."[105] By locating a settlement in an area of the property that was already a hub of activity, such as the acreage immediately surrounding the Farm Barn, Alec and Marilyn wished to preserve wide swaths of undeveloped acreage. They hoped that their alternative "Integrated Village Development" would complement the educational programs and partnership activities taking shape under the auspices of Shelburne Farms Resources by providing nearby homes for employees and consumers.[106]

Members of the Webb family debated various aspects of Alec and Marilyn's 1973 land use proposal for most of the next decade. Meanwhile, negotiations with the town selectboard for a property tax stabilization agreement, as well as the proposal to place a conservation easement on the core of the estate property, remained at a standstill.

However, in about 1974, discussions about the transfer of land outside of the estate gates to the town of Shelburne resumed when the Nature Conservancy, to which Derick had been introduced a few years earlier by Marilyn and her first husband, Jerry Leimenstoll, agreed to participate in the transaction. The parties ultimately settled on a compromise solution: a bargain sale of a smaller portion of the land, which would ensure its conservation and provide Derick with some financial relief at a price that the Conservancy and the town could afford. The Conservancy would permanently retain and conserve 107 acres, located along the shores of the LaPlatte River and McCabes Brook to the south of Bay Road. The Conservancy would temporarily own another 100 acres, located along Shelburne Bay to the north of Bay Road, until the town of Shelburne had raised the necessary funds to purchase it. As Derick explained to his children, the transaction was a logical compromise:

> *It appears obvious that it will be difficult if not almost impossible to retain our whole property without discovering & promptly securing new sources of income. To date no one has done this—mostly because purely commercial projects have been discarded by preferences of all concerned…I still own all the property and am trying to do what seems best as our decision must be made about current and long range problems concerning operation, management and eventual transfer of the property…I would rather lose the outside land, if absolutely necessary, to preserve the inside rather than run which I think might be too great a risk of losing it all.*[107]

At the end of 1976, Derick sold both parcels to the Nature Conservancy for $300,000, half of their appraised value. The town acquired its portion of the property from the Conservancy two years later, after the municipality was awarded a grant from the federal Bureau of Outdoor Recreation. The town used the $300,000 difference in the sale price donated by Derick as matching funds for the grant.[108]

Following the transfer of the land to the Nature Conservancy and the town of Shelburne, Derick was able to discharge some of his personal debts and expenses. However, the future of the remainder of the Shelburne Farms estate, which then totaled some 1,650 acres, remained tenuous. By the late 1970s, his annual property taxes had reached $50,000, and he would not reach agreement with the town of Shelburne on property tax stabilization for his lands until 1982. His accumulated debt continued to climb as a result of compounded interest on his remaining liabilities. By the early 1980s, Derick's debt totaled approximately $1 million.[109]

Between 1978 and 1982, Derick and his children finally settled on a plan for Shelburne Farms. After extensive internal deliberations and consultations with several sympathetic groups, including the Nature Conservancy, the American Farmlands Trust, the Ottauquechee Land Trust, Lake Champlain Islands Trust, and the Shelburne Selectboard, they ultimately developed a multifaceted solution utilizing several land use strategies.[110]

The key feature of the solution consisted of transferring ownership of the estate to a family organization similar to that which Alec and Marilyn had proposed several years earlier. Family members first considered a proposal for Shelburne Farms Resources to purchase the bulk of the land and expand its educational mission to assume management of the agricultural ventures. SFR would mount a major fundraising campaign to finance the purchase. Derick would then be able to immediately pay off both his debt and the capital gains taxes that would result from the transaction.

He would reserve only a small homestead parcel for himself: forty-six acres on Orchard Point surrounding his residence, Orchard House, as well as additional parcels for each of his six children to have as either year-round dwellings or places to stay when visiting. The siblings all agreed to the plan to legally cede their inheritance rights to the property at large.[111]

Family members and SFR board members investigated several means of raising the necessary funds, including outright grants from foundations and/or individuals and a possible loan from the Nature Conservancy. Shelburne Farms Resources needed to be able to raise an estimated $2.14 million to pay Derick's entire debt and capital gains taxes, and fund the property taxes for which the organization would then be responsible. When the costs of repairing the estate buildings and establishing an endowment to support the nonprofit's annual operating costs were factored in, the total amount that SFR's board members wished to raise ballooned to $4.45 million.[112]

One of Shelburne Farms Resources' financial hurdles was lessened when the Shelburne Selectboard agreed to complete a property tax stabilization agreement for the estate after the proposed sale occurred. Under the terms of the agreement, SFR's annual property tax bill would amount to $36,500, instead of the $50,000 Derick was then paying.[113]

However, the nonprofit faced two additional, significant obstacles. First, a major component of the project, the retirement of Derick's debt, was unappealing to potential donors. Second, benefactors were reluctant to give to an organization that had no prior experience in raising the large amount of money the project required and whose current financial situation was tenuous at best. In the early 1980s, SFR's annual operating budget totaled some $80,000, and the nonprofit generated just enough revenue to cover its costs. Would SFR be able to both sustain itself and conserve the estate in the long run? The organization's own board expressed some skepticism. In a meeting held in October 1979, board members asked, "What sort of burden will this create for SFR, which in itself is a fragile entity—debt wise? What about cash flow?"[114]

Faced with the reality that Shelburne Farms Resources was unlikely to be able to raise all of the necessary funds to complete the transfer within a short period of time, family members explored ways to reduce Derick's financial requirements and thus decrease the amount SFR would need to raise. At this point, they returned to the concept of establishing conservation easements. Between 1979 and 1982, Derick and Alec held discussions with the Lake Champlain Islands Trust and the town of Shelburne regarding the possibility of creating conservation easements for thirty shoreline acres between Quaker Smith Point and Orchard Point.[115]

The easement proposal was well timed. The town was experiencing significant growth, which resulted in a dwindling amount of undeveloped shoreline in the area and made the municipality less dependent on the revenue it received from Shelburne Farms' property taxes. Moreover, development of a portion of the Shelburne Farms property would require an increased burden on town services, such as public schools and police and fire departments, which would offset the revenue the town would have received from such development. Community residents proved receptive to the plan for Derick to donate the easements, and the agreements were finalized in 1982.[116]

Another opportunity for reducing Derick's debt load arose in 1980. Derick agreed to sell a forty-seven acre parcel of land as a residential leasehold to Shelburne Farms Resources' staff member and valued advisor Eileen Rockefeller. Located to the south of the Farm Barn and known as Valley View Farm, the parcel included a nineteenth-century brick farmhouse historically occupied by the estate farm managers and their families. In 1980, Rockefeller was renting one section of the house and had expressed interest in finding a permanent residence in the local area. Unlike a traditional

More than a mile of shoreline was permanently protected by a conservation easement in 1982. By Marshall C. Webb, 1976. Shelburne Farms Collections.

lease arrangement, in which tenants occupy property for a fixed period of time in exchange for regular payments, the transaction resulted in the permanent sale of the residential rights, with restrictions on future subdivision and new construction on the parcel. Rockefeller received the security of a permanent residence, while the Webb family received assurance that the parcel was protected from development. The leasehold arrangement held philosophical significance to family members; they felt that unlike a conventional subdivision, the land would continue to be viewed as a whole. Rockefeller offered her lawyer's services to help research and develop a prototype leasehold agreement. Following approval from the town selectboard for the leasehold concept, Rockefeller's purchase was finalized in August 1980.[117]

Yet even with a reduced purchase price made possible by Derick's sale of Valley View Farm and donation of conservation easements on the shoreline acres, Shelburne Farms Resources still faced a significant fundraising burden. Derick's debt, which was compounded by high interest rates, instilled the family with a sense of urgency. Other potential methods of raising funds from the property itself, which they had previously discussed, such as a larger-scale program of leaseholds or a carefully sited, denser residential development, would have required years of planning before any financial return was received. By 1981, it was clear that Shelburne Farms Resources would be unable to raise the necessary funds in a timely manner. Alec later reflected that the scheme was a "fantasy."[118]

Derick then turned to what many family members considered to be a last resort: the subdivision and sale of a major section of the property to raise enough funds to retire his debt. Once completed, he could afford to donate the remaining estate acreage to a new corporate entity formed to conserve and manage the remainder of the Shelburne Farms property, which would be known as Shelburne Farms, Inc. The Ottauquechee Land Trust would assist with the sale of the parcel to ensure its sensitive development and, it was planned, would eventually own the shares of the new organization.[119]

In 1982, a consortium of private buyers, led by Tom Cabot of the prominent Cabot family of Boston, Massachusetts, purchased a 500-acre parcel from Derick for $1.1 million. The parcel consisted of two lots: 175 acres located in the northwestern section of the Shelburne Farms estate, directly to the north of the north gate, and an additional 325 acres across Harbor Road to the east. Cabot created the Pheasant Hill Trust with a group of partners, pledged to build no more than eight sensitively sited residences on the smaller lot, and agreed to seek a way to place conservation easements on the larger lot, which would restrict its future use to agricultural purposes.[120]

With the sale, Derick relinquished the last of the land he owned outside of the estate gates, and Shelburne Farms declined in size by almost one-third, from 1,650 acres to 1,150. The decision was an agonizing one for many family members, but they were forced to conclude that it was the only viable method of preserving the bulk of the estate. As a journalist reported in early 1982,

> *The proposed sale has been the subject of some internal family controversy…It represents the last sacrifice the Webbs can make while still retaining the core property of the estate. Although the land in question has never been an integral part of the estate, it contributes to the visual integrity of the property and does have agricultural potential. Any sale of open farmland for development is bound to be controversial, especially to owners like the Webbs who have demonstrated a consistent dedication to the stewardship of the Farms.*[121]

Family members were certain that they had exhausted all other options for preserving the property as a whole. Derick stated, "If something like this hadn't worked out I would say we could have gone on the way we have been for at most a year…It had become all too clear that as the taxes increased if some solution weren't found it [the estate] would be broken up and its entire character changed. That was something none of us wanted."[122] Marshall later reflected that although the sale was heartbreaking, "We needed to survive."[123]

In the summer of 1982, soon after selling the 500 acres to the Pheasant Hill Trust, Derick incorporated Shelburne Farms, Inc. (SFI), with Hunter Lewis as its founding board chair, and transferred ownership of the bulk of his remaining 1,150 acres to the new corporation. He donated fifteen percent of his shares in SFI to the Ottauquechee Land Trust immediately and considered a pledge to transfer the remainder in annual increments over a period of several years to maximize his tax benefits. At the same time, he retained forty-five acres on Orchard Point as a residential leasehold for himself and reserved six additional leaseholds for his children, ranging in size from one to seven acres each. The children's parcels included Alec and Marilyn's and Marshall's existing homes, two small summer cottages near Shelburne House, and an undeveloped parcel near the former estate greenhouse and garden complex. Derick's transaction, which embraced key components of Alec and Marilyn's original land use proposal, was recognized as a national model for the preservation of large estates by the National Trust for Historic Preservation.[124]

However, during the next two years, Derick was reluctant to commit to donating the remainder of the SFI stock to the land trust. In a November 1983 letter to Alec and Marilyn, he wrote, "I guess we are trying to answer the question which I have actually been asked a number of times by interested people about what happens to the place if it fails in a year or two and has been pledged to OLT in its entirety. Should as much land be saved as possible even at the expense of abandoning programs? Or should some sensible compromise be worked out?"[125] He was more comfortable with Alec playing a lead role in developing such a compromise than he was with an organization dedicated solely to land conservation. In consideration of equity among the siblings and the possibility that future estate taxes might force land sales, Alec and Marilyn continued to put forward their generation's request that he bequeath Shelburne Farms to a nonprofit that would manage it for the benefit of the public.[126]

Derick died suddenly of a heart attack in March 1984. Unbeknown to any of his children, his will was consistent with their desire that the remainder of his property be left to a nonprofit organization. He bequeathed the contents of Shelburne House, the farm livestock and equipment, and all of the shares he owned in Shelburne Farms, Inc., which then amounted to eighty-two percent of the total, to Shelburne Farms Resources. Soon thereafter, SFR reached an agreement to acquire the eighteen percent of the shares that the Ottauquechee Land Trust owned in exchange for donating conservation easements on key agricultural and scenic lands along the main farm drive.[127]

After thirteen years of wrenching debate, negotiation, and compromise, Derick and his children had succeeded in preserving the core of Shelburne Farms as an agricultural estate with an educational purpose. Derick's receptiveness to his children's lofty, idealistic vision for the property, his willingness to incur substantial debt while land use solutions were sought, and his generosity in relinquishing private ownership of lands that his family had held for almost one hundred years made such a significant achievement possible.

The Webb family also benefited from good timing and a receptive local climate. Recently enacted state laws, as well as the support of the community of Shelburne, the Nature Conservancy, and the two local land trust organizations, allowed them to reach innovative solutions to an extremely challenging problem. Alec later reflected that the widespread community support for saving Shelburne Farms proved to be a major factor in the success of that effort.[128]

Southern Acres: A Family Partnership

After the deaths of Watson and Electra in 1960, their three sons, Sam, Watson Jr., and Harry, assumed joint ownership of Southern Acres Farm. During the decades of the 1970s and 1980s, the brothers faced similar challenges to those which Derick and his children experienced. Sam, Watson, and Harry wished to preserve Southern Acres as a private agricultural estate, but the realities of managing the property prompted them to question their ability to do so in keeping with their father's vision.

The three brothers operated Southern Acres entirely independently of their cousin Derick's ventures at Shelburne Farms. After the deaths of Vanderbilt and Watson Sr. in 1956 and 1960, respectively, their children remained on cordial, but mostly distant, terms with each other. With the exception of a close friendship between second cousins Mary and Laura Webb, the daughters of Derick and Harry, respectively, the members of the South-

A Southern Acres Farm Hereford bull in front of the Breeding Barn, c. 1960–70. Kitty Webb Harris.

ern Acres and Shelburne Farms branches of the family had little regular contact with each other. By the 1960s, there was almost no exchange between the two properties either for social or agricultural purposes. Just before Watson Sr.'s death in 1960, he and Derick had agreed to erect locked gates where the main drives crossed from Shelburne Farms to Southern Acres to discourage local poachers and trespassers from traveling from one property to the other. However, the gates also further reduced communication between the two farms. Sam explained another reason for the separation in 1979: "Southern Acres is an operation independent from Shelburne Farms and I'll tell you why. We must keep the roads clear in winter. If we attempted to share a snow plow, it can't be two places at once. When the grain is ripe, we'd both need the combine at the same time. So the operations are completely separate."[129]

The two branches of the family likely grew apart because of different philosophies toward preserving their properties. Watson's sons were staunch proponents of private land ownership, and they looked a little askance at Derick's children and their idealistic embrace of the environmental and back-to-the-land movements. In addition, Derick's deferral of building and road maintenance stood in contrast to Sam, Harry, and Watson's belief in maintaining Southern Acres as a manicured backdrop for their private residences. While the main drive at Shelburne Farms was deteriorating and filled with potholes, the corresponding roadway at Southern Acres was always freshly surfaced and ditched. One Webb family member later described the difference in appearance between the two farms as "night and day."[130]

But by 1973, the steer fattening business that the Webb brothers had introduced at Southern Acres Farm had proved to be a financial failure, and the brothers faced a growing monetary burden with each passing year. In the early 1960s, the first few years of their joint ownership, the farm had operated at an annual loss of $60,000 to $70,000. Like their cousin Derick, the brothers were required to show a profit for their estate at least two out of every five years in order to retain an agricultural deduction on their federal income taxes, and they did so by subsidizing its costs. However, the taxes and annual maintenance of the several additional properties each brother also owned consumed a significant share of their income, and their taxes for their holdings in Shelburne continued to climb. Moreover, American agriculture was in the midst of an economic decline caused by the ongoing energy crisis in the early 1970s.[131]

In 1973, each of the brothers contributed more than $36,000 to Southern Acres Farm to cover a total deficit of $109,000. By 1975, Watson would write, "I'm unwilling to participate in any further farm losses for any kind of farming—whether raising cattle or crops…My commitment is to maintaining…a generally decent appearance. Beyond that, I'm not interested in undertaking any activities which do not at least produce a break-even result."[132]

In 1974, Sam, Harry, and Watson decided to sell off their existing steers and remaining Hereford breeding stock. In the future, instead of purchasing cattle outright, they planned to contract with other farmers to raise their livestock at Southern Acres until it was ready for market. In doing so, the brothers hoped to maintain the property as an agricultural estate while greatly reducing their direct costs.[133]

In 1975, Harry Webb died at the age of fifty-three. His one-third interest in Southern Acres, as well as his own neighboring farms, descended to his three daughters, Kate ("Kitty") Harris (b. 1948), Laura Brown (b. 1950), and Dundeen ("Deenie") Galipeau (b. 1952). However, Harry's daughters were not interested or able to carry his former portion of the Southern Acres Farm expenses or manage the operation. Sam and Watson both felt that the Southern Acres Farm property was more of a burden than a pleasure, but they were sympathetic to their nieces' situation, and they still felt

The Breeding Barn, by Kitty Webb Harris, winter 1978. Courtesy of Kitty Webb Harris.

obligated to keep Southern Acres in family hands. By the early 1980s, the family members agreed to divide legal ownership of most of Southern Acres Farm. Sam and Watson retained joint title and control of 223 acres of the property, including the south gate and the Breeding Barn complex.[134]

However, despite the restructuring, Sam and Watson faced the same long-term issues regarding the high costs of the agricultural operations. Their property taxes and operating deficits continued to grow throughout the late 1970s and early 1980s. Around 1980, the annual deficit for Southern Acres Farm reached $120,000 even though the agricultural operations grossed over $1 million. Though the property's financial burden had seemed high when divided among three siblings, it was an even greater encumbrance for the two surviving brothers.[135]

In about 1980, Sam, Watson, and Sam's son, Samuel B. Webb Jr., who would soon return to the area to accept a position at the University of Vermont, began investigating their family's options for Southern Acres Farm. After reviewing the operations, Sam Jr. concluded that it would be extremely difficult to manage Southern Acres as a break-even or profitable venture. The family members considered the idea of selling some acreage in order to preserve the core components of the farm, yet they possessed conflicting emotions about a possible sale. In 1979, Sam Sr. stated, "Whatever takes place, my own desire and that of my family is to see Southern Acres remain forever pastoral."[136]

Sam and Watson were also reluctant to consider land use strategies for their property that would place restrictions on its future use or obligate them to provide public access. Therefore, they did not investigate the possibility of a tax stabilization agreement with the town of Shelburne, even though members of the selectboard had publicly expressed a desire to see the Southern Acres property preserved. Nor did the brothers investigate the possibility of conservation easements for the farm.[137]

Instead, in 1980, Sam and Sam Jr. began negotiating with the University of Vermont (UVM) to donate much of the acreage that Sam and Watson owned jointly to UVM for its research farm. Under their plan, they would also enter into a long-term lease with UVM for the remainder of their jointly held land. The Webbs stipulated that the university keep the land in agricultural use, preserve the Breeding Barn, and retain three Southern Acres Farm employees. The proposal appealed to university officials because it would allow them to consolidate their beef, dairy, and sheep operations, and horticultural and agricultural research projects, from several disparate sites to a single location. The consolidation was projected to increase efficiency and cost savings if the university invested in a new dairy barn at Southern Acres, among other major projects.[138]

In 1982, the university began a short-term lease of Southern Acres Farm for some of its agricultural operations while school officials and the Webbs continued to discuss the long-term disposition of the property. The Webbs leased the property to UVM free of charge with the understanding that the university would be responsible for maintaining the farm's buildings, fields, and roads. UVM began to use the property as a satellite facility for its dairy farm, stabling approximately 200 head of heifers and dry cows in the Breeding Barn and using the surrounding fields for pasture and for hay and corn production.[139]

Without a deed to the property, however, UVM officials were reluctant to invest funds in maintaining the large stock of existing buildings and infrastructure, and, furthermore, they were unable to construct the additional, modern facilities that their consolidation plans required. As a result, Southern Acres Farm began to suffer from significant deferred maintenance, and the university reconsidered its plans to consolidate its agricultural operations at Southern Acres. Meanwhile, the two Sam Webbs were unable to persuade Watson Webb to donate his portion of the farm to UVM, as he felt little personal connection to the school. Thus, the negotiations stalled.[140]

Since discussions with UVM had come to a standstill, Sam Jr. turned to the Shelburne Museum as a potential steward for the property. By the mid-1980s, he had convinced his father and uncle to donate the land and buildings that they owned jointly to the institution. In doing so, they would relieve themselves of their financial and managerial burden while assuring that the property would be owned by an organization with close ties to the Webb family. The museum had been founded by their mother and grandmother, and Sam Sr., Sam Jr., and Watson were all long-term members of the organization's board of trustees. The family members on the board all possessed an emotional attachment to Southern Acres and the desire to see it preserved if at all possible. At the same time, Watson also agreed to donate the Brick House and the approximately ten acres immediately surrounding it to the museum in exchange for life tenancy. Watson's gift of the Brick House to the Shelburne Museum was finalized in 1985, and the donation of Southern Acres Farm was completed two years later. The transactions were well timed, as Sam Sr. passed away at the age of seventy-six in 1988.[141]

CHAPTER 15

A FARM AND EDUCATION CENTER

The mission of Shelburne Farms is to cultivate a conservation ethic by teaching and demonstrating the stewardship of natural and agricultural resources. At the heart of what we do is the practice of sustainable rural land use and the care and sharing of Shelburne Farms as an historic landmark of exceptional natural and architectural beauty. Our program goals are to increase awareness and appreciation of natural and agricultural resources and the working landscape, and to inspire active stewardship of the environment. If we are successful in achieving our mission, a growing number of caring and ecologically literate citizens will make choices that contribute to a sustainable future.

— SHELBURNE FARMS MISSION STATEMENT, 2007[1]

BY THE END OF THE TWENTIETH CENTURY, Shelburne Farms and Southern Acres had moved full circle. The two properties, united in 1994 under the aegis of the family-founded nonprofit, were conserved for future generations. Owing to the initial generosity of family members and a wide community of supporters, the Webbs had achieved their goals of preserving Shelburne Farms and creating a vibrant, multifaceted organization dedicated to environmental education. Although no longer the private preserve of a wealthy family, Shelburne Farms reflected, perhaps more than ever, one of Seward and Lila Webb's most important goals for their estate: to serve as a model farm pioneering innovative practices for the benefit of the public. By 2000, Shelburne Farms—the place and the organization—served as a renowned, international leader in environmental education, agriculture, land conservation, and historic preservation.

SHELBURNE FARMS, 1984–1994: CULTIVATING A CONSERVATION ETHIC

Derick Webb's death in 1984 marked the beginning of a new era. Some 1,150 acres of Shelburne Farms, including pastures, woodlands, and more than twenty historic structures, were now entirely owned by a nonprofit organization and managed for the benefit of the public. The next ten years proved to be a period of significant growth, as Shelburne Farms Resources assumed oversight of the farming operations, expanded its educational programs, and launched major fundraising and rehabilitation efforts. Of the Webb family,

Marshall, Alec, and Marilyn played key roles in shepherding Shelburne Farms through the first few years of its full ownership by SFR. Alec continued to serve as general manager, a role he had held since 1979. He oversaw the day-to-day activities and finances of the agricultural and general property operations. Marilyn served as president of SFR from 1976 to 1988, supervising program and organizational development. Working with board chairmen Metcalfe Walling and Jake Callery, she led the first capital campaign and oversaw the rehabilitation and opening of Shelburne House as an inn in 1987. Alec succeeded Marilyn as president in 1988, when she left to pursue other interests prior to their divorce. Meanwhile, Marshall continued in his role as manager of the buildings, grounds, and woodlands. Apart from Alec's serving as president, the board became wholly independent of the Webb family in 1998, when Marshall resigned as a result of a new policy prohibiting neighboring property owners from serving on the board in order to avoid any potential conflicts of interest.[2]

In bequeathing Shelburne Farms to Shelburne Farms Resources, Derick expressed confidence in the organization's ability to manage and preserve the property. Since the organization's beginnings in the early 1970s, in fact, the board and staff had considered the property integral to their vision, and Shelburne Farms had served as a base from which their programs were developed. The Webb family's agricultural ventures and land management strategies were intertwined with the educational objectives of their nonprofit. In 1985, SFR revised its mission statement to more explicitly represent the integration of the estate and its agricultural operations into the organization's existing environmental education framework:

The goal of Shelburne Farms is to preserve, maintain, and adapt its historic buildings and landscape for teaching and demonstrating the stewardship of natural and agricultural resources. Shelburne Farms conducts educational, agricultural, and cultural programs in the belief that the quality of our living environment depends on the conservation of natural resources, a healthy agricultural base and a striving for cultural excellence.[3]

The core components of this new mission, "teaching" via educational programs and "demonstrating" via agriculture and other related ventures, would shape the direction of the organization, and Shelburne Farms itself, over the next twenty years and beyond. By the 1990s, the new unity of the organization and the property had resulted in an evolution of nomenclature: both were simply referred to as "Shelburne Farms."

While Derick's bequest was a momentous gift, it also presented the nonprofit organization with a huge challenge. In 1984, the year of Derick's death, the Farm was in a precarious financial position. For several years, it had faced considerable annual operating deficits; that year, the deficit amounted to some $79,000. The nonprofit had now acquired this additional financial burden along with the challenges of managing the agricultural ventures and a large amount of acreage. Board and staff members wished not only to continue farming on a similar scale, but to further expand the nonprofit's programs *and* to restore the key estate buildings. Such plans would require significant additional funds as well as considerable skill in managing the merger of two distinct operations and major organizational growth.[4]

Over the next few years, Shelburne Farms developed a three-pronged solution to its financial challenges. First, in order to generate immediate income, the organization sold a few additional residential leasehold properties using the model developed in 1980 for Eileen Rockefeller and Valley View Farm. As much as it pained those associated with the organization to part with more land, leasing carefully sited acreage to sympathetically minded individuals seemed to be an appropriate compromise to sustain the nonprofit. In 1985, Shelburne Farms sold four parcels, each with the potential for development as a single house site, to benefactors Philip and Crea Lintilhac. Located to the northeast of the pole barn along Lemrise Bay, and on Windmill Hill west of Lone Tree Hill, the leaseholds were sited in areas where they would have minimal impact on the core features of the property and its productive agricultural land. The Lintilhacs, along with Crea's parents, constructed private residences on two of the four leaseholds in 1987 and 1988.[5]

With the funds received from the sale of the leaseholds, Shelburne Farms' board and staff members were able to focus on longer-term strategies for generating income. However difficult Derick's sudden death was for his family members on a personal level, it both simplified the property's situation and significantly improved the organization's prospects for raising funds. Foundations and individuals were much more receptive to supporting programs and projects that were now wholly nonprofit in nature. The Lintilhacs had just established a family foundation when they purchased leaseholds from Shelburne Farms in 1985, and their foundation's pledge of $1 million later that year launched the first phase of the nonprofit's Centennial Capital Campaign. The campaign raised more than $6 million by 1993, supporting the publication of the first edition of an educational curriculum guide, the rehabilitation of the north gatehouse to serve as a new visitor center for public access, the rehabilitation of Shelburne House as the Inn at Shelburne Farms, preservation work at the Coach Barn, and the rehabilitation of portions of the Farm Barn to serve as a new education center. Moreover, the campaign, and the successful launch of the Inn, placed the nonprofit on a much more stable financial footing.[6]

Shelburne Farms' third major strategy for raising funds consisted of expanding the agricultural and forestry ventures and developing additional, income-generating enterprises in keeping with its goal of "teaching and demonstrating the stewardship of natural resources." By doing so, staff and board members hoped to improve the organization's self-sufficiency and further its mission of environmental education. They made Shelburne Farms, Inc. a new subsidiary of the nonprofit organization, creating an innovative new organizational structure. The subsidiary would manage the sale of cheddar cheese and other agricultural products, and the operating revenue from these and future ventures would serve as a major source of funds for the nonprofit's educational programs.[7]

To implement this strategy, board and staff members focused their energies between 1984 and 1994 on expanding the dairy and forestry and developing new enterprises that used some of the property's historic buildings as their bases. In keeping with Shelburne Farms' longstanding tradition of agricultural innovation, they introduced practices and systems that were then new to the industry at large.[8]

Dairy Operations

When Shelburne Farms Resources acquired the Shelburne Farms property and agricultural operations in 1984, the dairy was just beginning to recover from years of deficits and transitioning from the raw milk operation to cheese making. Over the next ten years, general manager Alec Webb, farm manager Buster Searles, Leonard Germain, who served as a consultant before succeeding Searles as farm manager, and cheese maker Bill Clapp continued their efforts to improve the quality of the Brown Swiss dairy herd and develop a premium cheddar cheese product.[9]

Shelburne Farms gradually refined breeding methods, replaced the poorer-performing cattle with superior young stock bred on the Farm, and revised pasturage and crop systems. They maintained a midsized herd that would produce a smaller yield of high-quality milk rather than a large herd that might produce a high volume of average-quality milk. Throughout the 1980s and

1990s, the Shelburne Farms dairy contained approximately 140 to 180 head, including about 90 milking cows at any given time.[10]

Staff members capitalized upon the large amount of available pasture at Shelburne Farms to improve the grasses that the Brown Swiss herd consumed. Around 1983, they began to implement a new system of "rotational grazing." Contrary to the conventional twentieth-century agricultural philosophy of housing cows indoors for all or most of the year and primarily feeding them grains—as espoused by former farm manager Frank Kendzior in the 1930s, among others—rotational grazing sought to maximize the amount of time cows spent pastured outdoors, eating fresh grasses. First developed in France in the 1950s and later refined in New Zealand, rotational grazing consists of frequently moving animals between pastures to allow grasses to rejuvenate quickly, thus creating a higher-quality feed. At Shelburne Farms, the system possessed the added benefit of keeping the pastures in excellent condition, which reduced the operation's negative environmental impact by decreasing agricultural runoff, erosion, and the need for fertilizers. In 1993, farm managers rotated the pastures every three to four weeks. In later years, they would revise the rotation schedule, reducing the amount of time the cows spent in each pasture area from days to hours.[11]

During the cooler months, the cows consumed a mixture of Farm-raised haylage, made from harvested grasses stored and aged in the trench silos, as well as corn and grains purchased from external suppliers. Staff members continued to restrict the use of pesticides and chemical fertilizers. In 1993, they began to supplement the trench silo system with a new method of producing haylage using large plastic-wrapped bales commonly referred to as "marshmallows." The bales reduced the amount of time and energy expended in feeding the cows by storing the haylage in a more easily transportable form.[12]

As the dairy staff worked to improve the quality of the milk that the Brown Swiss herd produced, Bill Clapp and other employees in Shelburne Farms' cheese department continued to refine their cheese making and marketing activities. In 1984, Clapp introduced a traditional English cheddar recipe that would prove central to the success of Shelburne Farms' cheese. That same year, the product was favorably reviewed in the *New York Times* as "a cheddar of great character, with a fine, full flavor and a distinctive bite."[13] Throughout the 1980s and 1990s, Clapp and his successors worked to enlarge the mail-order catalog, wholesale, and retail venues for Shelburne Farms' cheese. Approximately $200,000 was included in the organization's 1985 capital campaign to renovate and expand the north gatehouse to serve as a new farm store and visitor center, replacing the small facility that had operated in the Farm Barn since the early 1980s. The new facility, which became known as the "Welcome Center," opened in 1986.[14]

By the mid-1980s, the cheese venture was producing approximately 50,000 pounds annually and using about 40 percent of the dairy herd's total milk yield. By 1997, cheese production had increased to approximately 100,000 pounds and 60 percent. In later years, Clapp's successors would continue to expand production and introduce smoked and cloth-bound cheddar.[15]

Clapp and his successors made cheese a few days a week on a year-round basis. On other days, Shelburne Farms sold fluid milk from its dairy herd to the International Cheese Company in Hinesburg, Vermont. In addition, the Farm sold excess young cattle each spring to other dairy farmers needing replacement stock, to businesses seeking bulls for artificial insemination purposes, and to vendors of beef products. Dairy staff found a good market for heifers with Canadian farmers, and they also sent animals to several prominent cattle shows in the United States.[16]

During the 1980s and 1990s, the dairy continued to be housed in the pole barn complex. From 1982 to 1993, the cheese department occupied a converted section of the pole barn's milking parlor. In 1993, the cheese activities moved to a group of renovated spaces in the main and north ell areas of the Farm Barn. Also in 1993, a 20,000-gallon holding tank for storing whey, a byproduct of the cheese-making process, was buried in the field to the east of the Farm Barn. Subsequently, the whey was pumped from the tank and sprayed onto farm fields as a natural fertilizer.[17]

During the mid-1990s, Shelburne Farms also invested in improvements

Left: Cows pastured at Shelburne Farms, by Marshall C. Webb, c. 1985. Shelburne Farms Collections.

at the pole barn complex. In 1994, with support from the Natural Resources Conservation Service of the United States Department of Agriculture, the organization redesigned the manure handling and drainage systems at the pole barn complex to limit the negative environmental impact produced by the phosphorus in manure runoff. The manure pit was enlarged, allowing staff members to completely cease spreading manure in the fields when the ground was frozen and unable to absorb the phosphorus. Additionally, grasses that filtered runoff water before it reached nearby soils were planted near the holding barn. In 1995, Shelburne Farms Resources constructed a new milking parlor at the complex designed to both improve the efficiency of the milking process and facilitate educational programs occurring at the dairy. The new parlor featured an innovative greenhouse roof, which maximized the amount of natural light entering the structure. As then farm manager Leonard Germain explained, the roof was "a breakthrough in building construction design for a dairy."[18]

By the late 1980s, the Shelburne Farms dairy had achieved significant renown for the quality of both its Brown Swiss cattle and its cheddar cheese. In 1987, the Eastern Milk Producers Cooperative Association recognized Shelburne Farms for the quality of its milk, and the Farm's cow Shelburne Titan Elly was awarded grand champion of the Kentucky National Brown Swiss Show. Three years later, the National Brown Swiss Association named the Shelburne Farms dairy herd first in the nation among those of its size. Also in 1990, Shelburne Farms' cheese won the first of many blue ribbons it would receive at successive annual meetings of the American Cheese Society. And in 1991, seventeen-year-old Shelburne Farms Del became the Brown Swiss world record holder for lifetime milk production. By the time of her death the following year, she had produced a total of 313,391 pounds of milk containing 8,819 pounds of protein.[19]

Forestry

Meanwhile, Marshall Webb continued the efforts he had begun in the 1970s to restore the health and productivity of Shelburne Farms' forests, with the goal of conducting ecologically sensitive annual harvests that would generate income for Shelburne Farms and its educational programs. After 1982, when some 200 of the 600 forested acres on the property were included in the land sold to the Pheasant Hill Trust, Marshall managed approximately 400 acres of woodlands for Shelburne Farms. Despite years of work on the forests, he still faced numerous challenges in improving them, among them "too much brush growing up; too many young trees…destroyed by too many deer; and many of the mature trees suffering from ash dieback, maple decline, red rot, beech scale nectria and more."[20] Throughout the 1980s, Marshall continued to remove dead and dying elm trees decimated by Dutch elm disease. By the middle of the decade, virtually all of the estate's hundreds of elms had succumbed.[21]

During the 1980s and 1990s, Marshall focused upon improving approximately twenty acres of woodlands each year via selective logging, thinning, and brush clearing. By the early 1990s, his annual production amounted to about sixty cords of firewood, most of which was sold to external parties, and several thousand board feet of logs and lumber, most of which was retained for internal historic preservation and programmatic use. In keeping with Marshall's own longstanding philosophies and the mission of Shelburne Farms, the forestry activities were designed to minimize any negative environmental impact.[22]

The Inn at Shelburne Farms

As the dairy, cheese, and forestry operations developed, the board and staff members of Shelburne Farms also conceived a plan to rehabilitate Shelburne House to serve as an inn and restaurant for the general public. In doing so, they would both preserve the building for the future and use it in a way that directly benefited the organization's efforts to "teach and demonstrate the stewardship of natural and agricultural resources."

The nonprofit organization had successfully hosted programs at Shelburne House since 1974, and overnight accommodations for the public began in the late 1970s. However, during these years, the building had continued to deteriorate. The programs and events it hosted barely paid their own costs, let alone providing the significant funds needed to reverse the increasing dilapidation resulting from decades of deferred maintenance.

While still generally structurally sound, Shelburne House and its gardens were in extremely poor condition by the early 1980s. The building's roof and plumbing continued to leak; its exterior wooden elements were extremely deteriorated; its aging electrical, septic, and plumbing systems required significant upgrades; and it possessed none of the life safety systems required by modern building codes for a public structure of its kind. Moreover, despite some repairs and updates conducted in the late 1970s and early 1980s, the building's new functions necessitated considerable interior refurbishment. The condition of the servants' wing was most serious; in fact, the nonprofit seriously considered demolishing the wing in 1980. In the gardens, the original brick walls, stairs, and other structural elements were in poor condition, the planting beds were mostly overgrown, and the semicircular balustrade overlooking Lake Champlain had been structurally compromised by ongoing erosion.[23]

The Shelburne Farms board began to review options for the long-term use and preservation of Shelburne House by the early 1980s. Several board members advocated that the dwelling become a vehicle to generate funds for the organization, and an internal feasibility study completed in 1983 presented three possible scenarios. The first option, operating the building primarily as a house museum, was in keeping with a traditional course for the use of gracious historic houses across the United States and abroad. In fact, several Vanderbilt country residences designed for Lila Webb's siblings had been opened to the public for tours within the previous fifty years. At Shelburne Farms, the feasibility study determined that making Shelburne House available for regular tours would be "less profitable long term but easier to manage."[24]

The second and third options, hosting business meetings and conferences, and converting the facility into an inn, were also time-honored strategies for reusing historic houses. These options were deemed to require the greatest amount of up front resources, and some question remained as to whether the ventures would generate enough revenue in the long term to both recoup the enormous initial investment they would require and provide a recurring source of income for the organization. Not only would the building's structural, systems, and cosmetic problems need to be solved, but additional and ongoing investments in amenities and hotel and restaurant supplies would be required. Moreover, the ventures would add significant staffing costs for front desk, housekeeping, kitchen, wait staff, and other employees. Board members had only to review the case of Elm Court, a residence built by Lila Webb's sister Emily Vanderbilt Sloane in Lenox, Massachusetts, which was quite similar in size, style, and age to Shelburne House, to understand the challenges they potentially faced. Sloane's descendents had managed Elm Court as an inn for nine years in the late 1940s and 1950s before closing it because of a lack of profit and the considerable amount of oversight it required.[25]

In any case, the 1983 feasibility study suggested that Shelburne House continue to be used seasonally rather than year-round. Upgrading the existing, aged heating system, which had lain dormant since the late 1930s or early 1940s, would add significantly to the costs of renovating and operating the building, and it was unclear whether the Shelburne area attracted enough prospective clientele during the winter to recoup those costs. As the study stated, Shelburne House had "little potential as a winter site due to poor snow cover and distances from ski areas."[26]

After more than two years of deliberations, and with the urging of Shelburne Farms' board member Paul Hawken and president Marilyn Webb, the board of directors elected to gamble on converting Shelburne House into an inn open to the general public. Many felt that an inn was the most appropriate use for the dwelling, as it was most in keeping with the family's tradition of filling the rooms with guests each season. They also wished the house to be open to all rather than to a select group of individuals visiting as part of a conference or other private event. As Marilyn stated, "We…decided that since [Shelburne House] was originally designed as a guest house, that was the most natural use to put it to."[27] The capital campaign that Shelburne Farms launched in 1985 included $1.6 million earmarked to fund the rehabilitation of the dwelling and its formal gardens.[28]

Over the next two years, Marilyn oversaw both the fundraising efforts and the overall project at Shelburne House. Preservation architect Martin Tierney, board member Remo Pizzagalli, construction manager Mark Neagley, inn director Marnie Davis, and interior designer Linda Seavey also played instrumental roles. The work included restoration of the roof, flashing, chimneys, gutters, damaged window frames, other exterior elements, and interior plasterwork; reinforcement of failing structural supports; improvements to the plumbing, electrical, and telephone systems; refurbishment of the interiors; and installation of new fire alarm, sprinkler, and septic systems. While many original elements were restored or replaced in character, the project was not a strict restoration, but rather a rehabilitation in keeping with the building's new use. Several new bathrooms were installed to provide more bedrooms with private facilities, and the original furniture was reupholstered, rearranged, and supplemented with new pieces that fit the needs of the inn. While some original wallpapers were reproduced, the rooms were mostly redecorated in a scaled-down, lighter interpretation of the house's late Victorian style to appeal to a modern clientele. Similarly, work started on repairing some of the garden walls, and the beds were replanted in the spirit of Lila Webb's vision rather than exact replicas of the original designs.[29]

The Shelburne House project was fraught with challenges. In order to publicize the project and begin taking reservations, Shelburne Farms was obliged to set an opening date of July 1, 1987, before board and staff members had raised all of the necessary funds. However, the work could progress only as funds were available, and the organization could not afford to turn away the income received through the occasional programs that used the dwelling during its regular May to October season. Therefore, the bulk of the construction work occurred in less than six months during the winter of 1986–87. More than seventy contractors and craftsmen, and an equal number of volunteers, endured difficult working conditions, since despite the use of portable industrial heaters, the building remained frigid.[30]

In addition, the State of Vermont's standard building codes for fire protection and other life safety concerns were often at odds with the team's efforts to preserve the dwelling's historic character. As a result, Tierney spent a great deal of time seeking innovative solutions that provided the same level of safety without compromising the building's integrity. He explained, "If you put in too many metal doors [and] close off the flowing spaces…the building dies. The wonderful story of the family and people who lived there would have been lost."[31]

And as with any construction project involving a historic structure, the contractors often discovered that the deterioration was worse than initially expected once work began. Neagley recalled, "The plumbers had the worst job of anyone. They ran into headache after headache. They jumped through hoops fixing fixtures that hadn't been

Above left: The servants' wing at Shelburne House, shortly before demolition, by Courtney Fisher, 1986. Shelburne Farms Collections.

Above right: A contractor installing wallpaper in the third-floor hallway at Shelburne House, by Paul Boisvert, May 1987. Shelburne Farms Collections.

used in 50 years. There were times when they spent an entire day just trying to get one sink to work."[32]

The deteriorated servants' wing proved to be perhaps the most difficult issue. Just to stabilize it would have required an investment of $800,000 to $1 million, a considerable portion of the total project budget. Board members felt that Shelburne Farms was not in a position to raise the additional funds required for the structure's stabilization, let alone its rehabilitation. Concerned that allocating limited financial resources to saving the wing would jeopardize the organization's ability to pursue the vision for Shelburne Farms as a whole, they preferred to demolish it. However, Vermont's Division of Historic Preservation opposed the loss of the wing, which contained a large portion of Shelburne House's service areas and thus represented an important component of the dwelling's history. After lengthy discussion before and during the permitting process, the Division reluctantly agreed that the demolition was necessary to ensure that the majority of the building would be preserved. The servants' wing was demolished in 1986, and the area of the building where it had attached was rebuilt as it had been before the wing was constructed.[33]

The Inn at Shelburne Farms opened to the public on schedule, one hundred years to the day after Seward and Lila Webb had first broken ground on the earliest residence. It quickly proved successful, and as Marilyn later noted, the rehabilitation project was a "major turning point" in the financial viability of Shelburne Farms.[34] During the 1987 season, the Inn's gross revenue totaled approximately $555,000. In 1994, it grossed some $1.26 million. In 1988, Shelburne Farms was awarded the prestigious Presidents' Award for Historic Preservation for its successful and sensitive rehabilitation of Shelburne House.

Marilyn Webb accepting Shelburne Farms' President's Award for Historic Preservation, by Steve Stewart, 1988. Shelburne Farms Collections.

Marilyn and Crea Lintilhac traveled to Washington, DC, to accept the award from President Ronald Reagan.[35]

The Coach Barn

Soon after opening Shelburne House as an inn, Shelburne Farms' board of directors also began to consider renting selected areas of the Coach Barn for weddings and other special events as a method of raising additional revenue. Since the mid-1970s, the organization had utilized the building for educational programs and its own events, including the annual Harvest Festival. In 1987, designer and sculptor Paul Nowicki provided the inspiration and legwork to launch Shelburne Farms' annual art exhibition, known as "Envisioned in a Pastoral Setting," at the Coach Barn to benefit the nonprofit and enhance its educational programs. To encourage the use of the property for cultural and educational programs, in the 1970s the board instituted a policy specifically prohibiting weddings and other functions without direct links to the organization's mission at either the Coach Barn or Shelburne House. They felt that the occasions might displace mission-related activities or negatively impact the experience of guests attending Farm programs. In 1976, board members had even requested that Derick Webb and his second wife, Rusty, select another location for their marriage ceremony besides Shelburne House. In the late 1980s, however, board members approved as a test case the rental of the Coach Barn for a few private events held at times when the building was not in use for educational programs. In 1993, when the education department moved to new facilities in the Farm Barn, the board subsequently authorized the use of the Coach Barn as a site for both internal and external special events. In order to achieve a balance between hosting mission-related events and renting the building for external functions, board members set a limit on the annual number of weddings at twelve.[36]

Shelburne Farms' investment in revenue-generating enterprises to support its programs proved to be the catalyst of the organization's financial success. By 1989, four years after the organization began its plan for self-sufficiency, and two years after the Inn at Shelburne Farms opened, the nonprofit achieved a positive cash flow. As its 1989 annual report noted, "We are pleased to report a modest operating surplus for the first time in the history of this organization. The successful restoration of Shelburne House as an inn was largely responsible for turning a $100,000 deficit five years ago into a $32,000 surplus in 1989."[37] By the turn of the twenty-first century, the Inn and the other income-generating activities would produce approximately 65 percent of Shelburne Farms' annual revenue of more than $4,655,000. In 1994, the innovative organizational structure developed at Shelburne Farms was featured as a national model on a popular business television program hosted by Lou Dobbs on the Cable News Network (CNN). In 1993, Alec reflected,

> *This is a new kind of institution that there's not a word for yet. It still is a working farm, it has elements of a university farm, and of a real farm community, too. There are elements of a private school in this, in the educational programs. There are elements of a museum, of a historic site—it's kind of a historic attraction...But there are all these things we are trying to get to work together...It feels like the odds are so great for this not to happen. Each year it feels like an insurmountable challenge, but it's happening. It's amazing.*[38]

Nonprofit Programs

Alongside its income-generating enterprises, Shelburne Farms continued to develop and expand its nonprofit programs. By the early 1980s, the organization reached students, educators, and members of the general public with a diverse group of programs that were led both independently and in conjunction with multiple partners. With the leadership of Megan Camp, who joined the Farm's education staff in 1983 and succeeded David Barash as education director two years later, the 1980s and early 1990s brought considerable growth in the organization's education and public programs, along with significant external recognition of these activities.[39]

During the 1980s and 1990s, Shelburne Farms Resources continued to host its popular public tours, Harvest Festival, Vermont Mozart Festival performances, and countless additional programs and events for people of all ages. The organization also added a significant new component to its public activities: a network of walking trails winding through the property.

Just before Derick's death in 1984, Marilyn and Alec had vacationed in England's Lake District. Out of their experiences came the idea for a walking trail system at Shelburne Farms. After Derick died later that year, Marilyn proposed that a footpath leading from the rear of the Farm Barn to the crest of Lone Tree Hill be constructed in his honor. Family members were enthusiastic about the idea and suggested memorial gifts to a trail fund in lieu of flowers at his funeral. The trail opened to the public in May 1985, leading visitors to a semi-circular redstone memorial bench placed on the shoulder of Lone Tree Hill. Eventually, this path became part of five miles of public trails created between 1986 and 1992 that linked broad sections of Shelburne Farms. Developed by Marshall and

David Barash, the trails utilized secondary farm roads, most of them former carriage drives, logging routes, and mown paths through fields to link the Welcome Center, Farm Barn, garden, and Coach Barn. Along the way, walkers encountered some of Shelburne Farms' most beautiful scenery, from the panoramic views of Lake Champlain and the Adirondacks seen from the top of Lone Tree Hill to the forested glades of an area called Butternut Hill, located between the Farm Barn and the dairy complex.[40]

Meanwhile, the organization's ongoing educational programs for children and educators remained its central focus. It offered field trips throughout the school year that were grounded in seasonal themes and activities, such as local wildlife, dairy farming, gardening, forestry, and soils. In 1987, a sugar house was constructed at the base of the forested slopes of Lone Tree Hill to serve as the hub of a spring maple sugaring program.[41]

The success of the Farm's programs for educators led to the development of an innovative curriculum guide, *Project Seasons*. Published in 1986 with funds raised in the first phase of the nonprofit's capital campaign, *Project Seasons* was developed by staff members and local teachers who had participated in educational programs from the late 1970s to the mid-1980s. The curriculum guide brought national and international recognition to Shelburne Farms' educational programs. Over the next ten years, teacher workshops based upon the *Project Seasons* curriculum, and its seasonal ideas and activities for teaching science in the classroom, attracted participants from across the United States and as far away as Tasmania and Honduras. As the *Burlington Free Press* reported in 1988,

> *A statewide survey conducted by [Megan] Camp four years ago found that science was taught an average of 20 minutes a week in elementary schools. The survey also found that most elementary school teachers were uncomfortable teaching science…The guides are now distributed in 35 states and about 300 teachers have attended the workshops. The result has been more science in the classroom. According to Camp, teachers who have participated in the workshop teach science an average of 120 minutes per week.*[42]

Project Seasons led to important collaborative programs with regional, national, and international organizations, including training workshops developed as part of the Lake Champlain Basin Education Initiative and the United States Department of Agriculture's National Ag in the Classroom program. In the 1990s, Megan Camp, who was appointed vice president and program director in 1991, traveled to Central and Eastern Europe to present environmental education work-

Megan Camp tapping a maple during a Spring Project Seasons workshop, by Paul Boisvert, 1986. Shelburne Farms Collections.

A winter trekking field trip behind the Farm Barn, by Adam Riesner, 1993. Shelburne Farms Collections.

shops for a program sponsored by the Institute for Sustainable Communities and supported by the United States Environmental Protection Agency.[43]

By 1989, Shelburne Farms' environmental education programs were extraordinarily successful. That year, the organization reported, "Every available school field trip was booked through June 1990. Demand far exceeds currently available resources…Over 4,000 schoolchildren from 45 Vermont schools and over 500 teachers from 20 states participated in our programs. *Project Seasons* has been sold in over 30 states across the country."[44] Increasing demand for field trips led to the institution of a lottery system for program registration by the early 1990s. In 1995, Shelburne Farms published a second edition of *Project Seasons*.[45]

As a result of its success, and the organization's desire to offer programs for young children and families, the education department outgrew its existing space in the Coach Barn. Attention soon turned to the Farm Barn, which contained thousands of square feet of underutilized space. The rehabilitation of the Farm Barn to accommodate both the education department and the cheese department, which had outgrown its facility at the dairy, was in keeping with Shelburne Farms' long-term vision for the Farm Barn as a multipurpose hub for organizational and partnership activities.[46]

With the successful rehabilitation of Shelburne House as the Inn at Shelburne Farms, Shelburne Farms' board and staff members felt more confident in launching another ambitious fundraising and building project. Although the nonprofit had undertaken critical stopgap stabilization work since acquiring the Farm Barn in 1976, the structure's last complete reroofing had occurred in the 1930s, the south-facing shingles were deteriorated beyond saving, the miles of exterior trim badly needed repair and painting, and the west façade was in extremely poor condition as a result of water infiltration and rotting sills. The building lacked a central heating system, and occupants relied on wood heat during the long winter months. Its electrical wiring was antiquated and unsafe, its bathroom facilities were inadequate, and it did not possess fire protection systems.[47]

By 1990, plans were laid to rehabilitate the Farm Barn to provide a new home for an expanded education department, as well as additional administrative space and room for the cheese making, cheese aging, and mail order facilities. A three-year, $2.9 million fundraising effort led by board chairman Tom Pierce and inspired by the Farm's creative programs developed by Megan Camp and her education colleagues, the campaign was launched with a lead gift from the Burton Bettingen Corporation of Los Angeles. Work on the structure was completed in 1993. The project included installing a new copper roof and a central heating system featuring a wood-chip furnace and radiant-floor heating. The cheese department occupied newly converted space in the main block and north ell.[48]

The centerpiece of the Farm Barn rehabilitation project was a complex of spaces devoted to the education department and its programs. The McClure Center for School Programs, named in honor of local philanthropists J. Warren and Lois McClure, who donated $200,000 to assist in securing a Kresge Foundation challenge grant for the fundraising campaign, occupied most of the building's north wing. The new center now contained flexible gathering spaces for field trips and other programs, a library, and offices. Across the building's courtyard, the organization opened a Children's Farmyard to provide families with informal access to farm animals and to experiences

The Children's Farmyard, by Adam Riesner, 1994. Shelburne Farms Collections.

such as milking a cow, carding wool, and collecting eggs.[49]

By 1994, ten years after Derick's death, Shelburne Farms' programs and enterprises were flourishing. In 1985, the organization hosted approximately 25,000 annual visitors, employed some twenty-five year-round staff and five additional seasonal staff, and possessed an annual deficit of almost $100,000. In 1994, the organization hosted approximately 115,000, employed forty-six people, and possessed an operating surplus of $20,000. The previous year, Marshall reflected that the organization's success was "beyond our wildest dreams."[50] In 1995, the National Trust for Historic Preservation honored the Webb family and Shelburne Farms with its National Preservation Honor Award.[51]

Reunion

In the 1980s and early 1990s, Shelburne Farms blossomed. However, serious challenges remained at Southern Acres. The Shelburne Museum's acquisition of Southern Acres Farm may have averted the potential of estate taxes levied after the deaths of Sam and Watson Webb, but it did not resolve the intractable problem of the property's financial solvency.

During the late 1980s, the museum renewed the lease with the University of Vermont while its board of trustees sought long-term solutions. Board members felt that the property would continue to lose money if it remained an agricultural operation. Already facing financial difficulties, the museum did not have the funds to manage Southern Acres as a farm. The Brick House, the residence where museum founder Electra Webb had experimented with decorative ensembles of her collections, was the only portion of the property with a direct link to the museum's mission. Therefore, board members reluctantly investigated several strategies for leasing or selling Southern Acres for limited subdivision, hoping to discover options that would allow its two most significant buildings, the Brick House and the Breeding Barn, to be preserved for the future.[52]

Board members soon focused on the possibility of creating a limited, sensitively sited residential development containing a total of thirty to forty house lots on the property. Under this plan, the Brick House would be converted into either condominiums or a clubhouse for residents, and the Breeding Barn would serve as a recreational facility. The project was projected to realize $10 million to $20 million for the museum.[53]

In 1993, Shelburne Museum trustee and local philanthropist J. Warren McClure, concerned about the possible development of Southern Acres Farm, approached the museum and Shelburne Farms with a proposal. He offered $500,000 to assist in a sale of the property to Shelburne Farms, thus preserving the core of Southern Acres and rejoining the two segments of the Webb family estate. Both organizations strongly supported the proposal and began negotiations to complete the transaction. Shelburne Museum would lose a great deal of projected revenue, but its board members felt that the transfer would relieve them of the burden of Southern Acres in a way that ensured its long-term preservation. They agreed to the plan with the understanding that they would retain ownership of the Brick House, the portion of the property with a direct link to the museum's mission.

Shelburne Farms would significantly enlarge its property from 1,150 acres to some 1,500 acres—and its annual operating costs would increase proportionately. However, its board members agreed that the acquisition of the Southern Acres Farm property was worth the potential risks. As president Alec Webb and board chairman Chuck Ross wrote to the members of the nonprofit,

> *For Shelburne Farms the opportunity to acquire and conserve Southern Acres presented a once-in-a-lifetime opportunity to create an unequaled resource base for future program development. It also presents the daunting challenge of managing and sustaining more land and another immense facility. The Board considered these issues at length in the context of our mission and long-range planning and unanimously decided to move forward. Everyone felt strongly that the conservation ethic we are striving to cultivate is directly expressed by doing everything possible to conserve and creatively use this productive farmland and working landscape as a resource for environmental education.*[54]

In 1994, Shelburne Farms and Shelburne Museum finalized an agreement to transfer 330 acres of Southern Acres Farm to Shelburne Farms for

$500,000. At the same time, Sam Webb Sr.'s children, Sam Jr. and Holly, contributed 68 acres of land on Windmill Hill, the parcel that Vanderbilt had sold to Sam in 1947 for $1, to Shelburne Farms. In addition to the $500,000 received from the McClures, Shelburne Farms received grants of $500,000 from the Freeman Foundation and $200,000 from the Vermont Housing and Conservation Board for acquisition, maintenance, operations, and building stabilization costs. Significant support also came from local residents, who expressed strong enthusiasm for the transaction and authorized the Shelburne Selectboard to negotiate a revised tax stabilization agreement with Shelburne Farms that encompassed the Southern Acres property.[55]

Following its acquisition of the Southern Acres lands, Shelburne Farms worked with the Vermont Housing and Conservation Board and the Vermont Land Trust on a conservation easement and a pledge for granting a façade easement to the Preservation Trust of Vermont on the Breeding Barn. Finalized in 1996, the agreement identified approximately 300 acres of Southern Acres to be used in perpetuity for agricultural, forestry, open space, and educational purposes, and allowed for the future rehabilitation of the Breeding Barn complex to support the Farm's mission.[56]

Right: Roof restoration at the Breeding Barn, by Marshall C. Webb, 1997. Shelburne Farms Collections.

A Farm and Education Center

Since the reunion of Shelburne Farms and Southern Acres in 1994, the estate property has completed its rebirth as a modern farm and education center. The organization's programs have continued to thrive and serve as models for similar efforts in the United States and beyond. Its collaborations with partnership organizations have expanded with each passing year, and its Brown Swiss dairy and cheddar cheese have garnered numerous additional awards for excellence. Shelburne Farms has placed a total of approximately 700 of its 1,500 acres under conservation easements; conducted a landscape stewardship plan to preserve and restore key features of the historic landscape; and launched a land stewardship fund to reduce potential development on private inholdings and neighboring properties that were once part of the estate. In 2000, Shelburne Farms was awarded National Historic Landmark status. The organization's annual budget surpassed $8 million in 2007, and it now employs more than sixty year-round staff members. The nonprofit is working on the rehabilitation of the two main structures on the Southern Acres portion of the property: the Breeding Barn and the nearby dairy barn. The Breeding Barn will become a three-season gathering space for a variety of special events, including agricultural fairs, conferences, and musical performances. Plans have been developed to convert the dairy barn into a residential learning center hosting intensive educational programs.[57]

From its earliest incarnation as a Gilded Age country estate to its current manifestation as a nonprofit environmental education organization, Shel-

burne Farms has remained a place of astonishing beauty, grand scale, and innovation. Through the years, the individuals who have owned and managed Shelburne Farms have been united by the audacity of their ambitions to create and preserve the enormous property and its working landscape, by an enduring dedication to public service, and by a tradition of innovation.

Seward and Lila Webb founded a private estate of enormous size and ambitions; constructed buildings and systems incorporating the most modern features available at the time; developed a wide-ranging model farm to experiment with the latest breeding, technological, labor-saving, and record-keeping practices; enjoyed a lavish lifestyle and a plethora of country pursuits; and created a family corporation to carry the estate into the future. As the twentieth century continued, the Webbs carried on their tradition of innovation with the introduction of veterinary testing to eradicate cattle diseases and the adoption of modern agricultural equipment and building designs for barns, silos, and milking parlors. Under the management of Derick Webb and his children in the later decades of the century, Shelburne Farms was the focus of pioneering endeavors to conserve the property for future generations: new ventures to increase agricultural viability; efforts to minimize the Farm's environmental impact on the land; collaborations with conservation and land trust organizations; the implementation of conservation easements and leasehold strategies; the adaptive reuse of many historic structures on the property; and, perhaps most importantly, the creation of a nonprofit entity dedicated to teaching and demonstrating environmental stewardship. Today that nonprofit continues the tradition of innovation with its unique organizational structure, diverse programmatic and income-producing activities, and partnerships with other organizations across the country and the world.

At the time of this writing, a few Webb family

members maintain a presence at Shelburne Farms and Southern Acres. Derick's sons Marshall and Alec have dedicated themselves to the property for their entire lives. Marshall, Alec, and Megan Camp, who married Alec in 2006, continue to live at Shelburne Farms and hold key leadership positions in the nonprofit organization.

At Southern Acres, Sam Sr. and Watson Jr. passed away in 1988 and 2000, respectively. In the years following Sam's death, his children subdivided and sold the Quaker Smith Point property, which remains in private ownership. Watson continued to return to the Brick House for three months each year through 1998. After Watson's death, Shelburne Museum assumed occupancy of the Brick House, and in the succeeding years, the museum restored the dwelling to reflect Electra Webb's period of residence. In 2004, the building was opened to the public for tours, events, and limited use as a guesthouse. Harry Webb's daughters Kitty and Deenie, and Deenie's husband Steve Galipeau, continue to live at Southern Acres.[58]

As might be expected in an era of high property and estate taxes and continued development pressures, much of the outlying acreage once owned by members of the Webb family is in transition from open agricultural land to more intensive uses. While the core of Frederica's Sled Runner Point property remains privately owned as a single parcel, the majority of Shelburne Point has been subdivided and is a residential area with a number of private homes. In 1997, Electra and Dunbar Bostwick's descendants sold Bostwick Farm to the Meach Cove Trust, formed by John Abele, a cofounder of Boston Scientific, and his wife, the Rev. Mary Abele. At the time of this writing, the Abeles have constructed a private residence and interfaith chapel there and are exploring ways to conserve their significant property for philanthropic purposes.[59]

Additional portions of the outlying acreage have been successfully conserved. The adjoining Shelburne Bay Park, owned by the town of Shelburne, and the LaPlatte River Natural Area, owned by the Nature Conservancy, host recreational boaters and fishermen who use the public lake access, and hikers and runners who use the trails that crisscross the area. And since 2000, Shelburne Farms' land stewardship fund has assisted in the establishment of conservation easements on more than 150 acres of land to the east of the north gate.[60]

More than one hundred and twenty years have passed since Seward and Lila Webb founded Shelburne Farms in 1886. In some ways, the estate has changed tremendously. In others, it has survived relatively unchanged. At its largest point in the early twentieth century, Shelburne Farms comprised some 3,800 acres encompassing a grand country residence, a park-like landscape designed for the private pleasures for the Webb family and their guests, and an extensive model farm. A century later, Shelburne Farms consists of the 1,500 acres, the historic buildings and landscape features, and the working farm at the heart of the original property. Shelburne Farms now hosts thousands of visitors who come to enjoy a panoply of educational programs, cultural and special events, local foods, and beautiful accommodations.

Through the years, the Webb family and their vision for Shelburne Farms and Southern Acres have endured some criticism. Exceedingly wealthy and without previous ties to the area, Seward and Lila Webb changed the property and the local community forever. In place of a network of small, independent farms came a luxurious private residence and model farm created with well-intended yet paternalistic goals. Yet as the twentieth century progressed, the generosity and public-mindedness of the Webb family, along with the community's appreciation of the property's cultural, agricultural, and educational value, resulted in the conservation of a significant portion of the land. Ironically, had Seward and Lila not created their private estate, it is likely that the development pressures of the mid- and late twentieth century would have resulted in the subdivision and transformation of

A working landscape at Shelburne Farms, by Marshall C. Webb, c. 1990. Shelburne Farms Collections.

much of the property from agricultural to residential use. Instead, their legacy lives on in the form of a love of the land and of agriculture, and a vision of using Shelburne Farms to create a sustainable future.

AFTERWORD

When my brother Marshall filed the paperwork with the IRS that established the nonprofit organization "Shelburne Farms Resources" in 1972, I don't think any of us six siblings had a clear picture about how the vision for creating an education center at the Farm would actually play out.

We all shared the experience of growing up immersed in the life of the dairy here: helping with chores at the barn, milking, haying in the summer, bringing home the aroma of manure and silage on our clothes. Through the days we spent outdoors and on the lake, we developed a love and appreciation for the land, and felt deeply connected to it. And then as teenagers in the 1960s, with the war in Vietnam, the struggles of the civil rights movement, sprawl development threatening the countryside, and the growing degradation of natural resources, we became passionate about doing something to help improve the health of our environment and our society. It made sense to us to connect thinking about the future at Shelburne Farms with the future of the earth.

More than thirty-five years later, I feel amazed by and grateful for what Shelburne Farms has become. The dairy is the anchor for cheese making and other land-based enterprises. Throughout the year, the sounds of children are everywhere. We are buoyed by strong community relationships and organizational partnerships. We are collaborating with the Sustainability Academy at Lawrence Barnes School in Burlington and with educators as far away as China, Japan, and Italy on advancing education for sustainability. And major historic preservation and rehabilitation projects continue the long process of turning the former estate infrastructure into an equally beautiful new campus for learning and inspiration. We could never have imagined how moving it would feel to see all this happening.

Shelburne Farms could have become another string of subdivided lots. The fact that it didn't started with our simply trying to consider the impacts of our family decisions in a wider context. One lesson we have learned from what has happened here is that clear intention, persistence, and collaboration are key ingredients for shaping an alternative future. But intention is the starting point. Becoming more careful about how the choices we make affect ourselves, our communities, and the earth is at the heart of a conservation ethic that Shelburne Farms is working to cultivate today.

A century after its founding, Shelburne Farms has been conserved and transformed for an educational purpose. Its stewardship is now in the hands of the board of trustees. And the work goes on thanks to many wonderful supporters and volunteers—a community of people seeking a shift in values and consciousness that will lead to a sustainable future. The continuing story of Shelburne Farms will be told by those who are dedicated to learning how to live without diminishing resources and opportunities for the generations to follow.

— Alec Webb
President, Shelburne Farms
February 2010

FINAL ACKNOWLEDGMENT

THE ARCHIVES AT SHELBURNE FARMS exist today because of the foresight and effort of Emily Wadhams, Marilyn Webb Neagley, Patti Naritomi, David Barash, Megan Camp, Julie Bressor, Margaret Campbell, Erica Donnis, Cathy Quinn, and Julie Eldridge Edwards.

This book would not have been possible without the scholarship and perseverance of author Erica Donnis, who served as curator of collections from 1998 to 2002. The initial intent of this project was to research and document the history of Shelburne Farms leading up to the establishment of the nonprofit organization. The plan was to print a scholarly, thesis-like manuscript in a three-ring binder that would be available for reference in the archives, with a few copies available for sale. Board member Lola Van Wagenen encouraged us to expand the vision to a publication that would be more widely available, and she facilitated partnering with the great people affiliated with the Vermont Historical Society. The publication could also not have come to fruition without the professional guidance and wonderful support provided by the Farm's curator of collections, Julie Eldridge Edwards, and communications director, Holly Brough.

And finally, this book project honors the memory of J. Watson Webb Jr. and his love for the history and stories of Shelburne Farms.

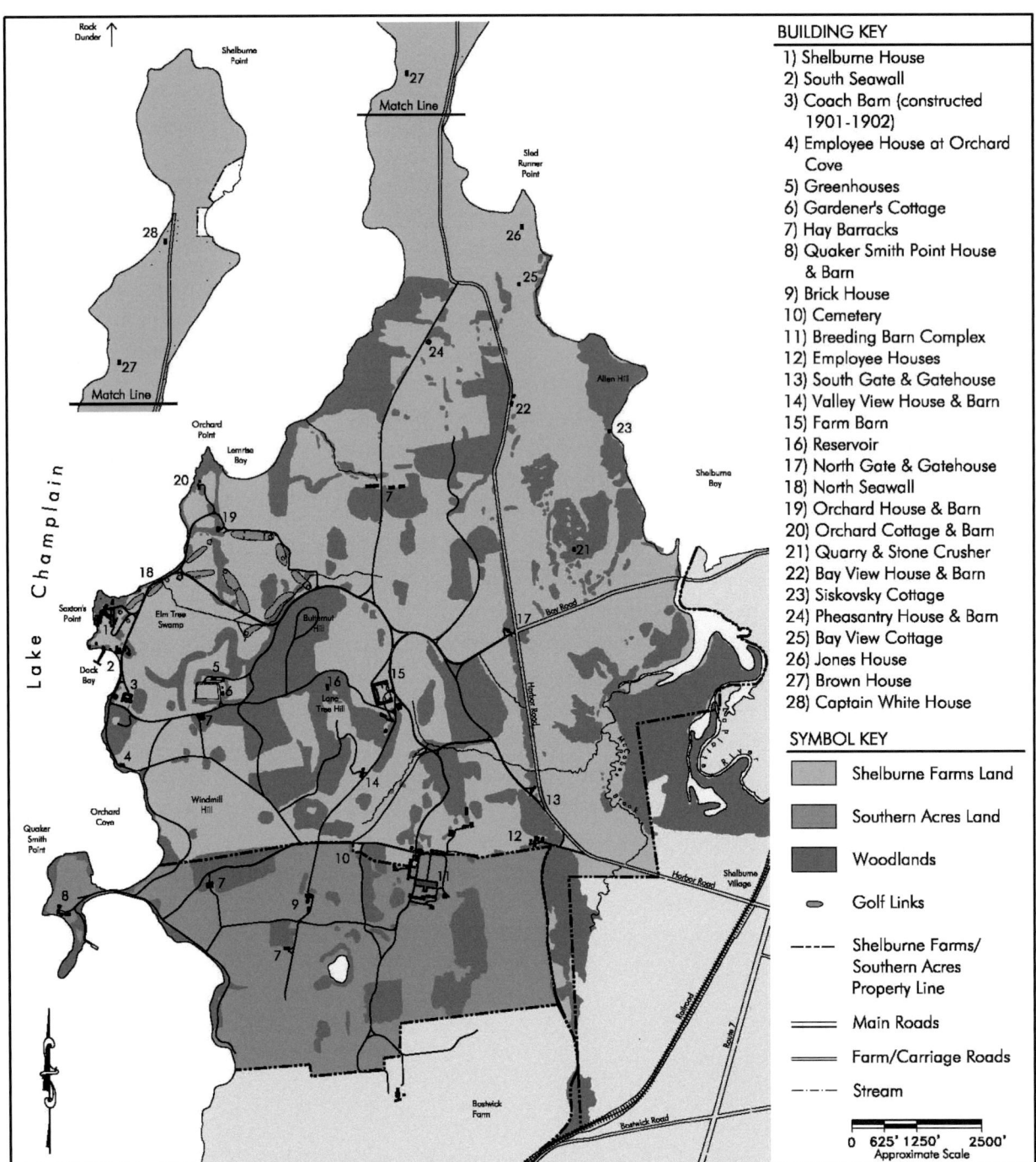

Shelburne Farms, 1886–1942 (left) and 2009 (right)

Sources: Soil Conservation Service, United States Department of Agriculture, aerial photograph depicting area in and around Shelburne Farms, Aug 25, 1942, numbered DCC-3-20 and DCC-3-24, original at National Archives, copies in SFC; F. W. Beers, Map of Shelburne, in *Atlas of Chittenden County, Vermont* (New York, 1869); Historic Photographs in the Print and Photograph Collection, SFC; Land, Genealogy, and Vital Records, STC; *Sanborn Fire Insurance Maps* of Burlington, VT, for Nov 1894 (sheet 28), Jan 1900 (s. 33), Mar 1906 (s. 38), Oct 1912 (s. 40), May 1919 (s. 39), Apr 1926 (s. 39), 1942 (s. 50), and 1942–60 (s. 50), Special Collections Department, Bailey/Howe Library, UVM; Marshall Webb, corr. and interviews with author,

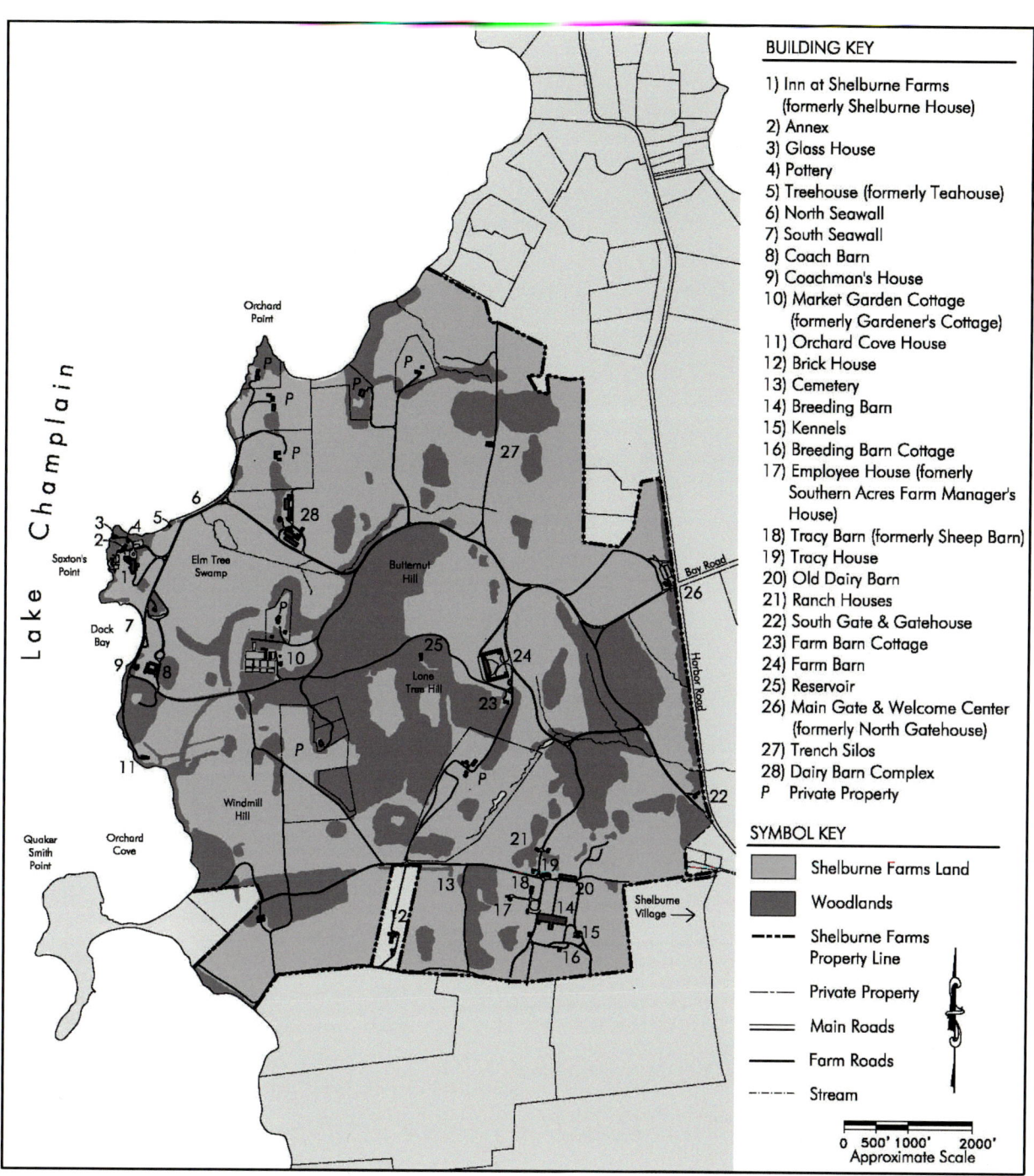

Mar–May 2009; and the following maps in APMI: Joseph P. Cotton, "A Topographical Map of Shelburne Farms, Shelburne, VT, The Property of W. S. Webb, Esq., Surveyed in 1886 by J. P. Cotton, C.E., Newport, R.I.," 1886; "Map of Land Owned by Dr. W. S. Webb on Shelburne Point showing names of original owners and areas purchased from each," surveyed May 1902, revised Dec 1935, 2004.3.21.7a, in Folder 6, FFD 7; McIntosh and Crandall, "Topographical Map of Shelburne Farms, Shelburne, Vermont," 1923, 2004.3.21.37, in Folder 3, FFD 8; "Original Purchases, Shelburne Farms, Shelburne Vermont," surveyed 1886–91, 2004.3.21.23.

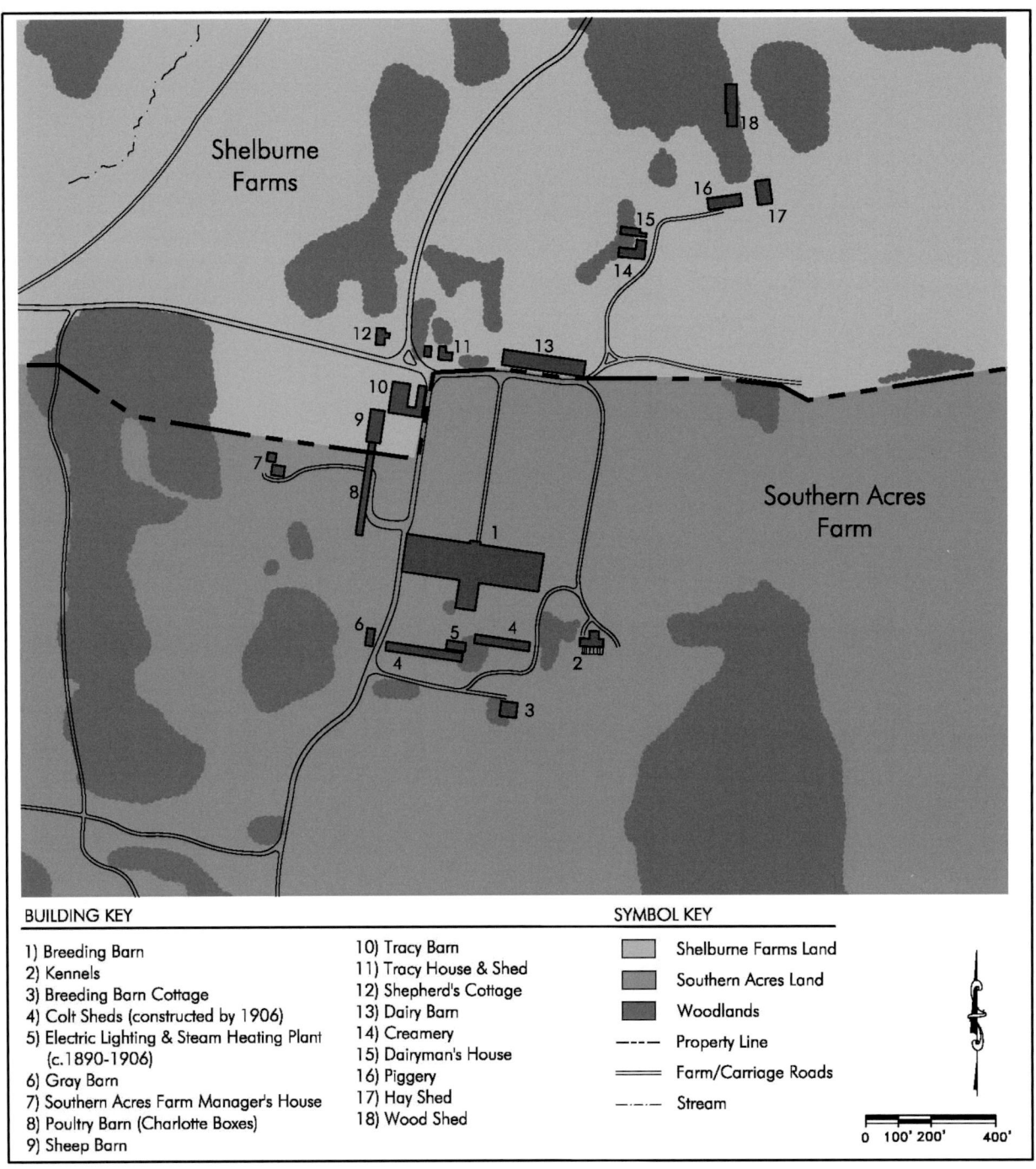

The Breeding Barn Complex (left) and Farm Barn and Surroundings (right), 1886–1942

Sources: Soil Conservation Service, United States Department of Agriculture, aerial photograph depicting area in and around Shelburne Farms, Aug 25, 1942, numbered DCC-3-20 and DCC-3-24, original at National Archives, copies in SFC; Historic Photographs in the Print and Photograph Collection, SFC; Land, Genealogy, and Vital Records, STC; *Sanborn Fire Insurance Maps* of Burlington, VT, for Nov 1894 (sheet 28), Jan 1900 (s. 33), Mar 1906 (s. 38), Oct 1912 (s. 40), May 1919 (s. 39), Apr 1926 (s. 39), 1942 (s. 50), and 1942–60 (s. 50), Special Collections Department, Bailey/Howe Library, UVM; Marshall Webb, corr. and interviews with author, Mar–May 2009, and interview with Jim St. George, c. May 29, 2009; and the following maps

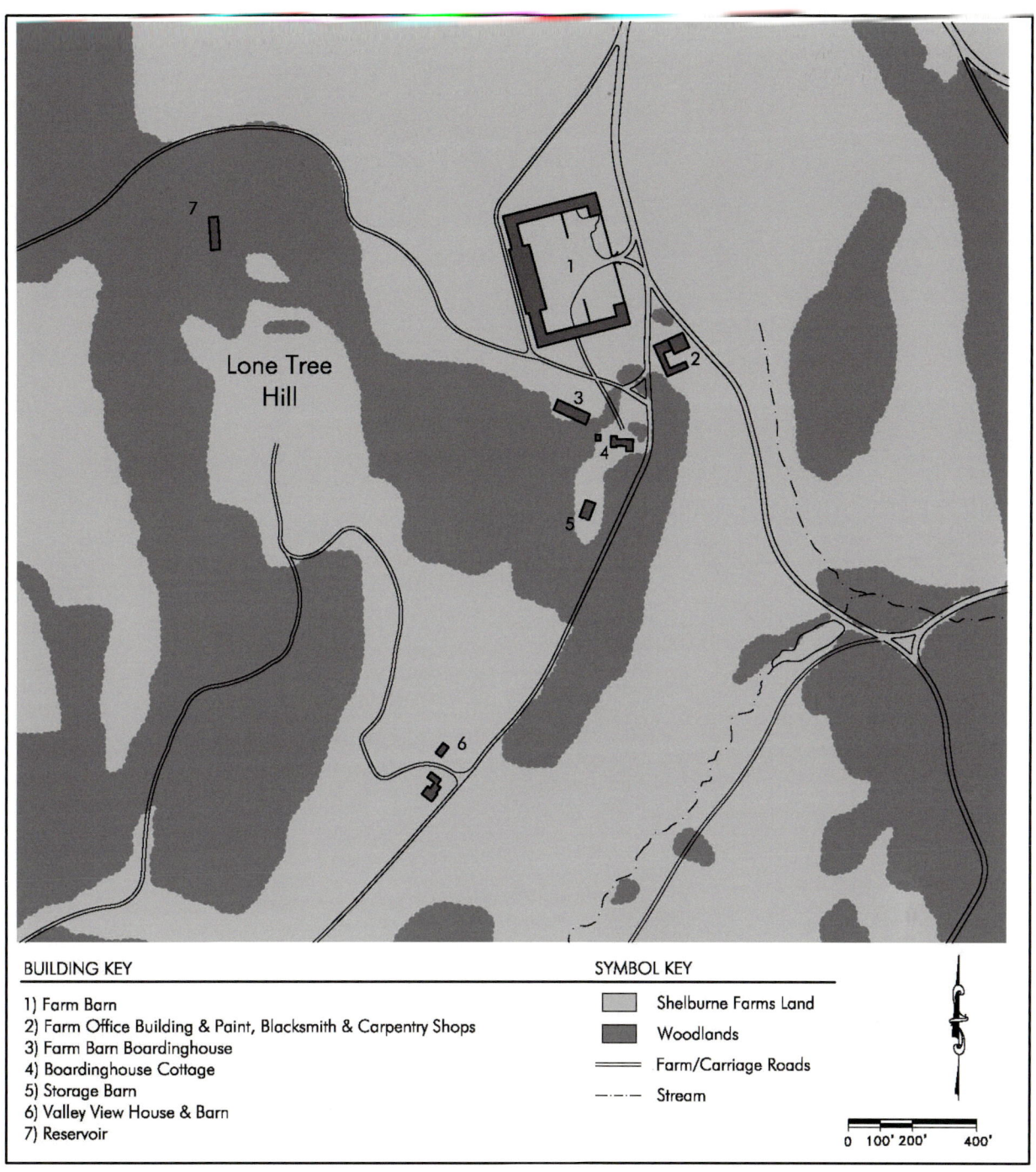

in APMI: McIntosh and Crandall, "Topographical Map of Shelburne Farms, Shelburne, Vermont," 1923, 2004.3.21.37, in Folder 3, FFD 8; "Southern Acres Farm, J. Watson Webb, Shelburne, Vermont," date unknown, 2004.3.37.9a, in Folder 2, FFD 18.

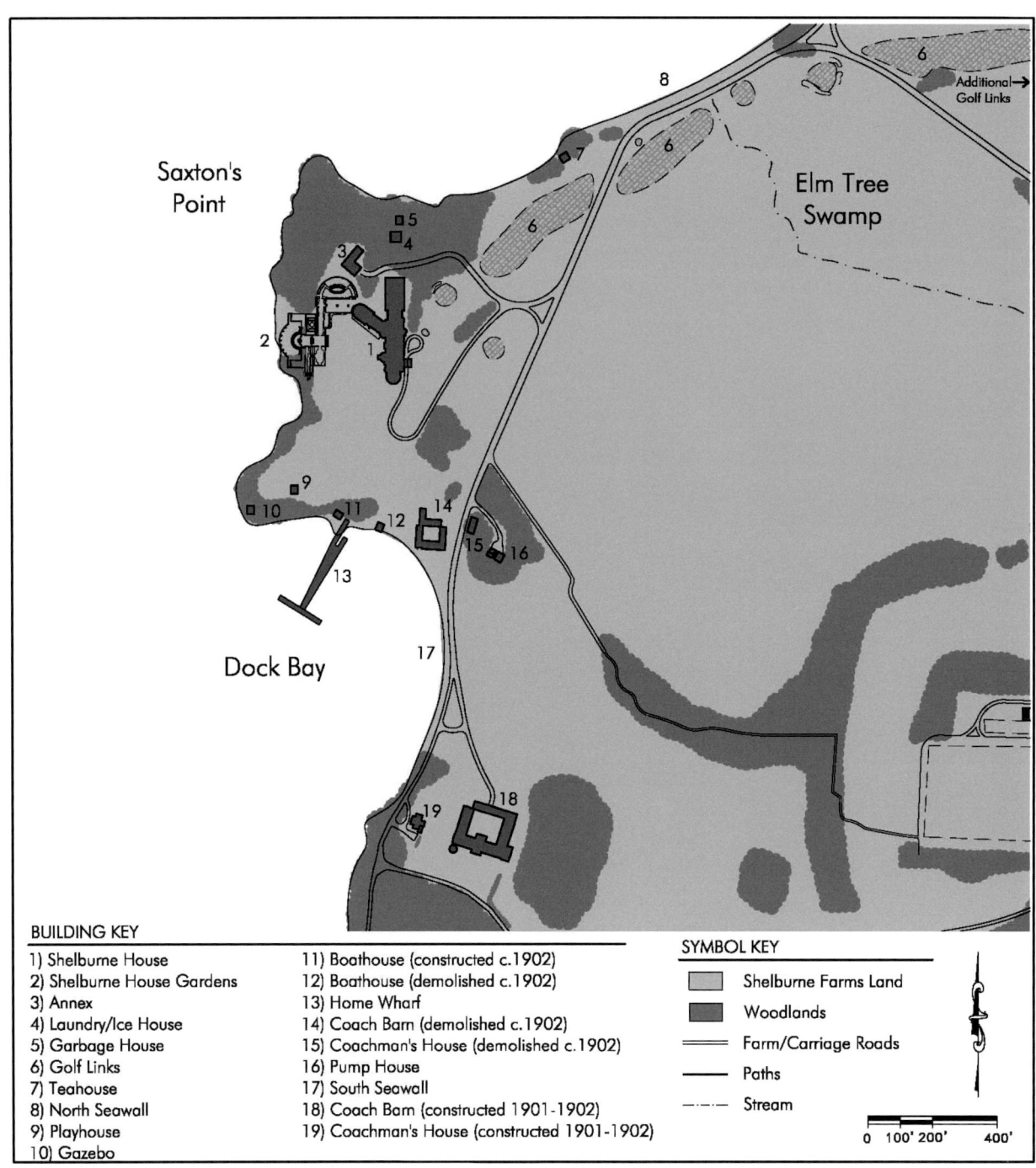

Shelburne House, the Coach Barn, and Surroundings, 1886–1942

Sources: Soil Conservation Service, United States Department of Agriculture, aerial photograph depicting area in and around Shelburne Farms, Aug 25, 1942, numbered DCC-3-20 and DCC-3-24, original at National Archives, copies in SFC; Historic Photographs in the Print and Photograph Collection, SFC; *Sanborn Fire Insurance Maps* of Burlington, VT, for Nov 1894 (sheet 28), Jan 1900 (s. 33), Mar 1906 (s. 38), Oct 1912 (s. 40), May 1919 (s. 39), Apr 1926 (s. 39), 1942 (s. 50), and 1942–60 (s. 50), Special Collections Department, Bailey/Howe Library, UVM; Marshall Webb, corr. and interviews with author, Mar–May 2009.

NOTES

Chapter 1

1. Jean (Jennie) Morehouse Edwards, "A Story for my Great Grandchildren," date unknown, Morehouse Family Papers Coll., MSA 247, Folder 6, VHS Library.
2. LOW to WSW, Apr 16, 1922, Folder 20, Deed Box Coll., LOW Papers.
3. This account of the geological and Native American history of the area, pages 3–5, is largely based on the following sources, with quotations and additional sources as noted: Christopher McGrory Klyza and Stephen C. Trombulak, *The Story of Vermont: A Natural and Cultural History* (Hanover, NH: University Press of New England, 1999); Jan Albers, *Hands on the Land: A History of the Vermont Landscape* (Cambridge, MA: MIT Press, 2000); William A. Haviland and Marjory W. Power, *The Original Vermonters: Native Inhabitants Past and Present* (Hanover, NH: University Press of New England, 1981); Michael Sherman, Gene Sessions, and P. Jeffrey Potash, *Freedom and Unity: A History of Vermont* (Barre, VT: Vermont Historical Society, 2004); Elizabeth H. Thompson and Eric R. Sorenson, *Wetland, Woodland, Wildland: A Guide to the Natural Communities of Vermont* (Hanover, NH: University Press of New England, The Nature Conservancy, and Vermont Department of Fish and Wildlife, 2000).
4. Klyza and Trombulak, 37.
5. Klyza and Trombulak, 29.
6. In addition, an 1869 map of Shelburne identifies an "Indian House" and "Indian House Bay" on the western shores of Shelburne Point (Frederick W. Beers, Map of Shelburne, in *Atlas of Chittenden County, Vermont* [New York: 1869]). Quote from Peter A. Thomas, Director of UVM's Consulting Archaeology Program, to Karen Freeman, VT Housing and Conservation Board, Oct 28, 1996, "Shelburne—Southern Acres Easement" Folder, Town of Shelburne Reference Files, VDHP. Also Giovanna Peebles, VT State Archaeologist, "Preliminary Archaeological Overview and Sensitivity Maps for the Town of Shelburne," Dec 1990, along with other reports, Archaeological Site Survey Forms, and corr. in the Shelburne Town Land Planning Folder, Town of Shelburne Reference Files, VDHP; Ida Monroe Simonds, "Reminiscences of Bygone Days," in Truman M. Webster, *Shelburne: Pieces of History* (Shelburne, VT: Shelburne Historic Sites Committee, 1994), 17; James B. Petersen, Jack A. Wolford, Nathan D. Hamilton, Laureen A. Labar, and Michael Heckenberger, "Archaeological Investigations in the Shelburne Pond Locality, Chittenden County, Vermont," May 1984, and N. Bazilchuk, C. Fastie, A. Heise, J. Kasmer, T. Naumann, R. Paul, D. Publicover, C. Savonen, S. Whidden, and K. Zimmerman, "The Physical Characteristics, Site of Discovery and Method of Preservation of a Dugout Canoe Found at Shelburne, Vermont," Apr 1, 1985, prepared for UVM Natural Areas program, both in Special Collections, Bailey/Howe Library, UVM.
7. Albers, 54.
8. Arthur B. Cohn, *Lake Champlain's Sailing Canal Boats: An Illustrated Journey from Burlington Bay to the Hudson River* (Basin Harbor, VT: Lake Champlain Maritime Museum, 2003), 9.
9. Sherman et al., 19, 30–31, 40; Klyza and Trombulak, 46–48.
10. Klyza and Trombulak, 48; Sherman et al., 62–63.
11. Shelburne town charter, quoted in Abby Hemenway, ed., *Vermont Historical Gazetteer: A Magazine* (Burlington, VT: A. M. Hemenway, 1868), vol. 1, 854–55.
12. Hemenway, vol. 1, 857; Sherman et al., 71–79, 125; Ralph Nading Hill, *Lake Champlain: Key to Liberty* (Woodstock, VT: Countryman Press, 1988), 144.
13. There is little evidence regarding the method of Ira Allen's acquisition of lands in Shelburne, and Hemenway speculates that he may have acquired them en masse illegally when the town was first chartered (Hemenway, vol. 1, 857). Ira Allen deed from William Hull to Silas Hathaway, Feb 16, 1799, Box 19, Folder 97, and Thomas Chittenden to Ira Allen, May 10, 1784, both in Box 6, Folder 21, Allen Family Papers, Special Collections, Bailey/Howe Library, UVM; Michael A. Bellesiles, *Revolutionary Outlaws: Ethan Allen and the Struggle for Independence on the Early American Frontier* (Charlottesville, VA: University Press of Virginia, 1995), 83–84; J. Kevin Graffagnino, "The Country My Soul Delighted In: The Onion River Land Company and the Vermont Frontier," *New England Quarterly* 65 (Mar 1992): 33; Marie Harding, *The History of Shelburne* (Excelsior Press and Shelburne Museum, 1963), frontispiece.
14. Hemenway, vol. 1, 856–61 (quote on 861). Also Cohn, 9; Ruth N. Roberts, "Facts and Fancies in History of Quaker Smith Point," 7, Smith Family Genealogy Records, STC; Lilian Baker Carlisle, ed., *Look Around St. George and Shelburne, Vermont* (Burlington, VT: Chittenden County Historical Society, 1975), 22; Jay Mack Holbrook, *Vermont 1771 Census* (Oxford, MA: Holbrook Research Institute, 1982), 52, 66, 67; Sherman et al., 101; Webster, 34, 54–55.
15. Contrary to Webb family lore, it does not appear that Brig. Gen. Samuel Blachley Webb, WSW's grandfather, received any portion of the town lands, including a plot encompassing Lone Tree Hill, as a land grant in recognition of his Revolutionary War service (Gerald P. Francis, "A Shelburne Farms Archives Research Note—Brigadier General Samuel Blachley Webb: Vermont Lands," Mar 31, 2008, passim, SFC). Hemenway, vol. 1, 870; Graffagnino, 42; United States Bureau of the Census, *Heads of Families at the First Census of the United States, Taken*

in the Year 1790: Vermont (Baltimore: Genealogical Publishing Co., Inc., 1992), 8–9.

16 This account of early settlers, pages 8–10, is largely based on records found in the Land Records, STC, with quotations and additional sources as noted. Hemenway, vol. 1, 859, 862; Comstock Family Genealogy Records, especially Mildred Kell to Mrs. Henry W. Tracy, Apr 5, 1970, STC; *Heads of Families 1790*, 27; Levi Comstock obituary, *BFP*, May 21, 1847; Polly Darnell, Shelburne Museum Archivist, to author, May 10, 2006.

17 Scott A. Bartley, ed., *Vermont Families in 1791* (Camden, ME: Picton Press, 1992), vol. 1, 176–78; Tracy genealogy and land claim notes in Legal Papers, Farm Manager's Papers (hereafter referred to as FM's Papers); Beers; Ezekiel Tracy death notice, *BFP*, Aug 14, 1873; Richard Tracy, corr. with author, May–Jun, 2004; Mary Twitchell, interview with author, Mar 2004; Doris Maeck, interview with author, Mar 5, 2004.

18 Although it was not unusual for Quakers to settle at some distance from established meetings, the Smiths may have had one or two particular reasons for doing so. William Smith supposedly "objected to the taxes in Shelburne Village and wanted to get as far away…as he could" (JWW Jr., "Pictorial History of the Webb Family," 51, JWW Jr. Coll.). Additionally, it appears that William and Elizabeth Smith were not legally married to each other (Nathan Perkins, *A Narrative of a Tour Through the State of Vermont from April 27 to June 12, 1789* [Rutland, VT: C. E. Tuttle Co., 1964], 32). "Sketch Made For Dr. William S. Webb, N. Y. City, of Certain Lands in Shelburne, Vt. April 1886," 2004.3.21.9, FFD 7, Folder 6, APMI; Hemenway, vol. 1, 858–59; Arthur L. and Frances P. Hyde, *Burial Grounds of Vermont* (Vermont Old Cemetery Association, 1991), 133; Roberts; Esther Monroe Swift, *Vermont Place Names: Footprints of History* (Camden, ME: Picton Press, 1996), 185; SBW Jr., interview with author, Aug 13, 2008. For more on Quakers in the area, see Thomas Bassett, "What Happened to Quakers in Chittenden County?" *Chittenden County Historical Society Bulletin* 17, No. 1 (Jan/Feb 1982); and Thomas Bassett, "Migration of Friends to the Upper Hudson and Champlain Valleys," in Hugh Barbour, ed., *Quaker Crosscurrents: Three Hundred Years of Friends in the New York Yearly Meetings* (Syracuse, NY: Syracuse University Press, 1995).

19 Hemenway, vol. 1, 505, 859; Saxton Family Genealogy Records, STC; and the following from Box 12, Allen Family Papers, Special Collections, Bailey/Howe Library, UVM: court orders to Chittenden County Sheriff "to seize Frederick Saxton to answer debt suit brought by Ira Allen," Jan 21 and 26, 1790 (Folders 5 and 6), agreement by Ira Allen and Frederick Saxton to exchange lands, Apr 8, 1790 (Folder 26), and deed from Frederick Saxton to Ira Allen, Jul 20, 1791 (Folder 111). While the Allen Papers and secondary sources consulted describe the land transaction as an exchange between Saxton and Allen, it was recorded in the Shelburne Town Land Records as a purchase (Deed, Ira Allen to Frederick Saxton, Jul 20, 1791, Land Records, vol. 1, 107, STC).

20 Edward S. and Sarah R. Saxton to William J. Van Arsdale, Jan 28, 1886, Box 1, Folder 3, Legal Papers, FM's Papers.

21 "Sturgis" and "Hyman" are also spelled "Sturges" and "Hymen" in some land transactions; the spellings found in genealogical records are used here. Philip G. Buffinton, Morehouse/Holabird family records and corr. with author, 2004–5. The author thanks Julie Eldridge Edwards for connecting her with Mr. Buffinton.

22 Hemenway, vol. 1, 859; Rev. Sylvester Nash, *The Nash Family: or, Records of the Descendants of Thomas Nash of New Haven, Connecticut, 1640* (Hartford, CT: Case, Tiffany and Company, 1853), 104, 175; U.S. Bureau of the Census, *Heads of Families at the Second Census of the United States, Taken in the Year 1800: Vermont* (Montpelier, VT: Vermont Historical Society, 1938), 62.

23 Cohn, 90. Also "Shelburne," in John J. Duffy, Samuel B. Hand, and Ralph H. Orth, eds., *The Vermont Encyclopedia* (Hanover, NH: University Press of New England, 2003), 265; Hemenway, vol. 1, 873–76; Hill, 144.

24 Klyza and Trombulak, 50; Sherman et al., 133.

25 Hemenway, vol. 1, 858.

26 Klyza and Trombulak, 74. According to MCW, Shelburne Farms' woodlands manager, only about 65 acres of land within the estate's remaining (core) 1,400 acres contain stands of trees that predate European settlement in the area. He believes that the core acreage was approximately 70% cleared by the early 19th century. It is likely that, in accordance with the terms of the town charter, the white pine on SF land was harvested and shipped to England for masts for the Royal Navy. MCW's estimate is corroborated by "Sketch Made for Dr. William S. Webb," which depicts only isolated stands of trees and orchards among the farmland purchased by WSW by Apr 1886. Also corr. and interviews between MCW and author, May 11 and 16, 2006; Klyza and Trombulak, 65–67; Robert E. Pike, *Tall Trees, Tough Men: An Anecdotal and Pictorial History of Logging and Log-Driving in New England* (New York: W. W. Norton, 1967), 38–46; Albers, 202–3.

27 Perkins, 31.

28 This account (p. 14–16) of agriculture in the Champlain Valley during the late 18th and early to mid-19th centuries is largely based on the following sources, with additional sources and quotations as noted: Cohn; Klyza and Trombulak; and Sherman et al. (quote here on 134).

29 Sherman et al., 160; Russell P. Bellico, *Sails and Steam in the Mountains: A Maritime and Military History of Lake George and Lake Champlain* (Fleischmanns, NY: Purple Mountain Press, 1992), 207, 211; Hill, 172.

30 The eastern section of the Erie Canal opened on the same date in 1823 as the Champlain Canal; however, the Erie would not be fully completed until 1825. Potash, or wood ashes, was used as a fertilizer and in the production of soap, glass, and textiles. Quote from Klyza and Trombulak, 70.

31 Entries for Shelburne, Chittenden County, in 1840 Vermont Census of Mines, Agriculture, Commerce and Manufacturing, Microfilm Reel #618, Bailey/Howe Library, UVM.

32 The following account (p. 16–20) of farming activities in the SF area is largely based on the following sources, with quotations and additional sources as noted: 1850, 1870, and 1880 Agricultural Census records for Shelburne, Chittenden County, VT, Microfilm #s 626, 628, and 629, and 1880 Federal Population Census for Shelburne, Chittenden County, VT, Microfilm #586, Reel 4, all in Bailey/Howe Library, UVM.

33 See, for instance, entries for Feb 2, Feb 4, Feb 5, Jul 8, and Nov 10, Franklin Morehouse Diary, 1857, Morehouse Family Papers Coll., MSA 247, Folder 5, VHS. Also Philip Buffinton genealogy records; corr. between Buffinton and author, 2004–5.

34 "Vermont Farm Notes," *BFP*, Apr 3, 1889.

35 Hemenway, vol. 1, 859; Holabird Family Genealogy Records, "Copies of Town Records," vol. 1, 3, and Land Records, passim,

all in STC; Deed, Mary and Hattie Holabird to WSW, May 2, 1888, Box 1, Folder 2, Deed, Charles E. and Mary S. Baker to Mary Holabird, Apr 16, 1888, Box 1, Folder 3, and WSW, memorandum of agreement, May 1, 1888, Box 2, Folder 6, all in Legal Papers, FM's Papers.

36 Based on the convergence of dates and other clues, references to "Louisa Nash," "Chany Louisa Nash," and "Louisa C. Nash" in genealogical, census, and legal records probably refer to the same person. Last Will & Testament of Asahel Nash [Jr.], Jul 17, 1878, vol. 11, 475–76, Land Records, STC.

37 In the early 1860s, Franklin Morehouse purchased a dictionary to further his children's education by bartering a "two horse load of potatoes" with a Burlington bookseller (note in Morehouse family dictionary, coll. of Philip Buffinton). Also Beers; Land and Vital Records, STC; Hemenway, vol. 1, 872–74; Kenneth M. Bessette Sr. and Melissa L. Cook, "Mysteries of History, or How the Shelburne Post Office Ended Up in the Shelburne Museum: A More or Less Accurate Account of the Real Past of the Tuckaway General Store," *Chittenden County Historical Society Bulletin* 31, No. 2 (Spring 1997): 8.

38 Franklin Morehouse to Roderick Morehouse, Jan 1, 1861, Morehouse Family Papers Coll., MSA 247, Folder 6, VHS. Also, for instance, Franklin Morehouse Diary, 1857, passim, in Folder 5, same location.

39 Klyza and Trombulak, 91.

40 Howard S. Russell, *A Long, Deep Furrow: Three Centuries of Farming in New England* (Hanover, NH: University Press of New England, 1982), 256. Also Albers, 204; Klyza and Trombulak, 72–73, 76–77.

41 Klyza and Trombulak, 74–79 (quote on 76).

42 Roberts; Deed, Lucinda D. Smith to William J. Van Arsdale, Feb 8, 1886, Box 1, Folder 3, Legal Papers, FM's Papers; Hamilton Child, *Gazetteer and Business Directory of Chittenden County, Vermont, for 1882–83* (Syracuse, NY: The Journal Office, 1882), 381.

43 The following are all in Legal Papers, Box 1, Folder 2, FM's Papers: Deed, John Nash to WSW, Feb 3, 1886, Deed, Edgar Nash to WSW, Jan 27, 1886, Deed, Louisa C. Nash to WSW, Jan 27, 1886, Deed, Elbert and Jane Nash to WSW, Feb 3, 1886, and Deed, Elbert and Jane Nash to WSW, Feb 21, 1889. Also Map, "Original Purchases, Shelburne Farms, Shelburne Vermont," surveyed 1886–1891, 2004.3.21.23, APMI. This map misidentifies Elbert and Jane Nash's holding near the LaPlatte River as belonging to "Albert" Nash.

44 Deed, Tracy family to Hamilton McK. Twombly, Nov 1, 1887, Box 1, Folder 3, Legal Papers, FM's Papers.

45 Holabird Family Genealogy Records, STC; Deed, Mary and Hattie Holabird to WSW, May 2, 1888, Box 1, Folder 2, Legal Papers, FM's Papers.

46 Klyza and Trombulak, 77.

47 Harding, 57; Philip Buffinton, Morehouse/Holabird genealogy records and land transaction notes; corr. between Buffinton and author, 2004–5; Edward Morehouse to Franklin Morehouse, Jul 18, 1864, transcribed by Hawley Morehouse on Dec 23, 1864, Morehouse Family Papers Coll., MSA 247, VHS; "Descendants of Asahel Nash," Nash Family Genealogy Records, STC.

48 Frederick Phisterer, *New York in the War of the Rebellion, 1861 to 1865*, Third Edition (Albany, NY: J. B. Lyon Company, 1912), 3646, 3652; Edward Morehouse to Franklin Morehouse, Jul 18, 1864, transcribed by Hawley Morehouse on Dec 23, 1864, and George C. Morehouse obituary, both in Morehouse Family Papers Coll., MSA 247, VHS; Philip Buffinton, Holabird/Morehouse genealogy records and corr. with author, 2004–6.

49 Lucia Morehouse Wells, "Another Letter From The Hub: Interesting Sights and Scenes in Boston, A Family Reunion After Thirty-One Years of Separation," 1890, courtesy Philip Buffinton and Nancy Buffinton Kelm. Also Jean (Jennie) Morehouse Edwards, "Childhood Memories & Girlhood Experiences," 1933, courtesy Buffinton and Kelm; and Buffinton, Holabird/Morehouse genealogy records and corr. with author, 2004–6.

50 Edwards, "Childhood Memories & Girlhood Experiences"; Hurlburt Family Genealogy Records, STC; Deed, Diana Satterley to William J. Van Arsdale, Feb 23, 1886, Box 1, Folder 3, and Deed, Hiram F. and Roxy J. Hurlburt to William J. Van Arsdale, Feb 23, 1886, Box 1, Folder 4, both in Legal Papers, FM's Papers.

51 Doris Maeck, interview with author, Mar 5, 2004, and corr. with author, May 20, 2006; Mary Twitchell, interview with author, Mar 2004; Richard Tracy, Tracy family genealogy records, Sep 2006; Deed, Lee Tracy to WSW, Oct 12, 1888, and Deed, Lee and Adeline A. Tracy to WSW, Feb 21, 1889, both in Box 1, Folder 4, Legal Papers, FM's Papers; Child, 381; Grand List for 1882, STC; Bessette and Cook, 9; Webster, 110–11.

Chapter 2

1 WSW, Jul 18, 1879, 1879 Journal, 85–86, WSW Papers.

2 Numerous sources state that WSW's first visit to VT occurred in the spring of 1881 on a trip undertaken for LOW's father, William Henry Vanderbilt, to scout out the feasibility of acquiring the Rutland Railroad. While he may well have made the journey in 1881, it is clear from the above citation that it was not his first visit to the area.

3 The biographical account of WSW and his family on pages 17–19 is largely based on the following sources, with quotations and additional sources as noted: James Crouthamel, *James Watson Webb: A Biography* (Middletown, CT: Wesleyan University Press, 1969); Ruth Lawrence, ed., *Webb and Allied Family Histories: A Documented Compilation of Genealogy and Biography* (New York: National Americana Society, 1937); Jerry Patterson, *The First Four Hundred: Mrs. Astor's New York in the Gilded Age* (New York: Rizzoli, 2000); transcripts of corr. from Gen. James Watson Webb and Laura Webb to their sons, passim, JWW Jr. Coll.; LOW, manuscript biography of WSW, Folder 32, Deed Box Coll., LOW Papers; F. A. P. Barnard, President of Columbia College, letter of recommendation, Oct 5, 1870, Folder 4, Deed Box Coll., LOW Papers; and "Dr. W. Seward Webb Dead In Vermont," *New York Times*, Oct 30, 1926. Also, for this paragraph, Gerald P. Francis, "A Shelburne Farms Archives Research Note—Brigadier General Samuel Blachley Webb: Vermont Lands," Mar 31, 2008, SFC.

4 Transcripts of corr. from Gen. James Watson Webb and Laura Webb to their sons, passim, JWW Jr. Coll.; "Warvie" Webb and Gen. James Watson Webb to WSW, Oct 23, 1864, Folder 3, "First Letters I Ever Received," Deed Box Coll., LOW Papers; "Pokahoe" clipping, source unknown, Oct 1889, Scrapbook vol. V, 167.

5 Gen. James Watson Webb to WSW, Jan 27, 1868, in transcripts of corr. from Gen. James Watson Webb and Laura Webb to their sons, passim, JWW Jr. Coll..

6 WSW to "Steve," Dec 28, 1871, WSW Personal Corr., WSW Papers.

7 Gen. James Watson Webb to WSW and H. Walter Webb, Aug 7, 1864; "Vermont Men of Today: Dr. William Seward Webb," *The Vermonter* 6, no. 8 (Mar 1901): 99; WSW's medical school records, WSW Papers; WSW's Columbia College diploma, #1999.818, Framed Works of Art Coll.

8 Barnard.

9 WSW, "Distemper of Pneumonia," "Treatment of Surfeit Mange," and "The Best Treatment for Distemper," *Forest and Stream*, 1876, Vanderbilt-Webb Clippings, vol. 1, 1870–1900, 5, JWW Jr. Coll.

10 Andrew Smith to Col. Emmet Clark, Sep 30, 1878, and George A. Peters to Col. Emmet Clark, Sep 11, 1878, both in Folder 4, LOW Deed Box Coll.; LOV, Apr 29, 1877, 1877 Journal, LOW Papers.

11 "But I am always called Lila, having christened myself by that name when a baby" (LOV, Jan 28, 1877, 1877 Diary, LOW Papers). Also John Foreman and Robbe Pierce Stimson, *The Vanderbilts and the Gilded Age: Architectural Aspirations, 1879–1901* (New York: St. Martin's Press, 1991), front pastedown.

12 Louis Auchincloss, *The Vanderbilt Era: Profiles of a Gilded Age* (New York: Scribner, 1989), 16–19; Jerry Patterson, *The Vanderbilts* (New York: Harry N. Abrams, 1989), 16–19, 25–27, 37–41; Arthur T. Vanderbilt II, *Fortune's Children: The Fall of the House of Vanderbilt* (New York: William Morrow and Company, 1989), 6–12, 21–23, 29–39.

13 John M. Bryan, *Biltmore Estate: The Most Distinguished Private Place* (New York: Rizzoli, 1994), 13; Foreman and Stimson, 14; Patterson, *The Vanderbilts*, 115, 212; Vanderbilt, 53.

14 LOV Journals and LOW Papers, passim; W. A. Croffut, *The Vanderbilts and the Story of Their Fortune* (Chicago: Belford, Clarke & Company, 1886), 61; Patterson, *The Vanderbilts*, 25; Robert A. M. Stern, Thomas Mellins, and David Fishman, *New York 1880: Architecture and Urbanism in the Gilded Age* (New York: Monacelli Press, 1999), 578; Vanderbilt, 14–17.

15 LOV, "Faithfulness Rewarded," "Maggie Martin," "Interest and Disinterestedness," and "The Philipps," LOW Papers. Also LOV Schoolbooks; LOV, Apr 29 and May 13, 1878, 1878 Diary; and LOV et al., "The Monogram Literary Club," title page, all in LOW Papers.

16 LOV, Jul 15, 1879, 1879 Journal, LOW Papers.

17 Both quotes from LOV, Jan 28, 1877, 1877 Diary, LOW Papers.

18 LOV, "Leaving School Forever," 1879–80 Journal, 8, LOW Papers.

19 LOV, "Harriman's Party Jun 12th 1875," 1875 Scrapbook, 97, LOW Papers.

20 LOV, Apr 29, 1877, 1877 Diary, LOW Papers.

21 LOV, 1878 Diary and "The Luzerne Party," 1879–80 Journal, 40–43, both in LOW Papers.

22 LOV, "The Luzerne Party," 1879–1880 Journal, 53–54, LOW Papers.

23 LOV to WSW, Nov 5, [1878], 1878 Journal, 299, LOW Papers.

24 LOV, 1879 Journal, LOW Papers. Also WSW, Sep 19, 1879, 1879 Journal, WSW Papers.

25 LOV, Jul 25, 1879, 1879 Journal, LOW Papers.

26 LOV, Jul 15, Jul 25, and Aug 14, 1879, 1879 Journal, LOW Papers.

27 LOV, Jul 8–9, Aug 12, 1879, and passim, 1879 Journal, LOW Papers. Also WSW, Jun 24–25, 1879, 1879 Journal, WSW Papers.

28 WSW, Aug 8, 1879, 1879 Journal, WSW Papers. Also 1878 letters in Folder 4, Deed Box Coll., LOW Papers; WSW's medical school records, WSW Papers. However, WSW did leave the possibility of returning to medical practice open: "I… registered at the City Hall as a physician under the new law" (WSW, Oct 1, 1880, 1880 Journal, WSW Papers).

29 WSW, Jun 24, Jun 26, Jul 10, Jul 15, Aug 9, Aug 11, Oct 13, and Oct 15, 1879, 1879 Journal, and May 9, Jul 2, and Oct 1, 1880, 1880 Journal, WSW Papers; Worden & Co., engraved announcement of WSW's admittance as partner, Jan 1, 1880, Folder 5, Deed Box Coll., LOW Papers; Lawrence, 92.

30 LOV, Apr 12, 1880, 1879–1880 Journal, LOW Papers; "A Vanderbilt Wedding: Dr. W. S. Webb United To Miss Leila [sic] Osgood Vanderbilt," *New York Times*, Dec 21, 1881.

31 Untitled and undated clippings, Vanderbilt-Webb Clippings, vol. 1, 1870–1900, JWW Jr. Coll.; William Henry Vanderbilt, "Last Will and Testament of William H. Vanderbilt," Sep 25, 1884, LOW Papers; "Webb, William Seward," residences, *New York City Directories*, 1881–90, Humanities Dept., New York Public Library; John Snook Contract Books, Architecture Department, New-York Historical Society; LOW to VW, Feb 20 [1913], VW Papers; Foreman and Stimson, passim.

32 Foreman and Stimson, 51–52. Also Jerry E. Patterson, *Fifth Avenue: The Best Address* (New York: Rizzoli, 1998), 118.

33 One of the greatest descriptions of this phenomenon appears in Edith Wharton's Pulitzer Prize–winning 1920 novel *The Age of Innocence*, in which the grand dowager Mrs. Manson Mingott reigns from one of the first townhouses in midtown Manhattan which, in the 1870s, was surrounded by "hoardings, quarries, one-story saloons, wooden green-houses in ragged gardens," and pastured goats [Wharton, *The Age of Innocence* (New York: Appleton, 1920), 24–25]. Also Eric Homberger, *Mrs. Astor's New York*, 73–76, 83–84, 103, 107, 257–58; Patterson, *The Vanderbilts*, 10–11, 75–93.

34 The ballroom of reigning society matron Mrs. Caroline Astor could accommodate 400 people, and the "Four Hundred" were those selected by "social arbiter" Ward McAllister to attend events held in the ballroom. Patterson, *The First Four Hundred*, 7, 133–35, 232.

35 LOW, "Which left the greatest impression on the history of the world, the Renaissance or the Reformation?," 1893–96, 1901, and 1904 Diary, 130–35, LOW Papers. Also "Mrs. Webb's Big Party," *New York Herald*, Jan 23, 1888, Scrapbook vol. V, 10; Foreman and Stimson, 23–27; Patterson, *The Vanderbilts*, 126–31; Vanderbilt, 120–24.

36 The names of these and additional clubs and societies to which WSW belonged may be found in WSW, entry for publication in *Matthews' American Armoury and Blue Book*, c. 1900, Folder 43, Deed Box Coll., LOW papers. Also *New York Post*, Apr 5, 1887, Scrapbook vol. IV, 141; "A Trio of Nabobs," *Savannah (GA) News*, Jan 9, 1887, Scrapbook vol. IV, 128; "Let's Go to the Club," *New York Journal*, Sep 7, 1890, Scrapbook vol. VI, 171; "The Opera Box-Holders," *New York World*, Nov 15, 1889, Scrapbook vol. V, 189; and Scrapbooks vols. V–IX, XII–XIII, passim.

37 WSW, quoted in "A Tribute to Vermont," *BFP*, Aug 6, 1895, Scrapbook vol. XIII, 41. Also Oakledge Farm/Shelburne House Guestbook, 1884–1928, 5–11.

38 See, for example, *Chicago Tribune*, Apr 12, 1885, Scrapbook vol. IV, 6; *New York Tribune*, Feb 12, 1885, Scrapbook vol. IV, 1; Editorial, *New York Truth*, Apr 21, 1887, Scrapbook vol. IV, 144; Editorial, *New York Truth*, Mar 29, 1889, Scrapbook vol. V, 84.

39 The Webbs' rented house, on the corner of Main and South Prospect Streets in Burlington, is now owned by UVM. EFG to

WSW, Apr 20, 1906, EFG Corr. with WSW, FM's Papers; Deed, Lawrence Barnes to WSW, Sep 10, 1883, and Deed, Home for Destitute Children to WSW, Oct 6, 1883, both in Box 1, Folder 4, Legal Papers, FM's Papers. The Oakledge deeds are also recorded in Land Records, General Index #15, 1883–1884 S–Z, vol. 20, City Clerk's Office, Burlington, VT.

40 "Dr. W. Seward Webb," *Albany (NY) Journal*, Feb 27, 1885, Scrapbook vol. IV, 0, and untitled article from *Keynote*, Sep 26, 1885, Scrapbook vol. IV, 60.

41 EFG to Dave H. Morris, Oct 6 and Oct 30, 1913, Folder M-4, FM's Papers; "Catalogue of the Oak Ledge Farm Herd Burlington, VT. Stoke Pogis-Rioter Blood," Box 12, FM's Papers; Oakledge photographs in "Estates—Oakledge" Folder, Print and Photograph Coll.; Stu Perry, "Oakledge History Passes to Bulldozers," *BFP*, May 13, 1975; "Training Exercise," *BFP*, Jun 5, 1975.

42 *New York Times*, Apr 3, 1887, Scrapbook vol. IV, 142. Also *New York Sun*, Dec 5, 1886, Scrapbook vol. IV, 120; *New York Sun*, Dec 13, 1887, Scrapbook vol. IV, 142.

43 Oakledge/Shelburne House Guestbook, Jul 1, 1884, 5; "The Children of Croesus," *New York Graphic*, Apr 9, 1888, Scrapbook vol. V, 33; photographs in JWW Jr. Coll., including #s E, I, and J; and Kenneth Edward Wheeling, *Horse-Drawn Vehicles at the Shelburne Museum* (Shelburne, VT: The Shelburne Museum, 1974), 12.

44 Betsy Beattie, "The Queen City Celebrates Winter: The Burlington Coasting Club and the Burlington Carnival of Winter Sports, 1886–1887," *Vermont History* 52 (Winter 1984): 6–7 (first quote); "Dr. W. Seward Webb," *Albany (NY) Journal*, Feb 27, 1885, Scrapbook vol. IV, 0 (second quote). Also David J. Blow, *Historic Guide to Burlington Neighborhoods*, vol. 1 (Burlington, VT: Chittenden County Historical Society, 1991), 85; undated and untitled clipping, c. Jan 1886, Scrapbook vol. IV, 79; *BFP*, Oct 7, 1886, Scrapbook vol. IV, 114; *BFP*, Jan 31, 1887, Scrapbook vol. IV, 132.

45 Mary Jane Capozzoli Ingui, *American History: 1877 to the Present* (Hauppauge, NY: Barron's, 1993), 25. Also Thomas J. Schlereth, *Victorian America: Transformations in Everyday Life, 1876 1915* (NY: HarperPerennial, 1991), 28–29.

46 Barr Ferree, *American Estates and Gardens* (1904), quoted in Clive Aslet, *The American Country House* (New Haven, CT: Yale University Press, 1990), v–vi.

47 Aslet, passim; Mark Alan Hewitt, *The Architect and the American Country House, 1890–1940* (New Haven, CT: Yale University Press, 1990), 12, 14.

48 Hewitt, 1, 10–14 (quote on 13).

49 LOV, Sep 4 and Sep 7, 1875, in journal section of "Sunday Stories for Little People" notebook, LOW Papers; Patterson, *The Vanderbilts*, 32, 70.

50 Bryan, 19–21; Foreman and Stimson, passim; G. W. Helfrich and Gladys O'Neil, *Lost Bar Harbor* (Camden, ME: Down East Books, 1982), 15; Robert B. King, *The Vanderbilt Homes* (New York: Rizzoli, 1989), passim; Patterson, *The Vanderbilts*, passim; Charles W. Snell, *Vanderbilt Mansion: National Historic Site* (Washington, DC: National Park Service, no date), 16.

51 Gen. James Watson Webb to WSW, undated, c. 1864–68, transcripts of corr. between Gen. James Watson Webb and Laura Webb and their sons, JWW Jr. Coll. Also WSW, Aug 22, 1879, 1879 Journal, WSW Papers; Crouthamel, 80.

52 WSW, Aug 22, 1879, 1879 Journal, WSW Papers.

53 WSW, Jul 18, 1880, 1880 Journal, WSW Papers; "A Vanderbilt Wedding," *New York Times*, Dec 21, 1881.

54 For quote, see chapter 2, note 1. President of the Champlain Transportation Company and later vice president of the Delaware & Hudson Canal Company, Col. Le Grand B. Cannon was both a business associate of the Webbs and a close friend. Cannon's 60-acre estate, Overlake, was sited on one of the highest points in Burlington, with views down to Lake Champlain and the Adirondacks. The core of the property is now owned by UVM. Publisher Henry Holt's Fairholt also stood in Burlington; his property currently belongs to the Burlington Country Club. Joseph Auld, *Picturesque Burlington: A Handbook of Burlington, Vermont and Lake Champlain* (Burlington: Free Press Association, 1893), 103, 163; Blow, vol. 2, 166–69; "Cannon, Le Grand," in John J. Duffy, Samuel B. Hand, and Ralph H. Orth, eds., *The Vermont Encyclopedia* (Hanover, NH: University Press of New England, 2003), 175–76; Peter Carlough, *Bygone Burlington: A Bicentenntial Barrage of Battles, Buildings & Beings* (Burlington, VT: Queen City Printing, 1976), 41; Bob Labbance, "Burlington's Ghosts of Golf," *Vermont Golf Journal and Directory* (1995), 57–59; James M. Moran, "An 'Unpractical Man' in Vermont: Frederick Law Olmsted and Fairholt," unpublished thesis, May 1997, Bailey/Howe Library, UVM; *Round About Burlington, Vt.* (Winooski, VT: Vermont Illustrating Co., 1900), n.p.

Chapter 3

1 RHR to FLO, Jun 17, 1886, Olmsted Associates Records, Series B, Job File 1031, Container B74, Reel 54, Frederick Law Olmsted Papers, Manuscript Division, Library of Congress (henceforth referred to as FLOP, LOC).

2 It is difficult to accurately estimate cost comparisons; the figure of $237 million, derived from "The Inflation Calculator" at www.westegg.com/inflation/, is a rough approximation only. William Henry Vanderbilt, "Last Will and Testament of William H. Vanderbilt," Sep 25, 1884, LOW Papers; Receipt and Release, JWW to Frederick W. Vanderbilt, Nov 13, 1936, Folder 4, Box 1, SBW Sr. Family Papers Collection; Jerry Patterson, *The Vanderbilts* (New York: Harry N. Abrams, 1989), 116.

3 The short period of time between William Henry Vanderbilt's death in Dec 1885 and the Webbs' first purchases in Shelburne in Jan 1886 has resulted in some speculation about whether the Webbs had previously researched possible land acquisitions and were waiting for the moment when LOW's inheritance was assured. Vanderbilt had begun to experience poor health in the year before his death, so the Webbs' anticipation seems plausible (MCW, comment on draft Chapter 3, Jan 2009; John Foreman and Robbe Pierce Stimson, *The Vanderbilts and the Gilded Age: Architectural Aspirations, 1879–1901* [New York: St. Martin's Press, 1991], 13–14). It is difficult to determine the exact number of farms the Webbs acquired for SF, as the land records do not always specify the contents or use of the parcels. Further research is necessary (Julie Eldridge Edwards to author, Jan 27, 2009). "Shelburne Farms Property Timeline," 2000; "Original Purchases, Shelburne Farms, Surveyed 1886–1891," Framed Works of Art Coll. #1999.850; "Map of Land Owned by Dr. W. S. Webb on Shelburne Point," May 1902, revised Dec 1935, 2004.3.21.7a, APMI; Legal Papers, passim, FM's Papers.

4 LOW, "Christmas Greeting," 1922, Box 2, Folder 2, Deed Box Coll., LOW Papers.

5 Sophie Bartlett Harmon, "The Story of the Bartlett Farm," in

Truman M. Webster, *Shelburne: Pieces of History* (Shelburne, VT: Shelburne Historic Sites Committee, 1994), 105–6. According to one researcher, another possible reason for WSW and LOW's selection of the Shelburne site for their estate is their erroneous belief that WSW's grandfather Samuel Blachley Webb had been granted a portion of the land that would become SF in recognition of his service in the Revolutionary War. At some point during the 1880s, the Webbs acquired a letter concerning S. B. Webb's inquiries into his father-in-law Richard Bancker's claims to land in Shelburne. It appears as if WSW and LOW misinterpreted this letter as documenting S.B. Webb's land grant. However, it remains unclear whether WSW and LOW had made this connection by 1886, when they began to purchase land in Shelburne (Gerald P. Francis, "A Shelburne Farms Archives Research Note—Brigadier General Samuel Blachley Webb: Vermont Lands," Mar 31, 2008, SFC)

6 John J. Flynn, Deposition, Feb 1939, Estate Papers Coll., LOW Papers.

7 Wales & Wales to Hamilton McK. Twombly, Dec 16, 1887, Folder 8, Box 1, and "GW Wales Abstracts of Title Shelburne Farms" and "Abstracts of Title" notebooks, Box 2, all in Legal Papers, FM's Papers.

8 Joe Sherman, *The House at Shelburne Farms: The Story of One of America's Great Country Estates* (Middlebury, VT: Paul S. Eriksson, 1986), 9. Also AOW, "Almost a Century," unpublished 1977 memoir, 27–28, SFC.

9 *New York Tribune*, Aug 29, 1886, Scrapbook vol. IV, 111. Also AOW, 28; Sherman, *The House at Shelburne Farms*, 9; "Now the Country," *New York Herald*, Jun 17, 1894, Scrapbook vol. XII, 89.

10 The following sources are all in Legal Papers, FM's Papers: Memorandum between WSW and Julia Value, Oct 31, 1887, Box 2, Folder 6; George W. Wales to Hamilton McK. Twombly, Dec 16, 1887, Box 1, Folder 8; and Deed, John J. Collamer to Hamilton McK. Twombly, Oct 31, 1887, Box 1, Folder 3. Also *Lewiston (ME) Journal*, Sep 30, 1886, Scrapbook vol. IV, 113; *Rochester (NY) Democrat Chronicle*, Feb 6, 1886, Scrapbook vol. IV, 80.

11 Wales to Twombly, Dec 16, 1887, Box 1, Folder 8, Legal Papers, FM's Papers.

12 *New York Tribune*, Aug 29, 1886, Scrapbook vol. IV, 111. Also Jan Albers, *Hands on the Land: A History of the Vermont Landscape* (Cambridge, MA: MIT Press, 2000), 202–11.

13 Sarah Bradford Landau, *Edward T. and William A. Potter: American Victorian Architects* (New York: Garland Publishing, 1979), 70–79; "Robertson, Robert Henderson," in *The National Cyclopaedia of American Biography*, Vol. VI (1896): 98; Henry F. and Elsie Rathburn Withey, "Robertson, Robert H.," in *Biographical Dictionary of American Architects (Deceased)* (Los Angeles: Hennessey & Ingalls, 1970), 516; Montgomery Schuyler, "The Works of R. H. Robertson," *Architectural Record* 6 (Oct–Dec 1896), 184.

14 Examples of RHR's country residence and estate work include the 1875 Theodore Timpson cottage in Seabright, New Jersey; "Hillside," built for Mrs. S. S. Adam in Oyster Bay, Long Island (1878); "Sunnymeade," built for Dr. Thomas Markoe in Southampton, Long Island (1886–87); "Hammersmith Farm," built for John W. Auchincloss in Newport, Rhode Island (1887); "Blantyre," built for Robert W. Paterson in Lenox, Massachusetts (1901–03); and RHR's own country house, "Wyndcote," in Southampton, Long Island (1887–88). Robert A. M. Stern, Thomas Mellins, and David Fishman, *New York 1880: Architecture and Urbanism in the Gilded Age* (New York: Monacelli Press, 1999), 300; Landau, *Edward T. and William A. Potter*, 70–79; Sarah Bradford Landau, "Potter & Robertson, William Appleton Potter, Robert Henderson Robertson," in Robert B. MacKay, Anthony Baker, and Carol A. Traynor, eds., *Long Island Country Houses and Their Architects, 1860–1940* (New York: W. W. Norton and Society for the Preservation of Long Island Antiquities, 1997), 365–68; Schuyler, passim; John T. Hopf, *Hammersmith Farm, Newport: A Summer White House, 1961–65* (East Passage Farm, 1987), 1; Carole Owens, *The Berkshire Cottages: A Vanishing Era* (Stockbridge, MA: Cottage Press, 1984), 168–70.

15 Stern et al., *New York 1880*, 213–214, 232, 962.

16 RHR designs in APMI and JWW Jr. Coll.

17 RHR to FLO, Jun 17, 1886, Olmsted Associates Records, Series B, Job File 1031, Container B74, Reel 54, FLOP, LOC; RHR, "A Country House," *American Architect and Building News* 21, no. 586 (Mar 19, 1887), 138ff; "Pictures of the Day," *New York Daily Graphic*, Jun 29, 1887, Scrapbook vol. IV, 155.

18 RHR to FLO, Jun 17, 1886, Olmsted Associates Records, Series B, Job File 1031, Container B74, Reel 54, FLOP, LOC.

19 This account of FLO and his work at SF, pages 35–41, is largely based on the following sources, with quotations and additional sources as noted: Charles E. Beveridge and Paul Rocheleau, *Frederick Law Olmsted: Designing the American Landscape* (New York: Universe Publishing, 1998); John M. Bryan, *Biltmore Estate: The Most Distinguished Private Place* (New York: Rizzoli, 1994); Alan Emmet, *So Fine a Prospect: Historic New England Gardens* (Hanover, NH: University Press of New England, 1996); Foreman and Stimson; Witold Rybczynski, *A Clearing in the Distance: Frederick Law Olmsted and America in the 19th Century* (New York: Simon & Schuster, 1999); Margaret Campbell, Erica Donnis, Patricia O'Donnell, and Catherine Quinn, *Shelburne Farms National Historic Landmark Nomination*, 2000, 38.

20 Beveridge and Rocheleau, 149. Also Bryan, 34–36, and Rybczynski, 368, 423–24. FLO's public landscape designs included Prospect Park in Brooklyn, New York (1865–95), designed with Vaux; Mont Royal Park in Montreal (1873–93); and the grounds for the U.S. Capital in Washington, DC (1875–92). While consulting for the Webbs on the SF landscape, FLO was also preparing plans for the Stanford University campus.

21 See, for instance, Foreman and Stimson, passim.

22 FLO, quoted in Beveridge and Rocheleau, 35. Also Patricia O'Donnell, "Chapter 1: Historic Landscape Assessment," in *Shelburne Farms Historic Resources Assessment Report*, Aug 2001, 22.

23 FLO to WSW, Jun 18, 1886, #374, Letterboxes Container 1, Olmsted Associates Series B, FLOP, LOC; Joseph P. Cotton to FLO, Sep 4, 1886, Records of Olmsted Associates Series B, Job File 1031, Container B74, Reel 54, FLOP, LOC; Joseph P. Cotton, "A Topographical Map of Shelburne Farms, Shelburne, VT, The Property of W. S. Webb, Esq., Surveyed in 1886 by J. P. Cotton, C.E., Newport, R.I.," 1886, APMI; Beers.

24 FLO to Charles Eliot, Jul 20, 1886, Container 44, Reel 39, FLOP, LOC.

25 FLO, quoted in Emmet, 149.

26 FLO, quoted in Emmet, 150.

27 FLO, "List of Trees and Shrubs Proposed to be Ordered for Dr. W. S. Webb 1887," Job #1031, Frederick Law Olmsted National Historic Site, National Park Service, hereafter referred to as FLO NHS.

28 WSW to FLO, Mar 26, 1887, FLOP, LOC.
29 "W. S. Webb's Country Home," *New York Tribune*, Feb 3, 1889, Scrapbook vol V, 68. Also FLO to WSW, Jun 14, 1887, #842 Letterboxes Container 1, Olmsted Associates Series A, FLOP, LOC; FLO, "List of Trees and Shrubs Proposed to be Ordered for Dr. W. S. Webb 1887," Job #1031, FLO NHS; WSW to FLO, Mar 26, 1887, FLOP, LOC; *BFP*, Aug 18, 1906, 7, and Aug 19, 1906, 7; David Webster and EWW, "Introduction," in William C. Lipke, ed., *Shelburne Farms: The History of an Agricultural Estate* (Burlington, VT: UVM, 1979), 18.
30 FLO to WSW, Jul 12, 1887, #887 Letterboxes Container 1, Olmsted Associates Series A, FLOP, LOC. Also FLO and James C. Olmsted, "Preliminary Study of Part of Plan for Laying Out the Shelburne Farms Estate of Dr. W. S. Webb," Plan # Z-19, Job #1031, FLO NHS.
31 FLO to Charles Eliot, Jul 20, 1886, Container 44, Reel 39, FLOP, LOC.
32 FLO to WSW, Jul 12, 1887, #603 Letterboxes Container 1, Olmsted Associates Series A, FLOP, LOC.
33 RHR to FLO, Mar 22, 1887, Records of Olmsted Associates Series B, Job File 1031, Container B75, Reel 54, FLOP, LOC.
34 MCW also wonders if the "pleasure derived from living on the lake at Oakledge" influenced their decision not to build on Windmill Hill, an inland location (MCW, comments on draft Chapter 3, Jan 2009). Emmet, 150.
35 Joseph P. Cotton to FLO, Sep 4, 1886, FLOP, LOC.
36 FLO to WSW, Apr 11, 1888, FLOP, LOC.
37 FLO and John Charles Olmsted to WSW, Jan 24, 1889, FLOP, LOC.
38 FLO Papers at FLOP, LOC, and FLO NHS.
39 Beveridge and Rocheleau, 118.
40 Bill Alexander and Stephanie Gardner, Biltmore Estate Company, to author, Dec 18, 2001.
41 WSW to FLO, Mar 9, 1887, Job File 1036, F. W. Vanderbilt, Rough Point, Newport, RI, FLOP, LOC.
42 "Mr. Archibald Taylor is foreman of the Farms and his is the controlling hand in the fulfillment of all plans; in person and manner he is a fine example of the old-time Scottish grieve or land steward, but improved by the spirit of scientific method" ("At Shelburne Farms," *BFP*, Oct 19, 1889, Scrapbook V, 178). Quote in text from Archibald Taylor obituary, *BFP*, Aug 18, 1908. Also "Catalogue of The Oak Ledge Farm Herd, Burlington, VT. Stoke Pogis-Rioter Blood," title page, Box 12, FM's Papers; advertisement for "Vermont Stock Farm," *BFP*, Jan 7, 1878; *Burlington City Directory* (Burlington, VT: Hiram S. Hart, 1882–83).
43 One contemporary noted that Taylor had "taken high honors as a landscape gardener, and his knowledge in regard to matters of this kind has been of immense assistance in the laying out of the grounds" (AHG. [A. H. Godfrey], "The Shelburne Farms," in Lipke, 26).

Chapter 4

1 LOW, Sep 6, 1903, 1903 Diary, and May 22–23, 1925, 1925 Diary, both in LOW Papers.
2 "Pictures of the Day," *New York Daily Graphic*, Jun 29, 1887, Scrapbook vol. IV, 155. Also RHR, "A Country House," *American Architect and Building News* 21, no. 586 (Mar 19, 1887), 138ff.
3 "Pictures of the Day," *New York Daily Graphic*, Jun 29, 1887, Scrapbook vol. IV, 155; RHR, architectural designs, APMI; Frederick Law Olmsted Sr., "Preliminary Study for Part of Plan for Laying Out the Shelburne Farms Estate of Dr. W. S. Webb," Jul 12, 1887, FLO NHS.
4 Oakledge/Shelburne House Guestbook, 17, 20; RHR, Elevations, "Residence for Dr. W. S. Webb, Burlington, Vt.," APMI; photographs in "Buildings—Shelburne House—Pre 1900" Folder, Print and Photograph Coll.
5 RHR, First Floor Plan, "Residence for Dr. W. S. Webb, Burlington, Vt.," APMI.
6 "Dr. Webb's Great Estate," *Troy (NY) Telegram*, Nov 10, 1891, Scrapbook vol. VI, 202. Another description of the house may be found in "W. S. Webb's Country Home," *New York Tribune*, Feb 3, 1889, Scrapbook vol. V, 68.
7 LOW recorded making a trip to the Boston decorating firm A. H. Davenport in Mar 1888 (LOW, Mar 23 and 24, 1888, 1888 Diary, LOW Papers). Quote from Lillian Wright, "Shelburne Farms: The Summer Home of Dr. William Seward Webb," *Boston Home Journal*, Nov 7, 1891, Folder 10, Deed Box Coll., LOW Papers.
8 RHR, "New Kitchen Wing for Dr. Seward Webb at Shelburne Vt.," elevations and floor plans, c. 1891, #s 2004.3.1.106-2004.3.1.110, 2004.3.1.112, APMI.
9 RHR, "Residence for W. S. Webb, Shelburne, Vt.," elevations and floor plans, #s 2004.3.26.1–2004.3.26.25, c. 1887–93, APMI; RHR, "Design for a Country House," *American Architect and Building News* 40 (May 20, 1893), 123ff; Architectural renderings of RHR's Beaux-Arts designs, #s 1999.762, 1999.764, 1999.765, 1999.766, Framed Works of Art Coll.; LOW, Shelburne House Inventory, c. 1920, 105, LOW Papers; "A Vermont Farm," *Boston Traveller*, Nov 6, 1889, Scrapbook vol. V, 185; "Seward Webb's Proposed Castle, The Largest Private Residence In America," *Chicago Post*, Sep 1, 1893, Scrapbook vol. XI, 121; "His Home To Be A Grand Palace: Dr. Webb's Plans for the Finest Residence In The World," *New York Press*, Jun 24, 1894, Scrapbook vol. XI, 103; Clive Aslet, *The American Country House* (New Haven, CT: Yale University Press, 1990), 29; Mark Alan Hewitt, *The Architect and the American Country House, 1890–1940* (New Haven, CT: Yale University Press, 1990), 71–97.
10 John Foreman and Robbe Pierce Stimson, *The Vanderbilts and the Gilded Age: Architectural Aspirations, 1879–1901* (New York: St. Martin's Press, 1991), passim; Richard Cheek and Tom Gannon, *Newport Mansions: The Gilded Age* (Little Compton, RI: Fort Church Publishers and Preservation Society of Newport County, 1995), 8–21, 68–79; Jerry Patterson, *The Vanderbilts* (New York: Harry N. Abrams, 1989), passim.
11 LOW, Jun 30, 1893, Diary containing entries from 1893–94, 1901, and 1904, LOW Papers.
12 One source (www.westegg.com/inflation/) calculates that $1.5 million to $3 million is approximately equivalent to $35.5 million to $73.7 million in 2008 dollars. "Seward Webb's Proposed Castle," *Chicago Post*; "His Home To Be A Grand Palace," *New York Press*; John M. Bryan, *Biltmore Estate: The Most Distinguished Private Place* (New York: Rizzoli, 1994), 17, 147; Foreman and Stimson, 295–97.
13 RHR, Shelburne House blueprints, c. 1895–98, APMI; JWW Jr., "Pictorial History," 66–67, JWW Jr. Coll.; RHR and R. Burnside Potter, "Proposed Squash Court for Dr. W. Seward Webb, Shelburne, Vt.," APMI; "Squash Court" entries in 1901 Ledger, 593–94 and 1902 Ledger, 474–75, FM's Papers; *Burlington (VT) Daily News*, Apr 10, 1895, Scrapbook vol. XIII,

26; RHR to EFG, Mar 26, 1901, Folder 87, EFG Corr., FM's Papers; LOW to VW, undated letter, VW Papers.

14 The figure of 40,000 square feet encompasses the first, second, and third floors of the main portion of the dwelling, including the south porch, as well as the 1899–1900 addition containing the formal entertaining spaces, including the conservatory. Incorporating the basement areas, attics, and servants' wing would increase the square footage to more than 55,000 (Julie Eldridge Edwards to author, May 15, 2009). RHR, Shelburne House blueprints, c. 1895–1901, APMI; Shelburne House photographs in Print and Photograph Coll.; Julie Eldridge Edwards, comments on draft Chapter 4, Jan 28, 2009.

15 Ibid.

16 LOW most likely served as the primary interior decorator for Shelburne House, since she selected the residence's furnishings after the turn of the 20th century. Prominent New York City decorating firms provided most of the new furnishings. W & J Sloane, a wholesale and retail company dealing in carpets and rugs that was owned by LOW's brother-in-law William Douglas Sloane, supplied the floor coverings for almost every new and renovated space, as well as draperies, upholstery materials, and window shades for the main rooms. LOW probably visited the company's New York showrooms, where she may have used the advisory services provided at Sloane's "Interior Decorating and Furnishing Department" to create interior ensembles. Other items were acquired from prominent firms such as William Baumgarten & Co., Fr. Beck & Co., H. B. Herts & Sons, and Carl Spring, of New York City; John H. Ragatz, of Philadelphia; and George E. Vernon, of Newport. The FM's Papers contain corr. between EFG and LOW that documents her detailed involvement with furnishing and redecorating Shelburne House c. 1905–36. See also LOW, Shelburne House Inventory, c. 1920, LOW Papers, and photographs of Shelburne House interiors in TEMC, Print and Photograph, and Photograph Album Colls.

17 The morning/smoking room is now known as the reception room. Quote from WSW Jr., inscription on back of a Thomas E. Marr photograph, #6620, TEMC. Also Marr photographs #s 3131, 3136, 3137, 4286, 6620, 6626, TEMC; images in "Shelburne House—Interiors" Folder, Print and Photograph Coll.; family photographs in Print and Photograph Coll. and Photograph Album Coll.; LOW, Sep 22, 1903, 1903 Diary, Jun 14, Jun 15, Jun 20, and Jul 18, 1904, 1904 Diary, and Sep 9, 1905, 1905 Diary, all in LOW Papers.

18 WSW's office is now known as the east dining room. Quote from "Shelburne Farms," *BFP*, Sep 20, 1899, Scrapbook vol. XXI, 30. Also MCW, comment on draft Chapter 4, Jan 2009.

19 MCW, comment on draft Chapter 4, Jan 2009; Thomas E. Marr photograph #3145, TEMC.

20 LOW, Shelburne House Inventory, passim; Thomas Marr photographs #s 3262, 3263, 3264, 3265, 3267, 3268, TEMC; images in "Buildings—Shelburne House—Interiors" Folder, Print and Photograph Coll.; "W. S. W.'s Trip to Wyoming 1896," Photograph Album Coll.

21 The corridor hall is now known as the tea room. Quote from EHW, in Lauren B. Hewes and Celia Y. Oliver, *To Collect in Earnest: The Life and Work of Electra Havemeyer Webb* (Shelburne, VT: Shelburne Museum, 1997), 10.

22 "Shelburne," *Burlington (VT) Daily News*, Dec 1, 1899, Scrapbook vol. XXI, 155. Also Thomas Marr photographs #s 3140, 3142, 3143, TEMC; images in "Events—Social" Folder, Print and Photograph Coll.; LOW, Nov 27, 1905, 1905 Diary and Dec 31, 1906, 1906 Diary, LOW Papers; Oakledge/Shelburne House Guestbook, 245.

23 Thomas Marr photograph #3258, TEMC. The north room is now known as the game room.

24 LOW, Shelburne House Inventory, passim.

25 The main stove in the kitchen was a model patented in 1880 by the Duparquet, Huot & Moneuse Company. Corr. between EFG and LOW, FM's Papers; LOW, Shelburne House Inventory, passim; "G. S. Blodgett Co. Heating and Ventilating Engineering, Burlington, Vt.," Shelburne House floor plan, c. 1895, APMI; View of Shelburne House in 1894 *Sanborn Fire Insurance Map*, sheet 28, Special Collections Department, Bailey/Howe Library, UVM; MCW, comment during Frank and Frederica Botala Oral History Interview, Jun 26, 2006, disk 2.

26 The heating system was supplemented by the 23 fireplaces located in living areas and bedrooms. There is no evidence to suggest that the "refrigerator room" included mechanical equipment; at the time, the term "refrigerator" referred to ice-cooled chambers. LOW, Shelburne House Inventory, passim; "G. S. Blodgett Co. Heating and Ventilating Engineering, Burlington, Vt.," Shelburne House floor plan, c. 1895, APMI; "W.S.W. Stock Account," 1890 Ledger, 5, FM's Papers; Shelburne Farms Bill Book, Mar 1898–Sep 1900, entry for Nov 27, 1899, 726, FM's Papers; "Dr. Webb's Phone System," *Milton (VT) Rays*, Mar 29, 1900, Scrapbook vol. XV, 137; corr. between MCW and author, Dec 21, 2001; MCW, comment in Botala Interview, disk 2; MCW, comments on draft Chapter 4, Jan 2009; Julie Eldridge Edwards, comments on draft Chapter 4, Jan 28, 2009.

27 For household employees, see "Maids' Wages" and Payroll/Time Books, c. 1903–38, Box 5, FM's Papers; LOW, Diaries, passim, LOW Papers; corr. between LOW and EFG, passim, FM's Papers; AOW, transcript of Oral History Interview with EWW, Sep 1, 1976, 12–15. For the Webbs' moving procedures, see corr. between LOW and EFG, FM's Papers, and, for example, LOW, May 9, 1904, 1904 Diary, LOW Papers.

28 Oakledge/Shelburne House Guestbook, passim; LOW, Aug 31, 1902, 1902–13 Diary/Scrapbook, LOW Papers; William Howard Taft to WSW, Jun 26, 1909, WSW Personal Corr., WSW Papers.

29 Pauline Robinson to Louise Crowninshield, undated [pre-1900], Accession 2374, Winterthur Collection of du Pont Family Papers, Record Group VI, Box 15, courtesy Hagley Museum & Library.

30 EHW, quoted in Hewes and Oliver, 5–6. Also AOW, "Almost a Century," 31, and AOW, Transcript of Oral History Interview, passim.

31 Berlin vehicles, developed in Europe in the 18th century, feature "large coach bod[ies] set upon double perches" (Edward Wheeling, *Horse-Drawn Vehicles at the Shelburne Museum* [Shelburne, VT: The Shelburne Museum, 1974], 40). JWW, Oct 14, 1905, 1905 Diary, JWW Jr. Coll.; EFG to LOW, Oct 10, 1905, Folder 12, EFG Corr., FM's Papers; "Pulitzer–Webb Wedding," New York Times, Oct 15, 1905.

32 AOW stated that the tea house was also used by WSW's brother J. Louis Webb as an artist's studio (AOW, Transcript of Oral History Interview, 15). The building is now known as the treehouse. "W. S. Webb Stock Account," 1890 Ledger, 3, FM's Papers; RHR, "Specification of Work and Materials to Be Employed in the Erection of a Tea House for Dr. W. S. Webb at Burlington, Vt.," undated, Folder 46, Deed Box Coll., LOW

Papers; LOW, Jul 9 and 18, 1893, and passim, Diary containing entries from 1893–96, 1901, and 1904, LOW Papers; "Play House Extension," 1890 Ledger, 498, FM's Papers; "Pictorial History," photograph #s 28, 29, JWW Jr. Coll.; JWW, Mar 30 and Apr 1, 1901, 1901 Diary, JWW Jr. Coll.

Chapter 5

1. "Shelburne Farms," *Burlington (VT) Farmer Advocate*, Jan 19, 1895, Scrapbook vol. XIII, 7.
2. John Martin Robinson, *Georgian Model Farms: A Study of Decorative and Model Farm Buildings in the Age of Improvement, 1700–1846* (Oxford: Clarendon Press, 1983), 14.
3. Jan Albers, *Hands on the Land: A History of the Vermont Landscape* (Cambridge, MA: MIT Press, 2000), 215. Also Witold Rybczynski, *A Clearing in the Distance: Frederick Law Olmsted and America in the 19th Century* (New York: Simon & Schuster, 1999), 60.
4. *New York Daily Graphic*, Jun 29, 1887, Scrapbook vol. IV, 154.
5. Oakledge Farm/Shelburne House Guestbook, 1884–1928, 20; MCW, interview with author, Dec 6, 2001; Bill Flynt, "Dr. William Seward Webb's Farm Barn at Shelburne Farms, Shelburne, Vt.," unpublished paper written for UVM Art History class, Dec 31, 1977, 1, Farm Barn Folder, SF Reference Files; Joseph P. Cotton, "A Topographical Map of Shelburne Farms, Shelburne, VT, The Property of W.S. Webb, Esq., Surveyed in 1886 by J. P. Cotton, C.E., Newport, R.I.," 1886, APMI; Deed, Mary and Hattie Holabird to WSW, May 2, 1888, Box 1, Folder 2, Legal Papers, FM's Papers.
6. The Holabird family house is now known as the "Farm Barn Cottage." It has also been referred to as the "Boarding House Cottage" and "St. George House." Deed, Mary and Hattie Holabird to WSW, May 2, 1888, Box 1, Folder 2, and WSW, memorandum of agreement, May 1, 1888, Box 2, Folder 6, both in Legal Papers, FM's Papers.
7. The redstone at SF is technically defined as Monkton quartzite. Quote from the inscription on the Farm Barn clock tower, Nov 6, 1888. Also "Barn Construction" account, 1888–89 Ledger, 90–95, FM's Papers; photographs of the Farm Barn, c. 1888–89, #669-23 and 669-24, Nitrate Negative Coll.; "New Bell for Shelburn [sic] Farms," *BFP*, Nov 16, 1888, Scrapbook vol. V, 59; Margaret Campbell, Erica Donnis, Patricia O'Donnell, and Catherine Quinn, *Shelburne Farms National Historic Landmark Nomination*, 2000, 9–10.
8. Within the first ten years of their completion, the turrets were lowered in height by several feet. One of the Webbs' grandchildren later wrote that WSW had concluded that the towers were out of proportion, "too imposing and too big for the structure" (JWW Jr., "Pictorial History of the Webb Family," 31–32, JWW Jr. Coll.). Also c. 1900 photographs of the Farm Barn by Thomas E. Marr, #s 3125, 3173, and 3178, TEMC.
9. AHG, "The Shelburne Farms," in William C. Lipke, ed., *Shelburne Farms: The History of an Agricultural Estate* (Burlington, VT: University of Vermont, 1979), 31.
10. There remains some question about the number of work mules housed in the Farm Barn. Evidence of 36 stalls remains in situ as of 2009 (MCW to author, Feb 4, 2009); AHG notes "70 or 80 head" (AHG, "The Shelburne Farms," in Lipke, 31); Pelham-Clinton notes that the stalls numbered "50 or 60" (C. S. Pelham-Clinton, "Biggest Barn in America: Dr. Seward Webb's Beautiful Estate at Shelburne Farms, Vt.," *Buffalo News*, Apr 22, 1895, Scrapbook vol. XIII, 29); and Powell notes "40 head" (Edwin C. Powell, "Shelburne Farms: An Ideal Country Place," *Country Life in America* 3, no. 4 [Feb 1903]: 153). During the construction of the Farm Barn, a group of shingled support structures was erected just to the south of the barn, adjoining the former Holabird farmhouse. The buildings, which included a small office, a structure containing blacksmith, paint, and carpentry shops, and several boarding houses, provided temporary work spaces and living quarters for construction crew members, agricultural workers, and office employees. Soon after the Farm Barn was completed, however, the office and shops were moved into its north wing. The vacated outbuildings, as well as most of the boarding houses, were demolished c. 1893–1900. One boarding house and the former Holabird house, which had been transformed into the boarding house cottage with a large new addition, were retained for use as employee residences. AHG, "The Shelburne Farms," in Lipke, 31–32; Photographs #s 60–77, JWW Jr. Coll.; "Office Construction" and "Outbuildings, Carp. Sh. Constr." accounts, 1888–90 Ledger, 100 & 120, FM's Papers; "At Shelburne Farms," *BFP*, Oct 19, 1889, Scrapbook vol. V, 178; RHR, "Office of Dr. W. S. Webb, Shelburne, Vt.," *American Architect and Building News* 24 (Dec 8, 1888): 266ff.
11. "At Shelburne Farms," *BFP*, Oct 19, 1889; "Shelburne Farms: Farm Department," *Burlington (VT) Farmer Advocate*, Feb 2, 1895, Scrapbook vol. XIII, 9; Flynt, 8–16, 30–38; Richard Derry, "Floor Plan Drawings Farm Barn At Shelburne Farms," Jun 30, 1991, APMI; *Sanborn Insurance Map* for Burlington, Vermont, Nov 1894, sheet 28, Special Collections Department, Bailey/Howe Library, UVM.
12. The barn was also equipped with passively ventilated drying areas for the grain in case it arrived from the fields too moist for immediate storage. MCW to author, Jan 29, 2009.
13. "Shelburne Farms: Farm Department," 9. "At His Country Home," *Albany (NY) Argus*, Aug 8, 1895, Scrapbook vol. XIII, 42; 1921 Weather Diary, FM's Papers; SF Employee Record Book, 108+, Box 20, FM's Papers; "E. F. Gebhardt Dies After Long Illness," *BFP*, Jan 5, 1942.
14. Flynt, 7.
15. Powell, 155. Also EFG to JWW, Jan 9, 1904, 1903–05 Folder, EFG Corr. with JWW, FM's Papers.
16. Mangelwurzel is a root vegetable grown for both livestock feed and human consumption. Ibid; 1920 Crop Record Book, FM's Papers.
17. FLO may in fact have suggested the drainage work while consulting on the estate landscape plan. He had experimented with drainage tile at his own farm on Staten Island in the 1850s, consulted drainage experts while traveling in England, and included tile installation for 500 acres of land in his Central Park design (Charles E. Beveridge and Paul Rocheleau, *Frederick Law Olmsted: Designing the American Landscape* [New York: Universe Publishing, 1998], 13, 53; Rybczynski, 86). "Irrigation Bed," APMI; "A Vermont Farm," *Boston Traveller*, Nov 6, 1889, Scrapbook vol. V, 185; MCW to author, Jan 29, 2009, and comments on draft Chapter 5, Jan 2009; and the following in the 1888–90 Ledger, FM's Papers: "Ditching" and "Draining on S.F." (78–79), and "Tile Stock" (341).
18. WSW to EFG, handwritten reply on EFG letter of Jan 26, 1911, EFG Corr. with WSW, FM's Papers.
19. EFG to WSW, Mar 7, 1911, EFG Corr. with WSW, FM's Papers.
20. In the 1920s, a few nut trees, including chestnuts, walnuts, and

pecans, were also planted. However, it is unclear whether the experiment was successful (EFG to WSW, Apr 1, 1920, and List of nut trees, c. 1920, both in "WH to WI" folder, FM's Papers, 1922–35). Powell, 154; "Shelburne Farms," *BFP*, Sep 20, 1899, Scrapbook vol. XXI, 30; "Shelburne," *Burlington (VT) Daily News*, Jun 20, 1900, Scrapbook vol. XV, 218; "At His Country Home," 42.

21 The following sources are all in EFG Corr., FM's Papers: Telegram to EFG, undated, EFG to A. E. Kline, Nov 28, 1902, and EFG to WSW, Jul 24, 1906, all in Folder 11; Folder 11, passim; and EFG to WSW Jr., Jan 30, 1905, Folder 319.

22 "Shelburn [sic] Farm: Hot Houses," Nov 1894 and Mar 1906 *Sanborn Insurance Maps*, Special Collections Department, Bailey/Howe Library, UVM. Also Hitchings & Co., "Sketch of Proposed Violet House for Shelburne Farms, Shelburne, Vt., Plan No. 1314," undated, "[Greenhouse] Plan for W. Seward Webb, Shelburne, Vt., Plan No. 1244," undated, and "W. Seward Webb, Estimate for Superstructure of New Violet House," Dec 1900, all in APMI; 1889–1900 Ledgers, passim, FM's Papers; images in "Gardens & Greenhouses" Folder, Print and Photograph Coll.; and Fred M. Abbey, "On the Bothy," *Gardenside Gossip* (March 1962), the newsletter of Gardenside Nurseries, Shelburne, VT, coll. in the possession of Harrison L. Flint, Lafayette, IN.

23 "Shelburne Farms," *New York Sun*, quoted in *BFP*, Sep 20, 1899, Scrapbook vol. XXI, 30.

24 Ibid. Also Abbey; Pelham-Clinton, 28; EFG to WSW, May 15, 1911, EFG Corr. with WSW, FM's Papers; Campbell et al., 14–15.

25 "At His Country Home," 42. Also Lillian Wright, "Shelburne Farms: The Summer Home of Dr. William Seward Webb," *Boston Home Journal*, Nov 7, 1891, Folder 10, LOW Deed Box Coll.

26 LOW to EFG, Dec 20, 1908, EFG Corr. with LOW, FM's Papers. Also, for example, LOW to EFG, Jan 6, 1905, Folder 12, EFG Corr., FM's Papers; EFG to Alexander Graham and T. Kinville, undated memorandum, EFG Corr. with LOW, FM's Papers; AOW, Transcript of Oral History Interview with EWW, 28–29; Abbey.

27 AHG, "The Shelburne Farms," in WSW, *Shelburne Farms Stud: Of English Hackneys, Harness and Saddle Horses, Ponies and Trotters* (New York: G. P. Putnam's Sons, 1893), 20.

28 LOW to EFG, Nov 3, 1910, EFG Corr. with LOW, FM's Papers. Also Wright, "Shelburne Farms."

29 LOW to EFG, Jan 11, 1906, EFG Corr. with LOW, FM's Papers. Also Abbey.

30 The following are all in FM's Papers: Folder 16, passim, EFG Corr.; LOW Corr. with EFG, passim, EFG Corr.; "Garden Produce," Dairy & Garden Produce Record Book, 2.

31 "Dr. W. Seward Webb's Stock Farm," *New York Times*, Jan 15, 1888, Scrapbook vol. V, 7.

32 "W.S. Webb's Country Home," *New York Tribune*, Feb 3, 1889, Scrapbook vol. V, 68; "Shelburne Farms: Farm Department," 9; RHR, "Yard View of West Elevation, Farm Barns for Dr. W.S. Webb, Burlington, Vt.," c. 1888, #200-144, APMI; "Steer Expense," "Steer Stock," and "Steer Farm Alt. & Rep.," 1898 Ledger, 34–39, 55, 194, FM's Papers.

33 *Catalogue of the Shelburne Farm's Herd, Shelburne, Chittenden Co., Vt., Stoke Pogis-Rioter Blood*, c. 1886–87, FM's Papers. Also "Dairy Stock" and "Dairy Stock and Implements" accounts in 1888–1900 Ledgers, FM's Papers; AHG, "The Shelburne Farms," in Lipke, 28; "W.S. Webb's Country Home," 68; and Harold Fisher Wilson, *The Hill Country of Northern New England: Its Social and Economic History, 1790–1930* (New York: AMS Press, Inc., 1967), 202.

34 The dairy's first location is unknown. "Shelburne Farms: Farm Department" states that it was "on the east side of the estate" (9). Also AHG, "The Shelburne Farms," in Lipke, 28; "W. S. Webb—Stock Account," 1890 Ledger, 3, and "New Dairy Barn," 1894 Ledger, 634–35, both in FM's Papers; "Shelburne Farms Corporation Plan of Cow Barn, Jan 1923," APMI; Campbell et al., 28–29. For later additions to the dairy barn, see also JWW Jr., "Pictorial History," 127, JWW Jr. Coll.; and *Sanborn Insurance Maps*, Nov 1894, Jan 1900, and Mar 1906, Special Collections Department, Bailey/Howe Library, UVM.

35 FK to JWW, Jul 27, 1927, GK Folder, FK Corr., FM's Papers; *Sanborn Insurance Map*, 1906; *Burlington (VT) Daily News*, Aug 28, 1902, Scrapbook vol. XVI, 128. The author thanks Julie Eldridge Edwards for bringing the latter source to her attention.

36 Dairy & Garden Produce Record Book, vols. 1 and 2, EFG to WSW, Mar 8, 1912, Folder 109, EFG Corr., and EFG to WW, Mar 8, 1912, Folder 108, EFG Corr., all in FM's Papers.

37 *Albany (NY) Journal*, Jan 22, 1889, Scrapbook vol. V, 66. Also "Distribution of Butter," Dairy & Garden Produce Record Book, 2–49, FM's Papers.

38 "Dairy Expense," 1890 Ledger, 185–91, FM's Papers.

39 Powell, 152–53. Also Julie Eldridge Edwards, "Did You Know…," *InFARMation*, Jun 13, 2008.

40 Powell, 153.

41 "Swinery Expense," 1897 Ledger, 174–75, EFG to L. W. Dow, Jul 18, 1914, Folder 108, EFG Corr., both in FM's Papers.

42 AHG, "The Shelburne Farms," in Lipke, 28; "Sheep and Poultry Farm—Construction," 1890 Ledger, 52, FM's Papers; Powell, 153; "Sheep and Poultry Farm Stock and Implements," 1891 Ledger, 62, FM's Papers; "W.S. Webb's Country Home," 68; *Sanborn Insurance Map*, 1900.

43 "Shelburne Farms: Farm Department," 9; AHG, "The Shelburne Farms," in Lipke, 28; Powell, 153; "Sheep and Poultry Farm Stock and Implements," 1891 Ledger, 62, FM's Papers; "W.S. Webb's Country Home," 68.

44 Powell, 153–54.

45 EFG to LOW, Aug 15, 1913, EFG Corr. with LOW, FM's Papers. Also "Sheep and Poultry Farm Stock and Implements," 1891 Ledger, 62, Telegram to EFG, undated, Folder 111, EFG Corr., Telegram to EFG, Feb 28 [year unknown], Folder 13, EFG Corr., all in FM's Papers.

46 GK to EFG, Dec 26, 1913, Folder 109, EFG Corr., FM's Papers. Also EFG corr. with WW and WSW in Folders 108 and 109, EFG Corr., FM's Papers.

47 JWW Jr., "Pictorial History," 52, JWW Jr. Coll.

48 Ibid; Photograph #149, JWW Jr. Coll.

49 The pheasantry was also known as the "Aviary." WSW also imported quail at least once ("Quails Imported Into Vermont," *New York Recorder*, Dec 7, 1891, Scrapbook vol. VIII, 150). The following sources are all in the 1891 Ledger, FM's Papers: "Wire-netting Fence @ Aviary," "Aviary Construction," "Aviary Barn," and "Shelter for Pheasants," 342–47, and "Aviary Expense," 502–6. Also "Shelburne Farms," *New York Sun*, quoted in *BFP*, Sep 20, 1899, Scrapbook vol. XXI, 30; Photographs #130–133, JWW Jr. Coll.

50 The following sources are in the FM's Papers: WSW to EFG, Nov 1, 1906, EFG Corr. with WSW; Game Records Book; and "List of Game Killed," Oct 1897–Nov 1906, Box 5. Also

LOW to VW, Nov 4, c. 1906–07, VW Papers; Powell, 154; Julie Eldridge Edwards, comments on draft Chapter 5, Jan 28, 2009.

51 WSW, "Letters To The Editor," *New York Tribune*, Jul 21, 1900, Scrapbook vol. XV, 250.
52 Powell, 156.
53 "The Shelburne Stallions," *(NY) Spirit of the Times*, Apr 28, 1888, Scrapbook vol. V, 34. Also Shelburne Farms Stud advertisement, c. May–Jun 1888, Scrapbook vol. V, 45.
54 WSW, *Catalogue Shelburne Farms Stud: Shelburne, Chittenden Co., Vermont* (New York: John Polhemus, 1891); WSW, *Shelburne Farms Stud* (1893); A. Nechaev to WSW, Feb 24, 1906, Folder #N-1, FM's Papers.
55 Clipping of unknown source, Mar 5, 1889, Scrapbook vol. V, 91.
56 Dr. James McLane to LOW, Sep 7, 1892, Folder 10, Deed Box Coll., LOW Papers. Also "Breeding Barn Stock and Implements," 1891 Ledger, 42–43, FM's Papers.
57 "New Blood for the Horse Show," *New York Herald*, Nov 12, 1899, Scrapbook vol. XXI, 141. Also WSW, *Shelburne Farms Stud* (1893), 10, 63; Tom Ryder, "The Versatile Hackney: Part Two," *The Carriage Journal* 38, no. 1 (March 2000): 25.
58 "The Hackney," *Honesdale (PA) Independent*, Jan 10, 1894, Scrapbook vol. XII, 7. Also Laurie Heise and Carolyn Christman, *American Minor Breeds Notebook* (Pittsboro, NC: American Minor Breeds Conservancy, 1989), 34; Tom Ryder, "The Versatile Hackney: Part One," *The Carriage Journal* 37, no. 4 (January 2000): 149.
59 AHG, "The Shelburne Farm," in WSW, *Shelburne Farms Stud* (1893), 27.
60 WSW, *Shelburne Farms Stud* (1893), 30.
61 "Dr. Webb and the Utility Horse," *Turf Field and Farm*, Jan 20, 1899, Scrapbook vol. XXI, 21. Also "Exhibit of Art In Dress," *New York Times*, Nov 16, 1894, Scrapbook vol. XII, 143; WSW, *Shelburne Farms Stud* (1893), 30.
62 WSW, letter to the editor, *Rider & Driver*, Sep 15, 1894, Scrapbook vol. XII, 121.
63 WSW, *Shelburne Farms Stud* (1893), 1–5, 15.
64 WSW, *Shelburne Farms Stud* (1893), xiii, 11.
65 WSW, *Shelburne Farms Stud* (1893), 3.
66 The annex also eventually contained feed storage rooms, but it is unclear when these spaces were added. "S.F. Breeding Barns (Construction)," 1888–91 Ledger, 114–16, FM's Papers; RHR, "Ground Plan," "Exercising Ring for Dr. W. Seward Webb, Shelburne, Vt.," #300-69, APMI; *Sanborn Insurance Map*, Nov 1894; AHG, "The Shelburne Farms," in Lipke, 34–37; Pelham-Clinton, 28.
67 This barn has also been referred to as the "Broodmare Barn," "Southern Acres Dairy Barn," and "Old Dairy Barn." It is most commonly known today as the latter. Quote from AHG, "The Shelburne Farms," in WSW, *Shelburne Farms Stud* (1893), 24.
68 The Tracy family's barn, which was constructed during the 19th century prior to the establishment of SF and later referred to as the "Sheep Barn," was destroyed by fire in the winter of 1962. The barn adjoining it directly to the south, now referred to as the "Tracy Barn," was designed by RHR and constructed between 1890 and 1892. AHG, "The Shelburne Farms," in WSW, *Shelburne Farms Stud* (1893), 23–24; *Sanborn Insurance Maps*, 1894, 1900, and 1906; *Shelburne Farms Breeding Barn Complex Conservation Plan*, Oct 31, 2004, III.36.
69 WSW, Introduction to *Catalogue of Shelburne Farms Stud* (1891), n.p.
70 AHG, "The Shelburne Farms," in WSW, *Shelburne Farms Stud* (1893), 24. Also Pelham-Clinton, 28.
71 The building supposedly possessed the "largest unsupported interior space in the United States for forty years after its construction," but this claim remains unsubstantiated (Campbell et al., 27–28 [quote on 27]). Quote in text from "At His Country Home," 42. Also "Shelburne Farms," *New York Sun*, quoted in *BFP*, Sep 20, 1899, Scrapbook vol. XXI, 30; Pelham-Clinton, 28; AHG, "The Shelburne Farms," in WSW, *Shelburne Farms Stud* (1893), 25–27; "Br. Barn Electric Lighting and Steam Heating Plant," 1891 Ledger, 680–81, FM's Papers; RHR, architectural plans for Breeding Barn, #s 300-57, 300-68, and 300-69, APMI; Julie Eldridge Edwards to author, Aug 7, 2009.
72 MCW, SF's woodlands manager, notes that "the forests [at SF] were more for aesthetic enjoyment and Nehasane [the Webbs' Adirondack estate] was all about lumber production and game" (MCW, comments on draft Chapter 5, Jan 2009). Quote in text from "At His Country Home," 42. Also Patricia O'Donnell, Chapter 1: Historic Landscape Assessment, in *Shelburne Farms Historic Resources Assessment Report*, 2001; MCW, interview with author, Feb 7, 2002.
73 John M. Bryan, *Biltmore Estate: The Most Distinguished Private Place* (New York: Rizzoli, 1994), 89–90.
74 AOW does mention Pinchot in her unpublished memoir, but as of yet no documentation by one of the parties directly involved has surfaced (AOW, "Almost a Century," unpublished 1977 memoir, 28, SFC). Former Chittenden County Forester Bill Hall, who has consulted on the woodlands at SF, has suggested that the juxtaposition of pine and spruce in the estate's forest plantations is a mark of Pinchot's involvement. Quote in text from Gifford Pinchot, *The Adirondack Spruce: A Study of the Forest in Ne-Ha-Sa-Ne Park* (New York: The Critic Co., 1898), v. Also Index of Names, Oakledge/Shelburne House Guestbook, 1884–1928; Pinchot diaries and corr., c. 1892–98, Gifford Pinchot Coll., Manuscript Division, LOC; MCW, comments on draft Chapter 5, Jan 2009.
75 "Forestry at Shelburne Farms," *Springfield (MA) Republican*, Apr 22, 1898, Scrapbook vol. XXI, 12; AHG, "The Shelburne Farms," in Lipke, 21; "Nursery Stock," 1896 Ledger, 84–85, "Forestry," and "Nursery" accounts, 1889–1900 Ledgers, all in FM's Papers.
76 "Pines for Shelburne Farms," *Burlington (VT) Daily News*, Apr 30, 1900, Scrapbook vol. XV, 169; "Pines for Shelburne Farms," *Burlington (VT) Daily News*, Mar 30, 1900, Scrapbook vol. XV, 139; "Western Pines," *Burlington (VT) Daily News*, Apr 11, 1900, Scrapbook vol. XV, 152.
77 MCW to author, Feb 7, 2002. Also "Burlington, Vt.," *Boston Morning Herald*, Jun 3, 1900, Scrapbook vol. XV, 199.
78 "Burlington, Vt.," 199.
79 EFG to LOW, Dec 15, 1902, EFG Corr. with LOW, FM's Papers. Also MCW, interview with author, Feb 7, 2002.
80 The following are all in FM's Papers. "Trans. Lg. Maples," 1896 Ledger Index; "Transplant Large Maples etc.," "Transplant Trees @ Roadsides," and "Webb, W.S., Set Large Trees @ Lawn," all in 1897 Ledger Index; "Webb, W.S., Set Lg. Elms @ Lawn," 1898 Ledger Index; "Set Trees @ No. Ent.," "Set Trees @ Roadsides," "Set Trees abt. Greenhouse," and "Set Trees @ W.S.W. Lawn," all in 1899 Ledger Index. Also "Transplanting Large Trees," *BFP*, Mar 23, 1899, Scrapbook vol. XXI, 24.

Chapter 6

1. AHG, "The Shelburne Farms," *Rider and Driver* 4, no. 7 (Oct 15, 1892): 8, Scrapbook vol. X, 20.
2. "Plan of Garden No. 1 Shelburne Farm [sic]," undated, APMI; Thomas Marr photographs #s 3120, 3135, TEMC; *Boston Home Journal*, Nov 14, 1890, Scrapbook vol. VI, 209; Susan Cady Hayward, "Historical Evolution of the Shelburne Farms Formal Gardens: Design Changes Through Time," unpublished paper prepared for Historic Preservation Program, UVM, May 10, 1984.
3. WSW to LOW, undated [c. 1910–19], Folder 12, Deed Box Coll., LOW Papers.
4. LOW to EFG, Mar 26, 1910, 1910 Folder, EFG Corr. with LOW, FM's Papers.
5. LOW, May 13, Aug 29, Aug 30, and Sep 30, 1904, 1904 Diary, and May 11, 1905, 1905 Diary, both in LOW Papers; corr. between EFG and LOW, passim, FM's Papers; EFG to Karl Heine, May 31 and Jun 2, 1904, and Karl Heine to EFG, Jun 1 and Jun 6, 1904, all in Folder 81, EFG Corr., FM's Papers; "The Garden of Mrs. W. Seward Webb, Shelburne Farms, Shelburne, Vt. on Lake Champlain," photographs by Isabelle H. Hardie, *Country Life in America* 31 (Oct 1917), 62–63.
6. LOW, Feb 1–Apr 12, 1907, 1907 Diary, LOW Papers; Charles Latham, *The Gardens of Italy* (New York: Charles Scribner's Sons, 1905), SFC# 2000.1006; Charles A. Platt, *Italian Gardens* (New York: Harper & Brothers, 1894), SFC# 2000.1046; Edith Wharton, *Italian Villas and Their Gardens*, illustrated by Maxfield Parrish (New York: Century Co., 1904), SFC# 2000.1057; Gertrude Jekyll, *Wall & Water Gardens*, Fourth Edition (London: Country Life, [c. 1910]), SFC# 2000.1034; Patricia O'Donnell, "Chapter 1: Historic Landscape Assessment," in *Shelburne Farms Historic Resources Assessment Report*, Aug 2001, 25–26.
7. LOW, May 13, 1911, 1911 Diary, LOW Papers; Farm Manager's Corr. with LOW re roses, 1925–26, Folder 2, FK and DNT Corr. with LOW, FM's Papers; historic photographs in "Landscape—Gardens" Folders, Print and Photograph Collection; "Shelburne House Gardens Timeline," 2000; Hayward, passim.
8. LOW to VW, Jul 27, 1911, VW Papers. Also "Management," Shelburne Farms Employee Record Book, 124, FM's Papers; Karl Heine to EFG, Feb 28, 1908, FM's Papers; Employee Record Book, 108ff, Box 20, FM's Papers; "E.F. Gebhardt Dies at Age of 83 After Long Illness," *BFP*, Jan 5, 1942.
9. LOW to EFG, Mar 17, 1907, 1907 Folder, EFG Corr. with LOW, FM's Papers.
10. LOW, Aug 30, 1904, 1904 Diary, LOW Papers.
11. LOW to EFG, Jun 11, 1908, 1908 Folder, EFG Corr. with LOW, FM's Papers.
12. LOW, Jul 23–24, 1926, 1926 LOW Diary, LOW Papers. Also historic photographs of Shelburne House Gardens, 1998.001, "Landscape—Gardens" Folder, Print and Photograph Coll.; Autochrome Coll.; "The Garden of Mrs. W. Seward Webb," 62–63; "The Gardens at Shelburne Farms, Mrs. Seward Webb's Home at Shelburne, Vermont," *Arts and Decoration* 11 (Jun 1919), 66–67; MCW, corr. with author, Jan 2, 2002.
13. One reporter also stated that the golf links were designed by "W.F. Davis, an Englishman," but this claim has not been substantiated (Ralph S. Bailey, "Estates of American Sportsmen: I. The country seat of Mr. Watson Webb at Shelburne Farms, Vermont," *Sportsman* 4 (Dec 1928): 39, in Album #80, JWW Jr. Coll.). Bob Labbance, "Willie Park Jr. in Northern New England," *Golfiana* 5 [1993]: 7–8, including quote from "Willie Park Tells of America," *Golfing* (1895), 7; Labbance, "Burlington's Ghosts of Golf," *Vermont Golf Journal and Directory* (1995): 59; John Reid, "The St. Andrew's Golf Club of America," 1898, reprinted in Mel Shapiro, Warren Dohn, and Leonard Berger, *Golf: A Turn-of-the-Century Treasury* (Secaucus, NJ: Castle, 1986), 413; "Golf Court," 1894 Ledger, 595–96, FM's Papers; "Golf Is Fashionable," *New York Press*, Jul 1, 1894, Scrapbook vol. XII, 100.
14. The outlines of a putting green and the first tee still exist on the lower slopes of the Shelburne House lawn. "Golf Is Fashionable," 100; "Shelburne Farms Links" Scorecard, SFC; Julie Bressor, corr. with author, Mar 16, 1999.
15. JWW to EFG, May 2, 1904, 1903–05 Folder, and WW to EFG, Mar 19, 1908, Jan–Apr 1908 Folder, both in EFG Corr. with JWW, FM's Papers.
16. It has been stated that the golf links was either the first or the third private course in the country, but, barring additional documentation, this claim does not appear to be accurate. Quote from *New York Sun*, quoted in "Shelburne Farms," *BFP*, Sep 20, 1899, Scrapbook vol. XXI, 30. Also Jerry Patterson, *The First Four Hundred: Mrs. Astor's New York in the Gilded Age* (New York: Rizzoli, 2000), 127–29; "Golf Is Fashionable," 100.
17. Patterson, *The First Four Hundred*, 134. Also AOW, Transcript of Oral History Interview with EWW, Sep 4, 1976, 20.
18. LOW, Sep 11, 1907, 1907 Diary, LOW Papers. Also EFG corr. with LOW, passim, FM's Papers; LOW Diaries, passim, LOW Papers.
19. LOW to VW, undated, starting, "What a walk over you gave St. Mark's…" VW Papers.
20. LOW to EFG, May 1, 1910, 1910 Folder, EFG Corr. with LOW, FM's Papers.
21. LOW, Nov 1, 1907, 1907 Diary, LOW Papers.
22. Ruth Wales du Pont to Ruth Hawks Wales, Jun 1917, Box A34, courtesy, The Winterthur Library: Winterthur Archives. Also LOW Diaries, passim, LOW Papers.
23. Photographs #s 298-309, 701-705, JWW Jr. Coll.; "Sues Her Mother-In-Law," *New York Evening World*, Jan 17, 1894, Scrapbook vol. XII, 13; EHW to VW, Dec 11, [c. 1911 or 1912], VW Papers; LOW, Jul 2, 1921, 1921 Diary, LOW Papers.
24. The *Elfrida* was also sometimes spelled *Elfrieda, Elfreda*, or *Elfreida*. "Yachts were measured both at the water line and by their maximum length. This would account for varying published measurements" (Julie Eldridge Edwards to author, Jan 28, 2009). Quote in text from "For Sale: Handsome Steam Yacht," *BFP*, Mar 14, 1889, Scrapbook vol. V, 74. Also "A Yacht's Long Voyage," *Boston Journal*, Jul 22, 1889, Scrapbook vol. V, 149; Lillian Wright, "Shelburne Farms: the Summer Home of Dr. William Seward Webb," *Boston Home Journal*, Nov 7, 1891, Scrapbook vol. VIII, 89; Captain E. W. Blodgett, *Elfrida I* Ship's Log, Oct 15, 1894, 1894 Log, Elfrida Log Book Coll.
25. Unidentified clipping, c. Jan 1886, Scrapbook vol. IV, 79; "A New Yacht," *Wilmington (DE) News*, Nov 6, 1888, Scrapbook vol. V, 58.
26. "Luxury in a Yacht," *Rutland (VT) Herald*, Jul 23, 1889, Scrapbook vol. V, 150; "A Yacht's Long Voyage," 149; "A New Yacht," 58; Harlan and Hollingsworth Company, "Proposed Steam Screw Yacht for Mr. W. Seward Webb," c. 1888, APMI.
27. "A True Patriot," *Troy (NY) Times*, Mar 30, 1898, Scrapbook vol. XXI, 12; "Yacht Elfrida in Governmental Service," *New*

York Press, Jul 17, 1898, Scrapbook vol. XXI, 15; Department of Commerce and Labor, United States Government, *Seagoing Vessels of the United States with Official Numbers and Signals* (Washington, DC: Government Printing Office, 1905), 76, Folder 945b, Trade Catalogue Coll., FM's Papers; "Elfrida," Department of the Navy, Naval Historical Center, http://www.history.navy.mil/danfs/e3/elfrida.htm. The author thanks Julie Eldridge Edwards for directing her to the latter source.

28 Gas Engine and Power Company and Charles L. Seabury Co., blueprints for "Steam Yacht Elfrida," 1899, APMI; Julie Bressor, "The Elfrieda," Fact Sheet, 1992, *Elfrida* Reference File; various newspaper articles in Scrapbooks, vols. XV, XVI, and XXI; EFG to LOW, Apr 7, 1905, EFG Corr. with LOW, FM's Papers.

29 *Lake Champlain Yacht Club: Centennial Celebration* (Lake Champlain Yacht Club, 1989), 1–2, 6. Also *Plattsburgh (NY) Telegram*, Sep 22, 1888, Scrapbook vol. V, 55; *BFP*, Oct 20, 1888, Scrapbook vol. V, 56; *BFP*, Oct 19, 1889, Scrapbook vol. V, 177.

30 Captain E. W. Blodgett, Jun 18, 1893, 1893 *Elfrida I* Ship's Log, *Elfrida* Log Book Coll. Also, in general, *Elfrida I* and *II* Log Books, passim, *Elfrida* Log Book Coll.

31 Captain E. W. Blodgett, Aug 7–10 and Aug 14, 1899, *Elfrida II* Ship's Log, and Sep 6, 1901, 1901 *Elfrida II* Ship's Log, *Elfrida* Log Book Coll.; Julie Eldridge Edwards to author, May 15, 2009.

32 "W.S. Webb's Country Home," *New York Tribune*, Feb 3, 1889, Scrapbook vol. V, 68; "New Boathouses and Docks Construction," 1891 Index to Ledger, and List of "Unfinished Work" inside rear cover of 1891 Ledger, both in FM's Papers; Photographs #s 1, 13, 14, and 18, JWW Jr. Coll.

33 Thomas E. Marr photographs of Dock Bay construction, c. 1901–02, TEMC; LOW to VW, Jun 11, [c. 1900–02], VW Papers.

34 C. S. Pelham-Clinton, "Biggest Barn in America: Dr. Seward Webb's Beautiful Estate at Shelburne Farms, Vt.," *Buffalo News*, Apr 22, 1895, Scrapbook vol. XIII, 28; "Coach Barn Harness Room Extension," 1890 Ledger, 294, "Coach Barn Extension," 1890 Ledger, 516, "Coach Barn Annex," 1891 Ledger, 638–40, and "Real Estate," Nov 1894 Ledger, 7, all in FM's Papers; AHG, "The Shelburne Farms," in WSW, *Shelburne Farms Stud: Of English Hackneys, Harness and Saddle Horses, Ponies and Trotters* (New York: G. P. Putnam's Sons, 1893), 20; Photographs #13, 16, 20–27, 30, 32, 166–73, JWW Jr. Coll.; Thomas E. Marr, Photograph #3115, TEMC; *Sanborn Insurance Map* for Burlington, Vermont, Nov 1894, sheet 28, Special Collections, Bailey/Howe Library, UVM.

35 "Destroy Old Coach Barn," 1902 Ledger, 482, and "Destroy Old Coach Barn Dwelling," 1902 Ledger, 519, FM's Papers.

36 The iron gates were wrought by the New York City firm J. L. Mott & Co. (see corr. with J. L. Mott & Co., c. 1899–1902, Folder 98, EFG Corr., FM's Papers). *New York Sun*, quoted in "Shelburne Farms," *BFP*, 30; RHR and R. Burnside Potter, "House Stables for W. Seward Webb," c. 1901 elevations and floor plans, APMI; Brooke Vincent, "The Coach Barn: Its Historical Context, Changing Uses and Current Function," unpublished essay for UVM class, Sep 1984, 11.

37 The drains were ordered from J. L. Mott & Co. (see note 36); the elevator was constructed by the James Murtaugh Company of NY, and the brick for the horse stalls was made by the Drury Brick Company in Essex Junction, VT. James B. Murtaugh to EFG, Oct 6 and Nov 15, 1905, Folder M-4, FM's Papers; "Dr. Webb's 'Phone System," *Milton (VT) Rays*, Mar 29, 1900, Scrapbook vol. XVI, 157; Vincent, "The Coach Barn," passim.

38 LOW to EFG, May 5, 1912, EFG Corr. with LOW, FM's Papers. Also "List of horses on Shelburne Farms Jul 18, 1900," in "Shelburne Horse Lists 1900 Etc.," 67–68, MS 416, vol. 2, SMA; Valerie Hunt, former curator of transportation, Shelburne Museum, materials prepared for public lecture "Horse-Drawn Vehicles from the Webb Estate," 2000; Edward Wheeling, *Horse-Drawn Vehicles at the Shelburne Museum* (Shelburne, VT: The Shelburne Museum, 1974), passim.

39 Edwin C. Powell, "Shelburne Farms: An Ideal Country Place," *Country Life in America* 3, no. 4 (Feb 1903): 155–56.

40 RHR and R. Burnside Potter, "Coachman's Cottage Dr. W. Seward Webb Shelburne, Vt.," elevations and floor plans, APMI; EFG to LOW, Aug 28, 1907, EFG Corr. with LOW, FM's Papers.

41 Margaret Campbell, Erica Donnis, Patricia O'Donnell, and Catherine Quinn, *Shelburne Farms National Historic Landmark Nomination*, 2000, 9.

42 LOW, Aug 31, 1902, 1902–13 Diary/Scrapbook, LOW Papers.

43 Kenneth Wheeling, "By Coach To Shelburne…" *The Carriage Journal* 39 (Jun 2001): 197. Also 1894 Coaching Club corr. and notes, WSW Personal Corr., WSW Papers.

44 JWW, Jun 26–29, 1901, 1901 Diary, JWW Jr. Coll.; LOW, May 3, 1903, 1902–13 Diary/Scrapbook, LOW Papers.

45 WSW to EFG, Dec 6, 1902, and WSW to EFG, undated, both in EFG Corr. with WSW, FM's Papers; Vincent, illustration 44; LOW to EFG, Aug 6, 1907, Sep 15, 1910, and May 10, 1914, EFG Corr. with LOW, FM's Papers; LOW, Jun 10 and Jun 12, 1907, 1907 Diary, May 15, 1914, 1914 Diary, and Nov 9, 1921, 1921 Diary, all in LOW Papers; EFG to GK, Jan 23, 1920, GK Folder, EFG Corr. with VW, FM's Papers; JWW, Jan 8, 1901, 1901 Diary, JWW Jr. Coll.; "Automobile Club's Run," *New York Times*, Nov 3, 1899, Scrapbook vol. XXI, 129; "Automobiles In Line," *New York Evening Mail and Express*, Nov 4, 1899, Scrapbook vol. XXI, 132; *New York Sun*, quoted in "Shelburne Farms," *BFP*, 30.

46 LOW, Sep 5, 1906, 1906 Diary, LOW Papers. Also EFG to LOW, Aug 8, 1907, EFG Corr. with LOW, FM's Papers.

47 EFG to WSW, Dec 14, 1905, EFG Corr. with WSW, and EFG to LOW, Apr 14, 1914, EFG Corr. with LOW, both in FM's Papers. Also MCW, interview with author, Jan 14, 2002; Vincent, 23.

48 This account of the Shelburne Depot and the Webbs' railroad activities, pages 90–93, is derived from the following sources: "Shelburne Depot," 1888–90 Ledger, 270–71, FM's Papers; Deeds, James E. White to WSW, Nov 26 and Dec 10, 1888, Legal Papers, FM's Papers; *Albany (NY) Press*, Jan 27, 1889, Scrapbook vol. V, 67; VW to FVPJ, Apr 29, 1943, FM's Corr., FM's Papers; Deed, CJ to Shelburne Museum, Inc., Oct 11, 1952, vol. 32, 357–58, Land Records, STC; RHR, LER, and Mackintosh & Crandall, Engineers, architectural and site plans for the depot and outbuildings, APMI; FK to GK, Mar 25, 1932, GK Folder, FK Corr. with VW, FM's Papers; Maggie Lidz and Jeff Groff, Winterthur Museum, corr. with author, Jan 28–29, 2009.

49 The Webbs allowed the railroad companies to use the depot at no charge until the mid-1930s. After that point, a lease was signed with the Rutland Railroad allowing use for $1 a year (VW to FVJ, Apr 29, 1943, VW's Shelburne Farms Corr., 1938–55, FM's Papers). Wagner Palace Car Company, "Wagner Palace Car Company Illustrated Descriptive List of Sleeping, Drawing-Room, Hotel, Private and Special Plan Cars, with Charter Rates for Private, Theatrical or Special Service, etc.,"

undated, Pullman Company Records, Case Pullman 09/00/03, Box 3, Newberry Library, Chicago; John H. White, Jr., *The American Railroad Passenger Car* (Baltimore, MD: Johns Hopkins University Press, 1991), 352–53; LER, "Shelburne Station, May 5, 1891" sketch, APMI; WSW, *California and Alaska and Over the Canadian Pacific Railway* (New York: G. P. Putnam's Sons, 1890).

50 Lori F. Wilson, *God With Us: A History of Trinity Episcopal Church, Shelburne, Vermont: 1790–1900* (Lori F. Wilson, 1990), 47, 50–51; Margaret McLeod Leef, "Lila Vanderbilt Webb: Dichotomous Patron of Trinity Episcopal Church," unpublished essay for UVM English class, c. 1995, passim.

51 *Burlington (VT) Daily News*, Aug 19, 1898, Scrapbook vol. XXI, 16.

52 Wilson, 64; "P.E. Society Cash Book," 1885–99, 22, Trinity Church Archives, loaned to SFC; EFG to WSW, Jan 24, 1903, EFG Corr. with WSW, FM's Papers; LOW, draft letter to Trinity parish, c. 1933, and DNT to LOW, Dec 17, 1933, both in Folder 16, Business Papers Coll., LOW Papers; LOW, Last Will and Testament, Jun 15, 1929, LOW Papers.

Chapter 7

1 C. S. Pelham-Clinton, "Biggest Barn in America: Dr. Seward Webb's Beautiful Estate at Shelburne Farms, Vt.," *Buffalo (NY) News*, Apr 22, 1895, Scrapbook vol. XIII, 28.

2 "At Shelburne Farms," *BFP*, Oct 19, 1889, Scrapbook vol. V, 178; MCW to author, Feb 19, 2002; MCW, "Shelburne Farms Road Inventory 10/98," Oct 1998, MCW Files.

3 Henry I. Hazelton, "Shelburne Farms," *New England Magazine* 25 (Nov 1901): 270. Also Charles E. Beveridge and Paul Rocheleau, *Frederick Law Olmsted: Designing the American Landscape* (New York: Universe Publishing, 1998), 44; Margaret Campbell, Erica Donnis, Patricia O'Donnell, and Catherine Quinn, *Shelburne Farms National Historic Landmark Nomination*, 2000, 6.

4 Contract between Elbert and Jane Nash and WSW, Feb 4, 1889, Box 1, Folder 2, and George W. Wales to WSW, Mar 2, 1889, Box 1, Folder 8, both in Legal Papers, FM's Papers; Campbell et al., 8.

5 "At Shelburne Farms," *BFP*, 178; Campbell et al., 8; W. J. Wilgus to EFG, Jul 7, 1902, EFG Corr., EFG to JWW, Jun 17, 1903, EFG Corr. with JWW, "Elm Swamp Sea Wall," 1898 Ledger, 585, and "New Sea Wall (South)," 1902 Ledger, 524, all in FM's Papers; Thomas E. Marr, photographs #s 3121, 3187, TEMC; MCW to author, Mar 5, 2002.

6 Bill Flynt, "Dr. William Seward Webb's Farm Barn at Shelburne Farms, Shelburne, Vt.," unpublished paper written for UVM Art History class, Dec 31, 1977, 8–16, 30–38; "Shelburne," *BFP*, May 23, 1899, Scrapbook vol. XXI, 26; "Stone Crusher" and "Stone Crushing," 1888–90 Ledger, 251 and 253, FM's Papers; Photographs #s 150, 151, JWW Jr. Coll.; WSW to EFG, May 9, 1911, EFG Corr. with WSW, FM's Papers.

7 "Ditching," "Drainage on SF," and "Stone Crushing," 1888–90 Ledger, 78–79, 253, FM's Papers.

8 Thomas E. Marr, photographs of Shelburne Farms drives, c. 1900, TEMC; Historic photographs, c. 1889–1900, "Landscape—Drives" Folder, Print and Photograph Coll.; Campbell et al., 8–9.

9 The roads were legally private, with one exception: the public retained the right to travel to and from the public cemetery, which predated the establishment of Shelburne Farms and was located near the Breeding Barn. Although the Webbs issued an open invitation for members of the public to drive throughout the property, at least some local residents felt too uncomfortable and/or unwelcome to take advantage of the offer, and, to them, the Webbs' efforts to close formerly public roads had the effect of creating a private preserve (Mary Twitchell, interview with author, Mar 2004). Quote from Lillian Wright, "Shelburne Farms: The Summer Home of Dr. William Seward Webb," *Boston Home Journal*, Nov 7, 1891, Folder 10, LOW Deed Box Coll. Also "Shelburne Farms," *Burlington (VT) Farmer Advocate*, Jan 19, 1895, Scrapbook vol. XIII, 7; Thomas E. Marr, Photograph #3206, TEMC.

10 "Entrance Lodge Alt. & Rep. Gates Etc.," 1896 Ledger, 309–11, "Entrance Lodge Gates Etc. Expense," and "No. Entrance Lodge Alt. & Rep." 1899 Ledger, 311–16, all in FM's Papers; Historic photographs, c. 1895–1940, "Landscape—Gates" Folder, Print and Photograph Coll.

11 The pump house was destroyed by fire on Jan 1, 1969 ("Shelburne Farms, Shelburne, Vermont, This Map Compiled from Aerial Survey…12-19-52 Revised Apr 21, 1969," 2004.3.21.59, FFD 8, Folder 10, APMI). Also "W.S. Webb's Country Home," *New York Tribune*, Feb 3, 1889, Scrapbook vol. V, 68; J. M. Pernham, "Plan of Water System Shelburne Farms Shelburne, Vt., Surveyed in Jul 1889," APMI; MCW, interview with author, Feb 14, 2002, and comments on draft Chapter 6, Jan 2009; ASW, handwritten note about water intake pipe, c. 1977, in "Water File," ASW Files.

12 The second reservoir was replaced by a third, concrete structure on the same site in 1988–89 (Campbell et al., 13). "Shelburne Farms," *New York Sun*, quoted in *BFP*, Sep 20, 1899, Scrapbook vol. XXI, 30. Also "W.S. Webb's Country Home," 68; Pernham; MCW, interview with author, Feb 14, 2002.

13 "Fire at Shelburne Farms," *BFP*, Oct 23, 1888, Scrapbook vol. V, 57. Also MCW, interview with author, Feb 14, 2002.

14 Most estate buildings were equipped with steam boilers; the Breeding Barn, however, possessed coal stoves (MCW to author, Jan 29, 2009, and comments on draft Chapter 6, Jan 2009). This account of lighting and heating systems, pages 101–2, is derived primarily from the following sources, with additional sources and quotes as noted: "Gaswork," 1888–90 Ledger, 221, "Gas Well," 1890 Ledger, 275–77, "Steam Heat Plant," 1890 Ledger, 480–81, "Steam Heating Construction," 1891 Ledger, 622, and "Breeding Barn Electric Lighting and Steam Heating Plant," 1892 Ledger, 474, all in FM's Papers; and *Sanborn Insurance Map*, Nov 1894, sheet 28, Special Collections Department, Bailey/Howe Library, UVM.

15 Quote from AHG, "The Shelburne Farms," in William C. Lipke, ed., *Shelburne Farms: The History of an Agricultural Estate* (Burlington, VT: University of Vermont, 1979), 38. Also, Flynt, 30–32.

16 While it is difficult to determine an accurate currency conversion rate, one source (www.westegg.com/inflation/) estimates that the $17,000 spent in 1892 is roughly equivalent to $402,000 in 2008 dollars. Merrit Ierley, *The Comforts of Home: The American House and the Evolution of Modern Convenience* (New York: Three Rivers Press, 1999), 139–40, 176; Ruth Morrow, Interview, "Shelburne, Vermont Historic Settlement Oral History Project," c. 2002, 7, Town of Shelburne Reference Files, VDHP.

17 Ierley, 196. Also "Green House—Stock & Expenses," 1890

Ledger, 178, and EFG to WSW, Aug 15, 1902, EFG Corr., Folder 316, both in FM's Papers.
18 EFG to WSW, Aug 15, 1902, EFG Corr., Folder 316, FM's Papers.
19 "LaPlatte Coal Docks & Sheds," 1893 Ledger, 608, FM's Papers; Edward Coleman, interview, in "Shelburne, Vermont Historic Settlement Oral History Project," c. 2002, 12; Frank and Frederica Botala, Oral History Interview, Jun 26, 2006, disk 1.
20 "Dr. Webb's 'Phone System," *Milton (VT) Rays*, Mar 29, 1900, Scrapbook vol. XV, 137. Also "Telephone S.F. Line," and "New England Telephone & Tel. Cy.," 24, 296, 1888–90 Ledger, FM's Papers.
21 AHG, "The Shelburne Farms," in Lipke, 38. Also "Telegraph Line, Dr.'s House to Depot," 1891 Ledger, 291, FM's Papers.
22 Western Union Messages, c. 1918–22, passim, and WSW to EFG, Aug 23, 1902, Folder 317, EFG Corr., both in FM's Papers.

Chapter 8

1 Archibald Taylor, General Order #82, Aug 15, 1898, General Order Book vol. 1, FM's Papers.
2 "A Vermont Farm," *Boston Traveller*, Nov 6, 1889, Scrapbook vol. V, 185; *Harper's New York*, Jan 25, 1888, Scrapbook vol. V, 13; "At Shelburne Farms," *BFP*, Oct 19, 1889, Scrapbook vol. V, 178; "At His Country Home," *Albany (NY) Argus*, Aug 8, 1895, Scrapbook vol. XIII, 42; *New York Sun*, quoted in "Shelburne Farms," *BFP*, Sep 20, 1899, Scrapbook vol. XXI, 30; JWW Jr., "Pictorial History of the Webb Family," 28, JWW Jr. Coll.
3 Starting and quitting times may have varied for each department in part so that office clerks would have time to record in detail the information about each employee's work hours or absences. This information was forwarded from each department at the beginning and end of each day (Archibald Taylor, "Notice," Apr 6, 1891, and General Order #106, Apr 15, 1901, both in General Order Book vol. 1, FM's Papers). Also Fred M. Abbey, "On the Bothy," *Gardenside Gossip* (March 1962), the newsletter of Gardenside Nurseries, Shelburne, VT, coll. in the possession of Harrison L. Flint, Lafayette, IN.
4 Stanley Johnson to SF, Aug 18, 1902, EFG Corr., FM's Papers.
5 W. E. Lay to EFG, Aug 29, 1902, EFG Corr., FM's Papers.
6 According to Webb family lore, WSW and LOW met and recruited WW in the late 1880s or early 1890s at Blenheim Palace, where their niece Consuelo, the Duchess of Marlborough, assigned him to be WSW's valet for the duration of his stay. However, no written documentation confirming the story has been discovered. Mrs. Woodgate was often referred to as "Nell" or "Nellie" (JWW Jr., "Pictorial History," 169–70, JWW Jr. Coll.; Julie Eldridge Edwards, comments on draft Chapter 7, Jan 28, 2009). In general, see "Pictorial History"; Social Security Administration, Social Security Death Index Entry for WW, Dec 1967, and Ellen Woodgate, United States Passport Application, Apr 23, 1923, both accessed on www.ancestry.com; entry for Tuffield Kinville, United States Population Census for Shelburne, VT, 1920; as well as the following, all in FM's Papers: LOW to EFG, Aug 10, 1907, EFG Corr. with LOW; LOW to VW, Mar 10, 1909, VW Papers; EFG to JWW, Jul 20, 1911, and JWW to EFG, Jul 26, 1911, both in Jul–Dec 1911 Folder, EFG Corr. with JWW; VW to Jacobs & Phillips, Aug 23, 1924, Folder 1, FK Corr. with VW; LOW to FK, Sep 7, 1930, Folder 3, FK and DNT Corr. with LOW.
7 FK to GK, Oct 8, 1925, GK Folder, FM's Corr. with VW, 1922–35, FM's Papers. Also Archibald Taylor, General Order #82.
8 The following are all from the FM's Papers: Archibald Taylor, "Notice," [before Nov 22, 1890], General Order Book vol. 1; FK, General Order #353, Dec 22, 1932, General Order Book vol. 2; SF Employee Record Book, 1893–1914, passim, Box 20; Maids' Wages Book, Jan 1903–May 1913, passim, Box 4; "Pay Roll Record House Servants From Apr 1903," passim, Box 4; and EFG to Frank Fitzsimmons, Jul 2, 1910, Folder "F to G," Box 2, FM's Corr., 1922–35. For comparison, see T. M. Adams, "Prices Paid By Farmers For Goods And Services And Received By Them For Farm Products, 1790–1871; Wages Of Farm Labor, 1780–1937," (Burlington, VT: Univ. of Vermont and State Agricultural College, Vermont Agricultural Experiment Station, 1939), passim; Madden's Employment Agency advertisements, *BFP*, Sep 2, 1910, Sep 2, 1915, Sep 21, 1915, Jan 2, 1920, and Jan 30, 1920.
9 EFG to LOW, Aug 29, 1913, EFG Corr. with LOW, FM's Papers.
10 Archibald Taylor, Aug 24, 1896, General Order #69, General Order Book vol. 1; EFG to JWW, Mar 8, 1910, 1910 Folder, EFG Corr. with JWW, both in FM's Papers.
11 "W.S. Webb's Country Home," *New York Tribune*, Feb 3, 1889, Scrapbook vol. V, 68.
12 LOW to EFG, Nov 28, 1916, EFG Corr. with LOW, FM's Papers.
13 EFG to LOW, Oct 4, 1915, EFG Corr. with LOW, FM's Papers. Also EFG to WSW, Aug 22, 1906, and EFG to WSW, Jan 23, 1908, EFG Corr. with WSW, FM's Papers.
14 See, for example, "W.S. Webb Stock Account," 1890 Ledger, 3, FM's Papers.
15 As the estate developed from 1890 to 1900, and staffing needs changed, four cottages of the group of eight were moved from their original sites to other sections of the property. In about 1894, two became residences for stock farm employees near the Breeding Barn. Two others were moved to the newly constructed north and south entrance gates for use as gatehouses (the south gatehouse in 1895 and the north gatehouse in 1898). DVW sold the remaining cottages in the late 1960s or early 1970s (Fred C. Koerner, "A Study Plan of a Portion of Land Owned by Derick V. Webb, Shelburne, Vermont," May 1969, 2004.3.21.17, FFD 7, Folder 8, APMI; MCW, interview with author, Jul 1, 2008). "Tenant Cottages Construction," 1890 Ledger, 314–17, "O.S. Nichols," 1890 Ledger, 346, 349, and "Entrance Lodge," 1895 Ledger, 611, all in FM's Papers; Margaret Campbell, "The South Gate Cottage and other Workers' Cottages of Shelburne Farms, Shelburne, Vermont," Dec 10, 1995, unpublished paper prepared for UVM Historic Preservation Program, 10–12; Julie Eldridge Edwards to author, Jan 6, 2009.
16 Campbell, "The South Gate Cottage," 10–11; "Chapel," 1888–90 Ledger, 72, FM's Papers; Francis E. Collette, *The Parish of St. Catherine of Siena, Shelburne: A History of Active Roman Catholicism in a Small Vermont Town* (Shelburne, VT: Parish of St. Catherine of Siena, 1995), 60–61; Marie Harding, *The History of Shelburne* 30; Truman M. Webster, *Shelburne: Pieces of History* (Shelburne, VT: Shelburne Historic Sites Committee, 1994), 121–22. Collette disputes the moving of the chapel to Shelburne Village (see pp. 61, 70), but the structures are very close in appearance, and the chapel disappears from SF maps and accounts after c. 1895.
17 LOW, Jul 4, 1905, 1905 Diary, LOW Papers.
18 "Was Host To A Village," *Baltimore Sun*, Dec 27, 1897,

Scrapbook vol. XXI, 4–5. Also LOW, 1913–15 Christmas Lists, Box 4, FM's Papers.
19 LOW, Aug 4–5, 1906, 1906 Diary, LOW Papers.
20 LOW to EFG, Jan 22 [c. 1910], EFG Corr. with LOW, FM's Papers. Also LOW, Jul 9, Dec 10, and Dec 13, 1907, 1907 Diary, and Apr 17, 1922, 1922 Diary, LOW Papers; corr. in Folder 10, Business Papers Coll., LOW Papers; and GK to FK, Feb 7, 1931, GK Folder, FK Corr. with VW, FM's Papers.
21 LOW to EFG, Aug 10, 1907, EFG Corr. with LOW, FM's Papers.
22 LOW to VW, Jan 29 [c. 1908], VW Papers.
23 Taylor did not officially step down as Farm Manager until 1908 (Karl Heine to EFG, Feb 28, 1908, Folder 82A, EFG Corr., FM's Papers). Quote from WSW to Archibald Taylor, Jan 14, 1904, EFG Corr. with WSW, FM's Papers. Also LOW, Nov 18, 1921, and Nov 24, 1921, 1921 Diary, LOW Papers; FK to LOW, Dec 22, 1927, Folder 2, and May 8, 1930, Folder 3, both in FK and DNT Corr. with LOW, FM's Papers.
24 LOW, Jan 11, 1925, 1925 Diary, LOW Papers.
25 LOW to GK, draft letter, undated [c. 1927], Estate Papers Coll., LOW Papers.
26 Ibid. Also GK to LOW, May 13 [c. 1927], same location.
27 GK and his wife were given a cottage in Shelburne by 1934. Corr. between GK and FK, GK Folder, FM's Corr. with VW, FM's Papers; LOW to FVJ, JWW, WSW Jr., and VW, Apr 21, 1929, Estate Papers Coll., LOW Papers.
28 WW to LOW, Mar 29, 1935, Folder 21, Business Papers Coll., LOW Papers.
29 The WWs spent each winter and spring in Santa Barbara, CA. After the dissolution of the trust following WW's death in 1967, the Webb family continued to support Mrs. Woodgate with $250 each month until she died in 1976 (corr. in Folder 21, Box 2, SBW Sr. Papers; Julie Eldridge Edwards to author, Jan 28, 2009). Also "Indenture between Eliza Osgood Webb and Morris Hadley and Vanderbilt Webb," Jun 15, 1929, LOW Papers; LOW to FVJ, JWW, WSW Jr., and VW, Apr 21, 1929, LOW Papers.

Chapter 9

1 LOW, "Christmas Greeting, 1922," Oakledge/Shelburne House Guestbook, 356.
2 Ruth Lawrence, ed., *Webb and Allied Family Histories: A Documented Compilation of Genealogy and Biography* (New York: National Americana Society, 1937), 93; "Dr. Webb Succeeds Cornelius Vanderbilt," *New York Journal*, Dec 21, 1899, Scrapbook vol. XXI, 162; "Webb for Vanderbilt's Place," *Pittsburgh (PA) Post*, Dec 21, 1899, Scrapbook vol. XXI, 162; various clippings in Scrapbook vol. XXI, 167–69; Henry A. Harter, *Fairy Tale Railroad: The Mohawk and Malone: From the Mohawk, through the Adirondacks to the St. Lawrence* (Utica, NY: North Country Books, 1979), 288–91; Jim Shaughnessy, *The Rutland Road* (San Diego, CA: Howell-North Books, 1981), 102.
3 Charles H. Burnett, *Conquering the Wilderness: The Building of the Adirondack & St. Lawrence Railroad by William Seward Webb* (Privately Printed, 1932), 65–66. Also WSW, entry for publication in *Matthews' American Armoury and Blue Book*, [c. 1900], Folder 43, Deed Box Coll., LOW Papers; Lawrence, 92–94; *New York Tribune*, Dec 1, 1888, Scrapbook vol. V, 60; "Dr. Webb at the Head of the Sons of the Revolution," *New York Sun*, Dec 8, 1889, Scrapbook vol. V, 201; "Webb, W. S. & Co.," *New York City Directory*, 1883/1884, New York Public Library; WSW, *California and Alaska and Over the Canadian Pacific Railway* (New York: G. P. Putnam's Sons, 1890); Samuel Blachley Webb, Worthington Chauncey Ford, ed., *Correspondence and Journals of Samuel Blachley Webb*, New York: [Lancaster, PA: Wickersham Press], 1893.
4 Editorial, *New York Truth*, Apr 21, 1887, Scrapbook vol. IV, 144. Also "Comfort in Night Travel," *Utica (NY) Daily Observer*, Mar 7, 1885, Scrapbook vol. IV, 3; Harter, passim; numerous newspaper clippings in Scrapbook vol. IV, 1–121; Editorial, *New York Truth*, Mar 29, 1899, Scrapbook vol. V, 84; "Wagner Palace Cars," *The Illustrated Buffalo Express*, Dec 6, 1891, Scrapbook vol. VIII, 149.
5 *Chicago Journal*, Oct 20, 1899, Scrapbook vol. XXI, 90. Also "Wagner Car Shops Will Probably Stay In Buffalo," *Buffalo Times*, Oct 22, 1899, "The Pullman-Wagner Consolidation," *New York Tribune*, Oct 22, 1899, and "Pullman Absorbs Wagner," *Philadelphia Times*, Oct 22, 1899, all in Scrapbook vol. XXI, 106.
6 The Adirondack and St. Lawrence Railroad was also known as the "Adirondack & St. Lawrence." The former version is used in this text because it appears in minutes of early board meetings and the May 1891 Articles of Consolidation. In about 1895, the company became known as the "St. Lawrence and Adirondack" or "St. Lawrence & Adirondack" (Julie Eldridge Edwards to author, Dec 4, 2008; records of the Adirondack and St. Lawrence Railroad, SFC). The details of the railroad project remain murky, and the primary and secondary sources often conflict each other or present biased perspectives. It is unclear, for instance, exactly how many acres WSW purchased for the undertaking. Further, more exhaustive research beyond the scope of this author's cursory investigations on this subject is much needed. The Adirondack and St. Lawrence Railroad was actually a conglomeration of two smaller existing railroads that were purchased by WSW (the Herkimer, Newport & Poland Railroad and the Mohawk & Malone Railroad) and connected with new sections of track. See, for example, "Northward Ho! The Vanderbilt Motto," *New York Herald*, May 7, 1891, Scrapbook vol. VII, 121.
7 "Webb Wants The Earth," *Buffalo Enquirer*, Aug 27, 1891, Scrapbook vol. VIII, 52. See also numerous newspaper clippings in Scrapbook vol. VII, 132–36, 190, 199; "Dr. Webb's Road: Work on the Adirondack & St. Lawrence Slower Than Was Expected," *New York Evening Advertiser*, Jul 13, 1891, Scrapbook vol. VIII, 11.
8 "Slaves On Webb's Road," *New York World*, Dec 15, 1891, Scrapbook vol. VIII, 161; "Treated Like Slaves," *Syracuse (NY) Standard*, Dec 18, 1891, Scrapbook vol. VIII, 174.
9 AOW, Transcript of Oral History Interview, Sep 4, 1976, 19. Also "Dr. Webb's Railroad," *Burlington (VT) Clipper*, Jul 9, 1891, Scrapbook VIII, 4; "The A. & St. L. R.R. Troubles," *Potsdam (NY) Herald*, Dec 18, 1891, Scrapbook VIII, 166.
10 Charles Burnett to Arthur R. Womrath, Inc., Jan 12, 1935, and Wilbur R. Tinney to Charles Burnett, Jan 28, 1935, Folder 14, Business Papers Coll., LOW Papers. Also corr. between LOW, Cyril Jones, Charles Burnett, and Plimpton Press, Folders 13 and 14, Business Papers Coll., LOW Papers.
11 Burnett, 40, 42.
12 SBW Jr. has stated that "Nehasane was originally 250,000 acres. Shortly after [WSW] purchased it the state of New York created a dam that flooded 100,000 acres. [WSW] sued the state and as a result that left 150,000 acres" (SBW Jr. to author,

Oct 15, 2006). Quote in text from Burnett, 55. Variations on the translation for the term Nehasane are "beaver crossing stream" ("A Lodge In The Woods," *New York Tribune*, Jul 15, 1893, Scrapbook vol. XI, 91) and "beaver falling off a log"; however, it is unclear if any of these translations accurately represent Native American meanings (MCW and Holly Brough, comments on draft Chapter 8, Jan 2009). Also Craig Gilborn, *Adirondack Camps: Homes Away From Home, 1850–1950* (Syracuse, NY: Adirondack Museum and Syracuse University Press, 2000), 226.

13 For general information about Nehasane, see historic photographs of Nehasane in TEMC and JWW Jr. Coll.; Scrapbook vols. VII and XII, passim; Gifford Pinchot, *The Adirondack Spruce: A Study of the Forest in Ne-Ha-Sa-Ne Park* (New York: The Critic Co., 1898); Florence Adele Sloane, *Maverick In Mauve: The Diary of a Romantic Age* (Garden City, NJ: Doubleday, 1983), 96–97; Robert B. King, *The Vanderbilt Homes* (New York: Rizzoli, 1989), 98–103; Gilborn, passim.

14 Inscription, Farm Barn clock tower, Nov 6, 1888; *St. Albans (VT) Messenger*, Nov 9, 1888, Scrapbook vol. V, 58; "A Grand Celebration," *BFP*, Nov 13, 1888, Scrapbook vol. V, 59; "New Bell for Shelburn [sic] Farms," *BFP*, Nov 16, 1888, Scrapbook vol. V, 59; "Shelburne," *BFP*, Oct 31, 1896, Scrapbook vol. XIII; LOW to Rev. Roelif H. Brooks, Feb 3, 1929, Folder 31, Family Papers Coll., LOW Papers.

15 "Mr. Cleveland's Trip," *New York Times*, May 23, 1887, Scrapbook vol. IV, 149; "The President In Albany," *Albany (NY) Journal*, Jun 10, 1887, Scrapbook vol. IV, 150–51; "The Revolution's Sons," *BFP*, Apr 3, 1889, Scrapbook vol. V, 90; "Dr. Webb at the Head of the Sons of the Revolution," *New York Sun*, Dec 8, 1889, Scrapbook vol. V, 201; J. G. McCullough to WSW, May 18, 1891, Folder 1, Family Papers Coll., LOW Papers; Charles Lacy, interviews with author, 2000 and 2003, and unpublished draft manuscript about Redfield Proctor and Fort Ethan Allen, 2000; unsigned letter on State of Vermont Adjutant and Inspector General's office stationery to Col. Charles S. Forbes, Apr 19, 1908, Folder 10, Deed Box Coll., LOW Papers; LOW, Jan 10, 1903, 1903 Diary, LOW Papers; LOW to VW, Jan 30, 1903, VW Papers; D. J. Foster to LOW, Oct 27, 1903, Folder 8, Family Papers Coll., LOW Papers; EFG to WSW, Nov 3, 1902, Folder 1, EFG Corr.; Michael Sherman, Gene Sessions, and P. Jeffrey Potash, *Freedom and Unity: A History of Vermont* (Barre, VT: Vermont Historical Society, 2004), 323, 343.

16 "A True Patriot," *Troy (NY) Times*, Mar 30, 1898, Scrapbook vol. XXI, 12. Also "Yacht Elfrida in Governmental Service," *New York Press*, Jul 17, 1898, Scrapbook vol. XXI, 15; Department of Commerce and Labor, United States Government, *Seagoing Vessels of the United States with Official Numbers and Signals* (Washington, DC: Government Printing Office, 1905), 76, Folder 945b, Trade Catalogue Coll., FM's Papers; "Report of the Secretary of the Navy," Summary Report, from *Annual Reports of the Navy Department for the Year 1898* (Washington, DC: Government Printing Office, 1898), accessed via Department of the Navy, Naval Historical Center, http://www.history.navy.mil/wars/spanam/sn98-12.htm.

17 "A Patriotic Proletariat" to WSW, Mar 20, 1898, WSW Personal Corr., WSW Papers.

18 According to Webb family oral history, Dewey presented WSW and LOW an eight-foot-long model ship in appreciation for the use of the *Elfrida*. The model ship was hung from the ceiling of the children's playroom on the third floor of Shelburne House (LOW, Shelburne House Inventory, c. 1920, 219, LOW Papers; clippings in Scrapbook vol. XXI, 33–56; JWW Jr., "Distribution Provisions," in "J. Watson Webb Jr. Family Trust" document, 9, Accession File for 2000.02, SFC). Between 1899 and 1918, the navy also loaned the *Elfrida* for use by various state militia groups (Department of the Navy, Naval Historical Center, "Elfrida," http://www.history.navy.mil/danfs/e3/elfrida.htm).

19 WSW, quoted in "Rich Men In Politics," *New York World*, Aug 30, 1896, Scrapbook vol. XIII, 109.

20 "The Man Who Would Be King," *(NY) Tammany Times*, May 10, 1902, Folder 11, Deed Box Coll., LOW Papers; *Worcester (MA) Gazette*, Aug 26, 1896, Scrapbook vol. XIII, 109; *Burlington (VT) Daily News*, Jul 28, 1896, Scrapbook vol. XIII, 107; "Webb for Speaker," *New York Herald*, Oct 4, 1896, Scrapbook vol. XIII, 115.

21 "Will It Be Senator Webb?" *New York Press*, Dec 27, 1897, Scrapbook vol. XXI, 5; JWW, Apr 21, 1904, 1904 Diary, JWW Jr. Coll.

22 EFG to LOW, Sep 3, 1902, FM's Papers. Also JWW, Jan 3, 1901, 1901 Diary, JWW Jr. Coll.

23 EFG to LOW, Apr 7, 1905, EFG Corr., FM's Papers.

24 "State Politics," *BFP*, Feb 3, 1898, Scrapbook vol. XXI, 8.

25 "The Way to the Governorship," *Hartford (CT) Courant*, Oct 1, 1895, Scrapbook vol. XIII, 50.

26 Paul M. Searls, *Two Vermonts: Geography and Identity, 1865–1910* (Hanover, NH: University Press of New England, 2000), 4–6, 76–83, 117–20, and passim.

27 Searls, 35, 117 (first part of quote), and 119 (second part of quote).

28 LOW to VW, Easter Sunday, 1910, VW Papers.

29 EFG to LOW, Apr 7, 1905, EFG Corr., FM's Papers.

30 LOW to EFG, Mar 17, 1907, EFG Corr., FM's Papers.

31 It is difficult to compare these financial statistics to today's dollars. One source, www.westegg.com/inflation/, estimates that $500,000 in 1889 is roughly equivalent to $11.8 million in 2008 dollars, $30 million in 1890 is roughly equivalent to $710 million, and $1.5 million is roughly equivalent to $35.5 million. *New York Journal*, Oct 13, 1889, Scrapbook vol. V, 172; "A Week's Income," *New York Evening World*, Feb 10, 1894, Scrapbook vol. XII, 21.

32 "Webb, W. S. & Co.," "Webb, W. S.," "Webb, H. Walter," "Webb, F. Edgerton," "Prall, John H.," and "Webb, Prall & Co.," *New York City Directories*, 1883/84–1887/88, New York Public Library; "F. Edgerton Webb, Banker, Dies At 83," *New York Times*, Feb 27, 1942.

33 Steven R. Weisman, *The Great Tax Wars: Lincoln to Wilson— The Fierce Battles over Money and Power That Transformed the Nation* (New York: Simon & Schuster, 2002), 4.

34 H. Walter Webb to WSW, Dec 23, 1895, Folder 10, Deed Box Coll., LOW Papers.

35 F. Edgerton Webb to WSW, May 20, 1897, Folder 10, Deed Box Coll., LOW Papers. Also Henry Sprague to WSW, Dec 18, 1897, Folder 10, Deed Box Coll., LOW Papers.

36 Burnett, 32–34.

37 WSW to EFG, Jan 14, 1904, EFG Corr. with WSW, FM's Papers.

38 "Dr. W. Seward Webb, In account with W. K. Vanderbilt," Jan 1, 1905, Folder 11, Deed Box Coll., LOW Papers; "Report of financial conditions when H.B.A. [Henry B. Anderson] took hold of matters, & loan from W.K.V. [William K. Vanderbilt]," 1905, Folder 9, Deed Box Coll., LOW Papers; "The Man Who Would Be King."

39 Ibid; "Bank Account of Dr. Webb Attached: Suit of Arthur L. Meyer for $400,000 Against Vanderbilt Son-in-Law," *New York World*, Apr 13, 1904, Scrapbook XVI, 208; Supreme Court of State of New York, Judgment for *Henry L. Sprague v. William S. Webb and Dominion Securities Company*, Jun 1915, Folder 11, Miscellaneous Papers Coll., LOW Papers.
40 WSW to LOW, May 21, 1903, Folder 8, Family Papers Coll., LOW Papers.
41 WSW to EFG, undated [c. 1903–04], EFG Corr. with WSW, FM's Papers.
42 Ibid. Also WSW to LOW, [illegible month] 21, 1903, Folder 8, Family Papers Coll., LOW Papers.
43 Supreme Court of State of New York. Also LOW to JWW, Jan 18, 1914, pasted in rear of 1914 JWW Diary, and JWW, Nov 23, 1914, 1914 Diary, both in JWW Jr. Coll.
44 WSW to EFG, undated, EFG Corr. with WSW, FM's Papers.
45 WSW to LOW, undated letter beginning "My dear Lila, I have made up my mind to spend 3 weeks at the sea shore this year…," Folder 53, Family Papers Coll., LOW Papers. Also "Trust Fund of Eliza O. Webb," c. Jan 1, 1937, Estate Papers Coll., LOW Papers.
46 JWW to VW, Apr 3, 1913, VW Papers; LOW to WSW, Apr 19, 1913, and E. D. Worcester to LOW, Jun 10, 1913, both in Folder 20, Family Papers Coll.; EFG to WSW, Mar 2, 1921, "WH to WI" Folder 2, FM's Papers.
47 WSW, Aug 13–16, 1879, 1879 Journal, WSW Papers. Also Barbara Hodgson, *Opium: A Portrait of the Heavenly Demon* (San Francisco: Chronicle Books, 1999), 1–2.
48 JWW to LOW, undated [Jan or Feb], 1898, starting "I just received the lovly [sic] things you sent me," Folder 2, Family Papers Coll., LOW Papers. This account of WSW's health problems, pages 128–132, is based on references found throughout the LOW Diaries, JWW Diaries, LOW Papers, FM's Papers, and VW Papers, with additional sources and quotations as noted.
49 *Burlington (VT) Daily News*, Mar 26, 1900, Scrapbook vol. XV, 133; *Milton (VT) Rays*, Jul 5, 1900, Scrapbook vol. XV, 242; "New York Society Notes," *New York Herald*, Jul 29, 1900, Scrapbook vol. XV, 252.
50 Otto Boeddiker, Apothecary invoice, Mar 1, 1904, and Walton Oxygen Works invoices, Mar 14 and Mar 31, 1904, all in Folder 69, Box 6, Shelburne Farms Bills, 1898–1935, FM's Papers. Also "Afflicted with Rheumatism and a Burn Last Fall," *Rutland (VT) Herald*, Mar 16, 1903, Scrapbook vol. XVI, 178.
51 Tellingly, as his bouts of illness became more regular, members of his family began to make note of his infrequent periods of *good* health as unusual. Quote from WSW to EFG, Feb 4, 1910, EFG Corr. with WSW, FM's Papers. Also AOW, Transcript of Oral History Interview, 21.
52 WSW to LOW, undated [after 1898, written at 3 a.m.], Folder 35, Deed Box Coll., LOW Papers.
53 David T. Courtwright, *Dark Paradise: A History of Opiate Addiction in America* (Cambridge, MA: Harvard University Press, 2001), 48. Also Parke, Davis & Company invoice, Feb 28, 1900, PARK Folder, 1900 Personal Bills Box, FM's Papers; WSW, Aug 16 1879, 1879 Journal, WSW Papers.
54 Henry Lawson, *Sciatica, Lumbago, and Brachialgia: Their Nature and Treatment, and Their Immediate Relief and Rapid Cure by Hypodermic Injection of Morphia* (London: Robert Hardwicke, 1872).
55 SBW Jr. believes that WSW's acquaintance with "Sir William Osler who was also a morphine addict but one of the lucky ones who kicked the habit" is good evidence that WSW was entirely aware of the addictive qualities of morphine (SBW Jr. to author, Oct 15, 2006). "Dr. McLane," 1897 Ledger Index, FM's Papers; Captain E. W. Blodgett, entries in 1901 *Elfrida II* Ship's Log, *Elfrida* Log Book Coll.
56 WSW to LOW, Sep 20–21, 1912, Folder 18, Family Papers Coll.
57 Courtwright, 36–49. Also Edith Wharton, *The Fruit of the Tree* (New York: Charles Scribner's Sons, 1907).
58 JWW to LOW, undated, Folder 53, Family Papers Coll., LOW Papers. Also AOW, Transcript of Oral History Interview, 18–19; "Is In Best of Health: Dr. W.S. Webb's Physician Says Cuban Trip Greatly Benefited Him," *Boston Morning Globe*, Mar 13, 1904, Scrapbook vol. XVI, 207.
59 It was not until 1991 that family papers documenting WSW's addiction to morphine were made available to historians. John Foreman and Robbe Stimson's account of WSW's problems with morphine in their book *The Vanderbilts and The Gilded Age* (see pp. 93–96) was the first public discussion of it (John Foreman and Robbe Pierce Stimson, *The Vanderbilts and the Gilded Age: Architectural Aspirations, 1879–1901* [New York: St. Martin's Press, 1991]). Also, for example, newspaper clippings in Scrapbook vol. XVI, 186–90; Robert W. Ganger, *Lila Vanderbilt Webb's Miradero: Window on an Era* (Palm Beach, FL: Historical Society of Palm Beach County, 2005), 115.
60 EFG to LOW, Apr 7, 1905, EFG Corr. with LOW, FM's Papers.

Chapter 10

1 WSW to EFG, Jul 14, 1903, EFG Corr. with WSW, FM's Papers; JWW, Jul 12, 1913, 1913 Diary, JWW Jr. Coll.
2 It is difficult to compare costs to today's dollars; however, one source (www.westegg.com/inflation/) estimates that $30,000 is roughly equivalent to $700,000 in 2008 dollars. Quote from EFG to WSW, Mar 10, 1903, EFG Corr. with WSW, FM's Papers. Also EFG to WSW, Jan 1, 1903, and Jan 2, 1905, and "Amounts Received from Dr. Webb For the Past Three Years," c. 1908–09, all in EFG Corr. with WSW, FM's Papers.
3 WSW to EFG, Jul 14, 1903, EFG Corr. with WSW, FM's Papers.
4 EFG to LOW, Nov 18, 1907, EFG Corr. with LOW, FM's Papers. Also WSW to EFG, Jan 14, 1904, EFG Corr. with WSW, FM's Papers; EFG to JWW, Jan 17, 1905, 1905 Folder, and Jan 18, 1908, Jan–Apr 1908 Folder, both in EFG Corr. with JWW, FM's Papers; JWW to LOW, Feb 17 and Mar 10, 1907, Folder 15, Family Papers Coll., LOW Papers.
5 EFG corr., 1903–17, passim, in EFG Corr. with LOW and EFG Corr. with WSW, both in FM's Papers; JWW, Oct 28, 1915, 1915 Diary, JWW Jr. Coll.; Coach Barn employee listings in Poultry and Employee Record Book, passim, Box 20, FM's Papers.
6 *Boston Herald*, Nov 10, 1897, Scrapbook vol. XXI, 3; WSW, "Letters To The Editor," *New York Tribune*, Jul 21, 1900, Scrapbook vol. XV, 250; "Statement of Pheasant Expenses," "Livestock Lists For Taxes 1912–1919" Folder, DVW Papers; WSW to EFG, Jun 11, 1903, Folder 9, EFG Corr., FM's Papers; Edwin C. Powell, "Shelburne Farms: An Ideal Country Place," *Country Life in America* 3, no. 4 (Feb 1903): 156.
7 EFG to JWW, Dec 16, 1915, Folder 313A, EFG Corr., FM's Papers.
8 EFG to JWW, Apr 4 and Apr 8, 1905, 1903–05 Folder, EFG Corr. with JWW, FM's Papers. Also JWW to EFG, Apr 6, 1905, 1903–05 Folder, and JWW to EFG, Feb 16, 1906, 1906 Folder, in same location.

9 EFG to JWW, Mar 16, 1911, Jan–Jun 1911 Folder, EFG Corr. with JWW, FM's Papers.
10 WSW, *Shelburne Farms Stud: Of English Hackneys, Harness and Saddle Horses, Ponies and Trotters* (New York: G. P. Putnam's Sons, 1893), 5, 9–11 (quote on 5). Also Paul M. Searls, *Two Vermonts: Geography and Identity, 1865–1910* (Hanover, NH: University Press of New England, 2000), 28, passim.
11 WSW, *Shelburne Farms Stud*, 5
12 JWW to James W. Appleton, Aug 18, 1911, Jul–Dec 1911 Folder, EFG Corr. with JWW, FM's Papers.
13 EFG to WSW, Jun 8, 1903, Box 1, Folder 2, EFG Corr. with WSW, FM's Papers. Also EFG to WSW, Jul 13, 1903, Box 1, Folder 2, EFG Corr. with WSW, FM's Papers; "$12,000 for a Hackney," *New York Sun*, Feb 4, 1897, Scrapbook vol. XIII, 127; "Big Sales of Harness Horses," *New York Sun*, Nov 20, 1899, Scrapbook vol. XXI, 149.
14 JWW to EFG, Jun 12, 1910, EFG Corr. with JWW, FM's Papers.
15 EFG to WSW, Feb 17, 1903, EFG Corr. with WSW, FM's Papers.
16 Ibid.
17 EFG to WSW, undated draft, starting "W.S.W. I was at A. attend [sic] a farm Tuesday," Box 2, Folder 6, EFG Corr. with WSW, FM's Papers.
18 A review of the Farm's financial accounts suggests that WSW and LOW spent approximately $450,000 on a renovated and expanded Shelburne House, rather than an estimated $1.5 million to $3 million for a more elaborate dwelling. Ledgers, 1895–1900, FM's Papers; "Seward Webb's Proposed Castle, The Largest Private Residence In America," *Chicago Post*, Sep 1, 1893, Scrapbook vol. XI, 121; "His Home To Be A Grand Palace: Dr. Webb's Plans for the Finest Residence In The World," *New York Press*, Jun 24, 1894, Scrapbook vol. XI, 103.
19 There is some indication that the *Elfrida* may have been sold to JWW in 1916, before it was sold out of the family. See 1903–18 letters in EFG Corr., EFG Corr. with JWW, and EFG Corr. with LOW, all in FM's Papers; JWW, various entries in 1912, 1913, and 1917 diaries, JWW Jr. Coll.; Joe Jackson, Librarian of New York Yacht Club, to author, Mar 13, 2000.
20 WSW to EFG, Feb 26, 1921, "WH to WI" Folder, FM's Papers. Also WSW to Mr. J. W. Wardlaw, General Manager of Central Vermont Railroad, Feb 4, 1920, same location.
21 *Springfield (MA) Union*, Oct 22, 1891, Scrapbook vol. VIII, 78; "Camp Col. Webb," *BFP*, Aug 17, 1896, Scrapbook vol. XIII, 108; David J. Blow, *Historic Guide to Burlington Neighborhoods*, vol. 1 (Burlington, VT: Chittenden County Historical Society, 1991), 85; and the following in FM's Papers: EFG to JWW, Dec 23, 1914, and Feb 8, 1915, Folder 313A, EFG Corr., EFG to Dave H. Morris, Esq., Oct 6 and 30, 1913, M-4 Folder, JWW to EFG, Jul 5, 1911, and EFG to JWW, Jul 5, 1911, both in Jul–Dec 1911 Folder, EFG Corr. with JWW.
22 EFG to LOW, Oct 31, 1905, Folder 12, and GK to EFG, Aug 15, 1905, Folder 13, and Folder 29, passim, all in EFG Corr., FM's Papers; EFG to WSW, Aug 22, 1905, EFG Corr. with WSW, FM's Papers; Jerry E. Patterson, *Fifth Avenue: The Best Address* (New York: Rizzoli, 1998), 147; Robert A. M. Stern, Gregory Gilmartin, and John Massengale, *New York 1900: Metropolitan Architecture and Urbanism 1890–1915* (New York: Rizzoli, 1995), 312.
23 Numerous architectural features were salvaged from the dwelling after the fire and reused in Shelburne House, the Brick House, and JWW and EHW's country house on Long Island (JWW to VW, Apr 28, 1913, and May 17, 1913, VW Papers, Edwin D. Worcester to LOW, May 1, 1913, and May 27, 1913, Folder 2, Business Papers Coll., LOW Papers; and Julie Eldridge Edwards, "The Evolution of Electra Havemeyer Webb's Country Estate, The Brick House, 1913–1917," unpublished master's thesis for the Masters Program in the History of Decorative Arts, Cooper-Hewitt, National Design Museum and Parsons School of Design, 15, 21). Quote in text from LOW, May 1, 1913, 1913 Diary, LOW Papers. Also unsigned Deed of Sale between LOW and John D. Rockefeller Jr., Feb 20, 1913, Folder 44, Deed Box Coll., LOW Papers; "Policeman Saves Dr. Webb From Fire," New York area newspaper, undated clipping, FM's Papers; LOW to EFG, passim, EFG Corr. with LOW, FM's Papers; LOW to VW, passim, 1912–13, VW Papers; JWW, various entries for Jan–Mar, 1913 Diary, JWW Jr. Coll.
24 LOW to VW, Easter Sunday, [1913], VW Papers. Also "Dr. Webb Has 10-Year Lease on $15,000 Flat," *New York Tribune*, Mar 23, 1913, FM's Papers; JWW, Mar 28, 1913, 1913 Diary, JWW Jr. Coll. The Webbs lived at 903 Park Avenue until 1923, when they moved to 270 Park Avenue (LOW, Apr 12, Jun 8, Jun 12, Aug 1–2, Sep 25–29, all in 1923 Diary, LOW Papers).
25 FK to American Jersey Cattle Club, Jul 28 and Jul 31, 1924, FK General Corr., 1924–32, FM's Papers. Also EFG to WSW, Jun 27, 1913, EFG Corr. with WSW, FM's Papers; "Pay Roll Record House Servants From Apr 1903," 15, Box 4, FM's Papers.
26 EFG to LOW, Nov 5, Nov 14, and Nov 16, 1910, and Aug 25, 1913, EFG Corr. with LOW, FM's Papers.
27 JWW, Jul 25, 1913, 1913 Diary. JWW attended Groton School in Groton, Massachusetts, from 1898 to 1904 and then attended Yale University from 1904 to 1907. He was employed by the Chicago & Northwestern Railroad in Milwaukee and Chicago from 1909 to 1910 (LOW, Jan 6, 1909, 1909 Diary, LOW Papers; Ruth Lawrence, ed., *Webb and Allied Family Histories: A Documented Compilation of Genealogy and Biography* (New York: National Americana Society, 1937), 103; JWW, Mar 10 and 24, 1913, 1913 Diary, JWW Jr. Coll.).
28 JWW to EFG, Mar 23, 1905, 1903–05 Folder, EFG Corr. with JWW, FM's Papers. Also JWW to EFG, Jan 26, 1907, Jan–Apr 1907 Folder, and EFG to WSW, Apr 10, 1908, Jan–Apr 1908 Folder, both in same location.
29 JWW to EFG, Oct 23, 1910, 1910 Folder, EFG Corr. with JWW, FM's Papers.
30 WSW to VW, Sep 29, 1904, VW Papers. Also A. Taylor to John McNabb, Sep 25, 1902, Folder 9, EFG Corr., FM's Papers; JWW, Jul 12, 1904, 1904 Diary, JWW Jr. Coll.; A. Henry Higginson and Julian Ingersoll Chamberlain, *Hunting in the United States and Canada* (Garden City, New Jersey: Doubleday, Doran & Company, 1928), 54–57; SBW Jr., Oral History Interview, Aug 26, 1997, rev. Oct 1997, Audio Recordings, SMA.
31 SBW Sr., quoted in Alexander Mackay-Smith, *Masters of Foxhounds* (Masters of Foxhounds Association of America, Inc., 1980), 105. A skilled left-handed player, JWW would continue to play polo into his forties, becoming "one of the great outstanding figures in the game of polo both in this country and in England…He played the No. 3 position for America on the victorious International Polo Team of 1921…He also played the No. 1 position against England on the winning United States International Teams of 1924 and 1927, then retiring from International Polo" (Lawrence, 103). JWW was named to the American Polo Hall of Fame in 1991. Higginson and Chamberlain, 54–57; JWW, Apr 18, Jun 29, and Jul 3, 1904, 1904 Diary, JWW Jr. Coll.; LOW, Jul 24, 1904, 1904

Diary, and Jun 18, 1921, 1921 Diary, both in LOW Papers; Julie Eldridge Edwards to author, Oct 1, 2004.

32 JWW to EFG, undated [1906], beginning, "I have sent back horse list which was nearly correct," Undated Folder, EFG Corr. with JWW, FM's Papers.

33 JWW to EFG, Apr 1907, Jan–Apr 1907 Folder, EFG Corr. with JWW, FM's Papers. Also JWW to LOW, Feb 17, 1907, Folder 15, Family Papers Coll., LOW Papers, and the following sources from EFG Corr. with JWW, FM's Papers: Arthur King to JWW, Feb 18, 1906, and JWW to EFG, Feb 21, 1906, 1906 Folder; EFG to JWW, Jan 30, 1907, Jan–Apr 1907 Folder; JWW to EFG, Jul 21, 1911, Jul–Dec 1911 Folder.

34 "Horses given to Mr. J. Watson Webb, by Dr. & Mrs. Webb, Oct 12th, & values of Jan 1, 1912," 1912 Folder, EFG Corr. with JWW, FM's Papers.

35 JWW to EFG, Apr 1907 letter beginning, "Dear Mr. Gebhardt, I hope every thing is going well on the farm," Jan–Apr 1907 Folder, EFG Corr. with JWW, FM's Papers.

36 EFG to JWW, Apr 15, 1907, Jan–Apr 1907 Folder, EFG Corr. with JWW, FM's Papers.

37 JWW to James W. Appleton, Aug 18, 1911, Jul–Dec 1911 Folder, EFG Corr. with JWW, FM's Papers.

38 JWW to EFG, Jan 8, 1911, Jan–Jun 1911 Folder, EFG Corr. with JWW, FM's Papers. Also, in general, EFG Corr. with JWW for 1911, FM's Papers.

39 JWW to EFG, Feb 5, 1912, 1912 Folder, EFG Corr. with JWW, FM's Papers.

40 JWW, Feb 15, 1916, 1916 Diary, JWW Jr. Coll. The 1913 personal income tax law authorized the collection of 5% of incomes between $100,000 and $250,000, 6% of incomes between $250,000 and $500,000, and 7% of incomes over $500,000. It is unclear exactly what WSW and LOW's annual income totaled at this time, but it is likely that they paid between $6,000 and $35,000 in taxes each year, certainly a substantial amount. Steven R. Weisman, *The Great Tax Wars: Lincoln to Wilson—The Fierce Battles over Money and Power That Transformed the Nation* (New York: Simon & Schuster, 2002), passim.

41 DNT to VW, Sep 18, 1941, FM's Corr. with VW, 1938–55, FM's Papers.

42 LOW to VW, Sep 11, 1919, Box 1, Folder 3, VW Papers.

43 JWW also served a term as state representative for Shelburne from 1921 to 1922 (Lawrence, 103; Lauren B. Hewes and Celia Y. Oliver, *To Collect in Earnest: The Life and Work of Electra Havemeyer Webb* [Shelburne, VT: Shelburne Museum, 1997], passim). JWW, Jan 3, 1910, 1910 Diary, Dec 8, 1912, 1912 Diary, and various diary entries through 1949, JWW Jr. Coll.; JWW to FK, Dec 5, 1923, Folder 3, "Some of Mr. J. W. Webb's Letters to Mr. Kendzior July 1923 to 1931 Originally Kept in Drawer of Mr. K's Desk," FM's Papers (hereafter referred to as "Some of Mr. J. W. Webb's Letters"); Edwards, "Evolution," 4–20, 22, 58–60; Hewes and Oliver, 1–2, 12; Frances Weitzenhoffer, *The Havemeyers: Impressionism Comes To America* (New York: Harry N. Abrams, 1986): 213; Freya Carlbom, "James W. O'Connor," in Robert B. MacKay, Anthony Baker, and Carol A. Traynor, eds., *Long Island Country Houses and Their Architects, 1860–1940* (New York: W. W. Norton and Society for the Preservation of Long Island Antiquities, 1997), 314; SBW Jr., comments on draft manuscript, Nov 15, 2006, and Transcript of Oral History Interview, SMA; Polly Darnell, comments on draft manuscript, May 1, 2007.

44 JWW, Jan 3, 1910, 1910 Diary, JWW Jr. Coll.

45 JWW, Sep 15, 1912, 1912 Diary, JWW Jr. Coll.

46 Deed, WSW and LOW to JWW, Apr 9, 1913, Misc. Papers Coll., LOW Papers. Also LOW to VW, Nov 4, 1912, VW Papers.

47 Lawrence, 104; "Webb Family Genealogy," 2001, SFC.

48 VW clerked at Root, Clark, Buckner, and Howland and later served as a partner in three successive firms: (1) Milbank, Tweed, Hope & Webb; (2) Curtis, Belknap & Webb; and (3) Patterson, Belknap & Webb. Lawrence, 104–105; "Webb Family Genealogy;" JWW, Sep 17, 1915, 1915 Diary, JWW Jr. Coll.; AOW, "Almost a Century," unpublished 1977 memoir, 27–28, passim, SFC; Princeton University, "Who was William Church Osborn?" http://www.princeton.edu/~arnold/other/william_church_osborn.htm; and MCW, comments on draft Chapter 9, Jan 2009. Also the following from FM's Corr. with VW, 1922–35, FM's Papers: VW to FK, Jul 16, 1924, VW Folder 1; VW to FK, Jun 9, 1925, Jun 12, 1925, and Jun 23, 1925, all in VW Folder 2; FK to VW, Jul 31, 1925, VW Folder 2; FK to VW, Jun 27 and Jul 6, 1931, VW Folder 3; VW to FK, Nov 13, 1933, VW Folder 4.

49 During the 1910s, it appears that Bay View House was also significantly renovated, or the original 19th-century farmhouse was possibly demolished and a new structure built in its place (JWW Jr., "Pictorial History," 87–89, JWW Jr. Coll.). Quote from AOW, "Almost A Century," 55. Also VW to LOW, Aug 31, 1927, Estate Papers Coll., LOW Papers; AOW, Transcript of Oral History Interview with EWW, 27.

50 AOW, Transcript of Oral History Interview, 27.

51 Ibid, 27–28.

52 WSW Jr. to VW, undated, Box 1, Folder 6, VW Papers. For VW's management of Orchard House and surrounding property, see VW to EFG, May 25, 1914, and Jun 14, 1914, Vaughan to VW, Jun 19, 1917, and VW to Vaughan, Jun 22, 1917, all in Folder 314, EFG Corr., FM's Papers; JWW, Jul 11, 1914, 1914 Diary and Apr 21, 1916, 1916 Diary, JWW Jr. Coll.

53 EFG to WSW Jr., Mar 13, 1919, Folder 319, EFG Corr., FM's Papers; LOW to VW, Sep 11, 1919, and Sep 17, 1919, Box 1, Folder 7, VW Papers; WSW Jr. to EFG, Feb 29 and Mar 6, 1920, and EFG to WSW Jr., Mar 3 and Mar 9, 1920, "WH to WI" Folder 1, FM's Papers.

54 Webb & Knapp allied with the architect Elliot B. Cross on real estate development projects (Michael Adams, "Cross & Cross, 1907–1940, John Walter Cross, 1878–1951, Eliot B. Cross, 1884–1949," in MacKay et al., 122). LOW, Mar 31, 1920, 1920 Diary, LOW Papers.

55 JWW, Oct 28, 1915, 1915 Diary, and Feb 6, Mar 1, Mar 2, and Mar 20, 1921, 1921 Diary, both in JWW Jr. Coll.; LOW to Ludvik Schwab, May 20, 1933, Folder 15, Business Papers Coll., LOW Papers; SBW Sr., "Statement," in William C. Lipke, ed., *Shelburne Farms: The History of an Agricultural Estate* (Burlington, VT: UVM, 1979), 52. Also the following from the FM's Papers: EFG to JWW, Apr 25, 1906, 1906 Folder, JWW to EFG, May 26, 1913, 1913 Folder, and JWW to EFG, Jan 9, 1914, 1914 Folder, all in EFG Corr. with JWW; VW to FK, Jan 11, 1926, VW Folder 2, FM's Corr. with VW, 1922–35; JWW to FK, May 6, 1929, Folder 4, FK Corr. with JWW; Invoice, E. F. Hodgson Co., Boston, MA, Jun 1922, EFG to WSW, Jul 3 and Nov 29, 1922, and Receipt, SF to Orchard Poultry Farm, Aug 31, 1922, all in "WH to WI" Folder 2, FK Corr.

56 "Ralph Pulitzer, 60, Dies In Hospital," *New York Times*, Jun 15, 1939; Freya Carlbom, "James W. O'Connor," Karen Morey Kennedy, "Walker & Gilette," and Keith N. Morgan, "Charles A. Platt, 1861–1933," all in MacKay et al., 314, 352, 423–24.

57 It remains unclear exactly why WSW and LOW sold Oakledge to FVP rather than giving the property to her. She occupied the house at Oakledge only during short visits to the area in 1921 and 1922, and she sold the estate to a consortium of Burlington businessmen in 1926. The main house was subsequently used as a private club and a hotel until c. 1970. The historic structures on the property were all demolished or burned as training exercises for the Burlington Fire Department in the 1970s (Blow, 85; Stu Perry, "Oakledge History Passes to Bulldozers," *BFP*, May 13, 1975; "Training Exercise," *BFP*, Jun 5, 1975). Draft deed of sale, LOW to FVP, Dec 1921, Box 1, Folder 6, Legal Papers, FM's Papers; LOW, Apr 23–24, Jun 4, and Jun 7, 1921, 1921 Diary, and Aug 2, 1922, 1922 Diary, LOW Papers; Carolyn Hodgdon and John Carpenter Colls., Oakledge Reference Files; and the following from the FM's Papers: VW and FK corr., Jan–Apr 1926, VW Folder 2, FK Corr. with VW; Charles F. Wolfe to FK, Apr 14, 1926, Folder WI to Z, FK Corr.

58 "Mrs. Ralph Pulitzer To Wed Son's Tutor," *New York Times*, Jun 29, 1924; "Mrs. Pulitzer Weds Cyril Jones Today," *New York Times*, Aug 12, 1924; "Mrs. Pulitzer Weds Cyril Hamlen Jones," *New York Times*, Aug 13, 1924; copies of materials from Milton Academy Archives, in "Jones, Cyril Hamlen" Reference File, especially "The Associate Head Master," *Milton Bulletin*, Feb 1941, 25.

59 JWW, Jul 6, 1912, 1912 Diary, JWW Jr. Coll. See also the entry for the following day, Jul 7.

60 JWW, entries for Jul and Aug 1912 (quote from Jul 6), 1912 Diary, JWW Jr. Coll.

61 JWW, Sep 22, 1908, 1908 Diary, JWW Jr. Coll. Also JWW, note on front endpaper, 1913 Diary, JWW Jr. Coll.; and Interest notesheet, c. 1890, Box 2, Folder 1, Legal Papers, FM's Papers. The author is grateful to Julie Eldridge Edwards for sharing her research about the Brick House, which greatly informed this discussion of the JWWs' use and modifications of the dwelling.

62 EHW, quoted in Julie Eldridge Edwards, "The Brick House, the Vermont Country House of Electra Havemeyer Webb," *The Magazine Antiques* CLXIII (Jan 2003), 194. Also EFG to JWW, Nov 14, 1908, May–Dec 1908 Folder, EFG Corr. with JWW, FM's Papers.

63 Edwards, "Evolution," 14–15 (quote on 15). Also EFG to JWW, Jul 9 and 22, 1913, and JWW to EFG, Aug 7, 1913, all in 1913 Folder, EFG Corr. with JWW, FM's Papers; JWW, Jul 9, 1912, and subsequent entries, 1912 Diary, JWW Jr. Coll.; Edwards, "The Brick House," 194; Adams, "Cross & Cross, …" in MacKay et al., 122–24; and the following from FFD 11, APMI: "Plan of McNeil's House, Shelburne Farms," 2004.3.31.12 and 2004.3.31.13 (Folder 2); Cross & Cross, "Alteration & Addition to the House of J.W. Webb Esq., Shelburne, Vt.," 2004.3.31.1 and 2004.3.31.2 (Folder 1).

64 JWW, Oct 5, 1913, 1913 Diary, JWW Jr. Coll. Also JWW to VW, Apr 28, 1913, VW Papers; JWW, Jun 1, Jun 9, Sep 13, Sep 16–20, and Nov 7–8, 1913, 1913 Diary, JWW Jr. Coll.; and the following in the FM's Papers: EFG to JWW, Apr 15, 1913, and JWW to EFG, Apr 28 and Aug 7, 1913, all in 1913 Folder, EFG Corr. with JWW; Folders 48 & 59, passim, EFG Corr.

65 Edwards, "Evolution," 22–25.

66 Edwards, "Evolution," 26–28; JWW, diary entries, passim, JWW Jr. Coll.

67 Ralph S. Bailey, "Estates of American Sportsmen: I. The country seat of Mr. Watson Webb at Shelburne Farms, Vermont," *Sportsman* 4 (Dec 1928): 42, in Album #80, JWW Jr. Coll.

68 EHW's collecting activities at the Brick House and elsewhere (she also decorated Westbury House in a similar manner to the Brick House) and their significance in the field of American decorative arts are explored in greater depth by Julie Eldridge Edwards in her thesis, "The Evolution of Electra Havemeyer Webb's Country Estate." See also Hewes and Oliver, 14–15; Weitzenhoffer, 213–14.

69 EHW, "What Started Me With The Museum," 1952, Box 1, Folder 2, EHW Papers, SMA. The Captain White House was most likely one of two dwellings owned by Capt. Lavater S. White that appear on the northern end of Shelburne Point in an 1869 Map of Shelburne (Frederick F. W. Beers, *Atlas of Chittenden County, Vermont* [New York, 1869]; a third house belonging to a member of the White family, the residence of Robert J. White, appears on the Beers map just to the south of the other two dwellings). Capt. White's grandson, Lavater E. White, described one of the two buildings as a "log block house" built by family ancestor Nathan White in the late eighteenth century, and the other as constructed c. 1816. Lavater E. White states that the latter house was demolished "a few years after the Webb's [sic] bought the property because it had been permitted to be run down to such an extent" (Lavater E. White to Ruth Roberts, Shelburne Town Clerk, Jun 28, 1933, White Family Folder, Genealogy Records, STC). It is possible that White misremembered the date of demolition, as the building known by members of the Webb family as the Captain White House remained extant, albeit in very poor condition, in 1929.

70 JWW, Mar 17, Oct 23, and Nov 6, 1913, 1913 Diary; Jul 18, 1914, 1914 Diary; May 17, 1915, 1915 Diary, and May 9, 1917, 1917 Diary, all in JWW Jr. Coll.; R. S. Towers to EFG, Jun 2, 1914, 1914 Folder, EFG Corr. with JWW, FM's Papers; Bailey, 42, 74.

71 Howard S. Russell, *A Long, Deep Furrow: Three Centuries of Farming in New England* (Hanover, NH: University Press of New England, 1982), 286, 357; Timothy Lathrop Miller, *History of Hereford Cattle, Proven Conclusively The Oldest of Improved Breeds* (Chillicothe, MO: T. F. B. Sotham, 1902), passim.

72 "Deaths and Funerals: Alexander Morrison," *BFP*, Mar 19, 1965.

73 In fact, "the cattle won everything where entered" at the Middlebury, VT, fair and "seven prizes out of eight entries" in the VT State Fair at White River Junction, both held in Sep 1915 (JWW, Sep 4, 1915, 1915 Diary, JWW Jr. Coll.). The following are all in JWW Jr. Coll.: JWW, Nov 21, 1915, 1915 Diary; Sep 13, Nov 26, Dec 17, and Dec 30, 1916, 1916 Diary; and Apr 9 and May 21–22, 1917, 1917 Diary; Mar 6, and Mar 19–20, 1921, 1921 Diary. The following are all in the FM's Papers: JWW to Fred Davis, Jan 23, 1923, Folder "D to E," Box 2, FM's Corr.; FK to E. S. Brigham, VT Commissioner of Agriculture, Feb 4, 1924, Folder "Bo-C," Box 2, FM's Corr.; Advertisement for Southern Acres Farm Herefords in *Hereford Journal*, 1923, Folder 4, "Some of Mr. J. W. Webb's Letters." Also "Vermont State Fair Opens Its Program To-Day," *BFP*, Sep 14, 1916; "17,000 People Present At Big Fair's Third Day," *BFP*, Sep 17, 1916; Bailey, 42.

74 JWW, *Hunters from Southern Acres Farm Shelburne, Vermont, 1915*, 2–3, KWH Coll.; JWW, Sep 30 and Dec 14, 1915, 1915 Diary, Dec 3, 1916, 1916 Diary, and Oct 30, 1934, 1934 Diary, all in JWW Jr. Coll.

75 JWW, Nov 20, 1933, 1933 Diary, JWW Jr. Coll.

76 JWW, "The Shelburne Terrier, a New Breed," *The Sportsman*

(Jul 1927): 76; J. Stanley Reeve, "The Country Gentleman and His Hounds," *Country Life*, LXVII, No. 1 (Nov 1934): 54; JWW, Sep 28–29, 1914, 1914 Diary, and Oct 24, 1915, 1915 Diary, JWW Jr. Coll.; Higginson and Chamberlain, 54–57.

77 SBW Jr. recalled that in later years, the Shelburne Foxhounds consisted of as many as 60 couples, or pairs: 30 couples of bitches and 30 couples of dogs, hunted separately (SBW Jr., comments on draft manuscript, Nov 15, 2006). Quote from JWW, "The Shelburne Terrier," 76. Also JWW, Nov 7, 1915, 1915 Diary, Jan 15, 1916, 1916 Diary, and Jan 12, 1930, 1930 Diary, all in JWW Jr. Coll.

78 Higginson and Chamberlain, 54–57.

79 See, for instance, JWW, Nov 6, 1914, 1914 Diary, Nov 16–17, 1915, 1915 Diary, and Jul 15, 16, and 25, 1916, 1916 Diary, JWW Jr. Coll.

80 JWW, Oct 27, 1928, 1928 Diary, JWW Jr. Coll. For additional accounts of foxhunting experiences, see JWW's *Shelburne Hounds Accounts of Runs*, 1906–10, KWH Coll.; JWW and EHW, *Hunting Journal*, 1922–32, JWW Jr. Coll.; and A. Henry Higginson, *Try Back: A Huntsman's Reminiscences* (New York: Huntington Press, 1931), 48–51.

81 FK to Free Press Association, Apr 9, 1923, Folder F to G, Box 2, FK Corr., FM's Papers. Also SBW Jr., Transcript of Oral History Interview, SMA; "Boundaries of the Country of the Shelburne Foxhounds," Jun 1939, 2004.3.22.21, and Map of Chittenden County with JWW notations of hunts, 1912–19, 2004.3.22.22, both in FFD 17, Folder 1, APMI; JWW, "Notice," in May–Dec 1908 Folder, EFG Corr. with JWW, FM's Papers; LOW, Nov 17, 1923, 1923 Diary, LOW Papers; JWW to "Friend," Oct 9, 1926, KWH Coll.; and JWW, Nov 21, 1930, 1930 Diary, JWW Jr. Coll.

82 FK to JWW, Sep 12, 1928, 1926–28, Folder 4, FK Corr. with JWW, FM's Papers. Also, Jim St. George, Interview, "Shelburne, Vermont, Historic Settlement Oral History Project," c. 2002, VDHP.

83 JWW to FK, Sep 19, 1928, Folder 4, FK Corr. with JWW, FM's Papers; SBW Jr., comments on draft manuscript, Nov 15, 2006.

84 JWW, Feb 22, 1914, 1914 Diary, JWW Jr. Coll.

85 JWW, Feb 1, 1935, 1935 Diary, JWW Jr. Coll. Also JWW, Feb 24, 1916, 1916 Diary, Sep 26, 1935, 1935 Diary, and Jul 3, 1936, 1936 Diary, all in JWW Jr. Coll.; Higginson and Chamberlain, 54–57.

86 Mackay-Smith, 101.

87 JWW, Apr 12, Apr 26, and Aug 21, 1914, 1914 Diary, Jan 1, May 23, and Nov 21, 1915, 1915 Diary, and Aug 18, 1917, 1917 Diary, all in JWW Jr. Coll.; SBW Jr., Oral History Interview, Oct 31, 2006; *Sanborn Insurance Map* for Burlington, VT, May 1919, sheet 39, Special Collections Dept., Bailey/Howe Library, UVM.

88 Bailey, 42. JWW also replaced the building's roof in 1915 (JWW to VW, Feb 29, 1932, Folder 4, FK Corr. with VW, FM's Papers). Also JWW, Sep 28 and Oct 6–7, 1913, 1913 Diary; Aug 22, Oct 16, and Oct 31, 1914, 1914 Diary; Oct 8, 1915, 1915 Diary; Jan 16 and Aug 7, 1916, 1916 Diary, all in JWW Jr. Coll.; JWW to FK, Mar 1 and Mar 7, 1923, Folder 3, "Some of Mr. J.W. Webb's Letters," and JWW to FK, [c. Dec 1926], Folder 4, FK Corr. with JWW, both in FM's Papers; SBW Jr., Oral History Interview, Oct 31, 2006.

89 Whippers-in typically serve under the huntsman and also often assist with controlling the foxhounds during the hunt. A section of the colt shed structure located behind the Breeding Barn may also have been used as a kennels until the 1928 building was erected (*Sanborn Insurance Maps* for Burlington, VT, May 1919, sheet 39, and Apr 1926, sheet 39, Special Collections Dept., Bailey/Howe Library, UVM). Bailey, 42; JWW, Oct 20 and Dec 8, 1912, 1912 Diary, Feb 8, 1913, 1913 Diary, JWW Jr. Coll.; EHW to VW Dec 11, 1912, VW Papers.

90 JWW, Sep 7, 1912, 1912 Diary, JWW Jr. Coll.. Also, for example, JWW to EFG, Feb 13, 1911, Jan–Jun 1911 Folder, Aug 15, 1912, and Sep 16, 1912, 1912 Folder, Jan 18, 1913, Apr 2, 1913, and Jun 20, 1913, 1913 Folder, all in EFG Corr. with JWW, FM's Papers; EFG to JWW, Apr 3 and Apr 15, 1913, 1913 Folder, EFG Corr. with JWW, FM's Papers.

91 FK to John Earley, Jan 18, 1926, Folder "E to F," Box 2, FM's Corr., FM's Papers. Also JWW to FK, Jan 3, 1923 [erroneously dated 1922], Folder 5, "Some of Mr. J.W. Webb's Letters," FM's Papers.

92 At the time of this writing, biographical information for R. S. Towers had yet to be located. SAF went without a farm manager several times between its establishment in 1913 and the 1950s; during these periods, JWW filled the role himself or asked the farm manager at SF to supervise. When FK was hired in 1923, for example, he assumed most managerial responsibilities for SAF as well as SF. JWW, Mar 17, 1913, 1913 Diary, and May 17, 1915, 1915 Diary, JWW Jr. Coll.; and the following from the FM's Papers: R. S. Towers to EFG, Jun 2, 1914, 1914 Folder, EFG Corr. with JWW; FK to R. S. Towers, Jan 23, 1923, Folder "T to U," FK Corr.; payroll information comparing Jul 1922 to Jul 1923, Folder 4, JWW to FK, Jan 3, 1923 [erroneously dated 1922], Folder 5, FK to JWW, Jan 15, 1923, Folder 8, and JWW and VW, general notice to farm employees re transfer of responsibility to FK, c. 1922, Folder 8, all in "Some of Mr. J.W. Webb's Letters," FM's Papers; JWW to Southern Acres Farm Managers, Aug 24, 1928, Folder 4, FK Corr. with JWW.

93 JWW to Horace Smith, Dec 21, 1955, Unprocessed Coll., flat file, KWH Coll. Also "Dies Suddenly While Exercising Horse," *BFP*, Jul 1, 1930; "Obituary: W. Harry Hopkins," *BFP*, Jul 2, 1930; "Obituary: Funerals Yesterday and Today," *BFP*, Jul 3, 1930; JWW to Horace Smith, Nov 15, 1955, and Horace Smith to JWW, Dec 1, 1955, both in Unprocessed Coll., Flat File, KWH Coll.; "Hopkins, W.H.," in "Breeding Barns," Employee Record Book, Box 20, 130 and 145, FM's Papers; JWW, Jun 30, 1930, 1930 Diary, Apr 10 and Jul 3, 1931, 1931 Diary, and Oct 14, 1932, 1932 Diary, all in JWW Jr. Coll.

94 JWW, Jul 17, 1916, 1916 Diary, JWW Jr. Coll.

95 JWW, Jul 12, 1913, 1913 Diary, JWW Jr. Coll..

96 According to SBW Jr., JWW also paid for the maintenance of Nehasane with his personal funds after he acquired the property in the 1930s (SBW Jr., Oral History Interview, Oct 31, 2006). Quote from JWW, Jan 13, 1916, 1916 Diary, JWW Jr. Coll.

97 JWW, Nov 23, 1933, 1933 Diary, JWW Jr. Coll.

98 JWW never fully retired from his insurance work but instead slowly decreased the amount of work he performed for his company until, in the last years of his life, he went into the office only rarely. See JWW diaries, passim, JWW Jr. Coll.; SBW Jr., comments on draft manuscript, Nov 15, 2006.

99 Lawrence, 103–5; AOW, "Almost A Century," 44–46.

100 JWW also participated in the Nassau County Home Defense League and Farm Bureau before he volunteered for military service. In 1917, the Committee on Convalescent Hospitals was disbanded, as it was decided not to rely upon private homes in case of war. Quote from unidentified author, possibly EFG,

undated typewritten manuscript filed between letters dated Jul 14 and Sep 5, 1917, EFG Corr. with LOW, FM's Papers. Also FVP to LOW, Aug 6–Aug 18, 1914, Folder 20, Family Papers Coll., LOW Papers; Lawrence, 103–5; JWW, 1917–1919 Diaries, JWW Jr. Coll.; and Committee on Convalescent Hospitals to LOW, Jun 14, 1916, LOW to Committee, c. Jun 20, 1916, LOW to Mrs. Edward McCauley Jr., Aug 23, 1916, and Mrs. Edward McCauley Jr. to LOW, Mar 15, 1917, all in Folder 3, Business Papers, LOW Papers.

101 LOW, Dec 25, 1917, 1914–19 Diary, LOW Papers.
102 LOW to EFG, Jan 20–21, 1918, EFG Corr. with LOW, FM's Papers.
103 EFG to WSW Jr., Feb 4, 1918, Folder 319, EFG Corr., FM's Papers. Also J. H. Lynch to EFG, Dec 15, 1917, and EFG to J. H. Lynch, Dec 19, 1917, both in Folder 313B, EFG Corr., FM's Papers.
104 EFG to VW, Aug 28, 1918, Folder 314, EFG Corr., FM's Papers.
105 EFG to LOW, Apr 20, 1918, EFG Corr. with LOW, FM's Papers.
106 LOW to EFG, Jan 20, 1918, EFG Corr. with LOW, FM's Papers.
107 EFG to GK, Dec 21, 1917, GK Folder, FM's Corr. with VW, 1922–35, FM's Papers.
108 John M. Barry, *The Great Influenza: The Epic Story of the Deadliest Plague in History* (New York: Viking, 2004), 234–39; Gina Kolata, *Flu: The Story of the Great Influenza Pandemic of 1918 and the Search for the Virus That Caused It* (New York: Farrar, Straus, and Giroux, 1999), passim.
109 EFG to LOW, Jan 6, 1919, EFG Corr. with LOW, FM's Papers. Also AOW, "Almost A Century," 47.
110 "Obituary: Howard S. Vosberg [sic]," *BFP*, Dec 23, 1918; and the following in the FM's Papers: EFG to AOW, Dec 24, 1918, Folder 314, EFG Corr.; EHW to EFG, Dec 28, 1918, Folder 313B, EFG Corr.; EFG to LOW, Jan 6 and Jan 22, 1919, EFG Corr. with LOW; "Vosburgh, Howard," Employee Record Book, 119, Box 20.

Chapter 11

1 LOW, "Christmas Greeting, 1922," Oakledge/Shelburne House Guestbook, 356.
2 LOW to JWW, Jan 16, 1921, Folder 24, LOW Family Papers. Also LOW to JWW, Jan 21, 1921, in same location.
3 VW to LOW, Aug 31, 1927, and LOW, Apr 17, 1922, 1922 Diary, both in LOW Papers; and the following from the FM's Papers: "Articles of Association of the Shelburne Farms Corporation," Apr 15, 1922, "Affidavit as to Proposed Issue of Capital Stock of Shelburne Farms Corporation," Apr 19, 1922, and By-laws of the Shelburne Farms Corporation, Apr 17, 1922, all in SF Corp. Records, 1922–39; VW to DNT, Sep 26, 1939, Box 2, Folder 9, Legal Papers; EFG to Wm. H. Caldwell, Secretary, American Guernsey Cattle Club, Aug 26, 1922; EFG to WSW, Nov 28, 1922, "WH to WI" Folder 2, FK Corr.; Guy M. Pageto to VW, Jul 22, 1922, Folder "PQ to R," FK Corr.; FK to John Lynch of Vander Poel, Pausner and Webb, Sep 10, 1931, Folder "T to U," FK Corr.; DNT, "Minutes of Meeting of Stockholders of Shelburne Farms Corporation," Nov 26, 1931, and "Minutes of Special Meeting of Directors of Shelburne Farms Corporation," Nov 26, 1931, both in Folder 3, FK Corr. with VW; VW to DNT, Sep 26, 1939, SF Corp. Corr., 1938–55.
4 DNT, "Minutes of Meeting," and "Minutes of Special Meeting," both in Folder 3, FK Corr. with VW, FM's Papers.
5 At this time, in the early 1920s, the family also began to consider the possibility of converting Shelburne House into a private club or inn after the elder Webbs' deaths. However, JWW considered the idea impractical, and it would be shelved until the early 1940s (Undated, typed scrap of paper, with note from JWW to VW at bottom, Folder 24 [1921], LOW Family Papers Coll., LOW Papers). EFG to F. S. Springer, Secretary, American Southdown Association, Aug 1, 1922, Folder "S-4", EFG Corr., FM's Papers; "Agreement Between Shelburne Farms Corporation and the Holders of the Common Stock Thereof," Jun 9, 1922, SF Corp. Records, 1922–39, FM's Papers; LOW to JWW, Jan 16, 22, and 24, 1921, and JWW to LOW, Feb 8, 1921, all in Folder 24, LOW Family Papers, LOW Papers; JWW, Feb 5, 1921, 1921 Diary, JWW Jr. Coll.
6 LOW to EFG, draft letter, c. 1922, Folder 17, Deed Box Coll., LOW Papers.
7 "E.F. Gebhardt Dies at Age of 83 After Long Illness," *BFP*, Jan 5, 1942.
8 At the time of this writing, little biographical information about FK (born about 1884–85) is known. For FK, see 1930 United States Population Census records for Shelburne, Chittenden County, VT, Microfilm #1479, Bailey/Howe Library, UVM; JWW and VW, general notice to farm employees re transfer of responsibility to FK, c. 1922, and JWW to James W. Hall, American Audit Company, Dec 29, 1922, both in Folder 8, "Some of Mr. J. W. Webb's Letters," FM's Papers; VW, letter of recommendation for FK, Sep 1935, SF Corp. Corr., 1933–55, FM's Papers. For interviews of other candidates for the position, see LOW, Apr 18, 1922, 1922 Diary, LOW Papers.
9 FK to VW, Jun 10, 1925, Folder 3, FK Corr. with VW, FM's Papers.
10 FK to W. H. Tomhave, Apr 4, 1923, Folder "T to U," FK Corr., FM's Papers. Also FK to E. S. Brigham, VT Commissioner of Agriculture, Jun 23, 1924, Folder "Bo–C," FK Corr., FM's Papers.
11 The following sources are all in FK Corr., FM's Papers: FK to J. Warner Bott, Jan 2, 1923, and FK to E. S. Brigham, VT Commissioner of Agriculture, Dec 29, 1923, both in Folder "Bo–C"; FK to W. O. Cutler, Supt. of Telegraph, Rutland, Jun 21, 1923, JWW to FK, Dec 30, 1924, Peter Connah to FK, Mar 7, 1925, and FK to Peter Connah, Mar 11, 1925, all in Folder "C to D"; FK to William Dean, Jan 27 and May 10, 1923, William M. Dean to FK, Mar 4, 1924, E. J. Davis Machine Co., Inc. to FK, Oct 29, 1924, and Charles Davis to FK, Jun 11, 1934, all in Folder "D to E"; FK to A. Goodrich, Dec 15, 1923, and FK to I. H. Gilfillan, Mar 25, 1924, both in Folder "G to H"; FK to H. M. Pearl, Jun 12, 1924, and FK to Earle Pillsbury, Oct 18, 1926, both in Folder "PQ to R"; FK to WSW, Jan 4, 1923, "WH to WI" Folder 2; FK to Robert Blastock, Jan 2, 1923, and FK to Alfred H. Blastock, Feb 8, 1923, both in general FK Corr. series, second folder; FK to Frank S. Springer, Secretary of American Southdown Association, Mar 7, 1923, general FK Corr. series, first folder; WSW to FK, Feb 5, Mar 15, Apr 26, and May 20, 1923, FK and DNT Corr. with LOW. Also the following in other series in the FM's Papers: JWW to FK, Jan 5, 8, and 9, 1923, Folder 8, "Some of Mr. J. W. Webb's Letters"; "Sheep and Poultry Farm Stock and Implements," 1891 Ledger, 62; Undated telegram to EFG, Folder 111, and Telegram to EFG, Feb 28 [year unknown], Folder 13, both in EFG Corr.; and EFG to LOW, Aug 15, 1913, EFG Corr. with LOW.
12 J. E. Cashman to FK, Apr 7, 1930, Folder "C to D," FK Corr., FM's Papers. Also the following in FK Corr., FM's Papers: FK

to Cashman, Apr 3, 1930, Folder "C to D"; A. J. Runnals to FK, Jun 25, 1924, and Runnals to FK, Mar 20 and 24, 1924, all in "R to S" Folder 2; FK to VT State Highway Board, Apr 2, 1925, FK to D. D. Snyder, Frissell & Snyder, Inc., Oct 7 and Dec 14, 1925, and Snyder to FK, Dec 18, 1926, all in "S to T" Folder 2.

13 FK to JWW, May 23, 1930, and JWW to FK, May 30 and Jun 2, 1930, all in Folder 3, FK Corr. with JWW, FM's Papers; FK to W. Fenwick, Jun 4, 1930, Folder "F to G," FK Corr., FM's Papers.

14 JWW to FK, Dec 16 [year unknown, c. 1927], Folder 1, "Some of Mr. J. W. Webb's Letters," FM's Papers.

15 FK to JWW, Nov 4, 1926, Folder 4, FK Corr. with JWW, FM's Papers.

16 The following sources are all in FK Corr. with JWW, FM's Papers: FK, "Repairs Programme for 1927," and FK, list of improvements made to Corporation, c. Nov 1926, both in Folder 4; FK to JWW, Nov 25, 1930, Folder 3; FK to JWW, Feb 18, 1931, Folder 1; FK to JWW, Sep 2, 1932, and FK to A. C. Hathorne Company, Sep 16, 1932, both in Folder 2. Also the following in FK Corr. with VW, FM's Papers: FK to VW, Oct 29, 1927, Folder 2; FK to VW, Feb 27, 1932, and William Shakespeare, Anaconda Roofing Company, to VW, Jul 13, 1932, both in Folder 4; VW to DNT, Sep 16, 1932, and Shakespeare to VW, Oct 29, 1932, both in Folder 3. Also the following from other series in the FM's Papers: DNT to FK, Oct 4, 1932, Folder "K to L," FK Corr., and FK to LOW, Oct 10, 1933, Folder 3, FK and DNT Corr. with LOW.

17 The following are all from FK and DNT Corr. with LOW, FM's Papers: DNT to LOW, Dec 4, 1925, Folder 2; FK to LOW, Nov 28 and Dec 3, 1923, Sep 9, 1925, and Aug 29, 1928; and LOW to FK, Dec 27, 1923. Also the following in other series in the FM's Papers: FK to Charles Patrick, Apr 4 and 8, 1932, Folder "PQ to R," FK Corr., and Frank S. Lanou & Son to DNT, Feb 25 and Sep 8, 1925, "L to M" Folder 1.

18 FK to LOW, Mar 20, 1925, FK and DNT Corr. with LOW, FM's Papers. James Torok was employed by Shelburne Farms from 1925 to 1932 (see the following, all in FM's Papers: FK to Torok, Mar 26, 1925, Folder "T to U"; FK to Dr. Allen, Brandon State School, Aug 5, 1932, Folder "A"; and T. W. Harvey Jr., Wee Burn Golf Course, to FK, Mar 18, 1925, "WH to WI" Folder 3).

19 FK to VW, Jun 9, 1925, FK and DNT Corr. with LOW, FM's Papers. Also FK to VW, Oct 29, 1927, Folder 6, FK Corr. with VW, FM's Papers.

20 FK to JWW, Sep 7, 1929, Folder 3, FK Corr. with JWW, FM's Papers. Also J. E. Howard, Turbine Equipment Company of New England, to FK, May 27, 1930, Folder 28, Deed Box Coll., LOW Papers; and the following from the FM's Papers: FK to VW, Jun 9, 1925, FK and DNT Corr. with LOW; JWW to Waring, Chapman & Farquhar, Civil Engineers, Sep 24, 1929, "WH to WI" Folder 1, FK Corr.; FK to JWW, Nov 30, 1928, Folder 3, and JWW to FK, Jan 28, 1933, Folder 2, both in FK Corr. with JWW; and FK, list of improvements made to corporation, c. Nov 1926, Folder 4, FK Corr. with JWW.

21 The following sources are all in FK Corr. with JWW, FM's Papers: FK to JWW, Jul 7, 1931, and JWW to FK, Jul 10, 1931, both in Folder 2; FK to JWW, Nov 21, 1934, and JWW to FK, Nov 21, 1934, both in Folder 1. Also JWW to FK, Oct 31, 1934, SF Corp. Corr., 1938–55, and JWW to FK, Feb 15, 1933, Webb & Lynch Folder 1, FK Corr. with VW, both in FM's Papers.

22 The following sources are all in the FM's Papers: FK to Mrs. J. W. Linsley, Jun 6, 1925, "L to M" Folder 2; JWW to FK, May 6, 1929, Folder 4, and FK to JWW, Nov 14, 1933, Folder 1, both in FK Corr. with JWW; FK to VW, Jan 19 and Apr 27, 1926, and VW to FK, Apr 9 and May 3, 1926, all in Folder 2, FK Corr. with VW. Also FK to VW, Jun 9, 1925, FK to LOW, Oct 15, 1932, LOW to Mr. Cadek, NY String Quartet, Nov 19, 1932, and LOW to FK, Dec 10, 1932, all in FK and DNT Corr. with LOW.

23 See Chapter 10, note 69, for further information about the Captain White house. The following sources are all in the FM's Papers: FK to JWW, Mar 21, Mar 28, and Apr 26, 1929, and JWW to FK, Mar 27, Apr 26, and Apr 29, 1929, all in Folder 4, FK Corr. with JWW; JWW to FK, May 16, 1927, Folder 1, "Some of Mr. J. W. Webb's Letters"; Memorandum of Agreement between SF Corp. and Charles Cross, Mar 14, 1927, Folder "C to D," FK Corr.; and James M. Frayer, City Milk Inspector, City of Burlington, to JWW, Oct 29, 1928, Folder "F to G," FK Corr. Also Julie Eldridge Edwards, "Did You Know …" InFARMation (Feb 1, 2008): 2.

24 JWW to FK, May 6, 1929, Folder 4, FK Corr. with JWW, FM's Papers.

25 FK to VW, Jun 9, 1925, FK and DNT Corr. with LOW, FM's Papers. Also FK, "Repairs Programme for 1927," c. Nov 1926, Folder 4, FK Corr. with JWW, FM's Papers.

26 The Boarding House's boiler system was salvaged and possibly moved to the Brick House (DNT to JWW, Nov 20, 1928, Folder 4, FK Corr. with JWW, FM's Papers). The following sources are all in the FM's Papers: FK to W. Fenwick, Shelburne, VT, Feb 3, 1928, Folder "F to G," FK Corr.; FK, "Repairs Programme for 1927," c. Nov 1926, Folder 4, FK Corr. with JWW; FK to VW, Oct 29, 1927, Folder 2, FK Corr. with VW; and JWW to FK, Mar 18, 1931, and FK to JWW, Mar 21, 1931, both in Folder 2, FK Corr. with JWW.

27 During FK's tenure, the corporation also produced field crops such as oats, alfalfa, silage corn, wheat, and barley to feed dairy cows and other livestock on the estate (all from FM's Papers: DNT to JWW, Apr 18, 1927, Folder 4, FK Corr. with JWW; FK to Walter Peel, Feb 18, 1929, Folder "PQ to R"; FK to Philip Suprenant, Feb 28, 1929, "S to T" Folder 2). The following sources are from FK Corr., FM's Papers: FK to C. J. Burke, Jan 17, 1923, Folder "Bo–C"; A. J. Gardner of Combination Cash Store to FK, Sep 17, 1925, and FK to Combination Cash Store, Sep 19, 1925, Folder "C to D"; B. H. Emery to FK, Jun 27, 1925, Folder "E to F"; FK to BFP Association, Jun 6, 1923, and Feb 23, 1925, both in Folder "F to G"; W. H. Green to FK, Mar 12, 1924, Folder "G to H"; FK to J. J. Hogan of Langwater Farms, Mar 3, 1924, and FK to The Lyman Farm, Jan 21, 1925, "L to M" Folder 2; FK to William Post & Son, Mar 5, 1924, Folder "PQ to R"; FK to John Tracy, Oct 30 and Nov 3, 1924, Folder "T to U"; Invoice dated Nov 21, 1929, recording apple sales from SF to M. M. Farrell & Sons, Burlington.

28 FK to VW, Aug 18, 1924, Folder 1, FK Corr. with VW, FM's Papers. Also FK to VW, Jan 2, 1924, in same location.

29 FK to Carey Brothers, Cheyenne, Wyoming, Jan 31, 1923, Folder "C to D," FK Corr., FM's Papers.

30 JWW to FK, Feb 5 [1924], Folder 2, "Some of Mr. J. W. Webb's Letters," FM's Papers. Also the following in FK Corr., FM's Papers: Donald D. Davis, American Hereford Cattle Breeders Association, to FK, Apr 6 and Jun 8, 1923, and FK to American Hereford Cattle Breeders Association, Jun 4, 1923, all in Folder 1; Arthur C. Johnson, Editor of Denver Daily Record Stockman, to FK, Mar 16, 1923, and FK to Johnson, Jun 4, 1923, both in Folder "IJ to K"; and FK to E. T. Springer, Cimarron, NM, May 15, 1923, "S to T" Folder 2.

31 FK to J. C. Cooley, Jul 17, 1923, Folder "C to D," FK Corr., FM's Papers. Also FK to E. S. Brigham, VT Commissioner of Agriculture, May 25, 1923, Folder "Bo–C," FK Corr., FM's Papers.

32 FK to E. S. Brigham, VT Commissioner of Agriculture, Sep 28, 1923, Folder "Bo–C," FK Corr., FM's Papers. Also FK to Brigham, Jun 29, 1923, in same location.

33 FK received a commission for his cattle-dealing activities (VW to JWW, Jan 26, 1934, SF Corp. Corr., 1938–55, FM's Papers). The following are all in FK Corr., FM's Papers: FK to A. Cutting, Oct 3, 1923, Folder "C" (quote); FK to County Agent, Clinton County Farm Bureau, Feb 29, 1924, Folder "C to D"; corr. between FK and I. H. Gilfillan, Folder "G to H"; and FK to A. J. Turner, Mar 17, 1924, Folder "T to U."

34 The following sources are all in the FM's Papers: FK to George T. Jarvis, Rutland Railroad Company, Sep 17 and Oct 15, 1923, Folder "IJ to K," FK Corr.; FK to JWW, Dec 21, 1923, Folder 5, FK Corr. with JWW; VW to FK, Jan 2, 1924, and FK to VW, Apr 30, 1925, Folder 1, FK Corr. with VW; FK to I. H. Gilfillan, May 21, 1924, Folder "G to H," FK Corr.

35 The following sources are all in the FM's Papers: FK to JWW, Dec 21, 1923, Folder 5, FK Corr. with JWW (quote); FK to George W. Bontwell, Apr 7, 1924, Folder "Bo–C," FK Corr.; FK to A. J. Turner, Mar 17, 1924, Folder "T to U," FK Corr. Also Harold Fisher Wilson, *The Hill Country of Northern New England: Its Social and Economic History, 1790–1930* (New York: AMS Press, Inc., 1967), 214, 301–26, 344.

36 FK to Waldo W. Clark, Sep 13, 1924, Folder "C to D," FK Corr., FM's Papers. Also FK to John Brechin, Mar 3, 1924, Folder "Bo–C," FK Corr., FM's Papers.

37 FK to The Lyman Farm, Mar 6, 1925, "L to M" Folder 2, FK Corr., FM's Papers.

38 FK to The Lyman Farm, May 6, 1925, "L to M" Folder 2, FK Corr., FM's Papers.

39 FK to JWW, Dec 21, 1923, Folder 5, FK Corr. with JWW, FM's Papers.

40 FK to VW, Feb 20, 1924, Folder 1, FK Corr. with VW, FM's Papers.

41 It is unclear exactly when the venture was fully abandoned. FK to BFP Association, Nov 10, 1924, Folder "F to G," FK Corr., FM's Papers; JWW to FK, Nov 8, 1924, Folder 5, "W to Z Letter File Farm Barn Office," DNT Corr., FM's Papers.

42 FK to Shelburne Cooperative Creamery, Jun 4, 1923, "S to T" Folder 1, FK Corr., FM's Papers. Also the following from the FM's Papers: FK to E .S. Brigham, VT Commissioner of Agriculture, Sep 28, 1923, Folder "Bo–C," FK Corr.; FK to JWW, Dec 21, 1923, Folder 5, FK Corr. with JWW; VW to FK, May 9, 1923, and FK to VW, Jun 11, 1923, in VW Folder 1, FK to VW, Jan 2 and Jan 30, 1924, both in Folder 3, all in FK Corr. with VW; and JWW to FK, Jan 5, 1923, Folder 8, "Some of Mr. J. W. Webb's Letters."

43 Carl B. Fletcher, Manager of the Shelburne Cooperative Creamery Co., to JWW, Feb 6, 1924, "S to T" Folder 1, FK Corr., FM's Papers. Also Shelburne Cooperative Creamery Co. to shareholders, Aug 1, 1924, in same location.

44 H. E. Bowman to FK, Feb 24, 1925, "Bo–C" Folder 3, FK Corr., FM's Papers.

45 FK to LOW, Mar 20, 1926, Folder 2, FK and DNT Corr. with LOW, FM's Papers.

46 *Shelburne Farms Breeding Barn Complex Conservation Plan*, Oct 31, 2004, III.23.

47 FK to JWW, Feb 12, 1927, Folder 4, FK Corr. with VW, FM's Papers. Also Wilson, *Hill Country*, 312–13.

48 The following are all in SF Corp. Corr., 1938–55, FM's Papers: DNT to VW, Sep 14, 1935; VW to DNT, Sep 27, 1935; Memorandum of Agreement between SF Corp. and L. E. Brigham, Jan 1, 1938, Folder "D-1-(a) L. E. Brigham." Also DVW, "Statement," in William C. Lipke, ed., *Shelburne Farms: The History of an Agricultural Estate* (Burlington, VT: University of Vermont, 1979), 59.

49 FK to Gillette Clipping Machine Co., Dec 28, 1925, and Jan 9, 1926, Folder "G to H," FM's Papers. Also "Shelburne Farms Corporation Plan of Cow Barn, Jan 1923," 2004.3.16.1, APMI; Wilson, *Hill Country*, 320, 324–25, 399; and the following in the FM's Papers: O. E. Wilder, Special Representative for the DeLaval Separator Company, to FK, Jun 28, 1927, Folder "D to E," FK to JWW, Jul 27, 1927, GK Folder, and JWW to FK, Jul 28 [1927], Folder 1, "Some of Mr. J. W. Webb's Letters."

50 FK to Editor of "The Field," London, Mar 23, 1926, Folder "F to G," FK Corr., FM's Papers.

51 FK, "Repairs Programme for 1927," c. Nov 1926, Folder 4, FK Corr. with JWW, FM's Papers. Also the following in FM's Papers: FK to JWW, Aug 1, 1929, and JWW to FK, Aug 6, 1929, Folder 3, both in FK Corr. with JWW; FK to L. E. Brigham, May 2, 1932, Folder "Bo–C," FK Corr.

52 FK to LOW, Oct 30, 1934, Folder 3, FK and DNT Corr. with LOW, FM's Papers.

53 Ibid. Also FK to Thomas Hooker, Jul 10, Jul 14, Jul 24, and Aug 14, 1925, "H to I" Folder 2, FK Corr., FM's Papers; FK to L. E. Brigham, Sep 8, 1934, Folder "Bo–C," FK Corr., FM's Papers.

54 FK to LOW, Oct 30, 1934, Folder 3, FK and DNT Corr. with LOW, FM's Papers.

55 L. E. Brigham Advertisement, c. 1934, Folder "Bo–C," FK Corr., FM's Papers.

56 FK to James W. Hall, Apr 26, 1926, "L to M" Folder 1, FK Corr., FM's Papers.

57 It is difficult to accurately compare these financial figures with today's dollars; however, according to one source (www.westegg.com/inflation/), $60,000 is roughly equivalent to $748,000 in 2008 dollars, and $20,000 is roughly equivalent to $250,000 in 2008 dollars. For quote, see VW to FK, Oct 17, 1927, Folder 1, FK Corr. with VW, FM's Papers.

58 In fact, the Webb family considered closing the dairy at least once, in 1924 (JWW to FK, Nov 8, 1924, Folder 5, "W to Z Letter File Farm Barn Office," DNT Corr., FM's Papers). Quote from VW to FK, Jul 2, 1925, Folder 1, FK Corr. with VW, FM's Papers. Also FK to VW, Jun 10, 1925, Folder 2, in same location.

59 FK to VW, Jun 9, 1925, FK and DNT Corr. with LOW, FM's Papers.

60 The following sources are all in the FM's Papers: LOW to FK, Jul 15, 1925, LOW to FK, Nov 30, 1928, and LOW to FK, undated, all in FK and DNT Corr. with LOW; JWW to DNT, Feb 23, 1930, DNT to JWW, Feb 23, 1930, JWW to FK, Mar 5, 1930, M. E. Walbridge to JWW, Apr 2, 1930, and JWW to Walbridge, Apr 3, 1930, all in Folder 3, FK Corr. with JWW; VW to FK, Sep 5, 1928, Folder 2, FK Corr. with VW; FK to JWW, Oct 23, 1931, Folder "F to G," FK Corr.; FK to D. A. Loomis, Champlain Transportation Company, May 19 and Jun 1, 1932, and Loomis to FK, Jun 8, 1932, all in Folder "C to D," FK Corr.; JWW to E. B. Smith, Dec 11, 1934, SF Corp. Corr., 1938–55. Also Deed, WSW and LOW to Clarence and Anna D. Morgan, Jul 30, 1910, vol. 17, 198–200, Land Records, STC; Lilian Baker Carlisle, ed., *Look Around St. George and Shelburne, Vermont* (Burlington, VT: Chittenden County

Historical Society, 1975), 60; "Map of Land Owned by Dr. W.S. Webb on Shelburne Point," 2004.3.21.7a, FFD 7, Folder 6, APMI.

61 DNT to FK, Feb 4, 1930, Folder "K to L," FK Corr., FM's Papers. Also DNT obituary, *BFP*, Sep 27, 1966.

62 Wages were reduced 5% in Feb 1931 and 5% in Jul 1931. See the following in the FM's Papers: FK to L. E. Brigham, Jan 12, 1931, and Memorandum of Agreement between Shelburne Farms Corporation and Brigham, Mar 13, 1931, both in Folder "Bo–C," FK Corr.; FK to JWW, Jan 12, Jan 27, and Feb 5, 1931, and JWW to FK, Feb 16, 1931, all in Folder 3, FK Corr. with JWW; JWW to FK, Jan 24, 1931, and Farm Managers' Forms addressed to Farm employees, Jan 1931, both in Folder 2, FK Corr. with JWW; FK to JWW, Mar 10, 1931, and FK to LOW, Feb 8, 1932, both in Folder 3, FK and DNT Corr. with LOW; FK to VW, Feb 2, 1933, Folder 3, FK Corr. with VW.

63 EHW to LOW, Apr 11, 1932, Folder 35, Family Papers Coll., LOW Papers. Also the following in the FM's Papers: WW to FK, Mar 5, 1932, Folder "WI to Z"; LOW to FK, May 12 and Nov 10, 1932, Folder 3, FK and DNT Corr. with FK; LOW to FK, Mar 21, 1935, Folder 1, FK and DNT Corr. with FK. Also GW to LOW, Apr 23 and May 13, 1932, Folder 35, Family Papers Coll., LOW Papers.

64 FK to VW, Feb 2, 1933, Folder 3, FK Corr. with VW, FM's Papers. Also the following in the FM's Papers: FK to LOW, Nov 5 and 11, 1931, Jan 28, Apr 15, and Dec 13, 1932, and Jan 18, 1933, all in Folder 3, FK and DNT Corr. with LOW; LOW to FK, Dec 14, 1934, Folder 1, FK and DNT Corr. with JWW; LOW to FK, Jan 28, 1932, Folder 3, FK and DNT Corr. with LOW; FK to Alfred C. Holland, Jan 24, 1933, "H to I" Folder 2, FK Corr.; FK to W. C. Fenwick, Apr 1, 1933, Folder "F to G," FK Corr.; DNT to JWW, Feb 7, 1933, Folder 2, FK Corr. with JWW; FK to Mrs. Charles Russell, Dec 8, 1931, "Inquiries from Men Looking for Employment" Folder, FK Corr. with VW; FK to C. A. Wilcox, Apr 1, 1933, Folder "WI to Z."

65 JWW to FK, Jul 10, 1931, Folder 2, FK Corr. with JWW, FM's Papers.

66 JWW to FK, Feb 9 [1933], Folder 2, FK Corr. with JWW, FM's Papers.

67 VW to FK, Feb 16, 1933, Folder 5, FK Corr. with VW, FM's Papers. Also JWW to FK, Feb 11, 1933, Folder 2, and FK to JWW, Feb 13, 1933, Folder 1, both in FK Corr. with JWW, FM's Papers; SBW Jr., Oral History Interview, Oct 31, 2006.

68 FK to VW, Feb 18, 1933, Folder 5, FK Corr. with VW, FM's Papers.

69 Ibid.

70 FK to James W. Hall, Apr 26, 1926, "L to M" Folder 1, FK Corr., FM's Papers.

71 FK to JWW, May 20, 1927, Folder 4, FK Corr. with JWW, FM's Papers.

72 JWW to VW, Dec 26, 1934, SF Corp. Corr., 1938–55, FM's Papers.

73 FK to James W. Hall, Apr 26, 1926, "L to M" Folder 1, FK Corr., FM's Papers. For fires see FK to JWW, Jul 24, 1930, FK to Vander Poel, Pausner & Webb, Sep 22, Sep 24, and Oct 10, 1930, and FK to JWW, Sep 22, 1930, all in "UV to W" Folder 2, FM's Papers.

74 FK to LOW, Oct 3, 1924, FK and DNT Corr. with LOW, FM's Papers.

75 LOW to FK, Jun 7, 1925, FK and DNT Corr. with LOW, FM's Papers.

76 FK to LOW, Jun 8, 1925, FK and DNT Corr. with LOW, FM's Papers.

77 FK to JWW, Dec 27, 1923, Folder 5, FK Corr. with JWW, FM's Papers.

78 The following sources are all in the FM's Papers: FK to GK, Oct 13, 1924, GK Folder, FK Corr. with VW; FK to John Earley, SAF, Jan 18, 1926, Folder "E to F," and FK to C. Stetson, May 2, 1927, "S to T" Folder 2, both in FK Corr.; and FK to VW, May 16, 1928, Folder 6, FK Corr. with VW.

79 FK to JWW, May 6, 1935, Folder 1, FK Corr. with JWW, FM's Papers. FK also made similar complaints in 1925; see FK to JWW, Jul 30, 1925, Folder 1, "Some of Mr. J. W. Webb's Letters," FM's Papers.

80 JWW to FK, May 28, 1935, SF Corp. Corr., 1938–55, FM's Papers. Also VW to FK, Jun 7, 1935, in same location.

81 It is unclear if FK was indeed guilty of embezzlement. After spending some time in South Africa, he eventually returned to England, where WW reported that he was operating a small farm of his own (WW to DNT, Jul 8 [1936 or 1937], Folder 2, DNT Corr., FM's Papers). JWW, May 7, Jul 28, Jul 30, Aug 2, Aug 3, and Oct 10, 1935, 1935 Diary, JWW Jr. Coll.; VW to FK, Jul 9, 1934; VW to FK, Jun 7, 1935; FK to VW, Jun 10, 1935; VW to FK, telegram, Jul 17, 1935; VW to WSW Jr., Jul 17, 1935; JWW to Burlington Trust Company, Aug 7, 1935; VW to FK, Aug 28, 1935; and VW to WSW Jr., Sep 25, 1935, all in SF Corp. Corr., 1938–55, FM's Papers; FK, typed note, Jul 19, 1935, Folder 1, FK Corr. with JWW, FM's Papers; General Order Book, Vol. 2, FM's Papers.

82 LOW to FK, May 24, 1929, Folder 3, FK and DNT Corr. with LOW, FM's Papers. Also the following in the FM's Papers: LOW to FK, Apr 12 and May 12, 1925, and LOW to FK, undated, both in FK and DNT Corr. with LOW; FK to G. C. Stafford, Mar 17 and Apr 9, 1928, "S to T" Folder 2, FK Corr.; William Lavilette to JWW, Dec 5, 1930, JWW to FK, Dec 8 and 20, 1930, and FK to JWW, Dec 11 and 29, 1930, all in Folder 3, FK Corr. with JWW; FK to LOW, Mar 8 and Apr 2, 1928 and LOW to FK, Mar 29, 1928, all in Folder 2, FK and DNT Corr. with LOW; FK to Charlie Kennison, Mar 23, 1928, Folder "K to L," FK Corr.

83 Susan Cady Hayward, "Historical Evolution of the Shelburne Farms Formal Gardens: Design Changes Through Time," unpublished paper prepared for Historic Preservation Program, UVM, May 10, 1984, 74.

84 The following sources are all in FK and DNT Corr. with LOW, FM's Papers: FK to LOW, Dec 10, 1925, LOW to FK, Jan 3, 1926, and LOW to FK, Aug 21, 1926, all in Folder 2; LOW to FK, Sep 7, 1930, Jan 4 and 12, 1931, all in Folder 3; FK to LOW, Dec 29, 1930, and Feb 18, 1931, in folder titled "Corr. re replacing new boiler Shelburne House, reduction of wages, change at vegetable garden—1930–1931."

85 The following sources are all in the FM's Papers: LOW to FK, undated, Aug 22, Aug 27, and Oct 21, 1926, and Jan 29, 1928, and FK to LOW, Dec 22, 1927, and Feb 3, 1928, all in Folder 2, FK and DNT Corr. with LOW; FK to LOW, Apr 4, 1929, Folder 3, FK and DNT Corr. with LOW; F. H. Horsford to FK, Apr 23 and Jul 2, 1923, and FK to Horsford, May 2 and Jul 5, 1923, all in "H to I" Folder 2, FK Corr.; FK to Fred Abbey, Apr 22, 1929, general FK Corr. series, first folder.

86 The following sources are all in the FM's Papers: Henry H. Salls to FK, Jul 8 and 21, 1931, and FK to Henry H. Salls, Jul 23, 1931, both in "S to T" Folder 1, FK Corr.; FK to George E. Wray, Lord & Burnham, Irvington, NY, Oct 27, 1927, "L to M"

Folder 2, FK Corr., J. J. Raine to FK, May 28, 1926, FK to LOW, Aug 20, 1926, May 8 and Nov 13, 1928, and Aug 5, 1929, G. S. Blodgett Co. to FK, Dec 30, 1930, and FK to G. S. Blodgett Co., Jan 8, 1931, all in Folder 2, FK and DNT Corr. with LOW; FK to LOW, Mar 28, 1929, Dec 30, 1930, Jan 26, Jun 3, Jun 16, and Nov 13, 1931, and LOW to FK, Apr 6, May 1, and Aug 27, 1929, and May 1, 1932, all in Folder 3, FK and DNT Corr. with LOW; FK to JWW, Feb 18, 1931, Folder 1, FK Corr. with JWW; FK to WSW Jr., Feb 1, 1935, Folder 4, FK Corr. with VW.

87 LOW, Oct 29, 1926, 1926 Diary, LOW Papers. Also LOW, Nov 30, 1925, 1925 Diary, and Jan 2 and Oct 25, 1926, 1926 Diary, LOW Papers; GK to DNT, Jan 15 [1926], and FK to GK, Jan 26, 1926, GK Folder, FK Corr. with VW, FM's Papers.

88 LOW, copy of Nehasane guestbook entry re death of WSW, JWW Jr. Coll. Also LOW to "the Employees of Shelburne Farms," Nov 7, 1926, Folder 2, FK and DNT Corr. with LOW, FM's Papers; Plot Plan and Record of Internments, Woodlawn Cemetery, c. 1936, Estate Papers Coll., LOW Papers.

89 LOW, Oct 30, Nov 1, Nov 3, and Dec 14, 1926, 1926 Diary, LOW Papers.

90 WW to FK, Feb 28 [1927], Folder "WI to Z," FK Corr., FM's Papers. Also WW to FK, Mar 15, 1927 and Feb 8 [1928], in same location.

91 LOW, diary entries for 1926–30, passim, LOW Papers.

92 JWW, Mar 17, 1932, 1932 Diary, JWW Jr. Coll.; LOW, Jun 17 and Nov 29–30, 1933, 1933 Diary, LOW Papers; WSW Jr. to LOW, May 1, 1933, Folder 38, Family Papers Coll., LOW Papers; LOW, Gulf Stream Corr., LOW Papers; SBW Jr., corr. with author, Oct 15, 2006; James B. Clark, Appraiser's Report, Sep 22, 1960, Folder 6, SBW Sr. Papers; Julie Eldridge Edwards, corr. with Robert Ganger, c. 2002–04, in "Miradero House— Bob Ganger" Reference File (the author thanks Edwards for bringing this material to her attention); Robert W. Ganger, *Lila Vanderbilt Webb's Miradero: Window on an Era* (Palm Beach, FL: Historical Society of Palm Beach County, 2005), passim.

93 AOW, "Almost a Century," unpublished 1977 memoir, 26. Also LOV, Sep 17, 1879, 1879 Journal, and LOW, Jan 21, 1906, 1906 Diary, both in LOW Papers.

94 Ganger noted that LOW "installed two acoustically magnified phone rooms [at Miradero] to mitigate her hearing problem" (Ganger, 145). Copious references to LOW's hearing problems are in the following: VW Papers; Folder 13, Business Papers Coll., LOW Papers; Folders 16 and 46, Family Papers Coll., LOW Papers; Folders 18–19, Deed Box Coll., LOW Papers; and LOW diary entries, 1909–34, passim, LOW Papers. Also LOW to VW, Apr 4 [1913], VW Papers; LOW to EFG, Jun 19, 1913, EFG Corr. with LOW, FM's Papers; LOW to FK, Nov 25, 1925, Folder 2, FK and DNT Corr. with LOW, FM's Papers; Harper Oriphone Company to LOW, Mar 24, 1913, FM's Papers; and AOW, Transcript of Oral History Interview with EWW, Sep 4, 1976, 19–20.

95 LOW, Oct 1, 1931, 1931 Diary, LOW Papers.

96 This account of LOW's health problems, pages 177–78, is largely based on the following sources, with additional sources and quotations as noted: Dr. Des Gennes, invoice and prescription, Folder 11, Business Papers, LOW Papers; VW to FK, Dec 19, 1928, Folder 2, FK Corr. with VW, FM's Papers; VW to FK, Feb 1, 1935, Folder 10, FK Corr. with VW, FM's Papers; VW to DNT, Feb 5, 1935, and VW to FK, Feb 28, 1935, both in Folder 4, FK Corr. with VW, FM's Papers; GK to FK, undated [c. late Feb 1935], GK Folder, and WW to DNT, Feb 18, 1935, Webb & Lynch Folder 2, both in FK Corr. with VW, FM's Papers; VW to DVW, Apr 17 [1936], Folder 3, Box 8, and AOW to DVW, Mar 3, 1935, Folder 5, Box 5, both in DVW Papers; LOW diary entries, 1921–36, passim, LOW Papers; JWW diary entries, 1935–36, passim, JWW Jr. Coll.

97 LOW, Jun 7, 1935, 1935 Diary, LOW Papers.

98 VW to FK, Mar 25, 1935, Folder 1, FK Corr., FM's Papers. Also the following sources in the FM's Papers: VW to DNT, Feb 5 and 17, 1935 and LOW to DNT, Feb 6, 1935, all in Folder 10, FK Corr. with VW; JWW to DNT, Feb 4 and 15, 1935, and LOW to FK, Mar 21, 1935, all in Folder 1, FK Corr. with JWW; WW to DNT, Feb 17 [1935], Folder "WI to Z," FK Corr.

99 JWW Jr., "Pictorial History of the Webb Family," 130–31, JWW Jr. Coll. Also JWW, Jul 9–10, 1936, 1936 Diary, JWW Jr. Coll.

100 JWW, Jul 12–14 and 16, 1936, 1936 Diary, JWW Jr. Coll.

101 JWW, Jul 17, 1936, 1936 Diary, JWW Jr. Coll.

102 CJ to LOW, Dec 20, 1929, Folder 31, Family Papers Coll., LOW Papers.

103 JWW, Jul 10, 1936, 1936 Diary, JWW Jr. Coll.

CHAPTER 12

1 VW to Henry du Pont, Jun 27, 1947, Box HF 434, courtesy The Winterthur Library: Winterthur Archives.

2 It is difficult to accurately compare these financial figures to today's dollars; however, one source (www.westegg.com/inflation/) calculates that $7,380,000 is roughly equivalent to $114,000,000 in 2008 dollars. The following sources are all in Chittenden County Probate Court records for the Estate of Eliza Osgood Webb, case #13400 (hereafter referred to as LOW Probate Court records): LOW, Last Will and Testament, signed Jun 15, 1929, filed Jul 14, 1936; Inventory and Warrant, Dec 24, 1936; Administration Account, Jul 14, 1937; and Decree of Distribution, Oct 23, 1939. See also "Trust Fund" document, c. 1936, Estate Papers Coll., LOW Papers; Receipt and Release, JWW to Frederick Vanderbilt, Nov 13, 1936, Folder 4, Box 1, SBW Sr. Papers.

3 LOW had leased rather than owned her New York City apartment, so it was not considered part of her estate. Under the terms of LOW's will, the Trinity Episcopal Church of Shelburne received a $50,000 endowment. Each of the Webb children received approximately one-fourth of the remainder (bulk) of LOW's property. FVJ received the additional gift of LOW's jewelry and clothing and 80 shares in the Shelburne Farms Corporation as opposed to the 40 shares each that her brothers received. This distribution resulted in FVJ and JWW each owning 80 corporation shares (20% interest) and WSW Jr. and VW each owning 120 shares (30% interest), as the 3 Webb sons had held shares since the corporation's establishment in 1922. Ibid.

4 SBW to VW, Sept 24, 1952, SF Corp. Corr., FM's Papers.

5 DVW, "Statement," in William C. Lipke, ed., *Shelburne Farms: The History of an Agricultural Estate* (Burlington, VT: UVM, 1979), 61; Unknown author [probably VW], "Objectives to be Obtained at Shelburne" and "Steps Which Might be Taken to Attain Foregoing Objectives," Sep 1937, SF Corp. Corr., FM's Papers.

6 VW to FVJ, Nov 29, 1944, SF Corp. Corr., FM's Papers.

7 VW to Richard Robbins, Sep 7, 1938, SF Corp. Corr., FM's Papers; VW, "Memorandum re Division of Shelburne and Ne-Ha-Sa-Ne Properties," Apr 24, 1939, Folder 1, Box 1, SBW Sr. Papers; DVW, "Statement," 61.

8 VW, "Memorandum re Division."
9 "Objectives to be Obtained" and "Steps Which Might be Taken"; VW, "Memorandum re Division."
10 VW to Internal Revenue Agent in Charge, Boston, MA, Jan 25, 1939, LOW Estate Papers, LOW Papers.
11 LOW to Mrs. Edward McCauley Jr., Committee on Convalescent Hospitals of the Woman's Section of the Navy League, Aug 23, 1916, Folder 3, Business Papers Coll., LOW Papers.
12 VW to Internal Revenue Agent in Charge, Boston, MA, Jan 25, 1939, LOW Estate Papers, LOW Papers. Also undated, typed scrap of paper, with note from JWW to VW at bottom, Folder 24 [1921], Family Papers Coll., LOW Papers.
13 VW, "Memorandum re Division."
14 Shelburne House was closed in the fall of 1936 and remained shuttered during the 1937 season. FVJ and VW reopened the building together in Jun 1938. In the summer of 1939, as the house officially changed hands, FVJ, JWW, and WSW Jr. retrieved items from the dwelling that they wished to acquire for themselves, with the mutual approval of all 4 siblings. The following are all in SF Corp. Corr., FM's Papers: DNT to WSW Jr., Sep 21, 1936; WW to DNT, Mar 20, 1937, and Feb 4, 1938; VW to DNT, Jun 6, 1938; and DNT to WSW Jr., Aug 10, 1939. Also FVJ, 1938 entry in Shelburne House Guestbook, vol. 2, 140; JWW, diary entries for Jul and Aug 1939, passim, 1939 Diary, JWW Jr. Coll.
15 One source (Harriet Patrick Dantzscher, "Sled Runner Point, Shelburne Bay," in Lilian Baker Carlisle, ed., *Look Around St. George and Shelburne, Vermont* [Burlington, VT: Chittenden County Historical Society, 1975], 51) states that FVJ had already obtained acreage in the area of Sled Runner Point as a wedding gift from her parents in 1925. However, this has yet to be confirmed.

As part of the Shelburne property they received, FVJ and VW jointly owned several plots in Shelburne Village, including the depot, the 3 employee cottages located near the depot, the Trinity Church rectory, and a portion of Shelburne Falls. Within the next few years, JWW, FVJ, and VW settled their affairs by completing a few additional land transactions related to their SF properties. FVJ reduced her holdings, and JWW and VW added to theirs. In 1940, FVJ sold a 94-acre parcel on Shelburne Point, which included the dilapidated Captain White house, to friends of VW and AOW's. In 1944, VW sold JWW an 8-acre parcel containing the Tracy Barn, which added to JWW's holdings in the area of the Breeding Barn complex and simplified the boundary line between SF and SAF in that area of the property. In 1946, FVJ sold VW some 400 acres on the southern boundary of her property on Shelburne Point. Finally, in 1948, FVJ and VW sold the 3 employee houses adjoining the depot to private individuals.

The 4 siblings attempted unsuccessfully to sell the Florida residence for their equal benefit before WSW Jr. volunteered to take the property as part of his portion of the inheritance. After WSW built his own residence nearby, the house was divided into 2 dwellings and rented to servicemen during the Second World War. After the war, it was sold to 2 different buyers.

The following sources are all in SF Corp. Corr., FM's Papers: "Objectives to be Obtained" and "Steps Which Might be Taken"; SF Corp. Meeting Minutes, Jul 28, 1939; JWW, Memorandum for Mr. Reardon, Sep 7, 1939; and List of property holdings, Sep 1, 1939, Folder "L & Mc Letter File Shelburne Farms Farm Barn Office 1940's." Also VW to DNT, Oct 30, 1944, Folder 4, "W to Z Letter File Farm Barn Office," DNT Corr., FM's Papers; JWW, Jun 22 and 25, 1939, 1939 Diary; Jan 11, 1940, 1940 Diary; and Mar 5, 1955, 1955 Diary; JWW Jr. Coll.; VW, "Memorandum re Division," Apr 24, 1939, and FVJ, JWW, WSW, and VW, Agreement for Division of LOW Estate [original name of document unknown, as first pages are missing], 1939, both in Folder 1, Box 1, SBW Sr. Papers; AOW, "Almost a Century," unpublished 1977 memoir, 29; LOW, Probate Court records; Robert W. Ganger, *Lila Vanderbilt Webb's Miradero: Window on an Era* (Palm Beach, FL: Historical Society of Palm Beach County, 2005), passim. Also numerous deeds dated 1939–48 and H. M. McIntosh, "Plan of a Portion of the Division Line between Properties of Frederica V. Jones and Vanderbilt Webb, Shelburne Farms, Shelburne, Vermont," Nov 1939, Book A, 59, all in Land Records, STC.
16 VW to FVJ, Nov 29, 1944, SF Corp. Corr., FM's Papers; ASW to author, Aug 6 and 13, 2009.
17 DVW, "Statement," 61; Obituary and Funeral Notice for DNT, *BFP*, Sep 27 and 29, 1966; Management & Office Employee Listing, c. 1908–12, Poultry and Employee Record Book, 160, Box 20, FM's Papers.
18 The following sources are all in DVW Papers: DVW to AOW, Feb 26, Mar 5, and Mar 11, 1928, Folder 2, and Dec 15, 1938, Folder 3, all in Box 3; Dr. George de Schweinitz to Dr. Conrad Berens, Mar 22, 1935, and Dr. William Holland Wilmer to Berens, Apr 12, 1935, both in Folder 2, Box 7; numerous letters to DVW from friends and family, c. Sep–Dec 1934, and "C.S.P. Summary of Activities During Senior Year, Together with Present Occupation and Address, Class of 1935," all in Folder 1, Box 6. Also LOW, Sep 22, 1934, 1934 Diary, LOW Papers; and MCW, comments on draft manuscript, Apr 19, 2007.
19 DVW to VW and AOW, beginning "Thursday," c. Nov 1935, Folder 5, Box 6, DVW Papers.
20 DVW to AOW, Mar 11, 1936, Folder 6, Box 6, DVW Papers. Also DVW to VW, Jan 9, 1936, Folder 7, Box 6, DVW Papers. For more on DVW's work in California, see DVW Corr., 1935–36, passim, especially letters to and from VW and AOW, DVW Papers.
21 DVW Corr., 1935–36, passim, especially letters to and from VW and AOW, DVW Papers.
22 DVW, "Statement," 59.
23 VW to Richard Robbins, Sep 7, 1938, SF Corp. Corr., 1938–55, FM's Papers. Also, in DVW Papers: DVW, Cornell class notes, and James McClure to VW, May 15, 1938, in Folder "Letters from Family & Friends Letters from DVW re Early Cattle Operation 1938–39 and undated," Box 7.
24 DVW, "Statement," 59.
25 The following sources are all in the FM's Papers: DNT to VW, Dec 6, 1938; DNT to VW, May 13, 1937, unlabeled Folder 12; DNT to JWW, Mar 22, 1937, unlabeled Folder 9.
26 JWW, Nov 6, 1938, JWW Diary, JWW Jr. Coll. Also the following in SF Corp. Corr., FM's Papers: DNT to VW, Sep 14, 1935; DNT to DWB, Dec 22, 1936; DNT to JWW, Jan 4, 1937; DNT to VW, Sep 4, 1937; Memorandum of Agreement between Shelburne Farms and Stanley Byington, Oct 21, 1937; Memorandum of Agreement between SF Corp. and L. E. Brigham, Jan 1, 1938, Folder "D-1-(a) L. E. Brigham"; DNT to VW, Jun 8, 1938; DVW to VW, Jun 6, 1939; DVW to DNT, Aug 12, 1940, Folder "D. V. Webb Letter File."
27 VW to DNT, Sep 21, 1938, SF Corp. Corr., FM's Papers.
28 Ibid.

29 Technically, the decision to diversify was made by the Webb family at large as joint stockholders in the SF Corp., because VW and FVJ did not acquire legal ownership of SF until the summer of 1939. VW to Richard Robbins, Sep 7, 1938, SF Corp. Corr.; JWW, Aug 30, 1938, 1938 Diary, JWW Jr. Coll.; JWW, "Rough Notes on Talk with Prof. Johnstone-Wallace and Dr. R. B. Hinman at Shelburne, On Aug. 30/38," VW to Richard Robbins, Sep 7, 1938, and DVW to Robbins, Jan 26, 1939, Folder "R-1 R. W. Robbins," DVW Corr., all in SF Corp. Corr., FM's Papers; DVW to Julian B. Clark, Jan 2, 1940, Folder "C-6 Misc.," SF Corr., FM's Papers.

30 VW to Richard Robbins, Sep 7, 1938, SF Corp. Corr., FM's Papers.

31 Herman I. Miller, "The Possibilities of Beef Cattle as a Source of Vermont Farm Income," UVM Agricultural Extension Service Circular 98, Jun 1939, Folder "B1-(d)-II Hereford Steers," DVW Corr., FM's Papers.

32 Aberdeen-Angus Breeders' Association Brochure, titled "Breeding and Management of Aberdeen-Angus Cattle in the East and Southeast," Folder "B1 (a) III Aberdeen-Angus—Misc.," FM's Papers; *The Story of Our Breed* (Webster City, IA: Aberdeen-Angus Breeders' Association, 1969), 138, 144.

33 The following sources are all in the FM's Papers: DVW to VW, Sep 13, 1938, SF Corp. Corr.; "Angus Purchases To Date," Feb 28, 1939, Folder "B1 (a) III Aberdeen-Angus—Misc.," DVW Corr.; DNT to R. B. Hinman, Mar 6, 1939, Folder "B-1-(e) Professor Hinman"; DVW to Andrew Anderson, Apr 8, 1939, Folder "B1 (a) II Hadley Angus Heifers."

34 DVW to VW, Sep 30, 1938, and DVW to AOW, Oct 7, 1938, SF Corp. Corr., FM's Papers; copies of DVW's typewritten diary entries, Oct 1938, bundled with DVW to AOW, Oct 18, 1938, Folder 4, Box 8, DVW Papers.

35 The last documented reference to Herefords dates to 1948 (H. S. Pierce, Burlingame, Field, Pierce & Browne, Inc., to DVW, Feb 4, 1949, SF Corp. Corr., FM's Papers). MCW believes the animals were phased out by the early 1950s (MCW, comment on draft Chapter 11, Jan 2009). Also the following in the FM's Papers: DNT to R. B. Hinman, Mar 6, 1939, Folder "B-1-(e) Professor Hinman"; DVW to Richard Robbins, Oct 2, 1939, VW Folder, SF Corp. Corr.; DVW to JWW, May 11, 1940, Folder "B-1-d III"; VW to DNT, Oct 24, 1945, Folder 2, "W to Z Letter File, Farm Barn Office," DNT Corr.

36 The following sources are in SF Corp. Corr., FM's Papers: DNT to R. B. Hinman, Mar 6, 1939, Folder "B-1-(e) Professor Hinman"; "Total Feed Consumed by 43 Hereford Steers from Nov 5, 1938 to Dec. 1, 1939," Folder "File Drawer A-Ba to Bl"; Farm inventory statement, Apr 1, 1941, VW Folder; and Farm inventory statement, Nov 19, 1941, Folder "A-4 Miscellaneous." The following sources are in DVW Corr., FM's Papers: DVW to Richard Robbins, Jul 20, 1940, Folder "R-1 R. W. Robbins"; DVW to VW, Oct 5, 1941, Folder 6, Box 8; "BEEF CATTLE Sept. 3, 1943," Folder "Beef Cattle Sales Fall 1943." Also Keenis Patterson, conversation with author, Jan 24, 2007; Clifford Gerald Bessette obituary, *BFP*, c. Feb 10, 1997; William Darcy Patterson obituary, *BFP*, Jun 24, 1978; Frank and Frederica Botala, Oral History Interview, Jun 26, 2006, disk 1.

37 Three vertical wooden silos were also placed behind the building and a trench silo constructed in the courtyard (MCW, conversation with author, Feb 26, 2007). For more on trench silos, see discussion of new dairy innovations in Chapter 13. MCW, comments on draft manuscript, Apr 10, 2007; DVW to VW, Dec 3, 1940, Folder "Letters from DVW re Early Farm Operation" Box 7, DVW Papers. Also the following in the FM's Papers: JWW, "Rough Notes," SF Corp. Corr.; DNT to VW, Nov 25, 1938, List of "Beef Cattle Pens and Yards," c. Aug 1940, Folder "File Drawer A Ba to Bl," Box 1, DNT Corr.; DVW to DNT, Jan 5, 1941, DVW Corr. with DNT, Folder 2; DNT to Charles Congdon, Jun 8, 1942, Folder "C-6 Misc."; DVW to DNT, Feb 19, 1942.

38 DVW, "Statement," 61.

39 The following sources are all in the FM's Papers: DVW to DNT, Feb 19, 1942, SF Corp. Corr.; "Attention Leo Aube: Work to be Done," Nov. 5, 1940, Folder "D. V. Webb Letter File," DVW Corr.; DVW to DNT, Jan 5, 1941, DVW Corr. with DNT, Folder 2.

40 DVW to Julian Clark, Jan 2, 1940, Folder "C-6 Misc.," SF Corr., FM's Papers.

41 J. L. Krall to DVW, Jun 22, 1945, Folder 3, "W to Z Letter File Farm Barn Office," DNT Corr., FM's Papers. Also DVW to VW, Sep 20, 1940, Folder "Letters from DVW re Early Farm Operation," Box 7, DVW Papers; Corr. in Folder "B-a-IV Sales," and "Beef Cattle Sales Fall 1944," Folder "B-3-Misc.," both in SF Corr., FM's Papers.

42 DVW to VW, May 2 and Aug 8, 1940, Folder 5, Box 8, DVW Papers; VW to Clifford Clevenger, Sep 9, 1943, FM's Papers; DVW, "Statement," 61.

43 SF also acquired some Yorkshire hogs at the same time but ultimately specialized in Duroc Jerseys. DVW to VW, Oct 5, 1941, Folder 6, Box 8, DVW Papers; DVW to Hosea Fuller, Nov 1, 1948, Folder "H-3 Hogs," DVW Corr., FM's Papers.

44 DVW to Richard Robbins, Sep 12 1940, Folder "R-1 R. W. Robbins," DVW Corr., FM's Papers.

45 DVW, "Statement," 61; DVW to VW, Oct 5, 1941, Folder "1959-60 Inventories," Box 8, and Inventory of Farm Barn Contents, Mar 29, 1960, 1959–60 Inventories Folder, both in DVW Papers; DVW to Brian Connor, Apr 27, 1942, and "Sale Fall Pigs" list, c. 1941–42, both in Folder "H-3 Hogs," FM's Papers; MCW, comments on draft Chapter 11, Jan 2009.

46 The following sources are all in the FM's Papers: DVW, "General Notice," Mar 23, 1942, John Boisvert to DVW, Dec 13, 1942, and DNT to DVW, Jan 22, 1942, Jan 4, 1943, and Feb 10, 1943, SF Corp. Corr.; DNT to DVW, Jan 13, 1944, DVW Corr. with DNT, Folder 2, DNT Corr.; "1946 Farm Plan—Vermont Agricultural Conservation Program" Form, Folder "1-AAA-(a)"; 1950 Agricultural Census Questionnaire, completed for SF, Second Folder "C-6 Misc.," SF Corr. Also MCW, comments on draft manuscript, Apr 10, 2007; Jane Boisvert, interview with author, May 7, 2007.

47 Frank Botala notes that a fire destroyed some or all of the piggery. However, the outline of the structure was depicted on the *Sanborn Insurance Maps* of 1942 and 1950, and Julie Eldridge Edwards notes that two local Shelburne residents were paid to dismantle the building in 1948–49. It is likely that Botala meant the creamery, which was destroyed by fire in 1942. Botala, disk 1; *Sanborn Insurance Maps* for Burlington, VT, 1942 (sheet 50) and 1942–1960 (sheet 50), Special Collections Department, Bailey/Howe Library, UVM; Julie Eldridge Edwards, "Did You Know…," *InFARMation*, Jun 13, 2008.

48 The following sources are all from the FM's Papers: DVW to DNT, Dec 21, 1941, and Jan 5, 1942, DNT to DVW, Jan 11 and 22, 1942, SF Corp. Corr.; DNT to DVW, May 8, 1942, DVW Corr. with DNT, Folder 2, DNT Corr. Also MCW, comments on draft manuscript, Apr 10, 2007; "History in a chicken house," *InFARMation*, Jun 4, 1993; DVW, "Statement," 61.

49 DVW, "Statement," 61.
50 Contrary to DVW's recollection that soybeans were not introduced to SF until c. 1948, farm records document the sowing of the crop by 1939. The following sources are in DVW Papers: DVW to AOW, Jun 4, 1939, Folder 4, Box 8; DVW to AOW, c. Sep 1939, and DVW to VW, Aug 8, 1940, both in Folder "Letters from DVW re Early Farm Operation," Box 7. Also DVW, "Statement," 61; Botala, disk 2.
51 "Summary of the 1938 A.A.A. Farm Program Northeast Region," USDA Regional Information Series Bulletin, c. Apr 1938, and Folder "1-AAA-(a)," passim, Box 9, DVW Papers.
52 DVW, "Statement," 61.
53 The following sources are in SF Corp. Corr., FM's Papers: DVW to Richard Robbins, Jul 20, 1940, Folder "R-1 R. W. Robbins"; and DNT to JWW, Nov 13, 1937, undated Folder 8. Also Botala, disk 1.
54 The following are all in SF Corp. Corr., FM's Papers: DNT to VW, Jan 25, 1937, Jun 8, 1938, and Sep 27, 1938; VW to DNT, Jan 27, 1937; and DVW to VW, Jun 6, 1939.
55 VW to FVJ, Nov 29, 1944, SF Corp. Corr., FM's Papers.
56 Deed, FVJ and CJ to VW, May 22, 1946, vol. 30, 123–124, Land Records, STC.
57 DVW to VW, May 19, 1941, Folder "Letters from DVW re Early Farm Operation," Box 7, DVW Papers.
58 MCW, comments on draft manuscript, Apr 10, 2007.
59 DVW to VW, Sep 27, 1942, Folder 6, Box 8, DVW Papers.
60 AOW to DVW, Jun 17, 1947, "Misc. Family Correspondence Folder," Box 8, DVW Papers.
61 WW died in 1967, but it is unclear exactly when he and his wife ceased to return to SF each summer. Sherman notes 1958; JWW recorded their presence at the annex though 1951; VW noted that they planned to return in the summer of 1953; MCW believes it was the early 1950s. MCW to author, Jan 25, 2007, and comments on draft manuscript, Apr 10, 2007; JWW diaries, passim, including Jun 23, 1951, JWW Jr. Coll.; VW to DVW, Mar 31, 1953, SF Corp. Corr., FM's Papers; Joe Sherman, *The House at Shelburne Farms: The Story of One of America's Great Country Estates* (Middlebury, VT: Paul S. Eriksson, 1986), 77, 79.
62 AOW, "Almost a Century," 65.
63 AOW and VW's domestic staff included butler Arthur Harris and Agnes Murphy, who served as cook and housekeeper. AOW, "Almost a Century," 33, 86 (quote on 33); AOW, Transcript of Oral History Interview with EWW, Sep 4, 1976, 35; VW to LOW, Jan 13, [c. 1932–34], Folder 29, Deed Box Coll., LOW Papers; Sherman, *The House at Shelburne Farms*, 78.
64 VW and AOW also made some changes to the house's plumbing system in order to facilitate water drainage from the pipes each fall to avoid damage while the house was unheated. Quote from AOW, "Almost a Century," 31–32. Also AOW, Transcript of Oral History Interview, 13-14.
65 VW and AOW also installed double exterior doors in the corridor hall leading out to the lawn (AOW, Transcript of Oral History Interview, 18). JWW to VW, Jun 7, 1938, FM's Papers; DVW to AOW, Jun 4, 1939, Folder 4, Box 8, DVW Papers; MCW, comments on draft manuscript, Apr 10, 2007; AOW, Transcript of Oral History Interview, 35.
66 DNT to JWW, Nov 16, 1936, unlabeled Folder 9, FM's Papers.
67 Charles Congdon to VW, Nov 3, 1941, and VW to Congdon, Nov 6, 1941, SF Corp. Corr., FM's Papers; AOW, Transcript of Oral History Interview, 13-14.
68 The laundry/icehouse building may have originally been built for laundry use during the late 19th c., before laundry facilities were available in the new servants' wing, and then converted for use as an icehouse. Once electric refrigeration was installed in Shelburne House in the late 1930s, the outbuilding's icehouse component was also increasingly unnecessary. In 1935, the laundry/icehouse's ceiling collapsed as a result of a local earthquake. It appears that the icehouse was stocked for the Webb family's use at least through the mid-1940s and then used for storage purposes. For servants' wing, see AOW, Transcript of Oral History Interview, 35; Sherman, *The House at Shelburne Farms*, 78; and SBW Jr., comments on draft manuscript, Apr 2, 2007. For garbage house, see DNT to VW, Jun 22, 1942, Folder 5, "W to Z Letter File Farm Barn Office," FM's Papers. For laundry/icehouse building, see "G. S. Blodgett Co. Heating and Ventilating Engineering, Burlington, Vt.," Shelburne House floor plan, c. 1895, APMI; WSW Jr. to DNT, Feb 8, 1946, Folder 2, "W to Z Letter File Farm Barn Office," FM's Papers; "Old Laundry & Ice House Area," Apr 4, 1960, "1959–60 Inventory" Folder, DVW Papers; MCW, comment during Botala, disk 2, and comments on draft manuscript, Apr 10, 2007; *Sanborn Fire Insurance Map* for Burlington, VT, 1942, Special Collections, Bailey/Howe Library, UVM.
69 JWW to DNT, Feb 2, 1937, undated Folder 8, FM's Papers. Also JWW to DNT, Feb 5, 1937, SF Corp. Corr., FM's Papers.
70 Ibid.
71 The greenhouse structures were re-erected at Gardenside Nurseries on Webster Road in Shelburne, where they remained at the time of this writing. Obituary for Alexander Graham, *BFP*, Jul 21, 1944. Also the following sources in the FM's Papers: A. J. LaBarge of LaBarge Flower Shop to DNT, Oct 26, 1936, unlabeled Folder 4; DNT to JWW, Feb 11, 1937; JWW to VW, May 8, 1938; DNT to Alexander Graham, Aug 29, 1938; and VW to DNT, May 29, 1939, all in SF Corp. Corr.; DNT to Dr. Oliver N. Eastman, Dec 8, 1938, and Eastman to DNT, Jan 8, 1939, both in unlabeled Folder 3; Eastman to DNT, Apr 24, 1939, and DNT to B. J. Fayette, May 16, 1939, and Feb 28, 1940, all in Folder "G Letter File Farm Barn Office Emptied 4/2/77," DNT Corr.; "Length of Service," Jul 1, 1939, Folder "E-F Letter File Farm Barn Office Emptied 4/2/77," DNT Corr.
72 WSW Jr. to DNT, Apr 8, 1936, Folder 2, DNT Corr., FM's Papers; DNT to unknown recipient, Jan 30, 1937, undated Folder 8, FM's Papers; Keenis Patterson, interview with author, Jan 24, 2007. MCW also recalls finding a "ground driven reel mower," which may have been used for the links and/or lawn areas near the main house (MCW, comments on draft manuscript, Apr 10, 2007).
73 Margaret Campbell, Erica Donnis, Patricia O'Donnell, and Catherine Quinn, *Shelburne Farms National Historic Landmark Nomination*, 2000, 23.
74 In more recent years, AOW's pottery studio has served as a potting shed, a staff apartment, and, most lately, a guest cottage. Campbell et al., 18, 20; "New room with a view," *InFARMation*, May 2, 1997; Julie Eldridge Edwards to author, May 15, 2009.
75 AOW, "Almost a Century," 67–70 (quote on 70).
76 Erica Donnis, AOW biography in Shelburne Farms Tour Guide Manual, c. 2000; "Aileen O. Webb, Leading Figure in National Crafts Movement, 87," *New York Times*, Aug 17, 1979.
77 The Jones's property at Sled Runner Point also included a garage, a tool shed, and, at some distance to the south of Allen Hill along the lakeshore, a simple summer cottage built for

Jaroslav Siskovsky, a violinist in the New York String Quartet for whom Frederica served as a patroness. Siskovsky had previously stayed at Bay View House, but by the late 1930s that dwelling's conditions were judged too antiquated to be satisfactory. JWW, Jan 2, 1938, 1938 Diary, JWW Jr. Coll.; DNT corr. with FVJ, 1938–45, Folder "IJK Letter File Farm Barn Emptied 4/2/77," DNT Corr., FM's Papers; FVJ to DVW, undated, Folder "Letters from Family & Friends 1938," Box 7, DVW Papers; FVJ, 1938 note in Shelburne House Guestbook, vol. 2, 140; Deed, John J. and Elizabeth C. Collamer to WSW, Aug 18, 1899, Folder 11, Legal Papers, FM's Papers; Wendy Joy Darby, "Wyeth & King, practiced 1930s–1940s, Marion Sims Wyeth, 1889–1982, and Frederick R. King," in Robert B. MacKay, Anthony Baker, and Carol A. Traynor, eds., *Long Island Country Houses and Their Architects, 1860–1940* (New York: W. W. Norton and Society for the Preservation of Long Island Antiquities, 1997), 444; Dantzscher, in Carlisle, ed., *Look Around St. George and Shelburne, Vermont*, 51; MCW, comments on draft manuscript, Apr 10, 2007.

78 The Botalas named two of their children Frederica and Cyril after Mr. and Mrs. Jones. Botala, disks 1 and 2; DNT to JWW, May 28, 1936, unlabeled Folder 9, FM's Papers.

79 The Browns demolished the Captain White house and reused the brick from the structure in their own new residence, which was constructed starting in the fall of 1940 (DVW to VW, Nov 21, 1940, Folder 5, Box 8, DVW Corr.). Deed, FVJ and CJ to Archibald W. Brown Jr. and Mary M. C. Brown, Aug 24, 1940, vol. 28, 165–67, Land Records, STC.

80 T. J. Allison to JWW, Jan 10, 1952, KWH Coll. Also JWW to Dennison Hull, Sep 29, 1950, KWH Coll.; JWW, Shelburne Fox Hounds record book, vol. 2, 1927–52, 403–24, Webb Family Papers, SMA; JWW diaries, passim, JWW Jr. Coll.

81 JWW, Nov 13, 1941, 1941 Diary and Sep 3, 1938, 1938 Diary, JWW Jr. Coll.

82 See, for example, JWW, Nov 5, 1938, 1938 Diary; Jan 9 and Nov 24, 1939, 1939 Diary; and Jul 30, 1943, 1943 Diary, all in JWW Jr. Coll.

83 JWW, diary entries, passim, JWW Jr. Coll.; George Edward Steen obituary, *BFP*, Jun 2, 1979.

84 JWW, diary entries, passim, including Dec 25, 1937, 1937 Diary; Mar 23, 1941, 1941 Diary; and Apr 6, 1943, 1943 Diary, JWW Jr. Coll.; DNT to JWW, Jan 1, 1938, undated Folder 8, FM's Papers; SBW Jr., Transcript of Oral History Interview, 8, SMA; Barbara Steen Paulman, corr. with author, Apr 7, 2007.

85 The following records are all in Land Records, STC: Deed, Sheepraise Corp. to EHW, Mar 31, 1932, vol. 22, 66; Deed, Sheepraise Corp. to JWW, Mar 31, 1932, vol. 22, 67; and Deed, VW to JWW, Oct 30, 1944, vol. 30, 10–12.

86 Deed, JWW and EHW to EWB, Jun 14, 1933, vol. 23, 85, Land Records, STC; JWW to FK, Mar 5, [c. 1932], JWW to Mrs. Ruth Roberts, Apr 13, 1932, and JWW memo, May 2, 1932, all in Folder 2, FK Corr. with JWW, FM's Papers. Also JWW, Mar 26, Apr 23, May 28, Jun 15, Jul 9, Jul 25, and Nov 23, 1932, 1932 Diary; Jan 28–29, Feb 5, and Jul 29, 1933, 1933 Diary; Jan 29, 1934, 1934 Diary; and Jul 3, 1935, 1935 Diary, all JWW Jr. Coll.

87 DWB to DNT, Apr 23, 1934, Folder "Bo-C," FM's Papers; FK to VW, Sep 5 and Sep 8, 1934, Folder 4, FK Corr. with VW, FM's Papers; "Trot Mark Broken by Nibble Hanover," *New York Times*, Sep 25, 1938; "To Retire Nibble Hanover," *New York Times*, May 24, 1942; "$100,000 Is Paid for Trotting Sire," *New York Times*, Sep 4, 1949; Deed, JWW to EWB, Mar 8, 1940, vol. 28, 79–81, Land Records, STC; "Division of Cost of Aerial Survey Made of Shelburne Farms, Southern Acres Farm and South End Farm by C. S. Robinson, Ithaca, N.Y.," Jan 15, 1940, SF Corp. Corr., FM's Papers; JWW, Nov 30, 1950, 1950 Diary, and Mar 6, 1951, 1951 Diary, JWW Jr. Coll.; "A Day in the Country, June 24th and 25th, 1953," *Proceedings of the New York Farmers*, Season 1952–53 (New York: 1953), 488, Shelburne Museum Library; Newspaper clipping from unidentified source, titled "Sheppard Pays $100,000 for Bostwick Stud," c. 1949, inserted in Brick House Guestbook, vol. 1, 1914–54, Webb Family Papers, SMA; Obituary for DWB, *BFP*, Jan 27, 2006.

88 In 1947, SBW Sr. demolished a section of the original farmhouse and constructed a large addition designed by architect Donald Ryan. JWW Sr. continued to pasture sheep on Quaker Smith Point into the 1950s. SBW Jr., conversations with author, Aug 30, 2006, and May 4, 2007; MCW, comments on draft manuscript, Apr 10, 2007; Deed, VW and AOW to SBW Sr., Jul 24, 1947, vol. 32, 14–16, and Deed, JWW to SBW Sr., Mar 31, 1949, vol. 32, 136–37, both in Land Records, STC; JWW, Nov 1, 1941, 1941 Diary and Mar 12, 1947, 1947 Diary, JWW Jr. Coll.; Civil Engineering Associates, "Property of Samuel B. Webb, Shelburne, Vermont," Aug 1975, 2004.3.21.62, FFD 8, Folder 10, APMI.

89 JWW, diary entries, passim, JWW Jr. Coll.; MCW, comments on draft manuscript, Apr 10, 2007; SBW Jr., comments on draft manuscript, Apr 2, 2007.

90 JWW to FK, Dec 20 [c. 1923–24], Folder 3, "Some of Mr. J. W. Webb's Letters," FM's Papers. Also JWW diaries, passim, JWW Jr. Coll.; and the following in the FM's Papers: DVW to DNT, Feb 17 and Dec 31, 1941, Folder 2; DVW Corr. with DNT; DVW to George Silvernail, Mar 31, 1941, Folder "B-1-d III"; JWW to DNT, Nov 22, 1943, Folder 4, "W to Z Letter File Farm Barn Office," DNT Corr.

91 GW to DNT, May 5, [1942 or 1943], Folder 4, "W to Z Letter File Farm Barn Office," DNT Corr., FM's Papers.

92 FVJ to DNT, Apr 23 and 29, 1941, and DNT to FVJ, Apr 27, 1941, both in Folder "IJK Letter File Farm Barn Office Emptied 4/2/77," DNT Corr., FM's Papers.

93 It is not entirely clear when the walls dividing the house were constructed, whether in the late 1930s, when VW and AOW were completing other work in WSW Sr.'s former office, or in 1941, in anticipation of WSW Jr.'s arrival. MCW to author, Jan 25, 2007, and comments on draft manuscript, Apr 10, 2007; AOW, Transcript of Oral History Interview, 33, 35; and the following in "W to Z Letter File Farm Barn Office," DNT Corr., FM's Papers: WW to DNT, Apr 30, 1941, and WSW Jr. to DNT, May 12, 1941, both in Folder 5, and DNT to WSW Jr., Apr 3, 1945, Folder 3.

94 The house was heated through at least the winter of 1938 and possibly into the early 1940s; DVW noted the lack of heat in the winter of 1945. JWW to VW, Jun 7, 1938, SF Corp. Corr., and DNT to VW, Mar 21, 1945, Folder 3, "W to Z Letter File, Farm Barn Office," DNT Corr., both in FM's Papers; MCW, conversation with author, Oct 12, 2006, and comments on draft manuscript, Apr 10, 2007.

95 After the war, WSW Jr.'s victory garden was abandoned, and employee Darcy Patterson cultivated a large vegetable garden for VW and AOW on the Coach Barn lawn. MCW, comments on draft manuscript, Apr 10, 2007; SBW Jr., interview with author, May 4, 2007; and the following in the FM's Papers: DNT to DVW, Apr 11, 1942, and VW to DNT, May 28, 1942,

both in SF Corp. Corr.; WSW Jr. to DNT, Mar 23, [1943], Folder 4, "W to Z Letter File Farm Barn Office"; GW to DNT, Mar 28, 1945, and WSW Jr. to DNT, Apr 30, 1945, both in Folder 3, "W to Z Letter File, Farm Barn Office," DNT Corr; FVJ to DNT, May 4, 1942, and CJ to DNT, Apr 5, 1943, both in Folder "IJK Letter File Farm Barn Office Emptied 4/2/77," DNT Corr.

96 SBW Jr., Oral History Interview, Oct 18, 2004; Keenis Patterson, interview with author, Jan 24, 2007.

97 AOW, "Almost a Century," 105–6.

98 JWW, Mar 8, 1942, 1942 Diary, JWW Jr. Coll.

99 AOW, "Almost a Century," 106; DWB obituary, BFP, Jan 27, 2006; MCW, comments on draft manuscript, Apr 10, 2007.

100 DVW, "To the Men of Shelburne Farms," Dec 13, 1941, General Order Book 2, FM's Papers. Also Barbara Kent Interview, 7, and Edward Coleman Interview, 16, in "Shelburne, Vermont Historic Settlement Oral History Project," c. 2002, VDHP; DNT to FVJ, Sep 22, 1944, Folder "IJK Letter File Farm Barn Office Emptied 4/2/77," DNT Corr., FM's Papers; Ginny Walters, "Couple Create Rich History: Colemans' Memories Paint Picture of Past," BFP, Apr 28, 1999; Barbara Steen Paulman, corr. with author, Apr 7, 2007.

101 The following sources are in DNT Corr., FM's Papers: unsigned letter to Mr. and Mrs. Edgarton, c. Sep 1942, DVW Corr. with DNT, Folder 2; Richard Webb to VW, Nov 15, 1943, Folder 4, "W to Z Letter File Farm Barn Office."

102 VW to F. B. Morrison, Feb 9, 1944, Folder "B-1-(d)-III," FM's Papers. For DVW's role, see, for instance, DVW to DNT, Feb 9, 1942, SF Corp. Corr., FM's Papers.

103 AOW, "Almost a Century," 108; Botala, disk 1; AOW, Transcript of Oral History Interview, 36; MCW, comments on draft manuscript, Apr 10, 2007, and Jan 2009.

104 See, for instance, Botala, disk 1; DNT to DVW, Mar 29, 1943, SF Corp. Corr., and CJ to DNT, Jun 9, 1942, Folder "IJK Letter File Farm Barn Office Emptied 4/2/77," DNT Corr., both in FM's Papers.

105 DVW, "General Notice," Mar 23, 1942, SF Corp. Corr., FM's Papers. Also MCW to author, Feb 4, 2009.

106 JWW, May 19 and 20, 1943, 1943 Diary, JWW Jr. Coll.

107 JWW, May 29, 1944, 1944 Diary, JWW Jr. Coll. See, in general, JWW diary entries for 1942 to 1945, JWW Jr. Coll.

108 JWW to T. G. Patterson and Ray Noonan, Nov 12, 1942, copy in Folder 4, "W to Z Letter File Farm Barn Office," DNT Corr., FM's Papers.

109 MCW, comments on draft manuscript, Apr 10, 2007.

110 The following sources are all in FM's Papers: DVW to DNT, Nov 25, 1942, and DVW, notice to employees, Jul 20, 1942, both in DVW Corr. with DNT, Folder 2, DNT Corr.; DNT to VW, Sep 30, 1944, Folder 4, "W to Z Letter File Farm Barn Office," DNT Corr.; R. C. Archer to VW, Oct 18, 1945, SF Corp. Corr.

111 DNT to Office of Price Administration, Montpelier, VT, Jul 16, 1946, Folder "N.O.P. Letter File Shelburne Farms Farm Barn Office," DNT Corr., FM's Papers. Also FVJ to DNT, May 31, Sep 5, Sep 11, 1945, Folder "IJK Letter File Farm Barn Office Emptied 4/2/77," DNT Corr., FM's Papers; "Twenty-Five Memorable Dates in 1945," newspaper clipping in rear of JWW 1945 diary, JWW Jr. Coll.

112 JWW, Sep 4, 1942, 1942 Diary, JWW Jr. Coll. See also entries for Nov 28 and 29, 1942.

113 JWW, Feb 6 and 7, 1943, 1943 Diary, JWW Jr. Coll.; HHW, "Summary" [of Shelburne Hunt], 1946, KWH Coll.

114 JWW, Jun 1, 1942, 1942 Diary, JWW Jr. Coll. See also DVW, "General Notice," Mar 23, 1942, SF Corp. Corr., FM's Papers; JWW, May 3, 1942, 1942 Diary, JWW Jr. Coll.

115 JWW, Aug 14, 1945, 1945 Diary, JWW Jr. Coll.

116 JWW, Aug 15, 1945, 1945 Diary, JWW Jr. Coll.

Chapter 13

1 Byron E. Colby, UVM Extension Specialist in Animal Husbandry, "A Vermont Pen Stable," *Proceedings of the New York Farmers*, Season 1952–53 (New York, 1953), 492, Shelburne Museum Library.

2 WOW obituary, *New York Times*, Mar 3, 2002; WOW biographical information, provided by Garrett Webb, Aug 1, 2007; "Sunapee Family Chosen NH Tree Farmers of the Year," *Concord (NH) Weekly Market Bulletin*, Nov 24, 1999; Richard Webb to author, Mar 3, 2008; Obituary for Barbara Webb Rockwell Henry, *Lebanon (NH) Valley News*, Nov 7, 1991; Obituary for Henry Benson Rockwell, *Brattleboro (VT) Reformer*, May 13, 1974; Martha Rockwell to author, Dec 6, 2007.

3 CJ took a leave of absence from Milton Academy during the 1946–47 school year and resigned in 1947. CJ to DNT, letters 1945–48, all in Folder "IJK Letter File Farm Barn Office Emptied 4/2/77," DNT Corr., FM's Papers; JWW, diary entries, 1946–49, especially Jul 17, 1946, Sep 22, 1946, Jul 8, 1947, and Feb 2, 1949, JWW Jr. Coll.; "Mrs. Cyril Jones, Vanderbilt Heir, 66," *The New York Times*, Feb 3, 1949; "The Associate Head Master," *Milton Bulletin*, Feb 1941, Milton Academy Archives, copy in CJ Reference File.

4 JWW, Oct 17, 1953, 1953 Diary, JWW Jr. Coll.; Deed, CJ to VW, Oct 11, 1952, and Deed, CJ to VW, Jul 10, 1954, both in Folder 17, Legal Papers, FM's Papers; newspaper clipping from unidentified source, titled "Sheppard Pays $100,000 for Bostwick Stud," c. 1949, inserted in Brick House Guestbook, vol. 1, 1914–54, Webb Family Papers, SMA. See also Deed, CJ to HWW, May 19, 1953, vol. 36, 253, other pertinent deeds, and Fred C. Koerner, "Plan of Land in Shelburne, Vt. to be Conveyed By Cyril H. Jones to Robert F. & Jane H. Patrick," Map Book A, 75, all in Land Records, STC.

5 VW may also have had rheumatoid arthritis (LOW to VW, Mar 13, [1913], VW Papers). "Vanderbilt Webb, Lawyer, Dies at 65," *New York World-Telegram*, Jun 18, 1956; AOW, "Almost a Century," unpublished 1977 memoir, 140; VW, Last Will and Testament, signed Mar 25, 1954, copy in Chittenden County Probate Court records for Estate of Vanderbilt Webb, case #16709; "W. Seward Webb, A Realty Man," *New York Times*, Jan 21, 1956.

6 DVW to VW, Apr 26, 1940, Folder "Letters from DVW re Early Farm Operation," Box 7, and DVW to VW, Dec 3, 1940, Folder 5, Box 8, both in DVW Papers; and the following in FM's Papers: DNT to SW, Jan 4, 1943; DVW to DNT, May 4, 1943, DVW Corr. with DNT, Folder 2, DNT Corr.; DNT to DVW, Feb 22 and 24, 1941, and DVW to DNT, Feb 24, 1941, Folder "D. V. Webb Letter File," DVW Corr.; Roger Smith to SF, Jan 12, 1943, Second Folder "C-6 Misc."; DVW to Clifford Clevenger, Feb 12, 1943, Folder "H-3 Hogs," DVW Corr. For context on artificial insemination, see R. H. Foote, Department of Animal Science, Cornell University, "The History of Artificial Insemination: Selected Notes and Notables," American Society of Animal Science, 2002, http://www.asas.org/Bios/Footehist.pdf.

7 DVW, "Statement," in William C. Lipke, ed., *Shelburne Farms: The History of an Agricultural Estate* (Burlington, VT: UVM, 1979), 62.
8 DVW to Lester T. Sawyer, HyCrest Farm, Leominster, MA, Dec 1, 1948, Folder "C-1 Cattle Misc.," DVW Corr., FM's Papers. Also DVW, "Statement," in Lipke, 62; DVW to VW, Nov 23, 1948, DVW Corr., FM's Papers; DVW to Lester T. Sawyer, HyCrest Farm, Leominster, MA, Mar 12, 1949, Folder "C-1 Cattle Misc.," DVW Corr., FM's Papers; MCW, comments on draft manuscript, Apr 10, 2007; Herman R. Purdy and R. John Dawes, *Breeds of Cattle* (New York: Chanticleer Press, 1987), 220.
9 DVW, "A Word About Shelburne Farms," and Harold C. Magnussen, "About Our Herd," both in *Shelburne Farms Annual Harvest Time Brown Swiss Sale and Champlain Picnic* brochure, Aug 29, 1964, ASW Files; MCW, comments on Erica Donnis, DVW biography, in Shelburne Farms Tour Guide Manual, c. 2000, and comments on draft manuscript, Apr 10, 2007; Obituary for Harold Magnussen, *Schenectady (NY) Daily Gazette*, Sep 10, 1990.
10 DVW, "Statement," in Lipke, 62–63. Also SBW Sr., "Statement," in Lipke, 52.
11 DVW, "Statement," in Lipke, 63–65. For context on pole barn design, see Thomas Visser, *A Field Guide to New England Barns and Farm Buildings* (Hanover, NH: University Press of New England, 1997): 102–3. For the creamery, see DNT, "Fire Loss, Dairy Creamery & Cellars 9:45 A.M. Sunday, Aug 9th, 1942," Folder "E-F Letter File Farm Barn Office Emptied 4/2/77," DVW Corr., FM's Papers; H. Talbot Jr. to DNT, Sep 21, 1942, and VW to FVJ, Sep 24, 1942, both in FM's Papers.
12 MCW notes that the new pole barn was not perfectly centrally located in the midst of the Farm's main pastures and cropland, and surmises that the barn's proximity to Orchard House was a major factor in its placement (MCW, comments on draft manuscript, Apr 10, 2007). Quote in text from Colby, "A Vermont Pen Stable," 490. Also Peter Woodside, "Shelburne Farms Milking Barn Complex (As-Built)," Aug 1978, 2004.3.15.10, FFD 7, Folder 1, APMI.
13 The trench silos were constructed in 1951, one year before the pole barn. Colby, "A Vermont Pen Stable," 490–91; DVW, "Statement," in Lipke, 63–65; JWW, Jul 7, 1951, 1951 Diary, JWW Jr. Coll.; ASW, interview with author, Feb 22, 2007; "A Day in the Country," Jun 24–25, 1953, *Proceedings of the New York Farmers*, Season 1952–53 (New York, 1953), 487. For context on bulk tanks, see Visser, 117; Michael Sherman, Gene Sessions, and P. Jeffrey Potash, *Freedom and Unity: A History of Vermont* (Barre, VT: Vermont Historical Society, 2004), 516–17.
14 DVW, "Statement," in Lipke, 63–65; VW to Harold Pierce, Burlingame, Field, Pierce & Browne, Inc., Jan 24, 1955, FM's Papers; Frank and Frederica Botala, Oral History Interview, Jun 26, 2006, disk 2; Margaret Campbell, Erica Donnis, Patricia O'Donnell, and Catherine Quinn, *Shelburne Farms National Historic Landmark Nomination*, 2000, 16–17, 26; MCW, comments on draft manuscript, Apr 10, 2007, and interview with author, May 16, 2007.
15 DNT to DVW, Jan 25, 1945, DVW Corr. with DNT, Folder 1, DNT Corr., FM's Papers.
16 Colby, "A Vermont Pen Stable," 492. Also DVW, "Statement," in Lipke, 65.
17 DVW, "Statement," in Lipke, 65; DVW, "A Word About Shelburne Farms," and Harold C. Magnussen, "About Our Herd."
18 Corr. in Folder "D-1 (f) Milk," DVW Corr., FM's Papers; DVW, "Statement," in Lipke, 62; MCW, comments on draft manuscript, Apr 10, 2007.
19 DVW, "Statement," in Lipke, 63–65.
20 Ibid, 62; ASW, interview with author, Feb 22, 2007; MCW, interview with author, Feb 26, 2007.
21 "Shelburne's Derick Webb Dies at 70," *BFP*, Mar 15, 1984; DVW's Vermont State Senator Campaign Brochure, Folder for Vermont State Senator Campaign Brochure, DVW Papers; Christie Carter, Vermont State Archives, to author, Mar 20, 2000, in "Webb, Derick" Reference File; Erica Donnis, DVW biography, in Shelburne Farms Tour Guide Manual, c. 2000; MCW, comments on draft Chapter 12, Jan 2009.
22 While certainly generous, DVW's efforts may have been a conscious attempt to sow goodwill among community members to ward off a contemplated rerouting of Route 7 to the west, potentially across his land. Lease, DVW to State of Vermont, Oct 24, 1957, and Deed, DVW to Town of Shelburne, Feb 1960, both in Folder 17, Legal Papers, FM's Papers; MCW and ASW, corr. with author, Apr 27, 2007.
23 At the time of this writing, biographical information for Herbert Stapleton had yet to be located. MCW, comments on draft manuscript, Apr 10, 2007, and comments on draft Chapter 11, Jan 2009; DVW, "Statement," in Lipke, 65; VW to DVW, Sep 10, 1954, DVW Corr., FM's Papers.
24 DVW apparently considered locating some portions of the dairy complex, including the holding and calf barns, on a site just north of the site of the former greenhouses, a location which would have sheltered at least some dairy activities from the view of the parkland section of the estate. This site may have been rejected because placing these activities away from the main dairy barn would have been less convenient for dairy staff and created additional labor costs. See William S. Cowles Jr., "SF Site Plan, Project No. 256," Jun 1954, 2004.3.15.15, FFD 7, Folder 2, APMI.
25 EHW, from "What Started Me With The Museum, By Electra Havemeyer Webb," Box 1, Folder 2, EHW Papers, SMA, quoted in Edwards, "The Evolution of Electra Havemeyer Webb's Country Estate: The Brick House, 1913-1947," unpublished thesis for the Masters Program in the History of the Decorative Arts, Cooper-Hewitt, National Design Museum and Parsons School of Design, 2002, 86. See also JWW Jr., introduction to Edward Wheeling, *Horse-Drawn Vehicles at the Shelburne Museum* (Shelburne, VT: The Shelburne Museum, 1974).
26 Lauren B. Hewes and Celia Y. Oliver, *To Collect in Earnest: The Life and Work of Electra Havemeyer Webb* (Shelburne, VT: Shelburne Museum, 1997), 27.
27 WSW Jr. to DNT, Feb 8, 1946, Folder 2, and WSW Jr. to DNT, Apr 20, [1946], Folder 1, "W to Z Letter File, Farm Barn Office," both in DNT Corr., FM's Papers; MCW to author, Jan 25, 2007.
28 AOW's 1960 residence has been variously referred to as the "Mrs. Vanderbilt Webb House," "Grandma's House," the "Summer House," the "Wildflower House," and the "Glass House." AOW, Transcript of Oral History Interview with EWW, Sep 4, 1976, 37–39; MCW to author, Jan 25, 2007; Campbell et al., 20; "Shelburne Farms Today=1982," map of property, 2004.21.75a, FFD 9, Folder 2, APMI.
29 ECWS, interview with author, May 2, 2007.
30 Prior to the war, DVW had made a home for himself first at the coachman's house, then known as the "Coach Barn

Cottage" (DVW to VW, Jan 14, 1939, and DVW to VW and AOW, Apr 3, 1939, Folder "Letters from Family & Friends Letters from D.V.W. re Early Cattle Operation 1938–1939," Box 7, DVW Papers), and then at Orchard House. He made minor modifications to Orchard House in the fall of 1940 when he moved into the house, including plumbing and heating repairs, painting, and upgrading the kitchen appliances. DVW to VW, Sep 8, 1940, Folder "Letters from Family & Friends Letters from DVW re Early Farm Operation," Box 7, DVW Papers; DVW to VW, Aug 8, 1940, Folder 5, Box 8, DVW Papers; VW to DVW, Nov 10, 1941, DVW Corr., FM's Papers; JWW, Oct 3, 1946, 1946 Diary, Apr 4, 1949, 1949 Diary, and Mar 11, 1950, 1950 Diary, JWW Jr. Coll.; MCW, comments on draft manuscript, Apr 10, 2007; ECWS, interview with author, May 2, 2007.

31 ASW, quoted in Marialisa Calta, "Gilded-Age Splendor: A Mansion's New Life," *New York Times*, Jun 4, 1987. Also AOW, Transcript of Oral History Interview, 37–38; ECWS, interview with author, May 2, 2007; MCW, comments on draft Chapter 12, Jan 2009; Tom McCormick, "Goodbye to the Gilded Age," *Wesleyan University Alumnus*, vol. LXXXI (Fall 1988): 23–27.

32 ASW, quoted in Calta, "Gilded-Age Splendor."

33 MCW to author, Jan 25, 2007, and comments on draft manuscript, Apr 10, 2007.

34 The broken water pipe was located in the basement of the main dwelling, under the north (game) room. Water ran downhill through the interconnected cellars into the servants' wing, where it collected until it spilled out of the wing's basement windows. MCW to author, Jan 25, 2007, comments on draft manuscript, Apr 10, 2007, and Jan 2009, and comments during Botala interview, disk 2.

35 Polly Darnell, Shelburne Museum Archivist, to author, Dec 20, 2006; Edwards, "Evolution," 61, 86; Hewes and Oliver, 26–27.

36 JWW, diary entries, passim, JWW Jr. Coll.

37 JWW, May 13, 1947, 1947 Diary, JWW Jr. Coll.

38 JWW, Jul 7, 1950, 1950 Diary, JWW Jr. Coll.

39 JWW, diary entries, passim, JWW Jr. Coll.

40 JWW, Nov 16, 1948, 1948 Diary, JWW Jr. Coll. See also SBW Sr., "Statement," in Lipke, 52; and HHW, "Summary," [of Shelburne Hunt], 1946, KWH Coll.

41 SBW Jr. maintains that the last hunt was conducted at Thanksgiving in 1952. SBW Sr. gives a date of 1955. However, the last hunt documented in JWW's papers occurred in 1949. JWW diaries, passim, including Sep 6, 1949, and Jul 6, 1954, JWW Jr. Coll.; JWW, Shelburne Fox Hounds Record Book, vol. 2, 1927–52, 444–45, 454–57, MS 335, Webb Family Papers, SMA; SBW Jr., in Alexander Mackay-Smith, *Masters of Foxhounds* (Masters of Foxhounds Association of America, Inc., 1980), 103; SBW Jr., Oral History Interview, Oct 18, 2004, and comments on draft manuscript, Apr 2, 2007.

42 SBW Sr. to VW, Sept 24, 1952, FM's Papers.

43 HHW's two farms in Charlotte were called High Acres Farm #1 and High Acres Farm #2, not to be confused with his High Acres Farm in Shelburne. In Dec 1974, just before Harry's death, he gave one of his Charlotte farms to his daughter Dundeen ("Deenie") (b. 1952). She and her new husband, Steven Galipeau, a former SAF employee, managed the farm from 1975 to 1980. Deed, JWW to HHW, Dec 2, 1950, vol. 32, 248–50, Land Records, STC; JWW, diary entries, passim, JWW Jr. Coll.; JWW Jr., Interview with Hope Alswang, Sep 1998, tape 3, Audio Recordings, SMA; KWH, interview with author, Mar 5, 2007; Dundeen and Steven Galipeau, interview with author, Dec 12, 2007; Obituary for Kate (Jennings) Webb Seemann, *BFP*, Feb 17, 2002.

44 Dundeen and Steven Galipeau, interview with author; KWH, interview with author, Jan 29, 2008; JWW, May 19, 1959, JWW Diary, JWW Jr. Papers; Lilian Baker Carlisle, ed., *Look Around St. George and Shelburne, Vermont* (Burlington, VT: Chittenden County Historical Society, 1975), 60. Also the following in Land Records, STC: Deed, Administration of Veterans' Affairs to HHW and Kate J. Webb, Apr 27, 1959, vol. 37, 8; Deed, HHW and Kate J. Webb to Shelburne Harbor Inn, Inc., May 21, 1959, vol. 37, 23.

45 SBW Sr. maintained a membership in Okeetee Club in South Carolina (the same hunting club to which JWW Sr. and EHW belonged), owned a salmon fishing camp in Quebec, and participated in a red grouse shooting club in Northumberland, England. After his parents' deaths in 1960, he acquired a portion of Nehasane and his father's interest in Moultrie Plantation in South Carolina. SBW Sr. to JWW Jr., Mar 17, 1975, and SBW Sr. to Frank L. Mallory, Apr 30, 1975, both in Shelburne Museum Administrative Records, Box 21, SMA-24, SMA; SBW Jr., comments on draft Chapter XI, Feb 21, 2008.

46 SBW Sr., "Statement," in Lipke, 55.

47 The transaction was delayed by the deaths of VW in 1956 and JWW and EHW in 1960. DVW officially sold the property to SBW Sr. and HHW, who then granted JWW Jr. a one-third interest in the parcel. SBW Sr. to VW, Sep 24, 1952, and VW to SBW Sr., Sep 29, 1952, both in FM's Papers; Deed, DVW and ECW to SBW Sr. and HHW, Mar 27, 1961, vol. 37, 301–2, and Deed, SBW Sr., Martha T. Webb, HHW, and Kate J. Webb to JWW Jr., Nov 20, 1961, vol. 39, 17–18, both in Land Records, STC; JWW, Aug 7, Sep 6, and Oct 28, 1958, 1958 Diary, JWW Jr. Coll.; Receipt and Acknowledgement, DVW to Executors of the Will of EHW, SBW Sr., and HHW, Mar 27, 1961, Folder 17, Legal Papers, FM's Papers.

48 JWW also bequeathed equal shares in Nehasane to his five children and equal shares in Moultrie Plantation in South Carolina to his three sons. In 1961, SBW Sr., HHW, EWB, and LWW purchased JWW Jr.'s interest in Nehasane, and SBW Sr. purchased JWW Jr.'s interest in Moultrie. The remaining owners divided the properties into separate, individually owned segments. JWW diaries, passim, JWW Jr. Coll.; "J. Watson Webb, Sportsman, Dies," *New York Times*, Mar 5, 1960; JWW, Copy of Last Will and Testament, Chittenden County Probate Records for Estate of JWW, case #17292; Estate of EHW, Final Accounting of Estate, May 1, 1964, Folder 5, Box 3, SBW Sr. Papers; SBW Sr. to JWW Jr., Mar 17, 1975, and SBW Sr. to Frank L. Mallory, Apr 30, 1975, both in Shelburne Museum Administrative Records, Box 21, SMA-24, SMA; SBW Jr., comments on draft Chapter XI, Feb 21, 2008.

49 JWW Jr. to SBW Sr., Mar 8, 1975, Shelburne Museum Administrative Records, Box 21, SMA-24, SMA. Also SBW Sr. to JWW Jr., Mar 17, 1975, in same location.

50 SBW Sr. to JWW Jr., Mar 17, 1975, Shelburne Museum Administrative Records, Box 21, SMA-24, SMA.

51 Deed, SBW Sr., Martha T. Webb, HHW, and Kate J. Webb to JWW Jr., Nov 28, 1961, vol. 39, 15–16, Land Records, STC; Campbell et al., 37; Barbara Steen Paulman to author, Apr 7, 2007; Polly Darnell, Shelburne Museum Archivist, to author, Sep 18, 2007, and interview with author, Sep 14, 2007; KWH, interview with author, Jan 29, 2008.

52 Dundeen and Steven Galipeau, interview with author; KWH and Frank Galipeau, Oral History Interview with Julie Eldridge

Edwards, Oct 14, 2004; SBW Sr. to JWW Jr., Mar 17, 1975, Shelburne Museum Administrative Records, Box 21, SMA-24, SMA.

53 A letter from VW to Museum Director Sterling Emerson of Oct 24, 1955, points to a regular pattern of borrowing staff, dating from JWW and EHW's time (Folder "Sterling Emerson Correspondence with Vanderbilt Webb," Shelburne Museum Administrative Records, Box 22, SMA-24, SMA). Shelburne Museum Invoice to Estate of EHW, Jan 21, 1961, Folder "Mr. J. Watson Webb Jr. Expenses 1955–1962" and Corr. with JWW, both in Shelburne Museum Financial Records, Box 10, SMA; SBW Sr. to JWW Jr., Mar 17, 1975, Shelburne Museum Administrative Records, Box 21, SMA-24, SMA; Obituary for John H. Brotz, *Shelburne (VT) News*, Jul 9, 1998, SMA; Dundeen and Steven Galipeau, interview with author; KWH and Frank Galipeau, Oral History Interview.

54 SBW Sr., "Statement," in Lipke, 51; KWH and Frank Galipeau, Oral History Interview.

55 According to Steven Galipeau, some Hereford breeding stock remained on the farm from 1967 to 1974. Quote from SBW Sr., "Statement," in Lipke, 55. Also KWH, interviews with author, Sep 5, 2007, and Jan 29, 2008; KWH and Frank Galipeau, Oral History Interview; Barbara Steen Paulman to author, Jun 5, 2007; KWH private photograph collection; Dundeen and Steven Galipeau, interview with author; Laura Webb Brown, interview with author, Jan 30, 2008; JWW Jr., "Pictorial History of the Webb Family," 47, JWW Jr. Coll.

56 During the winter months, the steers were housed in pens built in the interior of the Breeding Barn and in the former colt sheds behind the Breeding Barn. In 1968, many of the original horse stall partitions in the Breeding Barn were removed to provide additional space for the cattle and were subsequently burned. The dirt-floored interior was also covered with concrete to provide the livestock with more sanitary conditions. SBW Sr., "Statement," in Lipke, 55; KWH and Frank Galipeau, Oral History Interview; Dundeen and Steven Galipeau, interview with author; SBW Jr., interview with author, May 4, 2007.

Chapter 14

1 DVW, "Statement," in William C. Lipke, ed., *Shelburne Farms: The History of an Agricultural Estate* (Burlington, VT: UVM, 1979), 67.

2 Ibid.

3 MCW, "Notes taken by M.C.W. on a meeting with our Vermont and New York lawyers…" Apr 16, 1974, Folder "Farm Memos 1971–1979," MCW Files; MCW, interview with author, Feb 26, 2007, and comments on draft Chapter X, Apr 10, 2007; Gordon Paterson, Oral History Interview, Oct 12, 2006.

4 JWW, Apr 3, 1954, 1954 Diary, JWW Jr. Coll. Also MCW, comments on draft Chapter XI, Oct 31, 2007.

5 MCW, comments on draft Chapter X, Apr 10, 2007.

6 Ibid.

7 DVW, "Statement," in Lipke, 67. Also MCW, comments on draft Chapter X, Apr 10, 2007, and comments on draft Chapter XI, Oct 31, 2007; Margaret Campbell, Erica Donnis, Patricia O'Donnell, and Catherine Quinn, *Shelburne Farms National Historic Landmark Nomination*, 2000, 9; Frank and Frederica Botala, Oral History Interview, Jun 26, 2006, disk 1.

8 MCW, interview with author, May 3, 2007; Map of SF with notes indicating locations of dead trees, 1969, 2004.3.21.77, APMI.

9 It is difficult to make exact comparisons of property taxes for the SF property between the 1930s and the 1970s, as the amount of acreage and number of structures it contained fluctuated. VW owned about 1,400 acres in 1939, and DVW owned about 1,850 acres in 1969 and 1,650 acres in 1976. 1940 Agricultural Census Questionnaire, Second Folder "C-6 Misc.," FM's Papers; DVW, "Statement," in Lipke, 65; "Shelburne Farms Financial Plan, Spring 1974," Folder "Farm Memos 1971–1979," MCW Files; Michael Wool to ASW, Jul 10, 1975, "Meetings" Folder, MCW Files; Michael Sherman, Gene Sessions, and P. Jeffrey Potash, *Freedom and Unity: A History of Vermont* (Barre, VT: Vermont Historical Society, 2004), 607; Ed Myers, "Historic Shelburne, Though Growing Fast, Retaining Neighborhood Quality," *BFP*, Aug 10, 1967 (the author thanks Julie Eldridge Edwards for directing her to the latter source). Also entries for DVW and SF in Shelburne Grand Lists for 1969 (73–74) and 1976 (107), and Shelburne property tax rates, 1969 and 1976 Shelburne Town Reports, all in STC.

10 ASW, interview with author, Apr 17, 2007; MCW, interview with author, Apr 19, 2007.

11 Paterson, Oral History Interview, Oct 12, 2006, and interview with author, Apr 25, 2007.

12 DVW, "Statement," in Lipke, 67.

13 Unfortunately, little detailed documentation about Kiley's plans was known to exist at the time of this writing, as his office records were destroyed by fire shortly after his death. Dan Kiley, "Proposal for a State Park in Shelburne, Vermont; analysis of surrounding area," Jul 1967, 2004.3.21.64, and "Proposal for a State Park in Shelburne, Vermont; land use diagram," Jul 1967, 2004.3.21.65, both in FFD 8, Folder 10, APMI. Also Obituary for Daniel Urban Kiley, *BFP*, Feb 23, 2004; Dan Kiley and Jane Amidon, *Dan Kiley: The Complete Works of America's Master Landscape Architect* (Boston: Little, Brown and Company, 1999), 203, 211.

14 DVW, "Statement," in Lipke, 67; Paterson, interviews, Oct 12, 2006, and Apr 25, 2007; ASW, EWW, and MCW, "Shelburne Farms and the Future," undated typed manuscript [c. 1972], 10, MCW Files; ASW, interviews with author, Apr 17, 2007, and Jan 13, 2010; MCW, interview with author, Apr 19, 2007; Mrs. Gordon Paterson, Minutes of "Derick V. Webb Family Meeting," Aug 29, 1969, ASW Files; Lilian Baker Carlisle, ed., *Look Around Essex and Williston, Vermont* (Burlington, VT: Chittenden County Historical Society, 1973), 25.

15 DVW, quoted in Maggie Maurice, "Dining in Splendor," *BFP*, Aug 15, 1983.

16 DVW's eldest son, born Derick Osborn Webb and known during his early life as Derry, changed his first name to Quentyn in 1976. The meetings were held on the south porch (early to mid Aug 1969 and Jun 1970) and in the Farm Barn (Aug 29, 1969). Quote from Mrs. Gordon Paterson, Minutes of "Derick V. Webb Family Meeting." Also ASW, EWW, and MCW, "Shelburne Farms and the Future"; MCW, interview with author, Apr 19, 2007, and comments on draft Chapter XI, Oct 31, 2007; ASW to DVW, Dec 11, 1976, in Folder "DVW/ASW Fall '76," ASW Files.

17 DVW's house, which was first known by the Webb family as The Orchards, came to be called Orchard House by his children. Quote from ASW, in Craig Bailey, "Family Farm," *Business People Vermont*, Aug 1999, 2–7, 39–40. Also Mary and David Phillips to "Derry" [Quentyn Webb], May 1971, Folder

"Farm Memos 1971–1979," MCW Files; ECWS, interview with author, May 2, 2007; Mary Phillips Kelly, interview with author, Dec 11, 2007; Lisa and John Roberts, interview with author, Feb 26, 2008.

18 MCW, quoted in Bailey.
19 MCW, interview with author, Apr 19, 2007.
20 MCW recalls Erlich's *Population Bomb* (Paul R. Erlich, *The Population Bomb* [New York: Ballantine Books, 1968]) and Meadows's *Limits to Growth* (Donella H. Meadows, *The Limits to Growth: A Report for the Club of Rome's Project on the Predicament of Mankind* [New York: Universe Books, 1972]) as being particularly influential. Quote from ASW, in Ed Barna, "An Estate for Everyman: A Rejuvenated Shelburne Farms' New Mission for the 21st Century," *Vermont Magazine* 5 (May/June 1993): 36. Also ASW, EWW, and MCW, "Shelburne Farms and the Future;" MCW, interview with author, Apr 19, 2007, and comments on draft Chapter XI, Oct 31, 2007; ASW, comments on draft Chapter XI, Oct 29, 2007; MWN, interview with author, Feb 26, 2008; Aldo Leopold, *A Sand County Almanac, and Sketches Here and There* (New York: Oxford University Press, 1949); Rachel Carson, *Silent Spring* (Boston: Houghton Mifflin, 1962).
21 In 1970, DVW did sell one small parcel at the southeastern edge of his property, bordering Harbor Road, to the town of Shelburne so it could build a sewage treatment plant (DVW to Shelburne Fire District No. 2, Jul 1970, Folder 17, Legal Papers, FM's Papers). Quote from ASW, EWW, and MCW, "Shelburne Farms and the Future." Also ASW to DVW, Dec 11, 1976, Folder "DVW/ASW Fall '76," ASW Files.
22 MCW, comments on draft Chapter XI, Dec 10, 2007.
23 ASW, quoted in Barna, 36.
24 MCW, interview with author, Apr 19, 2007.
25 DVW, quoted in minutes of Webb family meeting, titled "5:00 PM Big House Library Sept 13 1972," in "Meetings" Folder, MCW Files. Also MCW, interview with author, Apr 19, 2007.
26 MCW, comments on draft Chapter XI, Dec 10, 2007.
27 ASW, interview with author, Apr 17, 2007, comments on draft Chapter XI, Oct 29 and Dec 4, 2007, and comments on draft Chapter 13, Nov 2009; MCW, interviews with author, Apr 19 and May 16, 2007, and comments on draft Chapter XI, Oct 31, 2007; Quentyn Webb, interview with author, Sep 5, 2007; Mary Phillips Kelly to author, Dec 6, 2007; Lisa and John Roberts, interview with author, Feb 26, 2008.
28 MCW, interview with author, Apr 19, 2007; ASW, comments on draft Chapter XI, Oct 29, 2007.
29 MCW, comments on draft Chapter XI, Dec 10, 2007. Also, for instance, "Minutes of Family Meeting," Dec 30, 1975, Folder "1975 Annual Meeting Marshall & Emily," MCW Files; DVW, Sep 8, 1975, "Meetings" Folder, MCW Files; MWN, interview with author, Feb 26, 2008.
30 DVW and ASW, "From Dad (and Alec) to the Family," Aug 5, 1975, "Meetings" Folder, MCW Files; MWN, interview with author, Feb 26, 2008.
31 ASW, interview with author, Mar 15, 2008, and comments on draft Chapter XI, Mar 31, 2008. Also MCW, comments on draft Chapter XI, Dec 10, 2007.
32 MWN, interviews with author, Sep 12, 2007, and Feb 26, 2008, and comments on draft Chapter 14, Nov 2009.
33 The Nature Conservancy, mission statement, at www.nature.org/aboutus. Also MWN, interviews with author, Sep 12, 2007, and Feb 26, 2008, and MWN to author, May 7, 2008.
34 MWN, interviews with author, Sep 12, 2007, and Feb 26, 2008; ASW, comments on draft Chapter XI, Jan 4, 2008.
35 The summer camp program was based out of an army surplus tent in the pheasantry pasture in 1970, was moved to the historic barn at Bay View in 1971, and was then located at the site of the original vegetable gardens and greenhouses in the center of the estate from 1972 to 1975. Quote from "At Shelburne Farms Camp," *Shelburne Newsletter*, vol. 6, no. 11 [c. spring 1974], ASW Files. Also MCW, IRS Application for Recognition of Exemption, [1972], and "Shelburne Farms Summer Camp" brochure, undated, both in "SFR" Folder, MCW Files; ASW, EWW, and MCW, "Shelburne Farms and the Future;" "Alec Webb, Background Notes for VCF, Aug 13, 2001," "Resumé" Folder, ASW Files; ASW, interview with author, Apr 17, 2007, comments on draft Chapter XI, Oct 29, 2007, and corr. with author, Jan 14, 2010; MCW, interview with author, Apr 19, 2007, and comments on draft Chapter XI, Oct 31, 2007.
36 ASW, Resumé, c. 1980, and Alternative Service reports, 1973–74, all in ASW Files; ASW, comments on draft Chapter XI, Oct 29, 2007.
37 MCW attended Groton School and then spent 3 years at Wesleyan University before withdrawing in 1969. He completed his undergraduate education at UVM. ASW, EWW, and MCW, "Shelburne Farms and the Future"; MCW, interviews with author, Apr 19, May 3, and May 16, 2007, and comments on draft Chapter XI, Oct 31, 2007.
38 MWN, quoted in Eric Loring, "Unique Shelburne Project to Focus on Ecological Values," *BFP*, Apr 30, 1971, Scrapbook vol. XXVII. Also ASW, Resumé, c. 1979, "Resumé" Folder, ASW Files; "Outdoor Crafts Program" publicity flyer, c. 1971, collection of MWN; Irene Zabytko, "Marilyn Webb: The Steward of Shelburne Farms," *Vermont Woman* (Apr 1988): 4–5; MWN, interviews with author, Sep 12, 2007, and Feb 26, 2008; ASW, comments on draft Chapter XI, Oct 29, 2007 and Jan 4, 2008.
39 SFR, Articles of Association, Jul 25, 1972, Board Minutes vol. 1, ASW Files. Also SFR Board Minutes, Aug 1972, Board Minutes vol. 1, ASW Files; MCW, IRS Application, "Shelburne Farms Resources—A Statement of Purpose—1972," and "Shelburne Farms Resources" brochure, all in "SFR" Folder, MCW Files.
40 "Notes on Meetings Concerning the Farm," Apr 2 [1972], "Meetings" Folder, MCW Files.
41 David Barash, "To The Trustees," Nov 1980, SFR, Inc. Binder, ASW Files. Also MCW to author, Dec 9, 2008.
42 Although the financial transaction was officially recorded in the board minutes as a loan of $6,000, ASW and MCW remember that a total of approximately $10,000 was effectively donated to SFR with "no expectations of being paid back" (MCW, comments on draft Chapter XI, Oct 31, 2007). Also ASW, interview with author, Dec 4, 2007; SFR Board Minutes, Aug 1972, Oct 5, 1972, and Nov 13, 1974, and Board Resolution, Dec 29, 1976, all in Board Minutes vol. 1, ASW Files; ASW, "Board Summary 10_03," ASW Files; MCW, IRS Application; MCW, interview with author, May 3, 2007.
43 SFR Board Minutes, Nov 13, 1974, and Jul 28, 1977, Board Minutes vol. 1, ASW Files; "The Baton Passes," *Shelburne Farms Newsletter*, Fall/Winter 1988, "Newsletters" Folder, SFR Coll.; MCW, interview with author, Apr 19, 2007; MWN to author, Feb 28, 2008.
44 MCW, comments on draft Chapter XI, Oct 31, 2007. Also MCW, quoted in SFR Board Minutes, May 4, 1973, Board Minutes vol. 1, ASW Files.
45 Shelburne Farms Annual Report, 2002, SFR Coll.; ASW,

"Board Summary 10_03," ASW Files; ASW, interviews with author, May 13, 2007, and Mar 15, 2008, and comments on draft Chapter 14, Nov 2009; MWN, interview with author, Feb 26, 2008, and comments on draft Chapter 14, Nov 2009.

46 SFR Board Minutes, Oct 2, 1974, Board Minutes vol. 1, ASW Files.

47 In 1972 and 1973, SFR expanded its programs at the Bay View area of the property to include an "alternative [outdoor] education course" managed by the local Champlain Valley Union High School, as well as garden plots available to local residents through Burlington Community Gardens. "Garden Plots at Shelburne Farms," and "Shelburne Farms Bayside Area is CVU's Summer Challenge Base," both in *Shelburne Newsletter*, vol. 6, no. 11 [c. spring 1974], ASW Files; Dorothy Pellett, "A Growing Enterprise: Community Gardening Groups That Took Root in 1970s are Still Sprouting New Offshoots," *BFP*, Apr 5, 2007; ASW to author, Apr 27, 2007.

48 After DVW and Elizabeth Webb's divorce in 1975, Elizabeth married photographer Clyde Smith, a longtime friend and neighbor who had rented Valley View House in the 1950s. MCW, interview with author, May 3, 2007; ERG, interview with author, Apr 23, 2007; SFR Board Minutes, Oct 5, 1972, Board Minutes vol. 1, ASW Files.

49 DVW to SFR, Inc., Jun 23, 1976, Board Minutes vol. 1, ASW Files. Also ASW to Mary and David Phillips, Aug 30, 1973, ASW Files; MCW, undated, handwritten document titled "Shelburne Farms," Folder "Farm Memos 1971–1979," MCW Files; Nancy Crowe, "Shelburne Farms: Laboratory for Agri(cultural) Ideas," *Barre (VT) Sunday Herald and Sunday Times Argus*, Nov 27, 1977, Scrapbook vol. XXVII; Edward Zimmerman to Director, Exempt Organization Division of Internal Revenue Service (IRS), Jun 20, 1980, SFR, Inc. Binder, ASW Files; SF Program and Facility Ideas, c. 1980, 2004.3.21.60, APMI; ASW, interview with author, Apr 17, 2007, and comments on draft Chapter XI, Oct 29, 2007.

50 Shelburne House was first opened for purposes related to the Webb siblings' educational programs and projects in 1972, when ASW arranged for permission from his parents to provide space for several meetings related to his work for the VT Department of Education (ASW, Alternative Service Report, Jul 16, 1973, ASW Files). SFR Board Minutes, Jan 20, 1975, and Mar 15, 1977, Board Minutes vol. 1, and Zimmerman to IRS, Jun 20, 1980, SFR, Inc. Binder, both in ASW Files; Paula Law-Killian, "How-To Series Touts Fresh Food for Health, Taste," *BFP*, Aug 19, 1977, Scrapbook vol. XXVII; "Doc Watson to Appear in Shelburne," *Middlebury (VT) Valley Voice*, Jul 19, 1978; "Jarrett Improvises in Vermont," *Vermont Educational Television Program Guide*, Aug 1978, Publicity Files; Tom Daniels, "Effort Made at Preservation of Country Property, Style," *BFP*, Jul 10, 1979; Maggie Maurice, "Music Camp," *BFP*, Jun 26, 1980; MCW, interview with author, May 3, 2007, and comments on draft Chapter XI, Oct 31, 2007.

51 MCW, interview with author, May 3, 2007; Vermont Mozart Festival, "History of the Vermont Mozart Festival," http://vtmozart.org/news_history.php; SFR Board Minutes, Nov. 27, 1974, and Mar 15, 1977, Board Minutes vol. 1, ASW Files.

52 Robin Green, "A Farm Is Saved—and Spreads Its Bounty," *New York Times*, Oct 17, 1979, Scrapbook vol. XXVII. Also Zimmerman to IRS, Jun 20, 1980, SFR, Inc. Binder, ASW Files; ERG, "The Shelburne Farms Bi-Monthly," Apr–May 1980, Folder "Staff—Job Descriptions," SFR Coll.

53 MWN, interview with author, Sep 12, 2007; ASW, comments on draft Chapter XI, Oct 29, 2007.

54 Active from 1972 to 1979, the Spinners group occupied space at the Farm Barn by 1975. Rockefeller, who became Eileen Growald after her marriage in 1980, operated her weaving studio in 1978 and 1979. Beeken and Downey arrived in 1980. Downey was succeeded by Jeff Parsons, with whom Beeken formed a partnership in 1983. Gardens For All occupied space at the Farm Barn from c. 1975 to 1977. O Bread opened its bakery in 1978. Of these ventures, Beeken/Parsons and O Bread continue to operate their businesses from the Farm Barn at the time of this writing. For Shelburne Spinners, see "Shelburne Farms: Stewardship in Practice" brochure, undated [before 1994], Folder "Stewardship in Practice," SFR Coll.; SFR Board Minutes, Nov 13, 1974, Board Minutes vol. 1, ASW Files; "The Wool Pool," *BFP*, Jun 11, 1977, Scrapbook vol. XXVII; "Shelburne Spinners to Spin Yarn and Tales at Reunion," *BFP*, Aug 27, 1987; Maggie Maurice, "Director Tries to Keep a Way of Life Alive," *BFP*, undated, Folder "Press Clippings 1982–1985 Inn," SFR Coll. For Gardens For All, see Maggie Maurice, "After Your Home Garden, It's in the Can," *BFP*, Jul 18, 1976. For O Bread, see Nancy Crowe, "'Organic' Sourdough Bread Bakers Set Up Shop in Shelburne Farms," *BFP*, Aug 13, 1978. Also ERG, interview with author, Apr 28, 2007; MCW, interview with author, May 3, 2007, and comments on draft Chapter 14, Nov 2009; Jeff Parsons to author, May 14, 2007; Peter Post, "Shelburne Farms: A Grand Past and an Active Present," *Middlebury (VT) Valley Voice*, Jul 13, 1977, and Crowe, "Shelburne Farms: Laboratory for Agri(cultural) Ideas," both in Scrapbook vol. XXVII.

55 At least one school field trip occurred in 1977, but the program was not formalized until the following year. "Putney School Field Trip," Mar 9, 1977, "SFR" Folder, MCW Files; "Field Trip Report, 1979–1980," and "School Program Report, 1980–1981," both in "Marshall Webb" Folder, MCW Files; "School Field Trips" mailing, c. 1980, and "A Guide to Supplement Your Class Trip at Shelburne Farms," c. 1980, both in MCW Files; ERG, interview with author, Apr 28, 2007; MWN, interview with author, Sep 12, 2007; ASW, comments on draft Chapter XI, Oct 29, 2007, and corr. with author, Jan 13, 2010; MCW, comments on draft Chapter XI, Oct 31, 2007.

56 David Barash, quoted in "SFR: Learning off the Land," *The Vermonter*, Sep 12, 1982, "General Property 1982–2001 Folder," Press Clippings Files. Also Post; ERG, interview with author, Apr 28, 2007; David Barash, interview with author, Apr 27, 2007.

57 Laura Hollowell, "Shelburne Farms Finds Kids Worldly," *Burlington (VT) Cynic* vol. CV (Apr 26, 1984), Scrapbook vol. XXVIII.

58 Ibid; "Harvest Festival Memorandum to all Employees," Sep 15, 1980, "Miscellaneous" Folder, SFR Coll.; ASW, comments on draft Chapter XI, Oct 29, 2007.

59 "Faculty Research at Shelburne Farms," memorandum for UVM faculty, c. 1977, Scrapbook vol. XXVII; MCW, interview with author, May 16, 2007; ASW, comments on draft Chapter 14, Nov 2009; Crowe, "Shelburne Farms: Laboratory for Agri(cultural) Ideas"; John Amadon, UVM College of Agriculture, to ASW, Nov 12, 1979, SFR, Inc. Binder, ASW Files; ERG, "The Shelburne Farms Bi-Monthly;" Castle Freeman Jr., "Shelburne Farms," *Country Journal* X, no. 6 (Jun 1983): 35.

60 Barash, interview with author, Apr 27, 2007; Green; L. Metcalf

Walling, "Shelburne Farms Has Access Policy," *BFP* Forum, undated [late Jul 1984, after Jul 18], Scrapbook vol. XXVIII; "Shelburne Farms Long Range Plan, May 1985," 67, Folder "Long Range Plan 1984–1985," SFR Coll.

61 MWN, "Statement," in Lipke, 73.

62 MWN, quoted in "Glimpse of Farm's Future Seen in Dartington Hall," *Shelburne (VT) South County News*, Oct 29, 1979, Scrapbook vol. XXVII, 1. Also MWN and ERG, "Summary of Management Structure at Dartington Hall," and Dartington Hall Interview Transcripts, both in SFR, Inc. Binder, ASW Files; MWN, report to SFR Board Re "SFR Business Plan and Budget," Oct 1980, "Marshall C. Webb" Folder, MCW Files; ASW, comments on draft Chapter XI, Oct 29, 2007; "That's Italian: Sharing our experience with organizations worldwide," *InFARMation*, Jan 19, 2001; *Dartington Hall: A Guide* (Totnes, Devon: Dartington Hall Trust, undated): passim; R. V. Denenberg, "Where Culture and Farming Thrive Jointly: Dartington Hall's 'Artistic Outpouring,'" *New York Times*, Jun 5, 1983, Scrapbook vol. XXVIII.

63 Ottauquechee Land Trust, "Shelburne Farms Long Range Plan, May 1985," Folder "Long Range Plan 1984–1985," SFR Coll.; SFR, "1984–1994 Annual Support, Attendance & General Fund Summaries," 1994–1995 Annual Report, 16.

64 MWN, quoted in SFR Board Minutes, Sep 19, 1974, Board Minutes vol. 1, ASW Files. Also MCW, "To all the family," undated memo, with subject line starting "This summer's work crew," Folder "Farm Memos 1971–1979," MCW Files; SFR Financial Statement, 1972–1974, and budget projections for 1975–1976, both in "SFR" Folder, MCW Files.

65 MCW, "To all the family;" MCW, interview with author, May 3, 2007, and comments on draft Chapter XI, Oct 31, 2007; "1980 Budget Summary," in "Marshall" Folder, MCW Files; Siliski, Murphy & Buzzell, SFR Financial Statements, Dec 31, 1980, MCW Files; Chris Granstrom, "A Pastoral Preserve Faces the Future: At Vermont's Shelburne Farms, a 19th Century Showplace Fulfills a Quest to Teach Love for the Land," *Smithsonian* 29 (May 1998): 94.

66 Lenore Broughton pledge document, Nov 28, 1975, Folder "1975 Annual Meeting Marshall & Emily," MCW Files; MWN to D'Ann C. Fago, Sep 22, 1976, Board Minutes vol. 1, "General Report" to Board of Directors, Jan 1980, SFR, Inc. Binder, and "Activity Report," c. 1980, SFR, Inc. Binder, all in ASW Files; "Shelburne Farms Buildings Projected Expenses and Income 1976–1978," c. 1976, and "Farm Barn Project" documents, c. 1976, all in "SFR Fundraising" Folder, MCW Files; ERG, "The Shelburne Farms Bi-Monthly"; Ann Ingerson, "Shelburne Farms: A New Resource Educational Center," *New England Farmer*, Jul 1982, Scrapbook vol. XXVIII; MWN, interview with author, Sep 12, 2007; ASW, comments on draft Chapter XI, Oct 29, 2007.

67 SFR Board Minutes, Jul 28, 1977, Board Minutes vol. 1, ASW Files. Also Barash, interview with author, Apr 27, 2007.

68 SFR Board Resolution, Dec 29, 1976, SFR Corporate Resolution, Jun 30, 1978, and SFR Board Minutes, Apr 14, 1980, all in SFR Binder, ASW Files; "1980 Budget Summary," in "Marshall" Folder, MCW Files; ASW, comments on draft Chapter XI, Dec 2, 2007.

69 ASW completed several accounting and management courses in the late 1970s to supplement his education and prepare himself for his positions at SF. "Shelburne Farms Employees '76," Folder "1975 Annual Meeting Marshall & Emily," MCW Files; ASW, resumé, c. 1979, "Resumé" Folder, ASW Files; MCW, interviews with author, Apr 19, May 3, and May 16, 2007; ASW, interview with author, May 13, 2007, and comments on draft Chapter XI, Oct 29, 2007; Quentyn Webb, interview with author, Sep 5, 2007; Mary Phillips Kelly to author, Dec 6, 2007, and interview with author, Dec 11, 2007; Lisa and John Roberts, interview with author, Feb 26, 2008; Campbell et al., 14.

70 MCW, "Statement: Alec Webb, Marilyn Webb, and Marshall Webb," in Lipke, 74. Also MCW, "To all the family," Apr 19, 1974, Folder "Farm Memos 1971–1979," MCW Files; "Minutes of Family Meeting," Dec 30, 1975, Folder "1975 Annual Meeting Marshall & Emily," MCW Files; Shelburne Farms Sawmill Brochure, undated [after 1978], "Activities" Folder, and Kate Green, "Marshall Webb Cutting Up at Lone Tree Lumber," *Shelburne (VT) South County News*, May 26, 1980, 1989 Press Clippings Binder, both in SFR Coll.; Map of SF with notes indicating locations of dead trees, 1969, 2004.3.21.77, APMI; Barna, 68; MCW, interview with author, May 3, 2007.

71 DVW, "To Alec and all the family," Nov 30, 1976, Folder "DVW/ASW Fall '76," ASW Files.

72 ASW, interview with author, May 13, 2007; Mary Phillips Kelly to author, Dec 6, 2007, and interview with author, Dec 11, 2007.

73 The Miskells rented the Market Garden site from 1981 to 2004. "Family Farm Employee Payroll" and "Non Family Farm Employee Payroll," Folder "Marshall & Emily 9/28/76," MCW Files; David Miskell to ASW and MWN, Sep 22, 1981, ASW Files; Post; Rux Martin, "Vermont Grows Gourmet," *BFP*, Jul 1, 1984, Scrapbook vol. XXVIII; ASW, comments on draft Chapter XI, Oct 29, 2007; MCW, comments on draft Chapter XI, Oct 31, 2007.

74 MCW, comments on draft Chapter XI, Oct 31, 2007. Also Mary and David Phillips to Quentyn Webb [and other Webb siblings], May 1971, Folder "Farm Memos 1971–1979," MCW Files; DVW, "Summary of Family Meetings 8–11, 18, 21," Aug 25, 1975, "Meetings" Folder, MCW Files; "Minutes of Family Meeting," Dec 30, 1975, Folder "1975 Annual Meeting Marshall & Emily," MCW Files; DVW to ASW, Nov 19, 1976, Folder "DVW/ASW Fall '76," ASW Files; MCW, interview with author, May 3, 2007; ASW, comments on draft Chapter XI, Oct 29, 2007; Mary Phillips Kelly, interview with author, Dec 11, 2007; Lisa and John Roberts, interview with author, Feb 26, 2008.

75 ASW, comments on draft Chapter XI, Oct 29, 2007; DVW to ASW, Nov 19, 1976, Folder "DVW/ASW Fall '76," ASW Files; MCW, interview with author, May 3, 2007; MWN, comments on draft Chapter 14, Nov 2009; Tom Daniels, "Shelburne Farms Joins the Ranks of Raw Milk Producers," *BFP*, date unknown [c. 1979], Scrapbook vol. XXVII.

76 Daniels, "Shelburne Farms Joins the Ranks of Raw Milk Producers." Also MCW, "Report on MCW's Meeting with DVW," Apr 11 [year unknown], Folder "Farm Memos 1971–1979," MCW Files; John Roberts, "Farm Newsletter," vol. 1, no. 1, Jul 25, 1975, "Farm Newsletters" Folder, MCW Files; Lisa and John Roberts, interview with author, Feb 26, 2008.

77 DVW, "Statement," in Lipke, 67. Also Paterson, interview with author, Apr 25, 2007; ASW, interview with author, Feb 22, 2007; MCW, comments on draft Chapter X, Apr 10, 2007, and interview with author, May 3, 2007.

78 DVW to ASW, Oct 11, 1976, copy in Folder "DVW/ASW Fall '76," ASW Files.

79 ASW has also noted that an analysis of SF's agricultural opera-

tions by Nortrust Farm Management, Inc., which was funded by ERG's father, David Rockefeller, and completed in 1980, "helped to clarify the long-term goals for the agricultural operations" (ASW, interview with author, Apr 1, 2008; Nortrust Farm Management, Inc., Report for Shelburne Farms, Feb 1980, ASW Files). Quote from "Shelburne Farms Agriculture," Dec 1979, SFR, Inc. Binder, ASW Files. Also MCW, interview with author, May 3, 2007; ASW, interview with author, May 13, 2007, and comments on draft Chapter XI, Oct 29, 2007; "Shelburne Farms: The Milk Primer" brochure, c. 1981, Folder "Education (Brochures, Maps, Handouts)," SFR Coll.

80 ASW, quoted in Freeman, 38. Also "Short Term Agricultural Plan," c. 1980, SFR, Inc. Binder, ASW Files; Sally Jacobs, "A New Era Begins," *BFP*, Sep 12, 1982, Folder "General Property 1982–2001," Press Clippings Files.

81 Bill Clapp, Oral History Interview, Jul 8, 2006, disk 1; MCW, "Remembering Bill," and "Sad News," both in *InFARMation*, Dec 5, 2008; Ingerson; Maurice, "Dining in Splendor."

82 Clapp, disk 1; MWN, interview with author, Feb 26, 2008; Daniels, "Shelburne Farms Joins the Ranks of Raw Milk Producers."

83 ASW, "Statement," in Lipke, 74. Also Clapp, disk 1; "Shelburne Farms Begins Farm Produce Distribution," *(Shelburne, VT) South County News*, Mar 1979; Jacobs.

84 The sale of raw milk was contemplated as early as 1973; see Minutes of Family Meeting, Apr 14, 1973, "Meetings" Folder, MCW Files. Also Clapp, disk 1; Daniels, "Shelburne Farms Joins the Ranks of Raw Milk Producers"; and "Spotlight on the Breeder: What Ever Became of You, Shelburne?" *Brown Swiss Bulletin*, Jun 1981, both in Scrapbook vol. XXVIII.

85 Ted Tedford, "Illness Outbreak Prompts Warning About Raw Milk," *BFP*, Oct 19, 1982; "Attention Shelburne Farms Milk Drinkers!" advertisement in *BFP*, Oct 20, 1982; Ted Tedford, "Raw Milk Cited in Twelve More Reported Illnesses," *BFP*, Oct 20, 1982; Ted Tedford, "Manager Disputes Raw Milk Finding," *BFP*, Oct. 30, 1982; and Eric Sorensen, "Raw Milk Sources Dry Up In Vt.," *BFP*, Nov 24, 1982; all in Scrapbook vol. XXVIII; ASW, comments on draft Chapter XI, Oct 29, 2007.

86 Clapp, disk 1; Sorensen; "Shelburne Farms, Inc. Revised Business Plan 1983–84," Feb 1983, Board of Directors Minutes Binder, May 1981–Oct 1983, ASW Files; ASW, comments on draft Chapter XI, Oct 29, 2007; MCW, comments on draft Chapter XI, Oct 31, 2007.

87 DVW to ASW, Oct 11, 1976, copy in Folder "DVW/ASW Fall '76," ASW Files.

88 ASW, "Statement," in Lipke, 74. Also Freeman, 35; "General Information" question and answer sheet about SF, c. June 1983, Board of Directors Minutes Binder, May 1981–Oct 1983, ASW Files.

89 Green, "A Farm Is Saved—and Spreads Its Bounty."

90 MCW, "Notes taken by M.C.W. on a meeting with our Vermont and New York lawyers"; ASW, interview with author, Apr 17, 2007; MCW, interview with author, Apr 19, 2007.

91 The Shelburne House contents sold by DVW included marble busts, an oriental rug, and several tapestries. DVW, memo to MCW, Mary Phillips Kelly, ASW, and Lisa Roberts, Dec 10, 1974, "Shelburne Farms Financial Plan, Spring 1974," and MCW, "Report on MCW's Meeting with DVW," Apr 11 [year unknown], all in Folder "Farm Memos 1971–1979," MCW Files; [MCW], handwritten notes entitled "Yearly Debt Payments," c. 1974, DVW to "The Family," May 14, 1976, and Michael Wool to ASW, Jul 10, 1975, all in "Meetings" Folder, MCW Files; DVW to ASW, Dec 12, 1976, Folder "DVW/ASW Fall '76," ASW Files; Mortgage, Burlington Savings Bank to DVW, Feb 4, 1976, vol. 56, 296–98, Land Records, STC; MCW, interview with author, Apr 19, 2007.

92 MCW, "Remembering Bill."

93 DVW actively considered potential options for conventional subdivision as late as 1973, when his advisor Gordon Paterson met with "land developers who are interested in discussing the possibility of a 300 unit development in Bayview and the Crusher" (Paterson, memo to DVW and ASW, Jun 4, 1973, in Folder "Town Agreement Land Use/Legal Planning," ASW Files. Also Minutes of Family Meeting, Apr 14, 1973, in "Meetings" Folder, MCW Files); MCW, "Notes taken by M.C.W. on a meeting with our Vermont and New York lawyers"; MWN, interview with author, Sep 12, 2007; ASW, interview with author, Aug 26, 2007, and comments on draft Chapter XI, Oct 29, 2007.

94 The appraised values listed here have been rounded to the nearest $100,000. SFR Board Minutes, Jan 19, 1981, Board Minutes vol. 1, ASW Files; Selectboard Minutes, Nov 1, Nov 14, and Dec 12, 1972, Selectboard Minutes vol. 3, STC.

95 Vermont State Law, Title 24 § 2741, in Legislative Council of the General Assembly for the State of Vermont, *Vermont Statues Annotated: Title 24, sections 1-3221* (Charlottesville, VA: LexisNexis, 2005), 341–42.

96 The 1975 agreement for the 3 buildings covered an initial term of 10 years. The 1982 agreement for the land covered an initial term of 3 years. Both have since been renewed and remain in place as of this writing. E. Wendell Aske, Shelburne Town Manager, to DVW, Dec 7, 1972, in Folder "Town Agreement Land Use/Legal Planning." ASW Files; Jack Tabaka, "Shelburne Farms Plan Still on Drawing Board," *BFP*, Jun 26, 1975; Agreement, Town of Shelburne and DVW, Dec 10, 1975, copy in Folder "Tax Stabilization Agreement/Town Farm Barn, Coach Barn, Shelburne House 1976–1986," ASW Files; ASW to Dick Spokes, Chairman of the Town of Shelburne's Shelburne Farms Ad Hoc Committee, Mar 20, 1980, SFR, Inc. Binder, ASW Files; Tax Stabilization Contract between Town of Shelburne and DVW, Aug 12, 1982, copy in Folder "Property Tax Agreements," ASW Files; ASW, interviews with author, Apr 17, 2007, and Mar 17, 2009. See also corr. and notes in ASW Files; Folder "Farm Memos 1971–1979," MCW Files; and Shelburne Selectboard Minutes, STC.

97 The 1969 state law, enacted to encourage the protection of farmland and natural areas from development, authorized the legal transfer of "rights or interests" to these lands to a state agency, municipality, or nonprofit organization. This law was followed in 1977 by one specifying the legal devices, including easements, that could be used to attain those goals (Vermont Statutes, Title 10 § 821–23 and 6301–9, http://www.leg.state.vt.us/statutes/statutes2.htm; Karin Marchetti and Jerry Cosgrove, "Conservation Easements in the First and Second Federal Circuits," in Julie Ann Gustanski and Roderick H. Squires, eds., *Protecting the Land: Conservation Easements Past, Present, and Future* (Washington, D.C.: Island Press, 2000), 96–7). Gordon Paterson to DVW, Aug 14, 1972, Aske to DVW, Dec 7, 1972, and "Memo to All Concerned re Draft Agreement Shelburne Farms/Town of Shelburne," Mar 22, 1974, all in Folder "Town Agreement Land Use/Legal Planning," ASW Files; Article 10 of Shelburne Town Meeting, Feb 1, 1974, in Town of Shelburne, VT, "Warnings and Proposed Budgets 1974–1975," 3, in Folder "Town/Taxes/PR," ASW Files.

98 SF, "To the Selectmen of the Town of Shelburne," Nov 1, 1973, and "The Shelburne Farms Proposal," Feb 22, 1974, both in "S.F. Town Prop." File, ASW Files.

99 Ibid; Article 10 of Shelburne Town Meeting, Feb 1, 1974, in Town of Shelburne, Vermont, "Warnings and Proposed Budgets 1974–1975," 3, and anonymous memo titled "To the Shelburne Community," Mar 1975, both in Folder "Town/Taxes/PR," ASW Files; MCW, "Notes taken by M.C.W. on a meeting with our Vermont and New York lawyers"; Tabaka; "200 Acres at Shelburne Bay Transferred to Conservancy," BFP, Dec 29, 1976; Maurice, "Director Tries to Keep A Way of Life Alive"; MWN to author, Feb 28, 2008, and interview with author, Sep 12, 2007; ASW, interview with author, Apr 9, 2009.

100 ASW, "Partnership Agreement Basic Points," c. Nov 1976 (first part of quote), and ASW to "Dad, Rusty, and Family," Dec 3, 1976 (second part of quote), both in Folder "DVW/ASW Fall '76," ASW Files. Also ASW to Mary and David Phillips, Aug 30, 1973, and ASW, SF property tax stabilization proposal, c. 1973, both in ASW Files; ASW, interview with author, Aug 26, 2007, and comments on draft Chapter XI, Oct 29, 2007.

101 ASW to "Family," Jul 13, 1976, Folder "Farm Memos 1971–1979," MCW Files; ASW, "Partnership Agreement Basic Points"; ASW, comments on draft Chapter XI, Oct 29, 2007.

102 ASW, "Partnership Agreement Basic Points." Also ASW, comments on draft Chapter XI, Oct 29, 2007.

103 ASW to DVW, Dec 11, 1976, Folder "DVW/ASW Fall '76," ASW Files.

104 MWN, quoted in Charles Bonenti, "Putting Land In Trust," Boston Sunday Globe, Apr 9, 1978, Press Clippings Files.

105 ASW to Mary and David Phillips, Aug 30, 1973, ASW Files. Also ASW, interview with author, Aug 26, 2007; Rob Eley, "Legal Device May Save Farm From Development," BFP, Aug 5, 1979, Scrapbook vol. XXVII.

106 ASW to Mary and David Phillips, Aug 30, 1973, and ASW and MWN for SFR, "The Regional Concept," 1981, both in ASW Files; ASW to "Family," Jul 13, 1973, Folder "Farm Memos 1971–1979," MCW Files; ASW, interview with author, Aug 26, 2007; MWN, interview with author, Sep 12, 2007.

107 DVW, "Notes re Alec's ultimatum," Dec 10, 1976, Folder "DVW/ASW Fall '76," ASW Files. Also SF, "To the Selectmen of the Town of Shelburne," Nov 1, 1973, and "The Shelburne Farms Proposal," Feb 22, 1974, both in "S.F. Town Prop." File, ASW Files.

108 The Nature Conservancy manages its portion of the land as the LaPlatte River Natural Area, and the town of Shelburne manages its portion as Shelburne Bay Park. The following sources are all in Land Records, STC: Deed, DVW to Nature Conservancy, Dec 21, 1976, vol. 58, 407–10; Agreement, DVW and Nature Conservancy, Dec 21, 1976, vol. 48, 237–43; Deed, Nature Conservancy to Town of Shelburne, Apr 17, 1978, vol. 62, 345–47; and Fred C. Koerner, Map of "Derick V. Webb Land to be Conveyed to the Nature Conservancy," Dec 1976, Map Glide 545A. Also SBW Sr. to DVW, Jan 25, 1977, Folder 13a, Box 6, SBW Sr. Papers; ASW to Spokes; "200 Acres at Shelburne Bay Transferred to Conservancy"; Bonenti; ASW, comments on draft Chapter XI, Oct 29, 2007.

109 DVW to ASW, Dec 12, 1976, Folder "DVW/ASW Fall '76," ASW Files; ASW, interview with author, Apr 17, 2007; Green, "A Farm Is Saved—and Spreads Its Bounty."

110 See, for instance, Davis Cherington, Massachusetts Farmland Trust, to ASW, MWN, and ERG, Mar 24, 1980, SFR, Inc. Binder, ASW Files.

111 DVW to "My Children: Quentyn, Marshall, Mary, Alec, Lisa, and Robert," Aug 28, 1979, Folder "Children's Memo/ER Note/Land Use," ASW Files; SFR Board Minutes, 1979–1981, passim, SFR, Inc. Binder and Board of Directors Minutes Binder, May 1981–Oct 1983; both in ASW Files; Eileen Rockefeller (ERG), "Shelburne Farms: Setting the Stage for Farmland Preservation," The Green Mountain Farmer 1, no. 4 (Jul–Aug 1980): 8, 1980 Folder, SF Publicity Files; ASW, comments on draft Chapter XI, Oct 29, 2007.

112 The following sources are all in ASW Files: SFR Board Minutes, Jul 30, Oct 15, and Nov 19, 1979, SFR, Inc. Binder; DVW to "My Children: Quentyn, Marshall, Mary, Alec, Lisa, and Robert"; ASW to Hunter Lewis, Mar 21, 1980, "Re: Shelburne Farms," SFR, Inc. Binder.

113 After the Pheasant Hill property was sold and the remaining land transferred to Shelburne Farms, Inc., the selectboard agreed to a phased property tax reduction from $26,768 for 1982 to $9,659 in 1985, without the original conservation easement provision. SFR Board Minutes, Jan 19, 1981, SFR, Inc. Binder, ASW Files; Don Melvin, "Shelburne Farms Gets Agricultural Tax Break," BFP, Aug 12, 1982, Scrapbook vol. XXVIII; Tax Stabilization Contract, Town of Shelburne and DVW, Aug 12, 1982, copy in Folder "Property Tax Agreements," ASW Files.

114 SFR Board Minutes, Oct 15, 1979, SFR, Inc. Binder, ASW Files. Also SFR Board Minutes, Jul 30, 1979, SFR, Inc. Binder, ASW Files; "1980 Budget Summary," in "Marshall" Folder, MCW Files; Siliski, Murphy & Buzzell; DVW to "My Children: Quentyn, Marshall, Mary, Alec, Lisa, and Robert"; ASW, interview with author, Sep 3, 2007.

115 The Lake Champlain Islands Trust later became the Lake Champlain Land Trust. The shoreline area for which conservation easements were created consisted of two parcels: one on Orchard Point and one between Quaker Smith Point and Saxton's Point. DVW to "My Children: Quentyn, Marshall, Mary, Alec, Lisa, and Robert"; ASW to Spokes; Eley; SFR Board Minutes, Aug 20, 1979, SFR, Inc. Binder, ASW Files; ASW, interviews with author, Apr 17 and Dec 4, 2007, and comments on draft Chapter XI, Oct 29, 2007.

116 Ibid. An easement covering the agricultural lands inside the estate gates, some 416 acres, was not finalized until 1986 (ASW to author, Mar 25, 2009).

117 Between the late 1880s and the mid-1950s, the Valley View house was occupied successively by SF farm managers Arthur Taylor, EFG, and DNT. Between the mid-1950s and 1980, the house was most often rented by a succession of private individuals and families who were friends of the Webbs. DVW's daughter Lisa and her husband, John Roberts, lived in the dwelling from 1974 to 1977 while John served as farm manager. ASW, interview with author, Apr 17, 2007, and comments on draft Chapter XI, Oct 29, 2007, and Mar 31, 2008; ERG, interview with author, Apr 23, 2007; Quentyn Webb, interview with author, Sep 5, 2007; Lisa and John Roberts, interview with author, Feb 26, 2008; Pat Elvin, "Shelburne Planners OK Webb Plan," source unknown, possibly Shelburne (VT) South County News or BFP, undated, c. 1981, Scrapbook vol. XXVIII; Campbell et al., 37–38.

118 ASW, interviews with author, Sep 3 and 11, 2007.

119 The Ottauquechee Land Trust later became the Vermont Land Trust. Darby Bradley, "Conservation and Limited Development Will Preserve Shelburne Farms," c. 1982, publication unknown, 1986 SF Press Clippings Binder; Jacobs.

120 Rod Griffin, "Shelburne Farms To Sell 500 Scenic Acres," *Burlington (VT) Vanguard Press*, Feb 5, 1982, Scrapbook vol. XXVIII; Jacobs; ASW, comments on draft Chapter XI, Oct 29, 2007.

121 The acreage numbers presented here and hereafter include the property leased to ERG in 1980. Quote from Griffin. Also MCW, interview with author, Apr 19, 2007.

122 DVW, quoted in Jacobs.

123 MCW, interview with author, Apr 19, 2007.

124 The parcels DVW reserved for family leaseholds consisted of Orchard House and acreage surrounding it; AOW's house on Saxton's Point; the teahouse/treehouse on Saxton's Point, the Orchard Cove House south of the Coach Barn, and two lots to the north of the former estate garden located in the vicinity of his defunct hog operation. At the time of this writing, the leaseholds for AOW's house, the Orchard Cove House, and the lots north of the garden have been acquired by SF, and the other two leaseholds remain privately owned. "Closing Memorandum for Derick V. Webb, Shelburne Farms, Inc., Ottauquechee Land Trust," Apr 9, 1982, "Report to Board of Directors," Sep 27, 1982, and Shelburne Farms, Inc., incorporation papers and By-laws, all in SFR Board Minutes Binder, May 1981–Oct 1983, ASW Files; ASW, interview with author, Apr 17, 2007, and comments on draft Chapter XI, Oct 29, 2007; Bradley; Jacobs; DVW, Copy of Last Will and Testament, in Chittenden County Probate Records for Estate of DVW, case #23349; National Trust for Historic Preservation, "Preserving Large Estates: Information: From the National Trust for Historic Preservation," Information Sheet #34, 1982.

125 DVW to ASW and MWN, Nov 18, 1983, ASW Files.

126 MWN, interview with author, Sep 12, 2007; ASW, comments on draft Chapter XI, Oct 29, 2007.

127 DVW, Copy of Last Will and Testament; ASW, interview with author, Apr 17, 2007, and comments on draft Chapter XI, Oct 29, 2007.

128 ASW, interview with author, Apr 17, 2007.

129 SBW Sr., "Statement," in Lipke, 55. Also KWH and Frank Galipeau, Oral History Interview with Julie Eldridge Edwards, Oct 14, 2004; SBW Jr., interview with author, Oct 31, 2006; Dundeen and Steven Galipeau, interview with author, Dec 12, 2007; Laura Webb Brown, interviews with author, Jan 30–31, 2008.

130 Steven Galipeau, interview with author, Dec 12, 2007. Also SBW Sr. to JWW Jr., Mar 17, 1975, Shelburne Museum Administrative Records, Box 21, SMA-24, SMA; Dundeen and Steven Galipeau, interview with author, Dec 12, 2007.

131 KWH and Frank Galipeau, Oral History Interview; SBW Jr., interview with author, May 4, 2007; JWW Jr. to SBW Sr., Mar 8, 1975, and SBW Sr. to JWW Jr., Mar 17, 1975, both in Shelburne Museum Administrative Records, Box 21, SMA-24, SMA.

132 JWW Jr. to SBW Sr., Mar 8, 1975, Shelburne Museum Administrative Records, Box 21, SMA-24, SMA. Also SBW Sr. to JWW Jr., Mar 17, 1975, in same location.

133 Corr. between JWW Jr., SBW Sr., and Frank L. Mallory, Mar 8 to May 14, 1975, Shelburne Museum Administrative Records, Box 21, SMA-24, SMA; SBW Sr., "Statement," in Lipke, 55.

134 Under the terms of the agreement, which was finalized in 1981, Sam Sr. added 88 acres neighboring his existing lands on and around Quaker Smith Point to his holdings, and Watson acquired 112 acres adjoining his Brick House parcel. KWH assumed ownership of Harry's High Acres Farm and additional land south of the Breeding Barn, for a total of 176 acres, and Dundeen acquired 135 acres to the southeast of the Breeding Barn, on which she and her husband built their own house in 1980. HHW's third daughter, Laura Brown, received interest in HHW's Adirondack property in lieu of a portion of Southern Acres. Dundeen and Steven Galipeau, interview with author, Dec 12, 2007; KWH, interview with author, Jan 29, 2008; Laura Webb Brown, interviews with author; "Final Plan Southern Acres Subdivision," Civil Engineering Associates, Aug 1980, approved by Shelburne Town Planning Commission on Jul 9, 1981, Slide 643A, and Final Decree of Distribution, Estate of HHW, Jun 12, 1981, copy in Land Records, vol. 73, 55–59, both in STC; Corr. between JWW Jr., SBW Sr., and Mallory, Mar 8–May 14, 1975, Shelburne Museum Administrative Records, Box 21, SMA-24, SMA.

135 SBW Jr., interview with author, May 4, 2007, and comments on draft Chapter XI, Feb 21, 2008; Dundeen and Steven Galipeau, interview with author, Dec 12, 2007.

136 SBW Sr., "Statement," in Lipke, 55. Also SBW Jr., interview with author, May 4, 2007; SBW Sr. to John Brotz, Aug 23, 1982, copy in "Southern Acres" Folder, Box 459, Lattie F. Coor Papers, RG 2, UVM Archives.

137 SBW Jr., interview with author, May 4, 2007.

138 "Potential for Having All Operations at Southern Acres," in "Southern Acres" Folder, Box 452, Lattie F. Coor Papers, RG 2, UVM Archives. Also, in general, Lattie Coor, UVM President, corr. and notes, 1980–86, in "Southern Acres" Folders, Boxes 452, 459, 467, 484, and 493, Lattie F. Coor Papers, RG 2, UVM Archives.

139 Lattie Coor, corr. and notes; SBW Jr., interviews with author, May 4, 2007, and Feb 21, 2008; Dundeen and Steven Galipeau, interview with author, Dec 12, 2007; Donald Maynard, interview with author, Apr 14, 2008.

140 Lattie Coor, corr. and notes; SBW Jr., interviews with author, May 4, 2007, and Feb 21, 2008; Dundeen and Steven Galipeau, interview with author, Dec 12, 2007.

141 SBW Sr.'s own property on and around Quaker Smith Point, then totaling some 200 acres, descended to his two children, SBW Jr. and Holly Froud (1936–2001). Deed, JWW Jr. to Shelburne Museum, Dec 27, 1985, Folder 20, Legal Papers, FM's Papers; Joint Use Agreement, SBW Sr. and Shelburne Museum, Feb 21, 1987, vol. 123, 429–36, Land Records, STC; KWH and Frank Galipeau, Oral History Interview; SBW Jr., interviews with author, May 4, 2007, and Feb 21, 2008; Polly Darnell, "Shelburne Museum List of Trustees," 2007, Office Files, SMA.

Chapter 15

1 The first version of this mission statement appeared in SF, Annual Report, 2004, SFR Coll. The version quoted here is from SF, Annual Report, 2007, SFR Coll.

2 MWN, interview with author, Sep 12, 2007; "The Baton Passes," *Shelburne Farms Newsletter*, Fall/Winter 1988, in "Newsletters" Folder, SFR Coll.; ASW, comments on draft Chapter XI, Oct 29, 2007, and Mar 31, 2008.

3 "Shelburne Farms Long Range Plan, May 1985," in Folder "Long Range Plan 1984–1985," SFR Coll.

4 Ibid.

5 ASW, interview with author, Sep 11, 2007, and comments on draft Chapter XI, Oct 29, 2007; Margaret Campbell, Erica

Donnis, Patricia O'Donnell, and Catherine Quinn, *Shelburne Farms National Historic Landmark Nomination*, 2000, 13–16; Property Ownership map, in Patricia O'Donnell and Heritage Landscapes, *Shelburne Farms Landscape Stewardship Plan*, 2004.

6. MCW, interview with author, Apr 19, 2007; MWN, interview with author, Sep 5, 2007; David Barash, interview with author, Apr 27, 2007; ASW, comments on draft Chapter XI, Oct 29, 2007; Centennial Campaign Phase III Brochure, c. 1988, and Centennial Campaign thank-you letter, Feb 1993, both in "Centennial Campaign" Folder, SFR Coll.
7. ASW, comments on draft Chapter XI, Oct 29, 2007.
8. Bill Clapp, Oral History Interview, Jul 8, 2006, disk 1.
9. "Sad news from the dairy," *InFARMation*, Jun 3, 1994, and SF, Annual Report, 1994–95, in Folder "Annual Reports 1995," both in SFR Coll.
10. "General Information" question and answer sheet, c. Jun 1983, Board of Directors Minutes Binder, May 1981–Oct 1983, ASW Files; "Shelburne Farms," *Brown Swiss Bulletin* 66 (Oct 1987): 11.
11. Ed Barna, "An Estate for Everyman: A Rejuvenated Shelburne Farms' New Mission for the 21st Century," *Vermont Magazine* 5 (May/June 1993): 68; "Shelburne Farms," *Brown Swiss Bulletin*, 11; SF, Annual Report, 1998, 5, in Folder "Annual Report 1998," SFR Coll.; Dan Undersander, Beth Albert, Dennis Cosgrove, Dennis Johnson, and Paul Peterson, "Pastures for Profit: A Guide to Rotational Grazing," (Madison, WI: University of Wisconsin Extension, 2002), http://learningstore.uwex.edu/pdf/A3529.pdf, passim.
12. "Shelburne Farms," *Brown Swiss Bulletin*, 12; "Mighty big marshmallows," *InFARMation*, Aug 13, 1993, SFR Coll.
13. Nancy Jenkins, "Food Notes," *New York Times*, Aug 15, 1984, Scrapbook vol. XXVIII.
14. "Shelburne Farms," *Brown Swiss Bulletin*, 15; "New Visitor Center Opens," *BFP*, Aug 11, 1986; Brochure for SF Centennial Campaign, Phase III, c. 1988, in Folder "Centennial Campaign," SFR Coll.; Campbell et al., 8; MWN, interview with author, Sep 12, 2007.
15. "Great milk," *InFARMation*, May 2, 1997, and "Shelburne Farms Long Range Plan, May 1985," both in SFR Coll. Also "Shelburne Farms, Inc. Revised Business Plan 1983–84," Feb 1983, Board of Directors Minutes Binder, May 1981–Oct 1983, ASW Files.
16. "Shelburne Farms," *Brown Swiss Bulletin*, 12–13; ASW, comments on draft Chapter XI, Oct 29, 2007.
17. Clapp, disk 1; *InFARMation*, 1993–1995 articles, passim, SFR Coll., notably "The first spreading," Jun 18, 1993; ASW, comments on draft Chapter XI, Oct 29, 2007.
18. Germain, quoted in "Just around the corner," *InFARMation*, Jan 13, 1995, SFR Coll. Also Clapp, disk 1, and the following in *InFARMation*, SFR Coll.: "Stewardship in practice," Aug 12, 1994, "Nature's filtration system," Sep 9, 1994, "The new parlor," Mar 24, 1995, and 1993–1995 articles, passim.
19. SF, Annual Report, 1987, in Folder "Annual Reports 1986–1989," SFR Coll.; *InFARMation*, May 22, 1992, SFR Coll.; Clapp, disk 1; Barna, 68; Deborah Straw, "Shelburne Farms Top Quality for Brown Swiss," *Eastern Milk Producer* (Feb 1988): 12–13.
20. Barna, 69. One of the most intractable issues proved to be a constantly expanding population of white-tailed deer at SF. Since the 1960s, local land suitable for deer habitat had dramatically declined owing to significant real estate development. As a result, more and more deer found a haven at SF, which by the 1990s was one of the last large undeveloped tracts in Shelburne, if not the greater Burlington area. The deer consumed new growth on the forest floor, interfering with the woodlands' ability to rejuvenate itself. In the late 1990s, MCW introduced an experimental and controversial deer hunt on the property in an effort to manage the population and reduce the damage they caused. See, for instance, "A plan to balance the herd," *InFARMation*, Sep 3, 1999, and "A successful pilot project," *InFARMation*, Oct 29, 1999, both in SFR Coll.
21. In fact, at the time of this writing, only one original elm remained standing on the property. MCW, interview with author, May 3, 2007.
22. "Woodlands as a resource," *InFARMation*, Jun 7, 1994, SFR Coll. Also Barna; "Some woodland facts and figures," *InFARMation*, Jun 7, 1994, SFR Coll.; MCW, comments on draft Chapter XI, Oct 31, 2007; MCW, interview with author, Jun 5, 2008.
23. The westernmost section of the garden balustrade fell into Lake Champlain in the early 1990s. "Shelburne Farms Long Range Plan, May 1985," 47–48. Also SFR Board Minutes, Aug 7, 1981, "Future Uses of Shelburne House," c. Jun 1983, and Alfred B. Burns, State of Vermont, to MWN, Sep 13, 1983, all in Board of Directors Minutes Binder, May 1981–Oct 1983, ASW Files; Maggie Maurice, "Shelburne Dowager Getting New Dress," *BFP*, date unknown, c. 1981, Scrapbook vol. XXVIII; MCW, comments on draft Chapter X, Apr 10, 2007; "Restoration Planned for Gardens at Shelburne," *Antiques and The Arts Weekly* XII, no. 33 (Aug 17, 1984): 50; MCW to Julie Eldridge Edwards, Oct 9, 2006, MCW Oral History Reference File (the author thanks Edwards for bringing this source to her attention); Karan Davis Cutler, "The Vermont Gardener: Make a Summer Visit to Lila Webb's Restored Shelburne Farms Garden," *Barre (VT) Sunday Herald and Sunday Times Argus*, Jul 26, 1987.
24. For example, Biltmore had been managed as a house museum by descendents of LOW's brother George Vanderbilt since 1930. The National Park Service acquired Frederick Vanderbilt's residence in Hyde Park, New York, in 1940. The nonprofit Preservation Society of Newport County had conducted tours at Cornelius Vanderbilt's The Breakers since 1948 and William K. Vanderbilt's Marble House since 1963. Quote from "Future Uses of Shelburne House." Also John Foreman and Robbe Pierce Stimson, *The Vanderbilts and the Gilded Age: Architectural Aspirations, 1879–1901* (New York: St. Martin's Press, 1991), 213–14, 239, 257, 299; MWN, interview with author, Sep 12, 2007.
25. Family members reopened Elm Court as an inn for a brief period c. 2003–05. It is now available for functions such as weddings. Foreman and Stimson, 147–48; "Future Uses of Shelburne House," and SFR Board Minutes, Jun 20, 1983, both in Board of Directors Minutes Binder, May 1981–Oct 1983, ASW Files.
26. "Future Uses of Shelburne House."
27. MWN, quoted in Jonathan Walters, "When a Grand Estate Goes Public," *Historic Preservation* (July/August 1987): 51. Also MWN, interview with author, Sep 12, 2007; ASW, comments on draft Chapter XI, Oct 29, 2007.
28. MWN, memo to SFR Board Members, Jul 8, 1983, and Lyman P. Wood to ASW and MWN, Oct 4, 1983, both in Board of Directors Minutes Binder, May 1981–Oct 1983, ASW Files; ASW, comments on draft Chapter XI, Oct 29, 2007.

29 Walters, 51; Marialisa Calta, "Gilded-Age Splendor: A Mansion's New Life," *New York Times*, Jun 4, 1987; Joe Sherman, "Restoring the Shelburne House," *Fine Homebuilding* (Dec 1988/Jan 1989): 64–68.
30 MWN, interview with author, Sep 12, 2007.
31 Martin Tierney, quoted in Walters, 51. Also MWN, interview with author, Sep 12, 2007; Tierney, interview with author, Jul 25, 2007.
32 Neagley, quoted in Walters, 51.
33 When the servants' wing was constructed in 1895, portions of the smaller appendage that predated the wing were covered over rather than removed. They were discovered intact when the wing was demolished in 1986 and were preserved. The remainder of the previous appendage was reconstructed according to plans drawn up by Martin Tierney. "Preservationists Oppose Razing Servants' Quarters," *BFP*, Jul 22, 1986; Sherman, "Restoring the Shelburne House," 64–68; ASW, comments on draft Chapter XI, Oct 29, 2007, and comments on draft Chapter 14, Jan 2009; MCW, comments on draft Chapter XI, Oct 31, 2007.
34 MWN, interview with author, Feb 26, 2008.
35 MWN, interview with author, Sep 12, 2007; "Presidential Award Recognizes Quality of Rehabilitation of Shelburne House," *Shelburne (VT) News*, Nov 1988, in Folder "Publicity 1988," Press Clippings Files; Tom Nold to author, Oct 3, 2007.
36 EWW, MCW, and MWN, "Report on the Subject of Building and Land Rental on Shelburne Farms," c. 1976, in "Meetings" Folder, MCW Files; Shelburne Farms Long-Range Plan, Nov 18, 1994, in Folder "Long Range Plan 1984–1985," SFR Coll.; "Coach Barn at Shelburne Farms Becomes Art Gallery in October," *Shelburne (VT) News*, Sep 1987, 19, in Folder "Publicity 1987," Press Clippings Files; ASW, comments on draft Chapter XI, Oct 29, 2007.
37 SF, Annual Report, 1989, in Folder "Annual Reports 1986–1989," SFR Coll.
38 ASW, quoted in Barna, 68. Also "The business side," *InFARMation*, Jul 29, 1994, and SF, Annual Report, 2000, in Folder "Annual Report 2000," both in SFR Coll.
39 ASW, comments on draft Chapter XI, Apr 6, 2008.
40 The walking trail network was considerably expanded in 1994–95, after SF's acquisition of Southern Acres, to a total of eight miles of trails. MWN, interview with author, Sep 12, 2007, and letter to author, Feb 28, 2008; Campbell et al., 9, 13; "Shelburne Farms Long Range Plan, May 1985," 8; SF, Newsletter and Annual Report, Spring/Summer 1985, in "Newsletters" Folder, SFR Coll.; SF, Annual Report, 1994–95, 5, in Folder "Annual Reports 1995," SFR Coll.; "Weekend Events Feel Brunt of Hurricane," *BFP*, Sep 29, 1985, Scrapbook vol. XXIX; ASW, comments on draft Chapter XI, Oct 29, 2007.
41 Chris Granstrom, "A Pastoral Preserve Faces the Future: At Vermont's Shelburne Farms, a 19th Century Showplace Fulfills a Quest to Teach Love for the Land," *Smithsonian* 29 (May 1998): 92–93; Amy Killinger, "A Laboratory Without Walls: Shelburne Farms Program Educates Young About Nature," *BFP*, May 9, 1988, in Folder "Publicity 1988," Press Clippings Files; Campbell et al., 14.
42 Killinger. Also Deborah Parella, *Project Seasons: Hands-On Activities for Discovering the Wonders of the World* (Shelburne, VT: Shelburne Farms, 1986); MWN, interview with author, Sep 12, 2007; ASW, comments on draft Chapter XI, Oct 29 and Dec 2, 2007; "Shelburne Farms Long Range Plan, May 1985," 66–68; Rosalyn Graham, "Honduran Teachers Learn New Ways to Teach About Nature, Environment," *Shelburne (VT) News*, Feb 14, 1990, in Folder "Publicity 1990," Press Clippings Files; Granstrom, 93; "Shelburne Farms: Stewardship in Practice" brochure, [before 1994], in Folder "Stewardship in Practice," SFR Coll.
43 Carolyn Battista, "New England–New York Consortium to Promote Agriculture in the Classroom," *Boston Globe*, Dec 6, 1987; *InFARMation*, Jun 18 and Sep 11, 1992, and May 20, 1994, SFR Coll.; ASW, comments on draft Chapter XI, Oct 29, 2007.
44 Shelburne Farms Newsletter, 1990, in "Newsletters" Folder, SFR Coll.
45 *InFARMation*, Jun 4, 1992, SFR Coll.; ASW, comments on draft Chapter XI, Oct 29, 2007.
46 "Shelburne Farms Long Range Plan, May 1985," 53–55; MCW, comments on draft Chapter XI, Oct 31, 2007.
47 "Shelburne Farms Long Range Plan, May 1985," 53–55; ASW, comments on draft Chapter XI, Oct 29, 2007; MCW, comments on draft Chapter XI, Oct 31, 2007.
48 The north and south turrets were the only sections of the building that were not reroofed; at the time of this writing, they still possessed the copper roofing installed in 1932. Campbell et al., 9–10; *InFARMation*, Jul 17, 1992, Jan 28, 1993, and Jun 4, 1993, all in SFR Coll.; ASW, comments on draft Chapter XI, Oct 29, 2007, and Mar 31, 2008.
49 Shelburne Farms Newsletter, 1990, in "Newsletters" Folder, SFR Coll.; ASW, comments on draft Chapter XI, Oct 29, 2007.
50 MCW, quoted in Granstrom, 96. Also "1985–1994 Annual Support, Attendance & General Fund Summaries," in SF, Annual Report, 1994–95, 16, SFR Coll.
51 Campbell et al., 38; MCW, comments on draft Chapter XI, Oct 31, 2007.
52 UVM continued to lease Southern Acres Farm until 1997. Lattie Coor and Ben Forsyth, corr. with SBW Sr. and SBW Jr., 1986, Box 493, Lattie Coor Papers, RG 2, UVM Archives; Donald Maynard, interview with author, Apr 14, 2008; SBW Jr., interview with author, May 4, 2007.
53 SBW Jr., interview with author, May 4, 2007, and comments on draft Chapter XI, Feb 21, 2008. Additional information about the proposed uses for the SAF property, including a previous plan to create a golfing resort, may be available in the future in the Shelburne Museum Board of Trustees' minutes and other materials in the SMA, which were not yet open for public access at the time of this writing.
54 Chuck Ross and ASW, "To Our Supporters," Sep 1994, in SF, Annual Report, 1993, in Folder "Annual Report 1993," SFR Coll.
55 "What an opportunity!" Mar 11, 1994, and "McClures give $500,000 to conserve historic farmland," Jul 1, 1994, both in *InFARMation*, SFR Coll.; "Cooperation Conserves Historic Acres," *Shelburne (VT) News*, Jul 4, 1994, 1, 20; Campbell et al., 38; ASW, comments on draft Chapter XI, Oct 29, 2007; SBW Jr., comments on draft Chapter XI, Feb 21, 2008.
56 Holly Brough to author, Jan 29, 2009. Also the following in ASW Files: undated document titled "Grant of Development Rights, Conservation Restrictions, Executory Interest and Right of First Refusal"; Vermont Land Trust, "Land Use Documentation Report: Shelburne Farms Property: Southern Acres, Shelburne, Vermont," Nov 1997; Shelburne Farms, the Vermont Housing and Conservation Board, and the Preservation Trust of Vermont, "Breeding Barn—Pledge Agreement," Dec 19, 1996.

57 Campbell et al., 38 and passim; *InFARMation*, 1994–2007 articles, passim, SFR Coll.; SF, Annual Reports, passim, SFR Coll.; "Shelburne Farms Chart of Acreages," 1998, 2004.3.21.21, APMI; ASW, comments on draft Chapter XI, Oct 29, 2007.

58 Sally Pollack, "Home Again: The Brick House Lovingly Restored to Electra's Eye," *BFP*, Jul 24, 2005; Shelburne Museum, "The Brick House," http://www.shelburnemuseum.org/brick_house/; Polly Darnell, Shelburne Museum Archivist, corr. with author, Apr 15, 2008.

59 For Shelburne Point, see, for instance, Matt Sutkoski, "Shelburne Point Carved Into House Lots," *BFP*, May 24, 2005. For Bostwick Farm, see for instance, Matt Sutkoski, "Vision for Shelburne Farmland Emphasizes Land, Accessibility," *BFP*, Jun 20, 2000; John Abele, "It's My Turn," *BFP*, May 11, 2007; "Local Update," *BFP*, Jun 13, 2004; Ashley Matthews, "Interfaith Gathering Dedicates Sanctuary," *BFP*, Oct 8, 2007.

60 SF, Annual Report, 2001, 6, and SF, Annual Report, 2002, 2–4, both in SFR Coll.

BIBLIOGRAPHY

MANUSCRIPT COLLECTIONS

At Shelburne Farms, Shelburne, VT.
Shelburne Farms Archives:

Autochrome Collection.
Architectural Plan and Map Inventory.
Botala, Frank and Frederica. Oral History Interview with Marshall Webb, June 26, 2006.
Bressor, Julie. "The *Elfrieda*," Fact Sheet, 1992. *Elfrida* Reference File.
Campbell, Margaret. "The South Gate Cottage and Other Workers' Cottages of Shelburne Farms, Shelburne, Vermont." Paper prepared for University of Vermont Historic Preservation Program, December 10, 1995. Employee Houses Reference File.
Campbell, Margaret, Erica Donnis, Patricia O'Donnell, Catherine Quinn, and Emily Wadhams. *Shelburne Farms National Historic Landmark Nomination*, 2000.
Clapp, Bill. Oral History Interview with Catie Camp and Joel Gardener, July 8, 2006.
Elfrida Log Book Collection.
Farm Managers' Papers.
Flynt, Bill. "Dr. William Seward Webb's Farm Barn at Shelburne Farms, Shelburne, Vt." Paper written for University of Vermont Art History class, December 31, 1977. Farm Barn Reference File.
Francis, Gerald P. "A Shelburne Farms Archives Research Note—Brigadier General Samuel Blatchley Webb: Vermont Lands." March 31, 2008.
Harris, Kitty Webb, and Frank Galipeau. Oral History Interview with Julie Eldridge Edwards, October 14, 2004.
Hayward, Susan Cady. "Historical Evolution of the Shelburne Farms Formal Gardens: Design Changes Through Time." Master's thesis prepared for Historic Preservation Program, University of Vermont, May 10, 1984.
Hunt, Valerie. Materials prepared for public lecture titled "Horse-Drawn Vehicles from the Webb Estate," 2000.
InFARMation. 1993–2010.
Jackson, Joe, Librarian of New York Yacht Club. Correspondence with Author. *Elfrida* Reference File.
Harris, Kitty Webb, Collection.
Leef, Margaret McLeod. "Lila Vanderbilt Webb: Dichotomous Patron of Trinity Episcopal Church." Paper for University of Vermont, c. 1995. Trinity Church Reference File.
Marr, Thomas E., Photograph Collection.
Nitrate Negative Collection.
Oakledge and Shelburne House Guestbooks.
O'Donnell, Patricia, and Heritage Landscapes. *Landscape Stewardship Plan, Shelburne Farms, Shelburne, VT*. June 2004.
Paterson, Gordon. Oral History Interview with Erica Donnis and Marshall Webb. October 12, 2006.
Photograph Album Collection.
Print and Photograph Collection.
Publicity Files.
Reference Files.
Scrapbook Collection.
Shelburne Farms Breeding Barn Complex Conservation Plan, October 31, 2004.
Shelburne Farms Historic Resources Assessment Report, August 2001.
"Shelburne Farms Property Timeline," 2000.
Shelburne Farms Resources, Inc. Collection.
Shelburne Farms Tour Guide Manual, c. 2000.
"Shelburne House Gardens Timeline," 2000.
Trade Catalogue Collection.
Vincent, Brooke. "The Coach Barn: Its Historical Context, Changing Uses and Current Function." Paper for University of Vermont class, September 1984. Coach Barn Reference File.
Webb, Aileen O. "Almost A Century." Unpublished Memoir, 1977.
Webb, Aileen O. Transcript of Oral History Interview with Emily Wadhams Webb, September 4, 1976.
Webb, Derick V., Papers.
Webb, Eliza (Lila) Osgood, Papers.
"Webb Family Genealogy," 2001.
Webb, James Watson, Jr., Collection.

Webb, Samuel B., Sr., Family Papers Collection.
Webb, Samuel B., Jr. Oral History Interview with Erica Donnis and Julie Eldridge Edwards, October 31, 2006.
Webb, Vanderbilt, Family Papers Collection.
Webb, Dr. William Seward, Papers.

At Shelburne Farms, Shelburne, VT. Shelburne Farms Collections:

Framed Works of Art Collection.
James Watson Webb Jr. "J. Watson Webb Jr. Family Trust" document. Accession File for 2000.02.

At Shelburne Farms, Shelburne, VT. Shelburne Farms Offices:

Webb, Alexander (Alec) S., Files.
Webb, Marshall C., Files.

At the Shelburne Museum, Shelburne, VT. Shelburne Museum Archives:

Audio Recordings.
"List of horses on Shelburne Farms July 18, 1900." In "Shelburne Horse Lists 1900 Etc.," 67–68. MS 416, vol. 2.
Shelburne Museum Administrative Records. SMA-24.
Shelburne Museum Financial Records.
Shelburne Museum Scrapbook. 1974–79.
Webb, Electra Havemeyer, Papers.
Webb Family Papers.

At the Shelburne Museum, Shelburne, VT. Office Files:

Darnell, Polly. "Shelburne Museum List of Trustees." 2007.

At the Bailey/Howe Library, University of Vermont, Burlington, VT. Microfilm Department:

United States Census Records for Shelburne, VT.

At the Bailey/Howe Library, University of Vermont, Burlington, VT. Special Collections Department:

Allen Family Papers.
Bazilchuck, N., C. Fastie, A. Heise, J. Kasmer, T. Naumann, R. Paul, D. Publicover, C. Savonen, S. Whidden, and K. Zimmerman. "The Physical Characteristics, Site of Discovery and Method of Preservation of a Dugout Canoe Found at Shelburne, Vermont." Prepared for University of Vermont Natural Areas Program, April 1, 1985.
Moran, James M. "An 'Unpractical Man' in Vermont: Frederick Law Olmsted and Fairholt." Master's thesis for Department of History, May 1997.
Petersen, James B., Jack A. Wolford, Nathan D. Hamilton, Laureen A. Labar, and Michael Heckenberger. "Archaeological Investigations in the Shelburne Pond Locality, Chittenden County, Vermont." Prepared for University of Vermont Natural Areas Program, May 1984.
Sanborn Fire Insurance Maps of Burlington, VT. November 1894 (sheet 28), January 1900 (s. 33), March 1906 (s. 38), October 1912 (s. 40), May 1919 (s. 39), April 1926 (s. 39), 1942 (s. 50), 1942–60 (s. 50), and 1978 (s. 50).

At the Bailey/Howe Library, University of Vermont, Burlington, VT. University of Vermont Archives:

Coor, Lattie F., Papers. RG 2.

At Chittenden County Probate Court, Burlington, VT:

Jones, Frederica Vanderbilt. Last Will and Testament and Estate Administration Paperwork. Case #15479.
Webb, Derick Vanderbilt. Last Will and Testament and Estate Administration Paperwork. Case #23349.
Webb, Eliza Osgood. Last Will and Testament and Estate Administration Paperwork. Case #13400.
Webb, James Watson. Last Will and Testament and Estate Administration Paperwork. Case #17292.
Webb, Vanderbilt. Copy of Last Will and Testament and Estate Administration Paperwork. Case #16709.
Webb, William Seward. Last Will and Testament and Estate Administration Paperwork. Case #11433.

At Shelburne Town Clerk's Office, Shelburne, VT:

Genealogy Records for Comstock, Holabird, Hurlburt, Nash, Saxton, and Smith Families.
Grand Lists.
Land Records.
Roberts, Ruth N. "Facts and Fancies in History of Quaker Smith Point." In Smith Family Genealogy Records.
Selectboard Meeting Minutes.
Town Reports.
Vital Records.

Additional Manuscript Sources:

Du Pont Family Correspondence. Winterthur Archives. Winterthur Museum & Library, Wilmington, DE.
Edwards, Julie Eldridge. "The Evolution of Electra Havemeyer Webb's Country Estate: The Brick House, 1913–1947." Unpublished Master's thesis for the

Masters Program in the History of the Decorative Arts, Cooper-Hewitt, National Design Museum and Parsons School of Design, 2002. Private collection of Julie Eldridge Edwards.

Harris, Kitty Webb. Private Collection.

Holabird and Morehouse Family Records. Private Collection of Philip G. Buffinton.

Materials related to Cyril Hamlen Jones. Including Correspondence, Milton Academy *Catalogues*, *Milton Bulletins*, and *The Milton Orange And Blue* Yearbooks. Milton Academy Archives, Milton, MA.

Land Records. City Clerk's Office. Burlington, VT.

Morehouse Family Papers Collection. MSA 247. Vermont Historical Society Library, Barre, VT.

Neagley, Marilyn Webb. Private Collection.

New York City Directories, 1881–90. On microfilm. Humanities Department. New York Public Library, New York City.

Olmsted, Frederick Law, Papers, Job #1031. Olmsted Archives. Frederick Law Olmsted National Historic Site, Brookline, MA.

Olmsted, Frederick Law, Papers and Olmsted Associates Records. Manuscript Division. Library of Congress, Washington, DC.

Pinchot, Gifford Collection. Manuscript Division. Library of Congress, Washington, DC.

Pullman Company Records. Newberry Library, Chicago, IL.

Snook, John. Contract Books. New-York Historical Society, New York, NY.

Social Security Administration. Social Security Death Index entry for Walter Woodgate, December 1967 (accessed at http://www.ancestry.com).

Town of Shelburne Reference Files. Vermont Division for Historic Preservation. State of Vermont, Montpelier, VT.

Winterthur Collection of du Pont Family Papers. Record Group VI, Box 15. Hagley Museum & Library, Wilmington, DE.

Woodgate, Ellen (Chorlette). United States Passport Application, April 23, 1923 (accessed at http://www.ancestry.com).

Newspapers

Albany (NY) Argus 1895
Albany (NY) Journal 1885–89
Albany (NY) Press 1889
Baltimore Sun 1897
Barre (VT) Sunday Herald and Sunday Times Argus 1977–87
Boston Herald 1897
Boston Home Journal 1890–91
Boston Globe 1987
Boston Journal 1889
Boston Morning Globe 1904
Boston Morning Herald 1900
Boston Sunday Globe 1978
Boston Traveller 1889
Brattleboro (VT) Clipper 1891
Brattleboro (VT) Reformer 1974
Burlington (VT) Cynic 1984
Burlington (VT) Daily News 1895–1902
Burlington (VT) Farmer Advocate 1895
Burlington (VT) Free Press 1847–2007
Burlington (VT) Vanguard Press 1982
Buffalo Enquirer 1891
Buffalo Illustrated Express 1891
Buffalo News 1895
Buffalo Times 1899
Chicago Journal 1899
Chicago Post 1893
Chicago Tribune 1885
Concord (NH) Weekly Market Bulletin 1999
Hartford (CT) Courant 1895
Honesdale (PA) Independent 1894
Lebanon (NH) Valley News 1991
Lewiston (ME) Journal 1886
Middlebury (VT) Valley Voice 1977–78
Milton (VT) Rays 1900
New York Daily Graphic 1887
New York Evening Advertiser 1891
New York Evening Mail and Express 1899
New York Evening World 1894
New York Graphic 1888
New York Herald 1888–1900
New York Journal 1890–99
New York Post 1887
New York Press 1894–98
New York Recorder 1891
New York Spirit of the Times 1888
New York Sun 1886–99
New York Tammany Times 1902
New York Times 1881–2002
New York Tribune 1886–1913
New York Truth 1887–99
New York World 1889–1904
New York World-Telegram 1956
Philadelphia Times 1899
Pittsburgh (PA) Post 1899
Plattsburgh (NY) Telegram 1888
Potsdam (NY) Herald 1891
Rochester (NY) Democrat Chronicle 1886
Rutland (VT) Herald 1889–1903
St. Albans (VT) Messenger 1888
St. Johnsbury Center (VT) New England Farmer 1982
Savannah (GA) News 1887

Schenectady (NY) Daily Gazette 1990
Shelburne (VT) News 1982–98
Shelburne (VT) South County News 1979–80
Springfield (MA) Republican 1898
Springfield (MA) Union 1891
Syracuse (NY) Standard 1891
Troy (NY) Telegram 1891
Troy (NY) Times 1898
Utica (NY) Daily Observer 1885
Wilmington (DE) News 1888
Worcester (MA) Gazette 1896

Notes from Personal Correspondence and Interviews, in the Possession of the Author

Alexander, Bill, and Stephanie Gardener, of the Biltmore Estate Archives.
Barash, David.
Bessette, Richard.
Boisvert, Jane.
Bressor, Julie.
Brown, Laura (Webb).
Buffinton, Philip G.
Darnell, Polly, of the Shelburne Museum Archives.
Edwards, Julie Eldridge, of Shelburne Farms.
Galipeau, Steven and Dundeen ("Deenie") (Webb).
Groff, Jeff, of the Winterthur Museum.
Growald, Eileen McGrath (Rockefeller).
Harris, Kate ("Kitty") (Webb).
Kelly, Mary (Webb) Phillips.
Lacy, Charles.
Lidz, Maggie, of the Winterthur Museum.
Maeck, Doris.
Maynard, Donald, of the University of Vermont.
Neagley, Marilyn (Thompson) Leimenstoll Webb.
Nold, Tom, of Shelburne Farms.
Parsons, Jeff, of Beekin/Parsons.
Paterson, Gordon.
Patterson, Keenis.
Paulman, Barbara Steen.
Roberts, John and Lisa (Webb).
Rockwell, Martha.
Smith, Elizabeth (Canfield) Webb.
Tracy, Richard.
Twitchell, Mary.
Webb, Alec, of Shelburne Farms.
Webb, Garrett.
Webb, Marshall, of Shelburne Farms.
Webb, Quentyn.
Webb, Richard.
Webb, Samuel B, Jr..
Webb, William Seward, IV.

Published Works

Abbey, Fred M. "On the Bothy." *Gardenside Gossip* (March 1962). Newsletter of Gardenside Nurseries, Shelburne, VT. Collection in the possession of Harrison L. Flint, Lafayette, IN.

Adams, T. M. "Prices Paid By Farmers For Goods And Services And Received By Them For Farm Products, 1790–1871; Wages Of Farm Labor, 1780–1937." Burlington, VT: University of Vermont and State Agricultural College, Vermont Agricultural Experiment Station, 1939.

Albers, Jan. *Hands on the Land: A History of the Vermont Landscape.* Cambridge, MA: MIT Press, 2000.

Aslet, Clive. *The American Country House.* New Haven, CT: Yale University Press, 1990.

Auchincloss, Louis. *The Vanderbilt Era: Profiles of a Gilded Age.* New York: Scribner, 1989.

Auld, Joseph. *Picturesque Burlington: A Handbook of Burlington, Vermont and Lake Champlain.* Burlington: Free Press Association, 1893.

Bailey, Craig. "Family Farm: Alec Webb and His Siblings Relinquished Claim to Some of the Most Beautiful Lakefront Property in the World for a Greater Good." *Business People Vermont* 16 (August 1999): 2–7, 39–40.

Bailey, Ralph S. "Estates of American Sportsmen: I. The Countryseat of Mr. Watson Webb at Shelburne Farms, Vermont." *Sportsman* 4 (December 1928): 39–42, 74.

Barna, Ed. "An Estate for Everyman: A Rejuvenated Shelburne Farms' New Mission for the 21st Century." *Vermont Magazine* 5 (May/June 1993): 34–39, 68–69.

Barry, John M. *The Great Influenza: The Epic Story of the Deadliest Plague in History.* New York: Viking, 2004.

Bartley, Scott A., ed. *Vermont Families in 1791.* Vol. 1. Camden, ME: Picton Press, 1992.

Bassett, Thomas. "Migration of Friends to the Upper Hudson and Champlain Valleys." In *Quaker Crosscurrents: Three Hundred Years of Friends in the New York Yearly Meetings.* Edited by Hugh Barbour. Syracuse, NY: Syracuse University Press, 1995.

———. "What Happened to Quakers In Chittenden County?" *Chittenden County Historical Society Bulletin* 17 (January/February 1982): 2–4.

Beattie, Betsy. "The Queen City Celebrates Winter: The Burlington Coasting Club and the Burlington Carnival of Winter Sports, 1886–1887." *Vermont History* 52 (Winter 1984): 5–16.

Beers, Frederick F. W. *Atlas of Chittenden County, Vermont.* New York, 1869.

Bellesiles, Michael A. *Revolutionary Outlaws: Ethan Allen and the Struggle for Independence on the Early American Frontier.* Charlottesville, VA: University Press of Virginia, 1995.

Bellico, Russell P. *Sails and Steam in the Mountains: A Maritime and Military History of Lake George and Lake Champlain.* Fleischmanns, NY: Purple Mountain Press, 1992.

Bernstein, Peter L. *The Wedding of the Waters: The Erie Canal and the Making of a Great Nation.* New York: W. W. Norton, 2005.

Bessette, Kenneth M., Sr., and Melissa L. Cook. "Mysteries of History, or How the Shelburne Post Office Ended Up In the Shelburne Museum: A More or Less Accurate Account of the Real Past of the Tuckaway General Store." *Chittenden County Historical Society Bulletin* 31 (Spring 1997): 1–10.

Beveridge, Charles E., and Paul Rocheleau. *Frederick Law Olmsted: Designing the American Landscape.* New York: Universe Publishing, 1998.

Blow, David J. *Historic Guide to Burlington Neighborhoods.* 3 vols. Burlington, VT: Chittenden County Historical Society, c. 1991–2003.

Bryan, John M. *Biltmore Estate: The Most Distinguished Private Place.* New York: Rizzoli, 1994.

Burlington City Directory. Burlington, VT: Hiram S. Hart, 1882–83.

Burnett, Charles H. *Conquering the Wilderness: The Building of the Adirondack & St. Lawrence Railroad by William Seward Webb.* Privately printed, 1932.

Capozzoli Ingui, Mary Jane. *American History: 1877 to the Present.* Hauppage, NY: Barron's, 1993.

Carlisle, Lilian Baker. *The Carriages at Shelburne Museum.* Shelburne, VT: The Shelburne Museum, 1956.

———, ed. *Look Around Essex and Williston, Vermont.* Burlington, VT: Chittenden County Historical Society, 1973.

———, ed. *Look Around St. George and Shelburne, Vermont.* Burlington, VT: Chittenden County Historical Society, 1975.

Carlough, Peter. *Bygone Burlington: A Bicentennial Barrage of Battles, Buildings & Beings.* Burlington, VT: Queen City Printing, 1976.

Carson, Rachel. *Silent Spring.* Boston: Houghton Mifflin, 1962.

Child, Hamilton. *Gazetteer and Business Directory of Chittenden County, Vermont for 1882–83.* Syracuse, NY: The Journal Office, 1882.

Cohn, Arthur B. *Lake Champlain's Sailing Canal Boats: An Illustrated Journey From Burlington Bay to the Hudson River.* Basin Harbor, VT: Lake Champlain Maritime Museum, 2003.

Collette, Francis E. *The Parish of St. Catherine of Siena, Shelburne: A History of Active Roman Catholicism in a Small Vermont Town.* Shelburne, VT: Parish of St. Catherine of Siena, 1995.

Courtwright, David T. *Dark Paradise: A History of Opiate Addiction in America.* Cambridge, MA: Harvard University Press, 2001.

Croffut, W. A. *The Vanderbilts and the Story of Their Fortune.* Chicago: Belford, Clarke & Company, 1886.

Crouthamel, James. *James Watson Webb: A Biography.* Middletown, CT: Wesleyan University Press, 1969.

Dartington Hall: A Guide. Totnes, Devon: Dartington Hall Trust, undated.

Duffy, John J., Samuel B. Hand, and Ralph H. Orth, eds. *The Vermont Encyclopedia.* Hanover, NH: University Press of New England, 2003.

Edwards, Julie Eldridge. "The Brick House: The Vermont Country House of Electra Havemeyer Webb." *The Magazine Antiques* CLXIII (January 2003): 192–201.

"Elfrida." Department of the Navy, Naval Historical Center. http://www.history.navy.mil/danfs/e3/elfrida.htm.

Elm Court Estate. http://www.elmcourt.com.

Emmet, Alan. *So Fine a Prospect: Historic New England Gardens.* Hanover, NH: University Press of New England, 1996.

Erlich, Paul R. *The Population Bomb.* New York: Ballantine Books, 1968.

Foote, R. H. "The History of Artificial Insemination: Selected Notes and Notables." American Society of Animal Science, 2002. http://www.asas.org/Bios/Footehist.pdf.

Foreman, John, and Robbe Pierce Stimson. *The Vanderbilts and the Gilded Age: Architectural Aspirations, 1879–1901.* New York: St. Martin's Press, 1991.

Freeman, Castle, Jr. "Shelburne Farms." *Country Journal* X, no. 6 (June 1983): 32–39.

Ganger, Robert W. *Lila Vanderbilt Webb's Miradero: Window on an Era.* Palm Beach, FL: Historical Society of Palm Beach County, 2005.

"The Garden of Mrs. W. Seward Webb, Shelburne Farms, Shelburne, Vt. on Lake Champlain." Photographs by Isabelle H. Hardie. *Country Life in America* 31 (October 1917): 62–63.

"The Gardens at Shelburne Farms, Mrs. Seward Webb's Home at Shelburne, Vermont." *Arts and Decoration* 11 (June 1919): 66–67.

Gilborn, Craig. *Adirondack Camps: Homes Away from Home, 1850–1950.* Syracuse, NY: Adirondack Museum and Syracuse University Press, 2000.

Godfrey, A. H. "The Shelburne Farms." *The Rider and Driver.* Part 1: vol. 4, no. 7 (October 15, 1892): 8–9. Part 2: vol. 4, no. 8 (October 22, 1892): 10–11.

Graffagnino, J. Kevin. "The Country My Soul Delighted In: The Onion River Land Company and the Vermont Frontier." *New England Quarterly* 65 (March 1992): 24–60.

Granstrom, Chris. "A Pastoral Preserve Faces The Future: At Vermont's Shelburne Farms, a 19th Century Showplace Fulfills a Quest to Teach Love for the Land." *Smithsonian* 29 (May 1998): 86–96.

Gustanski, Julie Ann, and Roderick H. Squires, eds. *Protecting the Land: Conservation Easements Past, Present, and Future*. Washington, DC: Island Press, 2000.

Harding, Marie. *The History of Shelburne*. Shelburne, VT: Excelsior Press and Shelburne Museum, 1963.

Harter, Henry A. *Fairy Tale Railroad: The Mohawk and Malone From the Mohawk, through the Adirondacks to the St. Lawrence*. Utica, NY: North Country Books, 1979.

Haviland, William A., and Marjory W. Power. *The Original Vermonters: Native Inhabitants Past and Present*. Hanover, NH: University Press of New England, 1981.

Hayward, Susan Cady. "Gardens of a Gilded Age: Vermont's Historic Estates are Flowering Once Again." *Vermont Life* XLII, no. 4 (Summer 1988): 3–9.

Hazelton, Henry I. "Shelburne Farms." *New England Magazine* 25 (November 1901): 273.

Heise, Laurie, and Carolyn Christman. *American Minor Breeds Notebook*. Pittsboro, NC: American Minor Breeds Conservancy, 1989.

Helfrich G. W., and Gladys O'Neil. *Lost Bar Harbor*. Camden, ME: Down East Books, 1982.

Hemenway, Abby, ed. *Vermont Historical Gazetteer: A Magazine*. Burlington, VT: A. M. Hemenway, 1868.

Hewes, Lauren B., and Celia Y. Oliver. *To Collect in Earnest: The Life and Work of Electra Havemeyer Webb*. Shelburne, VT: Shelburne Museum, 1997.

Hewitt, Mark Alan. *The Architect and the American Country House, 1890–1940*. New Haven, CT: Yale University Press, 1990.

Higginson, A. Henry. *Try Back: A Huntsman's Reminiscences*. New York: Huntington Press, 1931.

Higginson, A. Henry, and Julian Ingersoll Chamberlain. *Hunting in the United States and Canada*. Garden City, New Jersey: Doubleday, Doran & Company, 1928.

Hill, Ralph Nading. *Lake Champlain: Key to Liberty*. Woodstock, VT: Countryman Press, 1988.

Hodgson, Barbara. *Opium: A Portrait of the Heavenly Demon*. San Francisco: Chronicle Books, 1999.

Holbrook, Jay Mack. *Vermont 1771 Census*. Oxford, MA: Holbrook Research Institute, 1982.

Hoffman, Robert V. "Full-Length Portrait of a Country Gentleman VIII—James Watson Webb." *Country Life* LXVII, no. 1 (November 1934): 69–71, 96–98.

Homberger, Eric. *Mrs. Astor's New York: Money and Social Power in a Gilded Age*. New Haven, CT: Yale University Press, 2002.

Hopf, John T. *Hammersmith Farm, Newport: A Summer White House, 1961–1965*. East Passage Farm, 1987.

Hyde, Arthur L., and Frances P. Hyde. *Burial Grounds of Vermont*. Vermont Old Cemetery Association, 1991.

Ierley, Merrit. *The Comforts of Home: The American House and the Evolution of Modern Convenience*. New York: Three Rivers Press, 1999.

Inflation Calculator. http://www.westegg.com/inflation/.

Jackson, Richard S., Jr., and Cornelia Brooke Gilder. *Houses of the Berkshires, 1870–1930*. New York: Acanthus Press, 2006.

Jekyll, Gertrude. *Wall and Water Gardens*. 4th ed. London: Country Life, [c. 1910]. Shelburne House Library copy, # 2000.1034. Shelburne Farms Collections.

Kiley, Dan, and Jane Amidon. *Dan Kiley: The Complete Works of America's Master Landscape Architect*. Boston: Little, Brown and Company, 1999.

King, Robert B. *The Vanderbilt Homes*. New York: Rizzoli, 1989.

Klyza, Christopher McGrory, and Stephen C. Trombulak. *The Story of Vermont: A Natural and Cultural History*. Hanover, NH: University Press of New England, 1999.

Kolata, Gina. *Flu: The Story of the Great Influenza Pandemic of 1918 and the Search for the Virus That Caused It*. New York: Farrar, Straus, and Giroux, 1999.

Labbance, Bob. "Burlington's Ghosts of Golf." *Vermont Golf Journal and Directory* (1995): 56–61.

———. "Willie Park Jr. in Northern New England." *Golfiana* 5 (1993): 7–8.

Lake Champlain Yacht Club: Centennial Celebration. Lake Champlain Yacht Club, 1989.

Landau, Sarah Bradford. *Edward T. and William A. Potter: American Victorian Architects*. New York: Garland Publishing, 1979.

Latham, Charles. *The Gardens of Italy*. New York: Charles Scribner's Sons, 1905. Shelburne House Library copy, # 2000.1006. Shelburne Farms Collections.

Lawrence, Ruth, ed. *Webb and Allied Family Histories: A Documented Compilation of Genealogy and Biography*. New York: National Americana Society, 1937.

Lawson, Henry. *Sciatica, Lumbago, and Brachialgia: Their Nature and Treatment, and Their Immediate Relief and Rapid Cure by Hypodermic Injection of Morphia*. London: Robert Hardwicke, 1872.

Legislative Council of the General Assembly for the State of Vermont. *Vermont Statues Annotated: Title 24, sections 1–3221*. Charlottesville, VA: LexisNexis, 2005.

Leopold, Aldo. *A Sand County Almanac, and Sketches Here and There*. New York: Oxford University Press, 1949.

Lipke, William C., ed. *Shelburne Farms: The History of An Agricultural Estate*. Burlington, VT: University of Vermont, 1979.

MacKay, Robert B., Anthony Baker, and Carol A. Traynor, eds. *Long Island Country Houses and Their Architects, 1860–1940.* New York: W. W. Norton and Society for the Preservation of Long Island Antiquities, 1997.

Mackay-Smith, Alexander. *Masters of Foxhounds.* Masters of Foxhounds Association of America, 1980.

Martins, Susanna Wade. *The English Model Farm: Building the Agricultural Ideal, 1700–1914.* Cheshire, UK: Windgather Press, 2002.

McCormick, Tom. "Goodbye to the Gilded Age." *Wesleyan University Alumnus* LXXXI (Fall 1988): 23–27.

Meadows, Donella H. *The Limits to Growth: A Report for the Club of Rome's Project on the Predicament of Mankind.* New York: Universe Books, 1972.

Miller, Timothy Lathrop. *History of Hereford Cattle, Proven Conclusively the Oldest of Improved Breeds.* Chillicothe, MO: T.F.B. Sotham, 1902.

Nash, Rev. Sylvester. *The Nash Family; or, Records of the Descendants of Thomas Nash of New Haven, Connecticut, 1640.* Hartford, CT: Case, Tiffany and Company, 1853.

National Cyclopaedia of American Biography, The. Vol. VI. New York : J. T. White, 1896.

National Trust for Historic Preservation. "Preserving Large Estates: Information; From the National Trust for Historic Preservation." Information Sheet #34, 1982.

Nature Conservancy, The. Mission Statement. http://www.nature.org/aboutus.

Newport Mansions: The Gilded Age. Little Compton, RI: Fort Church Publishers and Preservation Society of Newport County, 1995.

Nickens, Eddie. "Family Farm: Descendants of its Founder have Transformed a Vermont Estate into a Center that Demonstrates the Best of Land Stewardship." *Historic Preservation* 48 (January/February 1996): 40–43.

Olmsted, Frederick Law, Jr., and Theodora Kimball. *Frederick Law Olmsted: Architect, 1822–1903.* New York: G. P. Putnam's Sons, 1922. Reprint, New York: Benjamin Blom, 1970.

Owens, Carole. *The Berkshire Cottages: A Vanishing Era.* Stockbridge, MA: Cottage Press, 1984.

Parella, Deborah. *Project Seasons: Hands-On Activities for Discovering the Wonders of the World.* Shelburne, VT: Shelburne Farms, 1986.

Patterson, Jerry. *Fifth Avenue: The Best Address.* New York: Rizzoli, 1998.

———, *The First Four Hundred: Mrs. Astor's New York in the Gilded Age.* New York: Rizzoli, 2000.

———, *The Vanderbilts.* New York: Harry N. Abrams, 1989.

Penfield, Wilder. "Halstead of Johns Hopkins: The Man and His Problem as Described in the Secret Records of William Osler." *Journal of the American Medical Association* 210 (December 22, 1969): 2214–18.

Perkins, Nathan. *A Narrative of a Tour through the State of Vermont from April 27 to June 12, 1789.* Rutland, VT: C. E. Tuttle Co., 1964.

Phisterer, Frederick. *New York in the War of the Rebellion, 1861 to 1865.* 3rd ed. Albany, NY: J. B. Lyon Company, 1912.

Pike, Robert E. *Tall Trees, Tough Men: An Anecdotal and Pictorial History of Logging and Log-Driving in New England.* New York: W. W. Norton, 1967.

Pinchot, Gifford. *The Adirondack Spruce: A Study of the Forest in Ne-Ha-Sa-Ne Park.* New York: The Critic Co., 1898.

Platt, Charles A. *Italian Gardens.* New York: Harper & Brothers, 1894. Shelburne House Library copy, # 2000.1046. Shelburne Farms Collections.

Powell, Edwin C. "Shelburne Farms: An Ideal Country Place." *Country Life In America* 3, no. 4 (February 1903): 152–56.

Princeton University. "Who Was William Church Osborn?" http://www.princeton.edu/~arnold/other/william_church_osborn.htm.

Proceedings of the New York Farmers. Season 1952–53. New York: 1953. Shelburne Museum Library.

Purdy, Herman R., and R. John Dawes. *Breeds of Cattle.* New York: Chanticleer Press, 1987.

Reeve, J. Stanley. "The Country Gentleman and His Hounds." *Country Life* LXVII, No. 1 (November 1934): 51–54, 98–100.

"Report of the Secretary of the Navy." Summary report from *Annual Reports of the Navy Department for the Year 1898.* Washington, DC: Government Printing Office, 1898. Accessed on Department of the Navy, Naval Historical Center, http://www.history.navy.mil/wars/spanam/sn98-12.htm.

"Restoration Planned for Gardens at Shelburne." *Antiques and The Arts Weekly* XII, no. 33 (August 17, 1984): 50.

Robertson, Robert H. "Country House. Mr. R. H. Robertson, Architect, New York, N.Y." *American Architect and Building News* 21, no. 586 (March 19, 1887): 138ff.

———. "Design for a Country House. Mr. R. H. Robertson, Architect, New York, N.Y." *American Architect and Building News* 40, no. 903 (May 20, 1893): 120ff.

———. "Dr. Webb's Office, Shelburne, Vt. Mr. R. H. Robertson, Architect, New York, N.Y." *American Architect and Building News* 24, no. 676 (December 8, 1888): 266ff.

Robinson, John Martin. *Georgian Model Farms: A Study of Decorative and Model Farm Buildings in the Age of Improvement, 1700–1846.* Oxford: Clarendon Press, 1983.

Rockefeller, Eileen. "Shelburne Farms: Setting the Stage for Farmland Preservation." *The Green Mountain Farmer* 1, no. 4 (July–August 1980): 8.

Round About Burlington, Vt. Winooski, VT: Vermont Illustrating Co., 1900.

Russell, Howard S. *A Long, Deep Furrow: Three Centuries of Farming in New England.* Hanover, NH: University Press of New England, 1982.

Rybczynski, Witold. *A Clearing in the Distance: Frederick Law Olmsted and America in the Nineteenth Century.* New York: Simon & Schuster, 1999.

Ryder, Tom. "The Versatile Hackney, Part One." *The Carriage Journal* 37, no. 4 (January 2000): 149–51.

———. "The Versatile Hackney, Part Two." *The Carriage Journal* 38, no. 1 (March 2000): 24–27.

Schlereth, Thomas J. *Victorian America: Transformations in Everyday Life, 1876–1915.* NY: Harper Perennial, 1991.

Schuyler, Montgomery. "The Works of R. H. Robertson." *Architectural Record* 6 (October–December 1896): 184–219.

Searls, Paul M. *Two Vermonts: Geography and Identity, 1865–1910.* Hanover, NH: University Press of New England, 2000.

Shapiro, Mel, Warren Dohn, and Leonard Berger, eds. *Golf: A Turn-of-the-Century Treasury.* Secaucus, NJ: Castle, 1986.

Shaughnessy, Jim. *The Rutland Road.* San Diego, CA: Howell-North Books, 1981.

"Shelburne Farms." *Brown Swiss Bulletin* 66 (October 1987): 11–15.

Shelburne Museum. "The Brick House." http://www.shelburnemuseum.org/brick_house/.

Sherman, Joe. *The House At Shelburne Farms: The Story of One of America's Great Country Estates.* Middlebury, VT: Paul S. Eriksson, 1986.

———. "Restoring the Shelburne House." *Fine Homebuilding* (December 1988/January 1989): 64–68.

Sherman, Michael, Gene Sessions, and P. Jeffrey Potash. *Freedom and Unity: A History of Vermont.* Barre, VT: Vermont Historical Society, 2004.

Slayton, Thomas. "Growing Trees—and Ideas at the Marsh-Billings-Rockefeller National Historical Park." *Vermont Life* LXI, no. 1 (Autumn 2006): 67–69.

Sloane, Florence Adele. *Maverick in Mauve: The Diary of a Romantic Age.* Garden City, NJ: Doubleday, 1983.

Snell, Charles W. *Vanderbilt Mansion: National Historic Site.* Washington, DC: National Park Service, undated.

"Spotlight on the Breeder: What Ever Became of You, Shelburne?" *Brown Swiss Bulletin* (June 1981).

Stern, Robert A. M., Gregory Gilmartin, and John Massengale. *New York 1900: Metropolitan Architecture and Urbanism 1890–1915.* New York: Rizzoli, 1983. First paperback edition, 1995.

Stern, Robert A. M., Thomas Mellins, and David Fishman. *New York 1880: Architecture and Urbanism in the Gilded Age.* New York: Monacelli Press, 1999.

The Story of Our Breed. Webster City, IA: Aberdeen-Angus Breeders' Association, 1969.

Straw, Deborah. "Shelburne Farms Top Quality for Brown Swiss." *Eastern Milk Producer* (February 1988): 12–13.

Swift, Esther Monroe. *Vermont Place Names: Footprints of History.* Camden, ME: Picton Press, 1996.

Thompson, Elizabeth H., and Eric R. Sorenson. *Wetland, Woodland, Wildland: A Guide to the Natural Communities of Vermont.* Hanover, NH: University Press of New England, The Nature Conservancy, and Vermont Department of Fish and Wildlife, 2000.

Undersander, Dan, Beth Albert, Dennis Cosgrove, Dennis Johnson, and Paul Peterson. "Pastures for Profit: A Guide to Rotational Grazing." Madison, WI: University of Wisconsin Extension, 2002. http://learningstore.uwex.edu/pdf/A3529.pdf.

United States Bureau of the Census. *Heads of Families at the First Census of the United States, Taken in the Year 1790: Vermont.* Baltimore, MD: Genealogical Publishing Co., 1992.

United States Bureau of the Census. *Heads of Families at the Second Census of the United States, Taken in the Year 1800: Vermont.* Montpelier, VT: Vermont Historical Society, 1938.

United States Department of Commerce and Labor. *Seagoing Vessels of the United States with Official Numbers and Signals.* Washington, DC: Government Printing Office, 1905.

Vanderbilt, Arthur T., II. *Fortune's Children: The Fall of the House of Vanderbilt.* New York: William Morrow and Company, 1989.

"Vermont Men of Today: Dr. William Seward Webb." *The Vermonter* 6, no. 8 (March 1901): 98–100.

Vermont Mozart Festival. "History of the Vermont Mozart Festival." http://vtmozart.org/news_history.php.

Vermont Statutes. Title 10 § 6301–6309. http://www.leg.state.vt.us/statutes/statutes2.htm.

Visser, Thomas Durant. *Field Guide to New England Barns and Farm Buildings.* Hanover, NH: University Press of New England, 1997.

Walters, Jonathan. "When a Grand Estate Goes Public," *Historic Preservation* (July/August 1987): 51.

Webb, James Watson. "The Shelburne Terrier: A New Breed." *The Sportsman* (July 1927): 76.

Webb, Samuel Blachley. Worthington Chauncey Ford, ed. *Correspondence and Journals of Samuel Blachley Webb.* New York: [Lancaster, PA: Wickersham Press], 1893.

Webb, William Seward. *California and Alaska and Over the Canadian Pacific Railway*. New York: G. P. Putnam's Sons, 1890.

———. *Catalogue Shelburne Farms Stud: Shelburne, Chittenden Co., Vermont*. New York: John Polhemus, 1891.

———. *Shelburne Farms Stud: Of English Hackneys, Harness and Saddle Horses, Ponies and Trotters*. New York: G. P. Putnam's Sons, 1893.

Webster, David S. "The Webb Barn." *Vermont Life* XVI, no. 1 (Autumn 1961): 46–49.

Webster, Truman M. *Shelburne: Pieces of History*. Shelburne, VT: Shelburne Historic Sites Committee, 1994.

Weisman, Steven R. *The Great Tax Wars: Lincoln to Wilson—The Fierce Battles over Money and Power That Transformed the Nation*. New York: Simon & Schuster, 2002.

Weitzenhoffer, Frances. *The Havemeyers: Impressionism Comes to America*. New York: Harry N. Abrams, 1986.

Wharton, Edith. *The Age of Innocence*. New York: Appleton, 1920.

———. *The Fruit of the Tree*. New York: Charles Scribner's Sons, 1907.

———. *Italian Villas and their Gardens*. New York: Century Co., 1904. Shelburne House Library copy, # 2000.1057. Shelburne Farms Collections.

Wheeling, Kenneth Edward. "By Coach To Shelburne…" *The Carriage Journal* 39 (June 2001): 197–99.

———. *Horse-Drawn Vehicles at the Shelburne Museum*. Shelburne, VT: Shelburne Museum, 1974.

White, John H., Jr. *The American Railroad Passenger Car*. Baltimore, MD: Johns Hopkins University Press, 1991.

Wilson, Harold Fisher. *The Hill Country of Northern New England: Its Social and Economic History, 1790–1930*. New York: AMS Press, 1967.

Wilson, Lori F. *God With Us: A History of Trinity Episcopal Church, Shelburne, Vermont; 1790–1900*. Shelburne, VT: Lori F. Wilson, 1990.

Withey, Henry F., and Elsie Rathburn Withey. *Biographical Dictionary of American Architects (Deceased)*. Los Angeles: Hennessey & Ingalls, 1970.

Zabytko, Irene. "Marilyn Webb: The Steward of Shelburne Farms." *Vermont Woman* III, no. 6 (April 1988): 4–5.

Zurborg, Carl E. *A History of Dairy Marketing in America*. Columbus, OH: National Dairy Shrine, 2005.

INDEX

Illustrations indicated in **bold**.

Abele, John and Mary, 272
Abenaki tribe, 4–5, 8
Adirondack and St. Lawrence Railroad, 118, 120–121, 126
Adirondack Mountains, 3, 5
agricultural census (1880), 11
agricultural operations: community and collaboration of, 199; models for, 239–240; during 1970s and 1980s, 227; at Southern Acres Farm, 253; Tower and, 213; Alec Webb and, 238; Derick Webb and, 206–207, 221, 227, 238; Marshall Webb and, 240; Mary Webb and, 240; *See also specific operations*
agricultural plans, 227–228
agricultural preservation, viii
agricultural research, 235
agriculture, in Vermont, 9–11, 14–15
Agriculture Conservation Program, 189
airstrip, **223**
Albers, Jan, 4
Allen, Ethan, 6
Allen, Helen "Rusty" (later Webb), 227, 243, 264
Allen, Ira, 6, 7, 8
Allen, Levi, 7
American Craft Council, 194
American Craft Museum, 194
American Estates and Gardens (Feree), 28
Annex, 46, 47, 101, 116, 176, 192
arboretum project, 37–38, 40, 75
archaeological sites, 4
art exhibitions, 264
Astor, John Jacob, 52
Atwood, Charles B., 23
automobiles, 90

Bang's Disease, 167–168, 185, 207
Barash, David, 231, 234, 236, 265, 266
Bay View: maintenance, 161–162; ownership, 142, 194, 206; photograph, **144**; use of, 144, 199
Bay View Cottage, 194
Beaudin, Hector, 189
Beaux-Arts architectural model, 46
Beeken, Bruce, xiii, 234

Belmont, August and Perry, 52
Benson, F. "Dad," **114**
Bessette, Clifford, 187
Bessette, Tom, 238
Biltmore estate, 36, 41
Blodgett, E. W., 85, 86
Boarding House Cottage, **112**; *See* Holabird family house
Boisvert, John, 189
Bostwick, Dunbar, 197, 201, 217
Bostwick, Electra Webb, 142, 197, 217
Bostwick Farm, 197, 201, 202–203, 272
Botala, John, Sr., 194–195, 200
Bourdett-Coutts, William, 71
Boutilier, Alan, 228
bovine tuberculosis, 129, 167, 207
Bowman, H. E., 165
Breeding Barn: description, 73–75; detail maps, **280-281**; employees in, **106**; as headquarters of Southern Acres, 149–150; photographs, **70**, **73**, **74**, **138**, **216**, **251**, **253**; preservation, 269, 270, **271**; size of, ix; J. Watson Webb, Sr. and, 139, 189
Brick House: photographs, **143**, **219**; preservation, 269, 272; Shelburne Museum and, 254, 269, 272; use of, 217; Electra Webb and, 145–147, 269; J. Watson Webb, Jr. and, 218, 272; J. Watson Webb, Sr. and, 145–147; WWII impact on, 203; *See* Comstock/McNeil family house
Brigham, Laughton Edward, 165, 168, 170, 185
Bronson, Frederic, 52
Brotz, John, 219
Broughton, Lenore "Norrie," 237
Brown, Archibald and Mary, 195, 214
Brown, Laura Havemeyer Webb, 252
Brown Swiss cattle: acquisition and herd size, 207, 212, 240, 257–258; cheeses from, xii, xiii; description, 207; feeding, xiii; photograph, **210**; quality of, 259, 260
brucellosis, 167–168, 185, 207
Burlington, Vermont, viii, 223
Burlington Coasting Club, 27
Burnett, Charles, 121
Burton Bettingen Corporation, 268
Butternut Hill, 266

Cabot, Tom, 250
Callery, Jake, 256
Cambridge Associates LLC, 231
Camp, Megan, 265, 266–267, **266**, 268, 272
camp, summer, xiv, 228–230
Canadian trade embargo, 9
Candido, Judy, 235
Canfield, Elizabeth (later Webb), 214–215, 224, 227, 232, 243
Cannon, LeGrand B., 33, 41
Cape Breton Railway, 126, **127**
Captain White house, 147, 162, 195
carriage collection, 213
Carter, Josh, xiii
Catalogue of the Shelburne Farm's Herd, 65
cattle: beef cattle, 186–188, 196, 211–212, 241; Brown Swiss cattle (*see* Brown Swiss cattle); dairy cattle, 164, **165**, 258; Durhams, 65; Farm Barn and, 187–188; feeding, 258–259; Herefords, 163, 196, **251**; Holsteins, 65; Jerseys, 65; Kendzior and, 163, 258; photograph, **258**; Derick Webb and, 186–188; *See also* dairy; livestock; steer fattening business
Champlain, Samuel de, 5
Champlain Canal, 10
Champlain Transportation Company, 169
Champlain Valley, 3–6, 8–9, 10
cheeses and cheese making: Brown Swiss cattle and, xii, xiv; cheddar cheese venture, 241–242, 257; Clapp and, **242**; in Farm Barn, 259, 267, 268; quality of, 260
Cherington, Davis, 228
Cherry Budd (cow), 65
chickens, 68, 188–189, 195, 200, 211; *See also* poultry department
Children's Farmyard, 268, **268**
Chittenden County, viii
Chorlette, Ellen (later Woodgate), 107, **115**, 116, 192
Church Woods, **96**
Cirillo, Jen, xii
Clapp, William, 241–242, **242**, 257, 259
Clarke, W. H., **41**
Cleveland, Grover, 122
Coach Barn: alterations, 222; architectural style, 86; as automobile garage, 90; description, 86–89; employees in, 88–89;

Harvest Festival and, 235; maintenance, 237; photographs, 87, **210**; preservation, 257; private events in, 264–265; Robertson design for, 86; Shelburne Farms Corporation and, 180; Shelburne Farms Resources and, 232, 234; as stable, 134, 187–188, 213
coaching, 86–90, **89**
coal, 101–102
Coleman, Robert, 201
communication systems, 102–103
Comstock, Daniel, 6
Comstock, Levi, 6, 14
Comstock, Lucia (later McNeil), **14**, 145
Comstock/McNeil family house, **143**, 145–146; *See* Brick House
Congdon, Charles, 194
Conquering the Wilderness (Burnett), 121
conservation easements, 248, 250, 251, 270, 271, 272
Correspondence and Journals of Samuel Blachley Webb, 118
Cotton, Joseph P., 36
Cowles, William S., Jr., 209, 211, 214
cows. *See* cattle
crafts program, 230
Cram, Laura Virginia (later Webb), 18, **18**
creamery, 65–66; *See also* milk and milking
crops, 60–61, **61**, 189–190
Cross, Eliot B., 146
Cross & Cross, 146

dairy: as agricultural focus, 240, 241; creamery, 65–66; dairy barn, 65, 74, 160, 166–167, 270; Kendzior and, 164–168; milk and milking, 65–66, 166–167, 211, 241–242, 259, 260; during 1970s, 238; photograph, **166**; production from, 65–66, 165; Shelburne Farms Corporation and, 164–168; under Shelburne Farms Resources, 257–260; Derick Webb and, 207–209, 211–213, 240; Derick (Quentyn) Webb and, 238; Lisa Webb and, 238; Marshall Webb and, 238, 240; Marilyn Webb and, 240; Mary Webb and, 238, 240; *See also* cattle
dairy barn, 65, 74, 160, 166–167, 270
Dairyman's Cottage, 65
Darling, Holly Webb, 270
Dartington Hall Trust of South Devon, 236
Davis, Leslie (later Webb), 224–227
Davis, Marnie, 262
Dewey, George, 52, 122–123, **123**
dining room car, **119**
Dock Bay, 86
Dominion Securities Company, 126
Downey, Tim, 234
du Pont, Henry Francis and Ruth Wales, 83
Dubel, Matt, xii–xiii
Dutch elm disease, 223, 238, 260

Earley, John, 151
Edgarton, Henry, 201–202
Education for Sustainability Institute, xii–xiii
educational programs, 227–230, 234–235, 264, 265, 266–267
Edwards, Jean "Jennie" Morehouse, 1–2, 11, **14**, 16
Edwards, Julie Eldridge, xvi, 146
Elfrida I (yacht), 84, 85, 123
Elfrida II (yacht), 84, **85**, 86, **108**, 135–136
Ellsmere (railroad car), **92**, 93, 136
Elm Court (residence), 36, 261
Elm Tree Swamp, 78, **78**
elm trees, 77–78, 233, 238, 260
Elmhirst, Leonard and Dorothy, 236
employees: in Breeding Barn, **106**; in Coach Barn, 88–89; compensation, 108–109; employer-employee relationships, 113; in Farm Barn, **107**; holidays, 109–110; multinational staff, 106–107; numbers of, 105; perquisites, 110–113, 160; photographs, **41**, **77**, **106–107**, **109**, **113–114**, **183**, **212**; Shelburne Farms Corporation and, 160; in Shelburne House, 52, **52**; at Southern Acres Farm, 219; supervision, 108; work schedules, 106; WWI impact on, 154; WWII impact on, 201
environmental sustainability, xii–xv
estate reductions, 133–135
Ethan Allen Child Care Center, 234
evergreen plantations, 76, **77**

Fago, D'Ann, 229, 231
Farm Barn: alterations, 222; beef cattle and, 187–188; cheese activities in, 259, 267, 268; construction, 57–59; description, ix; detail maps, **280-281**; as education center, 257, 267; employees in, **107**; maintenance, 237; O'Bread Bakery and, xiii, 234; photographs, **56-58**, **107**, **161**, **187**, **237**, **267**; poultry department and, 189; rehabilitation, 160, 267–268; Robertson design for, 56–57; Shelburne Farms Resources and, 232–233
farm valuations, in Vermont, 15
farmers' market, 228, **233**
Fay, Patrick, 107
Feree, Barr, 28
Fern Lodge, 176
flowers, 64, 193; *See also* formal gardens; greenhouses
flu (1918), 156
Flynn, John J., 33
food rationing, 203
Forest Lodge, **121**, 122
forests and forestry operations: development, ix, 75–76; elms and maples, 77–78, 223, 238, 260; evergreen plantations, 76; A. Taylor and, 75–76; Derick Webb and, 222–223; Marshall Webb and, 238, 260; *See also* lumber and logging
formal gardens, 79–82, **80**, 174–175, **175**, 193–194
Fort Ethan Allen, 122
Four Hundred social set, 25
foxes, 195
foxhounds, 138, 148–149, **152**, 195–196, 217
foxhunting, 138, 148–149, **153**, 196, 217
French and Indian Wars, 5

Galipeau, Dundeen "Deenie" Cromwll Webb, 252, 272
Galipeau, Steve, 272
Gamble, David, 201
Garden Way Associates, 228
gardens: formal gardens, 79–82, **80**, 174–175, **175**, 193–194; Gebhardt and, 80; market garden, 239; vegetable gardens, xiii, 62–63, 239; victory gardens, 200; Aileen Webb and, 194; Frederica Webb Jones and, 200; Lila Vanderbilt Webb and, 79–81
Gardens For All, 234
gates, entrance, 99–100, **100**
Gaynor, Gertrude (later Webb), **141**, 142, 143, 199
Gaynor, William, 142
Gebhardt, Edward F.: compensation, 109; daughter's illness, 113–114; death, 159; on employee holidays, 109; as employee supervisor, 108; on estate reductions, 134; on evergreen plantations, 76; as farm manager, 59, 137; gardens and, 80; greenhouses and, 156; photograph, **41**; retirement, 158–159; road system and, 95; on tractors, 61; J. Watson Webb, Sr. and, 150–151; as Seward Webb's political advisor, 124; on Seward Webb's run for governor, 125, 131–132; WWI impact on, 154–155
George III (king), 5
Germain, Leonard, 257, 260
golf links, x, 82–83, **83**, 172–173, 193–194, 203–204
Graham, Alexander, 107, 178, 193
Grant, Ulysses S., 23
Great Depression, 170–172
Green Mountains, 3, 5
greenhouses, 62–63, **62**, 155–156, 174–175, 193

Hall, Bill, 238
Handcraft Cooperative League of America, 194
Harris, Kate "Kitty" Brewster Webb, 252
Harrison, Benjamin, 58, 122
Harvest Festival, 235
Havemeyer, Electra. *See* Webb, Electra Havemeyer (daughter-in-law)
Hawken, Paul, 231, 234, 262

haying, **190**
Hemenway, Abby, 9
High Acres Farm, 217
Hill, Tom, 234
Hobart, Garrett, 86
hogs, 188–189, 211, 241; *See also* piggery
Holabird, Cassius, 13, 15, 57
Holabird, Harriet "Hattie," 13, 15–16, 57
Holabird, Mary (daughter), 15–16
Holabird, Mary (mother), 11, 13, 15–16, 57
Holabird, Oliver, 16
Holabird, William, 16
Holabird family house, **112**; *See also* Boarding House Cottage
Holden, Margie, 235
Home Estate, 158, 172, 174–176, 180, 192, 213–215
Hopkins, William H., 107, 139, 148–149, 151–152, **152**, **153**
horse breeding, 70–75, 134–135
horses, ix, 174, 190, 197; *See also* coaching; foxhunting; Shelburne Farms Stud; *individual horses*
Hurley, Dennis, **98**

Ierley, Merrit, 102
Indians, 4; *See also specific tribes*
influenza (1918), 156
infrastructure systems: communication systems, 102–103; entrance gates, 99–100; lighting and heating systems, 101–102; maintenance, 160; road system, 95–99; water system, 100–101
Ingleson, Fred, 148, 217
Inn at Shelburne Farms, 256, 257, 260–264
Integrated Village Development, 246
Iroquois tribe, 5

Jennings, Kate DeForest (later Webb), 217
Johnson, Elizabeth "Betty" (later Webb), 198, **202**
Johnson, Stanley, 106
Jones, Andrew, **114**
Jones, Cyril Hamlen, 145, 194, **195**, 200, 206
Jones, Frederica Webb. *See* Webb, Frederica (later Jones) (daughter)

Kendzior, Frank: cattle feeding and, 258; dairy and, 164–168; as employee supervisor, 108; farm finances and, 162–164, 168–169; firing of, 174; on golf links, 172–173; Great Depression and, 170–172; as manager Shelburne Farms Corporation, 159–162, 172–174; on Shelburne Hunt, 149
kennels, 150, **150**, 173, 203, 217; *See also* Shelburne Foxhounds
Kerr, Graham, 68, 115
Kiley, Daniel Urban, 224
Kiluna Farm, 145
King, Frederick Rhinelander, 194

Kinville, Tuffield, 107, 115
Kinzel, Amy, 229–230
Kinzel, Robert, 229–230, 231
Kissam, Maria Louisa (later Vanderbilt), 19, 36, 93
Klyza, Christopher, 3
Knickerbocker Club, 34
Kunhardt, Philip, 228

labor shortages, 201
Ladd, Bill, 228, 238, 239, 240
Laffin, Cricket, 239
Lake Champlain, 3, 5
Lake Lila, 122
land stewardship fund, 270, 272
land use plans, 227–228, 243–248
LaPlatte River, 4
Lay, W. E., 106–107
Lazarowski, Jack, 235
Leimenstoll, Jerry, 228
Leimenstoll, Marilyn Thompson. *See* Webb, Marilyn Thompson Leimenstoll (great granddaughter-in-law)
Lewis, Hunter, 250
lifestyle changes, 135–136, 154
lighting and heating systems, 101–102
Lintilhac, Philip and Crea, 257, 264
livestock: acquisitions, 64, 185–186; breeding programs, 64–65; economizing, 134, 159; Shelburne Farms Corporation and, 159, **165**; at Southern Acres Farm, 252; steer fattening business, 220, 252; J. Watson Webb, Sr. and, 196; *See also individual species*
logging and lumber, 238, 260
Lone Tree Hill, 3, 32, 57, 89, 101, 122, 200, 265, 266
Lone Tree Lumber, 238
lookout station, 200
lumber and logging, 238, 260
Lumière, August and Louis, 81
Lyman Farm, 162, 164

Magnussen, Harold, 207, 211
mail-order business, 242, 259
management transitions, 136–140
manure handling, 260
maple sugaring program, xiii, 266
maple trees, 77
Marble House, 46
market garden, 239
Matchless of Londesboro (horse), **70**, 72, 135
McCabes Brook, 4
McClure, J. Warren, 268, 269, 270
McClure, James, 184
McClure, Lois, 268, 270
McClure Center for School Programs, 268
McCullough, John, 122
McGee, Edward "Eddie," **114**
McKinley, William, 86
McNeil, Lucia Comstock, **14**, 145

McNeil, William, **14**, **145**
Meach Cove Trust, 272
Meyer, Alfred, 126–128
milk and milking, 65–66, 166–167, 211, 241–242, 259, 260
Miradero del Mar (house), **176**, 177
Miskell, David and Susan, 239
Missisquoi (steamboat), 84
model farms, 55
Mohawk tribe, 5
Moraine Farm, 36
Morehouse family, 1, 16
Morehouse, Clarke, 1–2, 16
Morehouse, Edward, 16
Morehouse, Franklin H., 7, 11, **11**, 13–14
Morehouse, George, 16
Morehouse, Hawley, 7, 16
Morehouse, Jean "Jennie" (later Edwards), 1–2, 11, **14**, 16
Morehouse, Lucia, 16
Morehouse, Maria, 11, 14, 16
Morehouse, Roderick, 16
Morehouse, Sturgis, 7
Morgan, Clarence, residence of, 217–218
morphine addictions, 130–131
Morrison, Alexander "Alec," 148
Mozart Festival, Vermont, 233–234, **245**

Nash, Asahel, Jr., 8, 13
Nash, Asahel, Sr., 7–9, 15
Nash, Betsy, 7–9, 15
Nash, Edgar, 11, 13, 16
Nash, Elbert, 15
Nash, Jane, 15
Nash, John, 8, 15
Nash, Louisa, 13, 15
Nash, Truman, 8
National Historic Landmark status, 270
National Preservation Honor Award, 268
National Register of Historic Places, 237
Native Americans, 3-4; *See also specific tribes*
Nature Conservancy, 226, 228, 247, 251
Neagley, Mark, 262
Nehasane Park, 76, 121–122, 128, 180
Nehasane Park Association, 180
New York Coaching Club, 89–90
Nibble Hanover (horse), 197
Nichols, O. S., 110
Nonprofit programs, 265–268
Norris and Ellyn Day Camp, 234
North Gate, 100
North Seawall, **103**
Nowicki, Paul, 264

Oakledge Farm, 25–27, **26**, 29–30, 136, 145
O'Bread Bakery, xiii, 234, 239
Ockert, Robert, **114**
Odzihozo, 5
Olmsted, Frederick Law, ix-x, 34–42, **35**, 44, 75, 95
Onion River Land Company, 6

Orchard Cottage, 214, 227
Orchard Cove House, 211, 227
Orchard House: description and location, 84; lack of use, 145; photograph, **143**; renovation, 214–215; Aileen and Vanderbilt Webb and, 142, 144; Derick Webb and, 248; Seward Webb, Jr. and, 144
Orchard Point, 8, 239, 248, 250
orchards, 61
Osborn, Aileen. *See* Webb, Aileen Osborn (daughter-in-law)
Osborn, Earl, 227
Osborn, William Church, 142
Osgood, Eliza, 19
Ottauquechee Land Trust, 250, 251

Panic of 1893, 126, 128
Park, Willie, Jr., 82
Parsons, Jeff, xiii, 234
pastoral myth, viii
Paterson, Gordon, 224
Patrick, Robert and Jane, 206
Patterson, Thomas, 203
Patterson, William Darcy, 187, 211
Perkins, Nathan, 9
Pheasant Hill Trust, 250
pheasant hunters, **69**
pheasantry, 68–70, 134
Phillips, David, 224, **225**, 227, 239, 240
Phillips, John C., 36
Pierce, Tom, 268
piggery, 66–67, **66**, 189; *See also* hogs
Pinchot, Gifford, 75–76, 122
Pizzagalli, Remo, 262
Point D'Acadie, 36
pole barn complex, **208**, 209, **209**, 211, 213, 259–260
Post, George, 34
Potter, Edward T., 34
Potter, Robert Burnside, 34
Potter, William Appleton, 34, 80, 93
poultry department, 68, 159, 174, 188–189; *See also* chickens
Prall, John H., 126
Proctor, Redfield, 122
programs, public, 227–228, 265
Project Seasons (curriculum guide), 266–267
property divisions, 140–145
property tax stabilization agreement, 244–245, 247, 248
public programs, 227–228, 265
public tours, 236
Pulitzer, Joseph, 145
Pulitzer, Ralph, 53, 145, 154
Pulitzer, Ralph, Jr., 145
Pulitzer, Seward, 145
Pump House, 100–101
Putnam County Products, 194

Quaker Smith Point, 6, 198, 272

quarry, 97

railroads, 10; *See also specific railroad companies*
Reagan, Ronald, 264, **264**
Red Cross volunteers, **155**
road roller, **98**, 159
road system, 95–99
Robbins, Richard, 185, 186, 187
Roberts, John, 227, 238, 239–240
Robertson, Robert Henderson: Coach Barn complex design, 86; education and career, 34; employee cottages design, 110–111, **111**; Farm Barn design, 56–57; Forest Lodge design, 122; photograph, **34**; St. Andrew's Golf Club and, 82; Shelburne Depot design, 91; Shelburne Farms commission, 34–35, 40; Shelburne Farms homes designs, 43, 44, **44**, 46; Sheperd's Cottage design, 67
Robins, Pat, 231
Rock Dunder, 4–5, **4**
Rockefeller, Eileen McGrath, 234, **235**, 236, 248–249
Rockefeller, John D., Jr., 136
Rockwell, H. Benson, 201, 205
Roosevelt, Theodore, 52, 86, 89, 123
Root, Elihu, 86
Ross, Chuck, 269
rotational grazing, xiii, 258–259
Rough Point, 36, 41
Rutland Railroad, 126

St. Andrew's Golf Club, 82
St. Catherine of Siena church, 111–112
St. Thomas Church, 23, **24**
Sappho (yacht), 27, 84
Sargent, Charles Sprague, 37
Sartori (chauffeur), 107, 114–115
Saxton, Edward Stevenson, 11, 13
Saxton, Frederick, 7, 13
Saxton, Sarah, 13
Saxton family house, **8**
Saxton's Point, 7, 44, **54**
School of American Craftsmen, 194
Searles, Gordon "Buster," 241, 257
Searls, Paul, 124
seasonal activities, 234
Seavey, Linda, 262
Seward, William Henry, 17
SFI. *See* Shelburne Farms Resources, Inc. (SFI)
Shaker Mountain School, 228
sheep, 67–68, **67**, 188–189, 211
Sheep and Poultry Farm, 67–68
Shelburne, Earl of, 6
Shelburne, Vermont: charter of, 5–6; industries in, 8; lot plans, 7; map, **12**; in mid-nineteenth century, 10–16; population (1960s), 223; settlement of, 6–9
Shelburne Bay Park, 272

Shelburne Cooperative Creamery, 164–165
Shelburne Depot, 90–93, **91**
Shelburne Farms: aerial view, **2**; conservation of, 246–247; decline of, x; disposition of, 182; early settlement, 6–8; establishment, vii–ix, 16; estate plan, **39**; family partnership (1939–1949), 182–186; finances, 185, 191, 223–224, 242–251, 256–257; land sales from, 257; landscape design, 35–42; main drive, 222, **222**, 252; maintenance, 236–237; maps, **37**, **278-282**; in mid-nineteenth century, 9, 10–16; as model farm, 55–56, 78; modern existence, vii, 1; 1960s, 221–227; 1970–1984, 227–251; as nonprofit corporation, xi–xii, 251, 257; ownership, 246; photographs, **2**, **42**, **273**; profitability, x–xi, 133; as scientific operation, ix; size of, ix, 250, 269, 272; Southern Acres Farm and, 198–199, 251–252, 255, 269–270; survey (1886–1891), **32**; taxes on, 223, 243–246, 247, 248
Shelburne Farms Corporation: economizing, 174–176; establishment, 157–159; finances, 162–164, 168–169; Great Depression and, 170–172; livestock and, 159, **165**; managerial tensions, 172–174; struggles, 168–170
Shelburne Farms Del (cow), 260
Shelburne Farms Resources, Inc. (SFI): articles of association, 230; budget, 248, 270; Coach Barn complex and, 232, 234; conservation easements, 248, 250, 251; educational programs, 228–230; establishment, 230; Farm Barn and, 232–233; financial struggles, 236; fund raising, 234, 237, 238, 247–248, 249, 257; incorporation, 250; leasehold agreement, 249, 250, 271; mission, 230–231, 255, 256; as nonprofit entity, 271; organizational structure, 264; Ottauquechee Land Trust and, 250; ownership, 255; Shelburne Farms and, 232; Shelburne House and, 232–233; uniqueness, 231; Vermont Mozart Festival and, 233–234; Derick Webb and, 256
Shelburne Farms Stud, 71, 134–135, 139
Shelburne Farms Stud (catalogue), 59, 70
Shelburne foxhounds, 138, 148–149, **152**; *See also* kennels; Shelburne Hunt
Shelburne Harbor Inn, 218
Shelburne House: aging and condition, 176, 181, 200, 215, 261; bedrooms, 49–50; description, vii; design work of, 44–46; detail map, **282**; domestic technology, 50–52; employees, 52, **52**; enlargements to, 47–48, 135; entertainment rooms, 50; family use of, 214, 215; guest rooms, 50; guests, 52–53, **53**; landscape, 54; library, **51**; location, 44; maintenance, 237; office of S. Webb, 49; ownership of, 192–193;

340 INDEX

photographs, **44**, **45**, **48**, **83**, **214**, **245**; refurbishment, xii; servants' wing, 215, 263, **263**; service areas, 50; Shelburne Farms Corporation and, 180; Shelburne Farms Resources and, 232–233; size of, 48; style of, 48–49; Aileen Webb and, 192, 199, 214; Alec Webb on, 215; after L. Webb's death, 181–182; Marshall Webb and, 233; Vanderbilt Webb and, 192
Shelburne Hunt, 138, 148–149, 173–174, 196, 203, 217; *See also* Shelburne foxhounds
Shelburne Museum, 147, 213, 215, 254, 269–270, 272
Shelburne Planning Commission, 228
Shelburne Point, viii, ix, 4, 6, 168, 272
Shelburne Spinners, 234
Shelburne Titan Elly (cow), 260
Shepard, Elliott, 21–22
Shepard, Margaret, 23, 34
Sheperd's Cottage, 67
Sims, Henry, 34
"Slaves on Webb's Road" (news article), 120
Sled Runner Point, 194–195, 206, 272
Sloane, Emily Vanderbilt, 21, 23, 36, 261
Sloane, William, 36
smallpox, 5
Smith, Edward, 124
Smith, Elizabeth, 6, 15
Smith, Isaac, 15
Smith, Lucinda, 15
Smith, William, 6, 15
Smith family house, **198**
Snook, John B., 23
South Gate, 99, **100**
Southern Acres Farm: advertisement, **147**; agricultural operations, 253; Breeding Barn and, 149–150; development, 147–148; employees, 219; as family partnership, 251–254; family use of, 142, 217; finances, 219–220, 252, 253, 269; foxhunting and, 148–149; W. H. Hopkins and, 151–152; labor shortages, 201; livestock, 252; maintenance, 215–216, 254; management, 150–151; ownership, 145, 251–254; Shelburne Farms and, 198–199, 251–252, 255, 269–270; Shelburne Museum and, 254; steer fattening business, 220, 252; University of Vermont and, 254; Alec Webb on, 269; Harry Webb and, 218–220, 251–252; J. Watson Webb, Sr. and, 142, 147–154, 173, 195–197, 215–216, 218; Sam Webb, Sr. and, 218, 251, 253–254; WWII impact on, 199, 202–203
Spencer, Stephanie, 234
Sprague, Henry, 127
Stapleton, Herbert, 213
Star of Gold (horse), **196**
steamboats, 53, 84
Steen, George Edward "Eddie," 197, 201

steer fattening business, 220, 252
stone crusher, 97, **98**, 99, 159–160
Street, William, 107
subdivision plans, 224–226, 246
sugar house, 266
summer house, 80
sustainability, environmental, xii–xiv

Taft, William Howard, 52, 131
Taylor, Archibald: birth and careers, 41; compensation, 109; as employee supervisor, 108; as farm manager, 41–42, 59; forestry operations and, 75–76; in honorary role, 115; as multinational staff, 107; photograph, **41**; road system and, 95
Teahouse, 54, 194; *See also* Waveledge
telegraph system, 102–104
telephones, 102
terriers, 195–196, 217, **217**
Thompson, Bryson "Tommy," 228, 234
Tierney, Martin, 262
Tiffany, Louis Comfort, 93
Tiffany & Co., 93
Torok, J. E., 160
tours, public, 236
Tower, Arunah, 201
Tower, David, 174, 182, 189, 193, 202, 213
Tower, Winfield, 201
Towers, R. S., 151, 189
tractors, 61, 190, 203
Tracy family, 15, 74
Tracy, Caroline, 13
Tracy, Dere Azro, 15
Tracy, Eunice, 6
Tracy, Ezekiel, 15, 182
Tracy, Guy, 11, 13
Tracy, Hannah, 16
Tracy, Henry, 16
Tracy, Hezekiah, 6, 13
Tracy House, 74
Tracy, Jennie, 13
Tracy, Julia, 15
Tracy, Julius, 16
Tracy, Lee, 16
Tracy, William, 16
Tracy Barn, 74, 187, 189, 197
"Treated Like Slaves" (news article), 120
tree nursery, 38
Trench silos, 209, 211, 259
Trinity Episcopal Church, 64, 93, **94**
Trombulak, Stephen, 3
Twombly, Florence, 23
Twombly, Hamilton McK., 33
Twombly residence, **24**

University of Vermont (UVM), 254, 269

Valley View Farm, 227, 248–249
Van Arsdale, William J., 33
Vanderbilt family, **20**
Vanderbilt, Alva, 25, 46
Vanderbilt, Cornelius, 19–20, **19**

Vanderbilt, Cornelius, II, 23, 31
Vanderbilt, Frederick, 21–22, 23, 36, 41
Vanderbilt, George, 36, 41
Vanderbilt, Lila Osgood. *See* Webb, Lila Osgood Vanderbilt
Vanderbilt, Louise, 36
Vanderbilt, Maria Louisa Kissam, 19, 36, 93
Vanderbilt, William Henry: death, 31; New York Coaching Club and, 30; Olmsted and, 36; residences commissioned by, 23; wealth of, 20; Lila Webb and, 19, 179; Seward Webb and, 22, 23
Vanderbilt, William K., 23, 25, 31, 46, 126
Vanderbilt Row, 23–24
Vaux, Calvert, 35, 36
vegetable gardens, xiii, 62–63, 239
Vermont (steamboat), 53
Vermont Mozart Festival, 233–234, **245**
Vermont's Own (product label), 228
Verret's grocery store, 189
victory gardens, 200
Vogelman, Hubert "Hub," 231
Vosburgh, Howard, 156

W. S. Webb & Company, 125
Wadhams, Emily, 224, **225**, 228
Wagner Palace Car Company, 25, 118
Wales, George W., 33
walking trails, 265–266
Walling, Lewis Metcalfe, 231, 256
War of 1812, 10
water system, 100–101, 160–161
Waveledge (painting studio), 194; *See also* Teahouse
Webb family, **18**
Webb, Aileen Osborn (daughter-in-law): crafts and, 194; gardens and, 194; marriage, 142; Orchard House and, 142, 144; photograph, **225**; Shelburne House use by, 192, 199, 214; subdivision plans and, 224; on Seward Webb, 121
Webb, Alexander "Alec" (great grandson): agricultural operations and, 238; dairy and, 240; education, 227, 228; on environment, xi; as farm manager, 238, 256, 257; inheritance, 227, 248; Integrated Village Development and, 246; land use plans and, 245–248, 250; military service and, 229; photographs, **225**, **229**; Shelburne Farms and, 227, 246, 250; Shelburne Farms Resources and, 228, 230–231, 256, 264, 272; on Shelburne House, 215; on Southern Acres Farm, 269; subdivision plans and, 224–228; walking trails and, 265
Webb, Alexander Stewart (grandson), 142, 156
Webb, Alexander Stewart (half-brother), 17
Webb, Barbara (granddaughter), 156, 205
Webb, Derick (grandson): agricultural operations and, 206–207, 221, 227, 238; air charter business, 224, 243; beef cattle

and, 186–188; careers, 183–184, 201; dairy and, 207–209, 211–213, 240; death, 251, 257; divorce, 232, 243; education, 183, 184; eye injury, 183; as farm manager, x, 180–181, 182, 191–192, 205–207, 213, 221–223, 238–239; finances, 243, 245, 247–249; forestry operations and, 222–223; land holdings, 206; land sold by, 247, 248, 249–250; marriages and family, 214–215, 264; name, 142; Orchard House and, 248; photographs, **183**, **202**, **208**, **212**, **223**, **225**; political activities, 212; residences, 214–215; on Shelburne Farms finances, 242; Shelburne Farms Resources and, 232–233, 256; subdivision plans and, 224–226, 249–250; taxes and, 245; WWII impact on, 201, 202

Webb, Derick Osborn "Quentyn" (great grandson): dairy and, 238; inheritance, 227, 248; living and working at Shelburne Farms, 227; photograph, **225**; Shelburne Farms Resources and, 230–231; subdivision plans and, 224–226

Webb, Dundeen "Deenie" Cromwell (later Galipeau) (great granddaughter), 252, 272

Webb, Electra Havemeyer (daughter-in-law): Brick House and, 145–147, 269; death, 218; Great Depression and, 170; inheritance and wealth of, 141, 153; marriage and family, 141; photographs, **114**, **141**; residences, 141–142, 154; Shelburne Museum and, 147, 213; WWII impact on, 201

Webb, Electra (later Bostwick) (granddaughter), 142, 197, 217

Webb, Elizabeth "Betty" Johnson (granddaughter-in-law), 198, **202**

Webb, Elizabeth Canfield (granddaughter-in-law), 214–215, 224, 227, 232, 243

Webb, Elizabeth "Lisa" (later Roberts) (great granddaughter): dairy and, 238; inheritance, 227, 248; photograph, **225**; Shelburne Farms, leaving of, 240; Shelburne Farms Resources and, 228, 230–231; subdivision plans and, 224–228; summer camp and, 230; Valley View farmhouse and, 227

Webb, Emily Wadhams (great granddaughter-in-law), 227, 228, 229–230, 231, 233

Webb, Frank Edgerton (brother), 126

Webb, Frederica (later Gamble) (granddaughter), 142, 197

Webb, Frederica (later Jones) (daughter): birth, 27; children, 137, 145; death, 205–206; as estate beneficiary, 179–180; health problems, 205–206; land holdings, 195; marriages, 53, 137, 145, 178; photographs, **27**, **28**, **29**, **123**, **141**, **183**, **195**; Shelburne Farms and, 180–181, 182, 191; Sled Runner Point and, 194–195; victory gardens and, 200; WWI impact on, 154; WWII impact on, 199

Webb, G. Creighton (brother), **82**

Webb, Gertrude Gaynor (daughter-in-law), **141**, 142, 143, 199

Webb, Gertrude (later Meades) (granddaughter), 142

Webb, H. Walter (brother), 125, 126

Webb, Harry Havemeyer (grandson), 196, 201, 217, 218–220, 251–252

Webb, Helen "Rusty" Allen (granddaughter-in-law), 227, 243, 264

Webb, Holly (later Darling) (great granddaughter), 270

Webb, J. Louis (brother), 126

Webb, Jacob Louis (grandson), 142

Webb, James Watson (father), 17–19, **18**, 27, 30

Webb, James Watson, Jr. (grandson), 142, 217, 218, **219**, 251, 253, 272

Webb, James Watson, Sr. (son): birth, 27; Breeding Barn and, 139, 189; Brick House and, 145–147; children, 142; death, 218, 251, 252; as estate beneficiary, 179–180; farm management and, 137; foxhunting and, 138, 217; Gebhardt and, 150–151; golf links and, 204; Great Depression and, 170; health problems, 216; Hopkins and, 151–152; horse activities, 138–139, 149; land holdings, 141–142, 197; livestock and, 196; marriage, 53; photographs, **27–29**, **53**, **114**, **137–138**, **141**, **153**, **217**; poultry and, 68, 189; Shelburne Farms and, 181; Shelburne Farms Corporation and, 158, 171; Shelburne Farms Stud and, 139; Southern Acres Farm and, 142, 147–154, 173, 195–197, 215–216, 218; Tracy Barn and, 189; WWI impact on, 154; WWII impact on, 201, 202–203

Webb, Kate DeForest Jennings, 217

Webb, Kate "Kitty" Brewster (later Harris) (great granddaughter), 252, 272

Webb, Laura Havemeyer (later Brown) (great granddaughter), 251, 252

Webb, Laura Virginia Cram (mother), 18, **18**

Webb, Leslie Davis (great granddaughter-in-law), 224–227

Webb, Lila Vanderbilt (later Wilmerding) (granddaughter), 142, 197, 217

Webb, Lila Osgood Vanderbilt: birth and early years, 19, 20–21, 29–30; Grover Cleveland and, 122; criticism of, 272; death, 93, 116, 178; as employer, 105–106; estate of, 179–180; farm purchases, 15, 16, 25, 31–33, 57; flowers and, 64; gardens and, 79–81; on Gebhardt's retirement, 158–159; as golfer, 83; Great Depression and, 170–172; health problems, 177; horses and, 30; inheritance and wealth, 31, 125, 128, 179; Manhattan townhouse, **24**, 136; New York social set and, 24–25; Oakledge Farm and, 25–27, 29–30; photographs, **21–22**, **27**, **29**, **46**, **53**, **82**, **177**; property sold by, 168–169; Theodore Roosevelt and, 89, 123; as sailor, 85; Shelburne Farms Corporation and, 157–158, 168; Shelburne Farms description by, 2–3; Shelburne Farms established by, 16; Seward Webb and, 21–22, 125, 176; as widow, 176; WWI impact on, 154

Webb, Marilyn Thompson Leimenstoll (later Neagley) (great granddaughter-in-law): dairy and, 240; educational programs and, 227, 230; Integrated Village Development and, 246; land use plans and, 245–248, 250; photograph, **264**; Shelburne Farms and, 227–228, 236, 250; Shelburne Farms Resources and, 231, 236, 256; walking trails and, 265

Webb, Marshall (great grandson): agricultural operations and, 240; cheese making and, 242; dairy and, 238, 240; education, 230; educational programs and, 230; forestry operations and, 238, 260; inheritance, 227, 248; photographs, **225**, **239**; Shelburne Farms and, 227, 236–237; on Shelburne Farms finances, 243; Shelburne Farms parcels owned by, 250; Shelburne Farms Resources and, 228, 230–231, 256, 272; Shelburne House and, 215, 233; subdivision plans and, 224–228; summer camp and, 229–230; walking trails and, 265

Webb, Mary (later Phillips Kelly) (great granddaughter): agricultural enterprises of, 239; agricultural operations and, 240; dairy and, 238, 240; inheritance, 227, 248; Orchard Cottage and, 227; photograph, **225**; Shelburne Farms, leaving of, 240; Shelburne Farms Resources and, 231; subdivision plans and, 224–227; Laura Webb and, 251

Webb, Osborn "Obbie" (grandson), 201, 205

Webb, Richard Humphrey (grandson), 142, 201, 202

Webb, Robert (great grandson), **212**, 224–227, **225**, 231, 248

Webb, Samuel Blachley (grandfather), 17

Webb, Samuel Blachley, Jr. (great grandson), 253–254, 270

Webb, Samuel Blachley, Sr. (grandson): death, 254, 272; inheritance, 197–198; military service and, 201; Quaker Smith Point and, 197–198, 200; Southern Acres Farm and, 218, 251, 253–254

Webb, Dr. W. Seward: birth and early years, 17, 18–19, 30; business affairs of, 117–118, 125–126; careers, 19, 25; criticism of, 120–121, 272; death, 93, 176; as employer, 105–106, 112–116, 120–121; as estate advisor, 136–137; farm purchases, 15, 16, 25, 31–33, 57; financial problems, 125–128; health problems, 128–132, 176; horses and, ix, 30; Manhattan townhouse, **24**, 136; morphine addiction, 129–132; New York social set and, 24–25; Oakledge Farm and, 25–27, 29–30; photographs, **18**, **23**, **29**, **119**, **120**, **122**, **129**; politics and political career, 110, 122–125; poultry and, 68; property sold by, 168–169; Theodore Roosevelt and, 123; as sailor, 85; Shelburne House office of, 49; Lila Webb and, 21–22

Webb, Vanderbilt (son): birth, 46; careers, 142, 206; carriage collection and, 213; death, 205–206, 214, 251; as estate beneficiary and executor, 179–180; golfing and, 83; health problems, 205–206; Home Estate and, 192; marriage and family, 142; Orchard House and, 142, 144; photographs, **46**, **53**, **101**, **141**, **180**, **183**; Shelburne Farms involvement, 143–144, 180–181, 182, 191, 206; Shelburne House and, 192, 214; wealth of, 192; Seward Webb, Jr. and, 145; WWI impact on, 143, 154; WWII impact on, 199–200, 202

Webb, William J. Gaynor (grandson), 142
Webb, William Osborn (grandson), 142
Webb, William Seward, III (grandson), 142
Webb, William Seward, Jr. (son): birth, 46; careers, 142; death, 206; as estate beneficiary, 179–180; finances of, 181; golfing and, 83; Great Depression and, 170; marriage and family, 142; Orchard House and, 144; photographs, **120**, **131**, **141**, **200**; Shelburne Farms Corporation and, 158; Shelburne Farms involvement, 143–144, 181; WWI impact on, 143, 154; WWII impact on, 199
Webb, Prall & Co., 125–126
"Webb Wants The Earth" (news article), 120
Welcome Center, 259
Wentworth, Benning, 5–6
West, William, **106**, **114**
Westbury estate, 141, 197, 215
Wetmore, W. Boerum, 84
Whippoorwill Farm, 142

White, Margaret, 13
White, Stanford, 80
Wickson children, **113**
Wilmerding, John, 201
Wilmerding, Lila Webb, 197, 217
Windmill Hill, 40, 47, 198, 257, 270
windrow turner, **229**
Wood, Lyman, 228, 231, 234
Woodgate, Ellen Chorlette, 107, **115**, 116, 192
Woodgate, Walter, 65, 83, 107, 115–116, 176, 192
woodlands. *See* forests and forestry operations
Woodside, Peter, 231
wool and wool production, 10, 15
World Crafts Council, 194
World War I, 143, 154–156
World War II, 199–204
Wright, Lillian, 99

yachting, 84–86
yachts: *Elfrida I*, 84, 85, 123; *Elfrida II*, 84, **85**, 86, **108**, 135–136; *Sappho*, 27, 84